KING LEOPOLD'S GHOSTWRITER

King Leopold's Ghostwriter

THE CREATION OF PERSONS AND STATES IN THE NINETEENTH CENTURY

Andrew Fitzmaurice

PRINCETON UNIVERSITY PRESS
PRINCETON & OXFORD

Copyright © 2021 by Princeton University Press

Princeton University Press is committed to the protection of copyright and the intellectual property our authors entrust to us. Copyright promotes the progress and integrity of knowledge. Thank you for supporting free speech and the global exchange of ideas by purchasing an authorized edition of this book. If you wish to reproduce or distribute any part of it in any form, please obtain permission.

Requests for permission to reproduce material from this work should be sent to permissions@press.princeton.edu

Published by Princeton University Press
41 William Street, Princeton, New Jersey 08540
6 Oxford Street, Woodstock, Oxfordshire OX20 1TR

press.princeton.edu

All Rights Reserved
ISBN 978-0-691-148694
ISBN (e-book) 978-0-691-220369

British Library Cataloging-in-Publication Data is available

Editorial: Ben Tate and Josh Drake
Production Editorial: Brigitte Pelner
Production: Danielle Amatucci
Publicity: Alyssa Sanford (US), Amy Stewart (UK)
Copyeditor: Patricia Fogarty

Jacket Image: Sir Travers Twiss, QC, FRS (engraving). Look and Learn / Illustrated Papers Collection / Bridgeman Images

This book has been composed in Miller

Printed on acid-free paper ∞

Printed in the United States of America

10 9 8 7 6 5 4 3 2 1

For Saliha

CONTENTS

Acknowledgements · ix

	Introduction	1
PART 1	Travers Twiss	29
	Travers Twiss in Society	29
	Oxford and King's College, London	55
	The Doctors' Commons, the Church of England, and the Admiralty	74
	Sovereignty in the Law of Nations and Ecclesiastical Law	89
	Catholic Reform and Tractarianism	94
PART 2	Metternich	108
	The Friendship between Twiss and Metternich	109
	Schleswig, Holstein, and Prussia	124
	Austria and Germany	128
	The German Confederation and the Austrian Empire	138
	Prussia and Germany	167
	"The Social Problem"	173
	Hungary and Public Opinion	178
	The Coup d'État in France	195
	The Crimean War	200
	Napoléon III and Italian Unification	212
	Global Revolution	221
PART 3	Agnes Willoughby and Pharaïlde van Lynseele	235
	Metamorphoses	235

	Agnes Willoughby	246
	Pharaïlde van Lynseele	302
PART 4	King Leopold and the Congo	392
	Revival through International Law	392
	The Standing of "Oriental Nations" in International Society	406
	Twiss and King Leopold	423
	Diplomatic Negotiations	447
	The Berlin Conference of 1884 and 1885	458
	The Congo Free State	475
PART 5	Civil Death	504
	Conclusion	530

Bibliography · 535
Index · 551

ACKNOWLEDGEMENTS

THIS BOOK WAS PRODUCED over more than ten years. More than anything I have written, it developed out of conversations with colleagues and friends. Many of those discussions concerned the need to build ties between intellectual history and the other fields of history, law, philosophy, and the social sciences in which my colleagues work. My debts reflect those concerns.

For many years, I have been engaged in a conversation with Chris Hilliard about how to write a history of "corrupt ideas." That exchange had a profound impact upon this book. I was also frequently pushed out of my comfort zone by colleagues including Barbara Caine, Marco Duranti, Nick Eckstein, Moira Gatens, Duncan Ivison, Kirsten McKenzie, Dirk Moses, Glenda Sluga, and Shane White.

There are numerous people who have aided me on various aspects of this project, and I will never recall them all, but they include Jan Bondeson, Angus Gowland, Rohan Howitt, Martti Koskenniemi, Randall Lessafer, Doreen Lustig, Mina Roces, Jan Vandersmissen, and Natasha Wheatley. Jennifer Pitts and I have been swapping notes on Twiss over many years. Michael Lobban also assisted on aspects of Twiss. Mayuko Sano has been helpful on the subject of Rutherford Alcock. Phil Stern and Phil Whithington helped me to think far more deeply about the political thought of corporations than I ever appreciated was necessary before I began talking with them on the subject. Robert Travers pointed me in the right direction for Awadh. Matthijs Lok made several very astute and useful suggestions. Susan James may not remember it, but she gave me courage to continue pursuing my ideas at an important moment.

Several people have read part or all of the manuscript. Jonathan Parry has been very generous with his ideas and extremely helpful with context and aspects of the argument. Ed Cavanagh and Sally Ghattas provided valuable feedback on an early draft. Shane White was an inspiration and an extremely agreeable neighbour for twenty years. His meticulous shredding of my prose required the investment of a considerable portion of his life and was more than I deserved.

Aspects of the argument have benefited from the hosts and audiences in various seminars and conferences. In Leuven in 2016, Inge Van Hulle and Randall Lessafer were excellent and generous hosts of the International Law in the Long Nineteenth Century conference, at which I presented some of the material. At Duke University, in 2017, I trialed the argument at Corporations and Empire, Rachel Brewster and Phil Stern's Sawyer Seminar, and received the warmest hospitality. In 2019, in Utrecht, I presented the case for the book to the participants in the Huizinga Institute Summer School. The discussion on that occasion greatly helped with sharpening the argument. The hosts, Camille Creighton, Boyd van Dijk, Annelien De Dijn, René Koekkoek, and Matthijs Lok, were extraordinarily kind and welcoming. I am grateful to the publishers Brill for permission to reproduce some passages from my chapter in Inge Van Hulle and Randall Lesaffer, eds., *International Law in the Long Nineteenth Century (1776–1914)* (Leiden, 2019).

If it were not for the passion and dedication of archivists, this book would not exist. Jennie De Protani, in the Athenaeum, provided completely unexpected material by pointing out various possibilities in the archive that were unknown to me. Robin Darwall-Smith made me understand how important University College was in Twiss's formation. To do so, he brought together an immense quantity of material in the University College archive that constituted a project in itself! Gustaaf Janssens, in the Royal Palace archive in Brussels, helped reveal the extent of the ties between Twiss and Leopold II. Marijke Vanwezzer provided crucial support with the State Archives, in Kortrijk, and the archivists of the Ministere des Affaires Etrangères, Brussels, were very efficient. The archivists of the Norfolk Record Office helped me to understand, over weeks, the boxes of Windham family papers and enabled me to reconstruct the life of Agnes Willoughby. The National Archives of the Czech Republic and the Bibliothèque nationale, Paris, assisted with the vast, and untapped, correspondence between Twiss and Metternich with great efficiency. Alice Millea, Anna Petre, and Elizabeth Back, in the Oxford University Archive, helped me solve a puzzle regarding Twiss and Rutherford Alcock. The staff of the National Archives in Kew, the London Metropolitan Archives, the Hammersmith and Fulham Archives, the Denbighshire Archives, in Ruthin, Wales, and the Manuscripts Room in the British Library were all unstintingly patient with my requests. Diana Manipud and Jessica Borge, in the archive of King's College, London, were very helpful and efficient. The archivists in Lambeth Palace bore with me for many days, over many years, and I am indebted to their cheerfulness and their deep knowledge of their holdings. Mary Person in the Harvard Law School Special Collections conducted a brilliant piece of detective work for me regarding the purchase of the eight manuscript volumes of Twiss's *Opinions*. She, Jane Kelly, and Lesley Schoenfeld, in the Law School Special Collections, very kindly assisted me in grappling with those volumes. The fact that many of these archivists have also assisted through a pandemic has further deepened my admiration for their work. For permission to reproduce images and documents, I am grateful to the Norfolk Records Office; the Master and Fellows of University College, Oxford; the Walters Art Museum; the Atkinson Art Gallery; the Harvard University, Law School Library; and the National Portrait Gallery, London.

It would be remiss not to mention Ian Malcolm. He is no longer at Princeton University Press, but the project only made the transformation from idea to book because he sought me out. He subsequently drew me out, now many years ago, over several long telephone conversations in which he helped crystalise what the book was about. I am tremendously grateful for his generosity. Ben Tate took over the project as editor and has been remarkably patient. He has also been unerringly encouraging and supportive. Brigitte Pelner has seen it through the final stages with great efficiency. Patricia Fogarty has been an extraordinarily careful and thorough copy-editor. I am very fortunate to work with such people.

I have some even deeper debts. Conal Condren helped shape my thoughts over a longer period than I can remember, and over numerous lunches, he patiently listened to and shaped the ideas in this book. Quentin Skinner has provided unwavering and unfathomable support over many years. This book builds from the foundation of his work. It is, I hope, an attempt to explore the potential of his methodological ideas. David Armitage has also been a fulcrum for me over three decades. The book began in a conversation between us more than ten years ago in the London Tube. I joined him immediately after having just read some remarkable letters between Twiss and Archbishop Tait in the Lambeth Palace archive. We were so lost in conversation that we went well beyond our station and arrived late for a bad play on Hobbes. Subsequently, he has provided almost daily encouragement and an endless stream of ideas and inspiration. Saliha Belmessous has born the greatest burden of this project, along with Ismaïl Belmessous and Yamin Belmessous. Ismaïl and Yamin have had to listen to Twiss stories for possibly as long as they can remember, and their forebearance has been surpassed only by their humour. Saliha examined the questions with me over many years, and read and corrected numerous drafts of the manuscript. She is the author of my best thoughts, and for that reason, and others, this book is dedicated to her.

KING LEOPOLD'S GHOSTWRITER

Introduction

MY AIM IN THIS BOOK is to explore how nineteenth-century persons experienced and understood metamorphoses of personhood. Each of the personal transformations in this account was connected to one man—the jurist Travers Twiss—and, although the analysis encompasses many persons, two are at the heart of my story. One was a woman, Pharaïlde van Lynseele, who married Twiss and, in doing so, changed herself from a London streetwalker into Lady Travers Twiss. The second was an artificial person, the International African Association, which Twiss helped King Leopold II of Belgium transform into the Congo Free State.

Many Victorians, notably jurists, understood that there were two kinds of persons: natural and artificial. Of course, there were Victorians and others subsequently who thought the idea of artificial persons, or corporate legal personality, to be confusing and misleading. It is true that nineteenth-century English philosophers, notably Jeremy Bentham, dismissed the notion of artificial persons, and it has been argued that the idea suffered a decline from the late eighteenth century.[1] According to this account, the concept of artificial persons was briefly revived in the late nineteenth century by Otto von Gierke. Inspired by German Romanticism, Gierke theorised the real existence of collective fellowships prior to their recognition in law. His work further inspired late-nineteenth-century and early-twentieth-century English legal historians and political theorists, notably F. W. Maitland, the Victorian historian of the common law, Harold Laski, and Ernest Barker.[2] Following this brief

---

1. For the Utilitarians' attack on the concept, see Quentin Skinner, "A Genealogy of the Modern State," *Proceedings of the British Academy*, vol. 162, (2009), 355–356.

2. David Runciman, *Pluralism and the Personality of the State* (Cambridge, 1997). For analysis of the debate over "real" personality versus artificial personality, see Ron Harris, "The Transplantation of the Legal Discourse on Corporate Personality Theories: From German Codification to British Political Pluralism and American Big Business," *Washington and Lee Law Review* (2006), 1421–1478.

revival, the notion of artificial personality is said to have once again declined as it came under attack from philosophers such as John Dewey, the American pragmatist.[3]

What such an account neglects is the fact that the concept of artificial personality flourished amongst lawyers in the nineteenth century, both on the Continent and in England. English jurists sought to respond to and accommodate the critiques of Bentham and his follower John Austin, and in this respect, their thought diverged from their Continental colleagues, but they nevertheless clung to the notion of artificial personality.[4] The concept flourished, in particular, amongst ecclesiastical lawyers, and amongst international lawyers who used it to understand the nature of the state and to think about relations between states.[5] In England, both international and ecclesiastical lawyers were, in common with their Continental colleagues, practitioners of

---

3. John Dewey, "The Historic Background of Corporate Legal Personality," *The Yale Law Journal*, vol. 35, no. 6 (April 1926), 655–673. Dewey was not entirely opposed to the idea of fictitious personality, but believed it became confused with the notion of associations having "real personality."

4. For the response of English international lawyers to Austin, see Michael Lobban, "English Approaches to International Law in the Nineteenth Century," in Matthew Craven, Malgosia Fitzmaurice, and Maria Vogiatzi, eds., *Time, History, and International Law* (Leiden, 2007), 66.

5. On the Continent, the concept of the artificial personality of the state was fundamental for international lawyers from the naturalists early in the century through to the generation of "liberal" jurists of the *Institut de droit international*. See, for example, in Germany, Jean-Louis [Johann Ludwig] Klüber, *Droit des gens moderne de l'Europe*, 2 vols., (Paris, 1834), 32, who argued that when a certain number of people united in a country with a fixed abode, they "formed a state," and their "union is considered to be a moral person"; Johann Kaspar Bluntschli, *The Theory of the State* (Oxford, 1895; first published in German in 1875), 22: "The recognition of the personality of the State is thus not less indispensable for Public Law (*Statsrecht*) than for International Law (*Völkerrecht*)." In France, Paul Pradier-Fodéré, in *Principes généraux de droit, de politique et de législation* (Paris, 1869), 187, argued that a "nation" was united "by ideas, by a soul, by all that makes a moral person"; and Frantz Despagnet, in *Cours de droit international public*, 2nd ed. (Paris, 1899), 77, wrote: "A state has two essential characteristics: juridical personality and sovereignty." In England, the civil lawyer George Bowyer could write: "All persons, whether natural or artificial, that is to say bodies politic, are capable . . . of taking under testamentary dispositions": Bowyer, *Commentaries on the Modern Civil Law* (London, 1848), 134. Travers Twiss, the subject of this study, wrote in his *The Law of Nations* (1884), 152: "De Wolff developed this doctrine more fully, perceiving that Nations were Composite Bodies, having in their collective capacities a Moral Being of their own." In Scotland, James Lorimer wrote of "jural persons, whether natural or artficial": Lorimer, *Institutes of the Law of Nations*, vol. 1 (Edinburgh, 1883), 134. In the Anglophone world, most international lawyers tried to accommodate Bentham and Austin's critiques. Henry Wheaton, for example, in the United States, citing Bentham and Austin, conceded the Utilitarians' point that international law was not law at all in the positive sense because it lacked a legislating sovereign: Wheaton, *Elements of International Law*, 6th ed. (Boston, 1855), 18–19; he nevertheless wrote about such sovereigns in terms that were strongly suggestive of an artificial personality, speaking

the civil law. In their understanding of artificial personality, they followed both Roman law, which had developed the idea in order to give legal status to groups of people, and early modern philosophers, such as Thomas Hobbes, who distinguished artificial persons from natural persons in order to describe the authority and agency of groups or representatives. "A Person," Hobbes wrote, "is he, *whose words or actions are considered, either as his own, or as representing the words or actions of an other man, or of any other thing to whom they are attributed, whether Truly or by Fiction*. When they are considered as his owne, then he is called a *Natural Person*: And when they are considered as representing the words and actions of an other, then he is a *Feigned* or *Artificial Person*."[6] Similarly, F. W. Maitland was able to observe, "Besides men or 'natural persons,' law knows persons of another kind ... Like the man, the corporation is ... a right-and-duty-bearing unit. Not all the legal propositions that are true of a man will be true of a corporation. For example, it can neither marry, nor be given in marriage, but in a vast number of cases you can make a legal statement about x and y which will hold good whether these symbols stand for two men or two corporations, or for a corporation and a man."[7] In fact, even marriage law could have a bearing upon the understanding of certain corporations.

Like Hobbes, Victorian lawyers believed that these two concepts of persons were connected. Their understanding of artificial persons, which included corporations such as the church, companies, and the state, was to a large degree analogically modelled upon natural persons. Their concept of natural persons was also shaped by the broader context in which personhood, natural and artificial, was understood, and so changes to the understanding of artificial persons could also have an impact upon natural persons. For example, when Victorians argued for emancipation, they also argued for the freedom of artificial persons, such as the church, from interference in its affairs by the state, and those debates informed arguments for the freedom of natural persons, as much as the reverse was true. It would seem, therefore, if one wants to understand personhood as Travers Twiss and his contemporaries understood it, that it would be desirable to reconstruct, as much as possible, all the multiple layers of thinking that surrounded that concept. A thorough approach to understanding natural persons could not neglect the broader context of artificial persons, nor could any account of artificial persons ignore the rich material on

---

of the "being of the state," which, in relation to the "society" of states, was "one and the same body" with a "perpetual" existence: *Elements of International Law*, 31.

6. Thomas Hobbes, *Leviathan*, ed. Richard Tuck (Cambridge, 1991), Ch. 16, 80 (111 in this edition). All underlining, italics, and strike-throughs are in the original texts unless otherwise stated.

7. F. W. Maitland, *The Collected Papers of F. W. Maitland*, ed. H.A.L. Fisher, Vol. 3 (Cambridge, 1911), 307.

natural persons. Nevertheless, the many excellent histories of persons, natural and artificial, tend to do precisely that: namely, ignore those broader contexts.

There are, however, some highly suggestive studies of the relations between natural and artificial persons, notably Ernst Kantorowicz's *The King's Two Bodies*. After F. W. Maitland had explored the legal fiction of the artificial person of the sovereign, Kantorowicz argued for the historical importance of the concept, "to bring into agreement the personal with the more impersonal concepts of government."[8] He showed how early modern sovereigns used the mystic fictions of the artificial person of the sovereign to maintain authority in an environment in which the person of the sovereign did not have a monopoly on the use of force nor the institutions to maintain authority available to modern states. Nevertheless, such fictions continued to play a role in maintaining authority into the nineteenth century (not to mention the twenty-first). In some extreme instances, such as of the Congo Free State, the element of fiction was initially more important, particularly to the act of the creation of the person of the state, than any real power. Medieval thinking thereby remained salient well into the epoch we consider modern, and it is perhaps, in this context, less strange that amongst his armory of mystic fictions employed to justify the creation of the Congo Free State from a private company, Travers Twiss appealed to the precedent of the Order of Knights of the Hospital of St John of Jerusalem, which had established sovereignty first over Rhodes and then Malta.

By acting in relation to each other, natural persons form societies. The artificial persons of sovereigns also act in relation to each other and similarly form societies: namely, societies of nations. In creating societies, however, persons natural and artificial establish rules about who can belong, including rules about how persons are created. During the nineteenth century, while those rules were exclusive, they were subject to debate and to changes about broadening membership. In Victorian England, for example, enfranchisement in political society was closely controlled along the lines of property and gender, but those restrictions were progressively liberalised over the course of the century. The categories of political society and the class-based concept of "Society" were closely aligned (albeit that "Society" could include women), and the liberalisation of one encouraged the liberalisation of the other.

One of the rules controlling membership in society, and the nature of membership, concerned how persons are created. There was a difference between a "natural person" in law and what we describe in the twenty-first century as a human being. Thomas Hobbes had written, in the seventeenth century, that natural persons excluded "Children, Fooles, and Mad-men that have no use of

---

8. Ernst Kantorowicz, *The King's Two Bodies: A Study in Medieval Political Theology* (Princeton, 1957), 5; Maitland, "The Corporation Sole," in *The Collected Papers of F. W. Maitland*, Vol. 3, 242–243.

reason."⁹ He was largely following the law with these categories. Women, while possessing personhood, had their legal personality incorporated into that of their husbands when they married. As William Blackstone put it: "By marriage, the husband and wife are one person in law."¹⁰ These rules of inclusion and exclusion persisted into the nineteenth century, but came under pressure to be more expansive. Pressure for the enfranchisement of women was first felt on the question of their separate legal personality, which would enable them, for example, to possess property apart from their husbands.¹¹ These expansions in the creation of natural persons were made by the Married Women's Property Acts of 1870 and 1882.

The judgement of insanity removed legal personality from people in the nineteenth century, but the growing, albeit small, numbers of people in asylums, and the development of state asylums, suggests that sanity was one area in which liberalisation made little progress.¹² The definition of insanity was shifting from a moral to a physiological question, reflected in Britain in the 1845 Lunacy Act, and while there were pressures for due process in the incarceration of allegedly insane people, the same Act removed the right of patients to use the law to contest their detention.¹³ Lunacy set limits upon liberalisation and personal transformations. Michel Foucault may have been wrong about the "great confinement"—his thesis that incarceration in state-run lunatic asylums expanded in the seventeenth and eighteenth centuries, with the rise of the modern state, excluding all who did not fit its definition of reason and enlightenment—but it is self-evident that any definition of liberty in a liberal state will set limits upon inclusion, although in Victorian Britain, proofs of insanity relied upon a very poor science of the mind.¹⁴ Indeed, two of the natural persons who are the subject of this book experienced the threat of losing legal personality through the judgement of lunacy—one was tried but

---

9. Hobbes, *Leviathan*, Ch. 16, 82 (113 in this edition).

10. Sir William Blackstone, *The Commentaries on the Laws of England*, 4 vols. (London, 1876), Vol.1, 418 (Ch. 15, iii).

11. Lee Holcombe, *Wives and Property: Reform of the Married Women's Property Law in Nineteenth-Century England* (Toronto, 1983); Mary Lyndon Shanley, *Feminism, Marriage, and the Law in Victorian England* (Princeton, 1989).

12. Roy Porter, *Madness: A Brief History* (Oxford, 2002), 94–95, 112; Thomas Knowles and Serena Trowbridge, eds., *Insanity and the Lunatic Asylum in the Nineteenth Century* (Abingdon, 2014); W. F. Bynum, Roy Porter, and Michael Shepherd, eds., *The Anatomy of Madness: Essays in the History of Psychiatry: Institutions and Society* (London, 1985).

13. Norman J. Finkel, *Insanity on Trial* (New York, 1988).

14. For problems with Foucault's "great confinement" thesis, notably that asylums prior to the mid-nineteenth century were generally private, see Edward Shorter, *A History of Psychiatry* (New York, 1997), 16–17; Roy Porter, *Mind-Forg'd Manacles: A History of Madness in England from the Restoration to the Regency* (London, 1987), 8; Serena Trowbridge and Thomas Knowles, "Introduction," in Thomas Knowles and Serena Trowbridge, eds., *Insanity and the Lunatic Asylum in the Nineteenth Century*, 3.

acquitted, and the other was incarcerated and lost her life. In each case, the perception of insanity was the cost of personal transformation or, one might say, a cost of overstepping the limits of liberal inclusiveness.

Despite such limits, the understanding of natural personality was expanding within Europe. There was similar pressure to expand the rules governing the creation of artificial persons. While nineteenth-century liberals did much to free individuals, they did not perceive the category of individuals and the rights that attached to them simply to be constituted entirely by natural persons. They were equally, if not more concerned with group personalities, and with the rights which attached to those communities, and when they sought to liberate individuals, they also sought to liberate those groups in their relations to the state as much as they sought to enfranchise natural persons. Since the Reformation, the state had jealously claimed a monopoly over the creation of artificial persons, particularly the church, with all such entities said to be the product of law. European states extended this understanding into the society that existed between them, the society of nations, claiming that they held a monopoly over who could be admitted to their society, while also insisting that all members must be states. In the nineteenth century, however, there was growing debate about whether artificial persons were subject to the state or could have an independent existence.[15] This debate was conducted in particular over religious associations during the course of the century. Within the Church of England, the group known as the Tractarians argued for less control of the church by the state, claiming that the church and its members were answerable to a higher power than the state. Similarly, the emancipation of Catholics and of the Catholic Church within England and Ireland led some to argue that the affairs of the church could be conducted alongside those of the state, and be determined outside the state by the Pope, rather than being subordinate to it. Travers Twiss contributed to these debates, taking the position that the Church of England, and the Catholic Church in England, were subject to the will of the state, reflecting the broader position that all artificial persons are created by the laws of the state. Late in the century, and in the early twentieth century, the "pluralists," led by F. W. Maitland, J. N. Figgis, G.D.H. Cole, and Harold Laski, argued for the rights of associations separately and not dependent upon the state.[16]

---

15. Harold J. Laski, *Studies in the Problem of Sovereignty* (New Haven, 1917); F. W. Maitland, *State, Trust and Corporation*, eds. David Runciman and Magnus Ryan (Cambridge, 2003). See also Runciman, *Pluralism and the Personality of the State*. The second half of the twentieth century witnessed a similar debate about whether natural persons possess legal personality outside the state in terms of their possession of human rights: Mark Mazower, "The Strange Triumph of Human Rights, 1933–1950," *Historical Journal*, vol. 47, no. 2 (2004); Samuel Moyn, *The Last Utopia* (Cambridge, Mass., 2010).

16. Runciman, *Pluralism and the Personality of the State*.

Just as there were arguments for relaxing and broadening the conventions governing both natural and artificial subjects of the state in the nineteenth century, so too was there pressure for the expansion of international society. In the eighteenth century, as sovereign states came to dominate global society, the law of nations made it clear that it would be "ridiculous," in the words of the eminent jurist Emer de Vattel, for any person other than a sovereign to claim membership in that society.[17] In practice, non-state organisations, including the church and chartered companies, such as the Dutch and English East India Companies, continued to wield power on the international stage, often with quasi-sovereign pretensions.[18] Sovereign states, however, jealously guarding their own authority, increasingly sought to restrict such powers in practice as well as theory, and the late eighteenth century and first half of the nineteenth century saw a rapid decline in the powers of those organisations. Questioning of this very restrictive understanding of international society in the nineteenth century included debate over whether non-state artificial persons, such as chartered companies and organisations like the International Red Cross, could be admitted once again to international society. By the twentieth century, this broadening of membership even encompassed natural persons who could be considered subjects of international society by virtue of their possession of human rights.[19]

The move towards a broader understanding of international society also included debates over whether non-European peoples could be admitted to membership. Since at least the sixteenth century, non-European peoples often had been included in the categories of either madmen or children in terms of their legal status. The sixteenth-century Spanish theologian Francesco de Vitoria had famously rejected the notion that non-Europeans were mad, and his judgement was celebrated by nineteenth-century jurists, but he concluded that the same people were very likely in the infancy of their civilisations and

---

17. Emer de Vattel, *The Law of Nations* (Northampton, Mass., 1805), bk. 2, §96. See also Travers Twiss, *The Oregon Territory* (London, 1846), 112–113.

18. For chartered companies with sovereign pretensions or as self-styled "commonwealths," see Andrew Fitzmaurice, *Humanism and America: An Intellectual History of English Colonisation, 1500–1625* (Cambridge, 2003); Philip J. Stern, *The Company-State: Corporate Sovereignty and the Early Modern Foundations of the British Empire in India* (Oxford, 2011); Edward Cavanagh, "A Company with Sovereignty and Subjects of Its Own? The Case of the Hudson's Bay Company, 1670–1763," *Canadian Journal of Law and Society*, vol. 26, no. 1 (2011). For the understanding of various kinds of non-state communities as bodies politic, including companies, church, and cities, see Phil Withington, *The Politics of Commonwealth: Citizens and Freemen in Early Modern England* (Cambridge, 2005). For studies building upon this insight, see Henry S. Turner, *The Corporate Commonwealth: Pluralism and Political Fictions in England, 1516–1651* (Chicago, 2016).

19. Astrid Kjeldgaard-Pederson, *The International Legal Personality of the Individual* (Oxford, 2018), 16–20.

so might be included in the category of children.[20] Victorians were inclined to come to the same conclusion—the infancy of non-Europeans fitted their progressive understandings of history—although they increasingly debated the possibility of admitting legal personality to non-European nations in international society. Nevertheless, just as the liberal state limited membership in the society of natural persons according to the possession of reason (amongst other attributes), so too liberal understandings of international society restricted membership to sovereign persons who were judged to be adult.[21]

These two movements in the transformation of membership of both societies, of natural and artificial persons, involved transformations in the status of the persons who were their subjects. Societies may broaden through two processes: that is, either because the definition of the society itself and who can be a member changes, or because the understanding of the potential member changes. In seeking to understand the expansion of society, we must consider both of these processes. Discussions of the expansion of political society in Victorian England often focus upon expansion of the franchise through measures such as the Reform Bills, which changed the definition of that society itself.[22] The understanding of political society was expanded when the bar of membership was lowered to include all householders in the Reform Act of 1867. A political society could expand, however, without necessarily changing the understanding of that society. Frequently, society expands when persons acquire the qualities that provide membership. Similarly, membership in "respectable society" could be broadened by changes in individuals' possession of the necessary qualities of respectability rather than changes in the idea of respectability itself.[23] The broadening of international society was also

---

20. For the celebration of Vitoria by nineteenth-century jurists, see Andrew Fitzmaurice, *Sovereignty, Property, and Empire, 1500–2000* (Cambridge, 2014), 254–255.

21. There are numerous studies on liberalism and international society. See, for example, Martti Koskenniemi, *The Gentle Civilizer of Nations: The Rise and Fall of International Law 1870–1960* (Cambridge, 2001); Uday Singh Mehta, *Liberalism and Empire: A Study in Nineteenth-Century British Liberal Thought* (Chicago, 1999); Antony Anghie, *Imperialism, Sovereignty and the Making of International Law* (Cambridge, 2005); Duncan Bell, *The Idea of Greater Britain: Empire and the Future of World Order, 1860–1900* (Princeton, 2007); Karuna Mantena, "The Crisis of Liberal Imperialism," in Duncan Bell, ed., *Victorian Visions of Global Order: Empire and International Relations in Nineteenth-Century Political Thought* (Cambridge, 2007); Jennifer Pitts, *A Turn to Empire: The Rise of Imperial Liberalism in Britain and France* (Princeton 2005); Jeanne Morefield, *"Covenants without Swords": Idealist Liberalism and the Spirit of Empire* (Princeton, 2005); and Fitzmaurice, *Sovereignty*.

22. Robert Saunders, "The Politics of the Reform and the Making of the Second Reform Act, 1848–1867," *Historical Journal*, vol. 50, no. 3 (2007), 571–591; Eugenio F. Biagini, *Liberty, Retrenchment and Reform: Popular Liberalism in the Age of Gladstone* (Cambridge, 1992).

23. Michael J. D. Roberts, *Making English Morals: Voluntary Association and Moral Reform in England, 1787–1886* (Cambridge, 2004), 206–207.

as much about who possessed the qualities for membership—for example, whether non-European peoples possessed statehood—as it was about changing the definition of those qualities—for example, whether statehood was a condition.

Given that society could expand through changes in the qualities of potential members, the expansion of any society—political society, respectable society, or international society—would require a certain kind of improvement (or, rather, what was represented as improvement) on the part of those members. For this reason, nineteenth-century European discourse was profoundly concerned with the question of improvement and personal transformation.[24] This book explores both processes of expansion: namely, that which required changing definitions of the various kinds of society, and that which emphasised the improvement and transformation of persons.

Travers Twiss is at the heart of this story. Twiss was not a particularly remarkable intellectual, but he had a long life—from 1809 to 1897—in which he engaged with many remarkable people and events. As a jurist, Twiss was certainly eminent, one of the leading international lawyers of his generation. His career began at Oxford, where he taught at University College. He then moved to a practice in civil law at the Doctors' Commons, the college of civilian lawyers in London. Prior to the college's decline in the 1860s, the jurists in the Doctors' Commons dealt with all matters of ecclesiastical law, including marriage law, as well as the law of nations. From this platform, Twiss was appointed to numerous offices in the church, including Chancellor, or judge, in the Consistory courts of several dioceses, as well as Vicar General, the most senior legal figure, to the Archbishop of Canterbury. Alongside this flourishing practice in ecclesiastical law, he worked in the Admiralty Courts, and in 1867, he was appointed Queen's Advocate General, effectively the Attorney General for international law. Fortunately, he was scrupulous, both as an Advocate in the Ecclesiastical Courts and Admiralty Courts and as Advocate General in the Admiralty Courts, in making copies of all his opinions during his career in the courts, from the 1840s to the '70s, which survive in eight manuscript volumes.[25]

Twiss never, however, reached the heights of male contemporaries such as John Stuart Mill, Thomas Babington Macaulay, Matthew Arnold, or Henry Maine, although he worked with many of the prominent intellectuals and politicians of his time—in England, and in Europe as well, particularly Austria

---

24. The classic study is Asa Briggs, *The Age of Improvement, 1783–1867* (Harlow, 1959), which is concerned not just with the Victorians' own belief in improvement but with what Briggs saw as the reality of improvement in social conditions. For representations of improvement, see Richard Foulkes, *Church and Stage in Victorian England* (Cambridge, 1997), 69–91.

25. [Travers Twiss], *Law Officer's Opinions, 1862–1886*, Harvard Law Library Historical and Special Collections, MS 1110, 8 vols.

and Belgium, and globally. He also had a deep involvement with what might be called London's demi-monde, and he attempted to bridge these different worlds in a number of ways.[26] He and others left a relatively detailed record of his dealings in all the domains in which he associated. His ordinariness is in itself useful.[27] He was an observer of events, although never just an observer—he also actively participated. He studied ideas closely, but he only ever understood them as part of political action. His changes of outlook reflect the tide of political thought in the nineteenth century. Conservatives, liberals, and radicals were polarised in the 1840s, divided between those who believed that reform was necessary and those, such as Twiss, who saw reform as a threat to the order of things. By the 1860s and until the '80s, a consensus between liberals and conservatives had grown, with a broad spectrum of support for reform, and Twiss pursued the new possibilities in a number of ways.

My account does not focus upon Twiss alone. Rather, it examines his web of relations with other persons and the transformations of those persons. In the first half of his life, Travers Twiss was ambivalent, at best, about his contemporaries' interest in social transformation. In particular, he was disturbed by the connection between such interest and the liberation of individuals through expansion of the franchise, as well as nationalist aspirations to liberate whole peoples from empires. His concerns about liberation movements reached their height at the time of the 1848 revolutions. He most fully explored his conservative approach to social change through the close friendship he developed with the exiled former Chancellor of Austria, Prince Klemens von Metternich. Metternich had been the architect of the Concert of Europe, which was the product of the Congress of Vienna in 1815, and as such, he was perhaps the most important European statesmen of the first half of the nineteenth century. The purpose of the Concert of Europe was to maintain a balance of the great powers in post-Napoléonic Europe. As far as Metternich was concerned, the cost of the stability and order of that balance would include suppressing liberal movements for change, such as that which exploded in revolutionary France in 1789 and destabilised Europe for the following twenty-five years. The Concert of Europe created a society of states and empires that was closed and resistant to change.

The 1848 revolutions threatened to demolish the Concert of Europe as they unleashed nationalist movements that could permanently alter the composition and balance of the great powers. Those revolutions sought two kinds of freedom: freedom of natural persons, through claims for political

---

26. Kellow Chesney, *Victorian Underworld* (Harmondsworth, 1970), 363. "Nothing formed so close a bond between the underworld and respectable society as prostitution."

27. For the usefulness of "middling figures" in intellectual history, see Emma Rothschild, "Language and Empire, c. 1800," *Historical Research*, vol. 78, no. 200 (May 2005), 209–210.

emancipation of middle- and working-class people, and freedom of artificial persons, particularly in the emancipation of nations within empires.[28] The two struggles were deeply connected, and it was difficult to support one without supporting the other, so that opposing nationalism, for example, would (and did) often also mean opposing the struggle for political rights. As a relatively young jurist, Travers Twiss was a great enthusiast for the stability provided by the Congress of Vienna, and when Metternich sought a collaborator who could voice opposition to the forces of liberalisation and nationalism, Twiss proved to be an enthusiastic partner. Metternich repeatedly stated that the struggle in 1848 and 1849 was the same as that which he had faced in 1813 and 1814: "Everything that we find in the question of Germany today and that is in play more generally in 1849 formed a great subject of meditation for me in the years 1813 and 1814. Everything that presents itself today to the eyes of the masses like a great discovery has for me no other value than strength and weaknesses which I already knew."[29] For ten years, the pair shared their ideas on how to deal with change, as well as their thoughts on all the major events following 1848, through the Crimean War, the Indian Rebellion, and the unification of Italy, and they left an extensive correspondence on those subjects. Fortunately, that correspondence survives in hundreds of letters held in the Bibliothèque nationale de France, Paris, and in Metternich's papers in the National Archives in Prague, and yet, surprisingly, they have been almost entirely ignored by historians, despite the rich portrait they provide of this dramatic period of history.[30]

Twiss frequently urged Metternich, a notorious reactionary, at least to appear to be liberal, or a "liberalist," as he put it. "Will you not," he asked, "add the word liberalist to your vocabulary?" He supported this plea with the apocryphal story that the theologian John Wesley justified the use of popular tunes for his hymns with the response that he "did not wish the Devil"—in this case the liberals—"to have all the good music." In this way, Twiss observed, Wesley "sanctified by use terms hitherto profane."[31] As this advice to the prince suggests, he had a Machiavellian appreciation that appearances in politics were as important as reality. He also proved himself sufficiently flexible in

---

28. Eric Hobsbawm, *The Age of Revolution: 1789–1848* (London, 2010; first published 1962); Douglas Moggach and Gareth Stedman Jones, eds., *The 1848 Revolutions and European Political Thought* (Cambridge, 2018).

29. Metternich to Twiss, Brighton, January 29, 1849, Bibliothèque nationale de France, Fol/ R.D./13810, 41v. See also Metternich to Twiss, Brighton, February 15, 1849, Bibliothèque nationale de France, Fol/ R.D./13810, 58: "Nothing that happens today seems to me to be a novelty. On the contrary, everything sends me back 35 years."

30. Twiss wrote to Metternich in both French and English, while Metternich wrote in French. All translations are mine.

31. Twiss to Metternich, December 2, 1848, National Archives of the Czech Republic, Prague, RAM-AC/ 10/ 774, 88–89.

his early career to support genuine reform in some circumstances, such as at the universities, but in the first half of his life, he nevertheless remained fundamentally conservative in his approach to the expansion of international society, political society, and even London "Society."

Twiss was himself transformed. While, for much of his early life, he held strong conservative instincts, sometimes concealed under the cloak of a liberal, in his later life, he supported events that fully embraced the possibilities of social transformation, and might even be described as radical, and yet he covered such alignments with a cloak of conservatism. His transformation occurred mid-century, corresponding with a broader shift in Victorian culture. Britain in the 1830s and '40s was troubled by religious conflict, with the Tractarian movement struggling for a return to pre-Reformation purity in the established church, as well as greater autonomy of the church from the state, while the enfranchisement of Catholics inspired fears of their disobedience to the state. The 1840s also brought famine, particularly in Ireland, with the repeated failure of crops. The consequent pressure to repeal the Corn Laws, and provide untaxed grain, deepened division between the landed aristocracy and the working and merchant classes of the cities. The revolutions of 1848 raised the possibility that autocratic governments throughout Europe would topple, while, at the same time, they threatened to tear apart the stability that had been established by the Concert of Europe. That wave of revolutionary sentiment was feared in Britain, particularly due to the resurgent demands of the Chartist movement.[32] It has often been argued that these conflicts receded rapidly in the 1850s, and that is true domestically, but conflict remained a serious problem for Britain in its empire and in the international sphere. It was engaged in the dispiriting Crimean War from 1853 to 1856, and just as that concluded, India rose in rebellion against British rule in 1857, while the struggle for Italian unification in 1859, aided by Napoléon III in France, renewed fear of expansionist Bonapartes. Nevertheless, the 1850s saw a shift in mood domestically, and by the early 1860s, the unrest of the previous decades had given way to what has been described as the Age of Equipoise, a time of conversation in politics rather than conflict, and a period in which liberal reform promised to resolve the causes of unrest.[33] Toleration of Catholics progressed, the Tractarian movement collapsed with the conversion of some of its leaders to Catholicism, Prime Minister Robert Peel

---

32. Margot Finn, *After Chartism: Class and Nation in English Radical Politics, 1848–1874* (Cambridge, 1993); John Saville, *1848: The British State and the Chartist Movement* (Cambridge, 1987).

33. Jonathan Parry, *The Politics of Patriotism: English Liberalism, National Identity, and Europe, 1830–1886* (Cambridge, 2006); Boyd Hilton, "Moral Disciplines," in Peter Mandler, ed., *Liberty and Authority in Victorian Britain* (Oxford, 2006), 224–246; W. L. Burn, *The Age of Equipoise: A Study of the Mid-Victorian Generation* (London, 1964); Saunders, "The Politics of Reform."

succeeded in repealing the Corn Laws, and the promise of political reform and expansion of the franchise was offered as a solution to working-class unrest. Under a liberal hegemony, society was to be governed not by the State but by the "moral action of individuals," who were to be guided by moral codes and non-State institutions.[34]

Having been conservative throughout the first fifty years of his life, by the early 1860s, Travers Twiss had embraced the notion that the moral action of individuals was the basis of political society, and he embraced the notion of individual improvement that made changes in the status of persons possible according to such an understanding of society and government. We could, therefore, see his transformation in thinking as symptomatic of the broader shift in mid-Victorian culture. A closer examination, however, of the events which defined his transformation reveals in a very specific way what the moral action of individuals could produce. Aided by Twiss, the actions of the different individuals with whom he engaged led to their own transformations. Those transformations shared common elements, not simply the common element of Twiss himself. Two such events in his life are salient, and they share a striking commonality: namely, while both involve the transformation of individuals through moral action, both pursue moral action in a way that broke the codes by which such action should be constrained.

While Twiss had close ties with many of the most eminent people of his time, figures such as Metternich and the Archbishop of Canterbury, he also had important relationships at the other end of society, amongst people who originated from the poorest classes. Notably, he had important relationships with two women who were at one time prostitutes—Agnes Willoughby and Pharaïlde van Lynseele.[35] Both of these women succeeded in transforming themselves. Lynseele was the daughter of peasant farmers in Belgium. Like many young women of her generation, she was drawn from rural poverty into urban prostitution, and to London, where many Belgian and French

---

34. Peter Mandler, "Introduction" to Mandler, ed., *Liberty and Authority in Victorian Britain*, 18. See also Roberts, *Making English Morals*.

35. There is debate in current scholarship regarding use of the terms "prostitute" and "prostitution." Many feminist historians now prefer the term "sex work," reflecting the contemporary "legitimisation of prostitution as a profession," while also recognising the agency of the women involved, while "prostitute" can be viewed as pejorative. Others, however, argue that in cases where poverty and unemployment force women into the profession—for example, in developing countries—the terms "prostitute" and "prostitution" more aptly reflect situations in which women's choices were constrained. I will follow those historians in using "prostitute" and "prostitution" because, although this book will explore the degree to which these women struggled against constraints and exercised some degree of agency, their choices in Victorian society were nevertheless driven by poverty and dependence. For these debates and the preference for the use of the word "prostitute" in the context of poverty and economic development, see Mina Roces, *Women's Movements and the Filipina, 1986–2008* (Honolulu, 2012), 2–3.

prostitutes worked.[36] There she met Twiss, and she subsequently adopted the persona of a parentless child of Dutch or Polish nobility (depending upon the version) in order to marry him. This book provides an account of her transformation, and of their marriage.

One of the assumptions of this book has been resisted by both social historians and intellectual historians alike: namely, the claim that supposedly elite figures and people from the bottom orders shared ways of thinking and shared concepts and behaviours in ordering the social and political world. It is a mistake to confine intellectual histories to the so-called elites, albeit that literate figures in the past often make the life of the historian easier by leaving clear statements of their thoughts. Moreover, by expanding the scope of intellectual history, we can address one of its greatest shortcomings. While intellectual history has advanced remarkably as a discipline in the past fifty years, it nevertheless remains largely, although not exclusively, confined to coherent, systematic treatises written by men because the great majority of manuscripts and printed texts, prior to the twentieth century, were written by men. If, however, intellectual history can take as its domain "the social imaginary, the complete range of the inherited symbols and representations that constitute the subjectivity of an age," then it must encompass representations beyond those that came from the printing press, including all forms of meaningful action by women.[37]

Women from the past often come to our attention because of their association with scandal, and this is true of Pharaïlde van Lynseele. As Judith Surkis remarked, "sensational stories" generate "troves" of archives.[38] Rather, however, than those scandals placing women on the margin of history, historians such as Natalie Zemon Davis have used the stories of women to place scandal in the "mainstream of history" by providing a bridge between representation and social and political life.[39] In Victorian Britain, prostitutes were often the cause of scandal because they "focused anxieties associated with industrialisation and capitalism more generally": they destabilised gendered understandings of morality; they were perceived as victims and agents, crystallising concerns about free will; and they were believed to carry disease, particularly sexual diseases.[40] In order to

---

36. Judith R. Walkowitz, *Prostitution and Victorian Society: Women, Class, and the State* (Cambridge, 1980); Judith R. Walkowitz, *City of Dreadful Delight: Narratives of Sexual Danger in Late-Victorian London* (Chicago, 1992), 22–23; Deborah Epstein Nord, *Walking the Victorian Streets: Women, Representation and the City* (Ithaca, 1995).

37. Quentin Skinner, "Motives, Intention, and Interpretation," in Skinner, *Visions of Politics. Vol. 1: Regarding Method* (Cambridge, 2002), 102.

38. Judith Surkis, "Of Scandals and Supplements: Relating Intellectual and Cultural History," in Darrin M. McMahon and Samuel Moyn, eds., *Rethinking Modern European Intellectual History* (Oxford, 2014), 94–95.

39. Surkis, "Of Scandals and Supplements," 94.

40. Mary Poovey, *Making a Social Body: British Cultural Formation, 1830–1864* (Chicago, 1995), 88.

evade prosecution and incarceration, prostitutes were adept at creating multiple identities, including several aliases and numerous addresses—both strategies that Lynseele had employed. Indeed, prostitutes invented new personalities for their very survival, while lawyers did so to create the fictions upon which the law depends. Where prostitutes surpassed lawyers was in their ability to perform this creative task outside the codes that governed society, or at least outside the codes of the law and polite society. In Lynseele's multiple personalities, Twiss encountered someone who ignored the trammels of social codes.

Lynseele and Twiss seized upon the potential for her metamorphosis from a streetwalker into a member of Victorian Society, a "lady by blood," as Twiss would later describe her. Even if the liberal spirit of the time inspired such an idea, it did not extend to welcoming prostitutes into Society. Lynseele and Twiss understood that artifice was necessary to enact transformation. The representation of a woman who was a Belgian-born prostitute as a Polish (or Dutch) noblewoman might well be classified as one of the notorious instances of imposture that are common to all ages but seemed to fascinate Victorians in particular.[41] It might not, that is, be described within the scope of moral action that aimed at emancipation or the improvement of the individual. One reason, however, that Victorians were so fond of such stories of imposture was that they were a species of the broader phenomenon of transformation which was so important to improvement. Imposters did not usually describe themselves as such—they were social climbers, seeking advancement (and for this reason, in part, I will avoid the language of imposture, as it was generally not employed in reference to Lynseele). Their main objective was to change their status rather than to deceive, but in order to do this they were obliged to break social codes. Deception was their method rather than their end. Victorian liberalism and scepticism of government did not unleash a state of license—society was governed by strict codes, including those based on class. Individuals at the bottom of society sometimes had to break those codes if they wished to rise to the top. The same restrictions applied when people in higher social classes, including at least one person in this study, wished to descend.[42]

---

41. Rohan McWilliam, "Unauthorised Identities: The Imposter, the Fake and the Secret History in Nineteenth-Century Britain," in Margot Finn, Michael Lobban, and Jenny Bourne Taylor, eds., *Legitimacy and Illegitimacy in Nineteenth-Century Law, Literature and History* (Basingstoke, 2010), 67–92; Rohan McWilliam, *The Tichborne Claimant: A Victorian Sensation* (London, 2007); Diane Atkinson, *Love and Dirt: The Marriage of Arthur Munby and Hannah Cullwick* (London, 2004); Kirsten McKenzie, *Imperial Underworld: An Escaped Convict and the Transformation of the British Colonial Order* (Cambridge, 2016). See also Natalie Zemon Davis, *The Return of Martin Guerre* (Cambridge, Mass., 1984).

42. For the tensions created by deliberate social descent, often through the performance of false identities, see Seth Koven, *Slumming: Sexual and Social Politics in Victorian London* (Princeton, 2004).

Breaking codes came with a social cost, and most people who pursued such a course tried to hide their actions.

The reinvention of Pharaïlde van Lynseele involved multiple layers of proofs, including the performance of rituals, around the marriage and her presentation to Society, that were essential to the creation of a new person. Lynseele and Twiss travelled separately to Dresden in 1862, where they married in the chapel of the British Legation, away from the public gaze.[43] Twiss was aware that marriages in legations were not subject to the same proofs of identity that were required in consulates by the Consular Marriage Act of 1849. There was no need for prior residence in the parish or a public declaration of the marriage. He knew this because he was Chancellor, the most senior legal officer, of the Consistory Court of the Diocese of London, the diocese that was responsible for chaplaincies on the continent. Proving the adage that the poacher makes the best gamekeeper, he subsequently sat on the 1868 Royal Commission on the Law of Marriage, which recommended closing the loophole.[44] Once married, Lynseele was transformed into a new legal person. Under the law of coverture, her legal personality was "incorporated," as William Blackstone put it, with that of her husband.[45]

When Mrs Twiss returned to London, she successfully joined Society. She was introduced to the Court of St James on May 16, 1863, and was presented by Lady Lucy Alcock to the Princess of Wales, who was standing in for the Queen, still in mourning for the death of Albert.[46] In 1867, on accepting the position of Queen's Advocate, Twiss was knighted.[47] Lady Twiss, as she was now, was again presented at court, completing her admission to social personality. Lynseele and Twiss had brilliantly, almost flawlessly, orchestrated her transformation into a member of Society. One of Lynseele's former clients, however, a poor lawyer called Alexander Chaffers, publicly denounced her as a prostitute. When Twiss and Lynseele's suit against him for libel collapsed in 1872, they were ruined, and Twiss was obliged to resign all of his many public offices.

It is difficult to explain why the couple, despite having taken great care with the reinvention of Lynseele, had pursued a course that was so dangerous not only for Twiss himself but also for Lynseele. It was not uncommon for men to have affective relationships with their mistresses, so emotion alone does not explain the need for the change in status. The moment of Lynseele's

---

43. "Certificate of Marriage for Travers Twiss and Pharaïlde Rosalinde van Linseele, August 29, 1862," National Archives, London, *General Register Office: Miscellaneous Foreign Marriage Returns*, Class: RG 34; Piece: 1.

44. *Report of the Royal Commission on the Laws of Marriage, Presented to Both Houses of Parliament by Command of Her Majesty* (London, 1868), 88.

45. Blackstone, *The Commentaries on the Laws of England*, Vol. 1, 418.

46. *The Times* (May 18, 1863), 5; *Morning Post* (May 18, 1863), 2.

47. *Western Daily Press* (August 20, 1867), 2; *Yorkshire Post and Leeds Intelligencer* (November 6, 1867), 3; *Alnwick Mercury* (November 16, 1867), 6.

metamorphosis is important: namely, the period of high liberalism between the 1850s and '70s, a moment of great social emancipation and expansion of the franchise. This was a movement in which all political interests shared— Liberals, Conservatives, Whigs, and Radicals—while disagreeing on the particular forms of emancipation.[48] Twiss's professional life was closely involved in the creation of new artificial persons in law, such as bishops, and questions of metamorphoses, such as the presence of Christ in the host. When he participated in Lynseele's transformation into a noblewoman, he took the phenomenon of social transformation to what was for him a new level, a radical act of creation, but it was an act that was consistent with the broader social and political mood for personal metamorphoses. Placing his behaviour in such a context may be said only to describe the act, rather than explain it, and that may be true, but the aspect whereby this act simultaneously fulfilled a creative impulse and pursued the contemporary concern with liberty may be said to, in fact, give as deep an understanding of motivation as we can expect from any account of social actions.[49]

One reason Victorians were fascinated by myths of metamorphosis was because their creative aspect made change possible in a society which increasingly valorised improvement and transformation. The moment was a time of increasing social mobility not only for men but also for women (for example, with the first of the Married Women's Property Acts, passed in 1870). William Gladstone described the moment as "the age of extended franchises."[50] At the same time, it should be said, measures such as the Contagious Diseases Acts, introduced shortly after Lynseele and Twiss's marriage, could make life for prostitutes and the poor extremely difficult.[51] The acts sought to control venereal disease and, as such, sought to control prostitutes, who were identified as the cause of the problem. Feminists and reformers such as Harriet Martineau and Florence Nightingale condemned the laws, although as Mary Lyndon Shanley has observed, nineteenth-century women's emancipation movements largely followed liberal principles and therefore sought the *legal* emancipation of women but did little to address the poverty of many women and class subordination.[52] For Lynseele, marriage would lead to both her legal obliteration,

48. Saunders, "The Politics of the Reform and the Making of the Second Reform Act, 1848–1867," 571–591; Boyd Hilton, "Moral Disciplines," 224–246; Burn, *The Age of Equipoise*.

49. Skinner, "Social Meaning and the Explanation of Social Actions," in *Visions of Politics: Vol. 1: Regarding Method*, 137.

50. Gladstone, cited in Saunders, "Politics of Reform," 582.

51. Walkowitz, *Prostitution and Victorian Society*; Walkowitz, *City of Dreadful Delight*, 22–23.

52. Walkowitz, *Prostitution and Victorian Society*, 75–77; Helen Rogers, "Women and Liberty," in Peter Mandler, ed., *Liberty and Authority in Victorian Britain*, 137–138; Shanley, *Feminism, Marriage, and the Law in Victorian England*, 12.

under the law of coverture, and to economic and social emancipation. She was prepared to trade her autonomous legal personality as a *feme sole* for material comfort and social elevation. The Married Women's Property Acts of 1870 and 1882 would restore her legal personality in England, but they did not protect her autonomy.

As is frequently the case, however, when examining the lives of people who left few written records of their own, it is more difficult to develop an understanding of Pharaïlde van Lynseele's life than it is to do the same for Twiss. The defamation trial which followed Alexander Chaffers's revelations is one of the most important sources on the life of Lynseele, and I discuss that trial and the events surrounding it in detail. Nevertheless, the reports of the trial and Twiss's own letters do not explain Lynseele's decisions. Accordingly, I have turned to a convention of micro-history whereby we may reconstruct one life by reference to the conventions which prevailed amongst people in similar situations in a similar time and place.[53] In this instance, I have done this by reference to the life of Agnes Willoughby (as she was generally known and generally chose to be known prior to her marriage), or Agnes Rogers. I have chosen Willoughby for this reason but also because she too was a prostitute who had Travers Twiss as her "protector" at one time. There are important differences between Willoughby and Lynseele—differences, in fact, that help shed light on Lynseele's story. But there are also important similarities, notably that Willoughby, too, transformed her status through marriage to an aristocrat. In her case, she did not take the precaution of changing her identity, and the consequence was disastrous for her new husband, William Windham, who was put through an insanity trial by his family in the Chancery Court. The published court record of the trial has been used in some accounts of Willoughby's life. There are further and untapped sources, however, that provide a vast amount of evidence for Willoughby's life and for the trial, and those are the papers of the Windham family in the Norfolk Record Office. The family hired lawyers to investigate both Willoughby and Windham, and their reports, as well as the papers of the various lawyers employed in the insanity trial, an unabridged transcript of the trial, and the letters of the family, of William Windham, and Agnes Willoughby herself, provide a rich account (again, not previously used by historians) of Willoughby's circumstances and the conventions by which her world was governed. They also provide insight into Lynseele's world.

Finally, amongst the people who were important in Twiss's life, I examine his relations with an artificial person, the International African Association, and his role in transforming that corporation into another kind of artificial person: namely, a state, the Congo Free State. King Leopold II of Belgium

---

53. Natalie Zemon Davis, "On the Lame," *American Historical Review*, vol. 93, no. 3 (June 1988), 572–603; "About an Inventory: A Conversation between Natalie Zemon Davis and Peter N. Miller," https://www.youtube.com/watch?v=hwiR3dz4Wg8.

established the Association in 1878 as a purportedly humanitarian organisation for ending the slave trade and bringing "civilisation" to the Congo, which was said to lack that attribute.[54] His real purpose was to create a vast personal empire. The Belgian government wanted nothing to do with his plans, fearing that its neutrality would be endangered. Leopold therefore determined to transform his company into an independent state, rather than a colony. He faced, however, a great obstacle: the system of states established by the Concert of Europe and the Congress of Vienna, and the corresponding understanding of the international order established in the law of nations in the eighteenth century. This society was highly inelastic, virtually closed to the admission of new members.

After he resigned from all his offices in 1872, Twiss vainly sought new roles, discovering that he was blocked from all positions in England. By 1877, however, he had found Leopold II, who needed a lawyer prepared to challenge the prevailing understanding of the international order. Correspondence in the Royal Palace in Brussels shows that Twiss worked for Leopold through the late 1870s and 1880s, laying down the path that could lead to the transformation of Leopold's private Association into a state, a path that triumphed over the very rules of international society that Twiss had championed in the first period of his career. His case rested upon three points. First, he argued for the admission of non-European states to international society (permitting African peoples to cede their sovereignty to private companies); second, he argued for the admission of certain "private corporations," as he put it, to that order (allowing those companies to receive cessions of sovereignty even when the companies were not themselves the agents of sovereigns); and, third, he claimed that such a corporation could be transformed into a new state. Such radical expansion of the understanding of international society necessitated a radical change in the status of an artificial person.

It is important to point out that there were many precedents for European corporations, notably chartered companies, assuming quasi-sovereign powers in the process of European expansion across the globe. Corporations such as the Virginia Company, the English and Dutch East India Companies, and the Hudson's Bay Company had for centuries employed their own armies and waged wars, signed treaties, established their own "commonwealths," and, above all, claimed to have established a certain kind of civil society that we associate with states.[55] In this sense, these corporations were actors in international society. But these "company-states," in Philip Stern's apt phrase, always acted with the sanction of their sovereigns. Sometimes that sanction only came

---

54. Adam Hochschild, *King Leopold's Ghost* (Boston, 1998).

55. For chartered companies as bodies politic, see Fitzmaurice, *Humanism and America*, and Stern, *The Company-State*; Cavanagh, "A Company with Sovereignty and Subjects of Its Own?"

retrospectively—for example, when conquests were approved by sovereigns as *faits accomplis*—but, once these corporations were established, sovereignty always followed. What Leopold and Twiss achieved in their transformation of the International African Association into the Congo Free State broke from this history of European colonising corporations. It was achieved without the sanction of any state. Although sovereign of Belgium, Leopold had acted as a private individual. The Association itself was not acting in Africa with the support of any state. When Twiss and Leopold succeeded in having the Association recognised as an actor on the international stage, the radical nature of this act was that it was unprecedented that a private person—albeit an artificial person—had been recognised as having standing in international society. It augured a dramatic transformation of international society itself in the twentieth century whereby various kinds of artificial persons were recognised to have standing in international society.[56] In this instance, where the law of artificial persons led, natural persons followed. Widening recognition of the status of artificial persons was succeeded by the recognition of the standing of natural persons in international society through twentieth-century human rights discourse.

Twiss's contribution to creating the Congo Free State was not simply discursive. In 1884, Prince Bismarck of Germany, in cooperation with the French, issued invitations to all the powers to come to Berlin to determine rules for the carve-up of Africa without deepening already festering conflicts between the great powers.[57] Britain reluctantly agreed to attend the conference. It assembled a delegation of experts. Twiss had never lost his status as one of the most eminent international lawyers of his generation and now was known for his expertise on Africa as well. What was not clear to the Foreign Office was the degree to which he was working for Leopold (it is only the letters in Leopold's private correspondence that reveal the true nature of Twiss's relationship with Leopold's plans). His recent publications on the status of "Oriental" nations and private associations in international law had been presented as contributions to theoretical debates, not as lawyer's briefs. They were all the more influential for their seeming impartiality. Twiss's old colleague and friend Lord Granville, who was once more Foreign Secretary, accordingly put Twiss forward as the legal advisor to the British delegation to the Berlin Conference,

---

56. For the rise of early-twentieth-century claims of international standing for artificial persons, see Natasha Wheatley, "Spectral Legal Personality in Interwar International Law: On Ways of not Being a State," *Law and History Review*, vol. 35, no. 3 (August 2017), 753–787.

57. S. E. Crowe, *The Berlin West Africa Conference, 1884–85* (London, 1942); Ronald Robinson and John Gallagher with Alice Denny, *Africa and the Victorians: The Official Mind of Imperialism* (London, 1965), 172–177; William Roger Louis, *Ends of British Imperialism: The Scramble for Empire, Suez, and Decolonization* (London, 2006), 75–126.

although he had no official status, possibly because the air of scandal still stuck to him.[58] Twiss gratefully accepted the invitation and the return to the performance of public duties for Britain. What the Foreign Office did not know, although later suspected, was that Twiss would be working for them *and* Leopold. The interests of the two parties were far from the same. Leopold, and his International African Association, were not invited to the Conference because it remained the case in 1884 that only sovereign states could talk to each other about matters of international life. Twiss's presence at the Conference was therefore crucial to Leopold.

Twiss chaired the committee on the occupation of territory and was in constant contact with the Foreign Office.[59] It quickly became apparent that none of the major powers wanted any of their rivals to gain control over the Congo—a territory the size of Western Europe itself. Bismarck accordingly realised that the best way to block the ambitions of all, while at the same time creating an entity that was a threat to nobody (nobody in Europe, that is), was to grant sovereignty to Leopold's company. This required a revision of who could participate in international society, and almost overnight, the great powers embraced Twiss's proposals. The Congo Free State was born. It was not a colony, because it had not been colonised by another state, and it was not quite like any other state either. It was an unfettered liberal individual for, as is now notoriously known, the sole purpose of extracting resources from the Congo, creating an economy in which the butchery of humans was not just an accident but a necessary part of its business. When the question of its constitution arose, Twiss produced one that he had written at Leopold's request the year before.[60] By this time, the Foreign Office realised his double role, but they accepted it phlegmatically.[61] They were not unhappy with the outcome of the Conference, and Twiss had served them well in other important respects. At the same time, he had helped establish a very important precedent in international law. From the late nineteenth century, and throughout the twentieth, private associations, such as the Red Cross, companies, and even individuals, in human rights discourse and in the prosecution of war crimes, progressively came to be accepted as potential subjects of international law. The last quarter of the nineteenth century even saw a resurgence of chartered companies

---

58. Telegram Malet to Granville, Berlin, 12 Nov 1884, National Archives, London, FO 84/1814/310; Granville to Malet, Foreign Office, 14 Nov 1884, National Archives, London, FO 84/1814/ 348.

59. On Twiss as chair of the sub-committee on occupation, see Malet to Granville, 19 January 1885, National Archives, London, FO 84/ 1820/ 58.

60. *Projet. La constitution de l'État—L'Afrique Equatoriale*, National Archives, London, FO 84/ 1814/ 220-221.

61. T. V. Lister, memo, Nov 23, 1884, National Archives, London, FO 84/ 1815/214; Julian Pauncefote, Memo, 6/11/84, National Archives, London, FO 84/ 1814/ 222.

making sovereign claims to territory.[62] The franchise of international society was greatly expanded.

Many contemporary international lawyers described Twiss's arguments as "judicial heresies."[63] The proposals broke the codes of international society. Part of the context for Twiss breaking social codes in the invention of new persons was his experience of his own marriage. Given that nineteenth-century Europeans closely associated the liberation of natural persons and the pursuit of individual rights with the liberation of nations, through nationalist movements, therefore cases of the transformation of the status of natural persons form part of the context for transformations in the status of artificial persons. The ties between these two kinds of personal metamorphoses are, above all, contextual.

Context is fundamental to understanding the meaning of any particular act or event, so we must cast our nets widely in the pursuit of meaning.[64] It has been argued on numerous occasions over the past fifty years that histories of ideas should encompass a broader understanding of context than historians have been inclined to do.[65] The foundational methodological statements for intellectual history following the "linguistic turn" always required breadth, but practice has generally fallen short of theory. Gareth Stedman Jones argued, more than twenty years ago, that "if there is a concept of discourse capable of unifying social and intellectual history it is not likely to develop from the 'new' social theory proclaimed by Foucault and his followers, but rather from an extension of the insights pioneered in intellectual and cultural history."[66] If change has been slow, it may be because, as Chris Bayly wrote, "Many intellectual historians continue to equivocate on the question of how to relate

---

62. Steven Press, *Rogue Empires* (Cambridge, Mass., 2017).

63. See, for example, Louis Delavaud, "La France et le Portugal au Congo," *Revue de géographie* (March 1883); Anon., *Sir Travers Twiss et le Congo: Réponse à la Revue de droit international et de législation comparée et au Law Magazine and Review, par un membre de la Société Royale de Géographie d'Anvers* (Bruxelles, Office de Publicité, 1884); "Politischer Tagesbericht," *Norddeutsche Allgemeine Zeitung* May 6, 1884; "O Congo e a 'Revista de Direito Internacional,'" *La Correspondencia de Portugal* (January 7, 1884); Edward Hertslet, *Private Treaties with African Chiefs*, January 16, 1884, National Archives, London, FO 84/ 1808/ 238–243.

64. I am following Quentin Skinner's argument, in particular, in making this case. The argument that context is fundamental to establishing meaning could be said to be a commonplace of historical practice. Skinner, however, provided a philosophical explanation for why context is fundamental to meaning. See, Quentin Skinner, *Visions of Politics: Vol. 1: Regarding Method* (Cambridge, 2002), in particular "Meaning and Understanding in the History of Ideas."

65. See, for example, Ellen Meiksins Wood, "Why It Matters," *London Review of Books*, vol. 30, no. 18 (September 25, 2008), 3–6.

66. Gareth Stedman Jones, "Anglo-Marxism, Neo-Marxism and the Discursive Approach to History," in *Was Bleibt von Marxistischen Persepktiven in der Geschichtsforschung?* (Göttingen, 1997), 185.

intellectual history to social and political history, for the good reason that this is an enormously difficult enterprise."[67] Such a broader approach is sometimes described as a social history of ideas or a rapprochement between ideological approaches to history and social theory.[68] Robert Darnton sought a similar reconciliation between intellectual and cultural history fifty years ago, using Clifford Geertz's anthropology as the common basis of interpretation, arguing that "digging downward in intellectual history calls for new methods and new materials, for grubbing in archives instead of contemplating philosophical treatises."[69] This study aims to broaden the use of context in the understanding of ideas in the way that such critics have suggested, grubbing in archives *and* dealing with philosophical, and legal, treatises.[70] One might ask what separates such a study from cultural history, particularly given that the two fields can draw upon similar materials and their boundary is unclear.[71] Cultural history will use an artefact, such as a book or a discourse, to identify and understand a deep structure that we call "culture," while intellectual history focuses upon what a person was doing when she or he wrote or spoke. I will avoid, therefore, describing this study as a "social history of ideas," if doing so might suggest that its protagonists shared a "mentality," an unconscious structure of ideas which accounts for the parallels in their inventions.[72] Such mentalities, a question which interested the Annales historians, may well have existed in some form, but what interests me are the conscious responses of the women and men in this story to the problems they faced and the degree to which their thoughts and actions compare, despite the differences of class

67. Chris Bayly, *The Birth of the Modern World, 1780–1914* (Oxford, 2004), 284.

68. Samuel Moyn, "Imaginary Intellectual History," in Darrin M. McMahon and Samuel Moyn, eds., *Rethinking Modern European Intellectual History* (Oxford, 2014), 112–140; William Sewell, *The Logics of History: Social Theory and Social Transformation* (Chicago, 2005); Quentin Skinner, "Motives, Intentions, and Interpretation," in Skinner, *Visions of Politics: Vol. 1*, 90–102. For the term "social history of ideas," see "Theories as Social Action: An Interview with Quentin Skinner," at Collège de France, Books and Ideas, https://booksandideas.net/Theories-as-Social-Action.html: "Many have argued, with some justification, that to concentrate on linguistic contexts is too narrow, and that what is needed is a more social history of ideas." Surkis, in "Of Scandals and Supplements," argues for the complementarity of intellectual and cultural history while resisting their fusion.

69. Robert Darnton, "The High Enlightenment and the Low-Life of Literature in Pre-Revolutionary France," *Past and Present*, vol. 51 (1971), 81.

70. As Darnton did, for example, in his essay on Rousseau: Robert Darnton, *The Great Cat Massacre and Other Episodes in French Cultural History* (London, 1984), 209–249.

71. Peter Gordon, 'What Is Intellectual History," Harvard Colloquium for Intellectual History (2012), https://projects.iq.harvard.edu/harvardcolloquium/pages/what-intellectual-history.

72. For the *"histoire des mentalités,"* see, for example, Lucien Febvre, *Le problème de l'incroyance au XVIᵉ siècle: La religion de Rabelais* (Paris, 1947). For a critique of such an approach, see Carlo Ginzburg, *The Cheese and the Worms: The Cosmos of a Sixteenth-Century Miller* (London, 1980), xix–xxiv.

which they attempted to overcome.⁷³ Carlo Ginzburg observed that his study of a sixteenth-century miller was dealing with a moment in which the gap between the cultures of social classes was widening and the possibility of common aspirations was being crushed.⁷⁴ In this study, by contrast, the central characters were attempting to bridge that gap, and in that context, the parallels in their ideas assume even greater importance. I prefer, therefore, to portray the reconstruction of context in this book as micro-intellectual history. Micro-history takes relatively minute events, or microcosms, and uses them to open up greater questions about history.⁷⁵ As Hamlet observed, "I could be bounded in a nutshell, and count myself a king of infinite space."

One might push back against this justification for micro-intellectual history by pointing out that there are good reasons why intellectual history has focused upon contextualising a canon of coherent systematic treatises which, for specific historical reasons, happen to have been written mainly by men. Political traditions remain meaningful, John Pocock argues, largely insofar as they are self-referential. For Pocock, a body of political thought can only be said to exist when a context "lasts long enough to give discourse some command over itself."⁷⁶ Conversations within and between cultures must be stable and durable in order to produce significant bodies of political thought. I hope to show, however, that, on a question such as the invention of persons, a vital question for political thought, non-canonical sources reveal that these conditions are met. Such sources, therefore, are both contexts and texts in the history of political thought. Pocock had earlier observed, "We need not therefore apologise for the unrepresentative elitism of studying only those readers whose responses were verbalized, recorded and presented. The *mentalité* of the silent and inarticulate majority should indeed be sought after and if possible recovered; it may have important information for us. But the history of *mentalités* is not identical with the history of discourse."⁷⁷ He is right, of course, that it is not the same, but nor was discourse—if by that we understand a conscious system of signs with command over itself—restricted to published texts.

While micro-intellectual history is frequently biographical, it is not biography. It provides an understanding of people who found themselves entangled in the events and ideas of the time in which they lived. An account of their lives can thereby become a perspective upon such events and also upon reasons why they adopted and moulded certain ideas to their purposes. Context enables us to understand the vast vocabulary, conventions, and practices that

---

73. Ginzburg, *The Cheese and the Worms*, xxiii.

74. Ginzburg, *The Cheese and the Worms*, xxiv.

75. Two classic studies are Davis, *The Return of Martin Guerre*, and Ginzburg, *The Cheese and the Worms*.

76. J.G.A. Pocock, "On the Unglobality of Contexts: Cambridge Methods and the History of Political Thought," *Global Intellectual History*, vol. 4, no. 1 (2019), 11.

77. J.G.A. Pocock, *Virtue, Commerce, and History* (Cambridge, 1985), 18.

can be brought to bear in order to understand any particular event, such as the transformation of the status of a person, natural or artificial. As Ludwig Wittgenstein observed, if we wish to understand a thing that we have not previously encountered—for example, a game of chess—we are obliged to bring our entire knowledge of games to bear upon the matter.[78] We must have a concept of games. It will help to have a concept of board games which have pieces. It will also help to have seen other people play board games, "and similar things."[79] Living in a world of such "language games," as Wittgenstein puts it, obliges us to understand all things, and to do all things, through processes of comparison and analogy.[80] Utterances acquire their meaning through association, through our comparison of them, with other things. When we wish to do something new, or to understand something new, we bring our almost infinitely complex store of language games to bear on the matter, searching for resemblances. It is for this reason that contextual intellectual history insists upon the recovery of context in order to understand the meaning of actions in the past. All we should add is that the kinds of things with which we compare in order to understand language games are almost limitless, as Wittgenstein showed, and certainly in cases such as personification, we must consider the strong "family resemblances" between the creation of natural and artificial persons.

In this particular instance, the micro-historical event upon which the rest of the study turns is the metamorphosis of Pharaïlde van Lynseele into a European noblewoman. That moment allows me to ask questions about transformations of persons, natural and artificial, more generally and to shed light upon the role played by transformation in Victorian culture and political thought. It then turns from the metamorphosis of Lynseele to the metamorphosis of the International African Association into the Congo Free State, in which Twiss also had a central role as a lawyer. The argument is that Lynseele's transformation provided part of the context for Twiss's understanding of changes in personhood that he brought to the case of the Congo association. This is not, however, to make a causal argument. We cannot say that Lynseele's transformation caused Twiss to perform a similar transformation in relation to the International African Association, even though the circumstances of the first moment had a causal role in pushing him towards the second. Indeed, while causes may have a role in historical explanation, the more important point made here is that in order to understand what a person meant by a particular action, we need to understand the broader range of discourses which could inform that action. In particular, we should understand discourses that belonged to a similar class

---

78. Ludwig Wittgenstein, *Philosophical Investigations*, trans. G.E.M. Anscombe (Oxford, 1953), 31.

79. Wittgenstein, *Philosophical Investigations*, 31.

80. For language games, see Wittgenstein, *Philosophical Investigations*, 21, 23.

of action as that they were performing.[81] There are connections between the different kinds of creations of persons, natural and artificial, in the lives of the people who performed them, and we, as historians, have ignored them.

Within the particular case of transformations of personal status, there are some very specific connections that Victorian jurists made between their understanding of artificial persons and natural persons. Twiss's marriage and his practice of international law were connected directly. His marriage scandal drove him into Leopold's arms, as the king proved to be the only person who was prepared to employ him in the 1870s and '80s. But there were deeper connections, which lay in the nature of the law itself. Having never been codified, English law contains many anomalies. Prior to, and to some degree even after, the Matrimonial Causes Act of 1857, one of the strangest of those anomalies was that marriage law, as a branch of ecclesiastical law, and the law of nations were unified in the practice of the civil lawyers who resided in the Doctors' Commons. Historians of international law in England have paid insufficient attention to the fact that, prior to the twentieth century, the lawyers who form the subject of their study were mainly employed in the pursuit of ecclesiastical law, and particularly marriage law. International law was a second string to their bows.[82] The reason marriage law and the law of nations were combined in this way was because both, in contrast to most law in England, had a common basis in Roman and civil law. When the Church of England broke from Rome in the sixteenth century, it retained Roman law as the basis of ecclesiastical law, while civil law provided a common language for legal relations between all European nations.[83]

One of the affinities between practicing in both those fields of law was in the creation of new legal persons. Every day in his legal practice, Twiss saw the potential for the transformation and creation of persons. He was responsible for the creation of the new person, or corporation, of bishops and archbishops. He ruled, as an ecclesiastical judge, on the correct interpretation of the creation of the body of Christ from the host. As Vicar General, he issued two-thirds of marriage licenses in England between 1852 and 1872—licenses that would, until the Married Women's Property Acts, transform the legal personality of both husband and wife as they became, as Blackstone put it, an incorporated whole. These were all conventional processes of metamorphoses, condoned and institutionalised by law. When he began to work for Leopold, however, he had to make a case for the metamorphosis of a person, a private corporation, into another kind of person, a state, that was not in any way condoned by law.

81. On cause and context, see Skinner, "'Social Meaning' and the Explanation of Social Action," in Skinner, *Visions of Politics: Vol. 1*, 128–144.

82. An exception is Lobban, "English Approaches to International Law in the Nineteenth Century," 66.

83. G. D. Squibb, *Doctors' Commons: A History of the College of Advocates and Doctors of Law* (Oxford, 1977).

It should be said that the formal conventions of law constitute only part of legal practice. Lawyers also work to a great degree through "informal law," which bridges the gap between the reality of legal practice and the forms of law. Prominent amongst the types of informal law are legal fictions. The jurist A. V. Dicey complained that, prior to reform, in the mid-nineteenth century, "every branch of the law teemed with fictions."[84] As J. H. Baker explained, "The object of legal fictions is that they allow the operation of the law to change while avoiding any outward alteration in the rules."[85] An early-twentieth-century example of legal fiction was the "curious phenomenon of the arranged divorce" prior to the reform of marriage law.[86] With mutual consent as an insufficient ground for divorce, adultery was "stage managed" in cases where it did not actually exist. The husband would be obliged to go through with a "kind of ceremony" with a woman with whom he was not actually having an affair—preferably in a Brighton hotel, if in England—where the act of adultery could be independently witnessed. The use of legal fictions was particularly prevalent until the mid-nineteenth century, when democratic pressure was brought to bear to eradicate such deceits by changes in statute, although fictions remain extremely important to the practice of law.[87] The object of legal fiction, to allow reality to change without outwardly altering the rules, fitted very closely the objective of the fiction of Lynseele's birth and noble heritage. The fiction enabled her, as a working-class woman, to become a part of English Society without altering any rules. It was a case in which the qualities of the potential member changed rather than the understanding of the society itself. While deceitful legal fictions allowed the law to work, they were deceits everybody involved in the theatre of the law understood and in which they participated. Lynseele and Twiss drew upon the practice of legal fictions, but they took such fictions to another level. While there were no obvious precedents in the law of nations for working outside recognised conventions and laws to create what Leopold required, Twiss's participation in the creation of the new person of Lady Twiss was salient. Moreover, Pharaïlde van Lynseele and Twiss had exploited the laws of marriage to facilitate her

84. A. V. Dicey, *Lectures on the Relation between Law and Public Opinion in England during the Nineteenth Century*, ed. Richard VandeWetering (Indianapolis, 2008), 66.
85. J. H. Baker, *The Law's Two Bodies: Some Evidentiary Problems in English Legal History* (Oxford, 2001), 35
86. Baker, *The Law's Two Bodies*, 36.
87. On the prevalence of legal fictions prior to the nineteenth-century reform, see Michael Lobban, "Legal Fictions before the Age of Reform," in Maksymilian Del Mar and William Twining, eds., *Legal Fictions in Theory and Practice* (Heidelberg, 2015), 199: "Very few indeed were those litigants whose case did not rest, in one form or another, on a legal fiction." For the contemporary salience of legal fictions, see Baker, *The Law's Two Bodies*, and Maksymilian Del Mar, "Legal Fictions and Legal Change in the Common Law Tradition," in Del Mar and Twining, eds., *Legal Fictions*, 225–254.

transformation. Following the Married Women's Property Acts, she regained a legal personality.

The eminent jurist Hersch Lauterpacht observed in 1927 that international law developed largely through analogies taken from private law, but we can extend that insight.[88] International law also developed through analogies based upon the understanding that states are persons. This was well understood by the seventeenth century. For Thomas Hobbes, the state was largely modelled upon the image of the autonomous, and aggressive, rights-bearing individual who lived in a state of nature.[89] International society was precisely such a state of nature. In 1849, Twiss had written to his friend Prince Metternich affirming his own Hobbesian understanding of that analogy: "I have always considered the life of the individual man to represent the life of nations."[90] Richard Tuck has observed, "It cannot be a coincidence ... that the modern idea of natural rights arose in the period in which European nations were engaged in their dramatic competition for the domination of the world."[91] The expanded Victorian understanding of the possibilities for personal transformation—the creation of new autonomous individuals—was an inspiration to international lawyers in their understanding of the person of the state. Such states pursued expansion beyond Europe perhaps more aggressively than ever before (with the Congo Free State taking aggression to a new and unfettered level, even for imperial states). In order to do so, they were modelled upon the most radical understanding of the autonomous individual that had been produced in liberal thought. Pharaïlde van Lynseele and the Congo Free State were two such individuals, and their lives would demonstrate the tragic limits as well as the possibilities of the liberal world of personal transformation.

---

88. Hersch Lauterpacht, *Private Law Sources and Analogies of International Law: With Special Reference to International Arbitration* (London, 1927); Randall Lesaffer, "Argument from Roman Law in Current International Law: Occupation and Acquisitive Prescription," *European Journal of International Law*, vol. 16, no. 1 (2005).

89. Richard Tuck, *The Rights of War and Peace: Political Thought and the International Order from Grotius to Kant* (Oxford, 1999), 14–15.

90. Travers Twiss to Prince Metternich, February 6, 1849, National Archives of the Czech Republic, Prague, RAM-AC/ 10/ 775, 103.

91. Tuck, *The Rights of War and Peace*, 14.

PART 1

Travers Twiss

"Nonsense, Steerforth!" I exclaimed. "You don't mean to say that there is any affinity between nautical matters and ecclesiastical matters?" "I don't, indeed, my dear boy," he returned; "but I mean to say that they are managed and decided by the same set of people, down in that same Doctors' Commons."

—CHARLES DICKENS, *DAVID COPPERFIELD*

Travers Twiss in Society

Fanny Walker and Robert Twiss married in 1805.[1] Fanny Twiss gave birth to her first child on March 19, 1809, and he was baptised in St George's Church in Hanover Square, Westminster, on April 15.[2] His name was Travers. His father, Robert Twiss, held degrees from Cambridge in both divinity and law and, on his mother's side, was a descendant of Welsh gentry, the Trevors of Trevalyn Hall, who later became the Travers and had been for centuries one of the most prominent families of Denbighshire County.[3] In the tenth century, Tudur Trevor was son-in-law to Hywel Dda, king of Deheubarth, in South Wales, while Trevor himself was king of the borderlands of North Wales.[4] By the sixteenth and seventeenth centuries, the Trevors had acquired numerous estates, including Trevalyn Hall, Plas Têg, and Brynkynallt, in Wales, and

---

1. Marriage of Reverend Robert Twiss and Fanny Walker, Church of England Marriages and Banns, 1754–1932, London Metropolitan Archives; DL/T/089/002, 678, entry 151.

2. Travers Twiss Baptism Record, London Metropolitan Archives, Church of England Parish Registers, 1538–1812, DL/T/089/005, 118.

3. Arthur Herbert Dodd, "Trevor Family, of Trevalun, Denbighshire, Plas Têg, Flintshire, and Glynde Sussex," *Dictionary of Welsh Biography* (1959).

4. Arthur Herbert Dodd, "Trevor Family of Brynkynallt, Denbighshire," *Dictionary of Welsh Biography* (1959).

Glynde Sussex in England, as well as leading the colonisation of Ireland. Sir Edward Trevor (died 1648) led expeditions in Ireland, while Sir Richard Trevor (1558–1638), a vice admiral, had been governor of Newry, Down, and Armagh. Sir John Trevor (1638–1717) had been Master of the Rolls, a member of the Privy Council, and Speaker of Parliament in the late seventeenth century, although it was said that he was so severely cross-eyed he caused confusion. No member was ever quite sure if he had caught the Speaker's eye and could address the house. Many of the Trevors were judges and bishops. Through Sir John Trevor's children, the Travers family were related to a number of aristocratic and gentry families, including that of the Duke of Wellington (whose mother was Anne Hill-Trevor, great-granddaughter of Sir John Trevor).

Robert Twiss grew up in Trevalyn Hall, where the family had lived since the sixteenth century, but he had no church benefice, no permanent means of income from the church, and was dependent upon the inheritance from his mother, Ann Twiss (born Ann Travers), of an estate in Hoseley, a property southeast of the village of Marford in Denbighshire, northeast Wales, on the England border.[5]

It would seem that Robert and Fanny Twiss were so grateful for this inheritance from Ann (who was also a witness at their marriage), while also anxious to make clear the connection with their gentry family, that they named their first-born son Travers after his paternal grandmother. His baptism is registered as "Travers, son of the Rev. Robert and Fanny Twiss."[6] When Twiss later provided the details for his own biographical entry in Edward Walford's *Men of the Time* (1862), he was careful to state his father's origins in "Trevallyn, Denbighshire," a seemingly minor fact notably missing from all other biographical sketches.[7] His aim here was to underline his genteel background, a common thread in much of what he wrote and did throughout his life, along with using that background

---

5. On Robert, see the entry for "Travers Twiss" in the *Dictionary of National Biography*, ed. Sidney Lee, Vol. 57 (London, 1899), 393.

6. See the baptism record for Travers Twiss at London Metropolitan Archives, St Gabriel Fenchurch, Composite register: baptisms and burials, 1709–1812, P69/GAB/A/003/MS05294. The name Travers Twiss would be a cause for various puns for much of the century. When it was Twiss's job, as Oxford's Regius Professor of Civil Law, to eulogise the candidates for honorary doctorates to audiences in the Sheldonian Theatre with Latin speeches—what were, in fact, raucous occasions, leading to the eventual exclusion of undergraduate students in 1875—the students would take great delight in his Latinisations, responding in one instance to the term "*extraordinarius*" with the shout "*Et cum Travers Twissimus*," and, in some accounts, with "*Traversissimus Twissimus*": "Close of the Grand Commemoration at Oxford," *Morning Post*, June 20, 1863, 5; "The Nemesis of Blackmail," *Brooklyn Daily Eagle*, August 13, 1882, 4; and for the exclusion of undergraduates from the ceremony, see *The Bath Chronicle*, February 18, 1875, 5.

7. See "Travers Twiss to Edward Walford," Doctors' Commons, August 26, 1861, MS letter (author's collection). See also Edward Walford, *Men of the Time: A Biographical Dictionary of Eminent Living Characters, including Women* (London, 1862), 760.

FIGURE 1. A nineteenth-century view of Trevalyn Hall, Denbighshire, by John Preston Neale.*

as a platform for developing webs of relations in arisocratic and genteel circles. Writing, however, to his friend Prince Metternich in 1849, Twiss claimed that he was from Shropshire, just across the border in England. On May 6, Metternich wrote to ask, "Is the Twiss who just died from your family?" Twiss responded, "Horace Twiss who has lately died was well known to me but no relation. His family was from Norfolk, mine from Shropshire."[8] When his father died, he drew attention to his gentility: "I have lost my father about six weeks ago ... he was a noble hearted generous man, one of the old school which is passing away around us and whose example we miss more and more every day."[9] For Metternich, as much as for Twiss, death was also an opportunity to contrast all that was wrong with the world with the virtues of the *Ancien Régime*: "The loss of a father is a hard blow to a son no matter what age he might be. You observed that the deceased was an adept of the 'Old School'; for that reason alone I have regrets at his passing. That School, my dear Twiss, will not perish because it is founded on reason and corroborated by experience."[10]

---

8. Metternich to Twiss, Richmond, May 6, 1849, Bibliothèque nationale de France, Fol/ R.D./13810, 90; Twiss to Metternich, May 10, 1849, National Archives of the Czech Republic, Prague, RAM-AC/ 10/ 775, 285. Why he would claim to originate from Shropshire when his family came from the adjoining county of Denbighshire, across the Welsh border, is unclear.

9. Twiss to Metternich, December 29, 1856, National Archives of the Czech Republic, Prague, RAM-AC/ 10/ 782, 30.

10. Metternich to Twiss, Vienna, January 1, 1857, Bibliothèque nationale de France, Fol/ R.D./13810, 147.

* From J. P. Neale, *Views of the Seats of Noblemen and Gentlemen, in England, Wales, Scotland, and Ireland*, 6 vols. [London, 1819–1823], Vol. 5, 264

Travers Twiss had a sister and two brothers.[11] The family spent a considerable amount of time on the family's North Wales estate, particularly when the children were young.[12] As early as 1809, however, when Travers was born, the family was living in Gloucester Place, Marylebone, in London.[13] Subsequently, they purchased a house at 39 Cambridge Terrace, on the east side of Regent's Park, and by the 1840s, the family was living at 35 Hamilton Terrace, in St John's Wood, North West London (a couple of blocks from Lord's Cricket Ground). Robert Twiss died in 1856 and left both properties to Travers, along with his Welsh real estate (while bequeathing use of the Hamilton Terrace property to Fanny while she remained alive).[14] Strikingly, he also left "to my said son Travers Twiss all my books on the Law of Nations and my three volumes of the Bible and New Testament with D'Oyly and Mant's annotations bound in Russia." It is notable that a vicar without benefice would have a collection of works on the law of nations, although Robert Twiss did have a degree in law, as well as divinity, from Cambridge.[15]

St John's Wood was, and still is, an affluent area, newly populated in the early years of the nineteenth century with freestanding villas rather than the terrace houses more characteristic of central London. Number 35 Hamilton Terrace still stands and is a handsome villa. The family stayed in this house for many years, and as late as 1861, Fanny Twiss lived there with two of her adult children, their families, and four female servants.[16] Travers Twiss, by this time, had reached great heights and had long left the family home. He lived in an "elegant" house in Park Lane, probably the most exclusive address in mid-nineteenth-century London, but much later in life, when he was ruined, he

---

11. His sister, Anne, was born in London in 1813. His brother Richard Twiss was born in 1815 and became a solicitor. According to the 1861 census, he was born in North Wales, presumably on the family estate. Travers's youngest brother, Edward Robert, was born in 1817 and followed his father into the church but died young in 1847. Call Number: DL/T/041/015, Board of Guardian Records, 1834–1906, and Church of England Parish Registers, 1813–1906, London Metropolitan Archives, London.

12. Robert Twiss's will, proved in 1856, reveals that the family kept "real estate" in Flint and Denbighshire until his death, at which time it was passed to Travers Twiss: "I give to my said son Travers Twiss his heirs and assigns for ever all my real estate whatsoever situate in the counties of Flint and Denbigh," Robert Twiss, Last Will and Testament, National Archives; Kew; Prerogative Court of Canterbury and Related Probate Jurisdictions: Will Registers; Class: PROB 11; Piece: 2243, 445.

13. "Travers Twiss," in the *Dictionary of National Biography*, 393.

14. Robert Twiss, Last Will and Testament, National Archives, London, Prerogative Court of Canterbury and Related Probate Jurisdictions: Will Registers; Class: PROB 11; Piece: 2243, 445.

15. "Clergymen Deceased," *Bucks Herald*, December 6, 1856, 3.

16. Her son Richard, now 46 years old, her daughter Anne, who was 48, her son-in-law George Marsden, her 11-year-old granddaughter Fanny: *Census Returns of England and Wales, 1861*, National Archives, London, Class: RG 9; Piece: 90; Folio: 91; Page: 12; GSU roll: 542571.

returned to Hamilton Terrace.[17] We find him there in the 1881 census, albeit at number 71, several doors down from where he grew up, and living with no family members, but with a housekeeper and a cook, both from the same Devon village.[18] The following year, in 1882, Twiss had moved and was living with Lady Twiss at 37 Hamilton Terrace, next door to his family's former home, but the 1889 Electoral Registers placed him again at number 71.[19] He did not die there, however, falling even further and ending life in 1897 in Fulham in a modest terrace at 6 Whittingstall Road.

Twiss was privately educated and then went to Oxford, where he matriculated—that is, where he was formally admitted—at the age of 17 on April 5, 1826.[20] He would remain a fellow until his marriage more than thirty years later. Having taken his degree in classics, he then studied mathematics and law.[21] He took his Bachelor of Civil Law at Oxford in 1835, and on February 19, 1835, he was admitted as a student at Lincoln's Inn. Prior to the 1850s, there was very little formal legal education in England. The common law was learned mainly through apprenticeship in the Inns of Court, and civil law was only taught in a "desultory" manner at Oxford and Cambridge.[22] The reform of this system was something to which Twiss himself contributed. He was admitted to the Bar at Lincoln's Inn in 1840 and became a Doctor of Civil Law at Oxford in 1841.[23] He would also, as we shall see, pursue a parallel career in political economy.

Contemporaries reported Travers Twiss to have a "grand personality" and even to be "a little mad."[24] He was certainly a man of great curiosity and energy, writing at one moment: "There is so much to be seen everywhere that a wise man need not much care in what direction he moves, if he only seeks relocation—only provided that he changes the scene, and breaks through his

---

17. For Twiss's Park Lane house as "elegant," see Goldwin Smith, *Reminiscences* (New York, 1910), 86–87.

18. *Census Returns of England and Wales, 1881*, National Archives, London, Class: RG11; Piece: 165; Folio: 83; Page: 23; GSU roll: 1341036.

19. "The Twiss Libel Case," *Lloyds Weekly*, April 30, 1882, 8; *Electoral Registers*, London Metropolitan Archives, MR/PER/B/045, 176.

20. University College Archive, Oxford, Registrum, Vol. 2, 1729–1842, April 5, 1826.

21. "Church and Universities," *West Kent Guardian*, December 15, 1838, 6: announcement that Twiss gained "Mathematical Honours."

22. Stefan Collini, *Public Moralists: Political Thought and Intellectual Life in Britain 1850–1930* (Oxford, 1991), 266.

23. See the entry for Travers Twiss in Joseph Foster, *Alumni Oxonienses*, Vol. 4 (Oxford, 1891), 1453. "Oxford," *Staffordshire Gazette and County Standard*, April 8, 1841, 4: announcement that, on April 3, Travers Twiss was granted the degree of Doctor of Civil Law on the last day of Lent Term at Oxford. See also Arches Court, Commission for the Admission of Travers Twiss, Doctor of Law, 2nd of November, 1841, Lambeth Palace Library, MS. KKK/11/29.

24. Anon., *Sir Travers Twiss et le Congo*, 39; Lambeth Palace Library Jackson MSS 33 ff.140-1, April 11 1871.

habits."[25] He held numerous offices, in the University of Oxford and the University of London, as well as in the church and in the law. He was known to be a connoisseur of wine and, according to a contemporary newspaper report, "a virtuoso in the matter of sherry."[26] The Bursar's records of University College, Oxford, give detailed accounts of the consumption of each fellow, including tea, biscuits, and wine. The records show that in the 1830s and early '40s, when Twiss was present in Oxford, he consistently consumed more wine than any of his colleagues and often twice as much as the next amongst the fellows.[27] Such consumption may also point to his sociability and hosting of guests. Nevertheless, he enjoyed a drink, writing at one point: "I have never recovered from my visit to the Duke of Nassau's cellar!"[28] Goldwin Smith, who held the Regius Professorship of Modern History at Oxford from 1858 to 1866 and was a fellow alongside Twiss at University College, recounted in his memoirs that he had "quaffed Cabinet Johannisberger" with Twiss in his Park Lane house on the night before his marriage in 1862.[29] The wine was produced on Metternich's German estate, given to him by the Austrian emperor for services performed at the Congress of Vienna.[30] Metternich gave Twiss a bottle of his wine, in turn, "for services to Austria." In the context of Twiss's own commitment to the international order established by the Vienna Congress, it was a richly appropriate reward. Twiss had visited the chateau a number of times and drank its wine regularly, writing at one time to Metternich to say, "I am having friends for dinner tonight . . . I propose that I place on the dinner table the 'Green Seal' [the Riesling] of 1846. It's the first time I will have tasted it since my visit to the chateau."[31]

25. Twiss to Metternich, July 26, 1851, National Archives of the Czech Republic, Prague, RAM-AC/ 10/ 777, 81.

26. *The Dundee Courier and Argus*, May 6, 1872,

27. In 1840–1841, for example, Twiss's wine bill was 30 pounds, 11 shillings, and 10 pence, while the next largest, for Mr Clampton, was 20 pounds, 12 shillings, and 9 pence, Mr Donkin 13.14.3, Mr Faber 10.12, and Mr Shadforth 11.18.7: Bursar's Ledger, 1840–41, University College, Oxford, UC: BU3/F3/19.

28. Twiss to Metternich, July 12, 1851, National Archives of the Czech Republic, Prague, RAM-AC/ 10/ 784, 10.

29. Smith, *Reminiscences*, 86–87. Given that Twiss was married in Dresden, Goldwin Smith may mean to say that it was the night before he left for his marriage.

30. For Metternich and the estate, see Schloss Johanissberg, http://www.schloss-johannisberg.de/en/history.htm.

31. Twiss to Metternich, December 19, 1851, National Archives of the Czech Republic, Prague, RAM-AC/ 10/ 777, 91. The Chateau Johannisberger Green Seal can be found on contemporary menus listed as "Hock." See, for example, the menu of Boston hotel Revere House in 1865, at NYPL Labs, "What's on the Menu?" http://menus.nypl.org/menu_pages/25827. On a subsequent visit to the chateau when Metternich was absent, Twiss reported, "I heard good news concerning the grapes": Twiss to Metternich, September 9, 1852, National Archives of the Czech Republic, Prague, RAM-AC/ 10/ 778, 22.

Twiss also spent many of his evenings dining out. His friend, the journalist Henry Reeve, recorded in his diary, "Dined at [Thomas] Longman's; nobody there but Twiss." The two men accordingly determined to find company and called upon Lady Andalusia Molesworth. Andalusia Molesworth had been a Covent Garden singer but had married Sir William Molesworth, the Radical politician, and had become a successful Society hostess; her guests included William Makepeace Thackeray, Charles Dickens, and Napoléon III, as well as many prominent British politicians.[32] When Twiss and Reeve called on her on the evening of February 23, 1853, Reeve reported that she was "in all the glory of Dukes and Cabinet ministers." Lord Aberdeen's government at the time was a coalition of Peelites, Whigs, and Free Traders, as well as the Radical Molesworth, and Reeve remarked upon the composition of Andalusia Molesworth's guests: "A coalition is an odd thing to see, and one laughed at Lord Aberdeen and Sidney Herbert talking to [Richard] Cobden and Milner Gibson."[33] Twiss's letters show that he enjoyed social life, and he valued the contacts he made with the intellectual and political elite, even while he frowned upon some, such as Cobden.

Twiss was a member of the Athenaeum, a club that combined aristocrats and intellectuals, and he was close to John Wilson Croker, one of its founders, no doubt due in part to Croker's own position as Secretary of the Admiralty.[34] Membership signified entry into the figurative "freemasonry" of the London intellectual elite.[35] Indeed, Twiss was one of the gatekeepers of that freemasonry as he sat on the club's committee for several years. It was a time-consuming but important service: "I had hoped to write a long letter, but have been occupied for several hours on the committee of the Athenaeum in selecting three candidates of distinguished eminence for election."[36] Ordinary members were elected by a ballot amongst the members, but every year nine men "of distinguished eminence in science, Literature, or the Arts, or for Public Service" were appointed by the club's Committee.[37] Many of the most eminent intellectuals of Victorian Britain were members of the club, including

---

32. "Molesworth [*née* Carstairs; other married name West], Andalusia Grant, Lady Molesworth," in *Oxford Dictionary of National Biography* (Oxford, 2019).

33. John Knox Laughton, *Memoirs of the Life and Correspondence of Henry Reeve*, Vol. 1 (London, 1989), 288.

34. Louis J. Jennings, ed., *The Croker Papers*, Vol. 3 (Cambridge, 2012; first published 1884), 231.

35. Collini, *Public Moralists*, 13–16. For a history of the club, see F. R. Cowell, *The Athenaeum: Club and Social Life in London 1824-1974* (London, 1975).

36. Twiss to Metternich, January 30, 1849, National Archives of the Czech Republic, Prague, RAM-AC/ 10/ 775, 72. On a separate occasion, Twiss excused himself to Metternich to say that he had been "very busy all day on a Library Committee of the Athenaeum Club": Twiss to Metternich, December 26, 1848, National Archives of the Czech Republic, Prague, RAM-AC/ 10/ 775, 206.

37. On "Rule 2," see Collini, *Public Moralists*, 13–16.

John Stuart Mill, Matthew Arnold, Henry Maine, J. R. Seeley, Leslie Stephen, and Walter Bagehot.[38]

Twiss was entered in the Book of Candidates for the Athenaeum on September 2, 1837. He was listed as follows: "Travers Twiss DCL Fellow of University College Ox."[39] A second line in different ink, added later, notes: "FRS Professor of Political Economy." The member who proposed Twiss was the sculptor Sir Francis Chantrey.[40] Twiss rapidly assumed an active role in the management of the club as well as being a frequent presence. He served on the General Committee for two terms, from 1848 to 1855.[41] He also made regular donations of his own works to the club's library.[42]

He ate regularly at the club prior to his marriage. Rule 29 of the club stipulated that members could write complaints on the back of their dinner bills, or receipts, and those complaints would be considered by the committee.[43] The members, including Twiss, made great use of this rule, at times writing short manifestos on the back of their bills. He complained about a meal in 1847, a year after the repeal of the Corn Laws and while the Irish Famine continued. The combination of crop failure, the collapse of the railway building boom

---

38. Collini, *Public Moralists*, 13–16.

39. "Travers Twiss," Athenaeum, Candidates Book, 1833-40, Mem/1/1/5, September 2, 1837, 1535.

40. The nature of his ties with Twiss are uncertain, but his presence in Oxford to receive an honourary DCL (Doctorate of Civil Law) may have been a cause of their meeting. Seven years after Chantrey's death, Twiss wrote to Prince Metternich to apologise for leaving Metternich's house in Brighton in haste but explained that he had to dine with Chantrey's widow, Lady Chantrey, at Twiss's hotel, the Bedford, so the ties were personal: Twiss to Metternich, December 26, 1848, National Archives of the Czech Republic, Prague, RAM-AC/ 10/ 774, 143. Chantrey was seconded in nominating Twiss by the antiquarian and bibliophile (a passion shared by Twiss) Sir Thomas Phillipps, who had been a student in Twiss's Oxford college prior to Twiss. Twiss was elected as a member on February 10, 1845, with 110 ayes and 2 blackballs: Athenaeum, Ballots 1843. Mem 1/4/1, Monday 10 February 1845. According to the club rules, "One blackball in ten shall exclude," Athenaeum, Mem 2/13: *Athenaeum. Rules and Regulations, List of Members, and Donations to the Library 1846* (London, 1847), 9.

41. Athenaeum, Minute Book 1854–55. Com 1/14, 200–206.

42. From 1847, when he donated *View of the Progress of Political Economy in Europe since the Sixteenth Century*, to his final year of membership, forty-three years later, in 1889, when he donated his *Le droit des gens ou des nations considerées comme communautés politiques indépendantes. I. Des droits et des devoirs des nations en temps de paix* (Paris, 1887): *Athenaeum. Rules and Regulations, List of Members, and Donations to the Library, 1848* (London, 1849), Mem 2/16, 140; Athenaeum. Donations to the library 1887–1910. Lib 3/1, February 22, 3. Most of the letters Twiss received from the club's committee were listed as "Thanks for presents," probably his books, but his name also appears in "Answer to complaints": Athenaeum, Letter Book, Sec 1/3, 93, 101, 131, 176, 177, 190, 203; Athenaeum, Letter Book, Sec 1/4, 53, 77, 169, 254.

43. Athenaeum, Mem 2/13: *Athenaeum, Rules and Regulations, List of Members, and Donations to the Library 1846* (London, 1847), 19.

of the 1840s, and the failure of numerous companies led to the Panic of 1847, with a plunge in markets. On June 17 of that year, Twiss ate veal and bacon with new potatoes while drinking a brandy and soda. On the back of his bill he wrote: "June 17. I beg with great respect to ask the committee whether it is not rather late in the day, when the markets are falling, to put the members of the club on rations of Stale Bread, and whether the change, though it may lead to a diminished consumption on the part of individual members, will not lead to an increased consumption in regard to the club itself."[44] The cynical but good-humoured tone was characteristic of the manners of other club members, giving an appearance "invariably that of the cool, *suave*, well-bred gentleman," as a satirical account of Thackeray, another club member, put it.[45]

Oxford was the centre of Twiss's early life, but from the 1840s until his fall in the 1870s, the Athenaeum was the hub through which he built his relationships, while in later life he focused upon international law.[46] He used the club to facilitate new offices; for example, Richard Jelf, the Principal of King's

---

44. Athenaeum, Marked Dinner Bills 1846–50, Travers Twiss, 17 June 1847. On December 15, 1849, for example, Twiss ate calf's head and complained that the "dining Room looks rather dark with the diminished lamps" and noted that his view was confirmed by "the opinion of my neighbours at dinner," thereby indicating the sociability of the dining room: Athenaeum, Marked Dinner Bills 1846–50, Travers Twiss, 15 December 1849. A year earlier, on March 6, 1848, at the moment the 1848 revolutions were breaking out, Twiss ate boiled beef, with which he drank port. He wrote on the back of his bill, "I beg to recommend to the committee that the cook be recommended to supply more than two pieces of puddings for the round of boiled beef": Athenaeum, Marked Dinner Bills 1846–50, Travers Twiss, 6 March 1848.

45. Edmund Yates, *Mr Thackeray, Mr Yates, and the Garrick Club: The Correspondence and the Facts* (printed for private circulation: London, 1859), 3.

46. He strengthened his ties in the Inns of Court by nominating a number of colleagues in the Inns, including Charles Cardwell of Lincoln's Inn in 1846 (Twiss's Inn apart from Doctors' Commons); and, in 1849, Arthur Bigge of the Inner Temple (as well as Fellow of All Souls Oxford): "Charles Cardwell," Athenaeum, Book of Candidates, 1841 to 1850, Mem 1/1/7, July 10, 1846, 2669; "Arthur Bigge," Athenaeum, Book of Candidates, 1841 to 1850, Mem 1/1/7, June 28, 1849, 3004. He used the club to reward people he worked with and to create networks of patronage—for example, when he nominated his colleague Arthur Waddilove from the Doctors' Commons for membership (he was elected in 1854), and when he nominated James Parker Deane from the Doctors' Commons (elected in 1854): "Arthur Waddilove," Athenaeum, Book of Candidates, 1841 to 1850, Mem 1/1/7, April 2, 1846, 2619; "James Deane," Athenaeum, Book of Candidates, 1841 to 1850, Mem 1/1/7, April 27, 1846, 2631. In 1857, Twiss proposed Thomas Tristram of the Doctors' Commons for membership, and he was elected in 1869: "Thomas Tristram," Athenaeum, Book of Candidates, 1850 to 1858, Mem 1/1/9, August 15, 1857, 4121. Twiss had two years earlier established Tristram's career and fortune, and he continued to promote Tristram through the Athenaeum. Of all Twiss's colleagues, Tristram would remain closest to him after Twiss was ruined by scandal. Twiss also proposed the more eminent Robert Phillimore for membership in 1865: "Robert Phillimore," Athenaeum, Book of Candidates, 1858, Mem 1/1/11, March 10, 1865, 5218. Given that Twiss had been passed over when Phillimore was made Queen's Advocate in 1862, his proposal indicates either generosity of spirit (consistent with his reputation) or a

College, London, met Twiss at the Athenaeum, and it was Jelf who proposed Twiss for his position at King's College in 1849 when both men were on the committee of the Athenaeum.[47]

Twiss proposed the politician Robert Lowe in 1850 immediately upon Lowe's return to England after several years as a member of the Legislative Council in the colony of New South Wales.[48] Lowe had been a student at University College in the early 1830s, when Twiss had just taken up his fellowship there.[49] His experience of Australia convinced him of the dangers of enfranchisement—he was particularly concerned by the demotic politics and unionism he encountered in Australia—and he became a prominent opponent of the Reform Acts.[50] His conservatism fitted Twiss's own inclinations at this point in his life. Twiss also used the Athenaeum to strengthen his ties with Oxford, proposing a number of fellows for membership.[51] Twiss also used the club to pay his debts within ecclesiastical law—his most lucrative professional practice. In 1869, he proposed James Atlay, the new Bishop of Hereford, as a member of the Athenaeum, and Atlay was duly elected the following day.[52] Since 1858, Twiss had been Chancellor of the Consistory Court of the Diocese

---

clear-eyed understanding that good relations with Phillimore, now listed as an Admiralty judge, were essential to his professional advancement.

47. In 1853, Twiss strengthened his ties at King's when he proposed the College's newly appointed professor of English literature and translator of Norse tales, George Webbe Dasent, for membership. "George Webbe Dasent," Athenaeum, Book of Candidates, 1850 to 1858, Mem 1/1/9, April 10, 1853.

48. "Robert Lowe," Athenaeum, Book of Candidates, 1841 to 1850, Mem 1/1/7, June 14, 1850, 3114. Lowe was elected to the Athenaeum in 1858 when he was noted in the Candidates Book as "Vice President of the Board of Trade," and in that position, he sponsored the Joint Stock Companies Act of 1856. For Lowe's return to England in May 1850, see A. Patchett Martin, *Life and Letters of the Right Honourable Robert Lowe Viscount Sherbrooke* 2 vols. (London, 1893), Vol. 2, 1.

49. Martin, *Life and Letters of the Right Honourable Robert Lowe*, Vol. 1, 20.

50. On universal manhood suffrage as "the norm in the Australian colonies" by 1861, and the pace of colonial reform generally running ahead of Britain as self-government was granted in the 1840s and '50s, see Parry, *The Politics of Patriotism*, 184–191; John Manning Ward, *Colonial Self-Government: The British Experience, 1759–1856* (London, 1976).

51. In 1851, he proposed George Bowen, an Oxford classicist, and James Ogle, the new Regius Professor of Medicine, for membership, although Ogle died before he could be elected: "George Bowen," Athenaeum, Book of Candidates, 1850 to 1858, Mem 1/1/9, December 10, 1851, 3284; "James Ogle," Athenaeum, Book of Candidates, 1850 to 1858, Mem 1/1/9, April 12, 1851, 3217. Ogle, like Twiss, was a supporter of reform at Oxford, while George Henry Sacherval Johnson, the Oxford Professor of Moral Philosophy, whom Twiss proposed for membership in the club in 1853, was, at the time Twiss put him up, one of the Royal Commissioners appointed to investigate reform of the University, an investigation in which Twiss, as we shall see, would play a partisan role: "George Henry Sacherval Johnson," Athenaeum, Book of Candidates, 1850 to 1858, Mem 1/1/9, January 17, 1853, 3453.

52. "James Atlay," Athenaeum, Book of Candidates, 1858, Mem 1/1/11, January 18, 1869, 5685.

of Hereford, and he clearly wished to maintain good relations with the new Bishop responsible for maintaining that lucrative position.

Importantly, the Athenaeum was a means by which Twiss developed his relations with the diplomat Rutherford Alcock, who was elected the year after Twiss.[53] When Alcock married, he and his wife would play a vital, albeit unwitting role, in bringing Twiss's wife into Society. Finally, Twiss used the club to cement the most important relationship of the first half of his life: namely, his friendship with Prince Metternich. When Metternich fled Vienna during the 1848 revolution, he was warmly received in London. On May 2, 1848, the Minute Book of the Committee shows that "Mr Brown" proposed Metternich for an honorary two-month membership (the standard term for visiting overseas members).[54] When Metternich was elected to an honorary membership for a second time, Travers Twiss was the member who proposed him. On April 21, 1849, Twiss wrote to Metternich to say, "Your name will be proposed to the committee of the Athenaeum on Tuesday."[55] Twiss wrote again days later to advise Metternich on club etiquette, as well as to inform him that the club secretary would be happy to "show you over the house."[56] At this moment, Twiss also recommended for membership both Count Colloredo, the Austrian ambassador at the Court of St James, and Count Eduard von Kielmansegge, who had been in the ministry of Hanover until 1848 and was now also an envoy to the United Kingdom. [57] Each of the men had interests in

---

53. "Rutherford Alcock," Athenaeum, Candidates Book, 1833–40, Mem/1/1/5, July 6, 1838, 1720.

54. Four Browns were members of the club at this time, but the likely proposer was Robert Brown, the botanist and Keeper of the Botanical Department at the British Museum, because the committee minutes record that Brown described Metternich simply as a "distinguished patron and promoter of science": Athenaeum. Honorary Members. Rule 13. 1830–1859, 14. Athenaeum: Minute Book. 1848-50, 11.

55. Twiss to Metternich, April 21, 1848, National Archives of the Czech Republic, Prague, RAM-AC/ 10/ 775, 272. The committee minutes for April 24, 1849, recorded that "a letter dated the 19th instant was read from Dr Twiss' recommendation for invitation His Highness Prince Metternich": Athenaeum: Minute Book. 1848-50, 206. Metternich apparently closely associated the club with Twiss because he kept his invitation to membership from the club secretary in the midst of his collection of letters from Twiss: Athenaeum Club to Metternich, April 24, 1849, National Archives of the Czech Republic, Prague, RAM-AC/ 10/ 775, 275.

56. Twiss to Metternich, April 27, 1848, National Archives of the Czech Republic, Prague, RAM-AC/ 10/ 775, 274. See also Twiss suggesting to Metternich that he contribute to the club's library: Twiss to Metternich, October 23, 1849, National Archives of the Czech Republic, Prague, RAM-AC/ 10/ 775, 443.

57. Twiss used the club to bring the three men together, explaining to Metternich, "Should you remain in London tomorrow ... I thought it would add to your satisfaction if you could have the opportunity of meeting Count Colloredo and Count Kielmansegge there [at the club] so I have proposed their names also": Twiss to Metternich, April 21, 1848, National Archives of the Czech Republic, Prague, RAM-AC/ 10/ 775, 272. He noted, "We

a counter-revolutionary political order in Europe and the perpetuation of the Concert of Europe, and Twiss's interest was in furthering that order.

With his friends, Twiss participated in coursing meetings—that is, in hunting with dogs, for example, as a guest, along with Baron William Brougham, of Sir Richard Tufton, Baron Hothfield, of Appleby Castle.[58] He wrote to Metternich: "I have several friends in the country to visit, one of whom I always go to see at this time of year, the representative of a class that does not exist elsewhere than in England. An ancient commoner family, having an ancient manor of Henry VII, with its hall, gallery, chapel, haunted room etc etc. Most of these families have been ennobled or made baronets, but there are some few exceptions and Mr Popham of Littlecote is one of these. He resides in Wiltshire."[59] Twiss was spending time each winter, then, in Littlecote House.[60]

---

are limited to 10 'distinguished strangers'" for temporary club membership. Laying bare his desire to augment his social capital, he added, "If you should see Count Colloredo perhaps you would be so good as to mention the circumstances": namely, of Twiss having been the means of bringing the men together.

58. *Carlisle Journal*, November 7, 1856, 5. Twiss was also a contributor to charities, including the Corporation of the Sons of the Clergy, a charity for children of the clergy who fell upon hard times, of which Twiss was elected governor in 1854: "Corporation of the sons of the clergy," *London Evening Standard*, November 10, 1854, 1. He was an enthusiastic scholar of medieval history, and along with Queen Victoria, he contributed £5 to the preservation of a statue of "Richard coeur de lion," which had been displayed at the Crystal Palace exhibition of 1851, and the sculpture was duly installed in the Old Palace Yard outside Westminster Palace, where it remains: *Morning Post*, June 29, 1853, 1. He was also an active member, and an appointed "Steward," along with famous contemporaries such as Charles Dickens, in the Royal Literary Fund, a charity which financed struggling writers, raising money through annual dinners: For the participation of Dickens and Twiss, see British Library, Literary Fund Anniversary Dinner Papers Loan 96 RLF 4/6: 1842–1843, Box 6; Loan 96 RLF 4/7: 1844–1845, Box 7; Loan 96 RLF 4/8, 1846–1847, Box 8; Loan 96 RLF 4/9: 1848–1849, Box 9; Loan 96 RLF 4/10: 1850–1851, Box 10. On the Literary Fund dinners and the role of Stewards, see Nigel Cross, *The Common Writer: Life in Nineteenth-Century Grub Street* (Cambridge, 1985), 8–37.

59. Twiss to Metternich, December 26, 1848, National Archives of the Czech Republic, Prague, RAM-AC/ 10/ 774, 146–147. Again, in March 1849, he wrote to Prince Metternich to say, "I went down to Littlecote on Saturday and had a day's hunting yesterday": Twiss to Metternich, March 13, 1848, National Archives of the Czech Republic, Prague, RAM-AC/ 10/ 775, 196. His visits to Littlecote at this time were regular, see also Twiss to Metternich, March 31, 1848, National Archives of the Czech Republic, Prague, RAM-AC/ 10/ 775, 243; Twiss to Metternich, July 27, 1849, National Archives of the Czech Republic, Prague, RAM-AC/ 10/ 775, 338; Twiss to Metternich, September 29, 1849, National Archives of the Czech Republic, Prague, RAM-AC/ 10/ 775, 408: "I purpose going to Littlecote for the rest of the break."

60. Popham's was not the only country house that Twiss visited. In autumn 1858, he wrote: "I have just returned from the Highlands of Scotland where I have been passing ten days at Brahan Castle in Ross shire, the seat of the Hon. Mrs Stewart Mckenzie. She is the 'Great Lady' of Scotland at the present time, the original of the Lady of the Lake of Sir Walter Scott": Twiss to Metternich, September 11, 1858, National Archives of the Czech Republic, Prague, RAM-AC/ 10/ 784, 11. He could also be found dining in country pubs, such as

The class which did not exist elsewhere than England was also to be found in Wales: notably, his own grandmother's family of Travers or Trevor. His observation that the Popham family was ancient but had not been ennobled was perhaps partly motivated by the parallel with the Trevors—while Sir John Popham had been speaker of the House of Commons in the sixteenth century, Sir John Trevor had held the same office in the seventeenth. Henry Reeve vividly portrayed the ancient respectability of Littlecote, with Twiss in the scene: "March 22nd [1856]. Went down to Littlecote House, near Hungerford, to see F. Popham. We found there Twiss, the Oxholms [General Valdemar Tully von Oxholm, the Danish ambassador to the Court of St James, and his wife, Marie Sophie Friderikke von Oxholm], and Sir F. Doyle [Francis Doyle, the poet], and had a very pleasant visit till the 25th. The house is the most perfect specimen of a medieval mansion I know in England—with the armour, the buff jackets, the arquebuses, the ghost-chamber, and the fish-ponds of the seventeenth century, all in complete preservation."[61]

Spending time at Littlecote included spending Christmas with his good friend Francis Popham. On December 26, 1854, Twiss wrote to Metternich, "From my address you can see that I am spending some days at my friend, Mr Popham's, in Wiltshire, where we are hunting all the animals [*tous les animaux*]. Today we chased a fox for three and a half hours on horseback."[62] He managed to connect this pursuit of the unfortunate fox with the broader contemporary context: "The fox hunt is the school of the heroes of Barraclava [*sic*.: Balaclava]! What combat! The affair of Inkerman is a veritable Thermopylae." By this time, Twiss had introduced his good friend Popham to his mentor Metternich. Popham was his "travelling companion," and when Twiss made one of his annual autumn tours of the continent in 1854, he travelled with Popham.[63] Initially, they visited Popham's ailing sister in Berlin, but they then came down to the resort town they knew as Marienbad (the Czech town of Mariánské Lázně), which was near to Metternich's Schloss Königswart, or Kynžvart Castle.[64] Popham subsequently maintained

---

the Black Horse Inn in Skipton, Yorkshire, on the occasion of a country fair, although his presence in Skipton may be due to the fact that Richard Tufton was also the proprietor of Skipton Castle: *Yorkshire Gazette*, September 20, 1856.

61. Laughton, *Memoirs of the Life and Correspondence of Henry Reeve*, Vol. 1, 261. Twiss probably came to know the Popham family first when he was Tutor to Francis Popham's younger brother, Alexander Hugh Leybourne Popham, at University College in 1840.

62. Twiss to Metternich, December 26, 1854, National Archives of the Czech Republic, Prague, RAM-AC/ 10/ 780, 40.

63. Twiss to Metternich, Frankfurt, September 10, 1854, National Archives of the Czech Republic, Prague, RAM-AC/ 10/ 780, 28: "I will have the pleasure to present you my travelling companion."

64. Twiss to Metternich, August 9, 1854, National Archives of the Czech Republic, Prague, RAM-AC/ 10/ 780, 20; Twiss to Metternich, September 10, 1854, National Archives of the Czech Republic, Prague, RAM-AC/ 10/ 780, 27. Popham showed his appreciation

FIGURE 2. Wild Dayrell.*

relations with the Metternich circle, and Twiss, as always, relished the role of mediator, writing: "Could you tell Count Paudar that Mr Popham's horse (Wild Dayrell) won at Newmarket against the Duke of Bedford and the Marquis of Exeter."[65] The horse was trained by Popham's hunting groom and achieved notoriety by surprising all expectations with its success.[66]

The horse's name was linked to the ghost story of Littlecote Hall: "If by chance you have a copy in your Vienna library of Sir Walter Scott's poem 'Rokeby' you will find in the notes of the fifth stanza an article on the White Lady of Littlecote Hall, and on the adventures of Wild Dayrell." Henry Reeve recorded that the friends celebrated Wild Dayrell's success with a dinner at Twiss's Park Lane house: "Popham's horse, Wild Dayrell, won the Derby. Dined with him next day at Twiss's."[67]

Popham sent manuscripts from the library of Littlecote as gifts for Metternich: "Mr Popham, who is next to me, asks me to say that he greatly desires to give you a note written by Charles I after the Battle of Reading for the museum of Königswart."[68] He may have judged that Metternich would have been sympathetic to the story of an autocratic ruler under siege from revolutionary forces. Twiss had written to Metternich about Popham's library for some years prior to the first meeting of the two men. In 1849, Twiss stayed at Littlecote in early January.[69] When he returned to London, he wrote to

---

to Metternich by sending gifts, including a "curious specimen of micrography that we can even see without the aid of a strong microscope" for Metternich's niece, the young Countess Pauline Sander, who would marry his son Richard: "I hope Mademoiselle the Countess does not hurt her beautiful eyes looking at it too frequently": Twiss to Metternich, October 28, 1854, National Archives of the Czech Republic, Prague, RAM-AC/ 10/ 780, 38.

65. Twiss to Metternich, October 1, 1854, National Archives of the Czech Republic, Prague, RAM-AC/ 10/ 780, 36.

66. "Wild Dayrell Winner of the Derby," *Bell's Life in Sydney and Sporting Reviewer*, September 8, 1855, 1.

67. Laughton, *Memoirs of the Life and Correspondence of Henry Reeve*, Vol. 1, 331. For horse racing as a pastime that brought the Victorian "underworld" and Society together, see Chesney, *Victorian Underworld*, 334.

68. Twiss to Metternich, December 26, 1854, National Archives of the Czech Republic, Prague, RAM-AC/ 10/ 780, 41.

69. Twiss to Metternich, January 3, 1849, National Archives of the Czech Republic, Prague, RAM-AC/ 10/ 775, 16: "I go to Littlecote near Hungerford tomorrow, and shall return to London on Monday."

* Wikimedia Commons, "Wild Dayrell and Earl of Craven.jpg," https://commons.wikimedia.org/w/index.php?curid=17966292

Metternich, "I hope you and the Princess have not suffered from the cold. It was very severe in the country—no hunting—and we had to amuse ourselves with a *chasse-au-cerf* [a deer hunt]."⁷⁰ He also fished: "I rather think your Highness has tasted some of my friend Mr Popham's trout, through Sir Minto Farquhar [Sir Walter Minto Townsend-Farquhar, a conservative politician]. There is a very curious stream in the garden where there are fish of ten pounds—a brace of which always grace the Waterloo Banquet at Apsley House [the annual celebration at the house of the Duke of Wellington of the defeat of Napoléon, which marked the debut to the Concert of Europe]." Due to the cold, however, Twiss and Popham spent most of their weekend reading manuscripts in the library of the house and, in particular, letters of "the Prince of Orange [William III] and his friends." They then proceeded in an "interesting occupation" of "comparing the account in the letters with Mr Macaulay's narrative." Twiss would have known Thomas Babington Macaulay from living next door to him in the Albany, and possibly also from the Athenaeum, but he was not positive about Macaulay's Whig politics. Macaulay's *The History of England from the Accession of James the Second* was published the previous year, and it provided a Whiggish account of the Glorious Revolution which Twiss and Popham found not to be entirely consistent with William III's letters. These were not the only letters of interest that Twiss uncovered in Littlecote's library. On a subsequent occasion, he wrote that, "on perusing a number of ms. letters at Littlecott," he had come across letters between Sir Robert Southwell and Edward Hyde, 1ˢᵗ Earl of Clarendon, recounting a dinner in which the Earl of Warwick said that "he was the first person who persuaded Charles II to sell Dunkirk to the French." The significance of the story was that it again contradicted Macaulay's Whig account of English history: "The adversary of the Stuarts, Macaulay, writes 'the sale of Dunkirk was justly imputed to him,' i.e., Ld. Clarendon."⁷¹ On yet another occasion, he informed Metternich that, at Littlecott, he had found letters of Richard Cromwell complaining to General George Monck, the leader of the English republic's army, about the debt Cromwell had inherited from his father, England's Lord Protector. Twiss reported that he had "sent off" these letters from the "Cromwellian period" to François Guizot, the former French Prime Minister, who was at that moment living in exile in London as another refugee of 1848.⁷² Guizot had written a number of histories of the English republic, and he was writing more on the subject. He had held ministerial offices throughout the period of the July Monarchy, including several years as Foreign Minister. As Prime Minister of France in the two years

70. Twiss to Metternich, January 10, 1849, National Archives of the Czech Republic, Prague, RAM-AC/ 10/ 775, 21.

71. Twiss to Metternich, October 13, 1849, National Archives of the Czech Republic, Prague, RAM-AC/ 10/ 775, 434–436.

72. Twiss to Metternich, September 29, 1849, National Archives of the Czech Republic, Prague, RAM-AC/ 10/ 775, 410.

immediately prior to 1848, he had collaborated closely with Metternich.[73] They were drawn together by a shared distrust of Palmerston, as well as a concern about Prussian power and Italian unification, and they shared a dislike for republics. Guizot now found himself in exile after the declaration of the French Second Republic. Metternich was very likely to have been the conduit for bringing Guizot and Twiss together.

Twiss took annual holidays on the Continent, usually in autumn or summer.[74] When he grew tired of the noise created by the "incessant passing of carriages" visiting the Crystal Palace exhibition in London, he decided to take a voyage up the Rhine to visit the "glaciers of Switzerland," possibly also motivated by his past writings on glaciers.[75] He also took regular holidays in Brighton, sometimes with his parents.[76] While there, Twiss reported: "I have found much benefit from the change of air. I ride for two or three hours on the downs," and he was surprised by the "highly cultivated valleys."[77] He commonly stayed in the Bedford Hotel. It was one of the most exclusive of the Brighton hotels favoured by aristocrats, but also intellectuals, and it was frequently booked out.[78] Charles Dickens, who said he "didn't in the abstract approve of Brighton," was nevertheless a frequent visitor at the Bedford. He stayed and ate there regularly from 1837 and throughout the 1840s and '50s. This was the hotel where he wrote *Dombey and Son* and where, in December 1848, he finished, according to his letters, *A Christmas Carol*.[79] Twiss stayed at the Bedford from at least 1844 and visited throughout the 1840s and '50s (at the same time that he subscribed, during the 1850s, to the first

---

73. Alan Palmer, *Metternich: Councillor of Europe* (London, 1972), 300–305.

74. See, for example, Twiss to Metternich, September 6, 1854, National Archives of the Czech Republic, Prague, RAM-AC/ 10/ 780, 25; Twiss to Metternich, July 8, 1855, National Archives of the Czech Republic, Prague, RAM-AC/ 10/ 781, 8; Twiss to Metternich, September 20, 1858, National Archives of the Czech Republic, Prague, RAM-AC/ 10/ 784, 14.

75. Twiss to Metternich, July 26, 1851, National Archives of the Czech Republic, Prague, RAM-AC/ 10/ 777, 80. While travelling up the Rhine, he stayed in Deutz, a suburb of Cologne, in the Hotel de Bellevue, and it is likely he was using his publisher John Murray's travel guide, which recommended the hotel as "comfortable, well conducted, airy, and quiet": Twiss to Metternich, August 26, 1851, National Archives of the Czech Republic, Prague, RAM-AC/ 10/ 777, 82; *Handbook for Northern Europe* (John Murray: London, 1848), 65.

76. They rented 1 Oriental Terrace (now Oriental Place), "close to the Bedford Hotel," during August and September 1849: Twiss to Metternich, August 17, 1849, National Archives of the Czech Republic, Prague, RAM-AC/ 10/ 775, 366.

77. Twiss to Metternich, August 22, 1849, National Archives of the Czech Republic, Prague, RAM-AC/ 10/ 775, 380.

78. On one occasion, Twiss and a friend arrived at the Bedford only find that the hotel was "so full" that rooms that they had booked "were not taken for us," so that they were obliged to find another hotel: Twiss to Metternich, December [no date], 1849, National Archives of the Czech Republic, Prague, RAM-AC/ 10/ 775, 456.

79. *The Letters of Charles Dickens*, Vol. 12, ed. Graham Story (Oxford, 2002), 615.

seventeen volumes of Dickens's *Household Words*).[80] He arrived there on Tuesday, April 27, 1858, at the same time as the Prussian ambassador, the Earl of Yarborough, and the Earl of Carnarvon, who was under-secretary of state for the colonies.[81] In August 9, 1853, he arrived at the hotel at the same moment as Countess Colloredo, the wife of the Austrian ambassador. The Countess had previously hosted Twiss, a defender of the Austrian Empire against the 1848 nationalist revolutions, at dinner parties and a ball in her London house.[82] He also travelled to Brighton to visit Metternich during the winter of 1848 and 1849.

Twiss was a member of several eminent societies. He was elected to the Ashmolean Society, the Oxford society for natural history, on December 4, 1843.[83] He was its President in 1844, according to a letter he wrote to the scientist Louis Agassiz on the movement of glaciers, which, Twiss said, was the subject of a forthcoming paper he would give to the Society. Agassiz was the first scientist to propose the idea of an Ice Age.[84] Twiss had previously read papers to the Society on the Roman theatre at Pula, in what is now Croatia, at a meeting of the society on March 4, 1836, which was then published in their proceedings, and a paper in 1842 on the "Sepulchral circles at Carrowmore" in Sligo, Ireland.[85] The two papers demonstrate an early interest in archaeology. In the pamphlet *On the Amphitheatre at Pola in Istria*, Twiss revealed that he had travelled extensively on the continent, examining, amongst other things, amphitheatres in France, Italy (in particular, Verona), and in the Balkans. He argued that these amphitheatres had been constructed earlier than previously thought, probably during the reign of Augustus. He conducted detailed measurements—for example, of seats, walls, and circumference—to show similarities of construction, thus pointing to their joint origin in time, and he compared the dimensions of Greek and Roman theatres.[86] Here he employed his skills in mathematics and his knowledge of classics and ancient history, showing that he was more than just a polymath; these were complementary and connected disciplines.

80. For Twiss's possession of the first seventeen volumes of *Household Words*, between 1850 and 1858, see *Catalogue of a Portion of the Miscellaneous Library of Sir Travers Twiss, Removed from Park Lane* (London, 1873), 24.

81. *Sussex Advertiser*, April 27, 1858, 3.

82. *Sussex Advertiser*, August 9, 1853, 3. For Twiss's visits to Brighton, see also *Sussex Advertiser*, September 24, 1844, 1; *Brighton Gazette*, August 25, 1853, 5; *Sussex Advertiser*, September 23, 1856, 5, listed as "Dr and Mrs Twiss." This is Mrs Twiss, his mother, Fanny Twiss. Robert Twiss, the father, died in 1856.

83. *Oxford University and City Herald*, December 8, 1843.

84. Travers Twiss to Louis Agassiz, January 24, 1843, Louis Agassiz and other correspondence, Houghton Library, Harvard University, MS. Am 1419, seq. 2264–2266.

85. "Irish Antiquities," *The Literary Gazette, and Journal of the Belles Lettres for the year 1842* (London, 1842), 52.

86. Travers Twiss, *On the Amphitheatre at Pola in Istria* (Oxford, 1836), 40.

He was elected to the Royal Society in 1838, regularly attending its meetings. He was, for example, present at the meeting on Saturday, February 21, 1846, in the mansion of the Marquee of Northampton, the Society President, in Piccadilly.[87] Prince Albert attended that meeting, as did Robert Peel, the Tory Prime Minister, and Lord John Russell, the leading Whig who would within months become Prime Minister. The members examined a system of signalling to avoid collisions at sea (a subject upon which Twiss, as an international lawyer, would later write), as well as Arthur Parsey's new compressed-air locomotive, although Parsey would prove to be no more successful as an engineer than he had been as a poet.[88] Three years later, Twiss wrote to Prince Metternich to say, "I was present at a remarkable meeting last night of the Royal Society, when the Archbishop of Canterbury & Lord John Russell (the Prime Minister) were admitted Fellows to the Society."[89] At other meetings of the society attended by Twiss, numerous aristocrats and intellectuals gathered to examine new systems of minting coins, new railway carriage wheels, and recently discovered medieval manuscripts.[90]

Twiss's interest in these meetings was driven by an enthusiasm for participating in the technological improvements and progress that prevailed at the time, but he was also frequently conscious of the connections between technological and political change, including the impact that such change could have on the world of diplomacy in which he was engaged. In 1853, for example, he wrote: "I was speaking the other day with Mr [Charles] Wheatstone, the inventor of the electric telegraph. He told me that, at the moment, we make great improvements in the method, and that in a short time, every government will have a telegraphic line, in every court of Europe, working expressly for the government... and we will be able to communicate with many more cities than we are able to at the moment."[91] When the plans for a trans-Atlantic telegraph cable were nearing a successful fruition in 1858, Twiss wrote, "We have had no adventure since the launching of the Leviathan."[92] This was Isambard Kingdom Brunel's ship the *Leviathan* (soon to be renamed the *Great Eastern*), the largest ship ever built, which Twiss believed would be used to lay the Atlantic cable. With a sceptical eye on the possibilities of improved communication between human communities, he believed that laying the cable would

87. "The Royal Society," *Morning Post*, February 23, 1846, 5.
88. See Arthur Parsey, "Inventors of Unconventional Forms of Motive Power," http://www.steamindex.com/people/unconventional.htm.
89. Twiss to Metternich, January 26, 1849, National Archives of the Czech Republic, Prague, RAM-AC/ 10/ 775, 68.
90. See, for example. "Royal Society," *Morning Post*, April 17, 1848, 6.
91. Twiss to Metternich, June 28, 1853, National Archives of the Czech Republic, Prague, RAM-AC/ 10/ 779, 20.
92. Twiss to Metternich, July 12, 1858, National Archives of the Czech Republic, Prague, RAM-AC/ 10/ 784, 8.

prove to be "as fruitless in regard to its direct object as that of the Tower of Babel." Nevertheless, twenty-seven years later, he would write on the necessity of protecting submarine cables during times of conflict. Those reflections contributed to a distinction he would draw between international, as opposed to neutral, legal spaces, which would prove to be important, in turn, to his argument for the need to internationalise certain rivers, including the Congo.[93]

Whether, however, the *Leviathan* would succeed in laying the cable, Twiss noted, "remains to be seen" (it was, in fact, another ship, the *Agamemnon*, that would perform the task, although the *Great Eastern* would lay a further cable in 1868). Asking Prince Metternich if he already had a "specimen of the cable," he offered, "if not, I will procure a portion for your collection."[94] Wheatstone, who was also involved in the building of the Atlantic cables, may have been his source for the artefact. Metternich responded a short time later to say, "The Königswart museum now possesses a specimen of the trans-Atlantic cable, and it thanks you for your excellent gesture."[95]

In 1853, Twiss was elected a fellow of the London Zoological Society, in which meetings were far less crowded than those of the Royal Society but were nevertheless attended by a mix of aristocrats and eminent intellectuals. He regularly attended its gatherings devoted to the collection of animals and plants from around the world.[96] In the same year, he was elected to the Royal Geographical Society, whose membership also included aristocrats and intellectuals, with the addition of foreign dignitaries and adventurers. On April 4, 1853, Twiss attended a Geographical Society meeting alongside the Poet Laureate Alfred Tennyson, at that moment at the height of his fame, and the Polish explorer Paweł Strzelecki, who had conducted extensive travels in Australia, including the discovery, to European eyes, of its highest mountain.[97] The meeting was largely consumed by discussions of Australian geography and maps. Twiss may well have already known Strzelecki from the Athenaeum, to which Strzelecki was elected in 1846 shortly after Twiss, and he later presented Strzelecki in the ceremony for honorary Doctorates of Civil Law at

---

93. Travers Twiss, "The International Protection of Submarine Telegraph Cables," *Association for the Reform and Codification of the Law of Nations: Report of the Eighth Annual Conference Held at Berne* (1880), 98–105.

94. Twiss to Metternich, July 12, 1858, National Archives of the Czech Republic, Prague, RAM-AC/ 10/ 784, 9.

95. Anticipating Twiss's imminent trip up the Rhine to visit Metternich at his Schloss Johannisberg, he added: "Don't take passage on the Leviathan, but content yourself with a modest steamer. What is certain is that the Leviathan will never reach the terrace of Johannisberg": Metternich to Twiss, Königswart, July 21, 1858, Bibliothèque nationale de France, Fol/ R.D./13810, 165.

96. *The Times*, June 3, 1853, 8; *Morning Chronicle*, June 3, 1853, 6; *Morning Chronicle*, July 11, 1853, 5.

97. "Geographical Soiree," *Morning Post*, April 7, 1853, 3.

Oxford, on June 20, 1860.[98] The following year, Twiss wrote to William Gladstone, at that time Chancellor of the Exchequer in Lord Palmerston's mixed government, regarding their mutual friend "Count Strzelecki." According to Twiss, Strzelecki had "mentioned to me that the idea had occurred to you of neutralizing by an Act of the European Powers the Isthmus through which the Canal must pass." The canal to which Twiss referred was the Suez, for which plans had been made several years previously and for which construction work had recently begun, although completion was ten years away. Twiss observed that he would be happy to share with Gladstone correspondence from Metternich, which Strzelecki had mentioned to Gladstone, in which Metternich had proved to be "a warm advocate of the canal and of its neutralization." Twiss astutely added, however, that "an English statesmen" may "hesitate to promote" the canal because its "effect upon the course of commerce between European and Asia may be prejudicial to the interests of British shipping." If, however, the canal was to be executed, then, he argued, there could be no doubt as to the "political wisdom of neutralising it," whether "we look to the common interests of the whole European family of nations" or to the "private interests of the Ottoman Empire." The neutralisation of Belgium and Switzerland, he continued, had saved the peoples of those countries from the ravages of war and the European powers from mutual hostilities.[99] Twiss's observations were prescient as the European powers would later enforce neutrality upon the canal, albeit briefly. His thoughts on the neutrality of rivers had been shaped by Metternich, and the neutralization of the Danube at the Congress of Vienna would prove to be crucial to his subsequent intervention, in the 1880s, in the debate over the Congo—a debate in which Gladstone would again play a part. For Twiss, neutralization was a means for the projection of European power.

Several years earlier, Twiss and Strzelecki had been present at the Royal Geographical Society's meeting on May 16, 1853, in which discussions were focused upon Arctic exploration in the presence of Captain William Kennedy. Kennedy had commanded the 1851 voyage sponsored by Lady Jane Franklin in search of her husband, John Franklin, who had been lost trying to find the Northwest Passage. Also present at this May meeting was French explorer Joseph René Bellot, who had participated in Kennedy's voyage. The meeting voted Bellot a member of the society in honour of his own impending voyage to communicate with the squadron taken by Edward Belcher to find Franklin.[100] He led the search party, in other words, in search of the search party. In April, Belcher's ships had

98. "University Intelligence," *The Standard*, June 21, 1860, 3. "Count P. de Strzelecki," Athenaeum, Candidates Book, 1841–50, Mem 1/1/7, January 10, 1846, 2562.

99. "Twiss to Gladstone," November 5, 1861: British Library, Gladstone Papers, Add. MS. 44397, fols. 170–171.

100. "Royal Geographical Society," *Morning Chronicle*, May 17, 1853, 5.

become frozen in ice in the Canadian Arctic archipelago. Three months after leaving this meeting in May, Bellot perished in ice in the Wellington Channel, while Belcher made his way back to England without his ships.

The range of eminent people with whom Twiss mixed was impressive and reflected the overlap between London "Society" and the Victorian intellectual elite: an intellectual elite, it should be said, that was drawn from a broad spectrum of professions and was engaged in practical affairs, not one shut off from the world.[101] He regularly attended the Queen's "Levees," ceremonies in which eminent members of government and military were presented to the Queen at St James's Palace.[102] He also regularly attended the presentation of senior clergy and church officials to the Queen.[103] He was a close friend of Archibald Tait, with whom he worked closely when Tait was Archbishop of Canterbury from 1868, although Twiss first worked with him when he was Bishop of London from 1856 and knew him earlier as a fellow at Oxford, where Tait was at Balliol College. He also worked closely with Tait's predecessors as Archbishop, Charles Longley (in office from 1862 to 1868) and John Sumner (in office from 1848 to 1862), with whom he dined at Lambeth Palace in the company of Prince Albert.[104] On Twiss's appointment as Regius Professor of Civil Law at Oxford in 1856, the Prime Minister, Lord Palmerston, presented Twiss again to the Queen.[105] In 1849, when Palmerson was Foreign Secretary, Twiss noted as an aside in a letter to Prince Metternich that "B. was not at Ld Palmerston's on Saturday."[106] He was again a guest at Lord Palmerston and Viscountess Palmerston's house two years later, when the large party included the Duke of Wellington, the man who had helped create the Congress of Vienna order that Twiss championed. Twiss, however, did not agree with Wellington on all issues.[107] Notably, as Prime Minister, Wellington had supported Catholic emancipation, as had Palmerston, a cause to which Twiss was opposed. Twiss also dined at Palmerston's house when he was Prime Minister in 1860.[108]

Twiss was regularly invited to attend dinners and balls at the residences of ministers and foreign ambassadors.[109] Prominent amongst these was

101. On the role of the intellectual in Victorian society, see Collini, *Public Moralists*, 28–29.

102. *London Evening Standard*, March 7, 1850; *Morning Post*, February 27, 1851, 5; *Morning Post*, March 4, 1852; "Her Majesty's Levee," *Morning Post*, March 13, 1856, 6.

103. See, for example, *Oxford University and City Herald*, June 27, 1857, 9.

104. *London Evening Standard*, June 1, 1854, 1.

105. *Oxford Journal*, March 15, 1856 , 5.

106. Twiss to Metternich, March 26, 1849, National Archives of the Czech Republic, Prague, RAM-AC/ 10/ 775, 224.

107. "Fashionable and Political Reunion," *Morning Post*, March 3, 1851, 5.

108. "Fashionable Entertainments," *Morning Post*, July 23, 1860, 5.

109. In 1851, he was a dinner guest of the Lord Chancellor, Thomas Wilde; other guests around the table included three further members of the government, George Howard, the Earl

the Countess of Colloredo (whom he would also have met in the Bedford Hotel in Brighton), wife of the Austrian ambassador, in the early 1850s, and later the Count and Countess D'Apponyi of the Austrian legation in Chandos House; he dined with both numerous times.[110] Twiss wrote a series of publications in support of the Austrian Empire in the late 1840s and early 1850s, at a time when it was being threatened by nationalist revolutions. The ambassador, Count Colloredo, carried letters between Twiss and Metternich when Metternich had returned, in 1852, to his residence in Vienna.[111] When Colloredo left London, he wrote: "Count Colloredo's departure will be regretted."[112] Subsequently, Metternich reproached Twiss for not keeping in close enough contact with Count Apponyi—not close enough, that is, to facilitate ties between Britain and Austria: "I learnt from Count Apponyi that you seldom meet. Please correct that situation. The march of the ambassador's spirit is as straight as your own and contact between two men of such quality is always useful."[113]

The reason Twiss moved in such elevated circles was partly because he held an extraordinary number of offices in various fields, including university, church, and the law. In writing to Victorian biographer Edward Walford on the information he provided for his own entry in Walford's *Men of the Time*,

---

of Carlisle, Henry Petty-Fitzmaurice, the Marquis of Lansdowne, and the solicitor general, Alexander Cockburn, as well as the Belgian and Prussian ambassadors: *Morning Post*, February 7, 1851, 5. He was the guest of another Lord Chancellor, John Campbell, in 1860: "The Lord Chancellor's Levee," *Lake's Falmouth Packet and Cornwall Advertiser*, November 10, 1860, 4. In 1853, he was a guest of the Earl of Clarendon, George Villiers, the Secretary of State for Foreign Affairs, and the Countess of Clarendon, in their official residence in Downing Street: "The Countess of Clarendon's Assembly," *Morning Post*, March 19, 1853, 5. In 1858, he stayed with the Bishop of Carlisle, "Lord Clarendon's brother," to discuss an ecclesiastical controversy, and "Lord Brougham came over from Brougham Hall to dine and talk over the matter on Monday. He was exceedingly wise and in great force and spirits": Twiss to Metternich, July 12, 1858, National Archives of the Czech Republic, Prague, RAM-AC/ 10/ 784, 13. In 1849, he attended the celebration of the opening of the new Prussian ambassador's house, and in 1853, he was present with many nobles and notables at the inauguration of the new residence of the Prussian embassy: "Inauguration of the new residence of the Prussian embassy," *Morning Post*, June 6, 1849, 6; *Morning Post*, February 14, 185, 5. He was also a guest at many other receptions given by the London legations, including the Americans and Swedes: For receptions given by the American legation, see "The American Legation," *Morning Post*, May 31, 1853, 5, and *Morning Post*, June 8, 1853, 5. For the Swedes, see *Morning Post*, March 15, 1860, 5.

110. See, for example, *Morning Post*, December 9, 1852, 5; "Grand All at Chandos House," *Morning Post*, May 27, 1853, 5; *Morning Post*, May 26, 1857, 5; *Morning Post*, July 14, 1858, 5.

111. Twiss to Metternich, November 29, 1852, National Archives of the Czech Republic, Prague, RAM-AC/ 10/ 778, 28; Twiss to Metternich, February 22, 1853, National Archives of the Czech Republic, Prague, RAM-AC/ 10/ 779, 7.

112. Twiss to Metternich, April 5, 1856, National Archives of the Czech Republic, Prague, RAM-AC/ 10/ 782, 7.

113. Metternich to Twiss, Vienna, March 10, 1857, Bibliothèque nationale de France, Fol/ R.D./13810, 152v.

Twiss declared that even he had been obliged to include in his list only the most important offices he had held.[114] His standing in such circles was due in part, by force of publication, to the influence of his voice on many of the most topical issues of his time. Moreover, he did not leave the reception of those publications to chance. Throughout his life, he sent copies of his latest works to influential figures as well as to his club. He corresponded with William Gladstone over many years, and he used that opportunity, on a number of occasions, to recommend his latest publications. In 1850, for example, he sent Gladstone, who was at that time an opposition member of parliament, his latest (anonymous) work on the 1848 revolutions: *Hungary: Its Constitution and Its Catastrophe*.[115] Similarly, four years earlier, in March 1846, he had sent the Prime Minister, Robert Peel, a copy of his work on the Oregon Territory.[116]

Twiss's political allegiances were described variously, with some accounts labelling him a Whig and others a "liberal conservative."[117] The liberal conservative label covers a broad spectrum, but it seems a fairer description of the first half of his career. In 1853, Twiss supported the re-election of William Gladstone, at this time Chancellor of the Exchequer, as one of the two members of parliament for Oxford University (the two universities, Oxford and Cambridge, were still at this time constituencies in themselves).[118] In the same contest, he opposed a "High Churchman, ritual and aesthetic to the verge of Popery."[119] This opposition to the proto-Catholic Oxford Movement would be consistent with his views more generally and would partly explain why he supported Gladstone, who was a defender of the Anglican Church, although Gladstone had agreed, at least until the early 1850s, with the wish of the Oxford Movement to make the established church the "determinant of national truth."[120]

In 1849, Twiss wrote, "I almost regret that I am not in the H. [House] of Commons but I cannot make up my mind to the dependency of a member of Parliament. It is an inversion of the normal order of things—'mind serving

---

114. See "Travers Twiss to Edward Walford," Doctors' Commons, August 26, 1861, MS letter (author's collection) to Edward Walford on his many offices. See also Edward Walford, *Men of the Time*, 760.

115. "Travers Twiss to William Gladstone," June 17, 1850, British Library, Gladstone Papers, Add. MS. 44369, fol. 278. For further letters to Gladstone on Twiss's latest publications, see also, for example, "Travers Twiss to William Gladstone," British Library, Gladstone Papers, Add. MS. 44370, fol. 18.

116. "Travers Twiss to Robert Peel," March 8, 1846, British Library, Peel Papers, Additional MS. 40586, ff.229, 231.

117. *Morning Chronicle*, January 23, 1854, 6.

118. "The Re-Elections," *Evening Mail*, January 12, 1853, 4.

119. *Evening Mail*, January 10, 1853, 8.

120. Boyd Hilton, "Moral Disciplines," in Mandler, ed., *Liberty and Authority in Victorian Britain*, 228.

matter.'"¹²¹ Soon after, however, he decided to stand. In 1854, the second Oxford MP, Robert Inglis, resigned, and Twiss was mooted as a candidate to stand for parliament.¹²² Before he could be asked, however, he appeared in Oxford soliciting an invitation. This was a break with the "old standing precedents" and, complained the *Oxford University and City Herald*, should have been "an effectual bar to any invitation." Nevertheless, the paper continued, "We should be very glad to hear whether he is a Tory or a Radical; for his friends seem to be rather doubtful on that point."¹²³ Twiss withdrew from the competition, "with no small reluctance," allowing the strongly protectionist and conservative Sir William Heathcote to win the contest.¹²⁴ One report portrayed Twiss as neither Tory nor Radical but an "extremist" Whig: "Some gentlemen of extreme views, who are dissatisfied with Sir William Heathcote's Conservative principles, contemplate bringing forward Dr Travers Twiss, of University. Dr Twiss is, as we stated some days ago, a 'Whig and something more,' and we should advise members of Convocation to make themselves fully acquainted with his views before promising him their votes."¹²⁵ Writing about his withdrawal shortly after, Twiss said: "A political party that had fought twice against Mr Gladstone held a grudge [*rancune*] against the government of which he was a member and wanted a candidate who sympathised with that grudge."¹²⁶ Lord Aberdeen's government, from 1852 to 1855, was a coalition of Peelites and Whigs, so the political party to which Twiss referred may be the Tories (with him running initially as an alternative conservative candidate to Heathcote), but it could also be the Whigs, as Gladstone was a Peelite at this time, although the Whigs were a part of the government. Twiss, however, was not strongly protectionist, nor a Free Trader—he believed that both positions were misplaced. "The Corn Law question," he wrote two years earlier, "has gained disproportionate importance from the prejudices of both parties reasoning on wrong grounds."¹²⁷ Not sharing the grudge against Aberdeen's government, he had "beat a retreat before the battle of Hastings and now, *voilà*, I am safe and sane and *nullius addictus iurare in verba magistri* [not

121. Twiss to Metternich, October 4, 1849, National Archives of the Czech Republic, Prague, RAM-AC/ 10/ 775, 414.

122. *Morning Chronicle*, January 17, 1854, 4.

123. *Oxford University and City Herald*, January 21, 1854, 9. See also "Oxford," *Reading Mercury*, January 21, 1854.

124. "Oxford University Election," *Oxford University and City Herald*, January 28, 1854, 9: Twiss declined the offer "with no small reluctance." See also *Inverness Courier*, January 26, 1854, 5. On Heathcote: *Inverness Courier*, January 26, 1854, 5.

125. "Oxford University Election," *Bell's Weekly Messenger*, January 23, 1854, 5.

126. Twiss to Metternich, February 7, 1854, National Archives of the Czech Republic, Prague, RAM-AC/ 10/ 780, 4.

127. Twiss to Metternich, March 3, 1852, National Archives of the Czech Republic, Prague, RAM-AC/ 10/ 778, 17.

obliged to swear allegiance to a master]."[128] He was again mooted for one of the Oxford University seats in 1859, but on that occasion he found himself in competition with the lawyer and politician Roundell Palmer. He again withdrew, possibly because he did not want be a rival to a man he described as a friend.[129] Palmer would go on to become Lord Chancellor and to have a role in Twiss's partial rehabilitation in the 1884–1885 Berlin Conference.[130]

To a large degree, while holding conservative views, Twiss stood apart from political allegiance, and his strongly held beliefs, until the 1860s, predominantly concerned what he believed to be the delusions of liberty, on the one hand, and the threat Catholics posed to the state, on the other. He was frequently sceptical of politicians—for example, when he observed: "Lord P. [Palmerston] will no doubt try to get through the session quietly, but his colleagues are not Solons in legislation."[131] In 1858, his aloofness was reflected in his judgement of the downfall of Palmerston's government: "The Palmerston ministry has come suddenly to an end. Men will agree more readily to destroy than to construct. Mr Gladstone has declined to join Lord Derby in forming an administration . . . The Peelites can hardly count themselves strong enough to act together. The sectional feeling is the predominant feeling of the day. Eclecticism in politics. The 'Girondists' reappear under various forms of political thought but it is essentially the same fault. Utopian theories."[132] While his political views were elusive, they can best be characterised by examining his ideas on some of the broader currents of the times rather than the party politics of England. He supported some moderate liberal reforms, and he was a passionate advocate of constitutional monarchy, but on questions such as rituals in the church, the balance of great powers, the nationalist revolutions of 1848, or, as we have seen, marriage law, he opposed change and innovation. It was later in life, after much upheaval, as we shall see, that he developed some radical ideas.

Twiss built up a very large income from his numerous offices as well as from his work as an Advocate in the Ecclesiastical and Admiralty courts. By the time he had to resign all those offices in 1872, the *South London Press* estimated his income at between £7,000 and £8,000 per year.[133] At the same

---

128. Twiss to Metternich, February 7, 1854, National Archives of the Czech Republic, Prague, RAM-AC/ 10/ 780, 4.

129. Twiss to Metternich, March 23, 1851, National Archives of the Czech Republic, Prague, RAM-AC/ 10/ 777, 52.

130. *Oxford Chronicle and Reading Gazette*, April 9, 1859, 5.

131. Twiss to Metternich, April 5, 1856, National Archives of the Czech Republic, Prague, RAM-AC/ 10/ 782, 6.

132. Twiss to Metternich, February 22, 1858, National Archives of the Czech Republic, Prague, RAM-AC/ 10/ 784, 4–5.

133. *The South London Press*, March 23, 1872, 2.

time, he had inherited two properties in London and real estate in Wales from his father in 1856, but he was nevertheless income-rich rather than asset-rich.[134] His prosperity was dependent upon the maintenance of his offices. He was dependent upon his wit, and reputation, rather than his fortune. In mid-nineteenth-century England, the average income of a successful barrister was approximately £3,000 per year, while those doing "second- or third-rate business" earned between £500 and £1,500 per year.[135] Only half of one per cent of the population maintained an income in excess of £1,000 per year, while £800 was sufficient for a "professional man" and his wife to live in an acceptable, if not "fashionable," neighbourhood of London, employ two servants, and generally "keep up appearances."[136] An eminent intellectual, such as John Stuart Mill, earned £2,000 per year from employment at the East India Company at the height of his career. Oxford and Cambridge fellows, whose duties were very light, earned from 300 to several hundreds of pounds per year, while the position of Tutor, a position Twiss held, could bring as much as £2,000 per year.[137] By any measure, therefore, Twiss was extremely well-off with £8,000 per year, and the size of his income is an indication of how much his wit and reputation served him. Putting this income together was the result of hard work. None of Twiss's offices alone brought a substantial income. In 1851, his fees from his role as judge in the Archdeacon's Court of Canterbury for granting probate were £32 and 10 shillings, while his fees in the Consistory Court of Canterbury were £139 and 12 shillings.[138] From such modest sums, it is clear why he felt the need to multiply these roles across several dioceses. Similarly, his posts at the universities also earned modest sums. In his published letter to the Vice Chancellor of Oxford concerning the study of law at the University, Twiss publicly complained about the insufficiency of his salary as Regius Professor of Civil Law. An annual emolument of £300 per year, he argued, was an unfitting reward for the chair once held by Alberico Gentili. It was, he said, with "some feeling of pain" that he was obliged to acknowledge the University placed "so low a value on the time and labour" of the person who was one of the "most distinguished advocates of the Civil Law Bar."[139]

---

134. Robert Twiss, Last Will and Testament, National Archives; Kew; Prerogative Court of Canterbury and Related Probate Jurisdictions: *Will Registers*; Class: PROB 11; Piece: 2243, 445.

135. Collini, *Public Moralists*, 44.

136. Collini, *Public Moralists*, 37.

137. Collini, *Public Moralists*, 43.

138. *Morning Post*, May 15, 1851, 7. In 1852, he was reported to have again earned £32 for being judge in the Archdeacon's Court of Canterbury, "Ecclesiastical Courts," *Morning Post*, November 16, 1852, 2.

139. Twiss, *Letter*, 24.

Oxford and King's College, London

Twiss's career commenced at university. He signed the admissions register of University College, Oxford, on April 5, 1826, at the age of 17.[140] The following year, on March 27, he was elected to the College's Bennet Scholarship.[141] The Bennet Scholarships differed from other scholarships offered by the College in that they were open to all students, whereas most scholarships specified that students must come from particular schools or counties. A further peculiarity was that only Bennet Scholars could be elected to the Bennet Fellowships. Master and fellows chose carefully from students of outstanding potential, as Bennet Scholars were likely to become senior members of the College. Early on, therefore, Twiss had been identified as a talent and provided with a career path.

He was duly elected to the Bennet Fellowship in 1830 and then faced the choice made by all Oxford fellows over whether to be a resident or non-resident fellow.[142] Non-resident fellows took the small College stipend as a supplement to professions in law, schools, or the church. Twiss chose residency, which offered a career in the teaching and administration of the College. He took this course with great enthusiasm and energy. Over the following dozen years, he held a series of positions in the College, including Moderator of junior and senior undergraduates, Bursar, Senior Bursar, Registrar, Tutor, Praelector in Greek, Praelector in Latin, and Dean.[143] Tutors were key figures in the College, at the centre of its life, responsible for day-to-day contact with students. Moderators and Praelectors gave lectures, the Registrar recorded all events and meetings of the College, and the Bursar kept the College accounts, keeping a ledger of each fellow's costs, including their biscuit consumption, as well as what they earned from student tuition and stipends. Each one of these positions attracted additional stipends.

Twiss gained a reputation as a polymath.[144] He was one of the few men in Oxford to speak German—a knowledge he used in the development of historical and legal methodology—and he became a Public Examiner in classics from 1835 to 1837 and an examiner in mathematics from 1838 to 1840.[145] These

---

140. University College, Oxford, Archive, Registrum, vol. 2, 1729–1842, April 5, 1826.

141. University College, Oxford, Archive, Registrum, vol. 2, 1729–1842, University College, Oxford: UC/ GB3/A1/ 27 March 1827.

142. University College, Oxford, Archive, Registrum, vol. 2, 1729–1842, University College, Oxford: UC/ GB3/A1/ 2/169.

143. Moderator of junior undergraduates for 1831/2–1836/7. Moderator of senior undergraduates for 1832/3–1836/7. Bursar for 1835/6, 1838/9 & 1841/2. Senior Bursar for 1843/4–1846/7. Registrar for 1835/6 & 1838/9. Praelector in Greek for 1837/8–1843/4. Dean for 1838/9–1843/4. Praelector in Latin for 1841/2.

144. Robin Darwall-Smith, *A History of University College* (Oxford, 2008), 348.

145. Joseph Foster, *Oxford Men and Their Colleges, 1880–1892*, 2 vols. (Oxford, 1893), Vol. 2, 30; Darwall-Smith, *A History of University College*, 348.

were the only two subjects prior to the 1850s that could lead students to Honours.[146] He would also later hold chairs of political economy and civil law. On top of these duties, Twiss was a College Tutor from 1836 to 1843. Tutors were selected by the Master and had more contact with the students than lecturing provided. Twiss was appointed Tutor immediately following the elevation of Frederick Plumptre to the Mastership, a position he occupied until 1870. Clearly, Plumptre held Twiss in high esteem, appointing him to the position of Tutor while he was still in his twenties. Plumptre guided the College through an epoch of reform.[147] He promoted Twiss as an instrument for the reform and opening of the College. Twiss introduced new interpretations of College statutes that enabled the selection of the best possible candidates for fellowships, rather than those who were seen best to fit very narrowly defined entry requirements. As a consequence of this avowedly liberal policy, the period in which Twiss was a constant presence in the life of the College, the 1830s and '40s, was one which saw the appointment of a series of highly talented fellows, many of them men who themselves had a reputation as liberal reformers. These included brilliant classicist John Conington, astronomer William Donkin, and two men close to Twiss: Goldwin Smith and Arthur Stanley. Smith, who Disraeli described as "a wild man of the cloister," became Regius Professor of History.[148]

Arthur Stanley was one of Oxford's leading theologians and was particularly indebted to Twiss, writing later in life of the kindness Twiss had shown him as a young man in Oxford.[149] In battles fought over College statutes, election of fellows, and access to the University, Twiss was on the side of reform, taking what he described as a "liberal" position. The election of Stanley to a fellowship illustrates his disposition and the complex tension between reform and conservatism that runs through his life. In 1838, University College sought to fill a fellowship which, like many positions, required candidates to come from a particular county—in this instance, Durham.[150] University College had a number of fellowships earmarked for candidates from North East England because its thirteenth-century founder had been William of Durham. Mark Pattison, a talented student at Oriel College who was also a Yorkshireman, applied for the position. He was dismayed, however, on the appointed day of the examination to find one of the other candidates was Arthur Stanley,

---

146. See Collini, *Public Moralists*, 207, on classics and mathematics in the Oxbridge curriculum.

147. Plumptre supported reform himself, albeit resisting outside attempts at reform, including the 1850 commission. On Plumptre as reformer, see Darwall-Smith, *A History of University College*, 351–366.

148. For the College fellowship in this period, see Darwall-Smith, *A History of University College*, 351–366.

149. Rowland E. Prothero and G. G. Bradley, *The Life and Correspondence of Arthur Penrhyn Stanley*, 2 vols. (New York, 1894), Vol. 1, 216.

150. Darwall-Smith, *A History of University College*, 356.

who was at Balliol and was one of the most brilliant students of his generation. Stanley would go on to become a leading liberal theologian of Victorian England and Dean of Westminster as well as a leader of Oxford reform. He had attended Rugby School, where he came under the influence of Thomas Arnold and, as a consequence, was not encouraged to apply for a fellowship at his own College, Balliol. Twiss had been his Tutor and persuaded him to apply for the vacant William of Durham Fellowship at University College.[151] He was not, however, from the North East and, according to Pattison, should not have been permitted to compete for the position, which he duly won. Twiss had persuaded the Master that the rules governing the fellowship should be interpreted to mean that it would be awarded to a man from the North East when no other merit separated the candidates.

Pattison went on to gain a Yorkshire Fellowship at Lincoln College, and in time he became Rector of Lincoln and a leading intellectual of the University. He was a follower of John Henry Newman and Edward Pusey, desiring a Catholic and pre-Reformation Church of England, for which many fellows at University College, certainly Twiss, would also have been glad not to see him elected. He deeply resented this episode and carried his bitterness towards Twiss to his grave. He died in 1884, but left a memoir and forbade his editors from changing a word of his manuscript where it concerned his "estimates of persons."[152] He settled a score with Twiss. Pattison wrote of his "amazement" at seeing the "well known figure of A. P. Stanley," "the most brilliant figure in the university," amongst the candidates for the University College fellowship. "It was impossible," he declared. "Stanley was not eligible by the statutes."[153] Pattison immediately suspected a plot in which the successful candidate was already decided, submitting the others to an unnecessary three-days' examination. He concluded that it was "Travers Twiss, who, I suppose, managed the plot."[154] He wrote a letter to the University, announcing his candidature, and alluded to his conclusion. Twiss, claimed Pattison, took this letter to the Provost of his College in a "rage." Here Pattison, from the safety of his grave, remarked upon Twiss's downfall but also his gift for simulation and dissimulation, observing, "Travers Twiss' subsequent performances before the world have been of a nature which, I think, justified me in thinking that the whole indignation was simulated by that astute lawyer."[155]

Twiss, having been humbled by scandal at this point—his "subsequent performances before the world"—was a soft target. He was not, however, averse to defending himself and his former colleagues, who by this point were almost all dead. He responded to Pattison—or, rather, to a review of Pattison's *Memoirs*

151. For this episode, see Darwall-Smith, *A History of University College*, 356.
152. Mark Pattison, *Memoirs* (London, 1885), Preface.
153. Pattison, *Memoirs*, 175.
154. Pattison, *Memoirs*, 175.
155. Pattison, *Memoirs*, 176–177. For this episode, see also Darwall-Smith, *A History of University College*, 348.

in *The Times*—with a letter pointing out that the stakes in this case were the reform of the University generally. The review, or "Notice," of Pattison's *Memoirs* in *The Times* embellished Pattison's version by stating that Twiss's "rage was as simulated as his honesty."[156] Twiss's letter set the record straight "as the last survivor who has a knowledge of the circumstances." He suggested of Pattison, that "having always a feeble memory he had to rely on this occasion on a morbid faculty of reproductive imagination." In his own memoirs, Twiss's friend from University College, the Regius Professor of Modern History, Goldwin Smith, wrote of the cruelty of Pattison's attack upon Twiss and dismissed him as highly talented but splenetic, a strong believer that universities were meant for research, not teaching, but "himself not a happy example of his system."[157] In his own defence, Twiss acknowledged, "I had prevailed on the Master and Fellows to adopt a liberal interpretation of the College statutes." Moreover, Twiss argued, he had no regrets about the appointment of Stanley, or the process, as his election formed "an epoch in the history of the University itself and of the College."[158]

This judgement about Stanley was no exaggeration. Following his election to the University College fellowship, Stanley had been the secretary to the Royal Commission on the University, and it was largely he who wrote its report in 1852. Twiss gave testimony to the Commission, albeit that his Master, Plumptre, refused. The Commission's report recommended the overhaul of the University's statutes, set down by Archbishop Laud in the seventeenth century, at the time part of Laud's broader entrenchment of the Church of England. The reforms recommended the opening of College fellowships and scholarships to a broad range of candidates, removing the local and religious requirements that were attached to most. These were, of course, reforms that had already been introduced at University College, led by Twiss and Plumptre, and from which Stanley himself had benefitted, as Pattison pointed out.[159] Indeed, the report stated that University College had "since the appointment of its present Master, made great efforts to free itself from the restrictions which statute or custom had imposed upon its elections."[160] The Commission's

---

156. "Mark Pattison's Memoirs," *The Times*, March 21, 1885, 5.

157. Smith, *Reminiscences*, 85–86.

158. He pointed out, however, that a precedent had been set for this "liberal" interpretation, one which opened fellowships to all candidates, when a previous applicant for a North Eastern fellowship had objected to an outside candidate a short time previously. On that occasion, the argument was won by Twiss and a junior member of the Chancery Bar, Roundell Palmer, who, as Twiss observed, went on to become the Lord Chancellor and remained so at the time of Twiss's letter to *The Times* in 1885 (having had a role in bringing Twiss into the British negotiations over the Berlin Conference of 1884 and the Congo Free State): Travers Twiss, "Letter," *The Times*, April 3, 1885, 4.

159. Darwall-Smith, *A History of University College*, 348–349.

160. Darwall-Smith, *A History of University College*, 368.

reforms also removed the requirement that students subscribe to the doctrine of the Church of England in order to matriculate. The facts that Twiss had been partly instrumental in introducing such ideas to University College, which became something of a model for the larger University reform, and that he had also been instrumental in selecting and promoting Stanley, indicate the degree to which he was prepared to promote liberal reforms—reforms he described as liberal himself.[161] Moreover, Twiss supported other reformers within the University, including George Henry Sacheverell Johnson, the professor of moral philosophy, who he successfully proposed for membership in the Athenaeum in 1853.[162] Johnson subsequently was appointed one of the University's commissioners by the 1854 Oxford University Act, charged with implementing the reforms recommended by the Royal Commission. Twiss would not always fall on the progressive side of reform, but this episode shows that ideas of a broader franchise—in this instance, the franchise for University and College membership—were attractive to him in certain circumstances.

During the 1830s and early '40s, Twiss had been a constant presence in University College.[163] By the mid-1840s, his presence in the College Register was diminishing, and in the first five years of the 1840s, he passed regularly between Oxford and his rooms in the Albany in Piccadilly, London.[164] It was not unusual for bright students to pursue a life in college for several years, followed by a career in the law. At University College, the model for this career path was William Scott, Lord Stowell (1745-1836). Stowell was an important presence, even in memory, at University College at the time Twiss was elected to his fellowship. Throwing himself into the life of the College for ten years,

---

161. Darwall-Smith, *A History of University College*, 367-369.

162. Athenaeum, Book of Candidates, 1850 to 1858, Mem 1/1/9, January 17, 1853.

163. The Registers record Twiss as present for significant College events, such as the election of fellows, on the following dates: 13 Jun 1831, 18 Jun 1833, 18 Feb 1836, 25 Oct 1836, 3 Dec 1836, 4 Feb 1837, 20 Mar 1837, 6 Jun 1837, & 16, 20 & 28 Nov 1837, 4 Jul 1838, 17 May 1839, 13 Jun 1840, 3 Dec 1840, 31 Oct 1843, 4 Jun 1844, 30 Oct 1844, 31 Oct 1846, 1 May 1847, 28 Oct 1850, 30 Jun 1851, 11 Dec 1851, 11 Dec 1852, 10 Jun 1856, 26 Mar 1858, 28 Oct 1858, 22 Mar 1859, 28 Oct 1859, 20 Mar 1860, 29 Oct 1860, 21 Mar 1861, 28 Oct 1861, 20 Mar 1862, & 28 Oct 1862. I am grateful to the University College archivist, Robin Darwall-Smith, for this information.

164. Twiss's ties with University College would be one of the few constants of his long life. He was obliged to resign his fellowship in 1862 because of his marriage, but in 1864, the College elected him an Honorary Fellow—a rare privilege, as he was at that time only the second person to have been elected to such a fellowship: Register, vol. 2, 1729-1842, University College, Oxford: UC/ GB3/A1/ 3/61. As late as 1892, at the age of 81, Twiss wrote to the College congratulating the Master on the grant of an honorary fellowship to Sir Edward Maunde Thompson, keeper of manuscripts at the British Museum (the best palaeographer in the country, as Twiss said) and Principal Librarian, who would become one of the central figures in the establishment of the modern British Library: Travers Twiss to James Franck Bright, June 17, 1892, University College Archive, Oxford, UC: GB6/ 1/ A3/4.

Stowell had held the posts of Tutor and Senior Tutor that Twiss himself later held and had a formidable reputation as a teacher.[165] He studied civil law and took a Doctorate of Civil Law, as would Twiss. He then moved to London and began a career in the Ecclesiastical Courts, holding the position of judge in the consistory court and Queen's Advocate General, as would Twiss. Stowell made his name in the law of nations, as would Twiss, and as the government Advocate in the Admiralty Courts, where Twiss also followed in 1862, although Stowell rose to the position of judge of the Admiralty Court, a position which was widely regarded as marked out for Twiss and which he was only denied as a result of the scandal in which he became entangled. It would be no exaggeration to say that Twiss had modelled his own career, to some degree, on Stowell, whom he described as "one of the most distinguished administrators of the Law of Nations."[166] Moreover, Stowell grappled with the question of the place of non-European peoples in the law of nations, and this question was one that was central to Twiss's own later thought and one upon which he cited Stowell admiringly.[167]

As a classicist, Twiss produced a two-volume *Epitome of Niebuhr's History of Rome*, in 1836 and 1837. This work was not, however, a product of disinterested classicism—nothing that Twiss produced was disinterested. Its perspective was, rather, foundational to his subsequent practice of law and to the kind of lawyer he would be. Born in 1776, Barthold Niebuhr was the most eminent historian of Rome in his time. According to a contemporary account, it was Twiss who introduced Niebuhr's work to the undergraduates of Oxford in the 1835 exams, to widespread "astonishment," although, as the same account observed, Niebuhr became to history what "Newton was to astronomy and geometry, Milton and Shakespeare to poetry."[168] Niebuhr, according to this account, stripped "obscurity" and "mythology" from Roman history, and Twiss made precisely the same claim in his introduction to the *Epitome*. Importantly, as Twiss also recounts, while travelling to Rome in 1816 to take a post as a diplomat, Niebuhr stopped at Verona on his way, and in the cathedral library, he discovered the lost manuscript of one of the important texts of Roman law, the

165. Darwall-Smith, *A History of University College*, 278–282.

166. Travers Twiss, *The Law of Nations Considered as Independent Political Communities: On the Rights and Duties of Nations in Time of Peace*, 2nd ed. (Oxford, 1884) 158. I am grateful to Robin Darwall-Smith for alerting me to the parallels between the careers of Twiss and Stowell.

167. For Twiss on Stowell, see Twiss, *The Law of Nations* (1884), 89, 158–162. For Stowell on the place of non-European peoples in the law of nations, see Jennifer Pitts, "Empire and Legal Universalisms in the Eighteenth Century," *American Historical Review*, vol. 117, no. 1 (February 2012), 105.

168. *Bell's Weekly Messenger*, June 26, 1852, 6. See also, for a review of the *Epitome*: *Morning Post*, March 26. 1836, 6. For Twiss's possession of numerous volumes by Niebhur, see *Catalogue of a Portion of the Miscellaneous Library of Sir Travers Twiss*, 10.

FIGURE 3. Twiss at University College.*

Institutes of Gaius.[169] Gaius was a second-century Roman jurist whose writings, alongside the sixth-century *Institutes of Justinian*, formed the foundation of Roman law but, by the nineteenth century, were only known through other sources. Niebuhr's discovery helped stimulate the development of an important new approach to the law, the historical school, led by Friedrich Carl von Savigny. It was Savigny who understood that the text Niebuhr discovered was the work of Gaius. The historical context which Gaius added to laws treated abstractly in Justinian's *Institutes* complemented Savigny's historicism.

169. Travers Twiss, *An Epitome of Niebuhr's History of Rome*, 2 vols. (London, 1836–1837), Vol. 1, xv.

* University College, Oxford, Archive, courtesy of the Master and Fellows of University College, Oxford

Medieval lawyers had believed Roman law to be *ratio scripta*, or written reason, while natural lawyers of the Enlightenment and even utilitarians, such as Jeremy Bentham, opposed to the idea of natural law, all sought a system of law based in reason. The German historical school argued, by contrast, that laws were the product of particular historical circumstances and national cultures, encouraging scepticism about the universality of law and thus scepticism about static codes of law, such as Napoléon's civil code. If law was a product of history, then it was also organic and should not be captured in static codes. This new perspective on the law spread rapidly beyond Germany. Within Britain, it marked several international lawyers, including James Lorimer in Scotland, who met Savigny, James Reddie, George Bowyer, Twiss's opponent on Catholic emancipation, and Twiss himself, as well as, most famously, inspiring the work of the English legal-historicists Henry Sumner Maine and John Westlake.[170] For some followers of the new legal historicism, the understanding that laws were culturally bound and locally significant nourished the celebration of national cultures. But this was not at all the perspective of Savigny, who was a "cosmopolitan humanist," uncomfortable with emerging German nationalism.[171] He regarded legal historicism as a means with which to revive the study of law and to provide jurists with better tools to guide the development of the law. Twiss, too, was no nationalist. He was extremely hostile to nationalism. He shared Savigny's conviction that the historical method could shed light on legal disputes and on the standing of the law more generally. He produced the *Epitome of Niebuhr* in part to provide a background to the understanding of the civil law, with its foundations in Roman law, in the study of which he was deeply immersed by this time and to the practice of which he would devote the rest of life as the foundation of both ecclesiastical law and the law of nations.

As early as 1837, at the age of 28, Twiss competed for the post of Drummond Chair of Political Economy, for which there were three candidates, Twiss, Hermann Merivale (later Permanent Under-Secretary for the colonies), and John Maurice of Exeter College. The candidates were distinguished according to their positions in relation to the Oxford Movement, or Tractarianism, which was at this moment at its peak. This movement sought to bring the Church of England into closer alignment with Catholicism through the reform of liturgy or church ritual and, in doing so, deeply divided the English educated classes in the mid-nineteenth century. Maurice was reported to "receive the zealous support" of the "Pusey Party"—that is, of the Tractarians. Twiss belonged to the "Old High Church Party, and moderates." Only Merivale was said to have political opinions which would "render nugatory his claims on the electors,"

---

170. See, for example, James Reddie, *Inquiries Elementary and Historical in the Science of Law* (London, 1840), 6, 88.

171. Koskenniemi, *The Gentle Civilizer of Nations*, 44.

although his "acquirements in Political Economy" were "very highly spoken of."[172] In a "spirited contest," Maurice withdrew, and the University's Convocation elected Merivale by a majority of six votes.[173] The election even inspired a florid poem, invoking Walter Scott's *Guy Mannering*:

> Vision / Of the result of the late Contest between Mr. Herman Merivale, of Baliol, and Mr Travers Twiss, of University College. / "Twist ye, twine ye, even so"—Guy Mannering. / University! Traverse, Twist, Twine as ye may, / His Dew falls on Hermon at close of the day. / But in contests so noble, by souls so inspir'd, / Ne'er will rankle the breasts such high feelings have fired; / Here the fame of the Victor ennobles defeat, / Since, to be next to him, is indeed to be great; / And the goal being touched—animosities end, / The Vanquish'd exulting, "My Rival's my Friend." Meg Merrilies[174]

While Merivale prevailed on this occasion and delivered an influential course of lectures on the British colonies (which Twiss would later have on his shelves), when the five-year appointment came to an end, Twiss ran for the position again in 1842.[175] This time, at the age of 33, he was successful, becoming the Drummond Professor of Political Economy at Oxford.[176] Several years later, Twiss and Merivale collaborated in having members of the Athenaeum elected.[177]

As the holder of the Drummond chair, Twiss lectured on diverse subjects, beginning, in 1843, with *On Money and Currency*, which he published only, he said, because the terms of his chair obliged him to, being unable to "pretend to any originality" in treating the subject.[178] In 1844, he published on machinery and, in 1845, on "certain tests of a thriving population," culminating in his lectures of 1846 and 1847: *View of the Progress of Political Economy in Europe*

---

172. *Oxford Chronicle and Reading Gazette*, February 18, 1837, 3.

173. "University Intelligence," *Morning Post*, March 4, 1837, 4.

174. "Of the Result of the Late Contest between Mr Herman Merivale, of Baliol, and Mr Travers Twiss, of University College," *Exeter and Plymouth Gazette*, March 18, 1837, 4.

175. For Twiss's copy of Merivale's *Lectures on Colonization and Colonies*, 2 vols., see *Catalogue of a Portion of the Miscellaneous Library of Sir Travers Twiss*, 9.

176. "Oxford," *Lancaster Gazette*, March 26, 1842, 4.

177. They nominated Arthur Waddilove, one of Twiss's colleagues in the Doctors' Commons, in 1846, and Waddilove was elected in 1854: "Arthur Waddilove," Athenaeum, Book of Candidates, 1841 to 1850, Mem 1/1/7, April 2, 1846, 2619; and also George Ferguson Bowen, who was elected in 1860: "George Bowen," Athenaeum, Book of Candidates, 1850 to 1858, Mem 1/1/9, December 10, 1851, 3284. Bowen was a classicist and fellow of Brasenose, President of the Ionian Academy on Corfu, and later the first governor of the newly established colony of Queensland in Australia.

178. Travers Twiss, *On Money and Currency* (Oxford, 1843), sig. B2. Twiss dedicated the Bodleian Library copy of these lectures to the Oxford mathematician Professor Baden Powell, a fellow member of the Ashmolean Society.

since the Sixteenth Century.[179] He emphasised the need to advance the study of political economy beyond the work of Adam Smith, who, Twiss pointed out, lived at a time prior to an understanding the full impact of industrialisation. He argued that machinery and industry were a factor that needed to be understood beyond capitalism itself.

Shortly after stepping down from the Drummond chair, Twiss took a new post in London. On January 19, 1849, Richard Jelf, Principal of King's College London, pointed out to the governing council of the College that "three Egyptian gentleman" had recently been admitted to the College "with the view of being educated as Diplomatists."[180] In fact, the College Calendar from 1849 reveals that there were in total, during the course of the year, "eight young Egyptians, sent over by the Viceroy of Egypt" to King's College to be trained for a career of "Diplomatic Service."[181] Since the expulsion of Napoléon in 1801, Egypt had exercised a great degree of autonomy from the Ottoman Empire under the rule of Muhammed Ali, who, until 1848, embarked upon a programme of modernisation combined with territorial expansion, a combination also characteristic of a number of nineteenth-century European states. That programme included sending students to Europe for training in industrial, military, and diplomatic arts. The policy was strongly supported by Britain, particularly with Viscount Palmerston as Foreign Secretary and Prime Minister, because it furthered Palmerston's vision of a strong Ottoman Empire which could serve as a bulwark against the Russian Empire, preventing its feared spread south as far as the Bosphorus or even further, through Syria, where it could imperil British trade routes to the East. Rather than seeking to influence the Ottomans through expensive direct controls, Palmerston and British policy more generally encouraged free trade and liberal reforms in the Ottoman Empire, including Egypt,

---

179. In accordance with the regulations of the professorship, Twiss again published portions of each of these courses of lectures. For the sale of Twiss's lectures on machinery at 2 shillings, see *Oxford University and City Herald*, April 20, 1844, 1. For his four lectures "On Certain Tests of a Thriving Population," delivered in Lent Term 1845, see "Advertisements and Notices," *Morning Chronicle*, May 21, 1845, 7. For advance notice of the publication of Twiss, *View of the Progress of Political Economy in Europe Since the Sixteenth Century: A Course of Lectures in Michaelmas Term 1846, and Lent Term 1847*, see *London Evening Standard*, June 25, 1847, 1. These announcements were repeated numerous times throughout the newspapers. While Twiss claimed no originality in these lectures, he nevertheless deemed them worthy of donation to the library of the Athenaeum: Athenaeum, Mem 2/16: *Athenaeum. Rules and Regulations, List of Members, and Donations to the Library 1848* (London, 1849), 140.

180. King's College, London, Archive, College Minutes, January 19, 1849, MS KA/IC/M5, 46–47. See also F.J.C. Hearnshaw, *The Centenary History of King's College London* (London, 1929), 180–181.

181. *The Calendar of King's College London for 1849–50* (London, 1849), 24.

which they believed would strengthen Ottoman power as well as advantage British trade.[182]

In 1848, Muhammed Ali had been replaced—first by his son and then by his grandson, Abbas I, who tried to undo many of his reforms—but in 1849, Egyptian students were still being trained in Europe, including eight sent to study the law of nations at King's College. The Principal of King's College argued accordingly that the College needed a chair of the law of nations in order to provide the necessary training for these and any other such students, and he proposed that Travers Twiss, "who until lately had filled the Chair of Political Economy at Oxford," was "a gentleman now in London who is fully competent to fill this Chair."[183] Jelf knew Twiss, as both had sat on the governing committee of the Athenaeum in 1849.[184] The council agreed to establish a "Professorship of the Law of Nations" and to offer the post to Twiss, who accepted by return post.[185] He remained in the position from 1849 until 1855. For Twiss, teaching was a duty and a means of influence, rather than a financial necessity: "I have been teaching all my life in one way or other. If it were not a duty, I should have long given it up, but toil in some shape or other is our lot and he toils least who toils to most purpose."[186]

The motives for the creation of this lectureship deserve comment. Histories of international law since the 1990s have rightly critiqued its purported universality. They point out that the discipline has European origins. Its originators frequently referred to it as the European law of nations and insisted that its application was only to "civilized" states—only, that is, to European states and to the recently formed United States of America. It is not surprising, therefore, that insofar as international law has been universalised it has often been as an instrument for the hegemony of European powers. However, this image of international law requires some nuance. At times, the law of nations was understood to apply beyond the concert of European states, with different authorities expressing different notions of its extent, and it would also appear that some non-Europeans showed an interest in international law as an instrument that could serve their own purposes. Twiss's views on the extent of the law of nations were not at one with all his contemporaries. Some

---

182. Robinson and Gallagher with Denny, *Africa and the Victorians*, 77–78; Martin Lynn, "British Policy, Trade, and Informal Empire in the Mid-Nineteenth Century," in Andrew Porter, ed., *The Oxford History of the British Empire: The Nineteenth Century* (Oxford, 1999), 111–113.

183. King's College Archive, College Minutes, January 19, 1849, MS KA/IC/M5, 46–47.

184. Athenaeum, London, Mem 2/16: *Athenaeum. Rules and Regulations, List of Members, and Donations to the Library 1848* (London, 1849), Committee of 1849–50.

185. "Travers Twiss to Richard Jelf," January 20, 1849, King's College Archive, KA/IC/T25.

186. Twiss to Metternich, April 12, 1849, National Archives of the Czech Republic, Prague, RAM-AC/ 10/ 775, 260–262.

of them, such as James Lorimer at the University of Edinburgh, had a very restrictive notion of the law of nations as exclusively European.[187] Following Lord Stowell, Twiss acknowledged, on more than one occasion, that its extent could include non-European powers. Given that his first professional post in the law of nations was created with precisely the purpose of training "Egyptian gentlemen" in diplomacy, he could hardly believe otherwise. To accept a post to train Egyptian diplomats was to accept the application of the law of nations to Egypt. Following the Crimean War and the 1856 Treaty of Paris, Twiss would explicitly state that the Ottoman Empire, which formally included Egypt, *was* a member of the society of nations. Clearly, for the Palmerstonians in Britain, there were strategic advantages to admitting the Ottomans into that society.

In 1855, Twiss published his King's College lectures. *Two Introductory Lectures on the Science of International Law* was his first general statement of the principles of international law. These may have been the lectures that the College *Annual Report* mentions Twiss "very kindly gave" to students in the Department of Civil Service and Commerce, and "to the public generally," in 1854.[188] He had first written these lectures in 1849, at the time he began his position and the Egyptian students their studies. In April 1849, he wrote to his friend and collaborator Prince Metternich, "I am writing an Introductory Lecture on the Law of Nations which I have promised to deliver at King's College the week after next."[189] He wanted Metternich's views represented: "If there are any views which as an old pupil of M. Koch [Christopher William Koch] your highness may think have not been properly set forth, pray let me have the benefit of your ideas." Koch's views, and Metternich's, favoured a balance between the great powers. This was what the Egyptian students would have to encounter as future diplomats, and it was also the system that in part sustained the Ottoman Empire. Britain needed the Ottomans as a bulwark against Russia, and Egypt autonomous within their empire.

Twiss delayed publication of the lectures. In May 1849, he informed Metternich, "I have been quite indisposed to write anything on any subject of late—partly I have been occupied with Court business . . . I have abandoned my lecture on the Law of Nations. I could not sit down in cold blood to write on the subject when I see it nowhere respected. I could get up to speak but not sit down deliberately to write."[190] At the time of his appointment to King's College, he believed that the Concert of Europe, which he understood to be

---

187. James Lorimer, *The Institutes of the Law of Nations*, 2 vols. (Edinburgh, 1884).

188. *The Calendar of King's College London for 1855-56* (London, 1849), 44-45.

189. Twiss to Metternich, April 21, 1849, National Archives of the Czech Republic, Prague, RAM-AC/ 10/ 775, 271.

190. Twiss to Metternich, May 31, 1849, National Archives of the Czech Republic, Prague, RAM-AC/ 10/ 775, 315.

founded on and also to uphold the law of nations, was crumbling in the wake of the 1848 revolutions. Nevertheless, he did indeed get up to speak in order to deliver his lectures.

When the *Two Introductory Lectures on the Science of International Law* was finally published, it was warmly reviewed.[191] Twiss regarded it as an outline of a future treatise, writing to Metternich that he begged "your acceptance of a short treatise on a subject which may interest you, as a 'Professor Emeritus' of the science of diplomacy. It is a sketch of a great subject and may serve as an introduction to a treatise on International Law, if I should ever have time and inclination to write such a work."[192] He must have been disappointed, therefore, with Metternich's response. Metternich began promisingly: "I read, as you would have no doubt, the work which you have just published. I had two reasons for doing so: one is because everything that comes from your spirit has a value for me; the other arises from the interest of the subject you have treated, an established master of the question. It goes without saying that everything you write conforms to my own convictions." Metternich's interest in the subject, however, was primarily as a sceptic. It is frequently argued that the Concert of Europe was based upon the *ius publicum Europaeum*, the public law of Europe that was itself drawn from the tradition of the European law of nations, in turn a product of early modern natural law and the Roman *ius gentium*. Twiss's *Two Introductory Lectures on the Science of International Law* summarised that genealogy. Given that Metternich was the chief architect of the Concert of Europe, we might expect his understanding of the rules governing the society of nations to conform to that account. In his response to Twiss, however, he entirely dismissed the perspective of the European law of nations. "Reading your work," he continued, "reminded me of discussions between Friedrich Gentz [Metternich's secretary and advisor from 1812] and myself in the first years after I took him into my department. I can't remember why I happened to say to him that, without wishing to say anything against the jus naturae and jus gentium, I did not know any other point of departure than the ius civile which I found in the Decalogue [Ten Commandments] and the Catechism, and to act according to the rules of conduct which are the only aegis for men to live in society. Putting all that aside, Gentz became furious and said to me bluntly: 'You understand nothing about the question! Occupy yourself with other matters.' Twenty years later, Gentz had the occasion, if my memory serves me correctly, to say to me: 'Do you remember our dispute about that matter? Well, I was unjust to you. Today I admit you were

---

191. For announcement of the publication, see *London Evening Standard*, January 25, 1856, 1. For a review: "Literature," *Morning Post*, April 15, 1856, 6: "This volume is entitled to the highest commendation."

192. Twiss to Metternich, April 5, 1856, National Archives of the Czech Republic, Prague, RAM-AC/ 10/ 782, 2–3.

right.'"[193] As with so many of the Socratic dialogues that Metternich included in his letters, this particular account ended with his adversary conceding that Metternich was absolutely right. Importantly, it also revealed that jurists, such as Twiss, were still struggling to convince diplomats and statesmen that their understanding of the law of nations had any bearing upon the actual conduct of states. If Twiss achieved anything in his career, it would be that he eventually prevailed in using law to change the reality of the world in which he lived. The human cost to the people of the Congo would be incalculable.

King's College had barely been established for twenty years and was a natural home for Twiss, having been inspired as an Anglican response to the secular London University (later University College London). In addition to catering for foreign students, the chair of international law was created as part of the more general reform of law in England in the 1850s, a reform in which Twiss enthusiastically took part. Since 1841, Twiss had had a flourishing practice in the civil law courts. The reason a Doctor in Civil Law would be appointed as a Professor of International Law is that the legal basis for international law, or the law of nations, was Roman and civil law. Much of the law of nations had been extrapolated from principles in private civil law; thus, for example, the concept of occupation in international law—that is, the claim that the first person who takes a territory becomes its owner—had been drawn from a private Roman law principle regarding property which declared that the first person to catch a wild animal or, for example, to pick up a seashell on the seashore becomes its owner. The reason for this analogous relationship between the two bodies of law was simply that while systems of private law had sovereigns who could provide sanctions behind principles, no such system of sovereignty existed in international law, so what might count as law required some degree of imagination. Civil law provided an important parallel system from which principles could be drawn. A lecturer in international law therefore needed a foundation in civil law, and indeed, in Europe as in England, all international lawyers were drawn from the ranks of civil law. In England, with its flourishing, and separate, system of the common law, this meant that civil lawyers and common lawyers were segregated into different worlds. Twiss had been concerned with questions of international law since his publication of *The Oregon Territory* in 1846, and his training in the principles of international law had started with the Bachelor of Civil Law in 1835 and continued until his Doctor of Civil Law in 1841. At King's College, he maintained this interest with lectures on "The Rights of War as to Belligerents and Neutrals" which, in June 1854, were advertised to members of the public. [194]

---

193. Metternich to Twiss, Vienna, April 20, 1856, Bibliothèque nationale de France, Fol/ R.D./13810, 133–134. For Gentz, see Brian Vick, *The Congress of Vienna: Power and Politics after Napoleon* (Cambridge, Mass., 2014), 124.

194. *Morning Chronicle*, June 14, 1854, 1.

The study of civil law at Oxford had been moribund for a very long time, and in 1855, the Regius Professorship of Civil Law, responsible for the delivery of lectures on the subject, had been held by Joseph Phillimore for nearly forty-five years.[195] In that year, Phillimore, now 80 and in virtual retirement, died at his home, Shiplake House, near Reading. Twiss was elected Regius Professor of Civil Law at Oxford and resigned his chair at King's College. He briefly considered the possibility of holding both positions but regretfully conceded in his resignation letter that "a limit must be set."[196] He travelled to Oxford in late October to accept the position.[197] Regius Professor was a prestigious title, but, as Twiss complained, he had very few students. In 1854, the year prior to his election, three students enrolled in the Bachelor of Civil Law.[198] The following year, there were two, and their attendance at lectures was not guaranteed. The professor was in the habit of delivering lectures to empty rooms—what were known as "wall lectures." In April 1856, Twiss explained to Metternich: "The post of Regius Professor of Civil Law is a kind of 'Blue Riband.' I go down to Oxford occasionally and give some public lectures, if so disposed, and if in the course of Academic Reform it shall be thought advisable to endow the Office and have a Resident Professor, I shall resign it."[199]

If he meant what he said about the consequences of reform, then he was bent upon a path of self-destruction, at least insofar as the Regius Professorship was concerned. With reform of the universities in full flow by the 1850s, Twiss took the occasion of his election to write and publish an open letter to the Oxford Vice Chancellor outlining an ambitious programme of reform not only for the teaching of civil law but for the role of civil law in society more generally. This was not the first time Twiss had called for University reform. In 1839, as a Tutor at University College, he had published anonymously a tract in the reforming spirit of the 1830s and '40s, calling for a radical overhaul of teaching at the universities. Across a spectrum of issues, Twiss often took a stance supporting the prevailing order, but this was not always the case, and his perspective changed. In this case, he complained that "a very large proportion [of students] quit the walls of this university without any apparent

---

195. *Oxford University and City Herald*, October 20, 1855, 8.

196. Travers Twiss, "Resignation letter": King's College Archive, KA/ICT25, T33.

197. Although he had rooms at University College, he had been resident for most of the past ten years in London. *Liverpool Daily Post*, June 11, 1855, 3; *London Evening Standard*, June 11, 1855, 3. "University Intelligence," *London Evening Standard*, October 18, 1855, 1: news that Twiss has accepted Chair and that "he is expected in Oxford at the end of the present week."

198. Travers Twiss, *A Letter to the Vice-Chancellor of the University of Oxford on Law Studies at the University* (London, 1856), 8.

199. Twiss to Metternich, April 5, 1856, National Archives of the Czech Republic, Prague, RAM-AC/ 10/ 782, 3.

benefit."[200] He scorned the "scanty attendance on the public lectures," a 50 per cent failure rate at exams, and the fact that "the lecture rooms of the Professors are almost deserted."[201] Even worse, Twiss pointed out, was that the universities provided students with "no theoretical preparation for their duties in the various departments of after-life"—by "after-life" he referred not to death but to the world outside Oxford.[202] "How far," he asked, did the present system "qualify a man for any department in life."[203] His own practice exhibited a deep commitment to bridging learning and a world of political and legal engagement. His proposed solution was to double the number of examinable subjects in the Bachelor of Arts from two, classics and mathematics, to four: namely, theology and moral philosophy; history and political philosophy, including law and antiquities; mathematics; and physics. Additionally, he argued that students should be required to reside at Oxford during the whole period of their studies and should be examined annually, obliging them to attend more than the occasional lectures.[204] He also called for a closer tie between lectures and exams so that students would see a benefit from attendance.

In his letter to the Vice Chancellor, Twiss argued that many of the problems of civil law stemmed from the prejudices of the great seventeenth-century common lawyer Edward Coke, who had claimed wrongly that principles of the civil law, which was associated in the minds of some with continental Catholicism, were inconsistent with the freedoms of the common law of England.[205] The recommendation from the 1846 Select Committee on Legal Education that more formal teaching of law should precede a student's training in a barrister's chamber, had provided an opportunity, according to Twiss, to revive the study of civil law. He argued that an education in the law in England could begin at university with the study of Roman law's *Institutes of Justinian*, the foundation of civil law, instead, as was the case, of the *Commentaries* of Blackstone, the foundation of the common law.[206] Indeed, even outside the university, common lawyers might profitably, he argued, draw upon the clear principles of civil law in order to resolve many of their problems. In England, the civil law only had an institutional role in the Ecclesiastical Courts, in marriage law and probate law (the law dealing with estates of deceased people), and in the Admiralty Courts, which, dealing as they did with conflicts at sea, were obliged to consider questions in the law of nations. Just one year after he wrote this letter, even these civil-law responsibilities would be drastically

---

200. A Tutor of a College [Travers Twiss], *Considerations of a Plan for Combining the Professorial System with the System of Public Exams in Oxford* (Oxford, 1839), 5.
   201. [Twiss], *Considerations of a Plan*, 6–7.
   202. [Twiss], *Considerations of a Plan*, 7, 13.
   203. [Twiss], *Considerations of a Plan*, 23.
   204. [Twiss], *Considerations of a Plan*, 16–18.
   205. Twiss, *A Letter to the Vice-Chancellor*, 4–5.
   206. Twiss, *A Letter to the Vice-Chancellor*, 6.

narrowed by the Probate and Divorce Acts of 1857, which transferred jurisdiction for marriage and probate to the common-law courts. Twiss was thus struggling against a strong tide in 1856 when he tried to revive the civil law. Where his hopes were realised, although perhaps not in the direction he initially anticipated, would be with the increasing institutionalisation and professionalization of international law throughout the second half of the century.

A further function performed by Twiss as Regius Professor was the presentation of candidates for honorary Doctorates in Civil Law (or DCLs) at the annual University commemoration ceremonies, or Encaenia, before what were usually large audiences in the Sheldonian Theatre. These occasions were accompanied by a Latin oration praising the virtues of the candidates and brought Twiss into contact with recipients who included nobles, diplomats, adventurers, and eminent military figures and intellectuals from throughout the Empire and the world. Often the awards were given to mark great events of the day.[207] In June 1856, Twiss awarded DCLs to representatives of the victorious powers in the just-concluded Crimean War. The recipients included Prince Frederick William of Prussia, the Prince of Baden, and the war hero Major-General Fenwick Williams, all of whom were cheered in the crowded auditorium. A further recipient was the ambassador Konstantinos Musurus Pasha, the representative of Britain's ally, the Ottoman Sultan.[208] Twiss presented Musurus Pasha to the audience in the Sheldonian as the "first Christian subject of the Porte" (that is, of the Ottoman empire) to have held the post of Ambassador, as well as praising the Sultan for having granted full privileges to his Christian subjects (the absence of which had been a pretext for the Russians to go to war in 1853). A call for cheers for the Sultan and Omar Pasha, the Ottoman general, reportedly "fell flat" because they "were rather abstract ideas."[209] It

---

207. Officially, the presentations and orations were supposed to be made by the University Orator, who, throughout this period, was Richard Michell (from 1848 to 1877), a fellow of Lincoln College. It would appear, however, that Twiss often relieved Michell from this duty, and he did this from the time he became Regius Professor. Newspaper reports even mistakenly referred to Twiss himself as the University Orator. In fact, Michel and Twiss appear to have been mutually indebted. The minutes of the newly established Hebdomadal Council, the University's governing body, reveal that, in 1857, the Council authorized Michel, who had been elected to the Council in 1854, to "employ an Actuary to ascertain the exact financial position" of the Regius Professorship of Civil Law: University of Oxford Archive, Minutes of the Hebdomadal Council, HC 1/2/1 fol. 130. Presumably, Michell was authorized because he raised the matter in the Council following Twiss's published complaint about the insufficiency of the Regius Professor's £300 stipend one year previously: Twiss, *A Letter to the Vice-Chancellor*, 24.

208. For Musurus, see Cemil Aydin, *The Idea of the Muslim World: A Global Intellectual History* (Cambridge Mass., 2017), 41, 52.

209. "The Oxford Commemoration," *Carlisle Patriot*, June 7, 1856, 5. For further reports on Twiss in this ceremony, see *London Evening Standard*, June 5, 1856, 1; *Oxford Journal*, June 7, 1856, 5.

was not only the audience who struggled with the novelty of the occasion. A week later, Twiss wrote to Prince Metternich: "I am sending you the English newspapers . . . to show you how Orientalism is making progress in England, as I have just presented the Ambassador of the Sultan for the Doctorate of Civil Law at Oxford. It's a strange thing [*drôle de chose*], but it's a symptom of a revolution accomplished and perhaps of a decadence to come. Of what? you say. But I don't know how to respond to the question, and if you did not ask it, it would be me who would propose it to Your Majesty [V.A., i.e., *Votre Altesse*]."[210] Although he found the situation bemusing, and potentially symptomatic of the luxury and effeminacy of commercial society (a long-held European fear of "Oriental" influence), Twiss apparently also believed that the change was inexorable. Both British and Austrian policy had for decades acknowledged the importance of the Ottoman Empire as a bulwark against the Russians, and that reality had been appreciated by Metternich, when he was Chancellor of the Austrian Empire, as much as it was by Palmerston in Britain.[211]

Despite his personal reservations, Twiss's encomium of the Turks on this occasion anticipated the publication, five years later, of his most important work on international law, *The Law of Nations*, in which he declared that the 1856 Treaty of Paris "may be considered as the formal Act of Reception of the Sublime Porte into the Fellowship of European Nations."[212] At issue here, for Twiss, as for his contemporaries, was the crucial question of the scope of international law. The Ottomans had been outside the 1815 Congress of Vienna despite the efforts of Metternich and Lord Castlereagh to persuade Mahmud II to send representatives to the meetings and to make territorial concessions in exchange for a guarantee of the empire's territorial integrity.[213] By virtue of the Treaty of Paris, however, as Twiss pointed out, the contracting powers had guaranteed the "independence and integrity of the Ottoman Empire" and its inclusion within international law. At the same time, the Ottomans had accepted that regulations established in the Congress of Vienna, governing open navigation of the great rivers of Europe, would include the Danube.[214]

---

210. Twiss to Metternich, June 16, 1856, National Archives of the Czech Republic, Prague, RAM-AC/ 10/ 782, 10.

211. Miroslav Šedivý, *Metternich, the Great Powers and the Eastern Question* (Pilsen, 2013), 33.

212. Travers Twiss, *The Law of Nations Considered as Independent Political Communities: On the Rights and Duties of Nations in Time of Peace* (Oxford, 1861), Vol. 1, 105. On the formal entry of the Ottoman Empire into the Concert of Europe at the Congress of Paris, see Aydin, *The Idea of the Muslim World*, 54.

213. Šedivý, *Metternich*, 40–43.

214. Twiss, *The Law of Nations* (1861), Vol. 1, 106. See Pitts, "Boundaries of Victorian International Law," 72, for an argument that Twiss limited the understanding of the law of nations to Europe; and Jennifer Pitts, in *Boundaries of the International: Law and Empire* (Cambridge, Mass., 2018), 170, argues that he was not prepared to recognise full equality for non-European nations.

For Twiss, the inclusion of the Danube in international law would permit the extension, for the first time, of western European influence through the mouth of the Danube into the Black Sea. These conventions regarding sovereignty over rivers would later become central to debates over the Congo, in which Twiss was also deeply involved.[215]

In July 1859, at the commemoration ceremony, Twiss presented DCLs and gave Latin orations on the feats of the "heroes" of the Indian Rebellion, what was termed at the time the Indian Mutiny and has also been called, from an Indian perspective, the first Indian war of independence. On this occasion, the recipients of the awards, survivors of the siege of Lucknow, were met with "thunderous cheers."[216] There is some piquancy to his role in the ceremony. Two years earlier, in February 1857, just months before the Indian Rebellion, he had provided an opinion to the ruler whom the English described as the "King of Oude"—he was, in fact, Wajid Ali Shah, the Nawab, or king, of Awadh, the northern Indian state between British India and the vestiges of the Mughal Empire. When the Nawab was deposed by the East India Company in 1856, he asked Twiss, as an authority on the law of nations, for his opinion on the legality of the conquest, and Twiss found in his favour. The unrest arising from the conquest of Awadh had been one of the causes of the Indian uprising. Twiss, however, never struggled to slide from one role into another. In his oration, he focused upon the feats of three British commanders in the war—Sir Archdale Wilson, Colonel Edward Greathed, and Sir John Lawrence—to whom he was awarding the DCL. It should not surprise us that holding different offices could lead a person to different positions regarding the same question, least of all a lawyer whose job it is to argue a case (although that was not the nature of the opinion Twiss offered to Wajid Ali Shah). Nevertheless, Twiss was remarkably supple over his lifetime, able to assume multiple and sometimes conflicting roles. His ability to adapt would be crucial to his reinvention and revival in later years.

---

215. Twiss's role in presenting the Doctorates of Civil Law at the annual commemoration ceremonies touched upon other aspects of his professional and personal life. In June 1860, he gave Latin encomia and presented the DCLs to recipients, including Paweł Strzelecki, whom he knew from the Royal Geographical Society meetings, and the ambassador for Sweden and Norway, at whose London residence Twiss had dined three months previously. *London Evening Standard*, June 21, 1860. 3. For the dinner with the ambassador, see *Morning Post*, March 15, 1860, 5. For Twiss performing this role, see also *Morning Chronicle*, November 18, 1859, 4. When the DCL presentations concluded, the Professor of Poetry, Matthew Arnold, whom Twiss would have known as a constant presence in the Athenaeum, then gave the Creweian Oration, recounting the events of the past year. While Arnold was, and still is, regarded as one of the great Victorian poets and essayists, the ceremony was so tumultuous that he was reported to have been "scarcely audible at any period of his harangue": *Birmingham Daily Post*, June 18, 1858, 1.

216. *Oxford Chronicle and Reading Gazette*, July 9, 1859, 2; and *Oxford University and City Herald*, July 9, 1859, 11, 12.

The ceremonies for DCL were often the occasion for celebrating officers and diplomats who had struggled for the empire. In 1863, Twiss awarded the DCL to Sir Rutherford Alcock, the British ambassador to Japan (and previously to China), who had only recently fought off attacks upon his embassy by Samurai.[217] Again, here, as we shall see in the next chapter, Twiss found himself rewarding a person whose life was interconnected with his own and, in this instance, connected with the extraordinary story of his marriage.

The Doctors' Commons, the Church of England, and the Admiralty

Shortly after his admission to the Bar at Lincoln's Inn in 1840 and his award of Doctor of Civil Law at Oxford in 1841, Twiss was admitted as a civilian lawyer in the Doctors' Commons, the College of Civilian Lawyers.[218] He then began a flourishing practice in civil law and moved to London, although he held the Drummond Professorship of Political Economy at Oxford from 1842 to 1847. He regularly travelled between London and Oxford, by coach until the early 1840s and by rail thereafter. The 1844 census shows Twiss at this time to be living in B5 in the Albany, off Piccadilly in Mayfair. Built in the 1770s, the Albany was the former home of Viscount Melbourne and then of George III's son, Prince Frederick. In the late 1820s, it was subdivided into sixty-nine apartments, or "sets." For anybody who had spent a long time living in college in Oxford, the Albany would have presented familiar surroundings. Women were not allowed, and the sets were staffed by porters. The Albany, in the heart of London, was, and remains, prestigious and fashionable. Twiss was in B5, while Oscar Wilde's fictional John "Ernest" Worthing, in *The Importance of Being Earnest*, was in B4.[219] Early Albany residents included Lord Byron and, just before Twiss moved in, William Gladstone. Thomas Babington Macaulay, the historian and Whig politician who held the posts of War Secretary and Paymaster General, lived there as well. Twiss would have also known him from the Athenaeum, which was just a short walk away off Pall Mall at the bottom of Regent Street. He described his daily routine at this time in a letter to Prince Metternich in 1849. Speaking of the Athenaeum, he wrote, "I generally call there about half past 4 o'clock on my way back from Doctors' Commons

---

217. Oxford University Archive, HC 1/2/1 fols 396–398.

218. Twiss was admitted as an Advocate on November 2, 1841: *The Jurist*, vol. 5 (London, 1842), 985; Squibb, *Doctors' Commons*, 202.

219. The notorious 1980s British MP Alan Clark was a more recent resident in Twiss's former set, B5, sharing not only the same rooms but a similar disposition to scandal. B5 was described, during Clark's time, as possessing "the straitened quarter of an Edwardian bachelor on his uppers." For Clarke, see *The Steeple Times*, "The Badgers of Albany," November 15, 2012, http://thesteepletimes.com/opulence-splendour/the-badgers-of-albany/.

[near Saint Paul's Cathedral], as I rise at 5 if the weather is fine."[220] He also entertained in his rooms at the Albany. His friend, journalist Henry Reeve, wrote in his journal in February 1853: "A pleasant dinner at Twiss's rooms at the Albany," where the guests, apart from Reeve himself, included Count Colloredo, the Austrian ambassador, "M. de Bille," a Danish diplomat, Viscount Edward Cardwell, the President of the Board of Trade, Judge William Erle (who Twiss would have known from when he was a fellow at Oxford), Pawel Strzelecki, the explorer, and "young Reventlow" from the aristocratic Danish family.[221] Cardwell talked of nothing but train crashes and the rapid growth of exports.

The Irish novelist Marmion Savage lampooned the Albany in the novel *The Bachelor of the Albany* while Twiss lived there. Savage wrote that the Albany was "the haunt of bachelors ... the dread of suspicious wives, the retreat of superannuated fops, the hospital for incurable oddities, a cluster of solitudes for social hermits, the home of homeless gentlemen, the diner-out and the diner-in, the place for the fashionable thrifty, the luxurious lonely, and the modish morose, the votaries of melancholy, and lovers of mutton-chops."[222] Like Prince Albert, who had set the fashion, Twiss was certainly a lover of mutton-chops, although he was not content with remaining a mere oddity or eccentric bachelor and would outgrow the Albany, as he had Oxford, although he remained there until the early 1850s. From 1854, he lived in Park Lane, and he stayed there until the 1870s, when, ruined by scandal, he was forced to sell.[223] The fact that Twiss was able to buy a house at this address was a reflection both of what by this time in his life was a very substantial income and also of his ambition and his desire to demonstrate to London Society that he was a personage of standing. Goldwin Smith commented that it was an "elegant little house" which Twiss purchased at "the summit of prosperity and reputation."[224]

From his set in the Albany and, later, his house in Park Lane, Twiss pursued an extraordinary career through the Doctors' Commons, the college of civil lawyers adjacent to the Inns of Court.[225] The Minute Book of the Doc-

220. Twiss to Metternich, April 27, 1848, National Archives of the Czech Republic, Prague, RAM-AC/ 10/ 775, 274.

221. Laughton, *Memoirs of the Life and Correspondence of Henry Reeve*, Vol. 1, 281–282.

222. Marmion Savage, *The Bachelor of the Albany* (New York, 1848), 33–34.

223. In 1853, he wrote to Metternich that he hoped to welcome his son, Prince Richard Metternich, at a new address: "I hope that Richard comes to London. Next year, I am going to establish myself in a house, no. 19 Park Lane, that gives onto Hyde Park, and there he will find himself perfectly at home": Twiss to Metternich, November 15, 1853, National Archives of the Czech Republic, Prague, RAM-AC/ 10/ 779, 36.

224. Smith, *Reminiscences*, 86–87.

225. It is possible that he was conscious of a sense of family tradition in entering the Doctors' Commons because Richard Trevor, of Trevalyn in Denbigh, had been admitted to the college in 1598 and had risen to become a judge of Admiralty (a position to which Twiss aspired but was denied due to his marriage scandal): Squibb, *Doctors' Commons*, 166;

tors' Commons shows that Twiss was present at its meetings several times a year for a quarter of a century, down to its last meeting on July 10, 1865.[226] Although the common law dominated English law, civil law was practiced in the Chancery Court, in matters dealing with equity, particularly contracts and property, that were unresolvable through the common law. Civil law was also practiced in the Ecclesiastical Courts, which, until 1857, had jurisdiction over marriage laws and probate, or wills, and finally in the Admiralty Courts. The Doctors' Commons, the civil law equivalent of the Inns of Court, provided buildings near St Paul's Cathedral in which the civil lawyers worked and could live, as well as housing the Arches Court for ecclesiastical matters. By the early nineteenth century, it had become clear that this separate system of civil law was in decline. The number of cases brought to the courts was diminishing, as were the number of lawyers who chose to specialise in this branch of the law. Charles Dickens, always keen to satirise Victorian law, was particularly scathing regarding the Chancery Court and the Doctors' Commons. *Bleak House* (a copy of which Twiss possessed) satirised the manner in which the Chancery Court consumed whole fortunes, but Dickens's portrayal of the Doctors' Commons was even more biting, perhaps because he worked there as a young reporter for five years from 1828 to 1833, several years prior to Twiss's arrival.[227]

Dickens devoted a chapter of his youthful essays *Sketches by Boz*, published in 1839, to the Doctors' Commons. He described arriving at the college: "Crossing a quiet and shady court-yard, paved with stone, and frowned upon by old red brick houses, on the doors of which were painted the names of sundry learned civilians."[228] In the court, he noticed "about a dozen solemn-looking gentlemen, in crimson gowns and wigs," and, "At a more elevated desk in the centre, sat a very fat and red-faced gentleman, in tortoise-shell spectacles, whose dignified appearance announced the judge." "We shall never be able to claim any credit as a physiognomist again, for, after a careful scrutiny of this gentleman's countenance, we had come to the conclusion that it bespoke nothing but conceit and silliness, when our friend with the silver staff whispered in our ear that he was no other than a doctor of civil law, and heaven knows what besides. So of course we were mistaken, and he must be a very talented man. He conceals it so well though—perhaps with the merciful view of not astonishing ordinary

---

Arthur Herbert Dodd, "Trevor Family, of Trevalun, Denbighshire, Plas Têg, Flintshire, and Glynde Sussex," *Dictionary of Welsh Biography* (1959).

226. "The Minute Book," Lambeth Palace Library MS. DC2, is the minutes of Doctors' Commons meetings from July 12, 1828, to July 10, 1865.

227. For Twiss's copy of *Bleak House*, see *Catalogue of a Portion of the Miscellaneous Library of Sir Travers Twiss*, 47.

228. Charles Dickens, *Sketches by Boz: Illustrative of Every-day Life and Every-day People* (London, 1854), 52.

people too much."[229] Dickens expanded on this sketch in *David Copperfield*, written in 1849 and 1850, when Twiss was installed in Doctors' Commons (Twiss kept a copy of *David Copperfield* in his library).[230] The central character, David, tells his friend Steerforth that his aunt suggests a career for him in the Doctors' Commons and asks him what that entails. Steerforth explains that it is a "a lazy old nook near St. Paul's Churchyard," "a little out-of-the-way place, where they administer what is called ecclesiastical law and play all kinds of tricks with obsolete old monsters of Acts of Parliament," and he goes on to observe that both marriage law and Admiralty law are practiced in this place. "Nonsense, Steerforth!," David responded, "You don't mean to say that there is any affinity between nautical matters and ecclesiastical matters?" Steerforth replied, "I don't, indeed, my dear boy . . . but I mean to say that they are managed and decided by the same set of people, down in that same Doctors' Commons."[231] Here Dickens commented upon the extraordinary fact that two seemingly disparate branches of law were isolated together in the same institution and, as a consequence, were closely wedded in English law. They were separated from the broader legal world through their common civil-law foundation, through their practitioners, and the place in which they were practiced.

This unlikely connection between marriage law, through ecclesiastical law, and the law of nations, through Admiralty law, lies at the heart of Travers Twiss's story. Twiss wed these two branches of law not only through his own legal practice but through his own life, and in this regard he was not unique. The cohabitation of the two branches of law in the Doctors' Commons, which Dickens claimed was not based on an affinity, other than their common civil-law foundation, nevertheless led to affinities. The law of nations developed through making analogies with private civil law.[232] That process was facilitated in England by the close institutional relationship between ecclesiastical law and the law of nations. Twiss, for example, at the time of the Scramble for Africa in the 1880s, took the concept of *territorium nullius* from canon law and introduced it into discussions of occupation in the law of nations.[233] He was very familiar with canon law through dealing with marriage in the English Ecclesiastical Courts. Not only, therefore, did he follow all civil lawyers in making such leaps, but he was instrumental in innovating them. He would do this again when he used the law to impersonate in marriage and to personify in the law of nations.

In *David Copperfield*, David follows his aunt's suggestion and determines to pursue a career in the Doctors' Commons. He accordingly describes his first

229. Dickens, *Sketches by Boz*, 53.
230. *Catalogue of a Portion of the Miscellaneous Library of Sir Travers Twiss*, 47.
231. Charles Dickens, *David Copperfield* (Philadelphia, 1850), Vol. 1, 390–391.
232. Hersch Lauterpacht, *Private Law Sources and Analogies in International Law*.
233. Fitzmaurice, *Sovereignty, Property, and Empire*.

visit to the college. It was, he said, to be "approached by a little low archway. Before we had taken many paces down the street beyond it, the noise of the city seemed to melt, as if by magic, into a softened distance."[234] David was to join the chambers of Spenlow and Jorkins as an articled clerk, and on their first meeting, Mr Spenlow conducted him on a tour of the college and the Court of Arches: "The upper part of this room was fenced off from the rest; and there, on the two sides of a raised platform of the horseshoe form, sitting on easy old-fashioned dining-room chairs, were sundry gentlemen in red gowns and grey wigs, whom I found to be the Doctors foresaid. Blinking over a little desk like a pulpit-desk, in the curve of the horseshoe, was an old gentleman, whom, if I had seen him in an aviary, I should certainly have taken for an owl, but who, I learned, was the presiding judge. In the space within the horseshoe, lower than these, that is to say on about the level of the floor, were sundry other gentlemen of Mr. Spenlow's rank, and dressed like him in black gowns with white fur upon them, sitting at a long green table ... The public, represented by a boy with a comforter, and a shabby-genteel man secretly eating crumbs out of his coat pockets, was warming itself at a stove in the centre of the Court. The languid stillness of the place was only broken by the chirping of this fire and by the voice of one of the Doctors, who was wandering slowly through a perfect library of evidence, and stopping to put up, from time to time, at little roadside inns of argument on the journey. Altogether, I have never, on any occasion, made one at such a cosey, dosey, old-fashioned, time-forgotten, sleepy-headed little family party in all my life; and I felt it would be quite a soothing opiate to belong to it in any character—except perhaps as a suitor."[235]

Dickens was not the only Victorian to notice that the Doctors' Commons was in need of reform. In 1833, the parliament established a select committee to inquire into the offices and duties of the Ecclesiastical Courts and the Admiralty Courts. The report of that committee found that "all the business of Doctors' Commons, in time of peace, is not sufficient to support a sufficiently numerous bar": that is, the number of "civilians," or civil lawyers, was declining and too low.[236] By the 1850s, it was clear that the future of the Doctors' Commons was limited, and the remaining members of the college realised that, in due course, they would have to give up their charter of incorporation. This would also mean selling the college buildings and the property on which they stood. These were very substantial assets, a city block in the heart of London, just below St Paul's churchyard, bounded by Addle Hill to the west and Knightrider Street to the north, with what is now Queen

234. Dickens, *David Copperfield*, Vol. 1, 397.
235. Dickens, *David Copperfield*, Vol. 1, 400.
236. Parliamentary Papers, *Reports from Committees*, session 2, February–24 August 1843 (London, 1843), Vol. 5, 90.

Victoria Street running straight through the block. Twiss's colleague in the College, Dr John Lee, wrote to him on March 20, 1854, to tell him that he was implacably opposed to the proposal to "the transfer of the testamentary jurisdiction to the court of Chancery . . . or of Matrimonial jurisdiction to the Courts of Common Law" (one of the early proposals to solve the problem of the civilian lawyers was to collapse all the courts into one, thus Ecclesiastical and Admiralty into Chancery, or vice versa). Lee concluded, "I never can agree to the dissolution of the College and the dividing its capital amongst the present members."[237] Twiss responded defensively by declaring, "I think you must have misunderstood the position which I maintained in our discussion [at the Doctors' Commons meeting] . . . I voted in our meetings in the negative about our property and the dissolution of the College, and after the petition had been agreed to it was placed in my hands to make some alterations on points on which I have objected."[238] For Twiss, who was perhaps the busiest of the Advocates in Doctors' Commons, and the most prolific officeholder, the dissolution of the college was potentially a financial disaster.

As there were only twenty-five civilian Advocates at this time, and they were the shareholders in the corporation of the Doctors' Commons, the very large sum of money from the sale of the college property—scores of thousands of pounds—would bring a small fortune for each member. There was, accordingly, a strong incentive for many of the members, particularly those less industrious than Twiss, to hasten their own demise and not to admit any new members to the college, as this would dilute the windfall. In this period, only Doctor Thomas Hutchinson Tristram was admitted to the college, in November 1855, at the request of Travers Twiss, who remained stubbornly optimistic about the future. For his £20 entrance fee, Tristram recouped £4,000 four years later on the sale of the college property. Unsurprisingly, perhaps, he remained a close friend to Twiss throughout his troubles.[239] It is only through Tristram's care that the letters from Metternich to Twiss in the Bibliothèque nationale de France have survived.[240]

237. "John Lee to Travers Twiss," March 20, 1854, Lambeth Palace Library, Lee Papers, MS 2876f.148.

238. "Travers Twiss to John Lee," March 27, 1854, Lambeth Palace Library, Lee Papers, MS 2876 148verso–149.

239. According to Tristram's son, writing in 1935, Twiss remained *"un ami très intime de mon père,"* even after his marriage scandal: "F .T. Tristram to Monsieur le Conservateur," June 1, 1935, Bibliothèque nationale de France, NAF 12629, 2.

240. Twiss left the letters to Tristram a few years before his death, forty years after Tristram's admission to the college. Tristram, in turn, left them to his wife when he died, and she left them to their son, F. T. Tristram; however, she "made me promise," F. T wrote, "that I would transmit them to my son." "But," he added in his note to the archivist in Paris in 1935, "he was killed in the war [the Great War]": "F. T. Tristram to Monsieur le Conservateur," June 1, 1935, Bibliothèque nationale de France, NAF 12629, 2.

Reform arrived eventually in 1857 with the Probate Act and the Matrimonial Causes Act, which, together, moved all matters concerned with wills and marriage to the common-law courts, while allowing the Advocates of the Doctors' Commons to continue to practice in those courts.[241] In the meeting of the college held on January 15, 1858, with twenty of twenty-six members present, Dr Alfred Waddilove (whom Twiss and Merivale had elected to the Athenaeum in 1854) moved a resolution: "By reason of the changes effected by the Probate and Divorce Acts, the position of this society is so essentially altered that it is no longer desirable that the Society should continue to remain a Corporate Body—that steps should therefore be taken towards surrendering the Charter of Incorporation and disposing by sale (or otherwise) of the property of the College for the common benefit of the present members thereof."[242] Although he withdrew the resolution, the college would not survive much longer. In 1865, the Advocates sold their property to the Metropolitan Board of Works for £83,950 and divided most of that sum between the twenty-six members. The Board of Works needed it for the Victoria Embankment project.[243] The Advocates did not, however, surrender their charter of incorporation, and the corporation therefore continued to exist until the death of the last Advocate, Dr Tristram, in 1912.[244] The affinity between marriage law and the law of nations survived the dissolution of the college, continuing in the Probate, Divorce and Admiralty Division of the High Court of Justice, in which barristers specialised in all three branches until 1970, when the Administration of Justice Act separated divorce into the Family Division and Admiralty into the Queen's Bench Division.[245]

241. Squibb, *Doctors' Commons*, 105. Even following this act, the members of the college remained deeply divided over whether to dissolve, as a further letter from Twiss to his ally Dr Lee reveals after a meeting to determine whether "we should offer the court to the judge of the Probate and Matrimonial causes." This matter was carried "merely by the casting vote of the judge, [and] that after a most stormed discussion." Twiss then revealed a plan to save the college: "We who wish to keep up the College and to practice if possible in Doctors' Commons, have also agreed to buy off those who wish to withdraw, if necessary, by giving them their shares": "Travers Twiss to John Lee," November 10, 1857, Lambeth Palace Library, Lee Papers, MS 2876ff, 156. The plan did not materialise, but it reveals the degree to which Twiss's fortunes had been made by his civil law practice, and it possibly explains why the charter of incorporation was never surrendered.

242. "Doctors' Commons: The Minute Book," Lambeth Palace Library MS. DC2 ff.217–220; "Arthur Waddilove," Athenaeum, Book of Candidates, 1841 to 1850, Mem 1/1/7, April 2, 1846, 2619.

243. The project was legislated in the Thames Embankment Act of 1862, claiming the marshy banks of the Thames as part of the city so that a new road, Queen Victoria Street, would link East and West London, running along the Embankment and then under St Paul's and directly through the block holding the college buildings and thus necessitating their demolition.

244. Squibb, *Doctors' Commons*.

245. Squibb, *Doctors' Commons*, 109.

The jurisdiction of the lawyers in the Doctors' Commons and the Ecclesiastical Courts over marriage law was something of a historical anomaly. It was a remnant of the pre-Reformation universal church, which governed all matters dealing with marriage. Divorce law remained largely consistent with pre-Reformation practice. England effectively maintained Catholic laws of marriage. It was extremely difficult for a husband to gain a divorce, and even more difficult for a wife. If a man wanted to divorce his wife, it was necessary for him to bring a criminal case in a common law court against another man for adultery with his wife. If he won this case, he would then have to petition for separation from an Ecclesiastical Court. If he won this second case, he would then have to apply to the House of Lords for a complete divorce. The Lords would hear the evidence from the previous two cases and, if they agreed, would send a recommendation to the House of Commons, who would hear the case again.[246] Every divorce required a separate act of parliament, effectively creating a new law in each instance. The costs of these proceedings were very high—approximately £150, but more if they were contested—and they were accordingly only accessible to very wealthy people. The whole process could take months or years. In 1856, only three such cases succeeded in England and Wales. Palmerston's aim in introducing the 1857 legislation was to alter marriage from being a sacrament to a contract, enabling the transfer of jurisdiction over marriage from ecclesiastical law and its arduous processes to a single common-law court.

The Matrimonial Causes Act can thus be placed in the context of broader emancipations for the middle classes in Victorian England. Opponents raised fears that easing divorce would undermine the institution of marriage, particularly amongst the "lower orders."[247] It would produce license rather than liberty. The existing laws were understood to protect the lower classes from corruption. An unhappy man, it was said, might simply sue for divorce. Other critics, such as William Gladstone, saw the Act as an attack upon the Church of England. Two-thirds of the clergy, in a petition from ten thousand parsons, opposed the Act because they did not want to marry men and women who had been divorced, prompting the Lords to respond that parsons were to follow the law of the land, not their consciences. Here were echoes of the divisions that had riven the church over the Tractarian movement, also portrayed partly as a contest over Erastianism, or the supremacy of the sovereign in religious matters. When the bill came to the House of Commons, it was held up for weeks in debate about what might constitute appropriate grounds for divorce. Would the "casual seduction of the chambermaid" make a man "liable to lose his wife and

---

246. Margaret K. Woodhouse, "The Marriage and Divorce Bill of 1857," *American Journal of Legal History*, vol. 3 (1959), 260–261; Shanley, *Feminism, Marriage, and the Law in Victorian England*, 39–44.

247. Woodhouse, "The Marriage and Divorce Bill of 1857," 263.

home"?[248] The Act was eventually passed and in the form Palmerston intended. Under it, men were required to prove adultery as the basis for divorce. Prior to 1857, women had been required to establish adultery as well as "exaggerated cruelty." The new legislation expanded the possible grounds to adultery plus either cruelty, bigamy, desertion, conviction for rape, or conviction for crimes against nature.[249] Divorce became more financially and legally accessible. However, all cases were restricted to one court in London—there would be no equivalent to a travelling assize court. Anybody who wished to divorce had to know the law and have the means to travel to London, as well as to pursue the matter through that court. Divorce was now possible for the middle classes but not for workers. The beneficiaries were those who were understood to be morally capable of dealing with divorce, or who were, as Samuel Wilberforce, the high church Bishop of Oxford, put it, already morally corrupt. Many of the fears, as well as aspirations, for the legislation were realised when, in the year after the Act, 300 cases, not three, were brought to the new court.

Despite, or perhaps even because of all this upheaval, Twiss's career flourished at Doctors' Commons. The diminishing number of civilian lawyers merely multiplied his lucrative offices. After nine years practicing as an Advocate in the Doctors' Commons, he was appointed in June 1849 to the office of Commissary-General of the city and diocese of Canterbury, in east Kent, meaning that Twiss was judge in all matrimonial and probate cases in the diocese.[250] In 1852, he was appointed as Vicar General to the Province of Canterbury, which made him responsible for issuing marriage licenses to the southern two-thirds of England.[251] Twiss therefore issued most marriage licenses in England between 1852 and his resignation in 1872. Clearly, this would be too many licenses for one man to deal with, so he appointed local surrogates to perform his role.[252]

Archibald Tait, who in 1852 was Dean of Carlisle and would later become Archbishop of Canterbury, was one of Twiss's strongest allies and supporters, and he commented acutely on the importance of these offices for Twiss. The two had met when Tait was also a student and fellow at Oxford. In 1852, Tait was on the Oxford Commission, to which Twiss gave evidence, and in this same year, Tait wrote to his wife about a meeting he had with Twiss: "I called this morning after church on Twiss. He has been in a great state of anxiety. If the Whigs had stood a day longer in office he was to have been made Queen's Advocate [i.e., Attorney General in the Ecclesiastical Courts] with a salary of about three thousand a year and come out as Sir Travers Twiss. The place

---

248. Woodhouse, "The Marriage and Divorce Bill of 1857," 271.
249. Woodhouse, "The Marriage and Divorce Bill of 1857," 273.
250. *London Evening Standard*, May 28, 1849, 1.
251. *The Times*, March 5, 1852, 4.
252. *South Eastern Gazette*, March 30, 1858, 5.

was vacant by Sir John Dodson's replacement [as Dean of Arches] of old Sir Herbert Jenner-Fust who is just dead. And hence it is very doubtful whether Lord Derby [the new Prime Minister] will confirm the appointment. This is certainly a trial, which he bears very well. I hope he may yet have the appointment. Meanwhile he has got one office vacant by Sir H. Fust's death—being appointed by the Archbishop of Canterbury Vicar General of the Province of Canterbury which is worth about 700 a year so that he will not starve. How I do wish he and Johnson provided for. He takes the whole state of matters very well."[253]

During the government turmoil of 1852, Twiss did indeed miss out on becoming Queen's Advocate and would have to wait until 1867 for the post. He certainly did his best to cover his disappointment when writing to Metternich: "The Archbishop of Canterbury named me, beginning this year, the 'Vicar General' of the Province of Canterbury."[254] He also explained the responsibilities of the office: "The Vicar General is the legal representative of the Archbishop," and his functions include "presiding at the convocation of the clergy in the absence of the Archbishop, and to do the same thing that the Speaker does in the House of Commons." He stated proudly that, on August 21, he would "go to St Paul's Cathedral and, after several legal ceremonies, I will prorogue the Convocation." He even spoke of himself in the third person as "V. G.": "If V. G. [Vicar General] stays in Vienna, I hope to see you at your house."[255] Similarly, Tait's letter is indicative not only of Twiss's ambition but also his fragility, revealing how the collection of offices was fundamental to the prosperity of a civil lawyer such as Twiss. It is also revealing of Tait's protective attitude to his friend, and when he became Bishop of London, and later Archbishop of Canterbury, Twiss received further offices. Their friendship was sorely tested by the scandal twenty years later. It was Tait who instructed Twiss to resign his offices and who declined future appeals for office from Twiss.

In March 1852, Twiss was appointed Commissary of the Archdeaconry of Suffolk.[256] In February 1856, he was made Chancellor of the Consistory Court of the Diocese of Hereford, including Herefordshire and parts of Shropshire and Worcestershire.[257] This meant he was the judge of the diocese in matters of ecclesiastical law. In November 1856, Bishop John Jackson, with whom Twiss would later work when Jackson was Bishop of London, made him

253. "Archibald Tait to Catharine Tait," February 19, 1852, Lambeth Palace Library, Tait Papers, Personal Letters of Catharine Tait, 1850–1878, 103, f.94verso.

254. Twiss to Metternich, July 7, 1852, National Archives of the Czech Republic, Prague, RAM-AC/ 10/ 778, 19.

255. Twiss to Metternich, July 7, 1852, National Archives of the Czech Republic, Prague, RAM-AC/ 10/ 778, 20.

256. *The Ipswich Journal*, March 6, 1852, 2.

257. *Evening Mail*, February 6, 1856, 3: Twiss appointed by the Bishop of Hereford to the Chancellorship of that diocese (which is also part of the Province of Canterbury).

Chancellor of the Diocese of Lincoln, covering Lincolnshire.[258] In July 1858, Bishop Tait made him Chancellor of the Diocese of London, including the City of London and Greater London north of the Thames.[259] In each of these jurisdictions—Suffolk, Canterbury, Hereford, Lincoln, and London—Twiss sat in judgement over matters concerning marriage and probate, although the timing of the 1857 Matrimonial Causes and Probate Acts could hardly have been worse for him. Nevertheless, he immediately set up a travelling probate court, with the Diocese of Lincoln, for example, regularly advertising in the *Hereford Journal* his arrival in Lincoln to hear cases.[260] Sitting as a judge in these courts over issues concerning marriage and divorce gave Twiss an expertise that would enable him to manage deftly the legal complexity of his own subsequent marriage. Similarly, with his experience issuing licenses, he knew how to manipulate the proofs of marriage. But the same responsibilies would also greatly amplify the scandal when it transpired that his own marriage was based upon an imposture. Perhaps no person is better placed to manipulate the law than a judge, but few could suffer as much for being discovered to have done so.

Indeed, Twiss, frequently judged the marriages and affairs of others.[261] Some cases were similar to his circumstances, particularly the celebrated Stepney Scandal. In this case, one of his Oxford colleagues, the Reverend James Bonwell, a fellow of Brasenose College and parish priest of St Philips Stepney, was charged with conducting an affair in his Stepney rooms with a young woman, Miss Elizabeth Yorath, a clergyman's daughter, until she became pregnant, while neglecting his invalid wife and child in Islington. Twiss was appointed Chief Commissioner of the Ecclesiastical Commission on the Reverend James Bonwell, held in the Doctors' Commons, to inquire into the case.[262] The affair and pregnancy were scandalous enough, and were

---

258. *London Evening Standard*, November 20, 1856, 2: Bishop of Lincoln, John Jackson, appoints Twiss to Chancellorship of Diocese of Lincoln; other accounts suggest Twiss's friend, Archibald Tait, now Bishop of London, was responsible: *Hertford Mercury and Reformer*, November 22, 1856, 2.

259. *Hertford Mercury and Reformer*, July 31, 1858, 3.

260. The notice declared that the "Worshipful Travers Twiss" would hold his "Probate Court at Ludlow on Tuesday the 12th," so that "all persons who have Wills to prove, Letters of Administration or Licenses to take out, or any other business to do, may then and there appear and have the same dispatched": *Hereford Journal*, July 23, 1856, 2; see also *Hereford Journal*, May 20, 1857: Twiss announces his Probate Court coming to Ludlow on May 26.

261. See, for example, "Law Intelligence," *London Daily News*, March 31, 1849, 6: a report on Twiss practising in the Ecclesiastical Court in a case of cruelty in marriage (a necessary condition for divorce), and the "custody of infants," representing the wife; "Court of Probate and Divorce," *Cambridge Chronicle and Journal*, January 19, 1861, 6: a case in which Eva Maria, the wife of the Reverend John Chippendale Montesquieu Bellew, conducted an affair with the Honourable Ashley Eden, a senior figure in the East India Office, with Bellew seeking "dissolution of marriage by reason of her adultery."

262. "Extraordinary Inquiry into the Conduct of a Gentleman," *Western Daily Press*, December 16, 1859, 2.

damaging to the reputation of the church, but the police became involved when it was discovered that the body of the dead baby had been "surreptitiously packed" into another person's coffin and "improperly buried" in Tower Hamlets Cemetery.[263] In his judgement, Twiss declared that "in respect of the scandal and evil report concerning the Rev. James Bonwell," there were "sufficient prima-facie grounds for instituting further proceedings," although he found that he was unable to determine whether Bonwell "had actual adulterous intercourse with the said Elizabeth Yorath within the said diocese" because the intercourse could have taken place elsewhere and thus outside his jurisdiction.[264] In this role, as in many others, Twiss was a moral, as well as a legal, guardian of the diocese and of several other dioceses in England and of the church.[265]

As Vicar General, Twiss was also obliged to attend upon the Archbishop of Canterbury at meetings of Convocation, the legislative assembly of the Province of Canterbury held in the sumptuous medieval Jerusalem Chamber in Westminster Abbey. These assemblies were held regularly throughout the year, with Twiss attending several times a year over his twenty years of office.[266] He again attended when Convocation, which included all the bishops in the Province of Canterbury, was presented annually to the Queen.[267] His authority in this role was such that he sometimes chaired the assembly, and when the Archbishop was absent, Twiss took his proxy.[268] He understood the role to be important to the union between church and state, writing in 1852: "I have had

---

263. "Ecclesiastical Commission on the Rev. James Bonwell," *Kentish Gazette*, December 20, 1859, 3. For some time, a question remained over whether the baby had died of natural causes, although that question was settled by an inquest.

264. "Ecclesiastical Commission on the Rev. James Bonwell," *Kentish Gazette*, December 20, 1859, 3; More detail to be found in "The Clerical Scandal at Stepney," *Manchester Courier and Lancashire General Advertiser*, December 17, 1859, 7; *South Eastern Gazette*, December 20, 1859, 8. In the subsequent proceedings in the Arches Court, Bonwell was deprived of his benefices.

265. *Essex Standard*, April 3, 1857, for Twiss on a commission to examine the dioceses. Other cases also contained elements that would later be found in his own, including the 1859 case of Elizabeth Green, who had run away to Gretna Green, across the Scottish border, to marry a man who subsequently denied the marriage. Scottish marriages did not require the same ceremony or proofs of marriage as had been required in England since the 1754 Marriage Act, and almost anybody—in Elizabeth Green's case, it was the Gretna Green blacksmith—could perform the ceremony, which, as the blacksmith said, was "as fast a marriage as if the Archbishop of Canterbury had done it": *London Evening Standard*, December 8, 1859, 6. For the 1753 Marriage Act and Gretna Green marriages, see Lawrence Stone, *The Family, Sex and Marriage in England 1500–1800* (Harmondsworth, 1977), 32.

266. "Meeting of Convocation," *Morning Post*, November 13, 1852, 6.

267. *London Evening Standard*, February 17, 1853; *London Evening Standard*, February 20, 1858, 2.

268. *Morning Post*, October 29, 1853, 3; "Church and Universities," *Liverpool Mail*, May 2, 1857, 2.

a good deal of work with the Convocation ... I hope, however, we shall keep up the union between the church and the state for some time to come. We are not mere Protestants as you well know, but have an historical basis of the three first centuries."[269]

Again as Vicar General, Twiss presided in the ceremonies swearing in new bishops. Bishops in the Church of England, as in the Catholic Church, were corporations. They might be corporations sole, so named because they were composed of only one person, or they might be corporations aggregate, which were comprised of two or more people. The corporation sole was a creation of medieval canon law that enabled the property of a church to be passed from one parson to another without ever becoming their personal property—the property remaining in the possession of the corporation, which the parson only assumed for his time in office.[270] The further advantage of this legal innovation was also to make church property a person in law, therefore enabling it to take actions against other persons and to have actions taken against it. The Bishop was therefore a legal impersonation, or personification, not simply in the literary sense but in constituting an artificial person. The corporation sole would, as Twiss's younger contemporary Frederic Maitland later observed, have remained a legal obscurity if it had not become the instrument for understanding the legal status of the crown.[271] The sovereign, too, was a corporation sole, a form of personification, and it was this artificial nature of the sovereign person that Hobbes would expand upon in his *Leviathan* to explain that the state was equivalent to neither the ruler nor the ruled.[272] As Vicar General, it was Twiss's job to perform the ceremony which created this legal person in the case of bishops. Corporations were created by the act of issuing of letters patent, and it was Twiss who performed that act. He was, therefore, an expert in the matter of personification. He understood that this process could apply to individuals, such as bishops and parsons, just as he also understood, as an international lawyer, that it applied to sovereigns. Here again, canon law and the law of nations drew upon common legal principles. This dual nature of personification—in its application to natural persons as well as to the creation of the artificial person of the state—would be fundamental to the dual personifications Twiss helped perform in later years: namely, the impersonation of his wife, incorporated into the legal personality of Twiss by marriage, and the personification of the Congo Free State.

269. Twiss to Metternich, November 29, 1852, National Archives of the Czech Republic, Prague, RAM-AC/ 10/ 778, 31.
270. Maitland, *State, Trust and Corporation*, 9–31.
271. Maitland, *State, Trust and Corporation*, 32–33.
272. Quentin Skinner, "A Genealogy of the Modern State," *Proceedings of the British Academy*, 162, (2009), 325–370; Runciman, *Pluralism and the Personality of the State*, 6–33.

Twiss would either personally grant the letters patent of incorporation to the new bishop or would instruct the Queen's Proctor to do so.[273] When the ceremony confirming John Jackson as the new Bishop of Lincoln was held in May 1853, Twiss instructed the Queen's Proctor to read the letters patent.[274] Three years later, Twiss became Chancellor over the diocese. When, in 1856, Archibald Tait was confirmed as Bishop of London, the ceremony was held in the Great Hall of the Doctors' Commons and in St Mary-le-Bow Church, Cheapside, with Twiss presiding. The ceremony began with morning prayers, followed by Twiss requesting the Proctor to read the letters patent. The Proctor then presented Tait to Twiss. Tait took the oaths of office, and then the Vicar General, Twiss, concluded the ceremony by reading and signing a "sentence" in excess of 500 words. He declared, amongst other things: "We, Travers Twiss, Doctor of Laws, Vicar-General, and Official Principal... having heard, seen, understood and discussed the merits and circumstances of a certain business of confirmation... of the person of the Very Rev. Archibald Campbell Tait... we have thought fit... to proceed to the giving our definitive sentence or final decree... a man both prudent and discreet, deservedly laudable for his life and conversation... there neither was nor is anything in the ecclesiastical laws that ought to obstruct or hinder his being confirmed... and we do commit unto the said Bishop elected and confirmed the care, government and administration of the spirituals of the said Bishopric of London; and we do pronounce, decree, and order... shall be induced into the real, actual, and corporal possession of the said Bishopric."[275] It was thus by speaking, to pronounce, decree, and order, that Twiss performed the act of creating the new legal person. This understanding that such signs perform the creation of persons constitutes a context for the later acts of creating both Lady Travers Twiss and the Congo Free State.

It is ironic that Twiss, who, as we shall see, would later implore Tait on more than one occasion to help him to regain any office, would at this moment confer office, legal personality, and "corporal possession," upon Tait himself. It was not always thus. Just days after Twiss incorporated Tait as Bishop of London, Tait granted Twiss the new office of Chancellor of the Diocese of Lincoln.[276] The relations of mutual assistance were seamless. When, for example,

---

273. *Morning Post*, May 19, 1857, 5: Twiss performed confirmation of the new Bishop of Norwich; "Home Intelligence," *The Ipswich Journal*, December 3, 1853, 3: Twiss participating in the ceremony consecrating colonial bishops in St Mary's Church, Lambeth; *Kentish Gazette*, December 5, 1854, 2: Twiss giving letters patent in consecration of bishops in St Mary's Church, Lambeth; *Hampshire Chronicle*, August 9, 1856, 8: Twiss in ceremony for consecrating bishops.

274. "Confirmation of the Bishop of Lincoln," *London Evening Standard*, May 4, 1853, 2.

275. *Evening Mail*, November 21, 1856, 7.

276. "The Lord Bishop of London Has Appointed Dr Travers Twiss to the Office": *Hertford Mercury and Reformer*, November 22, 1856, 2.

Tait was too sick in 1866 to give his annual "charge" to his synod, Twiss delivered it for him in St Paul's Cathedral.[277] Arthur Stanley, formerly Twiss's protégé at University College and now Dean of Westminster, was so impressed that he teased Tait that it "was his best Charge yet."

After the passing of the Matrimonial Causes and Probate Acts in 1857, Twiss became a Queen's Counsel in January 1858 so that he could work as a barrister in the Common Law Courts. On January 16, 1858, the new Court for Divorce and Matrimonial Causes met for the first time, Sir Cresswell Cresswell sitting as judge, and four advocates from Doctors' Commons, including Twiss, were "called within the bar."[278] Twiss similarly began immediately working as a barrister in the new Court of Probate, also presided over by Cresswell.[279] The new divorce and probate courts deprived the ecclesiastical Arches Court of the Province of Canterbury of much of its business. The Dean, or judge, of the Arches Court, Sir John Dodson, died in April 1858, leaving his depleted office vacant. Rumours immediately circulated that Twiss would be made the new Dean, obliging him to resign his position as Vicar General.[280] By late May, however, Twiss had declined the offer because the stipend was reduced to £30 a year by the creation of the new courts, "a very small allowance for the chief ecclesiastical judge of the Province of Canterbury."[281] One report declared of the humbled Arches Court: "No one cares to be its judge."[282]

Having entered the Doctors' Commons in 1841, Twiss pursued his practice not only in the Ecclesiastical Courts and, later, in the new Court for Divorce and Matrimonial Causes, but also in its other branch concerning "nautical matters," as Dickens put: that is, in the Admiralty Court. The Admiralty Court was not reformed until 1875, when it was reunited with probate and marriage in the Probate, Divorce and Admiralty Division of the High Court, after a brief separation since 1858. Admiralty law held great significance in an island-based maritime power with a vast empire. The Admiralty Court and its lawyers were particularly busy during times of war, deciding disputes over war prizes. Twiss took cases on collisions at sea (a subject on which he would later publish), salvage, and the capture of ships during war.[283] Most of his cases in the Admi-

277. Randall Thomas Davidson and William Benham, *Life of Archibald Campbell Tait, Archbishop of Canterbury*, 2 vols., 3rd ed. (London, 1891), Vol. 1, 472.

278. *Aris's Birmingham Gazette*, January 18, 1858, 2.

279. *Chelmsford Chronicle*, January 14, 1859, 2.

280. *London Evening Standard*, May 3, 1858, 5.

281. *Morning Chronicle*, May 20, 1858, 5.

282. *Morning Chronicle*, May 20, 1858, 5; By July, Twiss's colleague in the Doctors' Commons, Stephen Lushington, had accepted the office: *Evening Mail*, July 12, 1858, 8.

283. For Twiss's cases, see *Law Officer's Opinions, 1862–1886*, 8 vols., Harvard Law Library, MS 1110; See also *Hampshire Telegraph*, June 7, 1851, 5; *Morning Chronicle*, November 27, 1851, 7; and *Morning Chronicle*, December 1, 1851, 7; *Morning Chronicle*, December 3, 1851, 7: shows two more cases—collisions at sea (something Twiss later published on); "Law Intelligence," *Morning Post*, December 15, 1857, 6–7: Admiralty Court,

ralty Court arose in the context of managing Britain's informal empire, or its sphere of influence, in the Mediterranean and in Asia. He was also deeply engaged with writing and lecturing on the law of nations, and in delivering legal opinions, outside the institutional context of the Admiralty Court.

Sovereignty in the Law of Nations and Ecclesiastical Law

In the first half of his career, a concern that linked Twiss's thoughts on ecclesiastical matters, on the one hand, and the law of nations, on the other, was the supremacy of sovereign powers. Whether in regard to the controversy over the Oregon Territory, Catholic reform in England, or the 1848 revolutions, Twiss argued for the subordination of individuals and associations to the rights of sovereigns. Sovereigns were the supreme personifications, or artificial persons, those who made possible all other personification, particularly corporations such as the church. This was the position he would dramatically revise when he later came to argue for King Leopold's International African Association.

One of the earliest statements Twiss made on the supreme rights of sovereignty was in the debate over the Oregon Territory. On the matter of who can be admitted to international society, he changed his views radically over the course of his lifetime. In the period of his life with which we have been concerned so far, his position on this question was consistent with his conservatism on many other questions: that is, he maintained the view which coalesced in eighteenth-century works on the law of nations that the only persons who can be admitted to international society are states. This view dominated international law throughout the nineteenth century, only coming into question in the last quarter of that century and then to a large degree as a consequence of the efforts of Twiss himself. Prior to the 1870s, Twiss's thoughts were consistent with the prevailing view. Nowhere was this position made clearer than in his contribution to the debate over the Oregon Territory.

The Oregon Territory was the vast region in the northwest of the North American continent which was perceived in the early nineteenth century to be void of sovereignty, with the indigenous peoples of that region generally not being regarded by European powers as possessing political societies capable of sovereign rule. As such, the territory was, according to the conventions of the law of nations, open to be occupied by the first persons who chose to seize it.[284] This region was accordingly subject to intense rivalry over claims to sovereignty between various European powers and the newly formed United States of America. Since the sixteenth century, Spain had claimed to possess

---

case of La Plata, Twiss "for respondents"; *Cambridge Independent Press*, April 3, 1858, 8: Twiss argued in Admiralty Court that capture of Cagliari was contrary to the law of nations.

284. Fitzmaurice, *Sovereignty, Property, and Empire*, 203–214.

dominium over the entire west coast of America, but because it had not backed that claim up with occupations in the north, its arguments were not taken seriously. As early as the 1780s and '90s, Spain and Britain came into conflict over possession of Nootka Sound, a booming region for the fur trade on the west coast of what is now Vancouver Island, but the outcome of the conventions between the two powers was that both agreed to withdraw their claims.[285] Russia also made claims to the northwest, establishing colonies and trading posts from 1784, even more so after the foundation of the Russian American Company in 1799. These settlements extended from Alaska as far south as San Francisco Bay. This expansion led to the Russian ukase, or edict, of 1821 claiming property over the "whole of the north west coast of America," meaning north of 51 degrees (from the northern tip of Vancouver Island).[286] By the first decades of the nineteenth century, the British were pushing their North American interests west towards the Pacific, largely through the offices of the Hudson's Bay Company. At the same time, in 1823, President James Monroe of the United States declared that the New World should be closed to further influence and expansionism by corrupt Old World powers. Monroe was particularly concerned that a newly stable Europe, following the decline of Napoléon and the 1815 Vienna Congress, would once more turn its focus outward. Both he and Thomas Jefferson argued that the west of the North American continent should be colonised by people from the east who could establish their own independent states and choose themselves whether or not to join the United States. By the late 1820s, however, John Quincy Adams had already declared that all west coast settlements came under the sovereignty of the United States.[287]

In the 1830s and '40s, large numbers of migrants began crossing the Rocky Mountains on the Oregon Trail, and pressure built to resolve the problem of sovereignty over the northwest Pacific coast. Britain had not relinquished its claims to the territory, and the British and United States governments entered into negotiations for a treaty of partition. Those negotiations were enflamed, however, by the 1845 Inaugural Address of the new President, James Polk, who declared, "Our title to the country of the Oregon is clear and unquestionable, and already our people are preparing to perfect the title by occupying it with their wives and children . . . are already engaged in the blessings of self-government in valleys of which rivers flow to the Pacific."[288] Polk believed that the United States would extend its sovereignty over these communities, although the image he summoned

285. On the Nootka conventions, see Frederick Merk, *The Oregon Question* (Cambridge, Mass., 1967), 2–5.
286. "Rules Established for the Limits of Navigation and Order of Communication along the Coast of Eastern Siberia, the North-West Coast of America, and the Aleutian, Kurile, and Other Islands, under Russian Ukase of September 4/16, 1821," in *Proceedings of the Alaskan Boundary Tribunal* (Washington, 1904), Vol. 3, II, 19–27.
287. Merk, *The Oregon Question*, 117–119.
288. Merk, *The Oregon Question*, 282.

was one anticipated by Jefferson and Monroe of new claims to territory, and new societies established, by individuals in a state of nature. Similarly, Swiss-born Albert Gallatin, one of the most senior US diplomats in negotiations with Britain over Oregon in 1818 and again 1826, argued: "Whenever sufficiently numerous, they will decide whether it suits them best to be an independent nation or an integral part of our great Republic."[289] In January 1846, the US Congress debated whether Oregon should be immediately subject to United States sovereignty or whether the settlers could establish their own republics, which would then decide whether to join the union. Robert Winthrop, of Massachusetts, declared that he had "the most sincere desire to see that territory in the possession of such of our people as desire to occupy it—whether hereafter as an independent nation, as was originally suggested by a distinguished Senator from Missouri (Mr Benton,) and more recently by a no less distinguished member Senator from Massachusetts, (Mr. Webster), or as a portion of our own wide-spread and glorious Republic."[290] As early as May 1843, some of these aspirations had already been realised when the Provisional Government of Oregon was created by the settlers—a government independent, until the conclusion of the Oregon Treaty in August 1846, from the United States of America.

These developments, particularly President Polk's declaration and Democratic calls for annexation of all the territory as far north as the Russian colonies in Alaska, provoked England. A third war between Britain and the United States within seventy years began to appear a distinct possibility until the United States' invasion of Mexico, in April 1846, brought pressure for a negotiated agreement for a boundary at 49 degrees latitude. The American administration had no desire to fight two wars at the same time. It was at the height of this dispute, in January 1846, that Twiss, at this time holding the Drummond Chair of Political Economy in Oxford, published his 250-page book *The Oregon Territory*. He declared that he hoped it could contribute to a peaceful solution of the conflict. At the time of his writing, and for some months to come, negotiations for a treaty were being conducted between the British ambassador, Richard Pakenham, and the US Secretary of State, James Buchanan. Twiss believed he provided materials to assist in their negotiation. He sent a copy to the Prime Minister, Robert Peel.[291] Throughout his lifetime, he succeeded in having his voice heard in the highest circles.

289. Albert Gallatin, *The Oregon Question* (New York, 1846), 47–48. For Gallatin in the Oregon negotiations, see Merk, *The Oregon Question*, 38–43, 53–58, 65–71.
290. Robert Charles Winthrop, "Speech of Mr Winthrop of Massachusetts, on the Oregon Question Delivered in the House of Representatives of the United States," Jan. 3, 1846 (Washington, 1846), 13. For Benton, see Thomas Benton, "Speech of Mr Benton of Missouri on the Oregon Question, Delivered in the United States Senate," May 22, 25, 28, 1846 (Washington, 1846).
291. On March 8, 1846, Twiss sent Peel a list of printing errors in the original copy: Twiss to Peel, March 8, 1846: British Library, Peel Papers, Additional MS. 40686.

Twiss provided, as always, a history of the dispute, including its various treaties and conventions. At the centre of his book was a lengthy discussion of the principles in the law of nations governing the occupation of territory. One of his principal concerns was to address whether people can settle a territory void of property and sovereignty and establish there their own government, as, indeed, the settlers who established the Provisional Government of Oregon had done, and as statesmen from Jefferson until Gallatin had claimed they could. Twiss believed that such claims were an affront to the rights of sovereigns. The occupation of territory, he argued, was the privilege of sovereign powers, and next to them, the rights of all other individuals or associations in international society were baseless. He founded these views upon the work of Emer de Vattel, the most eminent authority of the previous century on the law of nations. He began his chapter on occupation by citing Vattel: "When a nation takes possession of a country to which no prior owner can lay claim, it is considered as acquiring the *empire* or sovereignty over it, at the same time with the *domain*." "When a nation," he argued, "occupies a vacant country, it imports its sovereignty with it, and its sovereignty entitles it not merely to a disposing power over all the property within it, which is termed its Eminent Domain, but likely to an exclusive right of command in all places of the country which it has taken possession of." Here Twiss was anxious to underline that in this respect a "nation differs from an individual" because "although an independent individual may settle in a country which he finds without an owner," as had individuals in Oregon, "and there possess an independent domain," that is, possess property, "yet he cannot arrogate to himself an exclusive right to the country, or to the empire over it." Only nations could transplant sovereignty; individuals could not. By a nation he meant a sovereign state: "Every nation that governs itself by its own authority and laws, without dependence on any foreign power, is a sovereign state; and when it acts as a nation, it acts in a sovereign capacity." The individuals who had transplanted themselves into Oregon could exploit nature and create property, but they were obliged to wait for the question of sovereignty over them to be settled by sovereign powers. Any such individuals' occupation of the "empire," or sovereignty, of such territory was "as against other nations, rash and ridiculous (Vattel, b.ii., §96)."[292]

It was, therefore, only a "nation" who could acquire sovereignty through occupation of a territory, and the claims of individuals, next to such nations, were "ridiculous." Twiss returned to this point in various ways throughout his treatise, repeating that "to constitute a valid territorial title by occupation ... the *state* must intend to take and maintain possession."[293] He agreed that a state may "delegate its sovereign authority" to individuals, or companies, for such purposes, and he conceded that such was often the case with colonies,

292. Twiss, *The Oregon Territory*, 111–112.
293. Twiss, *The Oregon Territory*, 114.

but he warned, "The colonists must be sent forth *by the public authority of the nation*, otherwise they will possess no national character, but will be considered a body of emigrants, who have abandoned their country."[294] Such, he implied, was the case for the Oregon settlers. Such also, he argued, was the case for the claim to prior discovery of the territory made by the United States: that is, the claim based upon the voyages to the Northwest in the 1790s by Captain Robert Gray in pursuit of the fur trade. Those voyages, declared Twiss, were "an act by a private citizen, without any commission from the state" and so could have no standing in the law of nations.[295]

Twiss's response to the Oregon crisis underlined two of the strongest characteristics of his thought. First, the question of who can be a legitimate actor in international society, to which he emphatically responded that only states, or people licensed by states, have international standing. Second, he insisted that only states, or their agents, can establish colonies in unoccupied territory. Both positions highlighted the primacy of sovereignty for Twiss; that was the salient feature of his thought until the 1870s, whether he was dealing with Catholic bishops, the 1848 revolutions, or colonies. Of all the forms of personality, of being a person, the sovereign was most important. In his rather Hobbesian view, all other forms of personality depended upon the sovereign. Indeed, Twiss's understanding of the primacy of the sovereign in international society exceeded that of Hobbes. He pointed out, in his 1856 *Introductory Lectures on the Science of International Law*, that for Hobbes, as for Grotius and Pufendorf, the law of nations was the law of nature applied to international society. That is to say that, as Hobbes pointed out, states faced each other in international society as individuals did in the state of nature. In both cases, there was no lawgiver to determine disputes. As Twiss put it: "Hobbes and Pufendorf both agreed that the Law of Nature, as applied to the relations of individual men as moral agents, underwent no necessary modification in application to states or nations."[296] The implication of this position was that moral agents other than states might conceivably engage in relations with nations, or with each other, in international society. Such, potentially, was the situation that Grotius had addressed when he examined the standing of a Dutch admiral who engaged, as a private individual and in international waters, with a ship, the *Santa Catarina*, under the flag of Portugal in the Straits of Malacca in 1601. Grotius believed the admiral, Jacob van Heemskerck, to be acting, even if indirectly, for the United States of Holland in a war fought against Spain and Portugal, but he also argued that even if the admiral did not have license from his sovereign, he was entitled to act as he had as a moral agent in a state

---

294. Twiss, *The Oregon Territory*, 112.
295. Twiss, *The Oregon Territory*, 243.
296. Travers Twiss, *Introductory Lectures on the Science of International Law* (London, 1856), 42.

of nature: that is, to act according to the needs of his self-preservation. In contrast to Hobbes, Grotius argued for the existence of a society between sovereigns, but Twiss believed both the Grotian and Hobbesian understandings of international society to be unacceptable. There must be, he insisted, a difference between individuals in a state of nature and states; otherwise, the doors to international society would be completely open. He argued that Wolff and Emer de Vattel had also recognised this problem and had accordingly argued that the "nature and essence" of the "moral being" of states must "necessarily differ in many respects from the nature and essence of the physical individuals or men of whom they are composed."[297] He concluded with Vattel, therefore, that "we are not to imagine that the Law of Nations is precisely and in every case the same as the Law of Nature . . . a state or civil society is a subject very different from an individual of the human race," and for this reason, individuals or private associations, such as the Dutch East India Company, could never pretend to sit in international society alongside states, no matter how much that society resembled the state of nature.[298]

It was this esteem for sovereignty that Twiss would revise in the years after his marriage scandal, when he worked for Leopold. That revision rested on two points: namely, the argument that private individuals or associations could have a standing in international society; and the argument that private individuals or associations could establish sovereignty in unoccupied territory. It consisted, therefore, of the reversal of the two positions central to his case for the Oregon Territory, and it also entailed a new understanding of personality, or moral agency. The sovereign was no longer supreme, and persons could be created independently of the sovereign. Twiss brought that newly creative understanding of personality to both his understanding of international society and his own domestic society. His newly creative understanding of personality cannot be comprehended apart from his marriage.

Catholic Reform and Tractarianism

In the 1840s, the most serious threat to sovereignty in England, as far as Twiss was concerned, was not on the international stage, at least not directly. Rather, it was a dual threat to the established church. On the one hand, some within the church were seeking independence from what they saw as government interference. On the other, Catholics, with encouragement from the Pope, sought greater religious and political freedom. For Twiss, the supremacy of the English sovereign was challenged by the Catholic Relief Act of 1829. The Duke of Wellington's government had acted because of fears of a revolution in Ireland, but in the wake of its passage, new fears arose that the Church

---

297. Twiss, *Introductory Lectures*, 43.
298. Twiss, *Introductory Lectures*, 44.

of England was moving closer to Catholicism. Those fears were realised by the Oxford Movement, or Tractarians, the group of high church members, led by Edward Pusey and John Henry Newman at Oxford, who explored reconciliation between the two churches based upon what they believed to be the proximity of their doctrines. Tractarianism, as Harold Laski put it, was "in its essence ... the plea of the corporate body which is distinct from the State to a separate and free existence."[299] Twiss was an expert in creating corporations, such as bishoprics, but in his early career, he was adamant that such corporations must be subject to the control of the state—they could have no free and separate political existence. As we have seen, he ran against a Pusey party candidate for the Drummond Chair of Political Economy in 1837, while he was identified with the "old" high church and "moderate" party. In a letter to Prince Metternich more than ten years later, while explaining the merits and faults of the various daily newspapers, Twiss declared: "I do not agree with any of them sufficiently ... The Times seems to have most strength in its articles, but it is capricious. I believe the people connected with it are personally hostile to myself as some of them were intimately connected with the Puseyite movement at the University, which is essentially democratic, though, strange to say, its forms have captivated many of the aristocratic ladies of Belgrave Square etc."[300] In a subsequent letter, he commented, "I have studied Puseyism as it is termed in this country, and found it produced some moral monstrosities."[301] "What can be more monstrous," he asked, "than a democrat high-churchman?" Such men "proposed to rehabilitate Christianity, to place it in accord with the new ideas, or in other words more truly to make the clergy the prophets of the new order of things."[302] The "present Pope," he said, had "adopted this idea," and Twiss himself saw no problem with the clergy pursuing "moral improvement," but he objected to the manner in which certain religious figures "sacrifice the means to the end." In particular, "one of the most dangerous symptoms of modern civilisation is its humanitarian tendencies."[303] He identified humanitarianism with democracy—what other motive could there be for extending the franchise. It was, of course, "impossible not to respect the sentiment," but humanitarianism should be distinguished from "humanity," and it was "above all things the office of the clergy to distinguish between the virtue and its counterfeit."

299. Laski, *Studies in the Problem of Sovereignty*, 108.

300. Twiss to Metternich, December 14, 1848, National Archives of the Czech Republic, Prague, RAM-AC/ 10/ 774, 141–142.

301. Twiss to Metternich, August 17, 1849, National Archives of the Czech Republic, Prague, RAM-AC/ 10/ 775, 367.

302. Twiss to Metternich, August 17, 1849, National Archives of the Czech Republic, Prague, RAM-AC/ 10/ 775, 368.

303. Twiss to Metternich, August 17, 1849, National Archives of the Czech Republic, Prague, RAM-AC/ 10/ 775, 369.

In 1841, Arthur Stanley wrote to Archibald Tait from Rome to say he had received "a private letter from Twiss to me" announcing that a "convulsive movement" will "not improbably take place, only equal to a moral Niagara ceasing to flow."[304] Stanley claimed he was "in a state of ferment beyond bounds" on receiving Twiss's news. He was referring to the latest pronouncements of the Oxford Movement. His reference to a moral Niagara ceasing to flow concerned Twiss's report of the publication of John Henry Newman's *Remarks on Certain Passages in the Thirty-Nine Articles*, or *Tract 90*, published in 1841, which argued that the Thirty-Nine Articles of 1563, which defined the doctrine of the Protestant Reformation as it was understood in the Church of England, was not a definitive break with Rome but merely a correction of errors of doctrine. The suggestion, therefore, of Newman, at this time, and the Oxford Movement which he led, was that the two churches should be reconciled. With three other Oxford Tutors, Tait published "Protest of the Four Tutors," a refutation of Newman's *Tract 90*. Stanley reported from Rome that the Pope had just issued a bull stating that the Thirty-Nine Articles were not inconsistent with the Decrees of Trent, the doctrinal statement of the Counter-Reformation.[305]

In October 1844, Twiss was a member of the committee that successfully ran Benjamin Symons as the new Vice Chancellor of Oxford. The aim of the committee appeared to be to block the Pusey party candidate from winning because, warned the *London Evening Standard*, if "the Tractarian candidate is permitted to succeed, the party will become more rampant and dictatorial than ever."[306] These tensions were exemplified by Prime Minister Lord John Russell's appointment of Renn Hampden as Bishop of Hereford in December 1847.[307] Russell was sympathetic to the Latitudinarians, which is to say that he accepted a broad interpretation and practice of religious doctrine. Hampden had for some years been singled out by the Tractarians for excessive liberalism in doctrine and Latitudinarianism. He represented "in the highest possible degree those latitudinarian principles against which the Oxford Movement was the incarnate protest."[308] The Tractarians had violently opposed his election to the Regius Professorship of Divinity at Oxford in 1836. Indeed, it had been Hampden's appointment to the professorship that had proved to be the catalyst for the Tractarians' transformation from "a scattered band of enthusiasts into a party."[309] They similarly opposed Russell's nomination of him as Bishop, which they perceived both in terms of an attempt to

---

304. Davidson and Benham, *Life of Archibald Campbell Tait, Archbishop of Canterbury*, Vol. 1, 93.
305. Davidson and Benham, *Life of Archibald Campbell Tait*, Vol. 1, 92.
306. "The Vice-Chancellorship of Oxford," *London Evening Standard*, October 2, 1844, 2.
307. On Hampden, see Laski, *Studies in the Problem of Sovereignty*, 77–80.
308. Laski, *Studies in the Problem of Sovereignty*, 97.
309. Laski, *Studies in the Problem of Sovereignty*, 97.

dilute doctrine and as an assertion of Erastianism, or the right of the state to interfere in matters of religion, a privilege claimed by sovereigns since the Reformation and, prior to that, asserted by Marsilius of Padua. The Dean of Hereford, John Merewether, wrote to Russell to tell him that "having fully counted the cost... I have come to the deliberate resolve that on Tuesday next no earthly consideration shall induce me to give my vote in the Chapter of Hereford Cathedral for Dr Hampden's elevation to the See of Hereford."[310] Russell's reply went to the heart of Twiss's concerns about the rise of Catholic sympathy, a single line stating ironically: "Sir, I have the honour to receive your letter of the 22nd inst. in which you intimate to me your intention to violate the law." As Dean, Merewether was necessary to the appointment ceremony of a new bishop in order to provide the seal of the chapter. Russell's reply underlined the fact that the appointment of bishops was a matter of state and not individual consciences. Days after this exchange of letters, Twiss signed a protest by members of the Convocation at the University of Oxford against the attempts to stop Hampden becoming Bishop of Hereford.[311] Eight years later, Hampden rewarded Twiss's loyalty by appointing him Chancellor of the Consistory Court of the Diocese of Hereford when that position became vacant. While Twiss, therefore, was closely associated within the church with what the Tractarians described as a "liberal" toleration of religious diversity, he was critical of the Tractarians for what he believed to be a "liberal" claim to autonomy from the state. At times, therefore, all sides in the debate criticised the excessively "liberal" ideas of their opponents. Boyd Hilton has observed that, in the 1820s, the term "liberal" was generally used negatively.[312] By 1848, it was more common to find positive appropriations of the term—a strategy Twiss attempted—but the negative associations persisted.

For Twiss, concerns about Tractarians and Catholics climaxed in 1850 when Pope Pious IX issued a brief (papal letter), *Universalis Ecclesiae*, re-establishing the Catholic hierarchy in England for the first time since the death of Queen Mary in 1558. Writing to Prince Metternich, he observed: "We are in a curious condition in regard to the Pope's Bull. The strong feeling, I should think, is really against the Tractarian school of English clergymen."[313] He pointed out that the Reformation in England had been "the work of the laity," and as a consequence, the "Laudian reaction" against the Reformation under Charles I had led to the "Puritan revolution against Laudism."[314] He

---

310. *Essex Standard*, December 31, 1847, 4.

311. *Essex Standard*, December 31, 1847, 4.

312. Boyd Hilton, *A Mad, Bad, and Dangerous People? England 1783–1846* (Oxford, 2006), 375.

313. Twiss to Metternich, November 19, 1850, National Archives of the Czech Republic, Prague, RAM-AC/ 10/ 776, 105.

314. Twiss to Metternich, November 19, 1850, National Archives of the Czech Republic, Prague, RAM-AC/ 10/ 776, 105.

clearly feared a similar backlash as a result of the rise of the Tractarians. A week later, he was more upset: "I have been carefully weighing the character and effect of the Brief of 14 September and I cannot but think that the creation of territorial sees within the realm of England" would be an "infringement of the Sovereignty of the Crown of England." In fact, he believed that the Pope had exceeded his authority in a manner that had not been seen anywhere in Europe, "in Catholic or Protestant countries," since the Reformation.[315] Twiss, who had deplored Pius's liberal ideas, nevertheless believed that, in this measure, he had exceeded his previous errors: "Of all the mistakes which the See of Rome has made, none has been attended with worse practical effects, than the attempt to set aside a lawful temporal authority."[316] By December 1850, he had decided to formally respond to this crisis: "I have much to do at present, having undertaken to investigate the legal question in Pope Pius's Apostolic letter."[317]

Anti-Catholic fear had grown since the Irish famine began in 1845, leading to a large influx of Irish Catholics into England, particularly Liverpool. As well, in 1845, John Henry Newman converted to Catholicism, just one of a wave of conversions amongst high church Anglicans. The growing number of Catholic subjects, combined with the liberalisation of religious worship in the Catholic Relief Act, made the reestablishment of the church hierarchy both desirable and possible. British sovereigns had long reigned over Catholic bishops in conquered territories, such as Quebec, but in England and Wales, the Catholic Church was only permitted "apostolic vicars," who governed in the name of the Pope but had no diocese. The introduction of thirteen bishops, and dioceses, in England and Wales, including an Archbishop of Westminster, caused a wave of anti-Catholic sentiment. For Twiss, that sentiment arose from a threat to the sovereignty of the crown. Incensed by the Papal brief, in 1851, Twiss published *The Letters Apostolic of the Pope Pius IX Considered with Reference to the Law of England and the Law of Europe*. He made it clear from the outset that he was concerned with law, not religion.[318] The Pope's brief, he argued, was "a direct violation of the Statute Law of the Land" because, in one instance, the Bishopric of St David's, it created a new See where there was an existing episcopal title, something that had been expressly prohibited by the Catholic Relief Act, because it would challenge the transfer of the original Catholic titles to the Church of England in the Reformation. More broadly, Twiss pointed out, the creation of Bishops' Sees,

---

315. Twiss to Metternich, November 26, 1850, National Archives of the Czech Republic, Prague, RAM-AC/ 10/ 776, 110.

316. Twiss to Metternich, November 26, 1850, National Archives of the Czech Republic, Prague, RAM-AC/ 10/ 776, 110.

317. Twiss to Metternich, December 28, 1850, National Archives of the Czech Republic, Prague, RAM-AC/ 10/ 776, 116.

318. Travers Twiss, *The Letters Apostolic of the Pope Pius IX Considered with Reference to the Law of England and the Law of Europe* (London, 1851), iii.

or domains of jurisdiction, contradicted long-standing practices which, in such matters, "constitute the law."[319] According to Twiss, this encroachment of the church upon temporal power was a consequence of the 1829 Catholic "Emancipation Act," as he called it, which left the question of church jurisdiction unresolved. Granting religious freedom did not, as he saw it, mean winding back the Reformation and allowing the church autonomy from the state. Moreover, given that the brief implied that Rome, a foreign power, could legislate questions of church jurisdiction within the borders of England, it constituted also "a glaring infringement of a branch of the law of Nations as regards the Sovereignty of the Crown of England."[320]

Twiss pointed out that Pius's brief re-introduced into England "the whole body of Canon Law sanctioned by the Popes," as distinct from the canon law that had been maintained by the Church of England. Employing that law, the new Archbishop, Cardinal Nicholas Wiseman, claimed to "govern" over his diocese "with ordinary jurisdiction."[321] Reading those words, Queen Victoria was reported to have declared, "Am I Queen of England or am I not?"[322] Twiss would have had her believe that her fears were justified. He went on to argue that Wiseman's distinction, and that of his defender, George Bowyer of the Middle Temple, between temporal and spiritual jurisdiction were false. Twiss, whose job it was to swear Bishops of the Church of England into office, knew better than most that the creation of every bishopric meant the creation of a legal person in temporal law, not simply in spiritual law. Wiseman and Bowyer, sounding very much like Reformation theologians, argued that the church exercised only spiritual rather than temporal jurisdiction and that ecclesiastical law was concerned only with the spiritual realm. Such claims were underlined by Pius having fled Rome only shortly before issuing his brief as a consequence of the revolution that had led to the creation of the Roman Republic in the Papal States in 1849. Nevertheless, Twiss responded that all ecclesiastical jurisdiction necessitates the exercise of temporal power, and consistent with the historical methodology he employed generally in examination of the law, he used over 150 pages of his book to analyse the historical and comparative bases for his argument. At the same time, he showed that, even in Catholic countries, the Pope always consulted sovereigns before creating new bishops.[323]

Bowyer responded to Twiss, in what was already an extensive pamphlet war, with *Observations on the Arguments of Dr Twiss respecting the New Catholic Hierarchy*, in which he reiterated that the Catholic Church sought no temporal jurisdiction in England and Wales and pointed out that the new Catholic

---

319. Twiss, *The Letters Apostolic*, iv.
320. Twiss, *The Letters Apostolic*, 2.
321. Twiss, *The Letters Apostolic*, 4–5.
322. Laski, *Studies in the Problem of Sovereignty*, 163.
323. Twiss, *The Letters Apostolic*, 8.

hierarchy was "unclothed with any temporal sanction."[324] While Bowyer was undoubtedly right that Wiseman was not challenging the temporal power of the crown, merely pushing the claims of spiritual jurisdiction as far as they could go, the exchange is illustrative of how concerned Twiss was at this stage in his career with the supremacy of sovereignty.[325] Sovereigns were the legal persons who created, directly or indirectly, all other legal persons, so it could not be possible for external powers to interfere in that process without compromising the sovereign. Although neither the Tractarians nor the Catholic Church claimed temporal power in England, both were pursuing their vision of the corporation of the church as a *perfecta societas*, and such a vision of corporate life threatened Twiss's understanding of the supremacy of sovereignty.[326] Moreover, commentary on the matter revealed that Twiss's fears about sovereignty were broadly shared. The *Leeds Intelligencer* declared that Twiss had published "decidedly the most elaborate and masterly" analysis of the "Pope's insolent and insidious attacks on our national independence."[327] The *Evening Mail* agreed with Twiss that creating bishops was a spiritual act, but in creating bishoprics, with territorial jurisdiction, the Pope "usurps an attribute of local sovereignty."[328]

The outpouring of such fears inspired anti-Catholic riots, particularly in Liverpool (where, because of the famine in Ireland, the Irish population had risen to 20 percent of the city), and a petition of 900,000 signatures to the Queen. As a consequence, the parliament immediately passed the Ecclesiastical Titles Act, sponsored by Prime Minister Lord John Russell in 1851. The new Act forbade the use of territorial titles by any non-Anglican bishop. The Act was ineffective, never leading to any prosecution, and it was repealed twenty years later under Prime Minister Gladstone. Twiss was, nevertheless, given a role in overseeing one of the important measures in policing the emancipation of Catholics: he was made one of the five members of the Maynooth Commission chaired by Dudley Ryder, the Earl of Harrowby, prominent as a staunch defender of the Church of England. St Patrick's College, in Maynooth, just west of Dublin, had been established in 1795 with the purpose of training Catholic clergy, but its annual grant from the British government was a meagre £8,000. Seeking to calm Irish discontent, Prime Minister Peel had increased that sum to £26,000 in 1845. On the one hand, the College was controversial in Ireland because it required the Oath of Allegiance from its members,

---

324. George Bowyer, *Observations on the Arguments of Dr Twiss respecting the New Catholic Hierarchy* (London, 1851), 7.

325. Laski, *Studies in the Problem of Sovereignty*, 163–164: on these fears being generated by a "mid-Victorian desire for unity."

326. On the corporation as *perfecta societas* in the understanding of the Tractarians, see Laski, *Studies in the Problem of Sovereignty*, 112.

327. *Leeds Intelligencer*, February 1, 1851, 4.

328. *Evening Mail*, February 5, 1851, 7. For similar commentary, see also *Bell's Weekly Messenger*, February 1, 1851, 6.

and on the other, it aroused further anti-Catholic feeling in England, with a coalition of Dissenting protestants and Anglicans questioning why the state should subsidise religious error, or even disloyalty to the crown.[329] The ostensible purpose of the Commission was to examine how effective the increased spending on the College had been, but it was clearly also concerned with the loyalty of Catholic subjects and institutions to the state. When Prime Minister Aberdeen established the Commission in 1853, he asked Twiss to be one of the commissioners.[330] He threw himself into the work of the Commission, writing of his "great interest" in its proceedings, while spending a comfortable autumn in the Vice Regal Lodge in Dublin.[331] The members of the committee returned the following summer to Dublin and submitted their report in 1855.[332] It reflected the prevailing anxieties about the fidelity of the Catholic subjects to a Protestant monarch. Questions for the professors of theology included: "What is the doctrine taught in Maynooth upon the question, whether the Pope can decide as to the right or duty of revolt against the civil power, so as to bind the consciences of Roman Catholics?"[333] Similarly, they were asked: "In what way do the Professors . . . execute the provision of the Statutes, c.5. s.3:—'Let the Professor of Dogmatic Theology strenuously exert himself to impress on his class, that the allegiance which they owe to the Royal Majesty cannot be relaxed or annulled by any power or authority whatsoever'? In what way is this doctrine specifically inculcated?"[334]

The College statutes recommended that, prior to admission, a student must deliver to the President of the College "the certificate of a public officer, testifying that he has taken the oath of allegiance to our august Monarch, and has also made a written promise that he neither belongs to, nor will join in any secret society," and a similar oath was required from all College officers.[335] Additionally, all of the students were required "during the year following their entrance, to take the oath of allegiance," but the commissioners found that because this ceremony was conducted at once for "the whole class, averaging about one hundred, standing in the court [of Maynooth Quarter Sessions],"

329. Parry, *The Politics of Patriotism*, 166–168.

330. "I have consented at Lord Aberdeen's request to act upon a Royal Commission of enquiry into the system of the College of Maynooth, in Ireland": Twiss to Metternich, September 4, 1853, National Archives of the Czech Republic, Prague, RAM-AC/ 10/ 779, 25.

331. "I have now been here for nearly six weeks with the Earl of Harrowby on a Royal Commission to enquire into the state of Maynooth College . . . the subject however is of great interest": Twiss to Metternich, Vice Regal Lodge, Dublin, October 23, 1853, National Archives of the Czech Republic, Prague, RAM-AC/ 10/ 779, 29–30.

332. Twiss to Metternich, June 12, 1854, National Archives of the Czech Republic, Prague, RAM-AC/ 10/ 780, 13.

333. *Report of her Majesty's Commissioners Appointed to Inquire into the Management and Government of the College of Maynooth* (Dublin, 1855), 43.

334. *Report . . . into . . . the College of Maynooth*, 43–44.

335. *Report . . . into . . . the College of Maynooth*, 19, 23.

they were "not fully satisfied" that the conditions were "best calculated to give the proper solemnity to the proceeding."[336] The report also touched upon the question of territorial titles for bishops. In his *Letters Apostolic*, Twiss conceded that Ireland had always had Catholic bishops appointed by the Pope. But he contrasted that situation with the rupture created by the Reformation in England.[337] And yet, four years later, in a letter written by Twiss to the House of Lords defending the report of the Commission, he declared that his committee had "unanimously decided to prevent, if possible, the use of any territorial title" attached to Irish bishops.[338]

Following the publication of the *Letters Apostolic*, Twiss sent a copy to Metternich, declaring, "I am disposed to think the argument is sound."[339] He hoped that he succeeded in substituting "a terminable for an interminable question—for although the political problem is most difficult, the religious problem is insoluble by legislation."[340] His prediction concerning the legislation would prove to be accurate. Nevertheless, while parliament debated the Ecclesiastical Titles Act, Twiss believed a moment of great crisis was at hand. "Political matters here," he wrote, "are in a very uncertain state. Every political party is said to be divided in itself upon the Papal Question."[341] The country, he said, was on the verge of a religious explosion which would "burst forth one way in England and another way in Ireland."[342] "What with free trade and protection, and Protestantism and popery," he mused, there might be "very serious conflicts," and the problems would extend well into the future: "I see this great question of the relation of the state to religion looming in giant proportions in the distant future."[343] He believed, however, that the cause of the problem was in the past, and specifically in the Catholic Relief Act. Lord John Russell had been one of the warmest supporters of the Relief Act. In 1828, the year prior to it passing, he had introduced the Sacramental Test Act, repealing the provision of the Corporations

---

336. *Report . . . into . . . the College of Maynooth*, 38.

337. Twiss, *The Letters Apostolic*, 131.

338. *Connaught Watchman*, May 23, 1855. See also Nigel Yate, *Anglican Ritualism and Victorian Britain 1830–1910* (Oxford, 1999), 227, for Twiss's participation in the Commission on Ritualism and his moderate position.

339. Twiss to Metternich, January 28, 1851, National Archives of the Czech Republic, Prague, RAM-AC/ 10/ 777, 8.

340. Twiss to Metternich, February 1, 1851, National Archives of the Czech Republic, Prague, RAM-AC/ 10/ 777, 11.

341. Twiss to Metternich, February 1, 1851, National Archives of the Czech Republic, Prague, RAM-AC/ 10/ 777, 17.

342. Twiss to Metternich, February 28, 1851, National Archives of the Czech Republic, Prague, RAM-AC/ 10/ 777, 27.

343. Twiss to Metternich, February 28, 1851, National Archives of the Czech Republic, Prague, RAM-AC/ 10/ 777, 27; Twiss to Metternich, March 23, 1851, National Archives of the Czech Republic, Prague, RAM-AC/ 10/ 777, 58. All underlining, italics, and strikethroughs are in the original texts unless otherwise stated.

Act that required officeholders to be members of the Church of England.[344] It was his government, twenty years later, with the support of Sir James Graham, that now tried to limit the implications of Pius's bull and the emancipation to which it responded. Twiss remarked upon the irony of Russell's struggle with the issue: "That element which, it was supposed, was appeased by the Relief Act in 1827 [sic.: 1829] has recovered its ancient strength."[345] Emancipation, Twiss seemed to say, could embolden rather than calm the causes of unrest.

His proposed solution to the crisis remained consistently Erastian, insofar as he insisted upon the submission of the church, an established church, to the state. He posed a rhetorical question to Metternich: "What are you inclined to think of the religious element; shall it be left to work alone or shall it be the yoke-fellow of the political element?"[346] But he was in no doubt about the answer. The Crown, he said, exercised "jus supreme" in religious matters "by maintaining an Established Church, and by keeping that Church in subordination to political considerations." At the same time, he said, "The fault which I find with the Papacy" was in its contradiction to the supremacy of the crown: "Cardinal Wiseman and the Holy See well know the municipal law, and they prepared a measure which deliberately violated it."[347] "I am rather in favour," he argued, "of the state establishing one form of religion, that of the majority, and protecting the rest . . . I am inclined to think that for the state, as such, to <u>ignore</u> religion is a political blunder."[348] One reason for the necessity of the state involving itself in religious matters was the treacherous nature of the clergy, and when Twiss spoke of treacherous clergy, he was thinking as much of the Puseyites as he was of the Catholics. "The clergy," he wrote, "are unfortunately unequal to the task of cooperating with the state—they will not be satisfied with a limited responsibility."[349] The problem with the clergy, he argued, was that they were inclined to make the same mistake in their understanding of religious diversity as the nationalists did in relation to the diversity of peoples.[350] Prior to the Reformation, the church had encompassed

344. Hilton, *A Mad, Bad, and Dangerous People*, 380–381.
345. Twiss to Metternich, February 28, 1851, National Archives of the Czech Republic, Prague, RAM-AC/ 10/ 777, 26.
346. Twiss to Metternich, March 10, 1851, National Archives of the Czech Republic, Prague, RAM-AC/ 10/ 777, 44.
347. Twiss to Metternich, February 1, 1851, National Archives of the Czech Republic, Prague, RAM-AC/ 10/ 777, 19.
348. Twiss to Metternich, March 10, 1851, National Archives of the Czech Republic, Prague, RAM-AC/ 10/ 777, 41.
349. Twiss to Metternich, March 10, 1851, National Archives of the Czech Republic, Prague, RAM-AC/ 10/ 777, 41.
350. "The great misfortune for mankind is that the clergy made the same mistake in their day of political power, which the laity are now doing; that of supposing uniformity necessary for unity": Twiss to Metternich, March 10, 1851, National Archives of the Czech Republic, Prague, RAM-AC/ 10/ 777, 41.

a great diversity, but subsequently the clergy pursued narrow understandings of religious doctrine: "There was a period when the Church, i.e., the universal assembly of faithful Christians, recognised a certain diversity of character in races, climates, countries, etc; at last they disregarded facts and made them subordinate to a theory. States are now doing the same thing."[351] States, of course, were doing the same thing in regard to nationalism, and this tendency caused problems in composite monarchies such as the United Kingdom, as well as empires such as Austria. Nationalism had not been a factor when Scotland and England unified in 1707, and there had been, as a consequence, no attempt to reduce Scottish customs and laws to a national standard, but "When England accomplished her union with Ireland this notion [of nationalism] was more developed than when she accomplished her union with Scotland. Hence there has been continual struggles between the two countries [England and Ireland], which end in the miserable result of sacrificing substantial unity for uniformity in matters of no importance [i.e., race, religion, culture]."[352]

At the same time that he argued for a tolerance of diversity, Twiss's Erastianism made him critical of the more extreme Latidudinarians, whose attachment to the established church was weak, and those who argued for the separation of church and state. "I consider," he argued, "the relations of religion to politics one of the most serious questions of the day—the tendency is to divorce them, but I am not satisfied as to the wisdom of this plan."[353] He questioned, in particular, the wisdom of Sir John Graham and the Peelites in opposing Lord John Russell in parliament: "They might object to the measure of Lord John itself—the *modus operandi*—But if they admit that the state is not to judge if a matter be spiritual or not, and is not to regulate the external status of a church," such a measure would be equivalent to claiming '*l'État est athée*' a pernicious doctrine."[354] Again, returning to his scepticism of the clergy, he continued, "the formidable phenomenon of the day is the alliance between the ministers of religion and the enemies (political) of the state—Piononon [Pius] and the republic, the archbishop of Paris and the barricades, the priests consecrating the trees of liberty etc etc." In 1848, hundreds of Liberty Trees had been planted in Paris, particularly in Place de la Bourse, in emulation of the Liberty Tree of the French Revolution, and they had been consecrated by priests with liberal sympathies.[355] Pius had initially shared those sympathies and helped

---

351. Twiss to Metternich, March 10, 1851, National Archives of the Czech Republic, Prague, RAM-AC/ 10/ 777, 41.

352. Twiss to Metternich, March 10, 1851, National Archives of the Czech Republic, Prague, RAM-AC/ 10/ 777, 41.

353. Twiss to Metternich, March 10, 1851, National Archives of the Czech Republic, Prague, RAM-AC/ 10/ 777, 40.

354. Twiss to Metternich, March 23, 1851, National Archives of the Czech Republic, Prague, RAM-AC/ 10/ 777, 60.

355. "Trees of Liberty in the Place de la Bourse," *Illustrated London News*, April 8, 1848, 226.

stoke the revolution in Italy before he had to flee it. Twiss was convinced that the clergy were in a broad alliance with revolutionaries and liberals. It was necessary, therefore, for the state to keep close control over religion, partly through the creation of an established church and partly through law. It was clearly in this light, therefore, that he understood the significance of the many legal offices that he held within the church. He nevertheless believed these tensions between church and state to remain as yet unresolved, particularly as emancipation and reform weakened the position of the established church: "The importance of the problem which representative systems must yet solve—'what part shall the state take in religion?.' Shall it keep aloof altogether, or must it for the sake of its own safety ally itself to the religion of the majority as the religion of the state, and of the Crown? It seems rather to be held that the religion of the Crown must be the religion of the nation, i.e., the majority—but it seems also an opinion likely to gain ground that the state should have no religion. I think this view very full of peril to the state."[356] He would spell out the nature of that peril in subsequent correspondence. Religion bound citizens to the state through motivations other than their material interests, and material interests, as he observed, rapidly abandoned sovereigns in times of revolution: "If the state is to keep aloof from religion, it must, I think, abdicate its care of moral interests, and it becomes reduced in its functions to the administration of material interests of the community, and as the King of Wurtenberg said, material interests slink away in the moment of trial, e.g. the National Guard. To you, as a statesman inclined to despair of the prospects of humanity, it must be consoling to see the 'principle of faith' is not extinct in the world."[357]

The duties of Vicar General included involvement in trials of the Anglican clergy in cases of improper doctrine. In 1856, Twiss had participated in the trial of George Denison, Archdeacon of Wells Cathedral, a high churchman vehemently opposed to progressive reforms. Denison was tried for having stated in a sermon that during the Eucharist, the giving of bread and wine to the congregation, "the body and blood of Christ being really present, after an immaterial and spiritual manner, in the consecrated bread and wine, are therein and thereby given to all." And this was true, he added, "for those who eat and drink worthily, and by those who eat and drink unworthily."[358] Denison was guilty, that is, of stating Catholic doctrine. There was much debate about the nature of the sacrament of the Eucharist amongst Christian denominations, and also within denominations, including the Anglicans. Medieval

---

356. Twiss to Metternich, March 13, 1851, National Archives of the Czech Republic, Prague, RAM-AC/ 10/ 777, 49.

357. Twiss to Metternich, March 23, 1851, National Archives of the Czech Republic, Prague, RAM-AC/ 10/ 777, 59–60.

358. "The Case of Archdeacon Denison," *North Devon Journal*, August 14, 1856, 8. See also "The Case of Archdeacon Denison," *Bath Chronicle and Weekly Gazette*, August 14, 1856, 8.

Catholic theologians had argued that in eating the bread and drinking the wine consecrated by the priest, the congregation eats the real flesh and drinks the real blood of Christ. This they described as the doctrine of transubstantiation, and they employed the Aristotelian distinction between the accidents of a thing, or its physical presence, and its substance, or its real nature, to explain how Christ was present in the substance of the bread and wine despite the appearance of its accidents. In the Reformation, Protestants maintained the Eucharist but rejected the Aristotelian explanation, which was foreign to scripture, instead reverting to the notion that the transformation was a mystery that was accessible only to those who had faith and were worthy. Denison's insistence that the bread and wine were flesh and blood for the unworthy as much as the worthy meant that he believed there was a real objective presence of Christ in the Eucharist (an idea also central to the thought of Edward Pusey at Oxford). The court found that he contravened the Thirty-Nine Articles of the Church of England, the theological doctrine of the church established in 1563, which explained the transformation of the bread and wine into flesh and blood as a mystery, but Denison was acquitted on a technicality. His trial was one of many occasions when Twiss found himself at the centre of the disputes between high Anglicans and the Oxford Movement, on the one hand, and the church hierarchy, on the other.

What is particularly significant in Denison's controversy, however, is that Twiss found himself in judgement over a case concerning the nature of personification. The Eucharist, even in the Anglican version, was a process whereby the person of Christ was made present in the bread and wine of the sacrament. Debate, in this instance, did not put that process of personification into doubt; it merely questioned whether it was a mystery or could be explained by Aristotelian philosophy. Personification was a trope found throughout Christian theology: for example, priests themselves were said to be *in persona Christi*—that is, in the person of Christ—when they performed the rituals of the church, including confession, and Reformation churches sometimes adapted this notion to Christ's presence in the congregation. We have already seen Twiss engaged in another process of personification: namely, that whereby an artificial person, a corporation, was created in order to possess the property of a diocese. It is perhaps hardly surprising that the same medieval theologians who developed the idea of transubstantiation also seized upon the idea of incorporation in order to solve the problem of the transfer of church property from one generation to another. In both cases, a person was created where none could be seen—a person in substance if not in accidents—in order to solve a problem. Jurists with a deep knowledge of canon law, such as Twiss, engaged on a daily basis with the processes of personification in order to explain matters as diverse as communion with God and Christ, the possession of property, and the creation of the state. These processes of personification were implemented in the creation of new subjects through emancipation. Nineteenth-century emancipation, we could say, had medieval roots. Importantly, however, in the case of the Eucharist, the question of personification was controversial as to whether a literal interpretation of the presence of the flesh and the blood should be taken, as was the case for Denison, or whether the presence was figurative, with a more elastic understanding of what it meant to personify and of how one thing could become another. In Denison's case, Twiss ruled in accordance with the views of his Archbishop, John Sumner, whose understanding of the Eucharist was figurative and therefore opposed to the Oxford Movement. Twiss held on his shelves a copy of Sumner's *Doctrine of the Real Presence*, published the year before the Denison trial.[359] For Twiss, however, it is clear that his understanding of personification in the Denison trial was not a view he expressed as Vicar General merely to please his superior. He took a similarly elastic, and even creative, understanding of personification into other areas of his life, notably to his understanding of states and also of his wife, but the earliest indications that he held such views are found in his rulings on the Eucharist.

359. *Catalogue of a Portion of the Miscellaneous Library of Sir Travers Twiss*, 13.

PART 2

Metternich

IN THE FIRST HALF OF HIS CAREER, Twiss's understanding of sovereignty was shaped by the 1815 Congress of Vienna and its aftermath. During this time, he formed a close friendship, and intellectual partnership, with Prince Klemens Wenzel von Metternich of Austria: a serendipitous relationship, given their mutual views upon sovereignty. Metternich was not only one of the leading enthusiasts for the international order established by the congress; he was also regarded as its chief architect. The congress was a meeting of the great powers following the defeat of Napoléon in 1814. It was held between September and June, even as Napoléon briefly returned from exile before his final defeat at Waterloo days after the congress concluded. Metternich hosted the congress, which sought to find a new order for Europe after many of its old boundaries had been disturbed by twenty years of revolutionary wars and Napoléon's conquests. The congress established the so-called Concert of Europe, whereby the four great powers—Austria, Russia, Prussia, and Britain—would combine in order to prevent the preponderance of any one. Such attempts to prevent universal monarchy had their origins in the sixteenth and seventeenth centuries and gave rise to the principles of non-interference in the Peace of Westphalia (1648) and the principle of the balance of power found in the Treaty of Utrecht (1713). At the same time that the Concert of Europe had secured international order and peace, it did so at the cost of maintaining authoritarian and repressive regimes through most of Europe. In France, the monarchy was restored; German and Italian principalities were generally autocratic; and, above all, the Austrian Empire, sprawling across central Europe, remained resistant to change and emancipation under Metternich's administration.

Twiss was a passionate advocate of this international order—a European legal order—based upon the supremacy and equality of sovereign powers, and whether or not such an order was mythical, he subordinated all other political questions, including emancipation, nationalism, or democracy, to the peace and stability he believed it provided. In this early stage of his career, he certainly would have found unimaginable the notion, which he later came to hold, that a private company or individual could exercise sovereign power. He had stated precisely the "preposterousness" of that notion in his 1846 treatise on the Oregon Territory. He had also bitterly opposed what he saw as a challenge to the sovereignty of the state represented by the Tractarians. Nor was he sympathetic to arguments for the transformation of the status of individuals, although precisely such a transformation would become central to his own life through his marriage. His political views, in this regard, were consistent with the conservatism of the time, but they were challenged by the wave of revolution that swept Europe in 1848, driven by nationalist and emancipist aspirations.

There are two salient points to Twiss's engagement with the 1848 revolutions. First, he was deeply committed to the defence of the international order established in 1815. Second, he opposed the emancipation of both natural persons and artificial persons. The conversations between Twiss and Metternich explored these two questions in great depth. It was a dialogue on the making and unmaking of persons, natural and artificial, at a moment of great volatility in both processes. They analysed in detail the plans to break up and reconfigure the sovereign entities that constituted the Concert of Europe, and they examined claims for emancipation across Europe which they condemned as fronts for nationalism. The bond between nationalism and freedom had been forged by the French Revolution—the 1848 revolutions, as they saw it, were a continuation of 1789. It is necessary to explore the conversation between Twiss and Metternich because it provides a measure for how far Twiss would transform his ideas and life from this counter-revolutionary moment between 1848 and Metternich's death, in 1859, to the period between the 1860s and 1880s, when he embraced ideas of transformation for both natural and artificial persons.

The Friendship between Twiss and Metternich

The Austrian Empire was at the heart of the 1848 revolutions. It had been formed in 1804 by Francis II, the Holy Roman Emperor, as a response to the collapse of the Holy Roman Empire under pressure from the Napoleonic wars. The Empire was a confederation of his former German territories and the Kingdom of Hungary, which he also ruled as the Habsburg monarch. As Foreign Minister from 1809, Prince Metternich used the Congress of Vienna to extend the Austrian Empire into the German Confederation to the north and south into northern Italy. As Chancellor of State from 1821, Metternich favored policies that were deeply conservative and directed at maintaining power over the Empire and the balance of power in Europe, rather than reforming the largely feudal societies making up the empire. For this reason, for many years, historians judged Metternich a tyrant stranding the peoples of the Austrian Empire in the past, playing them off against each other, impeding economic and political development, and implacably opposed to the aspirations of the French and American revolutions. He pursued an order rooted in the *Ancien Régime*.

Following the disastrous experience of war in the twentieth century, this judgement of a relatively peaceful period in Europe's history shifted, and Metternich began to be represented as a "wise maintainer of stability" and the "most important and successful diplomat of his time," under whom the Austrian Empire experienced "three decades of peace, prosperity, stability, cultural renewal and economic transformation."[1] The most recent studies of Metternich have taken this interpretation further. Wolfram Siemann is the only biographer to have examined his papers in Prague in depth (rather than relying upon the memoirs and eight volumes of letters and documents published by his son Richard).[2] Siemann, consistent with Metternich's rehabilitation, presents him as a "visionary" and master "strategist" whose main aim was to establish a peaceful order in Europe through the equilibrium of the great powers. He shows how, during his first visit to London in 1794, Metternich was influenced by the constitutionalism of Edmund Burke, and although he was unquestionably committed to order before liberty, a committment to the rule of law remained central to his thought throughout his life. Metternich's reputation, it would seem, fell victim to the historiography of the very nationalism that he fought against with Twiss in the years between 1848 and 1859.

The turn away from the historiography of the nation-state in the past thirty years has allowed more complex accounts of Metternich to emerge. Nevertheless, no account of Metternich has engaged with the hundreds of letters he exchanged with Twiss over the eleven years following the 1848 revolutions, nor have those letters been employed by historians more generally.[3] Even Siemann, who provides the most exhaustively archival account of Metternich, only mentions Twiss twice and briefly, once in a list of friends during Metternich's exile in England and again as somebody with whom he maintained "regular correspondence," but he makes no use of the correspondence between the two men.[4] Siemen's purpose is to provide an account of Metternich during

1. Eric Hobsbawm, *The Age of Revolution: 1789–1848*, 128, noting this shift with some scepticism; Alan Sked, "The Nationality Problem in the Habsburg Monarchy," in Douglas Moggach and Gareth Stedman Jones, eds., *The 1848 Revolutions*, 325; Alan Sked, *Metternich and Austria: An Evaluation* (Basingstoke, 2008), 246.

2. Wolfram Siemann, *Metternich: Stratege und Visionär: Eine Biografie* (Munich, 2016).

3. The only scholarly examination of the correspondence is a two-page note: Count Philipp Georg Gudenus, "Metternich as Ghostwriter," *Manuscripts*, vol. 40, no. 1 (Winter 1988), 41–42. Gudenus remarked upon the similarity between the content of the letters in the Bibliothèque nationale, Paris, and passages in Twiss's articles in the *Quarterly Review*, although he was apparently unaware of the far more extensive correspondence in National Archives of the Czech Republic, Prague. I am grateful to Dr Shirley Sands of the Manuscript Society for having provided a copy of Count Gudenus's article.

4. Siemann, *Metternich*, 842, 847.

his years in office, so the lacuna is consistent with his aims. At the same time, however, the correspondence between Metternich and Twiss provides an extraordinary commentary upon one of the most tumultuous periods of modern history. It is a dialogue between a man who shaped the events upon which he was commenting, and another who was of a more modest standing, at least when compared to Metternich, but whose life was shaped by the currents of the century. Moreover, although Metternich was no longer in formal office, his partnership with Twiss was not formed for the sole purpose of a mutual commentary on events from a distance. Metternich had not simply fled and retired—as appearances suggested (and as his biographers tend to assume). In addition to their correspondence, he and Twiss collaborated on a series of anonymous publications in order to intervene in the debates and contribute to the cause of counter-revolution. They also acted as conduits between their respective governments, providing information and trying to influence events.

In March 1848, as we have seen, revolution in the Austrian Empire led to Metternich's resignation. The wave of nationalist and liberal sentiment across Europe was led in Hungary by Lajos Batthyány and Lajos Kossuth. They demanded the creation of liberal constitutional government, including freedom of the press and freedom of association, the abolition of serfdom, and the dismantling of feudal taxes and land tenures. But they also used nationalist Magyar sentiment to demand the separation of Hungary from the Austrian Empire. The first set of demands partially succeeded, but neither the Austrian Empire nor other European powers, particularly the Russians, were prepared to accept the break-up of the empire. Nationalist separatism, once unleashed, threatened to undermine its own proponents, who found themselves challenged by numerous competing and overlapping ethnic and cultural groups.[5] Other peoples under the Empire also sought autonomy, including Ukrainians, Czechs, Poles, Croats, Slovaks, and Italians. Metternich complained to Twiss that the new Austrian government was "invested with the faculties of the Committee of Public Safety under the reign of terror in France." "Hungary and Transylvania," he lamented, "are today born in blood."[6] In 1849, the revolution in the Austrian Empire ended abruptly when Czar Nicholas invaded with 300,000 troops and restored the Emperor.

During the months that the Austrian Empire began to disintegrate under the forces of nationalism and emancipation, the same forces brought revolution to the numerous German principalities. Here, though, it was a centralising movement, not a fragmenting one.[7] The German Confederation established

---

5. Mike Rapport, *1848: Year of Revolution* (London, 2008).
6. Metternich to Twiss, December 6, Bibliothèque nationale de France, Fol/ R.D./13810, 10r-v.
7. Brian Vick, *Defining Germany: The Frankfurt Parliamentarians and National Identity* (Cambridge, Mass., 2002); Wolfram Siemann, *Die deutsche Revolution von 1848/49* (Frankfurt, 1985).

the Frankfurt Parliament in May 1848, overturning the conservative principles upon which it had been established and declaring, by December, "basic" rights, including freedoms of the press, of movement, and of religion. As in Hungary, the assembly was nationalist and called for German unification. The boundaries of that German state—which peoples it should encompass, including how much of the German-speaking territories of the Austrian Empire—were a main subject of debate. The Frankfurt Parliament vainly sought ways to bring the various German peoples under one sovereign. In Germany, the revolution halted in late 1848 when Prussian aristocrats returned to power in Berlin.

In response to the 1848 revolutions, Twiss embarked upon a vigorous campaign of publishing, urging respect for existing sovereign bodies. Between 1848 and 1851, he wrote books and essays on every centre of conflict in the revolutions. These publications included his 1848 *The Relations of the Duchies of Schleswig and Holstein to the Crown of Denmark and the Germanic Confederation* (also published in German translation in Leipzig in 1849 as *Beiträge zur Schleswig-Holsteinischen Frage*); the anonymous *Hungary: Its Constitution and Its Catastrophe* in 1850; and several essays in the *Quarterly Review*, the Liberal-Conservative rival to the Whig *Edinburgh Review*. In addition, Twiss exchanged hundreds of letters with Metternich (Metternich wrote to Twiss in French and Twiss to Metternich in both English and French) between May 20, 1848, and February 1859, shortly before Metternich's death in June, with the bulk written between 1848 and 1851.

Metternich was forced from power after almost forty years in office. The Emperor Ferdinand asked him to step down on March 13, 1848, in the face of growing riots and violence.[8] With his life in danger, Metternich fled with his family to England, where they arrived in April, after travelling for nine days in disguise.[9] They took a house in London at first, then in Brighton in September, and subsequently, from the spring of 1849, in Richmond. He remained in England until October 1849. He was first elected to a short-term membership at the Athenaeum in May 1848, and Twiss had him elected again on April 24, 1849. It is possible that Benjamin Disraeli, who had first met Metternich on May 17, had introduced him to Twiss.[10] Although many years distant from becoming Prime Minister, Disraeli was already a leading conservative voice. In parliament on August 18, 1848, while attacking Secretary of State Palmerston's policy on Italy, he denounced the "modern, newfangled, sentimental principle of nationality" evident in the revolutions.[11] In June 1848, Metternich wrote to Disraeli regarding *"notre homme,"* a man who would publish articles in the

---

8. Palmer, *Metternich*, 309–311.

9. Palmer, *Metternich*, 313–314.

10. For the first meeting of Disraeli and Metternich, see Benjamin Disraeli, *Letters: 1848–1851*, Vol. 5 (Toronto, 1993), 34.

11. Disraeli, *Letters*, Vol. 5, 91, n. 2.

Quarterly Review on the revolutions and who was consulting with not only Metternich but also Disraeli. Given the depth of collaboration between Twiss and Metternich on the writing of those articles, it would appear that "*notre homme*" was Twiss.[12] Twiss knew Disraeli, and some years later wrote, half-admiringly, of him to Metternich: "Disraeli . . . I look upon him as a juggler who will not exactly practice sleight of hand but attempt sleight of tongue."[13]

It is not easy to characterise the relationship between Twiss and Metternich, as it appears to be marked by both power and affection. Clearly, Twiss was Metternich's instrument, allowing him to present his interpretation of the events unfolding in the revolution but untainted by his name. Essays in Metternich's own name would not have been taken as neutral appraisals of the situation. But if Metternich was employing Twiss, he was doing so on a subject upon which Twiss was in enthusiastic agreement. We know from Twiss's earlier publications—for example, on the Oregon Territory—that his views on sovereignty were already clear. He was not simply Metternich's mouthpiece, although he was prepared to play that role. Metternich was evidently pleased to find a powerful but independent voice. He wrote to Twiss: "I find myself at ease with you because your spirit marches straight: I never could get on with those who take the opposite direction. To get on, men must above all have understanding between them."[14] In their early collaboration, Twiss sometimes simply paraphrased Metternich's own writings and thoughts. But the relationship matured. After almost two years of working together, Twiss still sought guidance, but he began to assert his own voice. When Metternich moved from London to Brussels, Twiss wrote to him with a draft of his new, forthcoming publication on Hungary. By this time, because of fear that their letters could be intercepted, their correspondence was increasingly coded. In this instance, Twiss referred to himself in the third person as "the artist," meaning the author of the manuscript: "Perhaps under the circumstances 'the artist' may be left to himself, but should the picture be at all untrue it would be as well to have the corrections suggested. I rather think the artist would prefer to say that there is nobody's hand in the picture but his own."[15] Distance made collaboration difficult, but it is also clear that Twiss now wanted to be more than a ghostwriter.

12. "*Notre homme*" could also have been Edward Cheney, although the appearance of his collaborative article with Metternich in the 1850 *Quarterly Review* makes it more likely that this 1848 letter refers to Twiss, who published in the *Quarterly Review* in 1848 and '49. On Cheney, see Disraeli, *Letters*, Vol. 5, 34, n. 2.

13. Twiss to Metternich, March 2, 1852, National Archives of the Czech Republic, Prague, RAM-AC/ 10/ 778, 17.

14. Metternich to Twiss, December 7, 1848, National Archives of the Czech Republic, Prague, RAM-AC/ 10/ 774, 110.

15. Twiss to Metternich, February 15, 1850, National Archives of the Czech Republic, Prague, RAM-AC/ 10/ 776, 12–13.

Twiss, like Disraeli, took the role of student to Metternich as mentor—Disraeli commented that Metternich tended to lecture but said that did not bother him.[16] Twiss's correspondence with Metternich at times betrays a similar tendency, particularly in their early years of collaboration. The day after Christmas in 1848, Twiss wrote to apologise for having left Metternich's house in Brighton in haste. He explained "I was exceedingly sorry that I could not venture to remain until you had concluded the paper which you were so kind as to read to me, but I was engaged to dine with Lady Chantrey at the Bedford at ½ past 6 and, as it was, I did not arrive till 7."[17] The following day Metternich responded: "I believe that you can find the response to all that you would like to know about the individuality of Napoléon in what I was able to tell you during your last visit. We will recommence that lecture and if there are questions you would like to clarify I will provide you with everything at my disposal."[18] Although Metternich and Twiss lent each other many papers to read, Metternich apparently sometimes preferred to read out his thoughts. The collaboration between Twiss and Metternich far exceeded that Metternich had with Disraeli. The two became very close, meeting frequently in Brighton, and later in Metternich's residence in Richmond, as well as London. Metternich's house on Brunswick Terrace in Brighton was only a block down the seafront from the Bedford Hotel, where Twiss stayed. The first letter from Metternich to Twiss was written from Brighton in November 1848, opening with "*Mon cher Travers*" and continuing, "I am impatiently waiting for you at the end of this week," suggesting they were already familiar. Six months later, Twiss would write of "the many agreeable hours I have passed with Your Highness," and by May 1849, Twiss could write: "Your Highness has been so kind on so many occasions that I cannot but address you as my feelings prompt me, for I venture to regard you as a friend whose acquaintance a fortunate chance has enabled me to make rather than as an illustrious stranger who has filled so great a part in the world's history."[19] When, in October 1849, Metternich left London for Brussels, Twiss wrote: "I regret much that you are about to leave our shore ... For my own part I cannot but regret that a literary intercourse, so valuable to myself, for large historical questions on international subjects, are difficult to penetrate even with the aid of memoires, should be broken off."[20] "It has been

---

16. For Disraeli in the role of student to the mentor Metternich, see Disraeli, *Letters*, xiv; and on Metternich lecturing, Disraeli, *Letters*, 41.

17. Twiss to Metternich, December 26, 1848, National Archives of the Czech Republic, Prague, RAM-AC/ 10/ 774, 143.

18. Metternich to Twiss, December 27, 1848, Bibliothèque nationale de France, Fol/ R.D./13810, 18–19.

19. Twiss to Metternich, July 27, 1849, National Archives of the Czech Republic, Prague, RAM-AC/ 10/ 775, 339; Twiss to Metternich, May 31, 1849, National Archives of the Czech Republic, Prague, RAM-AC/ 10/ 775, 310.

20. Twiss to Metternich, October 4, 1849, National Archives of the Czech Republic, Prague, RAM-AC/ 10/ 775, 415–416.

most agreeable and profitable to me," he added, "to hold converse with one of the actors in the greatest drama of modern times."[21]

When Metternich was able to return to Austria following his English and Belgian exile, Twiss stayed with him every year at one of his chateaus, either at Königswart in Bohemia or Johannisberg on the Rhine, near Mainz.[22] In the summer of 1854, Metternich wrote to ask Twiss to come and stay at Königswart, where he would be residing from June to September: "If you come to see me you will be received with open arms by me and what remains of my family," and repeating, "Do come and stay either under my roof or that nearby [in Marienbad], I do not need to tell you that I would prefer the first of those choices."[23] During this visit, Metternich gave Twiss a medallion, of which Twiss wrote: "It is good to have a memory [*souvenir*] of a friend that one can touch."[24] Perhaps encouraged by the thought, Metternich then gave him a statue of himself, transported from Vienna to Twiss's library in Park Lane with some difficulty.[25]

Twiss had dealt with representations of Metternich on previous occasions, reporting several years earlier that on his way to the Athenaeum, he had taken the opportunity of "paying a visit to Mr Philipps and seeing your portrait in its finished state."[26] He added, "I think it is a good likeness and hope you are pleased with it." This was the 1849 portrait of Metternich by artist Henry Wyndham Phillips, which is now held in the Walters Art Museum.[27] Some months later, Twiss reported, "Your portrait by Mr Phillips has been making

---

21. Twiss to Metternich, "London ¼ before 2," second letter of October 4, 1849, National Archives of the Czech Republic, Prague, RAM-AC/ 10/ 775, 419–420.

22. Twiss to Metternich, September 6, 1854, National Archives of the Czech Republic, Prague, RAM-AC/ 10/ 780, 26; Twiss to Metternich, August 22, 1855, National Archives of the Czech Republic, Prague, RAM-AC/ 10/ 781, 11 for "*un petit voyage*" to Calais, Brussels, Rotterdam, Amsterdam, Hamberg, Copenhagen, Berlin, and from there to Königswart; Twiss to Metternich, October 14, 1856, National Archives of the Czech Republic, Prague, RAM-AC/ 10/ 782, 24—"let me thank you for a most agreeable visit"; Twiss to Metternich, August 29, 1857, National Archives of the Czech Republic, Prague, RAM-AC/ 10/ 783, 7.

23. Metternich to Twiss, June 16, 1854, National Archives of the Czech Republic, Prague, RAM-AC/ 10/ 780, 17.

24. Twiss to Metternich, September 16, 1854, National Archives of the Czech Republic, Prague, RAM-AC/ 10/ 780, 32.

25. Twiss to Metternich, December 29, 1857, National Archives of the Czech Republic, Prague, RAM-AC/ 10/ 783, 14; Twiss to Metternich, February 22, 1858, National Archives of the Czech Republic, Prague, RAM-AC/ 10/ 784, 3; Twiss to Metternich, July 12, 1858, National Archives of the Czech Republic, Prague, RAM-AC/ 10/ 784, 8.

26. Twiss to Metternich, March 15, 1849, National Archives of the Czech Republic, Prague, RAM-AC/ 10/ 775, 206.

27. The Walters Art Museum, "His Excellency the Prince Metternich," https://art.thewalters.org/detail/1576/his-excellency-the-prince-metternich/.

FIGURE 4. Portrait of Metternich, 1849, by Henry Wyndham Phillips.*

a provincial tour."[28] Metternich's pose recalls the famous portrait of him by Sir Thomas Lawrence, in 1815, which celebrated him as the architect of the Vienna Congress and the post-Napoléonic order. The objective of the 1848

28. Twiss to Metternich, February 15, 1849, National Archives of the Czech Republic, Prague, RAM-AC/ 10/ 776, 13.

* The Walters Art Museum, "His Excellency the Prince Metternich," https://art.thewalters.org/detail/1576/his-excellency-the-prince-metternich/

portrait, therefore, was consistent with the purpose of Twiss and Metternich's collaboration: that is, it was counter-revolutionary insofar as it perpetuated the myth of Metternich as the coachman of Europe. Phillips, however, added his own touches, producing a sombre portrait in a darkened room, with shadows under Metternich's eyes, and a kneeling figure on an inkstand in the background with her fingers to her lips, symbolising Metternich's possession of the *arcana imperii*.

In the later years of their friendship, the two men continued their rich dialogue on contemporary society and politics, but their rapport was now based upon a strong mutual affection rather than power. Metternich repeatedly wrote to Twiss urging him to come to stay in the summers, declaring, for example, in 1857: "I don't know where I will be this summer but wherever it is I wish above all to see you"; and the following summer, "Your letter made me hope that I would have the satisfaction of receiving you on my mountain [Schloss Johannisberg] and I don't need to tell you how much that desire is genuine."[29]

The warmth Metternich expressed towards Twiss was reflected more broadly across his family. Twiss and Richard Metternich, the Prince's son, established a friendship, with Twiss being invited to the wedding between Richard and his niece, Pauline.[30] Metternich insisted repeatedly that Twiss attend the wedding: "I hope to see you at my home [*chez moi*] this year... I would be delighted to count you amongst the witnesses [*témoins*] at Richard's wedding."[31] Twiss visited Richard in Dresden and Paris at his diplomatic postings, while Richard stayed with Twiss in his house in Park Lane.[32]

Metternich's third wife, Melanie, did not like or trust many of his visitors, particularly not while in England, but Twiss was one of few exceptions.[33] She wrote during the family's exile in Brussels: "Twiss (formerly a lawyer of

---

29. Metternich to Twiss, Vienna, March 10, 1857, Bibliothèque nationale de France, Fol/ R.D./13810, 152v; Metternich to Twiss, Königswart, July 21, 1858, Bibliothèque nationale de France, Fol/ R.D./13810, 163v.

30. "I must tell you, my dear Twiss, that in a couple of weeks Richard will marry. He has chosen his niece, the little Pauline Sandor, who, from being a little girl, becomes my daughter in law. The marriage arranged itself out of the blue, because the idea had not occurred to anyone in the family": Metternich to Twiss, Vienna, April 7, 1856, Bibliothèque nationale de France, Fol/ R.D./13810, 130v. In the following decades, Pauline von Metternich would become one of the most influential socialites in Europe, a patron of Wagner and Liszt, and a subject for paintings by Degas and Boudin, as well aiding in the development of *haute couture*; she held a prominent place in the court of Napoléon III, to which Richard became ambassador, and she subsequently became prominent in Vienna Society: Princess Pauline Metternich, *My Years in Paris* (London, 1922).

31. Metternich to Twiss, Vienna, April 20, 1856, Bibliothèque nationale de France, Fol/ R.D./13810, 135v.

32. See, for example, Twiss to Metternich, October 1, 1854, National Archives of the Czech Republic, Prague, RAM-AC/ 10/ 780, 33.

33. Palmer, *Metternich*, 315–323.

the English crown) also arrived. His visits give pleasure to Clement [Metternich], who, in general, likes people who spread, in public, good principles and salutary things, and Twiss is one of those people."[34] A year later, Metternich had returned to his German estate, Johannisberg, where he received various statesmen and dignitaries, including Prussia's envoy to the Frankfurt Parliament, Otto von Bismarck, and the Austrian King. During this period, Twiss came to stay with Metternich on the estate, and the Countess wrote: "Our English friend, Monsieur Travers Twiss, has left us, on the 9th [of September], after having passed an extended period with us [*chez nous*]."[35] On subsequent visits to the continent, Twiss also stayed with the Metternichs in their "suburban villa" in Vienna.[36] He had become almost part of the family, as Metternich remarked: "You have promised me an oral conversation and it will take place [in summer] either at Königswart or on the banks of the Rhine [at Schloss Johannisberg]. I'll let you know whether I will be in one place or the other when I fix it for myself . . . you can be assured that it is not in the middle of my family that you would play the role of a stranger; it's been a long time since you lost that character."[37]

    34. Klemens von Metternich, *Mémoires, documents, et écrits divers laissés par le Prince de Metternich*, 8 vols. (Paris, 1884), Vol. 8, 77.
    35. Metternich, *Mémoires, documents, et écrits divers*, Vol. 8, 109.
    36. Twiss to Metternich, July 7, 1852, National Archives of the Czech Republic, Prague, RAM-AC/ 10/ 778, 18.
    37. Metternich to Twiss, Vienna, June 18, 1856, Bibliothèque nationale de France, Fol/ R.D./13810, 138. In numerous letters, Twiss not only asked after the Countess Melanie, "her Highness," but also provided information for her. On more than one occasion, he acknowledged letters from her, offering "kind respects to the Princess Metternich and thanks for her letter": Twiss to Metternich, July 27, 1849, National Archives of the Czech Republic, Prague, RAM-AC/ 10/ 775, 341. He also wrote to express appreciation for gifts, including gloves, received from the Princess: Twiss to Metternich, October 19, 1852, National Archives of the Czech Republic, Prague, RAM-AC/ 10/ 778, 27. He apologised in one letter, in January 1849, for not having "yet had an opportunity of enquiring about *Mildred Vernon*, but I have not forgot my promise to her Highness": Twiss to Metternich, January 18, 1849, National Archives of the Czech Republic, Prague, RAM-AC/ 10/ 775, 45. *Mildred Vernon* was a novel in three volumes describing life for the nobility in Paris just prior to the fall of the July Monarchy in 1848, so its subject matter was unsurprisingly of interest to a Hungarian noblewoman exiled by the same revolutions. The novel was written under the nom de plume Hamilton Murray and published in 1848: Hamilton Murray, *Mildred Vernon: A Tale of Parisian Life in the Last Days of the Monarchy*, 3 vols. (London, 1848). Twiss's promise was to discover the true author of the novel, so his next letter began with news: "The authoress of Mildred Vernon is said to be Madame Blaise de Berry née Stuart (Scotch)," followed by anecdotes of her "intimate" relationship with Lord Brougham, the former Lord Chancellor. Twiss to Metternich, January 20, 1849, National Archives of the Czech Republic, Prague, RAM-AC/ 10/ 775, 53. In fact, she was Rose Stuart, rumoured to be Brougham's illegitimate daughter, who grew up in Paris and married Henry Blaze de Bury, becoming Marie Pauline Rose Blaze de Bury in 1844 and establishing a literary salon. Twiss knew Brougham from at least one prior occasion when they dined together in the Bishop of Carlisle's house. He then passed on to stories regarding Countess Daun

Gossip was one of the important topics in correspondence with Metternich. Twiss would report scandals. In one instance, he was fascinated by a Russian woman of peasant origin who had passed herself off as a noblewoman: "I must beg you to give M. Montenegro a little bit of news. The soi-disant Princess Korsakoff-Remsky [Sofya Vasilievna Rimskaya-Korsakova] of Baden notoriety is not a princess at all! Her husband is a lieutenant. The father was a Russian proprietor who grew poor as his steward grew rich. 'Naturally,' you will say. However, the Steward had a daughter. The son of the proprietor married the daughter of the Steward, and so the fortune (not above 30,000 roubles per an) returned to the family. This fortune as you may suppose does not suffice for the annual expenditure of a Grande Dame Russe—hence an occasional 'changement de domicile' without a liquidation des debts, and the sudden departure from Baden was only an instance ... The most amazing fact is that she has forced herself uninvited into the salons of St Petersburg."[38] The striking characteristic of the story is its parallel with the reinvention of a woman, whose origin was in Belgian peasantry, as a Dutch noblewoman and as the wife of Travers Twiss, a process that would commence within two years of his account of Sofya Vasilievna Rimskaya-Korsakova. Metternich should not have been shocked by such stories, unless it was by the element of class. Recent accounts of the Congress of Vienna have underlined the degree to which it was conducted as much through balls and dancing, liaisons, salons, vast and lavish dinners, as it was through the formal diplomatic negotiations.[39] Metternich was himself occupied during the congress with trying to win the favour of Princess Wilhelmine, the Duchess of Sagan. She hosted one of the most influential salons in Vienna and is believed to have shaped the hardening of Metternich's attitudes to Napoléon, as well as alienating him, according to Austrian spies, from the Tsar Alexander.[40]

Certainly, Twiss's friendship with Metternich and the several hundreds of letters they exchanged over ten years from 1848 had great personal value to him. Extraordinarily, although he was a probate lawyer and judge of probate, he left no will. It is true that, at the end of his life, he had little left to leave and few to whom he could leave what little remained. The letters from

---

d'Auersperg—"Her history is far more romantic"—as he had discovered hundreds of her letters at his friend Mr Popham's house, at Littlecote, and Countess Melanie subsequently filled in details of the story. Twiss to Metternich, July 27, 1849, National Archives of the Czech Republic, Prague, RAM-AC/ 10/ 775, 338. For a recommendation to Princess Melanie of Joseph Marryat, *A History of Pottery and Porcelain* (London, 1850), published by John Murray, see Twiss to Metternich, August 20, 1850, National Archives of the Czech Republic, Prague, RAM-AC/ 10/ 776, 81.

38. Twiss to Metternich, October 14, 1857, National Archives of the Czech Republic, Prague, RAM-AC/ 10/ 782, 23–24.

39. See, for example, Vick, *The Congress of Vienna*; Glenda Sluga, "Women at the Congress of Vienna," *Eurozine* (January 2015).

40. Sluga, "Women at the Congress of Vienna."

Metternich are the only object for which he produced a testament of any kind. He left a note, attached to them, instructing that they should be given to Thomas Tristram, the last civilian to be admitted to the Doctors' Commons, on Twiss's recommendation: "The Metternich letters may be given to Dr T. Hutchinson Tristram who will value them. 10 April, 89."[41] Far more numerous than the letters from Metternich to Twiss, mostly held in the Bibliothèque nationale de France, Paris, are those from Twiss to Metternich, now in the National Archives in Prague. Indeed, the letters from Twiss to Metternich record numerous instances in which Twiss thanks Metternich for his last letter, providing the date, for which no corresponding letter survives in Twiss's collection of Metternich's letters. As much as Twiss valued the correspondence, therefore, it is evident that he lost more than half of the letters Metternich sent to him, while Metternich's record keeping was scrupulous. The combined archives provide, therefore, a somewhat lopsided image of the correspondence, with Twiss's voice outweighing Metternich's, albeit Metternich's words can frequently be heard echoing in Twiss's responses. The reason so many of the letters Twiss valued were lost may be because they passed through several hands before arriving in the Bibliothèque nationale. But the reason may also partly lie, by Twiss's own account, in the terrible state of his rooms in both the Doctors' Commons and in the Albany, with papers piled high and disordered. It was not only Twiss's rooms that were disordered. Such was the dreadful nature of Twiss's handwriting, but also the apparent value Metternich placed upon this correspondence, that Metternich had one of his secretaries transcribe some of the letters into a legible form (as well as making copies of some of his own letters). Metternich's problems with reading may have been in part due to the fact that Twiss generally wrote in the evenings, and therefore in the dark: "I fear you will have some difficulty in reading my writing, as I write by candle light, but I hope not."[42] On another occasion, Twiss lamented: "I write to you a very miserable letter at one in the morning."[43] The problem, he said, was that he was "so much occupied" that he was obliged to "seize an irregular moment." He was also often buried in papers: "Excuse my rambling note, but I am writing in the midst of law papers at the Doctors' Commons."[44] Days later he wrote: "I shall commence my version of events at Vienna this evening. The most valuable part of my day is generally occupied with business in Court so that I have only the evenings

---

41. "Travers Twiss—note, " April 10, 1889, Bibliothèque nationale de France, Fol/ R.D./13810, 3.

42. Twiss to Metternich, January 16, 1850, National Archives of the Czech Republic, Prague, RAM-AC/ 10/ 776, 9.

43. Twiss to Metternich, January 28, 1851, National Archives of the Czech Republic, Prague, RAM-AC/ 10/ 777, 9–10.

44. Twiss to Metternich, December 2, 1848, National Archives of the Czech Republic, Prague, RAM-AC/ 10/ 774, 87.

to write in." He was primarily occupied by his work as a lawyer.[45] Court, for Twiss, could be both the Court of Arches for ecclesiastical matters, or the Admiralty Court. His multiplying ecclesiastical offices now absorbed most of his time, more than his professorships at King's College and then Oxford. All that he published at this stage of his career, including his work on international law, had to be written at night.

Some degree of secrecy attached to the letters, no doubt in part because Metternich's role in Twiss's publications on the 1848 revolutions had to be disguised. There is no question that although Metternich had formally retired from public affairs in 1848, his position remained sensitive. In June 1848, the newly free press in Vienna had accused Metternich of having been extraordinarily corrupt while in office, and of having betrayed the country by being in the pay of the Russians.[46] The Austrian government was obliged to investigate the accusations, and the inquiry, which ultimately found no proof for the charges, lasted until 1850. Metternich's vast properties in Austria were sequestered during this period, so that any debts could be charged against them. Bad publicity, or evidence of meddling in Austrian affairs, could have potentially endangered both his property and his ability to return from exile.

While most letters were sent through the post, many were delivered by hand because the pair did not trust the post: "As I have an opportunity of sending this by a private hand, I shall write more fully than I could otherwise have done."[47] Even the hand-delivered letters were somewhat shrouded in mystery. Late in 1850, Twiss and Metternich exchanged several letters in which they referred to their sponsoring of the translation into English of a work published on the continent. At no point did they name the author or reveal the identity of the book, while they used enigmatical terms such as "I was glad to find that the 'tall book' has reached your hands."[48] All that can be concluded is that their collaboration extended beyond works that have been identified.[49] In 1849, Twiss wrote to Metternich: "I send you the address of a relative who will oblige me by taking care of anything. If I should have time today I shall write a note by the Post for 'our mutual friend' to read. I do not think any of the letters addressed to me have been read by him—so that he made a sad mistake

---

45. "I hope to be able to send the remainder of the proof sheets this evening. I have been occupied in Court all day and have not had time to write": Twiss to Metternich, December 12, 1848, National Archives of the Czech Republic, Prague, RAM-AC/ 10/ 774, 123.

46. Palmer, *Metternich*, 318.

47. Twiss to Metternich, March 3, 1850, National Archives of the Czech Republic, Prague, RAM-AC/ 10/ 778, 2.

48. Twiss to Metternich, November 12, 1850, National Archives of the Czech Republic, Prague, RAM-AC/ 10/ 776, 98.

49. See also Twiss to Metternich, November 8, 1850, National Archives of the Czech Republic, Prague, RAM-AC/ 10/ 776, 94; Twiss to Metternich, November 19, 1850, National Archives of the Czech Republic, Prague, RAM-AC/ 10/ 776, 102.

in the choice, and his curiosity is the more unreasonable."[50] The reference to their "mutual friend" is obscure, but clearly they feared for the security of their correspondence.[51] Shortly after, Twiss wrote again, this time, he said, at the behest of Baron August Koller, an Austrian diplomat resident in London. Koller, Twiss reported, was "very anxious" about the location of a letter that he had sent to Metternich.[52] The letter had been included in a parcel that Twiss had sent for them both through a "Danish gentleman" who worked for the Danish legation. Koller had "not heard of their [the letters'] safe arrival and distrusts the surety of my messenger." Twiss himself, however, would have understood the lack of trust, as he conceded that "my letter was rather enigmatical" albeit that "I have no doubt that you did not require the aid of a Sphinx [a dealer in riddles] to interpret it." Nevertheless, it is striking that he felt it was necessary to be secretive in case the letters fell into the wrong hands.

In 1850, Twiss wrote in French to Metternich in Brussels but in such coded language that his meaning was not always clear. He had recently received from Metternich a corrected draft of an article on which the two men had been collaborating. Twiss referred to the manuscript as a "present"—he commented, "your present arrived"—and then used the metaphors of a painting to refer to aspects of the work: "Concerning the picture I spoke to you about—it has been decided that . . . it can have the grandeur of the original design, and something more as well."[53] The elaborate pretence appears to have been caused by the use of the postal service because in Twiss's next letter, which was hand-delivered by a mutual acquaintance, a prince, Twiss observed, "I may write freely" and then apologised for his previous obscurity: "I dare say you were a little puzzled by a French letter which I wrote to you in rather enigmatical language, as I did not know how many hands it would pass through. I do not think any letter to me would be read here, from what I have seen of them, but I did not know how far at Brussels there may be an over curious zeal amongst the officials."[54] Metternich, however, apparently did not share Twiss's confidence regarding the confidentiality of correspondence sent to England. Secrecy flowed, also,

---

50. Twiss to Metternich, October 4, 1849, National Archives of the Czech Republic, Prague, RAM-AC/ 10/ 775, 414.

51. On another occasion, Twiss took the opportunity of a visit by his father to Brussels to send a copy of a book to Metternich, by that time resident there, and yet despite the personal mode of delivery, he noted that the bookseller had written a name, presumably Twiss's, on the "outside" of the book "which I shall caution him against doing the next time": Twiss to Metternich, October 23, 1849, National Archives of the Czech Republic, Prague, RAM-AC/ 10/ 775, 439.

52. Twiss to Metternich, February 17, 1850, National Archives of the Czech Republic, Prague, RAM-AC/ 10/ 776, 14–15.

53. Twiss to Metternich, March 13, 1850, National Archives of the Czech Republic, Prague, RAM-AC/ 10/ 776, 20.

54. Twiss to Metternich, April 1, 1850, National Archives of the Czech Republic, Prague, RAM-AC/ 10/ 776, 24 and 30–31.

with correspondence in the other direction, with Twiss writing to Metternich in Brussels: "I delivered all the letters. Lord Melbourne was at Brocket Hall. I received a letter acknowledging the letters, which I enclosed under cover to him. So I have not broken the ice, but only thrown a stone upon the surface."[55] Again, the meaning here is obscure. This was not Lord Melbourne, the former Prime Minister, who had died in 1848, but his younger brother Frederick Lamb, the third viscount, who had moved into the hall his brother vacated. Lamb had been the British ambassador to Austria for ten years until 1841, so he would have been well known to Metternich, but why the veil of secrecy was necessary over the correspondence is unclear. Nor does Twiss clarify what ice had not been broken. Some light, however, may be shed on this reference by another opaque letter Twiss wrote later the same year in which he alerted Metternich to the fact that a "great change" had come over the Foreign Office, that a more pro-Austrian policy was to be pursued, and that Twiss had been authorised to inform Metternich of that fact.[56] He added, "An old friend of your Highness, who is better acquainted with Austrian, and German, affairs than any other person in England" was "satisfied with his father-in-law." Metternich wrote "Lord Melbourne" in the margin to the transcribed version of this letter, and Frederick Lamb's sister, Emily, was married to Lord Palmerston, the Foreign Minister.[57]

Twiss's dialogue with Metternich is testament to the suppleness of his character and his willingness to submit to a powerful figure, but it also reveals the force of his ideas and personality and his understanding of the complexity of the issues confronting Europe. While Metternich remained in England, his frequent visitors included the Duke of Wellington, Lord Palmerston, and Disraeli, so Twiss found himself in the company of the leading statesmen of the time. Indeed, we learn from the letters of John Wilson Croker that Twiss mediated access to Metternich while he stayed in England. Croker was an influential figure in the Admiralty, and could have known Twiss through that channel, although he was also one of the founders of Twiss's club, the Athenaeum.[58] Croker was writing a review for the *Quarterly* on the posthumous memoirs of the Whig politician Henry Vassal-Fox, Lord Holland, which had just been published in 1850. Holland had given a damning account of Metternich as a "cruel" criminal, guilty of "horrid acts of power," and "hardly qualified by any superior genius to assume the ascendancy in the councils of his own

---

55. Twiss to Metternich, January 16, 1850, National Archives of the Czech Republic, Prague, RAM-AC/ 10/ 776, 4.

56. Twiss to Metternich, November 26, 1850, National Archives of the Czech Republic, Prague, RAM-AC/ 10/ 776, 107-108.

57. Twiss to Metternich, November 26 (transcription), 1850, National Archives of the Czech Republic, Prague, RAM-AC/ 10/ 776, 111.

58. On Croker in the Admiralty, see C. I. Hamilton, "John Wilson Croker: Patronage and Clientage at the Admiralty, 1809–1857," *Historical Journal*, vol. 31, no. 1 (2000), 49–77.

and neighbouring nations, which common rumour has for some years attributed to him."[59] Croker took it upon himself to expose Holland's "posthumous libel," writing to a friend: "I had access to Prince Metternich myself, through the medium of Dr Twiss, who sent me some observations of the Prince's on Lord Holland's book."[60] Above all, their collaboration was based upon their shared conviction that "order," the balance of great powers and the supremacy of sovereignty, should take precedence over nationalism, emancipation, and democracy, as well as upon their shared determination to continue to project that vision of Europe against the forces of change.

Schleswig, Holstein, and Prussia

In January 1848, the Danish King, Christian VIII, died, leading to widespread demands for the establishment of a constitutional monarchy to replace the authoritarian system that had prevailed since the seventeenth century. The self-described "liberals" succeeded in their demands, but the new constitution did not include the Duchies of Schleswig and Holstein, lying between Denmark and Prussia, which the new liberal government announced they would integrate into Denmark. The Duchies were ruled by the Danish crown but were populated by both Danes and Germans. On the announcement of the policy of integration, the German population of the Duchies rose in arms. They were aided by an invasion of the Prussian army, partly provoked into action by the nationalist demands of the Frankfurt Parliament, establishing a provisional government of Schleswig-Holstein and declaring "they would not suffer a German country to be given up to the Danes."[61] Twiss responded rapidly to this event, publishing by July an account of the treaties between the great powers over centuries that had established the Duchies as territories of the Danish sovereign. It is improbable that Metternich had a hand in this work. It is possible that Twiss and Metternich had met as early as June, but as this treatise was published in July, it is unlikely that Metternich was involved in its production, and there is no correspondence between Twiss and Metternich relating to it. As it was published shortly after Metternich's arrival

---

59. Henry Richard Lord Holland, *Foreign Reminiscences* (New York, 1851), 110–112.

60. Louis J. Jennings, ed., *The Croker Papers*, Vol. 3 (Cambridge, 2012; first published 1884), 231. Ironically, Twiss complained to Metternich in 1850 that one of his own articles had been pushed back from publication in the *Quarterly Review* because Croker had exercised his right, as one of its founders, to include an article at the last moment: Twiss to Metternich, January 16, 1850, National Archives of the Czech Republic, Prague, RAM-AC/10/ 776, 7.

61. Travers Twiss, *The Relations of the Duchies of Schleswig and Holstein to the Crown of Denmark and the Germanic Confederation* (London, 1848), 171. For the broader context to the conflict, see Jonathan Sperber, *The European Revolutions, 1848–1851* (Cambridge, 1994), 213–214.

in England, it may have brought Twiss to Metternich's attention. Certainly, Metternich could have read the copy in the Athenaeum library that Twiss had donated.[62]

In this treatise, Twiss used his historical methodology to refute the German claim that the Duchies were independent states, and he insisted that the treaties and guaranties that had established them as Danish must be respected. In particular, both Britain and France had provided guaranties for the treaties establishing Denmark's sovereignty over Schleswig-Holstein. Guaranties were a form of treaty whereby a third party, or parties, commit to aid one or both states who form a treaty when the enjoyment of their rights from the contract is threatened. Quoting Vattel, Twiss pointed out that a guaranty is "an engagement into which no sovereign ought to enter into lightly" and that they seldom did, unless they had "an indirect interest in the observance of the treaty."[63] In the case of Britain, the sovereign, who was also the Elector of Hanover, had signed the Treaty of Gottorp in June 1715, as part of the Treaty of Utrecht. In doing so, he had also received, in consideration from the King of Denmark, the Duchies of Bremen and Verden. The Treaty of Gottorp thus declared: "His royal majesty in Great Britain engages and obliges himself, his heirs and successors, to maintain King Frederick IV [of Denmark], his heirs and successors, in the occupation, enjoyment, and possession of the ducal part of the Duchy of Schleswig."[64] According to Twiss, respect for such treaties was essential to the sovereign's self-preservation because they were made, as Vattel had pointed out, from self-interest and their violation entailed breaking ties of mutual obligation and preservation that underpinned the system established by the Vienna Congress and, before it, the Treaty of Westphalia. Nationalism and irredentist movements threatened that system.

The prevailing understanding of international law, the *ius publicum Europaeum*, reflected the system of great powers. When Twiss gave his lectures at King's College in 1851, the understanding of international law that he endorsed was Grotian insofar as he agreed that international society existed and, as such, that society was governed by law. He therefore rejected sceptics of international law such as John Austin, on the one hand, while at the same time rejecting what he described as the "Utopian" cosmopolitanism of Kantians, on the other.[65] For Twiss, as for seventeenth-century natural law theorists, the fundamental law of international society was self-preservation, which was itself the reason for establishing society, whether a society of natural

---

62. Athenaeum, Mem 2/16: *Athenaeum. Rules and Regulations, List of Members, and Donations to the Library 1850* (London, 1851), 55.
63. Twiss, *The Relations of the Duchies of Schleswig and Holstein*, 121.
64. Twiss, *The Relations of the Duchies of Schleswig and Holstein*, 125.
65. Twiss, *Two Introductory Lectures on the Science of International Law*, 49.

persons who created a state, or a society of artificial persons, such as states. According to this view, sovereigns entered into agreements with each other as part of a social contract to ensure their preservation in international society (just as natural persons made a social contract for their preservation under a sovereign). Any failure to respect such agreements endangered not only the existence of that sovereign but the whole society itself.

Writing to Prince Metternich the following April, Twiss nevertheless conceded that the nature of treaties of guaranty were problematic.[66] He distinguished between specific guaranties, which entailed limited actions in specific circumstances, and unlimited guaranties, in which the bounds were unclear. Such "general" guaranties were "of no practical use to the party guaranteed, but only to the guaranteeing party as furnishing a pretext for intervention." If the meaning of such "compacts" was "not settled," he argued, "the bona fides of a state may be impugned." He feared that "treaties so called of Guaranty specify frequently the modus operandi positive, without any qualification or extension of notion of a Guaranty." He could not escape the conclusion that "guaranties are out of date in this age, like treaties generally!"[67] By this time, the war between Prussia and Denmark over Schleswig had reignited, and he lamented that the "poor Danes have made a bad beginning," reporting that he had dined with the Secretary of the Danish Embassy and "two Admirals" (as might be expected for a lawyer who worked in the Admiralty Courts) who had criticised Danish naval tactics at the Battle of Eckernförde.[68]

Despite unpublished doubts about treaties of guaranty, Twiss's arguments met, as was often the case, very favourable reports in the press amid calls for the British government to respect its treaty engagements, underlined by Twiss, and to take a firmer line against Prussia.[69] In the short term, Twiss's side of the argument prevailed, both in terms of public opinion in Britain and because the Danish army re-established control over the Duchies. In the long term, as also was often the case with Twiss's views at this stage of his career, his arguments ran against the grain of a changing international order and rising nationalism. When the Prussians invaded Schleswig-Holstein again in 1864, the Duchies were incorporated into the German Confederation and then into the German Empire in 1871.

Twiss is also credited by the *Wellesley Index* with an article, "The Germanic States," in the September 1848 issue of the *Quarterly Review*, and

---

66. Twiss to Metternich, April 12, 1849, National Archives of the Czech Republic, Prague, RAM-AC/ 10/ 775, 263.

67. Twiss to Metternich, April 12, 1849, National Archives of the Czech Republic, Prague, RAM-AC/ 10/ 775, 266.

68. Twiss to Metternich, April 12, 1849, National Archives of the Czech Republic, Prague, RAM-AC/ 10/ 775, 260.

69. *Morning Post*, August 7, 1848, 4; *Evening Mail*, February 23, 1849, 4.

according to the *Index*, Metternich was his collaborator on that publication.[70] If so, this would be their first collaboration. The surviving correspondence between Twiss and Metternich, however, while containing detailed plans for their later publications, begins in November 1848. It is clear from the November correspondence that the two men were already acquainted, so it is not impossible that they had collaborated between June and September, but there is no evidence for Metternich's contribution to "The Germanic States." The article itself lacked the polemical force of Twiss's later collaborations with Metternich. It assumed the form of a narrative of the background to the 1848 revolutions in the confederation of German states. Twiss's pro-Austrian bias was evident primarily in the treacherous role in which Prussia was cast. According to his account, the Holy Roman Empire collapsed when Prussia was the first German state to abandon its commitments, signing a separate peace treaty with Napoléon. Austria was left to fight alone until also obliged to adopt the principle of "every man for himself."[71] Similarly, when the War of the Second Coalition began in 1798, "Prussia remained neutral, and Austria completed the sacrifice of the Germanic Empire."[72] Prussia's neutrality nevertheless excited the jealousy of Napoléon, and it was drawn once again into a humiliating war.[73] When Napoléon was defeated in Russia in 1812, national feeling began to develop in Prussia along with plans, inspired by Baron Heinrich vom Stein, for a newly established Prussian constitutional monarchy along the lines of the British constitution. The Prussians, however, according to Twiss, also wished to impose their liberal constitution upon the smaller German principalities which were not ready for such a system of government.[74] "One might almost suppose," he conjectured, "that the spirit of Stein breathes at the present moment in the breasts of some of the members of the Francfort parliament."[75] He proceeded to recount how German unification was avoided in 1815 by the creation of the German Confederation, and from this moment, "Prussia seems to have become alienated from Austria," assuming that the Confederation was an Austrian "machine."[76] This background, for Twiss, then explained why, when the revolution came in 1848, Prussia did not come to the aid of Austria and seized the opportunity to propose itself at the head of a movement for a united German nation. The members of the Frankfurt Parliament, he said,

70. "Travers Twiss," in *The Wellesley Index to Victorian Periodicals, 1824–1900* (2006–2019).
71. [Travers Twiss], "The Germanic States," *Quarterly Review* (September 1848), 453–454.
72. [Twiss], "The Germanic States," 455.
73. [Twiss], "The Germanic States," 458.
74. [Twiss], "The Germanic States," 462.
75. [Twiss], "The Germanic States," 466.
76. [Twiss], "The Germanic States," 471.

"resolved unanimously that the freedom, unity, independence, and honour of the German Nation" must be established.[77] On March 21, "a proclamation 'to the Prussian people and the German nation' announced that the King of Prussia had . . . adopted the Ancient German National colours," declaring "'from this day forward Prussia is fused in Germany.'"[78] For Twiss, nationalism was destructive, a threat to the system of great powers and the self-preservation of the sovereigns within it.

Austria and Germany

The first joint publication for which correspondence survives showing that Twiss and Metternich collaborated was the December 1848 *Quarterly Review* essay "Austria and Germany." In this article, written as the events of the revolutions unfolded, the disease in both cases was said to be the same: namely, nationalism. Nationalism was dangerous to empires. For Twiss, the threat to the Austrian Empire was also a threat to the British Empire: "To myself I confess the welfare of the Austrian Empire is second to that only of the British Empire."[79] "The word *Nation*," he argued, has two senses, "it represents a political idea and a historical fact." In the first sense, it signified "an independent political society united by common political institutions—in other words, a State." In the second sense, it denoted "an aggregate mass of persons . . . who are connected by the ties of blood and lineage, and perhaps by a common language."[80] "It is of the utmost importance," he continued, that the two different ideas "should be kept distinct," but this was not the case. Their confusion had "given birth to the modern doctrine of *Nationalism*, which, while it involves an absurdity in its conception, is essentially aggressive in its application."[81] For Twiss, the idea of a "nation-state"—the term he used—was crucial to the stability and prosperity of the international order. It was, as he saw it, the fundamental unit of political society established by the system created by the Treaty of Westphalia and ratified by the Congress of Vienna. But nation-states should not be confused, he insisted, with nationalities. Indeed, "Nations," in the sense that they were synonymous with "States," may well be empires, such as the Austrian Empire, that comprise many nations in the cultural sense. As for Disraeli and Metternich, for Twiss nationalism was a destructive and revolutionary force, and the force, moreover, that was responsible for the 1848 revolutions.

77. [Twiss], "The Germanic States," 474.
78. [Twiss], "The Germanic States," 477.
79. Twiss to Metternich, October 4, 1849, National Archives of the Czech Republic, Prague, RAM-AC/ 10/ 775, 417.
80. [Travers Twiss], "Austria and Germany," *Quarterly Review* (December 1848), 186.
81. [Twiss], "Austria and Germany," 186.

Mid-Victorian liberals were generally critical of the "principle of nationality," which conservatives attacked as the inspiration of the revolutions.[82] If, therefore, liberals did not endorse the "principle of nationality," the question arises as to why conservatives associated them with that cause. Many British liberals expressed sympathy with the continental revolutionaries. In Hungary, Germany, and Italy, the revolutions were struggles for both emancipation, in terms of manhood suffrage, but also as national liberation and freedom from oppressive empires, in the case of Austria, or feudal principalities, in the case of Germany. Victorian liberals may have been more interested in emancipation understood in terms of suffrage, freedom of the press, and freedom of assembly, but conservatives were not averse to tarring them with the same brush of nationalism that they used for the revolutionaries.[83] This, at least, was Twiss and Metternich's perspective. It was reflected, for example, in an assessment Twiss made of Richard Cobden, the liberal exponent of free trade. In 1849, despite his relatively optimistic view of Russia, Cobden had denounced the possibility of a loan being made to that Empire at the time of its intervention in the Hungarian revolution in support of Austria. In a series of speeches made at the London Tavern in 1849, he also condemned loans to the Austrians. He was strongly sympathetic with the Magyar revolution and declared in his speech on the Russian loan that the inhabitants of London "were indifferent to the fate of Hungary, or to the designs of those despots who are making an attack upon her liberties and independence."[84] "The people of a separate and independent nation," he declared, "should be able to regulate their own affairs."[85] The Hungarians were "a noble people struggling for its liberties."[86] "Will any man dare," he asked, "to lend his money, to pay for cutting the throats of an innocent people?"[87] By January 1850, however, it was clear that the Russians wanted the money to invest in railways, and Barings bank was prepared to lend it to them.

Twiss attacked Cobden, as he attacked all friends of the Hungarian nationalists, commenting to Metternich, "Mr Cobden, by the by, has damaged

---

82. Georgios Varouxakis, "1848 and British Political Thought on 'The Principle of Nationality,'" in Douglas Moggach and Gareth Stedman Jones, eds., *The 1848 Revolutions*, 140–161.

83. Sperber, *The European Revolutions, 1848–1851*, 209, shows that, while nationalist and liberal ambitions were ostensibly aligned, many nationalists forgot their liberal princples when they aligned themselves with fellow nationals engaged in suppressing the liberties of non-nationals.

84. Richard Cobden, "Speech on Russia," in *Speeches of Richard Cobden, esq., M.P., on Peace, Financial Reform, Colonial Reform and Other Subjects: Delivered during 1849* (London, 1849), 125.

85. Cobden, "Speech on Russia," 126.

86. Cobden, "Speech on Russia," 132.

87. Cobden, "Speech on Russia," 130.

himself by interfering with the Russian loan."⁸⁸ Twiss, however, decided to take the question beyond the issue of the Russian loan and questioned the credibility of Cobden as leader of the free trade movement, suggesting that the credit for the campaign against the Corn Laws belonged to the aristocrat Charles Villiers: "There is a feeling growing up against him, as having stolen the laurels which properly belonged to Mr Charles Villiers, which his interference with the monied interests is likely to exasperate." He conceded that Cobden "helped to excite the feeling which carried the abolition of the Corn Laws," but concluded, "He is one of the imposters of the day" and suffered from "an exaggerated notion of his own influence and importance."⁸⁹ Such attacks upon liberals did not, however, prevent Twiss from appropriating their arguments or even their title.

Just one month prior to Twiss's publication of his observations on nationalism in the *Quarterly Review*, he wrote, on November 18, the first of his surviving letters to Metternich. At this stage, his tone was still formal.⁹⁰ He assumed Metternich knew that he was writing an essay, or essays, on the 1848 revolutions. The letter also acknowledged Metternich's role in assisting with Twiss's writing: "It has occurred to me that it will be more convenient to discuss the administrative system of Austria in a separate memoir." He then turned to the questions he would discuss in a sentence Metternich heavily underlined: "I should then propose to discuss the doctrine of Nationality or Nationalism, as propounded of late in Germany as the basis upon which an independent political society should be set up showing its inherent defects as a political bond and its peculiar inapplicability to Germany." A year later, Twiss similarly identified that in Hungary the "principle of most mischief is the doctrine of nationality," and Metternich again underlined the passage.⁹¹

Metternich responded two days later, on November 20, with a letter containing very similar views to those Twiss would publish in the essay as well as offering his own observations as material. "The question of 'nationalities' and of 'nationalism,'" wrote Metternich. "I'll tell you what I think of that question and you make what you will of my observations." He expanded: "The distinction you make between the substantive nationality and the added syllable 'ism,' shows us that you admit the justice of the difference that I make as a

---

88. "Twiss to Metternich," January 16, 1850, National Archives of the Czech Republic, Prague, RAM-AC/ 10/ 776, 8.

89. "Twiss to Metternich," January 16, 1850, National Archives of the Czech Republic, Prague, RAM-AC/ 10/ 776, 9.

90. "In accordance with your kind permission, I take an early opportunity of addressing to your highness a few remarks on the subject of the conversation with which you were so obliging as to favour me": "Twiss to Metternich," November 18, 1848, National Archives of the Czech Republic, Prague, RAM-AC/ 10/ 774, 2.

91. "Twiss to Metternich," September 10, 1849, National Archives of the Czech Republic, Prague, RAM-AC/ 10/ 775, 397–398.

general rule between the proper denomination of things and the inflexions that open the door to the false application of things."[92] These distinctions were consistent with a view that Metternich had stated since 1814. At that time, he had recognised the need to deal with the reality of rising national sentiments which had been encouraged by Napoléon. His attitude was that "events which cannot be hindered must be led."[93] He accordingly struggled with the Emperor Francis's desire to impose administration divisions within the Austrian Empire that were modelled upon German provinces. Metternich argued that the Empire must constitute a family of nations and that it must not be perceived as alien to the peoples under its authority.[94] They should therefore be enabled to develop their own institutions. This recognition of nationality, however, was intended to hinder nationalism and the pressure for nation-states.

Twiss transposed Metternich's discussion of nationalism directly into his essay. Similarly, a week later, he wrote: "I should be obliged for your sketch of Joseph II at your earliest convenience. I drew a character of him last night and shall be glad to make it more complete."[95] Metternich duly responded, "My dear Travers! Here is my short sketch [*esquisse*] of the person and acts of Joseph II." "Tell yourself with certainty," Metternich assured him, "that the judgement that I give on this prince and his short rule fully conforms with the facts." He then continued, "Joseph II was an amalgam of qualities and faults, of good intentions and a lack of knowledge, of tendencies close to despotism and a desire for popularity."[96] Twiss's discussion of Joseph's rule that comes at the beginning of the *Quarterly* essay on Austria and Germany followed this portrait. We might, he wrote, be disposed to praise Joseph "for his political liberality," but "his system was essentially despotic, his method revolutionary ... With an abundance of excellent intentions, but with a total want of practical sense, he pulled down the edifice of the state."[97]

Metternich returned repeatedly to discussion of the dangers of nationalism in the months and years to come. In Germany, he argued, nationalism had been awakened by the humiliation of Napoléon's invasion and the need to rebuild: "Between the years 1808 and 1813, the Prussians, crushed by the French colossus, searched in the awakening of German national patriotism for

---

92. Metternich to Twiss, November 20, 1848, Bibliothèque nationale de France, Fol/R.D./13810, 7v.

93. Metternich, cited in Arthur G. Haas, "Metternich and the Slavs," *Austrian History Yearbook*, Vol. 4 (January 1968), 121.

94. Haas, "Metternich and the Slavs," 122.

95. Twiss to Metternich, November 27, 1848, National Archives of the Czech Republic, Prague, RAM-AC/ 10/ 774, 71.

96. Metternich to Twiss, November 29, 1848, National Archives of the Czech Republic, Prague, RAM-AC/ 10/ 774, 49.

97. [Twiss], "Austria and Germany," 191.

support for their own reconstruction."⁹⁸ At the same time, he constantly reiterated that nationalism, in whichever country—whether Prussia or Hungary, for example—was a mask for the pursuit of other interests.⁹⁹ Peter Mandler observes: "The principal effect of 1848, then, for most of the intellectual and political Establishment was to confirm their sense that nationalism was an atavism from which England had providentially escaped and to reinforce their consciousness of England as the directive centre of a multi-national kingdom and empire, precisely the form that advanced civilizations should take."¹⁰⁰ Austria was another such multi-national empire, and it was precisely that consciousness that would lead to the warm welcome Metternich received in England as well as the elaborate arrangements made, which included Twiss, for him to project his understanding of multi-national empires.

The collaborative writing project was conducted as interviews through the letters as well as in person. On November 23, Twiss established an agenda for their Saturday meeting.¹⁰¹ The following day, he sent Metternich a fur-

---

98. Metternich to Twiss, Brighton, February 11, 1849, Bibliothèque nationale de France, Fol/ R.D./13810, 50.

99. While the Frankfurt Parliament deliberated the future constitution of Germany, he wrote: "The leading article in the Morning Chronicle today is remarkably well done. It characterises perfectly the position in Frankfurt. Analysing that position reveals the following elements: [First] a real interest, the national idea, reduced to the role of a masque destined to cover false politics and personal ambition. [Second] Executing a program conceived by adventurers and surrendered into the hands of ignorant people and armed with that presumption which gives men the passion of their ignorance": Metternich to Twiss, Brighton, January 29, 1849, Bibliothèque nationale de France, Fol/ R.D./13810, 41.

100. Peter Mandler, "'Race' and 'Nation' in mid-Victorian Thought," in Stefan Collini, Richard Whatmore, and Brian Young, eds., *History, Religion, and Culture: British Intellectual History 1750-1950* (Cambridge, 2000), 230.

101. He wrote that he hoped "to avail myself on Saturday of your permission to call upon you": "Twiss to Metternich," November 23, 1848, National Archives of the Czech Republic, Prague, RAM-AC/ 10/ 774, 10-12. He then set out a series of questions for discussion: "Would you be so kind as to consider the different plans suggested in 1815 for the reconstruction of the German Empire? 1. A single monarchy. Would you object to the Emperor Francis' [Francis II] objection to this being made known? 2. A North and South Germany divided by the Maine. 3. The plan of the four great powers to establish five states; Austria, Prussia, Hanover, Bavaria, and Württemberg." He continued: "I should be further obliged to you to consider the objections to a federal state" both including and excluding Austria. By this point, it was clear that Twiss was speculating about 1848 rather than 1815: "This latter [a federal state] is at present the plan which seems most likely to be proposed." He concluded, "I have, I think, exhausted the possible combinations as I conceive a Republic to be impracticable." He progressed to a discussion of Italy and whether a northern Italian state could be established and then followed with statements from press reports on the revolutions, asking whether certain facts were correct, concluding the letter with the question: "May Nationalism be regarded as a reaction against the centralism of Joseph II in its origin, and against the Imperialism of Napoléon in its present development?": "Twiss to Metternich," November 23, 1848, National Archives of the Czech Republic, Prague, RAM-AC/ 10/ 774, 16.

ther series of questions, generally questions of fact, and announced he would arrive in "London tomorrow by the 12 o'clock train." Next amongst Metternich's papers is a 4,000-word treatise, or "exposé," written in French in the hand of Metternich's secretary and delivered to Twiss on November 25. The opening pages of Twiss's essay in the *Quarterly Review* are at times translated verbatim or otherwise paraphrased from this work by Metternich. The rest of the 12,000-word *Quarterly Review* essay is woven together from the questions and answers that passed between the two men over the following weeks.[102] On December 6, 1848, for example, when describing the new leaders of the Hungarian government, Metternich wrote to Twiss: "Kossuth & Batthyani were named (if you like), or rather imposed, as Ministers to the King of Hungary. They are the two men who have the most *savoir faire* in the kingdom. Both are equally revolutionaries and separatists. Kossuth is a bandit and rebel *[homme de sac et de corde]*. Batthyani, on the other hand, is an aristocrat in contradiction with himself. Between them there is an implacable hatred."[103] Days later, Twiss's essay appeared in the *Quarterly* with a paraphrased version of Metternich's portrait: "The Diet at Pesth now threw itself into the arms of Kossuth, and voted him unlimited powers, with the title of President of the Committee of National Defence. Batthyani thereupon withdrew altogether . . . Kossuth and Batthyani had never been cordially united; they had indeed acted for some time together in the ministry which the events of March had imposed upon the King of Hungary being both revolutionists and both separatists. They were, perhaps, the only two individuals of the ultra-Magyar party who had sufficient knowledge of public business to carry on the government; but they were in other respects essentially discordant in character. Batthyani, for instance, was an inconsistent aristocrat; Kossuth, a consistent democrat."[104]

102. Exposé. Remis le 25 Nov. 1848 à M. Travers Twiss, National Archives of the Czech Republic, Prague, RAM-AC/ 10/ 774, 49.
103. Metternich to Twiss, December 6, Bibliothèque nationale de France, Fol/ R.D./13810, 10.
104. [Twiss], "Austria and Germany," 215. These methods are repeated throughout the correspondence. In his December 2 letter, Twiss noted that he would move onto "a brief review of events since the Diet transferred its functions to the Franckfurt Assembly." He then turned to a series of further questions for Metternich: "1. What is the correct legal view of this assembly? Is it a tradition from the old Diet or not? 2. I should be obliged to you for a little skeleton of facts connected to the Viennese insurrection and the Hungarian rising. I mean only a skeleton. I will set the bones together, if any of them should be detached. 3. Is there any certainty to the Poles and Hungarian Jews being the leaders of the emeute? 4. Have the Poles a separate organisation, or are they a band of the tribe of red republicans." He also asked "If you have any facts connected with the Viennese affair which it is desirable to make known, I should be very much obliged if I did receive them in a note on Wednesday next": Twiss to Metternich, December 2, 1848, National Archives of the Czech Republic, Prague, RAM-AC/ 10/ 774, 86–89.

Similarly, Twiss proceeded, in the article on Austria and Germany, to provide and analyse a detailed statistical table on the numerous nationalities that made up the Empire, on the one hand, and the German Confederation, on the other. Again, we find Metternich's hand in the publication, when he wrote to Twiss, on November 20, that he had requested demographic information from an aide that would "put you in possession of the most complete statistics on the Austrian Empire. You would do well to adjourn just until the arrival of that material."[105] Having received the information, Twiss proceeded to break down each territory in the Austrian Empire into its constituent peoples, showing there were not one but several, or more, nationalities for each territory. Transylvania alone he broke down into "Magyars, Szecklers, Saxons, Wallachians, Gipsies, Armenians, Bulgarians."[106] He concluded, therefore, that "territorial distinctions according to nationalities" could only be admissible in the Austrian Empire in what he described as the political sense of "nation," and not in the cultural sense—only, that is, as a body politic, or *"corps d'empire,"* which was framed to the interests of the "various populations."[107]

Metternich was, therefore, at least the co-author of this work, even though he consistently referred to it as *"votre travail"* and *"votre article."* Subsequent letters reveal that Twiss sent the proofs of the article to Metternich, who returned corrections on those proofs.[108] He had "hesitated for a moment" to accept Metternich's offer due to his fear that there could be delays to printing, but concluded: "Pray make any note which may occur to you." Twiss then explained the nature of the *Quarterly* and its publisher, John Murray III, pointing out that the editor could make changes to the article. Responding to a question about how much the *Quarterly* would pay for the article, he stated: "I think 1£ per page sufficiently liberal. I think that is the rate at which my labor is estimated."[109] He noted that some authors received £10 per page, but added, "I take whatever is sent without enquiry on the same principle upon which we act at the Bar in respect of fees. They are settled by those who give them and we ask no questions." Metternich's corrections to the proofs of the article were minor—a copy of the corrected proofs is still amongst his papers—and Twiss incorporated them all.[110]

---

105. Metternich to Twiss, November 20, Bibliothèque nationale de France, Fol/R.D./13810, 7.

106. [Twiss], "Austria and Germany," 190. On the multiplication of central European nationalities during the revolution strengthening the argument for the centralisation of power around the empire, see Sperber, *The European Revolutions*, 134–135.

107. [Twiss], "Austria and Germany," 188.

108. "I am very much obliged for your kind offer to look at the proof sheets": Twiss to Metternich, December 11, 1848, National Archives of the Czech Republic, Prague, RAM-AC/ 10/ 774, 115–122, transcribed by Metternich's secretary at 163–167.

109. Twiss to Metternich, December 11, 1848, National Archives of the Czech Republic, Prague, RAM-AC/ 10/ 774, 166.

110. For the corrected proofs, see National Archives of the Czech Republic, Prague, RAM-AC/ 10/ 786, 1–25.

At times, Metternich imposed his views. In a December 13 letter, Twiss opened, "Your criticisms are just."[111] The following day, he wrote that he had "availed myself of your kind corrections" and asked, "Do you think I may say 'An act of mutiny as it were,' instead of 'lèse-majesté' against the empire?"[112] When the essay was published, Metternich requested a copy. He asked: "Do you think you could place at my disposition a copy of your article in the Q.R. [*Quarterly Review*], some copies entirely detached from the volume in order to facilitate their transmission to the Continent?"[113] Twiss replied, almost apologetically, "You will have received by this time copies of the Quarterly, and I have no doubt your accurate eye will have detected some slight alterations in the text—a little spice here and there, more pungent than I use myself."[114] The changes, he claimed, were the "Editors additions." "This is meant for your private ear," he added. "I dare say Mr Murray will be anxious to hear your opinion of the number."[115] Murray had an important role in commissioning the articles, with Twiss commenting some weeks later: "As for the latest Q.R. . . . I saw the editor today and he has promised to let me know what topic he thinks most suitable."[116]

This exchange indicates that the collaboration between Metternich and Twiss, while kept secret from the public, involved others apart from Disraeli. It appears to have been a coordinated effort, including the publisher Murray, to oppose the central ideas, particularly the nationalism, of the 1848 revolutions. Moreover, as Metternich revealed, the objective was, in part, to transmit the article to Europe, presumably as a propaganda tool. Other collaborators were involved and revealed that the objective was more precise than simply opposing the revolution. Their aim, in particular, was to establish stronger sympathy for the Austrians, widely perceived to be the most conservative force in European politics, at a time when many in the British government supported the Prussians and the objectives of the Frankfurt Parliament.[117] During the years

---

111. Twiss to Metternich, December 13, 1848, National Archives of the Czech Republic, Prague, RAM-AC/ 10/ 774, 127.

112. Twiss to Metternich, December 14, 1848, National Archives of the Czech Republic, Prague, RAM-AC/ 10/ 774, 138.

113. Metternich to Twiss, December 27, 1848, Bibliothèque nationale de France, Fol/ R.D./13810, 19.

114. Twiss to Metternich, December 30, 1848, National Archives of the Czech Republic, Prague, RAM-AC/ 10/ 774, 69.

115. Metternich responded, "I received the copies of the Quarterly Review from Mr Murray and, in reading the article, I observed the alterations which are not important and neither add nor subtract from it": Metternich to Twiss, January 1, 1849, Bibliothèque nationale de France, Fol/ R.D./13810, 21.

116. Twiss to Metternich, January 23, 1849, National Archives of the Czech Republic, Prague, RAM-AC/ 10/ 775, 66.

117. Frank Lorenz Müller, *Britain and the German Question: Perceptions of Nationalism and Political Reform, 1830–63* (Basingstoke, 2002), 108–133.

1849 and 1850, the Prussians and Austrians struggled for control over the German federation, and Twiss was enlisted in the cause of aiding Austria. One letter that Twiss kept amongst his letters from Metternich was from a correspondent who was clearly assisting with the preparation of the articles for the *Quarterly Review* (the signature on the letter is illegible, but it is not Murray). This author wrote to Twiss: "My anxiety as to the next article would be to give it that direction which under all the circumstances of Europe the P [Prince] should think most likely to serve the cause of good understanding and mutual support between Austria and England. Much—almost everything, I should fancy—will depend on the result of the next few weeks, or days, on the fate of Prussia. In whatever way the question pending may be settled, one can't but foresee a more general revolution in the general arrangements of Europe than there has been since Bonaparte consolidated his Empire and there is no man now living whom I should hold so qualified and auspicate to the probable developments as the P.M. [Prince Metternich]. Already he has arrived at conclusions which will be valuable for your guidance if you compose (as I trust you will) a third article for the next Q.R."[118] The author, who appears to have some connection with the *Quarterly Review*, clearly believed that the stakes in this conflict could not be higher, and that the outcome in these early months of the revolution was in the balance. It is evident that a group of British conservatives enlisted Twiss to work with Metternich to help tip the balance of the turmoil in favour of Austria, with the purpose of maintaining the Concert of Europe and, through it, order.

At the same time that Twiss continued with the dialogue, he enthusiastically played the role of apologist for Metternich's rule and the order that he believed that Metternich had ensured. On November 27, with a new series of questions, he wrote to Metternich from the Bedford Hotel: "I should be glad to have an opportunity of contradicting indirectly some 3 or 4 falsehoods respecting the system of Prince Metternich—if any occur to you which are easily to be explored."[119] He then digressed into the nature of rule: "I quite agree with you that it is impossible for a great statesman to set himself right with his contemporaries ... but it is always most desirable that there should be a correct public opinion in the world ... If public opinion can be indirectly affected, the object is frequently gained without the trouble of doing anything directly. Again, a false public opinion leads to false conclusions ... Therefore, it can never be too soon to correct a false public opinion—a new school of thinkers can never be formed too soon. Excuse my discussion, but I wished to explain my motives in wishing indirectly to strike down two or three falsehoods."[120]

118. Letter to Twiss, January 26, 1849, Bibliothèque nationale de France, Fol/R.D./13810, 38v–39.

119. Twiss to Metternich, November 27, 1848, National Archives of the Czech Republic, Prague, RAM-AC/ 10/ 774, 157.

120. Twiss to Metternich, November 27, 1848, National Archives of the Czech Republic, Prague, RAM-AC/ 10/ 774, 74.

This was one of Twiss's most explicit explanations of what his role was in collaborating with Metternich. It is a theme to which he returned repeatedly. Writing in 1849, he pointed out to Metternich that Prussia had established a good reputation in Britain at Austria's expense: "It should be remembered that Prussia has been working for many years to popularize herself with England, but she has only half succeeded, whilst Austria has looked on with folded arms. Now it should be otherwise."[121] As is paradoxically the case for conservatives, Twiss understood that continuity with the past demanded innovation, partly because of the necessity of inventing the past, but also because, invented or not, the volatility of the present and future changed the meaning of the past. He perceived himself to be a shaper of public opinion—that most potent of social forces, according to nineteenth-century accounts.

Despite the strength of Metternich's presence in these letters, Twiss consistently pressed his own views, and as conservative as Twiss was himself, he attempted to bend Metternich to the new environment of the post-1848 world. In his letter to Twiss on November 20, Metternich declared, "Believe me, I was always full of liberality while at the same time an adversary of liberalism, full of respect for the rights due to nationalities and of reserve in face of the pretentions of nationalism."[122] Metternich had indeed tried to push the Emperor Francis to grant greater autonomy to the numerous nationalities in the Austrian Empire in the years after 1814, but his repeated plans had failed.[123] While Metternich announced his opposition to liberalism, Twiss tried to convince him, two weeks later, to describe himself as a liberal or, at least, a "liberalist": "Will you add the word liberalist to your vocabulary. Wesley, the founder of Methodism, did not wish the Devil to have all the good music, so he sanctified by use terms hitherto profane. So with ideas, we must not allow them to be profaned by the improper use of words, and I should suggest the 'parti libéraliste' being distinguished from the 'parti liberal.'"[124] This extraordinary recommendation underlines how capacious the concept of liberalism could be, while at the same time indicating that he was potentially able to see himself as a liberal or, at least, a "liberalist." Some months later, Twiss noted that "we agreed to distinguish liberality from liberalism."[125] He certainly showed himself to be sensitive to the need to adapt to a new political language and a new political environment—a potential for metamorphosis that was itself within liberalism. That adaptability would

---

121. Twiss to Metternich, December 22, 1849, National Archives of the Czech Republic, Prague, RAM-AC/ 10/ 775, 448.

122. Metternich to Twiss, November 20, 1848, Bibliothèque nationale de France, Fol/ R.D./13810, 7v.

123. Haas, "Metternich and the Slavs," 126–127.

124. Twiss to Metternich, December 2, 1848, National Archives of the Czech Republic, Prague, RAM-AC/ 10/ 774, 88–89.

125. Twiss to Metternich, August 17, 1849, National Archives of the Czech Republic, Prague, RAM-AC/ 10/ 775, 369.

prove throughout his long life to endure even more than the conservatism that he articlutated in his correspondence with Metternich.

Even as Twiss and Metternich were collaborating on their first article in December 1848, they were anticipating new projects together. On December 7, Metternich first suggested the idea for what would be the March 1849 *Quarterly Review* essay on the Austrian Empire: "I'll let you know when you come to see me about an idea for an essay for the first issue of 1849 which I believe to be very important, to cast the daylight of truth upon reality of Austrian power stripped of all makeup. I hope you already know enough to know what I want."[126] The concluding remark reflects the fact that Metternich largely directed the subjects upon which the pair collaborated. Nevertheless, while deferential, Twiss put his own views on the future projects, writing on December 26, when the first *Quarterly* article had been completed, "How much there is to think of at present if one looks for a moment at the great social problems involved in the fermentation of ideas ... You say that the civilisation of the age is false. Will it soon be otherwise? Is not this part of the trial of this world? But this is one of the questions which I shall be happy to try to fathom with you."[127] Certainly scepticism about the rhetoric of civilisation was common in the nineteenth century, if not as common as the rhetoric itself.[128]

The German Confederation and the Austrian Empire

The new year brought optimism with it. At least, Metternich concluded, it could not be as bad as 1848, from which, he said, he "had learnt nothing," but "it must have taught something to many others. The year which we have entered will provide the proof of the signficance [*la portée*] of their lesson."[129] Nevertheless, at stake, he observed a week later, was "the life and the existence of the Austrian Empire," so there was still work to do.[130] "I will provide you," he promised, "with my theses which always presented themselves to me instinctively, but which

---

126. Metternich to Twiss, December 7, Bibliothèque nationale de France, Fol/R.D./13810, 13.

127. Twiss to Metternich, December 26, 1848, National Archives of the Czech Republic, Prague, RAM-AC/ 10/ 774, 151. The following day Metternich responded: "What will be necessary will be to prepare for the next term a complementary essay in which the development will employ events that provide a rich texture": Metternich to Twiss, December 27, 1848, Bibliothèque nationale de France, Fol/ R.D./13810, 18.

128. Andrew Fitzmaurice, "Scepticism of the Civilizing Mission in International Law," in Martti Koskenniemi, Walter Rech, and Manuel Jiménez Fonseca, eds., *International Law and Empire: Historical Explorations* (Oxford, 2017).

129. Metternich to Twiss, January 1, 1849, Bibliothèque nationale de France, Fol/ R.D./13810, 22v.

130. Metternich to Twiss, January 10, 1849, Bibliothèque nationale de France, Fol/ R.D./13810, 25.

one does not reveal in written form due to the force of circumstances. With such theses, as with all truths, the sense of the moment and the opportunity obliges one to <u>express</u> them. The subdivision of the spirit which gives rise to the ideas of <u>nation</u> and <u>nationality</u>, taken from a <u>historical</u> and <u>political</u> point of view, is an example of what I am talking about. The need to establish that difference only made itself felt to me when I took up my quil to address the subject."[131]

Twiss, in response, offered his best wishes for the new year to Metternich and "Madame la Princesse," suggesting that, even if "dark clouds hover about," there were "infinite grounds for congratulations of the brightening of the political horizon." Building an argument for the next essay in the *Quarterly*, he wrote on the essential role of the Austrian Empire in holding Europe together, as well as the bridge it formed between Europe and "Asia": "It will be interesting to examine the position which Austria has occupied as the 'cement' between the Asiatic and the European civilisation ... Of course, western Europe with its constitutional habits is prejudiced against absolute forms of government ... We are satisfied that government should <u>direct</u>, not <u>control</u>. The state on the other hand compels individuals to act for themselves, and so forces them to acquire habits of conduct, which become by degrees more difficult to break than laws."[132] His point was not that the liberal system whereby individuals governed themselves should be introduced to Austria. It was, rather, that regardless of the type of government, Europe needed the stability of the Austrian Empire.

On January 23, Twiss wrote saying he had been "occupied all day in the Admiralty Courts" but was now catching up with the latest news from Vienna and the European newspapers. Having summarised various articles, he continued: "The editor [Murray] seems to wish <u>rather an article that should treat of principles than facts</u> ... Will you consider this? I shall be happy to come to Brighton on Saturday night."[133] Metternich, however, was not interested in Murray's preferences, responding with his own prudential views on the question of principles: "In the passages of the Alpes the path that shows us to our destination is marked for voyagers by milestones [*jalons*] placed from time to time. Those milestones are posts twenty feet high which rise above the snow. The snow can obscure the route and the voyager should stop, in that case, and the milestones which he can see will not prevent him from falling into the precipice which is found on the right, or on the left, or on both sides of the path. Principles function in the moral world like milestones; they are not the point of arrival,

---

131. Metternich to Twiss, January 1, 1849, Bibliothèque nationale de France, Fol/R.D./13810, 22.

132. Twiss to Metternich, January 3, 1849, National Archives of the Czech Republic, Prague, RAM-AC/ 10/ 775, 15.

133. Twiss to Metternich, January 23, 1849, National Archives of the Czech Republic, Prague, RAM-AC/ 10/ 775, 66. It appears to be Metternich who added the underlined emphasis.

but they mark the path."[134] On the other hand, he was a great enthusiast for "facts": "Do not see me as pleading my personal cause, a cause which in reality is nothing but one of the practical application of principles, which can therefore be attacked without being defeated. I have behind me fifty years of facts; facts are submitted to other rules than ideas, they carry within them elements of accusation and of their defense, and it is history that is the sole competent tribunal to pronounce the verdict, guilty or not guilty."[135] Facts were discovered through experience, and Metternich never wasted an opportunity to underline the fact that he was one of the most enduring statesmen in Europe.

A week later, Twiss turned to the question of which kinds of monarchy would be best for Austria, and he distinguished between "Pure" and "Mixed," with further subdivisions of "Pure" into "absolute and constitutional," while the divisions of "Mixed" were unlimited.[136] The following day, he delved further into the various kinds of constitution and stated his desire to "'rehabilitate' as it were (*réhabiliter*) the term monarchy."[137] Furthermore, he added, "I should wish also if possible to rescue the word Republic," returning again to the anecdote of Wesley not wishing the Devil to have all the good music.[138] "So," he argued, "with many terms. They become debased by usage, and it may be desirable to rescue if possible the term 'Republic' from democracy."[139] He pointed out that "even Rousseau" had called any state governed by law to be a republic. "In this sense of the word," he concluded, "a constitutional monarchy would be one variety of republic."[140] Having previously urged Metternich to adopt the mantle of a liberal, he now suggested he also present himself as a republican. Even at this stage of his career, he was ideologically nimble, appropriating liberal language to a conservative cause. He declared, "So with the word monarchy it has been brought into disrepute undeservedly as if it were inconsistent with the well-being of individuals."[141] The opposition of

---

134. Metternich to Twiss, Brighton, January 25, 1849, Bibliothèque nationale de France, Fol/ R.D./13810, 32v–33.

135. Metternich to Twiss, January 10, 1849, Bibliothèque nationale de France, Fol/ R.D./13810, 25v.

136. Twiss to Metternich, January 30, 1849, National Archives of the Czech Republic, Prague, RAM-AC/ 10/ 775, 72.

137. Twiss to Metternich, January 31, 1849, National Archives of the Czech Republic, Prague, RAM-AC/ 10/ 775, 78.

138. Twiss to Metternich, January 31, 1849, National Archives of the Czech Republic, Prague, RAM-AC/ 10/ 775, 79.

139. Twiss to Metternich, January 31, 1849, National Archives of the Czech Republic, Prague, RAM-AC/ 10/ 775, 79.

140. Twiss to Metternich, January 31, 1849, National Archives of the Czech Republic, Prague, RAM-AC/ 10/ 775, 84 (there is confusion in the pagination here—page 79 should be followed by 84).

141. Twiss to Metternich, January 31, 1849, National Archives of the Czech Republic, Prague, RAM-AC/ 10/ 775, 85.

monarchy and democracy "we were saved from in 1688" because at the time of the Glorious Revolution the English had "no United States of America to mislead superficial observers." The American system, he conceded, might "suit the wants of a population like that of the states yet be totally unsuitable to the circumstances of most European communities." Moreover, the European revolutionaries supposed that because the United States was democratic and antimonarchical, democracy was the "antidote of monarchy."[142]

One of the salient issues for Twiss and Metternich, in the early days of 1849, was the political form that Germany would take: namely, whether it would unify into a single empire or state, or remain a confederation. The decisive question was whether Austria would be included in the new political body or not. If Austria was excluded, it would be possible to create a German state or empire. If Austria was included, the Germans of the Austrian Empire could not be absorbed into a German state, so a confederation would remain.[143] Metternich had championed the existing federation, which he regarded as his own creation, and was implacably opposed to the notion of national unity. The existing forms of sovereignty and order were to take precedence over the forces of nationalism. The principal purpose of the collaboration with Twiss was to promote that vision.[144] The correct path was federal union: "German unity cannot be achieved except with the aid of completely turning everything upside down [*bouleversement complet*], while in union we can find a pledge to develop national strength in peaceful and conservative routes."[145] Metternich described the German Confederation, as it had been established by the Congress of Vienna, as the "Système Metternich."[146]

Twiss responded that he wished to know more about the Système Metternich, while once again returning to the task of defending Metternich: "I

---

142. Twiss to Metternich, January 31, 1849, National Archives of the Czech Republic, Prague, RAM-AC/ 10/ 775, 86.

143. For this debate, see Sperber, *The European Revolutions, 1848-1851*, 226-227.

144. With a characteristic certainty in his own convictions, Metternich wrote: "When one day the acts of the years I have been citing come to be placed before the public view, the outcome which awaits me will be that which gives to me a spirit of divination to which I have no pretension. It will be found that I understood that $2+2=4$ is a truth and what we know surpassed divination. I knew, and definitely did not divine, that between the ideas of unity and union there is more than one difference, that there is opposition": Metternich to Twiss, January 10, 1849, Bibliothèque nationale de France, Fol/ R.D./13810, 27v-28.

145. Metternich to Twiss, January 10, 1849, Bibliothèque nationale de France, Fol/ R.D./13810, 27v-28.

146. Referring to himself in the third person, he declared: "Examined up close, the System Metternich was a cult of things while that of his adversaries was . . . to replace things . . . with an abstract formula . . . One voice has made itself heard at Frankfurt until now by the exclamation 'We will condemn to shame the attempt at justification of the System Metternich' . . . I abstain [from declaring] . . . that facts have a greater value than exclamation": Metternich to Twiss, January 10, 1849, Bibliothèque nationale de France, Fol/ R.D./13810, 28-28v.

should like to discuss the so-called Système M. [Metternich] showing that it is not a <u>personal</u> system but an *état des choses*" and adding, "there are three or four points on which I would like to set the opinion of the world right."[147] This would include "the Confederation of 1815," the German Confederation, because "the idea of such an union was most appropriate." "I quite appreciate," he added, "the distinction which you have marked out between <u>unity</u> and <u>union</u>." Defending Metternich would also mean that "it might be convenient to show what view the Emperor Francis and his minister P.M. [Prince Metternich] took of the renewal of the Empire in 1815." "All this," he noted, would come "under the second head of the 'Relations of Austria to Germany.'" The argument would be that Austria "is pre-eminently the Conservative Power, her mission has been 'the maintenance of peace in Europe.'"[148] At the same time, Twiss warned Metternich that the age of empires was drawing to a close. He returned to "the distinction between <u>unity</u> and <u>union</u>." We might say the first corresponded to the state, and the second to empire, although he did not speak in those terms in this discussion because, for Twiss, the idea of the state could embrace a number of political forms, including empire. "It seems to be of the greatest importance," he continued, "that these two ideas should not be confused as we are entering upon an era when the <u>person</u> of the common sovereign will cease in so many states to be the great connecting link between different races or lands."[149] "For instance," he observed, "it is patent on the face of things, that the English constitution is not suitable to Ireland in practice—this therefore is a 'make-believe,' and when the time of trial arrives it is of necessity superseded by another pro-tempore arrangement."[150] This is a point to which he repeatedly returned in the following years: "We have made one great political blunder in trying to govern Ireland by the same laws as England. It should be a lesson to the laws of <u>unity</u>. We made a <u>Union</u> and we endeavour to make out of it a <u>unity</u>, but in vain. *Naturam expellas furca, tamen usque recurret* [you may drive nature out with a pitchfork but she will keep coming back]."[151]

In his thoughts on political union, he revealed his understanding that sovereignty is a fiction, or make-believe. That understanding arose from his training in law and political philosophy. He then sought to break down the opposition drawn between representative and absolute government, arguing

---

147. Twiss to Metternich, February 1, 1849, National Archives of the Czech Republic, Prague, RAM-AC/ 10/ 775, 90.

148. Twiss to Metternich, February 1, 1849, National Archives of the Czech Republic, Prague, RAM-AC/ 10/ 775, 91.

149. Twiss to Metternich, February 1, 1849, National Archives of the Czech Republic, Prague, RAM-AC/ 10/ 775, 93.

150. Twiss to Metternich, February 1, 1849, National Archives of the Czech Republic, Prague, RAM-AC/ 10/ 775, 94.

151. Twiss to Metternich, February 28, 1851, National Archives of the Czech Republic, Prague, RAM-AC/ 10/ 777, 27–28.

that "the same institutions cannot be expected to produce the same result when the circumstances are essentially different. But there is a disposition to put implicit faith in a representative legislature, as being the opposite to an absolute monarchy."[152] Democracy, therefore, while effective in some circumstances, would fail in others. At the same time, "absolute monarchy, like any other form of <u>pure</u> government may be expected to fail when applied to a very complicated and extensive system, because it cannot be all-sufficient." Similarly, "representative institutions are in their way not a panacea for political difficulties." While Metternich had been condemned as a supporter of the *Ancien Régime* and an absolutist, Twiss sought to break down the oppositions between the old and the new, but he also anticipated that European empires would not last, including the empire of Great Britain itself. They suffered, as he saw it, from the same problems as representative systems: that is, no system could adapt to changing circumstances.

Metternich examined the idea inspiring the desire for unity and the interests that were served by that idea. The idea was the nation, but the interest, he was certain, was Prussian power, a particular interest, while the Germans' true interest should be in a federal union: "The question of German unity is a question of interest and sentiment. The interest is not found in the unity but in the union of the parties which compose the German body. It is sentiment—for some, a romantic idea, for others, a factional calculation—that, even so, excites them to pronounce in favour of unity. It is the ideologues of the head and the heart who, in their pursuit of the object [nationalism] play another role ... [namely] the enlargement of Prussia by its pretended fusion in Germany, which in their [the Prussians'] eyes will be <u>the conquest of the various German states by the Prussians through pacific, political, and legislative means,</u> and will at the same time be useful for advancing a radical Utopia."[153] The radical utopia that he had in mind was a liberal state, but, for Metternich, all plans to promote such liberal states were necessarily tied to nationalism, and his opposition to liberal ideas was to a large degree driven by his opposition to nationalism.[154]

---

152. Twiss to Metternich, February 1, 1849, National Archives of the Czech Republic, Prague, RAM-AC/ 10/ 775, 94.

153. Metternich to Twiss, Brighton, February 3, 1849, Bibliothèque nationale de France, Fol/ R.D./13810, 44v–45.

154. Responding two days later, Twiss shared the most recent news from the continent, and his most recent reading on the events, including an article on Prussia in the *North American Review*, which he judged not "worth your buying" because it presented a "<u>Romantic</u> view of Germany and of the 19th century," which he dismissed with the observation that "<u>sentiment</u> is transient, that of <u>interest</u> somewhat permanent": Twiss to Metternich, February 5, 1849, National Archives of the Czech Republic, Prague, RAM-AC/ 10/ 775, 96–97. It was unsurprising that Twiss, or Metternich, as anti-nationalists, would be fundamentally opposed to the Romanticism that fed it.

Twiss again tried to move Metternich by degrees to a new position. He conceded that "I have always looked for a common interest for a united Germany, and failed in discovering such . . . But I have thought, I must confess, that some of the Confederate states were too small for the convenience of their neighbours or their own."[155] While he agreed that the settlement of 1815 was necessary to protect "vested interests," he wondered if it was not now "in their own interests to make parts of larger societies rather than to stand alone." He expanded upon this idea before commenting, "The fault which is usually found in England with reference to Austria is that her policy with respect of Germany was too repressive."[156] Such repression, it was said, would lead to "either the stifling of the political life of all individuals, or an explosion of a mischievous, possibly dangerous, kind." "No provision," he concluded, in a tone that now sounded more like Twiss himself than putative English critics, "was made for training the political thought of the Germans by improving their political institutions, and accustoming them to political action in accordance with such institutions."[157] "How are such objections to be met," he asked, "so as to satisfy a reasonable English mind." He had now shifted from an argument about the size and number of the German states under the Confederation to a claim about the need for political reform, although the two questions were not unrelated—one reason that the small principalities and cities of Germany were maintained in 1815 was to keep their ruling families in power and so to remain attached to the *Ancien Régime* and oppose what were seen as revolutionary forces. Twiss, at least, showed that he recognised the need for some reform.

He followed up these concerns two weeks later by asking Metternich if there was a problem with respecting sovereignty—one of the objectives of the Concert of Europe—and, at the same time, constraining liberty: that is, how could sovereign peoples of the German Confederation be respected if they were not able to pursue their own political objectives, even if those objectives included being dissolved into a larger state. Metternich argued in reply: "The question which you have addressed me regarding 'what is more important: to leave the rights of sovereigns entirely free or to not incur the risks of the consequence of that liberty' is posed in a manner too categorical . . . the consequences are inseparable between the respect of the rights of sovereignty and the rejection of those rights." The same question arose, he said, in 1813 when "Austria wanted to respect the rights of sovereignty of the German princes and she therefore insisted upon their union in a federal system, that is to say in a Staatenbund [confederation]. The word bundestaat,

155. Twiss to Metternich, February 5, 1849, National Archives of the Czech Republic, Prague, RAM-AC/ 10/ 775, 98.
156. Twiss to Metternich, February 5, 1849, National Archives of the Czech Republic, Prague, RAM-AC/ 10/ 775, 99.
157. Twiss to Metternich, February 5, 1849, National Archives of the Czech Republic, Prague, RAM-AC/ 10/ 775, 99.

to which it has been reduced, is indefinable ... it is a new invention and destined to mask the mediatisation of sovereignties to combine them into one sovereignty, <u>into that of the German people</u>."[158] In 1813, the question was one between "a federation of sovereign states and an empire in which individual sovereignty could find no place," and the situation in 1848 had not changed. Effectively, Metternich was arguing that the artificial person of the sovereign, as much as a natural person, was not free to self-destruct, while at the same time, those sovereigns had to be forced to be free through their inclusion in the confederation.

In early 1849, Twiss also speculated on what would follow the revolution in terms of a "Counter Revolution": "The fever having passed away, strength returns to the body, only however on the supposition that there is a vital energy in the body which reproduces strength."[159] That vital energy, he suggested, would be maintained by strong institutions and customs. He was particularly concerned that "there is an element in modern societies which cannot be well neglected," namely: "the population of large towns. There will always be a fermentation in it which will produce wine or vinegar." The difference would be made by "municipal institutions," which were an "instrument of education" and by which "an orderly organisation may be maintained."[160] Key amongst these were corporations: "As you well observed, corporations, as opposed to associations, are an aristocratical institution." A strong state, therefore, and one which could re-establish itself after revolution, would be one in which corporations multiplied the conventions of rule and the aristocratic character of the state itself. For this reason, when Metternich wrote to Twiss four weeks later to note the establishment of the new Austrian constitution, he identified one of its weaknesses as a failure to establish "representative corporations" within the empire: that is, corporations which could perform the role of representing interests rather than having those interests directly represented.[161] Twiss argued that the education of a young state through such municipal corporations was essential to its strength in later years, just as the strength of an adult person draws upon that person's education. He drew a Hobbesian and Grotian analogy: "I have always considered the life of the individual man to represent the life of nations to a certain extent."[162] He would remark upon this

---

158. Metternich to Twiss, Brighton, February 21, 1849, Bibliothèque nationale de France, Fol/ R.D./13810, 65–66.

159. Twiss to Metternich, February 6, 1849, National Archives of the Czech Republic, Prague, RAM-AC/ 10/ 775, 101.

160. Twiss to Metternich, February 6, 1849, National Archives of the Czech Republic, Prague, RAM-AC/ 10/ 775, 102.

161. Metternich to Twiss, March 13, 1849, National Archives of the Czech Republic, Prague, RAM-AC/ 10/ 775, 194–195.

162. Twiss to Metternich, February 6, 1849, National Archives of the Czech Republic, Prague, RAM-AC/ 10/ 775, 103.

parallel repeatedly in his correspondence and publications: "How strange it is that states should have the passions of mortal men!"[163] Lacking any legislating sovereign, international law was developed in the nineteenth century by drawing analogies from private civil law, so for an international lawyer such as Twiss, it was inevitable that he would think of states as persons comparable with natural persons. He qualified this idea, however, with the observation that "nations do not grow like men equally fast in point of time."[164] When he worked to transform King Leopold's private corporation into a state, he would even revise that aspect of the analogy.

Twiss frequently expressed a very Hobbesian view of self-preservation and the primacy of order as a political good, and he returned to these themes in reflecting upon the revolutions from the relative calm of October 1849: "Hobbes considered the state of nature to be a state of war, and the crude natural man seems to be the same today as he was in bygone times . . . I thought at one time an invasion of moral barbarism was at hand."[165] He revealed here that, as much as his contemporaries, there had been moments during these years, such as when the Chartists met in their hundreds of thousands in London in April 1848, when he feared that the revolutions would traverse the English Channel and could not be contained.[166] That fear alone provided abundant motivation for his collaboration with Metternich. For Hobbes, the state of nature, in addition to being characteristic of international society, could be reached through civil war, which destroyed sociability, and for this reason, Hobbes admired Thucydides's analysis of the catastrophic consequences of civil war. Unsurprisingly, therefore, Twiss immediately followed his observations on Hobbes with praise for Thucydides: "Never was more truth told than by Thucydides in his sketch of man as a political being."[167] Twiss would only add, as we shall see, to his Hobbesian and Thucydidean analysis an element of class. The cause of the breakdown of civil society, he would argue, was not so much a "political" conflict as a "social" conflict, a conflict between the orders. His solution to that conflict was conservative, but it entailed the appropriation by conservatives of a number of liberal reforms and a more fluid understanding of class, arguing for a moral aristocracy to which somebody such as he himself could belong. Although he had not reached the kinds of

---

163. Twiss to Metternich, January 28, 1851, National Archives of the Czech Republic, Prague, RAM-AC/ 10/ 775, 10.

164. Twiss to Metternich, February 6, 1849, National Archives of the Czech Republic, Prague, RAM-AC/ 10/ 775, 103.

165. Twiss to Metternich, October 4, 1849, National Archives of the Czech Republic, Prague, RAM-AC/ 10/ 775, 417.

166. On the "apocalyptic" mood in England in the immediate aftermath of the 1848 revolutions, see Parry, *The Politics of Patriotism*, 172.

167. Twiss to Metternich, October 4, 1849, National Archives of the Czech Republic, Prague, RAM-AC/ 10/ 775, 417.

radical ideas regarding metamorphosis across the social orders that he would subsequently embrace for membership in international society, as well as for some individuals, notably his wife, he nevertheless had begun to accept that social status must be fluid.

On February 7, Twiss wrote to Metternich once again with his thoughts on his latest reading, and prefiguring the next publication: "I rather think the distinction between 'unity' and 'union' may form the counterpart in the next number to that between Historical and Political Nationalities. How much discord and misery would have been spared the world, if men could have been content with the 'unity of the spirit' and 'the union of the body.'"[168] He wrote for a second time the same day to say, in response to the latest letter from Metternich, that it enabled him to "appreciate the System M. in a new light."[169] It was a "Federal System as opposed to the Unitary System, and the policy of P.M. was directed not to prevent the development but the change of the Federal System." Twiss confessed that, while he knew that "respect for legality" was a "dominant trait in the character of the Minister [Metternich]," he nevertheless had held "doubts, whether his [Metternich's] views were not too pure, too scientific."[170] But now, he declared, continuing to refer to Metternich in the third person, even if he was the recipient of the letter, "I understand better his position. He was in the presence of an enemy." The "enemy" were the "minority," who were "seeking from time to time to supersede the Federal System."[171] This, he observed, had been "the common struggle in all federal systems," including the Swiss and the "Americans in which the southern states and their leaders" also sought their own ends.[172] Metternich heavily underlined in red all of Twiss's remarks retracting his previously critical statements.

Twiss followed his apology with a statement of the plan for the next essay. "It should be shown," he reasoned, "that the System M. was federal and the antisystem is 'Unitarian.' The next point to be established clearly is that the Unitarian System is impracticable for Germany, therefore the conclusion follows that the System M. was right and the P.M. the friend of Germany, not its enemy."[173] While, days earlier, Twiss had attempted to introduce some nuance

---

168. Twiss to Metternich, February 7, 1849, National Archives of the Czech Republic, Prague, RAM-AC/ 10/ 775, 107.

169. Twiss to Metternich, February 7 (second letter), 1849, National Archives of the Czech Republic, Prague, RAM-AC/ 10/ 775, 108.

170. Twiss to Metternich, February 7 (second letter), 1849, National Archives of the Czech Republic, Prague, RAM-AC/ 10/ 775, 109.

171. Twiss to Metternich, February 7 (second letter), 1849, National Archives of the Czech Republic, Prague, RAM-AC/ 10/ 775, 109.

172. Twiss to Metternich, February 7 (second letter), 1849, National Archives of the Czech Republic, Prague, RAM-AC/ 10/ 775, 110.

173. Twiss to Metternich, February 7 (second letter), 1849, National Archives of the Czech Republic, Prague, RAM-AC/ 10/ 775, 113.

into the analysis of the Austrian Empire and the German Confederation, seeking concessions regarding the size of member states and the need for political reform, Metternich had made it plain that such nuance was impossible in the face of the "enemy," and their case returned to a simple opposition between nationalistic states and multi-ethnic federal empires. As the apprentice, Twiss retreated.

Metternich disagreed with his critics that he was a reactionary, but without taking up Twiss's ideas of reform: "You are absolutely right that the respect for legality has always influenced my march. I find myself in that regard in perfect agreement with the sentiment of Europe and the principles of government . . . I have been accused by the opportunists to have been stationary. I don't know how to be stationary other than in principles . . . I know how to march and to stop depending upon the circumstances but I never believed that a fast train was something that governments should follow."[174] At the same time, he excused his policies by the necessity of opposing nationalist forces that threatened the existing sovereignties of central Europe: "You say very justly 'He was in the presence of an enemy, the Unitarian spirit of a minority, reaching from time to time to supersede the federal system.' To complete the truth of that thesis, it is necessary to consider certain measures which are the result of the difference between 1820 and 1848. In the first of those years, unitarism was supported by enthusiasm; in the second [1848] by politics—that which is revolutionary."[175] Again, in his thinking, national unity and liberalism, or revolutionary politics, were closely bound together. He returned to the idea that the nationalism that drove the idea of German unification was a cover for deeper interests—namely, Prussian expansionism—and suggested that national goals could more successfully be realised within a confederation: "I wanted to serve the principle of federation in Germany, not that I was looking, in its application, for the summum bonum, which I know definitely does not exist in any human institution, but because I was following my clear conviction that that system is truly rational and satisfies, at the same time, the interests of Germany and the good of political peace, while the unitary system does not take account of the national spirit which it subordinates to the spirit of a coterie and covers their ambitions."[176] "The nature of the Germany [political] body," he added, "is anti-unitary, and to act against the nature of a body is to follow a false route."[177] He pushed Twiss towards simply oppos-

---

174. Metternich to Twiss, Brighton, February 11, 1849, Bibliothèque nationale de France, Fol/ R.D./13810, 49.

175. Metternich to Twiss, Brighton, February 11, 1849, Bibliothèque nationale de France, Fol/ R.D./13810, 49v.

176. Metternich to Twiss, Brighton, February 11, 1849, Bibliothèque nationale de France, Fol/ R.D./13810, 47v.

177. Metternich to Twiss, Brighton, February 11, 1849, Bibliothèque nationale de France, Fol/ R.D./13810, 48.

ing the pursuit of national unity rather than discussion of possible reform: "You are in the true characterisation of the situation: a struggle between the principles of unity and federation. The so-called 'System Metternich' is in fact not a system but an order of things."[178] Here Metternich also revealed that his highest objective was the pursuit of order and stability, and it was for this reason he opposed both nationalism and the pursuit of a German state. Peace would prevail, Metternich concluded, "if the great political body which is placed at the centre of the continent of Europe is placed under a federal regime rather than a unitary regime." Federation was not an end in itself but a means of assuring order, to which all other political goods were subordinate. Even in his last years, in the aftermath of the Crimean War, he observed: "You know the march of my spirit and the calm in my soul, you would not doubt that I am above all a man who likes order, and who does not believe that order can be assured by the elements of disorder." Such a belief was only possible "when phantasmagoric [visions] replace reality in the public understanding. That is my conviction and I am too old to change it."[179]

Metternich also warned Twiss not to refer to him by name, and not to defend his "system" as his own invention: "What remains for me to ask you is that my name does not appear in the article you are writing. Speak of things but not of me."[180] He repeated this plea just days later: "Avoid naming me ... not for personal reasons, but in the interests of the cause that I serve and which cannot be diminished by a personification."[181] His fear was that overt attempts to defend him would play into the hands of his "enemies," who used personal politics to attack the order he had established: "To diminish the cause, they raise the person. If I was a fact I couldn't do anything further against such a procedure." Twiss reassured him: "I shall be careful not to speak of the P.M. and as little as possible of the system M. by that name." [182] Instead, he would substitute "the Cabinet of Vienna, or the Austrian Cabinet." Metternich did not want their publications to be perceived as a blatant attempt to clear his name. Twiss noted that he had never, "in any work of value," read "attacks against the personal character of P.M. but only against the system." The strategy, therefore, was to defend Metternich's system rather than Metternich himself. At the same time, he therefore reasoned that "if the system ceases to be

---

178. Metternich to Twiss, Brighton, February 11, 1849, Bibliothèque nationale de France, Fol/ R.D./13810, 47.

179. Metternich to Twiss, Königswart, October 18, 1856, Bibliothèque nationale de France, Fol/ R.D./13810, 144–144v.

180. Metternich to Twiss, Brighton, February 11, 1849, Bibliothèque nationale de France, Fol/ R.D./13810, 55v–56.

181. Metternich to Twiss, Brighton, February 15, 1849, Bibliothèque nationale de France, Fol/ R.D./13810, 62v.

182. Twiss to Metternich, February 13, 1849, National Archives of the Czech Republic, Prague, RAM-AC/ 10/ 775, 117.

misunderstood," then Metternich would be perceived as *"sans reproche."*[183] With this objective, he judged that the first task, for English readers, would be to explain the "Governmental organisation of the Austrian Empire."[184] In particular, he thought it was important for readers to understand the nature of government through councils rather than ministers. His suggestion was that in the "pure monarchy" of Austria, the councils performed a similar role to the parliament in the "mixed monarchy" of England. He claimed, however, that English people were "at a loss to know how the government was carried on" in Austria. "They believe," he added, "P.M. [Metternich] directed everything according to a rule of his own."[185] By explaining that Austria, in fact, had a complex system of government, Metternich could be absolved of the blame for the problems that had evolved prior to 1848. At the same time, he could take credit for "how the Austrian system has lasted, why it is durable."

While Twiss had previously used the concept of interest to question the "sentiment" behind nationalism, arguing that interest was the more powerful motivator, he now found interest in itself to be insufficient as a basis for government. "I noted," he continued, "an observation in your Character of Napoléon as to his estimate of Mankind, that they were to be governed through their <u>interests</u>."[186] A mixed monarchy, however, "seeks to govern them by <u>principles</u>." "Napoléon's system of government," on the other hand, "would resolve itself into the art of gratifying the selfish feelings of individuals." Those individuals, at the same time, would conduct themselves according to their "own gain or loss—which would be destructive of the community." "The true art of government," he concluded, would "consist in furthering the interests of individuals so far as it is not at variance with principles which must be observed to maintain the existence of the state."[187] While prepared to accept the logic of individualism, Twiss placed the state above the individual. Within a state, he argued, "there are various races etc. without a common interest." The integrity of the state, not the "selfish" interest of the individual, must therefore be the highest good.

As always, Twiss focused upon the role that ideas had in shaping social and political life, but in this letter, he was concerned that ideas could also be out of step with their context. "The great objection to the German universities,"

---

183. Twiss to Metternich, February 13, 1849, National Archives of the Czech Republic, Prague, RAM-AC/ 10/ 775, 117.

184. Twiss to Metternich, February 13, 1849, National Archives of the Czech Republic, Prague, RAM-AC/ 10/ 775, 118.

185. Twiss to Metternich, February 13, 1849, National Archives of the Czech Republic, Prague, RAM-AC/ 10/ 775, 118.

186. Twiss to Metternich, February 13, 1849, National Archives of the Czech Republic, Prague, RAM-AC/ 10/ 775, 119.

187. Twiss to Metternich, February 13, 1849, National Archives of the Czech Republic, Prague, RAM-AC/ 10/ 775, 119.

he argued, "in respect of the Confederation, was that they scattered political ideas about which were far in advance of the political habits of the country."[188] Romantic nationalism, he wished to say, did not sit well with the German Confederation. Similarly, Prussia had made the "great practical mistake" of supposing that the education which "she gave to the intellect of her people" would "necessarily fit them for the enjoyment of political power."[189]

On February 15, Twiss promised that he was collecting "*matériel de guerre*." He once more turned to the praise of mixed constitutions, arguing, "We do not consider representation necessarily democratic—as I generally observe German diplomatists combine these two expressions." It was possible, therefore, for a "representative system" to be embedded into a monarchy which "serves to bring the morbid poisons to the surface at an early stage of the disease, when they may be treated more certainly and safely."[190] He added, "If of course this is overdone as in a democratic republic there is a kind of political erysipelas [severe skin infection]." The virtue of emancipation, therefore, was not that it recognised natural freedoms, but that it prevented popular unrest fermenting away from view. On the other hand, a popular state was simply an uncontrolled infection of popular sentiment.

The following day, Twiss wrote again, suggesting that one analogy that might explain the situation in Austria and Germany to Englishmen was the situation of Ireland within Britain. "We have," he said, "the Irish Association with O'Connell at its head working by constitutional means" and by "constitutional agitation" in order to "carry some great modifications in the civil state of Irishmen."[191] Twiss appeared to be conflating Daniel O'Connell's Catholic Association, established in 1823, which had pursued Catholic emancipation in Britain, and O'Connell's subsequent Repeal Association, which had sought the repeal of the 1803 Act of Union, with Queen Victoria as the head of an independent Irish state. He recounted that "then came a new party 'Young Ireland,'" which did not seek the repeal of the Union as an "end" but as a "means to obtain further civil modifications" and "bent upon making a great political change."[192] Indeed, in July 1848, inspired by events on the continent, the Young Ireland movement attempted an uprising, but its leaders had been arrested and transported to Van Diemen's Land (Australia). "This last

188. Twiss to Metternich, February 13, 1849, National Archives of the Czech Republic, Prague, RAM-AC/ 10/ 775, 120.

189. Twiss to Metternich, February 13, 1849, National Archives of the Czech Republic, Prague, RAM-AC/ 10/ 775, 121.

190. Twiss to Metternich, February 15, 1849, National Archives of the Czech Republic, Prague, RAM-AC/ 10/ 775, 127.

191. Twiss to Metternich, February 16, 1849, National Archives of the Czech Republic, Prague, RAM-AC/ 10/ 775, 142.

192. Twiss to Metternich, February 16, 1849, National Archives of the Czech Republic, Prague, RAM-AC/ 10/ 775, 142.

party," Twiss declared, "does not hesitate to establish anarchy as a transition stage."[193] The threat of the internal rebellion of the Irish might bring home to English people the dangers of supporting the freedoms that many of them had admired in the speeches of leaders such as Kossuth: "I think I might be able by some such illustration to make Englishmen understand the position of the governments in Germany."[194] In addition to these concerns internal to the state, he added, "Then there is this further difference that makes it a matter of international interest," namely, "that the proposed changes are at variance with the sovereignty and independence of the German states and the treaty arrangement of the European powers." Again, the sovereignty of states came before the liberty of individuals.

On February 20, writing as he usually did from his rooms in the Albany, Twiss said he would try to come to Brighton the following Saturday. He now visited Metternich in Brighton every week or two. He announced, after so many letters laying out ideas, that "I am happy to say that I have begun writing."[195] "The difficulty," he said, "is to think for any time consecutively amidst the petty distractions of term business"—by this time, he was lecturing at King's College. As he was now writing, however, he would be "strongly for the publication of 'Facts'—there is so much misrepresentation, that what with false data and incorrect reasoning half the world are in an atmosphere of gross error."[196] The clear form that the article was now taking was to present an apology for the German Confederation: that is, to explain why Germany had not, in 1815, been formed as one or two "unitary" states. That apology would then form the basis in the second part of the article for explaining why Metternich defended the order established in 1815 and also why the Revolution of 1848 should be resisted on the same grounds. At the same time, he still had doubts about whether the settlements of 1815 had been satisfactory: "Do you think, as matters have turned out, that it would have been better to have left the sovereign rights of each state of the Confederation perfectly unshackled as far as its <u>internal</u> policy was concerned or that this would have led to so much diversity that it would have been a cause of disruption."[197]

193. Twiss to Metternich, February 16, 1849, National Archives of the Czech Republic, Prague, RAM-AC/ 10/ 775, 143.

194. Twiss to Metternich, February 16, 1849, National Archives of the Czech Republic, Prague, RAM-AC/ 10/ 775, 143. On the "enormous" popularity of Kossuth in England, see Cecil M. Knatchbull-Hugessen, *The Political Evolution of the Hungarian Nation*, 2 vols. (London, 1908), Vol. 2, 159; Zsuzsanna Lada, "The Invention of a Hero: Lajos Kossuth in England (1851)," *European History Quarterly*, vol. 43, no. 1 (2013), 5–26.

195. Twiss to Metternich, February 20, 1849, National Archives of the Czech Republic, Prague, RAM-AC/ 10/ 775, 146.

196. Twiss to Metternich, February 20, 1849, National Archives of the Czech Republic, Prague, RAM-AC/ 10/ 775, 148.

197. Twiss to Metternich, February 22, 1849, National Archives of the Czech Republic, Prague, RAM-AC/ 10/ 775, 149. In a further series of letters and notes written in late

By March 3, he reported that he had very nearly completed the full manuscript and sought only "some points on which I would beg your attention."[198] Accurately previewing the final form of the article, Twiss wrote to say that he believed it was essential that the article conclude with "a notice respecting the Treaties of 1815."[199] It was important, he said, "to put the Treaty Engagement of the European Powers before the English public," and he wished to know if Metternich agreed. These treaties, he argued, were "the basis of international obligations between the European Powers."[200] He proceeded to write a series of letters over the next week on aspects of the treaties and the nature of the protection they engaged.[201] For Twiss, as an international lawyer, such obligations were "sacred," as he would state in his writings on the law of nations. Maintaining those obligations would, of course, mean maintaining Prussia and Austria in their current form. He was untroubled by the circularity of the argument: namely,

---

February, Twiss reported on his writing habits and his specific plan for the article, and posed a series of questions. On February 23, he asked: "Have the goodness to consider this statement 'The good sense of the Emperor Francis recoiled from setting up a sham Empire,'" and this phrase duly appeared verbatim in the published article: Twiss to Metternich, February 23, 1849, National Archives of the Czech Republic, Prague, RAM-AC/ 10/ 775, 152; [Travers Twiss], "The German Confederation and the Austrian Empire," *Quarterly Review* (1849), 427. In the same letter, he invited himself to dinner the following day: "I shall come down tomorrow and be with you about half past five, and if you will allow me, to dine with you." In a following note, he added, "I shall ask you to be kind enough to look at the MS," and in a further note, he outlined the final plan to which the published article would be true: "1. The Federal Arrangement of 1815; 2. The growth of the Burschenschaft [the nationalist and liberal student movement banned by Metternich in the 1819 Carlsbad Decrees] and its unitarian views; 3. Austria's position in three points of view—Europe, Germany, Austrian Empire; 4. Policy of Prussia; 4. Recent events—Revolution not reform, Republic not Constitutional Monarchy": Twiss to Metternich (no date), 1849, National Archives of the Czech Republic, Prague, RAM-AC/ 10/ 775, 155–156.

198. Twiss to Metternich, March 3, 1849, National Archives of the Czech Republic, Prague, RAM-AC/ 10/ 775, 165–167. In particular, he had ventured to criticise Article 13 of the Act of the German Confederation. This was the article that stated all states of the Confederation must have a constitution based upon the provincial estates. It was a vague basis for a constitution, but Twiss nevertheless wished to criticise it "as attempting to substitute an impracticble uniformity" and sought advice on whether "my view is really untenable" and whether perhaps "it is unjust to criticise such measures from a totally different point of view from that which their authors occupied."

199. Twiss to Metternich, March 4, 1849, National Archives of the Czech Republic, Prague, RAM-AC/ 10/ 775, 174.

200. Twiss to Metternich, March 4, 1849, National Archives of the Czech Republic, Prague, RAM-AC/ 10/ 775, 176.

201. Twiss to Metternich, March 5, 1849, National Archives of the Czech Republic, Prague, RAM-AC/ 10/ 775, 179; Twiss to Metternich, March 7, 1849, National Archives of the Czech Republic, Prague, RAM-AC/ 10/ 775, 182; Twiss to Metternich, March 7 (second letter), 1849, National Archives of the Czech Republic, Prague, RAM-AC/ 10/ 775, 183.

that the Concert of Europe should not be disturbed because its constituent powers had agreed that it should not be disturbed.

He finally announced that the article had been sent to the press, but it would still be possible to "correct the proof sheets."[202] Two days later, it became apparent that some changes would be necessary on the subject of the Free City of Krakow. The city had been established as a semi-autonomous republic at the Congress of Vienna, under the protection of the three neighbouring powers, Russia, Prussia, and Austria. At the Congress, Metternich had opposed the division of Poland, preferring the idea of a peaceful Polish state as a neighbour to Austria rather than an aggressive Russia, but he did not prevail with that particular design.[203] Following a popular uprising in 1846, however, Metternich's government annexed Krakow, dissolving the republican government and establishing it as a duchy within the Austrian Empire. This act was difficult to reconcile for anybody, such as Twiss or Metternich, who regarded themselves as champions of the established order of the Concert of Europe, nor, given that the city's status was protected by treaty, was it consistent with the sacred status of treaties that Twiss espoused. He had resolved to address this hypocrisy head-on, but Metternich was not comfortable with the argument. Twiss responded that he had determined to "dismiss the fiction of Cracow being an indulgence" of "sentiment."[204] He reassured Metternich, "I had already made some considerable modifications in the general train of reasoning," and he wished now to "venture to trouble you" with the "passage as it last stands if you have any remarks to make upon it." He feared it would be "the part of the article which will be most likely to provoke criticism and I am anxious therefore to put the case before the reader in the manner the least exceptionable."[205]

The argument, in fact, was one which strained Twiss's own views, and in that sense, he was his own critical reader. His strategy was to argue that the treaty establishing Krakow in the first place was flawed and that its protected status meant that it possessed no real sovereignty that could be violated. By way of illustration, he compared Krakow with the "treaties of protection with the Indian states," although he conceded, in his correspondence at least, that there was a great variety in those treaties.[206] In the final version of the article, he argued that the "Three Powers" were "virtually sovereign" over Krakow "in

---

202. Twiss to Metternich, March 8, 1849, National Archives of the Czech Republic, Prague, RAM-AC/ 10/ 775, 184.

203. Haas, "Metternich and the Slavs," 122–123.

204. Twiss to Metternich, March 10, 1849, National Archives of the Czech Republic, Prague, RAM-AC/ 10/ 775, 185.

205. Twiss to Metternich, March 10, 1849, National Archives of the Czech Republic, Prague, RAM-AC/ 10/ 775, 186.

206. Twiss to Metternich, March 10, 1849, National Archives of the Czech Republic, Prague, RAM-AC/ 10/ 775, 186.

some such manner as the East India Company is supreme and virtually sovereign over the protected Sikh and Hill states in Upper India."[207] In fact, just prior to the Indian uprising in 1857, Twiss would present a more nuanced view of sovereignty in India, but nuance was not going to extract Metternich from the hypocrisy of his situation. He wrote to Metternich, "The quotation from Lord Hastings [the Governor General of India] struck me as apposite."[208] In the final version of the article, Twiss cited Hastings, declaring that when the ruler of a state "has been induced . . . to rely upon a foreign power for protection," then that ruler can "only in a very qualified sense" be referred to as "independent."[209] Twiss added: "It would be as well that the term *Protection* should not find a place in the vocabulary of the Law of Nations." Almost thirty years later, at the Berlin Conference, he helped the British government argue for the idea of the "Protectorate," establishing a distinction between colonial occupation and the Protectorate in the law of nations, and insisting, against Prince Bismarck, who wished to see all colonial dominions treated equally, that different obligations attended in each case.

Metternich responded to this letter the following day, declaring, "You are absolutely right regarding protection as a subject which opens an avenue to polemic."[210] "But it is for that reason," he added, "that it is bristling with spikes" and "one must say as little as possible." Protection, he continued, "is neither dependence, nor complete submission, and for that reason it cannot be defined in all its occurences." The "ladder [*échelle*] of comparison" was not the same "between different situations," and it was therefore impossible to compare the situation of the Ionian Islands under the British crown and the position of Krakow in relation to its "three creators."[211] A week earlier, Metternich had argued that the "suppression" of Krakow was conducted in the spirit of the treaties arising from the Congress of Vienna, not against them: "The question of Cracow does not at all pose a difficulty for the appreciation of the treaties of 1815. The suppression of that little state was not at all made in violation of those treaties, but [was] rather a necessary consequence of the precepts of order in the spirit of which all the arrangements of 1815 were made and desired. The predominant fact in the question of Crakow was that of 'the value or absence of value of the engagements made.'" The citizens of Krakow had not respected their side of the bargain: "The three powers who established the relative independence of the Republic of Cracow linked to

207. [Twiss], "The German Confederation and the Austrian Empire," 458.
208. Twiss to Metternich, March 10, 1849, National Archives of the Czech Republic, Prague, RAM-AC/ 10/ 775, 186.
209. [Twiss], "The German Confederation and the Austrian Empire," 459.
210. Metternich to Twiss, "*La Protection*," March 11, 1849, National Archives of the Czech Republic, Prague, RAM-AC/ 10/ 775, 188.
211. Metternich to Twiss, "*La Protection*," March 11, 1849, National Archives of the Czech Republic, Prague, RAM-AC/ 10/ 775, 188.

their gift conditions that the little state did not only not observe but, in a long series of events, violated with impunity. What the givers gave they took back because the favoured party did not take account of the conditions attached to the donation. The question, and the entire question, is whether in a contract it is permissible for one of the contacting parties to violate with impunity the conditions of the contract and the answer to that question is not in doubt."[212]

Metternich pointed out that the Ionian Islands, "existed under" the sovereignty of France prior to 1815, at which point they were placed under British sovereignty. "The state of Cracow," on the other hand, "never existed prior to its creation by the three powers. In creating it those three powers emancipated it from their sovereignty, which they had excercised collectively, and in declaring it free they no less imposed a connection with themselves under the title of protection."[213] It was impossible to compare islands under "royal governance" and a city that "governed itself." The reason for the impossibility was that "protection is an in-between; between subjection and political independence; between sovereignty and the freedom of the political body and that of the protector. The word 'protection' does not draw a definitive line between rights of the first [the protected body] and the duties of the second [the protector]."[214] The three powers, he continued, could not wish, by the "emmanicpation of their sovereignty" to create a "movement directed against the internal peace of their own domains by creating a field of retreat for a band of conspirators determined to risk all in order to shuffle the cards." Metternich's argument was that emancipation was accompanied by duties and obligations, and this is a theme to which Twiss returned, many years later, in his discussion of the emancipation of "Oriental" states. Metternich's defence effectively stated that treaties could be put aside when sovereignty and peace were at risk: a matter of reason of state. He concluded, "If you want more detailed information on the question of Cracow, I can provide it," but he warned, "I believe that in the article that you have under the pen, you must avoid anything that could aid an attack," so the question of Krakow was to be avoided, despite his purported confidence in his defence.[215]

After a long weekend of hunting at Littlecote, Twiss responded, "I perfectly assent to your general view and also to your particular application of it."[216] He

---

212. Metternich to Twiss, Brighton, March 5, 1849, Bibliothèque nationale de France, Fol/ R.D./13810, 71.

213. Metternich to Twiss, "*La Protection*," March 11, 1849, National Archives of the Czech Republic, Prague, RAM-AC/ 10/ 775, 189.

214. Metternich to Twiss, "*La Protection*," March 11, 1849, National Archives of the Czech Republic, Prague, RAM-AC/ 10/ 775, 190.

215. Metternich to Twiss, "*La Protection*," March 11, 1849, National Archives of the Czech Republic, Prague, RAM-AC/ 10/ 775, 190.

216. Twiss to Metternich, March 13, 1849, National Archives of the Czech Republic, Prague, RAM-AC/ 10/ 775, 196.

agreed to omit, when "correcting the proof tonight," his discussion of the British protection of the Ionian Islands and to limit his discussion of the Indian states. He conceded "as you have doubts," somebody of a "different character of mind would have strong objections" to the comparisons.[217] Metternich clearly did not want to dwell on the subject of protection and the Free City of Krakow because no construction could be put on the events of 1846 that did not reflect badly upon his celebrated defence of the order established by the Congress of Vienna.

In this letter, Twiss had not mentioned the fact that the day was the first anniversary of the demonstrations in Vienna and Metternich's resignation from the position of Chancellor. Metternich, however, did not fail to mark the passing of the anniversary and wrote to Twiss the same day, remarking upon it with precision: "This evening at eleven o'clock, it will have been one year since I withdrew from the post that I held for 38 years and 9 months, marking the end of an order of things and the beginning of another order."[218] The "other" order, in fact, proved to be an intermediary stage prior to the "new order," which had been ushered in by the news from the previous day that the Austrian Empire had promulgated a new constitution on March 7. The new constitution re-established strong authority in the Emperor and revoked the laws of Hungary's revolutionary government. Metternich celebrated: "Yesterday we learnt that on the seventh of this month a line was drawn between the chaos and a new order for which chaos was the starting point."[219] The "intermediary epoch," he said, had been a period of nothing other than "destruction" in which "nothing was created." Creation could only begin when "chaos ceases." He tempered his pleasure in the new constitution with the thought that "all constitutions that come from revolutions are a bad thing; the product finds itself impregnated with the elements of their origin," and this, he said, was true of "the constitution in question."[220] Nevertheless, he concluded, that "from the point of view of necessity," the outcome was the "least worst" in the situation in which the Empire found itself in 1849, a situation in which "true good was not in the power of men."

Twiss responded the following day: "The 13th must have been an anniversary to you, even at this distance, suggestive of many contending emotions."[221] He moved on to business, observing that the editor of the *Quarterly Review*

---

217. Twiss to Metternich, March 13, 1849, National Archives of the Czech Republic, Prague, RAM-AC/ 10/ 775, 197.

218. Metternich to Twiss, March 13, 1849, National Archives of the Czech Republic, Prague, RAM-AC/ 10/ 775, 193.

219. Metternich to Twiss, March 13, 1849, National Archives of the Czech Republic, Prague, RAM-AC/ 10/ 775, 193.

220. Metternich to Twiss, March 13, 1849, National Archives of the Czech Republic, Prague, RAM-AC/ 10/ 775, 194.

221. Twiss to Metternich, March 14, 1849, National Archives of the Czech Republic, Prague, RAM-AC/ 10/ 775, 200.

had requested him to add "a paragraph on the new Austrian constitution," and he therefore asked Metternich if there was "anything which occurs to you worth putting forward prominently."²²² The following day, he sent Metternich not simply a paragraph but an "epilogue" on the constitution, which duly appeared after the conclusion of the *Quarterly Review* article.²²³ He noted that, while this epilogue was "in type," it was not too late to include any "remarks" Metternich might wish to make.

Twiss acknowledged receipt of Metternich's final corrections on March 17, while recounting that he had seen "an Austrian watchmaker this morning."²²⁴ The watchmaker had news from Vienna, including from a Hungarian brother-in-law who reported "dissatisfaction" with the military crackdown upon the deputies in the revolutionary parliament as "rather too sharp practice," adding, "I merely mention this as amongst the 'straw' which it is good to watch in the 'wind.'" The watchmaker reported that the "lower orders" in Vienna were "quite changed in character." They had become "surly and sulky."²²⁵ This, he said, was "to be expected after the disorder through which they have passed," although he added, "I do not know them." The absence of order, rather than liberty, was once again the diagnosis of the problem, but Twiss did not ignore liberty, immediately turning to the question "What shall be the machine for regulating the liberty of the subject."²²⁶

The article that appeared in the *Quarterly Review* in March followed the plan laid out in the previous months' correspondence, and began with an explanation for the "Federal arrangement" adopted for Germany in 1815. We know from the correspondence that, throughout the article, Twiss had substituted "the Cabinet of Vienna" for the name of Metternich himself. He

---

222. Twiss to Metternich, March 14, 1849, National Archives of the Czech Republic, Prague, RAM-AC/ 10/ 775, 201.

223. Twiss to Metternich, March 15, 1849, National Archives of the Czech Republic, Prague, RAM-AC/ 10/ 775, 205.

224. Twiss to Metternich, March 17, 1849, National Archives of the Czech Republic, Prague, RAM-AC/ 10/ 775, 210.

225. Twiss to Metternich, March 17, 1849, National Archives of the Czech Republic, Prague, RAM-AC/ 10/ 775, 211.

226. Twiss to Metternich, March 17, 1849, National Archives of the Czech Republic, Prague, RAM-AC/ 10/ 775, 213–214. The question of liberty brought him directly to which "tribunal" would "administer the law of libel in reference to the press." Metternich had a long record of suppressing freedom of the press, and Twiss now took him into the history of English laws licensing and restricting press freedoms, beginning with the Bill of Rights of the Glorious Revolution, which, he noted, was "silent on the press," and he concluded, presumably in relation to the new Austrian constitution: "I think there was no alternative but to declare the press free, subject in some way to 'opinion.'" Nevertheless, public opinion was not quite supreme because it was subject to the question "Can this opinion be made to act rightly." One manner in which it could be shaped was through publishing, as Twiss had already argued several times, but he also had something more concrete in mind: namely, a law of libel "against treason and sedition, including publications."

accordingly recounted that the "voice" of the "Cabinet of Vienna" was "most influential in deciding the question of the reconstitution of Germany" in 1815.[227] That voice argued for the "application of the federal principle," the creation of the German Confederation, as the "only sure means of combining internal peace with external security." The powers who signed the Treaty of Westphalia, Twiss explained, had "indirectly declared the *political unity* of Germany to be inconsistent with the general interests of Europe." Such a state would have been "inconsistent with a real and durable balance of power in Europe." At the same time, it was necessary to "avoid establishing in the heart of Germany" a state whose "power of aggression would be out of all proportion to the means of resistance" offered by the smaller German principalities. The consequence of such a system would be to force those smaller states to seek outside assistance and so disturb "the European balance."[228] The means to avoid these problems was "a Confederation of States, properly adjusted." History had shown, he argued, that "the Germanic body is essentially anti-Unitarian in its nature." Such a view may, he conceded, clash with the Romantic nationalism of the poet Ernst Arndt, a champion of German unity and a member of the Frankfurt Parliament, but Arndt's vision, he argued, was in conflict with history, and Twiss proceeded into an account of the disunity of the Holy Roman Empire since the Middle Ages to prove his point.

The next objective of this essay was to show that the negotiations over the form of the German Confederation had been fraught and that Metternich did not simply get his own way. Austria and Prussia had jointly argued for a "minimum of political rights" to be "fixed by the Federal Act," but, according to this account, they were vetoed by Bavaria and Wurtemberg, who "objected most vehemently" to the proposal because it interfered with "the plenitude of their newly-acquired sovereignty."[229] It was customary, Twiss continued, "to suppose" that Austria and Prussia were "on this occasion advocates of absolutist principles of government—whereas Austria, in the person of the President of the Congress [i.e., Metternich], declared that the subjects of every German State under the ancient Empire possessed rights against their sovereign, which had of late been disregarded—but that such disregard must be rendered impossible for the future." Austria (meaning Metternich) was obliged, however, to make "concessions" to the other German states, notably to Hanover and the "despotic character" of the King of Wurtemberg, preventing these ancient rights being safeguarded in the constitution of the confederation. With Hanover and Wurtemberg on one side and, on the other, Heinrich vom Stein of Prussia "and his friends," who wanted to "pledge the Confederation" to

---

227. [Twiss], "The German Confederation and the Austrian Empire," 428.
228. [Twiss], "The German Confederation and the Austrian Empire," 429.
229. [Twiss], "The German Confederation and the Austrian Empire," 432.

popular representation and unity, "a middle course was at last adopted." The pursuit of the middle course was "chiefly through the influence of Austria," and committed the states of the confederation to "no very definite" result in terms of the nature of their constitutions. By this point in the article, it was apparent that Twiss had succeeded in convincing Metternich to portray himself as a champion of a moderate form of liberal constitution in addition to his existing reputation as pragmatic negotiator. There is a long-standing debate over whether Metternich was a despotic conservative or a brilliant diplomat dealing with the political realities of his time, but what the correspondence with Twiss reveals is that, regardless of which portrait may be most accurate, he was a careful manipulator of his own reputation.

Twiss now turned to the second part of the plan agreed with Metternich, an account of the development of the Burschenschaft. Whether these student societies were "already essentially revolutionary" prior to the 1820s was, he said, a moot point, but there was no question that, in 1832, they "publicly declared war against the Federal system of Germany" by announcing that they would pursue "the unity and freedom of Germany by revolutionary means."[230] Twiss now had to cleanse Metternich's reputation from having put down this movement in favour of liberal constitutions, and he did so by using the analogy of the Young Ireland movement he had prefigured in his letters. It was "the duty of German governments to put it down," just as it had been for the British to suppress "the criminal excesses of 'Young Ireland.'"[231] The "statesmen," he explained, who had maintained the "federal arrangement of 1815 during the life of an entire generation of men" had been engaged in a "struggle between Unitarian and the Federal principles." Those statesmen carried on their work "in the face of an enemy—namely the Unitarian spirit of an active minority seeking to supersede the Federal system."[232]

Twiss argued that sovereignty "remains in favour of individual states" who make up confederations. This was the best system for the geographical position of Germany, which was placed between "Democracy on her western frontier, and Absolute Monarchy on her eastern."[233] The system of confederation enabled "proportionate shades of political thought and political habits" across that space. These considerations, he continued, which applied to Germany were "applicable in a still more forcible manner to the Austrian Empire." That empire, he pointed out, included several nationalities "differing in their origin, their history, their language, their habits, and their mode of annexation to the empire," and yet that Empire was a "single political body."[234]

230. [Twiss], "The German Confederation and the Austrian Empire," 435.
231. [Twiss], "The German Confederation and the Austrian Empire," 435.
232. [Twiss], "The German Confederation and the Austrian Empire," 436.
233. [Twiss], "The German Confederation and the Austrian Empire," 436-437.
234. [Twiss], "The German Confederation and the Austrian Empire," 438.

The essay moved on to Austria's relations with Europe, with Germany, and with its empire. In its external relations with Europe, Austria was "an essentially pacific Power" because it was already "saturated" with "territorial dominion" and was therefore conservative of both her own interests and "for other Powers."[235] In relation to Germany, or the "German Nation," Austria played a role of regulating and steadying, which was why the "mantle" of Roman Emperor fell upon the Emperor of Austria and not Prussia. Austria could separate from Germany "with much less inconvenience" than if Germany separated from Austria, a situation in which the smaller German states would become prey to Prussia.[236] In relation to her own empire, Austria sat in a web of complexity that surpassed that of all other European states in terms of the "unity of government and the diversity of administration." "The absence of unity" meant, for example, that when the capital, Vienna, was occupied by invaders such as Napoléon, the "action of the empire" was not "paralysed." "More unity of government" in the future would be "a great calamity to the Austrian empire."[237]

Having dismissed the ambition for a unified state, or the breaking of the Empire in preference for a series of national states, Twiss addressed himself to the entanglement of those nationalist ambitions with the movement for emancipation and popular sovereignty. "The Austrian Cabinet," he argued, possibly still using code for "Metternich," "would have been considerably embarrassed" if the recent "attempt to abolish by way of revolution all *objective sovereignty* had been successful." By "objective sovereignty" he meant the fact of sovereignty, thereby reminding his readers that an aim of the revolution was the dissolution of the Empire itself. "It is hardly necessary to point out," he continued, "that the so-called 'Sovereignty of the People' is a doctrine, not a fact; that it reduces all sovereignty to subjective sovereignty: that in any other view of sovereignty it involves a contradiction of ideas, or resolves itself into a palpable truism." By "subjective sovereignty" he presumably meant a regime of rights. He reasoned that the pursuit of a regime based entirely upon the rule of individual rights, in which those individuals did not give up any of their freedom, was inconsistent with the idea of sovereignty itself, which required such sacrifice and was therefore inherently contradictory.[238] He assumed that the creation of all societies involved individuals giving up some portion of their sovereignty over themselves, or their rights, to the sovereign. He made precisely this point in relation to the individual states who join confederations, and the point was no less true for natural persons as it was for artificial persons.[239]

235. [Twiss], "The German Confederation and the Austrian Empire," 440.
236. [Twiss], "The German Confederation and the Austrian Empire," 442.
237. [Twiss], "The German Confederation and the Austrian Empire," 449.
238. [Twiss], "The German Confederation and the Austrian Empire," 451.
239. [Twiss], "The German Confederation and the Austrian Empire," 436.

Writing two weeks later to Metternich, he explained further: "What I meant in the Quarterly Review"—that "sovereignty of the people" involved "either a contradiction of ideas or a palpable truism"—had reference to the fact that the existence of a "sovereign" implies "subjects." It therefore involved a "contradiction of ideas to say that the people collectively is sovereign over the people collectively for that is to say that the sovereign and the subject are identical, and it is a palpable truism to say that the people collectively is sovereign over the people collectively for that were to say that the will of the community must control the will of the individual, a first principle in every political society."[240] Here, rather than state his opposition to the fundamental principles of liberal thought, as he had done previously, Twiss observed merely that they did not take one very far in determining the best form of government.

Fortunately, however, Twiss observed, the "destructive" tendency of the revolution "has been checked," so that "the sovereignty of the Crown remains unimpaired." It would be possible therefore to "reconstruct" the empire, maintaining "unity of government" and creating a legislative power that was representative and not merely administrative. This was the challenge now facing the new cabinet. In defence of Metternich, he pointed out that the "Austrian cabinet" was, as was "well known," already engaged in creating precisely such a representative system when the "French revolution of February [1848] broke out."[241] Metternich, he was anxious to stress, had been sympathetic to moderate liberal reform but was prevented by circumstances from realising his ambitions.

The last section of the essay turned the reader's attention to the future. Even in the case of "simply homogenous states," Twiss warned, the creation of a "central representative body" had proved to be "a most difficult problem of statesmanship," and it would be much more so "in the case of a composite state."[242] The task was made more complex by the already existing "local representative institutions." The continued existence of those bodies could "create discord and disunion," while their suppression would be seen as a "retrograde step in political life." The local bodies would therefore need to be maintained but made "subordinate" to the central body, while the central body must be formed with "deputies from the provincial bodies."[243] Such an arrangement, he hoped, would address "the spirit of the awakened nationalities of the Austrian empire," which "requires to be soothed." Moreover, "existing rights must be maintained," and that entailed respecting "historical diversity" of the "various parts" of the empire. He cited Alexis de Tocqueville several times in this

---

240. Twiss to Metternich, April 12, 1849, National Archives of the Czech Republic, Prague, RAM-AC/ 10/ 775, 257.
241. [Twiss], "The German Confederation and the Austrian Empire," 451.
242. [Twiss], "The German Confederation and the Austrian Empire," 451.
243. [Twiss], "The German Confederation and the Austrian Empire," 452.

essay on the virtues of federal systems and, in this instance, quoted him, arguing that the citizens of the two nations with the highest degree of provincial liberty, England and the United States, attributed their greatness and prosperity to that liberty.[244]

Returning to the proposals for confederation in 1814 and 1815, Twiss noted Baron vom Stein's desire to include in the Federal Act of the Confederation a clause which stated that "popular representation shall be introduced into every Federal State."[245] "Austria" had opposed this proposal, he explained, because "all the ancient portions of the Empire" contained constitutions "of very varied character" according to their "State-peculiarities." Stein's resolution, therefore, would have "been to revolutionise, and not to restore, the Germanic body of States" and therefore to "disturb" Germany "instead of tranquilising it." Instead, Article 57 of the Federal Act stipulated: "The existing constitutions of the states . . . cannot be changed other than by constitutional means." Twiss cited Metternich's correspondence as Foreign Minister in 1820, explaining that the meaning of Article 57 was that "every order of things which has once legally existed . . . contains materials for a better system." Change, Metternich explained, could only happen over time, so the German states should maintain the "legal foundations of their existing constitutions and defend them with vigour and wisdom against all individual attacks."[246] "The great reproach of the Austrian cabinet [i.e., Metternich]," Twiss triumphantly concluded, "has been its scrupulous respect for legality."

Twiss reminded the readers of the heavy penalties which would be visited upon any state that broke treaty engagements, particularly treaties as weighty as the Act of the Congress of Vienna, which had established the order of Europe. The creation of a "Unitarian State, with Austria at its head" from the German Confederation would, he pointed out, violate that Act in numerous ways, and the powers who agreed to it would lose the numerous other advantages and territories they had gained from the same treaty.[247] By way of illustration of the penalties incurred upon breaking treaties, he pointed out that Russia, France, and Britain had intervened in the 1827 war between Turkey and Greece out of "political sentiment" inspired by nationalist philhellenism and that "the sequel," the war between Russia and Turkey, "illustrates in a remarkable manner how the violation of a right leads invariably to moral, if not material, mischief."[248]

The violation, however, of treaty agreements obliged Twiss to address the awkward case of Krakow, as prefigured in the correspondence with

---

244. [Twiss], "The German Confederation and the Austrian Empire," 452.
245. [Twiss], "The German Confederation and the Austrian Empire," 452.
246. [Twiss], "The German Confederation and the Austrian Empire," 454.
247. [Twiss], "The German Confederation and the Austrian Empire," 456–457.
248. [Twiss], "The German Confederation and the Austrian Empire," 457.

Metternich. The "last event" which had "attracted attention" to the treaties of 1815 had been "the re-incorporation in 1846 of the territory and city of Cracow into the Austrian dominions."[249] How could this act be reconciled with respect for treaties? Twiss explained that the three powers, Austria, Prussia, and Russia, who had been responsible for the "joint Protection" of Krakow, had judged "the express conditions of the arrangement to have been violated on the part of Cracow." He did not specify the nature of this violation, but presumably he and Metternich believed that the popular uprising had not conformed to Article 57 of the Federal Act stipulating that constitutional change could only proceed through constitutional means. The violation permitted the three powers to "revoke and suppress their reciprocal obligations under the Treaties of 3rd May, 1815, and Cracow consequently reverted to Austria." As previewed, Twiss proceeded to claim that, in any case, Krakow's independence had been "counterfeit"—a fiction agreed to merely to please the "fancy" of the Russian emperor Alexander.[250] In reality, it was "the creature of the Three Powers" who retained "joint supremacy and were "virtually sovereign over it, in some such manner," he added, "as the East India Company is supreme and virtually sovereign over the protected Sikh and Hill states of Upper India." As promised, he made no mention of the Ionian Islands. His case was not, however, finished, as he now lamented that the powers had made a mistake in ever agreeing to the independence of Krakow—a necessary conclusion from his argument—and the consequence was that "some of the Signatories of the Act [of the Congress of Vienna]" had noted the "departure" of the three powers from its provisions.[251] Now Twiss was able to reach his conclusion that, in order that such difficulties not arise, the term "protection" should be banished from the law of nations, a conclusion, as I have noted, that he would reverse in the subsequent context of the carve-up of Africa.

Twiss completed the essay, with a warning that the "nineteenth century" must avoid the errors committed by the "eighteenth": namely, adopting a "spirit of generalised ideas and sentiments," which was "the enemy of civilization as of political liberty, both of which are plants of slow growth."[252] "The general interests of Europe," he declared, "are paramount at the present moment to any considerations of local interest. Above all, respect for the peace of Europe dictates the sacrifice of some opinions, and the abandonment of some interests."[253] Freedom was an opinion, and nation was an interest. The order established by the Congress of Vienna guaranteed sovereignty, and sovereignty guaranteed peace. He saw no inconsistency in his opposition to the

---

249. [Twiss], "The German Confederation and the Austrian Empire," 458.
250. [Twiss], "The German Confederation and the Austrian Empire," 458.
251. [Twiss], "The German Confederation and the Austrian Empire," 459.
252. [Twiss], "The German Confederation and the Austrian Empire," 459.
253. [Twiss], "The German Confederation and the Austrian Empire," 459.

fragmentation of the Austrian Empire, on the one hand, and his opposition to the consolidation of the German Confederation, on the other. The problem was not centralisation or fragmentation; it was the necessity to respect law, to respect the agreements of sovereign powers and to subordinate all other "local" concerns to supremacy of the society of sovereign states.

The essay's epilogue on the new constitution was dated March 17 and summarised events in the year since, as Twiss put it, the "Ides of March" of 1848—whether the comparison was with what he saw as the betrayal of Metternich, or of Metternich with Caesar, or both, is not clear.[254] "The interval," he observed, "has been rife with anarchy," but the new year offered hope. The "transition" was drawing to a close, and a new constitution, and a new emperor, Franz Joseph I, revealed that the "Crown" was still "the fountain from which law and justice spring forth." Some "political writers," he conceded, had complained that the new constitution had been issued "without the concurrence of the Subject." There might be "weight in such an objection, if such a concurrence on the part of the subject were needed to found a legal basis for the new order of things, which is notoriously not the fact." It should "never be forgotten," he observed, that a "Royal charter" was the "fundamental law" of the "liberties of the subject England." The new constitution for Austria similarly established "an unimpeachable basis of legality." It combined "due respect for the diversity" of the Empire with "a necessary provision for Unity of Government."[255] This was only the "starting point" for the "new order of things," but the "vessel of the New State is launched," and it was "steering in the right course." He need hardly have added that the cause of his satisfaction was that the new order of things was planted firmly upon the old order of things.

Metternich was less sanguine than Twiss about the new Austrian constitution. "From the depth of my conscience," he wrote, "all charters that come from revolutions are bad things; the product will be discovered to be impregnated with elements of its origin, and this is the case with the charter in question."[256] He had, however, frequently appealed to necessity in order to justify measures taken during his rule, and he was consistent, in that respect, in his analysis of the system that had replaced him: "Considered from the point of view of necessity, I accord it the value of a work which is the least worst possible in the situation of the empire and the government of the empire, and I would even say that, in the world of 1849, the situation is such that the <u>true good</u> is not at all in the power of men."[257]

---

254. [Twiss], "The German Confederation and the Austrian Empire," 460.

255. [Twiss], "The German Confederation and the Austrian Empire," 461.

256. Metternich to Twiss, Brighton, March 13, 1849, Bibliothèque nationale de France, Fol/ R.D./13810, 75v.

257. Metternich to Twiss, Brighton, March 13, 1849, Bibliothèque nationale de France, Fol/ R.D./13810, 75v–76. He even conceded that the new empire had some redeeming features: "Three points I consider to be vital and were not lost to the view of the authors of

Twiss and Metternich argued that order and peace were more valuable than freedom and Romantic attachments to nation, and they believed that the means for maintaining order was to respect and defend law. They opposed emancipation and nationalism because both encouraged revolution, which, they believed, overturned law. They also perceived that there was a close connection between emancipation and nationalism, for example, in the Burschenschaft movement. Some of the moderate figures arguing for emancipation were prepared to pursue their goals through the existing federal German Confederation and Austrian Empire and their constituent states, ruled as constitutional monarchies, and they perceived arguments for break-up of the empires as endangering the chance for liberty.[258] But the more radical voices in 1848 certainly pursued both freedom and the replacement of the empires with nation-states. Rejecting these calls, Metternich explained that liberty could never be enjoyed without order: "Three great epochs mark history. The appearance of Christianity and, with it, true liberty. The French Revolution which made a caricature of liberty. We live in the third epoch which is responsible for as much revolution. What is the difference between the epochs? If we were to believe the promoters of monuments, it is liberty which drives the evolution [between epochs]. That pretension is false: liberty is, at the same time, an aim and also a product; a product of order."[259] Rather than securing liberty, therefore, the French Revolution had destroyed the conditions under which liberty could be enjoyed: "Christianity created the only foundation from which liberty can be grasped; a moral foundation. It [Christianity] proclaimed the duties and distilled the rights in equality before God. The Revolution turned the moral order upside down and replaced duties with the *Déclaration des droits de l'homme et du citoyen*. The present epoch is the logical and practical result of order being turned upside down."[260] As might be expected from an apologist for the *Ancien Régime*, true liberty was found in duties as much as rights.

For Twiss and Metternich, arguments for emancipation, even when pursued constitutionally, were to be distrusted as leading almost inevitably to nationalism and therefore challenging the federal system of government. This connection was not merely accidental. Both emancipation and nationalism were underpinned by a spirit of transformation, and self-realisation

---

the charter. One is the question of the subdivision of the empire . . . Another is the creation of corporations representing the parts of the empire of which the empire is composed and the formation of central representation, not by the aid of direct election but through the means of deputising individual corporations. The third point appears to my eyes to be that the sense and the text of the act is careful to place in evidence the source of power."

258. Rapport, *1848: Year of Revolution*, 29.

259. Metternich to Twiss, Richmond, May 6, 1849, Bibliothèque nationale de France, Fol/ R.D./13810, 87v.

260. Metternich to Twiss, Richmond, May 6, 1849, Bibliothèque nationale de France, Fol/ R.D./13810, 87v–88.

and self-invention.²⁶¹ Nation-states were understood to be artificial persons, and they could therefore, like natural persons, seek to free themselves from the *Ancien Régime*, which was epitomised, in the case of natural persons, by unrepresentative government and, in the case of nation-states, by their suppression within empires. The image of the modern state was, as Richard Tuck has observed, largely developed by analogy from the aggressive right-bearing individual of early modern natural law theories.²⁶² Twiss and Metternich tried to stem this tide of emancipating both nations and natural persons, although as we have seen, Twiss was not entirely averse to appropriating some degree of liberal rhetoric, and he possessed some interest in the possibilities of personal transformation (for both individuals and states). Those interests were restrained at this point in his career but they would develop over the next thirty to forty years. He never, however, developed any enthusiasm for nationalism. As his interest in the transformation of natural persons progressed, he did develop a corresponding interest in the emancipation of artificial persons, but that interest was directed to corporations and non-European states rather than nations.

Prussia and Germany

In May 1848, the deputies in the Frankfurt Parliament had resolved to create an Imperial Constitution that would stipulate the basic rights, including freedom of speech, assembly, religion, movement, and the abolishing of class privileges, which were to be adopted by all German states. They also resolved upon the need for a German emperor, and they agreed, in January 1849, that he should be elected from amongst the German princes. Progress on the constitution was slow, however, and a draft did not come to a vote in parliament until late March and April 1849. At the same time, rebellion had spread to Italy, and the King of Sardinia led a struggle against the Austrian Empire, notably in the battle of Novara on March 22 and 23. Twiss and Metternich followed the developments in Frankfurt and Italy, as well as the rumours, on a daily basis, while they carefully read and shared copies of the German press, particularly *Deutsche Beitung*. On March 24, possibly with news already of the result of the Battle of Novara, Twiss reported, "The feeling here seems very general against Sardinia."²⁶³ Referring to the manifesto of alliance between France

---

261. Benedict Anderson points to this mid-nineteenth-century connection between emancipation and nations as one whereby the appeal to a people to form a nation-state led to inclusiveness: "If 'Hungarians' deserved a national state, then that meant Hungarians, all of them": Benedict Anderson, *Imagined Communities: Reflections on the Origins and Spread of Nationalism* (London, 2006; first published 1983), 81–82.

262. Tuck, *The Rights of War and Peace*, 14, 15, 234.

263. Twiss to Metternich, March 24, 1849, National Archives of the Czech Republic, Prague, RAM-AC/ 10/ 775, 221.

and Piedmont, he declared, "The manifesto deserves no mercy." On March 26, he wrote that Frankfurt deputy Carl Welcker's attempt to push through the constitution of the German Empire several days previously should have been rejected, and it was, because it "shews the utter absence of materials to constitute an unitarian monarchical state."[264] At the same time, he declared, "I think the King of Prussia sufficiently discredited" by the vote, although the King, Frederick William IV, would be elected head of state two days later. "I would be sorry to see him in the situation of the King of Sardinia," Twiss observed, as the Sardinian king had fled to Portugal after the Battle of Novara. Revealing his antipathy to the liberal and nationalist ambitions of the Frankfurt Parliament, he concluded: "I think it desirable that the unpractical character of the Frankfurt projects should be confessed by their own acts."[265]

In the last days of March, the parliament prepared to offer the crown for the German Empire to Frederick William IV, even while support for the parliament amongst the German states was dwindling as the popular movements in those states were being suppressed. Frederick William held to the doctrine of divine right, so the opportunity of accepting election to head of state, while attractive on the face it, placed him in a dilemma in regard to his own principles. Even prior to that event, Metternich had drily observed: "In 1848 the revolution offered the German crown to the King of Prussia through a method which must make that prince reflect ... The Prussian crown has a known value while that offered by the assembly constituted in Germany ... was strongly doubtful ... It is a crown with a neutral value and, in that sense, the question is open between a crown and the hat of a president. The current situation would appear to be in favour of the bonnet of a Doge of Venice."[266] Metternich could not understand how any monarch would transform her- or himself from a hereditary ruler to an elected one. Twiss revelled in the situation. "What," he asked, would the King of Prussia have "gained practically" by refusing the crown? His "good faith" might have had "an opportunity of exhibiting itself."[267] He might have "kept his word" in refusing a crown that "the Princes of Germany had not consented to offer him": that is, Twiss was pointing out, the crown of Germany was not in the gift of the liberal deputies of the Frankfurt Parliament but in the German princes, as it had been

---

264. Twiss to Metternich, March 26, 1849, National Archives of the Czech Republic, Prague, RAM-AC/ 10/ 775, 223.

265. Twiss to Metternich, March 26, 1849, National Archives of the Czech Republic, Prague, RAM-AC/ 10/ 775, 224.

266. Metternich to Twiss, Brighton, February 11, 1849, Bibliothèque nationale de France, Fol/ R.D./13810, 50v–51. The humour of the King declining the offer from the Frankfurt Parliament was widely appreciated: Sperber, *The European Revolutions, 1848–1851*, 2, and on his indecision, 229.

267. Twiss to Metternich, March 27, 1849, National Archives of the Czech Republic, Prague, RAM-AC/ 10/ 775, 227.

for the Holy Roman Empire. The problem with such a principled stand for the King, he pointed out, was that "his love for the crown would have been disowned." "I do not wish to impugn his integrity of purpose," Twiss wryly remarked, "but I would sooner rather not have it put to the test."[268] He was not certain, in any case, that the king's refusal of the crown "would have established the incompatibility of monarchy with a Bundestaat [a federal state]." It would only have "established his belief that the Crown of Prussia was better 'in the hand' than the imperial 'bird in the bush.'" In any case, he concluded, the parliament was in disarray, having voted against its own constitution. The deputy Heinrich von Gagern, who had argued for German unity—"the mainspring of the Bundestaat"—had "broken down."[269] Metternich held Gagern in higher esteem than most of the Frankfurt deputies (probably because Gagern opposed the break-up of Austria), albeit evaluating him in a typically imperious manner: "M Gagern evidently does not lack means and I regard him as the most practical spirit amongst all those present in Frankfurt. Today he regards his duty as a challenge that he wants to win blow by blow. I don't know him personally and, even if I saw him [in the past], he was in a situation so subaltern that my gaze passed over him."[270] At the same time, he shared Twiss's sense of the absurdity of the offer made by the parliament to Frederick William IV, complaining, in particular, about an article just published in a Cologne gazette which "does not state a wish nor a counsel for the Prussian King; it pronounces an order. The King must, it says, do certain things; he may express reserves but those reserves will be put to the will of the Frankfurt assembly. It will be parliament that will decide what is convenient to allow or what to regulate among the scruples of His Majesty of Prussia. It is not for the King to determine whether he accepts or rejects the offer of the Imperial Crown, he must obey his election."[271] Although Metternich consistently protested that he was a constitutionalist, he was deeply troubled by the notion that monarchs could hold their positions at the will of their subjects.

"The King says," Twiss laughed, "Gentlemen, I do not accept the Imperial Crown, at least not from your hands, but remember you have committed yourselves to the offer."[272] At the same time, the King reasoned, "I do not allow you

---

268. Twiss to Metternich, March 27, 1849, National Archives of the Czech Republic, Prague, RAM-AC/ 10/ 775, 228.

269. Twiss to Metternich, March 27, 1849, National Archives of the Czech Republic, Prague, RAM-AC/ 10/ 775, 229.

270. Metternich to Twiss, Brighton, February 15, 1849, Bibliothèque nationale de France, Fol/ R.D./13810, 60. For Gagern on Austria, see Vick, *Defining Germany*, 164, and Frank Eyck, *The Frankfurt Parliament 1848-1849* (London, 1968), 108, 345.

271. Metternich to Twiss, Brighton, April 7, 1848, Bibliothèque nationale de France, Fol/ R.D./13810, 79-79v.

272. Twiss to Metternich, April 11, 1849, National Archives of the Czech Republic, Prague, RAM-AC/ 10/ 775, 253-254.

to withdraw" the offer, because the parliament were never "entitled to make it." He continued, "I acknowledge the sense of your election" of himself to the Imperial Crown, even while he denied their power to elect, and he therefore concluded, "Accordingly I shall take measures to place myself at the head of the new Federal State." Gagern's response, Twiss observed, was, "Your Majesty has misunderstood us. We did not make the offer in the sense assumed by your M. but categorically and unconditionally. Accept it or refuse it without reserve." "It is not," Gagern would say, "an offer of marriage which you may accept subject to your friends' approval, but the offer of a crown in virtue of a constitution."[273] In this imaginary exchange, Twiss was as able to perceive the struggle from the perspective of the liberals as he was from that of a prince who adhered to divine right. Writing three weeks later, on April 21, he struck a more troubled tone on the King's dilemma. He would soon learn that this was the day that Frederick William finally rejected the Imperial Crown, effectively bringing an end to the German constitution and the revolution, but, as Twiss wrote, the question was still in the balance, and the danger, as he saw it, was that the King would seek the Berlin assembly's approval for accepting the crown. "If the King of Prussia," he wrote, "allows the assembly at Berlin a voice in the question, there is an end of the Prussian Monarchy for the time."[274]

Despite such fears, he asked, "Has not the bubble of nationality burst?," and had not "identity of race, and of language, failed before diversity of interest." "The World of Germany," he triumphantly concluded, "remains a paper world." Nevertheless, there was still work to do: "Chaos is still chaos." "Western Europe," however, would "cease to regard Prussia as the chosen leader of modern Germany. Prussia has been rejected."[275] The question remained: "What Power" would be "elected" so as to give "reality to the new order of things." The answer was that "none can be found" and the German states would not "elect a mistress in Austria." By default, "We come to a Directory—in other words a Confederation. In other words Germany will remain Germany and will not be superseded by any creation of the Frankfurt Assembly."

Over the summer, Metternich used the Frankfurt Parliament to write an essay to Twiss on "The German Question." "Everything is possible," he declared. "The struggle has commenced between the principle of royal sovereignty and that of the people."[276] The "very strange thing," he observed, was that, in contrast to the past, the verdict upon that struggle was being put to a

273. Twiss to Metternich, April 11, 1849, National Archives of the Czech Republic, Prague, RAM-AC/ 10/ 775, 255.

274. Twiss to Metternich, April 21, 1849, National Archives of the Czech Republic, Prague, RAM-AC/ 10/ 775, 269.

275. Twiss to Metternich, March 27, 1849, National Archives of the Czech Republic, Prague, RAM-AC/ 10/ 775, 230.

276. Metternich to Twiss, "The German Question," August 11, 1849, National Archives of the Czech Republic, Prague, RAM-AC/ 10/ 775, 248.

"third party [*un tiers*]." In the past, "the prince and his subjects resolved the question between them."²⁷⁷ In this case, the subjects, in the form of the Frankfurt Parliament, had asked the Prussian King, Frederick William, to declare a verdict upon their sovereignty by making an offer to him as a third party. "If," Metternich noted, "that offer had been made to an individual enjoying an independent situation, the acceptance of the offer would present fewer difficulties than is the case for a king who, not long ago, determined the question of rights [*tranché la question du droit*] in his own country." "Reduced to its simplest terms," he continued, "it is necessary to have the judgement of Frederick William upon the principle of sovereignty. The crown that he already wears is based upon princely sovereignty; that which he is offered is based upon the sovereignty of the people. Can the same head wear the two crowns?"²⁷⁸ His question, at least in part, was not whether the same person could be monarch over two different, albeit overlapping domains, but whether the same person could be a princely monarch in one domain and a constitutional monarch in another. In any case, he argued, replying to his own question, the answer would be "idle" because the "true embarrassment would not be in the accumulation of two crowns, but in the fusion of two countries": that is, in the fusion, presumably, of Prussia with Germany more generally. In the situation in which those "countries" were fused, he asked, which sovereignty would prevail: "Royal sovereignty would dissolve into the sovereignty of the people, or vice versa? Would the Prussian king wish for the first, the Frankfurt assembly perhaps wishing for the second?"²⁷⁹

Metternich now inserted a sub-title in his letter, which had developed into an essay, "The Sovereignty of the People," in order to examine this question from the point of view of political theory. Under this title, he began, "I recommend to you the brochure of M. de Barante," which "contains some excellent things."²⁸⁰ This was Prosper Brugière, Baron de Barante's treatise *Questions constitutionnelles*, which had been published the same year. Barante was a member of the *doctrinaires*, a group of French Royalist thinkers who aimed to reconcile monarchy with the objectives of the French Revolution. He was a friend of Benjamin Constant and described himself as a liberal.²⁸¹ During the Bourbon restoration (1813–1840), he was a councillor of state, and he

---

277. Metternich to Twiss, "The German Question," August 11, 1849, National Archives of the Czech Republic, Prague, RAM-AC/ 10/ 775, 248.

278. Metternich to Twiss, "The German Question," August 11, 1849, National Archives of the Czech Republic, Prague, RAM-AC/ 10/ 775, 249.

279. Metternich to Twiss, "The German Question," August 11, 1849, National Archives of the Czech Republic, Prague, RAM-AC/ 10/ 775, 250.

280. Metternich to Twiss, "The German Question," August 11, 1849, National Archives of the Czech Republic, Prague, RAM-AC/ 10/ 775, 250.

281. Aurelian Crăiuțu, *Liberalism Under Siege: The Political Thought of the French Doctrinaires* (Lanham, 2003), 29–30.

continued to hold office after the July Revolution of 1830, but, like Metternich, he found himself removed from power by the 1848 revolution. According to Metternich, the first chapter of *Questions constitutionnelles* argued that the sovereignty of the people was a fiction, and it was this concept, in particular, that Metternich enjoyed.[282] For political philosophers such as Hobbes or Rousseau, all sovereignty was artificial, and even Hobbes at times used the terms "artificial" and "fictional" interchangeably.[283] For Hobbes, the artificiality of sovereignty was constituted by its personification of the will of the people who covenanted to create the state. The authority in that covenant, although established by an artifice, was nevertheless real and formidable. Metternich, however, used Barante to distinguish between popular sovereignty, which was "fictional," and the sovereignty of a monarch, which was not a fiction because it could be located in the person of the monarch.

He interpreted Barante as follows: "1. Sovereignty of the people is perhaps just a fiction and this is because the idea of sovereignty is indubitably one of supreme power and that power cannot be exercised by the people, it must be delegated by them to somebody else other than the sovereign. Therefore, what remains if it passes into other hands? *Fiction*! 2. This fiction acquires the value of a necessity in a republican regime."[284] This was a rather partial account of Barante's thesis. Barante had stated that the "sovereignty of the people is an incontestable principle, but an abstract principle."[285] And he had indeed concluded that "the people have no means to really exercise sovereignty; to delegate is to lose it."[286] On the other hand, he argued, if all power was placed in the hands of a prince, such as a Bonaparte, there was a grave risk of tyranny. He argued that it was necessary to divide sovereignty between the people, constituted in an assembly, the executive, and a monarch. When power was not shared and "confined uniquely to the assembly," the "fear of tyranny" again arose.[287] It was essential for the "good of the people" that no authority should be absolute.[288]

Metternich's distortion of Barante served his larger purpose: namely, to distinguish what he argued to be the fictional nature of sovereignty exercised in republics from what should be the real sovereignty exercised in the person of a monarch. If the sovereignty of the monarch was perceived as "fictional," or artificial, he argued, this perception became a cause of "weakening

282. Prosper Barante, *Questions constitutionnelles* (Paris, 1849), 1–17.
283. Quentin Skinner, "The Purely Artificial Person of the State," in Skinner, *Visions of Politics. Vol. 3:Hobbes and Civil Science* (Cambridge, 2002), 188–197.
284. Metternich to Twiss, "The German Question," August 11, 1849, National Archives of the Czech Republic, Prague, RAM-AC/ 10/ 775, 251.
285. Barante, *Questions constitutionnelles*, 4.
286. Barante, *Questions constitutionnelles*, 6–7.
287. Barante, *Questions constitutionnelles*, 16.
288. Barante, *Questions constitutionnelles*, 5.

[*affaiblissement*]" and "splitting [*fractionnement*]" of "authority," which was "contrary to the safety of all associations."[289] For Metternich, as for Twiss, sovereignty must be strong and undivided (a paradoxical thought from somebody who had governed the Austrian Empire, but not inconsistent with a Grotian account of sovereignty as unitary but nevertheless capable of being divided amongst the parts of an empire). A further assumption behind his distinction between the sovereignty of republics and monarchies was that some forms of power were personified, and exercised remotely from the people who authorised that power, while others were real and exercised directly. Metternich's scepticism of personification complemented Twiss's own rather rigid views at this time. Twiss certainly understood that various kinds of personification were necessary to social and political life, perhaps more so than Metternich, but he understood and practiced those conventions within strict limits imposed by society, church, and state.

Throughout May 1849, events in Europe generally moved in a direction that gave Metternich and Twiss hope. The Frankfurt Parliament, in particular, foundered, and the hopes for a German Empire came to an end for the moment. Frankfurt was a portrait of "'dissolving views,'" as Twiss put it, because "just as the outline threatens to become quite clear, the picture fades away into air."[290] By the middle of the month, he was rejoicing that "the Frankfurt assembly has almost burst asunder . . . in infinite small atoms."[291] Metternich, by this time, had moved from Brighton to Richmond, and Twiss was riding down to visit him there.

"The Social Problem"

By the close of 1849, Twiss was confident that order was returning to Europe: "The democratic party in Europe is discredited, if not demoralised. 'Order' is the watchword."[292] Even by May of that year, he felt able to reflect on how "history" would judge the events of 1848 and 1849.[293] Venturing to "guess at your meaning," he questioned whether Metternich believed there was a "policy" which would have "prevented these revolutionary outbreaks." "Or do you go so far as to say" that "statesmanship" could not have prevented but only

---

289. Metternich to Twiss, "The German Question," August 11, 1849, National Archives of the Czech Republic, Prague, RAM-AC/ 10/ 775, 251.

290. Twiss to Metternich, May 2, 1849, National Archives of the Czech Republic, Prague, RAM-AC/ 10/ 775, 281.

291. Twiss to Metternich, May 16, 1849, National Archives of the Czech Republic, Prague, RAM-AC/ 10/ 775, 289.

292. Twiss to Metternich, December 22, 1849, National Archives of the Czech Republic, Prague, RAM-AC/ 10/ 775, 452.

293. Twiss to Metternich, May 25, 1849, National Archives of the Czech Republic, Prague, RAM-AC/ 10/ 775, 300.

"deferred" the "late results: that they are in fact the legitimate fruits of the revolutionary elements of 1792."[294] This was quite a substantial concession from a conservative point of view: namely, that the liberal revolutions were inevitable and perhaps even "legitimate." "This," Twiss continued, "is of course possible. The arrangements of 1815 may perhaps have been considered by the statesmen of that period, who had fathomed the question, to be only provisional—a sort of compromise between the past and the future, a transition in fact." He wrote almost as if the person he was addressing was not one of the most important amongst those statesmen. Now, he was not merely suggesting that Metternich might think of himself as a liberal, but that Metternich, and the statesmen of 1815, might also think of themselves as the architects of the revolutions of 1848! Nevertheless, even if the revolutions had been anticipated, and the post-1815 order had been intended as a transition, the key question, Twiss noted, was: "But to what?"[295] "Socialism," he observed, "is merely systematised sansculottism. It is in fact the philosophy of sans-culottism": that is, it pursued the most radical and egalitarian vision to arise from the French revolution.[296] The transition, therefore, had to be to some other vision "but in what order? Shall it be in continuation? Or opposition?"[297] Prussia, he argued, was well placed to provide leadership. After "strong positive disturbing forces," there was a need for positive leadership, and Prussia could take that role. This, too, was a significant concession from a pro-Austrian perspective. One of the "great moral difficulties of the age," he continued, was to respond in a positive way to a "strong positive disturbing force." If no direct political solution could be found, then it was necessary to find "artificial" means of stimulating "society" because when a "sound stimulus is not given, society has recourse to an unsound one." If "physicians" did not prescribe medicine, people had recourse to "charlatans."[298] What then were "healthy stimuli"? "Commerce and local institutions" provide the "natural excitement for the masses." Where they did not exist, "they should be created." Such institutions provided the "masses" with something to work for; otherwise, they "will be against."[299] "Much of the English system," he concluded, "seems to be constructed with some such view

294. Twiss to Metternich, May 25, 1849, National Archives of the Czech Republic, Prague, RAM-AC/ 10/ 775, 300.

295. Twiss to Metternich, May 25, 1849, National Archives of the Czech Republic, Prague, RAM-AC/ 10/ 775, 300.

296. Twiss to Metternich, May 25, 1849, National Archives of the Czech Republic, Prague, RAM-AC/ 10/ 775, 300–301.

297. Twiss to Metternich, May 25, 1849, National Archives of the Czech Republic, Prague, RAM-AC/ 10/ 775, 301.

298. Twiss to Metternich, May 25, 1849, National Archives of the Czech Republic, Prague, RAM-AC/ 10/ 775, 301.

299. Twiss to Metternich, May 25, 1849, National Archives of the Czech Republic, Prague, RAM-AC/ 10/ 775, 301–302.

as this."³⁰⁰ Twiss was sure that Metternich's "predilection for local institutions" inclined him to "such views as Englishmen." The church provided some of the most useful local institutions into which the masses could put their energy. "Parish offices," he declared, "are wonderful safety valves for villages." From Machiavelli to Rousseau, such notions of civil religion had been perceived as essential to social order and civic virtue, but it is nevertheless striking to find these notions espoused by a man holding so many senior offices in the Church of England.

Metternich replied to these questions, as he frequently did, by appealing to his notions of political reality rather than Twiss's "abstract" ideas.³⁰¹ He noted that Twiss asked in what way Austria's, or Metternich's, "plan" had "not been executed." Metternich responded that the word "principles" should be substituted for "plan." Any plan worthy of the name, he observed, should be based upon "definable ends." The end which the Imperial court of Austria had pursued since 1814, he said, was "respect for law." It had pursued that end "without deviation" and, as such, had established the "order" within which "true freedom and peace" were enjoyed.³⁰² "Myself, my dear Twiss," he continued, "who had a great part in the development of public affairs, I would justify by what you have just read . . . I wanted political peace, not by following abstract ideas but by following calculation [*un calcul*]."³⁰³ When we speak, he said, "of my conscience, nothing would make me change the direction that my conscience indicated." "Surrounded" by men who, "seeing the peace," thought revolution was "extinguished," he asked himself in "what direction governments should search their force. Was it in despotism or in liberalism?" His answer was that it was neither. "All I ever knew," he continued, "was good government and progress."³⁰⁴ By this he did not mean "illusory" progress, implicitly the progress of the revolutionaries and liberals, but "true progress" which took as its guide "justice, reason, and lawfulness."³⁰⁵ "Future historians" could "confirm" his judgement or could otherwise "deny it" with the "values of a utopia." At the same time, "if I am not mistaken," he added, "the Utopians have not discovered within which camp I pitched my tent." Correcting Twiss, he observed that the

---

300. Twiss to Metternich, May 25, 1849, National Archives of the Czech Republic, Prague, RAM-AC/ 10/ 775, 302.

301. Metternich to Twiss, "Richmond Mai," 1849, National Archives of the Czech Republic, Prague, RAM-AC/ 10/ 775, 304. Another copy of this letter is Metternich to Twiss, Richmond, May 31, 1849, Bibliothèque nationale de France, Fol/ R.D./13810, 92.

302. Metternich to Twiss, "Richmond Mai," 1849, National Archives of the Czech Republic, Prague, RAM-AC/ 10/ 775, 304.

303. Metternich to Twiss, "Richmond Mai," 1849, National Archives of the Czech Republic, Prague, RAM-AC/ 10/ 775, 307.

304. Metternich to Twiss, "Richmond Mai," 1849, National Archives of the Czech Republic, Prague, RAM-AC/ 10/ 775, 307.

305. Metternich to Twiss, "Richmond Mai," 1849, National Archives of the Czech Republic, Prague, RAM-AC/ 10/ 775, 308.

"arrangement of 1815" was never "provisionary," but he conceded that it was a "compromise between the past and the future."[306] But the past, he said, could not be "annulled." The past should be maintained in order to assure the future, a future that was based upon the "elements of justice, reason, and respect for legality." Metternich, therefore, stuck to his conservative position, albeit that he insisted that he was no despot and that he valued both progress and the rule of law. Twiss had not succeeded in persuading him to describe himself as a "liberalist," but, at the same time, his assumption of the mantle of progress and the appeal to the rule of law showed that he was prepared to appropriate liberal discourse—or elements in common between competing political discourses—in order to legitimate his pragmatic conservatism.

Twiss replied with an apology for using the word "plan," but excused it as the habit of an Englishman who "as you well know, is in most cases, painfully practical, and is not well satisfied with principles, unless applied to action."[307] This was, in fact, a fair representation of Twiss's engagement with political and legal ideas—they were tools for action. Henry Cavendish, he pointed out, had first understood the use of steam as an agent, but his name would not be heard "once in a thousand times" compared to James Watt, who had applied the discovery to the steam engine.[308] Returning to the questions of where the revolutions of 1848 would lead, and their origin in the French Revolution of 1789, he observed, "We now are led to the Old French Revolution which was a social phenomenon dominated by the genius of Napoléon." By a social phenomenon, Twiss meant a class struggle, or a conflict between orders. Ironically, Karl Marx was also, at this time, arguing that the revolutions were a class struggle.[309] Six months later, while still convinced that the recent revolutions were a struggle between the orders, Twiss questioned whether they might, as such, be merely the prelude to greater changes: "Time only will show whether the events of 1848–9 are an epilogue of the drama of 1789, or an 'entre-acte,' an interlude as it were between two great dramas—a political and a social one."[310] Again, Marx would have agreed, and the revolutions did prelude long-term change, although much of that was gradual rather than revolutionary.

Twiss found, however, that there were problems within the revolutionary aspirations for equality: "*Égalité* was thought to be sufficient to secure its [the revolution's] social character, but *égalité* was found to be a name instead of a

306. Metternich to Twiss, "Richmond Mai," 1849, National Archives of the Czech Republic, Prague, RAM-AC/ 10/ 775, 308.

307. Twiss to Metternich, May 31, 1849, National Archives of the Czech Republic, Prague, RAM-AC/ 10/ 775, 312.

308. Twiss to Metternich, May 31, 1849, National Archives of the Czech Republic, Prague, RAM-AC/ 10/ 775, 312.

309. Sperber, *The European Revolutions, 1848–1851*, 200.

310. Twiss to Metternich, October 4, 1849, National Archives of the Czech Republic, Prague, RAM-AC/ 10/ 775, 415–416.

thing, as it will always prove to be." The problem was the revolutionaries' pursuit of "absolute instead of proportionate" equality. "The latter element," proportionate equality, "is not destructive—on the contrary, states have perished where it has not been preserved." "'À chacun selon son œuvre'—'He that hath much shall receive much' but not of the same thing that he already possesses. To the rich man honor to the poor man subsistence."[311] His point was that the inequalities that had led to the revolutions were inequalities of kind as well as wealth. The solution to inequality, therefore, could not be found by treating all people in the same way. From the point of view of a nineteenth-century liberal, the most generous construction that could be placed upon his meaning was that equality should be pursued through distinguishing the needs of different social orders. At the same time, he could be suspected of using the strategy he had recommended to Metternich of employing the vocabulary of liberals and revolutionaries to pursue conservative ends—in this instance, establishing an argument for maintaining distinctions between orders by describing those differences, such as honor and subsistence, as "equality." Nevertheless, "the social problem," he said, "must be analysed by the philosopher, must be solved by the statesman, or the next generation will rue the consequences."[312] Over the coming months, as the threat of the revolutions subsided, he returned repeatedly to the "social problem" and to the role of political philosophy in addressing it. "Europe for the moment," he wrote, "is spared but it is clear that the grave questions of the day are social not political . . . These are questions partly for the moralist but political philosophy cannot ignore them."[313] Though he regarded events with a conservative eye, he certainly confronted the central problem of the moment and correctly anticipated the period of reform and social change that would ensue, and in which he would take part, in a variety of ways, over the following decades.

Looking forward, Twiss promised, "I must take up this social problem this autumn when I shall have leisure to take up my quill again."[314] In studying "*l'avenir de l'Europe*," he was relieved to find that "more materials will survive than I at one time expected": that is, he could see that the revolutions had not completely undone the old social orders. But where, he asked, "will be the cement."[315] "There is no cement for the future," he argued, "but self-interest

---

311. Twiss to Metternich, May 31, 1849, National Archives of the Czech Republic, Prague, RAM-AC/ 10/ 775, 313.

312. Twiss to Metternich, May 31, 1849, National Archives of the Czech Republic, Prague, RAM-AC/ 10/ 775, 314.

313. Twiss to Metternich, October 4, 1849, National Archives of the Czech Republic, Prague, RAM-AC/ 10/ 775, 417–418. The passage was underlined by Metternich in red ink.

314. Twiss to Metternich, May 31, 1849, National Archives of the Czech Republic, Prague, RAM-AC/ 10/ 775, 315.

315. Twiss to Metternich, May 31, 1849, National Archives of the Czech Republic, Prague, RAM-AC/ 10/ 775, 316.

and the problem is to substitute a healthy for a morbid self-interest." Healthy self-interest was solidarity between the classes, while morbid self-interest was expressed through "individualism": "If this solidarity can be established, if the mutual relationship can be once more restored in the place of the selfish individualism which prevails in France and elsewhere, the links in the network of society may be joined once more."[316] The pursuit of healthy self-interest would lead "man" and "society" to "acquiesce in the true principles of justice, reason, and legality."[317] The "English mind," in particular, rightly appreciated self-interest, an understanding, he speculated, that "results from commercial dealing, or is the latter the effect rather than the cause?" Twiss was not at all hostile to modern political philosophy. His vision of a commercial society, governed by justice, reason, and the rule of law, and driven by self-interest, was consistent with the contract theories of seventeenth- and eighteenth-century political thought that had underpinned the modern revolutions. He was trying to wed that vision, however, with an aristocratic attachment to the social order of the *Ancien Régime*.

Hungary and Public Opinion

In the early days of the collaboration between Metternich and Twiss, Metternich advised: "I would like you to pay attention to everything the press produces regarding Hungary. It is becoming for me a great interest."[318] In March 1849, Twiss worried: "Is the course of events in Hungary as satisfying as might have been expected?" After Ferdinand I had abdicated the Austrian throne in favour of Franz Joseph I, in December 1848, relations between the Austrian Empire and Hungary deteriorated. The Hungarian revolutionary army had rapid and unexpected success against the Austrians, although by July 1849, they had fought a series of bloody battles over the Danube fort town of Komárom, halfway between Vienna and Buda, which had led to the complete destruction of that town and their eventual defeat.[319] Twiss anticipated this outcome, commenting at a distance: "Comora [Komárom] will give trouble. What a pity to have it destroyed but *che sera, sera!*"[320] The correspondence

---

316. Twiss to Metternich, May 31, 1849, National Archives of the Czech Republic, Prague, RAM-AC/ 10/ 775, 316.

317. Twiss to Metternich, May 31, 1849, National Archives of the Czech Republic, Prague, RAM-AC/ 10/ 775, 317.

318. Metternich to Twiss, Brighton, January 29, 1849, Bibliothèque nationale de France, Fol/ R.D./13810, 42.

319. For a narrative of the Hungarian revolution, see Knatchbull-Hugessen, *The Political Evolution of the Hungarian Nation*, Vol. 2, and for the defeat at Komárom, Vol. 2., 130–131.

320. Twiss to Metternich, March 27, 1849, National Archives of the Czech Republic, Prague, RAM-AC/ 10/ 775, 230.

contains a number of examples of such dispassionate, and ironic, analysis of human suffering, the tone fitting the *raison d'état* used by advocates of the balance of great powers.[321]

In May 1849, Hungary remained rebellious, while Metternich dispassionately evaluated the moment: "Attacked by all political and socialist parties, it is her nature that prevails. What does she seek in the two directions: does she pursue politics or simple conservatism? What will happen to her in this enormous confusion? We will see more clearly in two months' time."[322] Twiss confessed to him, "I am a little puzzled by the serenity which you displayed . . . in regard to Austrian affairs."[323] That serenity, however, may have been due in part to Czar Nicholas I's pledge of Russian soldiers to help the Emperor Franz Joseph end the revolt.[324] Moreover, Austria, as Twiss observed, was "now concentrating her energies for a military operation" not against "insurgents" but "in the field," where it held an advantage.[325] Kossuth "proclaiming the dethronement of the Habsburg House" was "bold," Twiss observed, and it was the "necessary sequel of his course of conduct," but it would "induce" the Bohemians and the "non-Magyar" population of Hungary to be "more warm in support of the cause of the Emperor."[326] For his part, Metternich was ambivalent about the involvement of the Russians: "It is not the old Hungary that is the object of the struggle. It is drawn into the route of crass revolution and of Polonism, in that plague which today appears everywhere as an ulcer which forms on the social body, and by the fact that it engages the Russian power in the struggle which covers the continent, placing it [Russia] on the social and political terrain, which at least has the value of an episode in the great drama of the epoch."[327]

---

321. Just days later, Twiss reported that he had received a note from "Prince Louis Lucien Bonaparte," Napoléon's nephew, who was born in England and spent many years in London but was at this moment a deputy in the Assembly in Paris, representing Corsica, and corresponding with Twiss. Bonaparte reported "alarm at Paris about the cholera": Twiss to Metternich, April 7, 1849, National Archives of the Czech Republic, Prague, RAM-AC/ 10/ 775, 247. The pandemic would kill thousands not only in Paris but also London. Twiss commented to Metternich: "It is just as well perhaps that it should be so as a 'development,'" presumably meaning that news of the cholera was better than news of any new revolutionary outbursts.

322. Metternich to Twiss, Richmond, May 6, 1849, Bibliothèque nationale de France, Fol/ R.D./13810, 90.

323. Twiss to Metternich, May 16, 1849, National Archives of the Czech Republic, Prague, RAM-AC/ 10/ 775, 288.

324. Sperber, *The European Revolutions, 1848–1851*, 228.

325. Twiss to Metternich, May 2, 1849, National Archives of the Czech Republic, Prague, RAM-AC/ 10/ 775, 280–281.

326. Twiss to Metternich, May 10, 1849, National Archives of the Czech Republic, Prague, RAM-AC/ 10/ 775, 283–284.

327. Metternich to Twiss, Richmond, May 6, 1849, Bibliothèque nationale de France, Fol/ R.D./13810, 89v.

In August 1849, General Görgei, the leader of the Hungarian army, had surrendered to the Russians, and Twiss wrote to Metternich in celebration.[328] He anticipated, however, a new battle, a battle in the struggle over public opinion: "After the material struggle is over, you will, I am sure, think that a moral struggle must be commenced and the great object of the Cabinet of Vienna should be to 'rehabilitate' [*réhabiliter*] Austria morally in the opinion of her subjects, and of Europe. The representative system of government has one great convenience, that it admits of corrections being supplied in time to public opinion without the government abandoning its vantage ground of presumption."[329] During 1849, as the "material" threat, as Twiss put it, of the revolutions began to recede, he was much occupied with this question of how to shape public opinion, ideally in order to prevent a resurgence of revolutionary ideas. His emphasis upon the importance of public opinion reflected a broader Victorian idea that, in the absence of interventionist government, society was governed by public opinion.[330] It has been pointed out, however, that public opinion, particularly in the period from 1792 to 1848, was far from monolithic and that the claim to act in the name of public opinion was largely rhetorical.[331] Twiss was very much aware of the fractured nature of public opinion, and it is for this reason that his many discussions of the subject emphasised the need to win the contests over opinion. Metternich was far more ambivalent, at best, about the idea of public opinion. "Publicity [*publicité*] is a relative idea," he wrote, "applied to facts, everywhere it excites because nobody can do anything against it . . . and at the same time it exists everywhere." Moreover, he pointed out, public opinion did not perform the same role throughout Europe as it did in Britian: "Publicity understood in the sense of publication varies with the mode of government which, on the other hand, is not simply the product of whim but has its motivation [*raison*] in other causes which, by their nature, can be good or bad." Due to such variations in government "publication is strongly restrained in Germany." "It arises from these facts," he concluded, "that the life of statesmen in countries submitted to a regime of silence must pass under different conditions to those of their colleagues in the countries of publicity."[332]

Metternich also responded to Twiss's celebration of the defeat of the Hungarian revolution with a more sober assessment and with disdain for the

---

328. For the surrender: Knatchbull-Hugessen, *The Political Evolution of the Hungarian Nation*, Vol. 2, 130–131.

329. Twiss to Metternich, August 22, 1849, National Archives of the Czech Republic, Prague, RAM-AC/ 10/ 775, 377–378.

330. This was a position articulated a generation later in Dicey, *Lectures on the Relation between Law and Public Opinion in England*.

331. Hilton, *A Mad, Bad, and Dangerous People*, 311.

332. Metternich to Twiss, Brighton, January 10, 1849, Bibliothèque nationale de France, Fol/ R.D./13810, 26.

democratic ambitions of Kossuth and the other revolutionaries: "The country lacks all foundation for the elements of democracy. The revolution took place in a region that is not native [*indigène*] but was introduced with a mask and with the aid of lures which the uncultivated and ignorant mass trusted. The truth of the situation is becoming obvious and it will be proved that thousands of men got themselves killed in the ranks of the rebels believing themselves to be defending the rights of the crown."[333] Once again, for Metternich the cause of unrest was nationalism, but nationalism was, as always, a mask for other interests: "It is the same with the struggles between nationalities; those which are burdened with the greatest fury have endured for centuries, either placed alongside each other, or mixed together, and in complete peace. It is <u>nationalism</u>, that newly introduced fruit, which has served as the means of excitement by the demagogues to arrive at ends which are not national but revolutionary. The revolution in the German parts of the Empire was made by professors and students and a small number of dupes in the region of the states. The revolution in Hungary has followed an opposite route. It is discussed by everyone. It was the nobles, who wanted liberalism alone, who put it in motion and it is a gang of demagogues from the middle class who made the revolution with the aid of a group of the Hungarian population."[334] He was confident, however, that the Hungarian people would once more support the empire: "Engaged in combat, the people continued the struggle because they are brave. Tomorrow they will fight for the emperor just as yesterday they fought against him."[335] In fact, faced with the difficult choice between Magyar nationalism and fidelity to the crown, half of the Hungarian officers in the imperial army had remained loyal to Franz Joseph during the war.[336]

Although Twiss believed that Hungary should be maintained within the Austrian Empire, he allowed more scope for reform than Metternich: "If the majority of the Magyars are loyal, I should advise Hungary not to be broken up. The old system admits of much improvement, but it is worth mending if it will hold together ... I am not quite certain that Hungary is not the mainstay, physically speaking, of the Austrian Empire. I should like much to discuss fully the European position of Hungary, and the Magyar element, as well as the Slavonic."[337] The pair continued to share all information on the progress of the

333. Metternich to Twiss, Richmond, August 25, 1849, Bibliothèque nationale de France, Fol/ R.D./13810, 110v–111.

334. Metternich to Twiss, Richmond, August 25, 1849, Bibliothèque nationale de France, Fol/ R.D./13810, 111v–112.

335. Metternich to Twiss, Richmond, August 25, 1849, Bibliothèque nationale de France, Fol/ R.D./13810, 112v–113.

336. István Deák, *Beyond Nationalism: A Social and Political History of the Habsburg Officer Corp, 1848–1918* (New York, 1990), ix.

337. Twiss to Metternich, January 16, 1849, National Archives of the Czech Republic, Prague, RAM-AC/ 10/ 775, 36–37.

revolutions, and, particularly, they paid close attention to how reports would shape public opinion. On January 18, 1849, Twiss wrote about various journals received and then noted, "I hear that an English history of Hungary will appear in a few days—on the side of Kossuth's friends, I believe."[338] Implicitly, as Twiss had previously written, it was necessary to provide a counter-narrative, and here he effectively prefigured his treatise of the following year on Hungary. The counter-narrative was necessary not only for propaganda purposes on the Continent but also to influence English government policy. The Whig Foreign Secretary, Lord Palmerston, supported revolutionaries in 1848, in defence of the ideals of liberal constitutionalism, even while he adhered to the notion of the balance of great powers. Most members of his own government, as well as the conservative opposition, were frustrated by his position. Twiss accordingly wrote to Metternich, "Lord Palmerston is disposed to withdraw as much as possible from any interference in foreign international questions. His policy is certainly not happy nor is it calculated to please any person but himself."[339]

In this same letter, Twiss progressed to speculate on how the Austrian Empire could be "reorganised to be a confederation of states under one supreme head."[340] He argued that the Magyars might accept this compromise if their "administration could be satisfactorily organised," but that it was "impossible that the King of Hungary will remain a distinct person from the Emperor." This was a prescient judgement given that the rule of Emperor Franz Joseph I, who came to power in December 1848, survived the split between Austria and Hungary in 1867 as dual monarch. At the same time, he put the rule of Franz Joseph in question, arguing that the "fundamental laws of Hungary" limited the earliest majority for a king to the age of 20, while Franz Joseph was still only 18. He then observed that the Hungarian constitution would be "an interesting subject to discuss"—its virtues and defects, and how it might be made to work "in harmony with a state-confederation."[341] He was outlining not merely a future conversation but his treatise on the subject.

Twiss's engagement with the participants in the revolutions extended beyond Metternich. He wrote on January 26: "The two persons whose names I mentioned in my last are in London and were introduced to me at my desire. They are no doubt agents of Kossuth's."[342] He pointed out that these two

---

338. Twiss to Metternich, January 18, 1849, National Archives of the Czech Republic, Prague, RAM-AC/ 10/ 775, 46–47.

339. Twiss to Metternich, January 18, 1849, National Archives of the Czech Republic, Prague, RAM-AC/ 10/ 775, 48.

340. Twiss to Metternich, January 18, 1849, National Archives of the Czech Republic, Prague, RAM-AC/ 10/ 775, 49.

341. Twiss to Metternich, January 18, 1849, National Archives of the Czech Republic, Prague, RAM-AC/ 10/ 775, 50.

342. Twiss to Metternich, January 26, 1849, National Archives of the Czech Republic, Prague, RAM-AC/ 10/ 775, 69.

men had accompanied Kossuth on trips to Vienna and elsewhere. He then observed, "They seemed to found all their hopes on the Chartists." The high point of Chartist protest was between April and June 1848, with hundreds of thousands of workers meeting in Kennington Park, south of the Thames, and a petition of millions (how many is contested) presented to parliament by the Chartist leaders demanding universal suffrage for men.[343] Just six months later, when Twiss wrote, the failure of the Chartists' demands had diminished the perceived threat, and many Chartists turned to plans for insurrection.[344] His antagonism to the Hungarian revolution was contained within a broader opposition to the internationalisation of the 1848 revolutions. Kossuth's agents extended that internationalisation into Britain. Twiss deceived those agents by concealing his work for Metternich.[345] He followed his observations on them by declaring, "Austria appears to me to have at this moment the highest vocation which almost ever fell to the lot of a state."[346] "She may freely lay," he continued, "the basis of the political organisation of a constitutional monarchy which shall serve as a model for other states and form the best practical refutation of the republican creed."

The republic he had in mind was the Second Republic in France, which had followed the bloody revolution of the previous year and was now led by the populist Louis-Napoléon Bonaparte, the nephew of Napoléon I: "A strange vision seems to be stealing over the minds of the friends of order in this country: that in order to neutralise the cry which will be raised for household suffrage, they must advocate universal suffrage. Is this the prompting of despair or of sound calculation? Was it instinct or folly that made men vote for Louis-Napoléon? I do not like to jump in the dark, I confess: it may be very safe, but I prefer to be satisfied a priori of the probable connection of cause and effect."[347] Since 1838, some members of parliament, such as the Radical Joseph Hume, had responded to the demands for universal suffrage from the Chartists, with a proposal for household suffrage which would restrict the vote to rate-payers. "The Legislature," Hume argued in parliament, "could put an end to these demands of the Chartists" if they were to "grant household suffrage on an extensive scale."[348] The Chartists

---

343. John Saville, *1848: The British State and the Chartist Movement*, 102-129.

344. David Goodway, *London Chartism, 1838-1848* (Cambridge, 1982).

345. Twiss to Metternich, January 26, 1849, National Archives of the Czech Republic, Prague, RAM-AC/ 10/ 775, 69. He commented that he was "extremely struck with the Tatar cheek bones of the two Magyars."

346. Twiss to Metternich, January 26, 1849, National Archives of the Czech Republic, Prague, RAM-AC/ 10/ 775, 70.

347. Twiss to Metternich, January 26, 1849, National Archives of the Czech Republic, Prague, RAM-AC/ 10/ 775, 71.

348. Joseph Hume, *On Household Suffrage: The Speech of Joseph Hume in the House of Commons on the 21st of March 1839* (London, 1839), 18.

were never far from Twiss's thoughts. His argument was that the pressure for household suffrage would give way to universal suffrage, and his fear was that the granting of universal suffrage would lead inexorably to the creation of a republic. This would be the chain of cause and effect. Now it was clear that his opposition to revolutions abroad, and his collaboration with Metternich, were partly driven by his fears for Britain itself, while the successful resistance to international revolution lay in the possibility of establishing a constitutional monarchy in Austria.

Undeterred by Metternich's doubts about the importance of public opinion, Twiss focused many of the discussions on Hungary, both on the question of how the Austrian Empire could win over its Magyar population, and also on how the battle over sympathy for the Magyars could be won in Britain itself. Kossuth toured Britain in the hope that public sympathy would lead to British intervention in favour of the Magyar cause.[349] Twiss was particularly concerned with the dilemma that "the truth" and "the facts," as he had said in previous letters, should be heard and that they could only be heard if right-minded people such as Metternich and himself published, but that, at the same time, restrictions had to be placed upon the press to prevent the publication of untruths. "Between secrecy and publicity," he wrote, "between a strict censorship and the absence of all restriction, as such, I do not see a safe halting place."[350]

The cause of falsehood, ironically, was enlightenment: "We have opened on a period in the world's history where men have begun to think who never used to think, i.e., whose predecessors never <u>thought</u> as they do. They have reached a certain stage in the process, an <u>imperfect</u> one, and they must be hurried on to a more <u>perfect</u> stage."[351] Again here, we find Twiss, in conversation with Metternich, articulating a remarkably progressive vision of history in which all classes work towards improvement. This vision implies acceptance of reform and change. What restrains it, however, from being a fully liberal outlook is the matter of who should be the guardians and drivers of change: namely, the aristocracy or "the most influential class." He continued: "The 'Spectator' observes that 'the political sovereignty of every state is vested in the most influential class.' Again, formerly those who had property

---

349. Knatchbull-Hugessen, *The Political Evolution of the Hungarian Nation*, Vol. 2, 159.

350. Twiss to Metternich, June 4, 1849, National Archives of the Czech Republic, Prague, RAM-AC/ 10/ 775, 328–329. One solution to the abuse of the press would be good libel laws: "Abuse of publicity and unrestrained speech may be restrained . . . falsehood or calumny on the one hand, libel or slander on the other may be punished." "We never appear," he noted, "to have had a definite law of libel in this country." This was a thought he would return to twenty years later when entangled in the libel trial that would transform his life.

351. Twiss to Metternich, June 4, 1849, National Archives of the Czech Republic, Prague, RAM-AC/ 10/ 775, 329–330.

carried swords ... they are no longer the fighting class but the men of order and propriety—but as their ancestors were the most influential by reason of their swords, so their descendants must be such by reason of their tongues or their pens. They must morally control the thoughts of the community. How is this to be done? Can it be done except by the Press and the Tribune?"[352] He repeated these thoughts throughout his letters on Hungary in 1849. "Public opinion," he wrote, "is a force independent of every government, in fact above the government, whether it is corporeally embodied in an army of soldiers, a bureaucratic hierarchy, a chamber, or an anonymous army of writers."[353] The necessary conclusion, therefore, was that "it is a much more simple method to govern through the Press, but it requires tact ... hence the bureaucrat must shirk from the idea, but the statesman may welcome it."[354] The press, therefore, had to be nominally free but, in order to prevent license and anarchy, it had to be "morally controlled" by the aristocracy. Moral control was precisely what Twiss and Metternich were seeking through their collaboration with the publisher John Murray. In April 1849, he remarked, "I much prefer not writing anonymously, yet the circulation of the Q.R. [*Quarterly Review*] at nearly 10,000 is important and I wish to command it at any time if I please."[355] He wished merely "to put the truth before the world," so that the public would have no "excuse" for being "left in the dark."

Although they were seeking moral control, Twiss hastened to point out that they were losing the moral struggle even while the material struggle was being won on the battlefield. Sympathy for the Magyars was high in Britain, while distrust of the Russians, who had intervened on the side of Austria, was deep—Russia was perceived to be a strategic threat to Britain in part because of the threat it posed to the Ottoman Empire and therefore to British access to its eastern Empire (which was through nominally Ottoman dominions). Twiss warned Metternich that "it deserves attention from the friends of Austria that at the present moment a very considerable number of the Journals and Periodicals in England are warmly enlisted on the side of the Magyars. The direct intervention of Russia has necessarily given a new aspect to the struggle and caused uneasiness in Western Europe, symptoms of which have exhibited in the Times and Morning Chronicle newspapers. But the friends of the Magyars have been exceedingly active in advantaging their cause by

---

352. Twiss to Metternich, June 4, 1849, National Archives of the Czech Republic, Prague, RAM-AC/ 10/ 775, 330–331.

353. Twiss to Metternich, October 23, 1849, National Archives of the Czech Republic, Prague, RAM-AC/ 10/ 775, 441.

354. Twiss to Metternich, October 23, 1849, National Archives of the Czech Republic, Prague, RAM-AC/ 10/ 775, 442.

355. Twiss to Metternich, April 12, 1849, National Archives of the Czech Republic, Prague, RAM-AC/ 10/ 775, 260–262.

statements highly unfavourable to Austria."[356] He complained that articles "giving the Magyar version of Hungarian affairs" were being published in French, German, and English, while "no counter statements are put forth." As evidence, he then listed all the English-language publications which were sympathetic to the Hungarians, while citing their political affiliations: "The Daily News (Radical), Globe (Liberal), and Standard (Protectionist) daily newspapers; The Examiner (Radical), Spectator (Liberal), Observer (Radical-Liberal), weekly newspapers with others of minor note advocate strongly the Magyar views. The Edinburgh Quarterly Review (Liberal), Westminster Quarterly Review (Radical), North British Quarterly Review (Liberal), Tait's monthly magazine (Liberal), and Frazer's monthly magazine (Moderate), have articles of similar tendency and some of them have admitted papers avowedly written by Magyars. All the above publications are of a superior stamp and circulate amongst the superior classes. Those of a lower grade are likely to take a line similar to that taken by a meeting in Marylebone Parish, to which, however, no great importance is to be attached, as it represented little more than a section of Radicals and Chartists."[357] The Chartist threat had, by this time, subsided, but Twiss still believed that "men of steady judgement and moderate feelings," as well as "practical conservatives," and "persons . . . adverse to strict government restraint" were being excited to sympathy with the "rights and liberties of Hungary." At the same time, "well intentioned" people were upset by the sufferings of Protestant Magyars, while "minds which are strongly alive to material interests, and which form a growing influential class in England" were concerned about questions of free commerce. All of these people deserved "to be set right by correct information."[358] The correct manipulation of public opinion could be a force for international peace: "If states are not to go to war, are not to control one another by the actual exercise of their power, they can only attain such a result by their influence, their moral weight as it were. A state has often to go to war to recover moral influence . . . but it is better to prevent such a result—if a state has become morally depreciated, I do not see why she should not recover her moral weight by influencing opinion in some other way than by an exercise of physical force."[359] The correction of public opinion was an even more pressing internal issue, however, than a matter of maintaining international peace. There was, Twiss argued, an even worse "system growing up" than that of

356. Twiss to Metternich, August 7, 1849, National Archives of the Czech Republic, Prague, RAM-AC/ 10/ 775, 346.

357. Twiss to Metternich, August 7, 1849, National Archives of the Czech Republic, Prague, RAM-AC/ 10/ 775, 346–347.

358. Twiss to Metternich, August 7, 1849, National Archives of the Czech Republic, Prague, RAM-AC/ 10/ 775, 348.

359. Twiss to Metternich, December 22, 1849, National Archives of the Czech Republic, Prague, RAM-AC/ 10/ 775, 450.

making war: "namely, fostering dissension at home," and such civil conflict must be "guarded against by influencing public opinion."³⁶⁰ Such influencing of public opinion was particularly necessary for the "government of a country where a representative system prevails."

Further anticipating the moral rather than the military struggle, Twiss discussed additional ways in which the minds of Hungarians could be set on the right course, apart from governing through the press. Of great importance were strong institutions, including constitutional monarchy and strong educational institutions and these two were closely tied. Reflecting upon England's own constitutional monarchy and system of public schools and universities, he advised Metternich: "What I think is this—that in states where representative institutions are being introduced, it is important that public educational institutions for the rearing of a <u>moral</u> aristocracy should exist."³⁶¹ The failure of the revolution merely underlined the need for introducing reform and representative government. But representative government depended upon a moral aristocracy and such governors could only be formed by a certain kind of education: "<u>Private</u> education will rarely produce public men. It may produce talkers or writers but not actors, or rarely so. You must learn to act well by acting your part for yourself. The art of government is better learnt than taught . . . The duties of a citizen . . . are learnt in public schools and universities."³⁶² "If Lord Aberdeen," he observed, "were to come into office tomorrow, two thirds of his cabinet would be recruited from Eton and Harrow schools."³⁶³ While Twiss's outlook remained firmly aristocratic, he argued for an aristocracy that should be formed, as he had been formed, rather than an inherited aristocracy. Such a system would not only support a representative constitution but also promote greatness.³⁶⁴

The task of reform in Hungary was heightened by the fact that the country was, in his view, still held in the grip of a feudal and oligarchical culture. "We are obliged," he argued, "to speak of Oriental feudalism when we would illustrate the constitution of the Hungarian nobles."³⁶⁵ Planning the next

---

360. Twiss to Metternich, December 22, 1849, National Archives of the Czech Republic, Prague, RAM-AC/ 10/ 775, 450.

361. Twiss to Metternich, September 5, 1849, National Archives of the Czech Republic, Prague, RAM-AC/ 10/ 775, 392.

362. Twiss to Metternich, September 5, 1849, National Archives of the Czech Republic, Prague, RAM-AC/ 10/ 775, 390.

363. Twiss to Metternich, September 5, 1849, National Archives of the Czech Republic, Prague, RAM-AC/ 10/ 775, 392.

364. "It is the interest of every state that wishes to secure the permanence of its greatness to provide for the recruitment of its <u>aristocracy</u> by its educational institutions": Twiss to Metternich, September 5, 1849, National Archives of the Czech Republic, Prague, RAM-AC/ 10/ 775, 389.

365. Twiss to Metternich, August 17, 1849, National Archives of the Czech Republic, Prague, RAM-AC/ 10/ 775, 362.

collaborative publication with the purpose of winning the moral struggle and shaping opinion public, Twiss suggested: "The utter unsuitableness of the old oligarchical system of Hungary to the exigence of modern times might be shown and the defects of its administrative and judicial systems exposed."[366] As had become apparent throughout their correspondence, neither Twiss nor Metternich believed that the state of Europe could be returned to what it had been prior to 1848, let alone to the *Ancien Régime*. "As far as I understand the old Hungarian constitution," Twiss argued, "the element of decentralisation, if one may so speak, seems to have been in excess."[367] "How and when," he asked, "did the nobles succeed in depriving (if so?) the deputies of the towns of the right of voting in the Diet? Was it always the fact that the deputies received instructions how they were to vote, and that they were never a deliberative assembly in the proper sense of the word?"[368] Clearly, he felt that representative institutions had to take the place of the oligarchical government that had prevailed. For this reason, he was ambivalent about the role played by Kossuth. On the one hand, he declared, "I rather regard Kossuth as a fanatic, and that it was his fanatical spirit that carried away the people about him."[369] At the same time, he shrank from the idea of publicly attacking Kossuth, or at least doing so in full measure: "I do not think Kossuth and Co have been treated with half the severity they deserve, but they were fools, and it is no good to call them so."[370] Similarly, he pleaded for leniency towards the rebellious Magyar aristocrats: "I should like very much to see voluntary exile substituted for imprisonment in the case of the Magyar nobles—in the way of commutation—there being some kind of mutual understanding, say foreign travel for five years ... you will perhaps smile at my importing humanitarianism into my practice, but we have to deal with a moral epidemic."[371] This plea, in August 1849, followed days after General Görgei's surrender to the Russians. The Austrian government was unmoved by appeals to clemency for Görgei's commanders, nor was it moved by the terms of the surrender which guaranteed their safety. The Austrian general Julius Jacob von Haynau hung and shot fourteen of the leaders on October 6, along with Prime Minister Lajos Batthyány and 120

---

366. Twiss to Metternich, August 7, 1849, National Archives of the Czech Republic, Prague, RAM-AC/ 10/ 775, 343.

367. Twiss to Metternich, September 19, 1849, National Archives of the Czech Republic, Prague, RAM-AC/ 10/ 775, 401.

368. Twiss to Metternich, September 19, 1849, National Archives of the Czech Republic, Prague, RAM-AC/ 10/ 775, 402.

369. Twiss to Metternich, February 17, 1850, National Archives of the Czech Republic, Prague, RAM-AC/ 10/ 776, 17.

370. Twiss to Metternich, January 16, 1850, National Archives of the Czech Republic, Prague, RAM-AC/ 10/ 776, 3.

371. Twiss to Metternich, August 22, 1849, National Archives of the Czech Republic, Prague, RAM-AC/ 10/ 775, 379.

others, as well as publicly stripping and flogging women.³⁷² The Austrian government had different notions of how to deal with the epidemic than Twiss. A further 1,500 revolutionaries were imprisoned for long periods, while Kossuth escaped.³⁷³ Twiss even went so far as to argue that Kossuth had played a positive role: "I should say that there are elements in the Magyar constitution that are worth preserving and imitating. The abolition of the ancient constitution by M. Kossuth has made innovation easy. He has indirectly served the Austrian Empire immensely, if I am not mistaken."³⁷⁴ Revolution was never a good thing, but in this instance, it had helped clear away the old order. The new order, for Twiss, would not, of course, be a democratic republic but a constitutional monarchy. Constitutional monarchies were adapted to reform, while republics were revolutionary: "It could be shown that the monarchical element has been the reforming element in all these matters, all over Europe . . . At the present time, there is a disposition to discredit monarchy as an institution, and to point to America as the land of promise, and the model state."³⁷⁵ The future of Hungary, however, would be served by monarchy "established on a firm independent basis of law."³⁷⁶

Having established the necessity of shaping public opinion and having agreed upon the diagnosis of Hungary's ills as well as a prescription for its future, Twiss set about outlining the next publication.³⁷⁷ Public opinion needed correction on the state of Hungary more than any of the other European crises.³⁷⁸ He concluded: "I cannot but think that an exceedingly careful paper might be drawn out giving accurate details as to Hungarian affairs, and passing on from facts to theories . . . I should like to discuss the Hungarian subject thoroughly in all its bearings." In August 1849, he turned seriously to the matter of research, even asking Metternich whether he should travel to Vienna "with a peep at Buda-Pesth."³⁷⁹ Metternich advised him against wandering

---

372. Knatchbull-Hugessen, *The Political Evolution of the Hungarian Nation*, Vol. 2, 131–132.

373. Rapport, *1848*, 376–377; István Deák, *The Lawful Revolution: Louis Kossuth and the Hungarians, 1848-1849* (New York, 1979); Deák, *Beyond Nationalism*, 37–38.

374. Twiss to Metternich, December 22, 1849, National Archives of the Czech Republic, Prague, RAM-AC/ 10/ 775, 453.

375. Twiss to Metternich, September 5, 1849, National Archives of the Czech Republic, Prague, RAM-AC/ 10/ 775, 395.

376. Twiss to Metternich, September 5, 1849, National Archives of the Czech Republic, Prague, RAM-AC/ 10/ 775, 396.

377. "We are rather bewildered by the mass of statements circulated and I cannot but think a publication would be opportune on the principle of *audi alteram partem* [listen to the other side]": Twiss to Metternich, August 7, 1849, National Archives of the Czech Republic, Prague, RAM-AC/ 10/ 775, 345.

378. "The European Subject of most interest upon which correct information is most needed is the real state of Hungary": Twiss to Metternich, September 10, 1849, National Archives of the Czech Republic, Prague, RAM-AC/ 10/ 775, 397–398.

379. Twiss to Metternich, August 9, 1849, National Archives of the Czech Republic, Prague, RAM-AC/ 10/ 775, 351.

into a revolution, and to stay away at least until "Comorn [Komárom] has surrendered."[380] Twiss therefore returned to his method of posing questions.[381]

Metternich responded to Twiss's requests for information with a copy of his "Aphorisms" on the matter: "Today you will receive in the post a copy of my aphorisms on the Hungarian situation at the end of 1844 which I brought with me for my private use in the form of a brochure. It was not to the public that I was speaking [in this brochure] in 1844; it was the Council of Ministers and the heads of the Hungarian conservative party to whom I addressed my impressions on this important question. If it had been my intention to address the public, I would have given the development of the argument a very different form than that which it has."[382] Despite the private nature of these insights, Metternich had decided that it was time the information became public. This brochure, Metternich declared, contained the truth about Hungary, and that truth was that it had been established as a constitutional monarchy for centuries: "The truth in relation to affairs in Hungary is contained in the following facts: a) For centuries the kingdom was placed under a constitutional regime which, like all regimes worthy of the name, was the fruit of certain laws . . . b) The Hungarian constitution was asleep during the long reign of Marie Thérèse. It was Joseph II who, after the centralisation of the Empire, in the path of liberalism, looked for progress through the philosophism of the eighteenth century which reawakened the drowsy constitutional spirit . . . 3) [*sic*.: c)] The thought of Francis I, during the whole period of his long reign, was never directed towards the abolition of the constitutional regime. It was towards practical reform and, for that matter useful, that he turned his will."[383] All these efforts to make enlightened and liberal reforms to the Empire had been set back by the French Revolution and Napoléon.[384] If

---

380. Twiss to Metternich, August 13, 1849, National Archives of the Czech Republic, Prague, RAM-AC/ 10/ 775, 351.

381. "As to Hungary, what is known as to the intentions of the Austrian ministry . . . during the life time of the Emperor Francis? What may be said or spoken of, as understood amongst the well-informed. Are there any facts which it is desirable to disclose incidentally?": Twiss to Metternich, September 29, 1849, National Archives of the Czech Republic, Prague, RAM-AC/ 10/ 775, 409.

382. Metternich to Twiss, February 25, 1850, Bibliothèque nationale de France, Fol/ R.D./13810, 115.

383. Metternich to Twiss, February 25, 1850, Bibliothèque nationale de France, Fol/ R.D./13810, 116–117.

384. "The first years following the general peace were not advantageous for the purposes of reform . . . The 22 years of struggle with the French conquerors had exhausted the public finances of the Empire . . . the truth, and all the truth, resides in the fact that the Emperors Francis and Ferdinand wanted to reform the Hungarian constitution in the path of legality and it was the opposition that accused the government of aiming to destroy the constitution . . . These, my dear Twiss, are the truths which without taking the risk of deceiving, you can support in the interests of history": Metternich to Twiss, February 25, 1850, Bibliothèque nationale de France, Fol/ R.D./13810, 117v–118v.

insufficient progress had been made, it was not because the rulers of the Austrian Empire lacked the will for reform; it was because they lacked the means.

Turning from a discussion of the internal reforms necessary to Hungary, Twiss suggested that his article would also return to the necessity of the Austrian Empire to European stability: "This might be discussed in relation to Germany, Lombardy, and Hungary."[385] It would argue, moreover, for "the impossibility of any system but a confederation." Such an empire would fill the "necessity of a power to counterbalance France," while pointing to "the impracticability of a Magyar-Slavonian state; the suicidal results of independence surrounded by more powerful states." From October, Twiss worked steadily on the article, abandoning a trip to Normandy to maintain the progress, and drafts passed back and forth between London and Brussels, where Metternich now resided.[386] By late October, he had produced an outline of the chapters that resembled the final work.[387] In January, he sent a copy of the article asking Metternich if he could "run your eye over the pages" in order to point out "errors of statement."[388] At the same time, he noted, "About one fifth of the original article has been excerpted by Mr Lockhardt, very judiciously, being materials interesting to those already acquainted with the constitution of Hungary rather than to the general reader."[389] The editors of the *Quarterly Review* were apparently having doubts about whether Twiss and Metternich's writings would appeal to a broad audience. Those concerns were confirmed by April 1850, when Twiss announced that John Murray had decided not to publish the article in the journal but to issue it as a separate pamphlet: "'The article on Hungary' is appearing as a pamphlet published by Mr Murray 'Hungary: Its constitution and its catastrophe by Corvinus.'" Murray's enthusiasm for the cause, however, appeared to be undiminished, as he had published the pamphlet "at his own expense."[390] The license of publishing it outside the journal allowed Twiss to expand the discussion to 100 pages: "It will be fuller

---

385. "The idea has passed through my mind that the subject which required to be treated might be stated thus. 'The maintenance of the Austrian Empire in its existing integrity is a European necessity.'": Twiss to Metternich, August 29, 1849, National Archives of the Czech Republic, Prague, RAM-AC/ 10/ 775, 382.

386. "You will receive enclosed with this note a sketch of the mode of treating the question, as at present proposed, numbered according to divisions, which seem convenient": Twiss to Metternich, October 13, 1849, National Archives of the Czech Republic, Prague, RAM-AC/ 10/ 775, 434.

387. Twiss to Metternich, October 13, 1849, National Archives of the Czech Republic, Prague, RAM-AC/ 10/ 775, 438.

388. Twiss to Metternich, January 16, 1850, National Archives of the Czech Republic, Prague, RAM-AC/ 10/ 776, 3.

389. Twiss to Metternich, January 16, 1850, National Archives of the Czech Republic, Prague, RAM-AC/ 10/ 776, 2.

390. Twiss to Metternich, undated, 1850, National Archives of the Czech Republic, Prague, RAM-AC/ 10/ 776, 118.

both in the legal part and in the political narrative. They thought it was not quite amusing enough for ordinary readers—and perhaps they know the class of reader whom the circulation depends upon . . . What the reviews like is a fair allowance of <u>personality</u> which I cannot indulge in."[391]

The reviews would prove to be a disappointment, but Twiss was not prepared to leave the reception of the pamphlet entirely to reviewers. He suggested to Metternich that "I shall buy about 50," while Murray would distribute between thirty and fifty for free, to journals but also "to Peers and MPs."[392] "If we can only correct public opinion in England," he reasoned, "it will have a great effect on the Continent through the House of Commons." In addition to having the pamphlet "noticed in some of the papers," he would employ "private recommendation in Society." On top of these efforts within England, he would send copies to Copenhagen, Berlin, Paris, and Vienna.[393] Such promotion was partly hampered by publishing anonymously, and Twiss clearly had some regrets about that decision. "If the pamphlet should be attacked," he mused, "I should probably attach my name to a second edition." He justified the decision to write anonymously, however, in the vaguest terms: "It was a rather <u>small</u> affair, and there were some reasons why it should appear as it does now."[394] The pamphlet would indeed be attacked, but no second edition would appear.

The anonymous pamphlet *Hungary: Its Constitution and Its Catastrophe* was the last of the publications to come from the collaboration with Metternich.[395] The tract moved systematically through the topics Twiss and Metternich had discussed over the previous twelve months of correspondence: namely, the Hungarian constitution and its laws, the role of the Diet and the crown, a narrative of Hungary's recent history, and an account of the revolution. Twiss denounced the "Magyar" revolution as having been based upon the false premise of an ancient Hungarian constitution. The nation which the revolutionaries claimed to champion had no legal or constitutional basis. Moreover, Twiss pointed out that, while arguing for universal suffrage and emancipation, the revolutionaries appealed to a past that was profoundly

---

391. Twiss to Metternich, April 1, 1850, National Archives of the Czech Republic, Prague, RAM-AC/ 10/ 776, 26–27.

392. Twiss to Metternich, undated, 1850, National Archives of the Czech Republic, Prague, RAM-AC/ 10/ 776, 118–119.

393. Twiss to Metternich, undated, 1850, National Archives of the Czech Republic, Prague, RAM-AC/ 10/ 776, 119–120.

394. Twiss to Metternich, undated, 1850, National Archives of the Czech Republic, Prague, RAM-AC/ 10/ 776, 120.

395. Corvinus [Travers Twiss], *Hungary: Its Constitution and Its Catastrophe* (London: John Murray, 1850). For the mid-April publication, see Twiss to Metternich, April 15, 1850, National Archives of the Czech Republic, Prague, RAM-AC/ 10/ 776, 42.

feudal. He again used his historical methodology, and archival material provided through Metternich's good offices, to make his case, arguing that all historical attempts to establish Hungary separately from Austria had resulted in disaster. Without the Austrian Empire, he concluded, all the nations who inhabited central Europe would be in a permanent war of all against all—not merely a "series of civil wars" but a "warfare of extermination"—because no one nation was sufficiently powerful to "impose its supremacy."[396]

American historian Robert Carter, an admirer of the Hungarian revolution, wrote with some justification, in 1852, that this anonymous work was written by an "Austrian agent" or "paid advocate of Metternich."[397] Reviews of the tract in the press were mixed. The *Evening Standard* described it as "ample and interesting," but at the same time it was "Austrian all over."[398] *The Times*, which Twiss did not trust, was more generous, taking a position on the conflict that was entirely in sympathy with the Austrian Empire. The reviewer, without naming Twiss, revealed that his identity was not a well-guarded secret: "a pamphlet . . . which bears the *nom de guerre* of 'Corvinus' but which is generally attributed to the pen of an accomplished civilian, who has, on several former occasions, elucidated the legal bearings of some important questions of foreign policy."[399] It was necessary, the reviewer continued, to distinguish between "the cause of practical reform in Hungary" and the "fury of a revolution" which had "plunged the nation into the horrors of civil war and foreign invasion." At the same time, the reviewer agreed with Twiss that the revolutionaries mounted their claims upon a national past that was based upon "laws so effete, institutions so perplexing, liberties so exclusive" while at the same time overturning the same constitution. On the other hand, in a review covering three pages, the *Examiner*, a Radical weekly, condemned Twiss's pamphlet in the strongest terms: "This pamphlet is a piece of pretentious and very paltry special pleading . . . it contains so strange an assemblage of erroneous statements, confused dates, and most sophistical arguments, that had it not been made the groundwork of some very unfair remarks in *The Times*, we should not have thought it worthy even a passing notice."[400] "For the martyrs of this holy cause," the reviewer lamented, "*The Times* has not one word of sympathy; for their murderers, not one word of blame." "Men of peace and order," the *Examiner* argued, rejoiced at the failure of the revolution in Hungary as "the fall of disorder

---

396. Corvinus [Twiss], *Hungary*, 89–91.

397. Robert Carter, *The Hungarian Controversy: An Exposure of the Falsifications and Perversions of the Slanderers of Hungary* (Boston, 1852), 25.

398. "Hungary: Its Constitution and Its Catastrophe," *London Evening Standard*, May 2, 1850, 3.

399. "Review," *The Times*, April 20, 1850, 5.

400. "The Literary Examiner," *The Examiner*, May 4, 1850, 276.

and social ruin." The revolutionaries themselves had been partly to blame for such fears because they had "injudiciously" sought sympathy from "every shade of political opinion, no matter how red."[401] Nevertheless, the fears had been groundless, and the Magyars had proved their "peaceable, orderly, moderate tendency." *The Times*, however, as "the organ of the monied interest," took the side "most likely to please its friends," in this case Twiss. *The Times* and Corvinus cheered on the "bloodhounds to a slaughter from which the Russians themselves have turned away with horror and disgust; and iniquities that revolted even the barbarous hordes of [Tsar] Nicholas."[402] The *London Daily News*, also a Radical newspaper, was similarly trenchant and concluded that "Corvinus" must be a disreputable English writer who had been recruited by Austrian agents: "Here we see Austrian agents come over to England, to enlist writers in the defense of Austria, furnishing them with dates and figures of doubtful correctness. These are accepted as truths by correspondents of the illiberal press ... But respectable writers naturally decline to lend their name to such assertions. Such publications ... are either anonymous or presented to the public under a borrowed name."[403] The critic rightly understood Twiss's strategy of appropriating liberal rhetoric in order to advance a conservative cause: "All the publications of this kind bear, of course, the appearance of liberalism, of moderation, and of fairness; but to look into them is to detect at once their inspiration and their purpose." The review also pointed out that Twiss's aim was to show that the Magyar revolution "was not a movement in defence of the ancient constitution of Hungary" and dismissed this notion as tantamount to claiming that the Reform Bill and free trade had "abrogated the Ancient Constitution in England."[404]

Twiss duly forwarded the reviews to Metternich.[405] Unworried by the trenchant tone, or wishing to seem so, he treated their views as predictable. "The Examiner amused me very much," he wrote, while "the Economist notices Corvinus somewhat adversely, as was to be expected."[406] On the other hand, he alluded to unpublished reports which were more positive: "Corvinus has reached the highest quarters and been read with much satisfaction. If I could see you, I could say more." The mysterious tone was consistent with much of the correspondence while Metternich was in Brussels.

401. "The Literary Examiner," *The Examiner*, May 4, 1850, 277.
402. "The Literary Examiner," *The Examiner*, May 4, 1850, 278.
403. "Literature," *London Daily News*, May 16, 1850, 2.
404. "Literature," *London Daily News*, May 16, 1850, 2.
405. Twiss to Metternich, May 9, 1850, National Archives of the Czech Republic, Prague, RAM-AC/ 10/ 776, 63.
406. Twiss to Metternich, May 9, 1850, National Archives of the Czech Republic, Prague, RAM-AC/ 10/ 776, 64.

The Coup d'État in France

Twiss and Metternich had not been corresponding when the initial revolution occurred in France in March 1848—it had been the fallout from those events that had led to Metternich's own flight from Vienna. They had regularly exchanged views, in retrospect, on various manifestations of the instability and untrustworthiness of France, but we have no record of their thoughts as the events unfolded. Such was not the case, however, for Louis-Napoléon's *coup d'état* in December 1851.[407] Throughout 1851, Twiss and Metternich became increasingly concerned with matters in France, and for Twiss, in that year only the matter of Pope Pius's creation of territorial sees for Catholic bishops in England loomed as a more important issue. Two salient points emerge from that correspondence. First, that the republic, at least as it was constituted in 1848, was an unstable form of constitution and the expanded (male) franchise contributed to that instability. Second, the instability in France provided an occasion to discuss the best form of a constitution.

As early as January 1851, it was clear that the situation in France was temporary. Metternich somberly observed: "France today is before something and that thing, whatever it is, is a dream and not an order of things resting on a foundation that could provide stability. Disorder reigns where that foundation contains faults and a great state like France cannot become prey [*proie*, i.e., prey to others] without menacing order in all other states."[408] Disorder in France threatened instability throughout Europe, as it had after the first revolution. Twiss pointed to the broader ideological instability: "Nothing gives me so helpless an idea of France than the writings of so many persons clearly hostile to the provisional state of things, although to what party they belong is not clear." These persons "criticise the critics of the *ancien régime* . . . In their view all the institutions of modern times are false."[409] Twiss was not referring to the writings of radicals or socialists, such as Pierre-Joseph Prouhdon, who was particularly active in journalism during the Second Republic. Rather he had been reading the *Lettres de Beauséant*, by Baron de Syon, and Auguste Romieu's *L'ère des Césars*. Syon was a follower of Joseph de Maistre's doctrines of absolute monarchy.[410] His treatise was described at the time it was published as "the declared enemy of all that is called liberalism." He was said to "detest all revolutions, the old and the new, that of 1789 like that of 1848, he would not even pardon the American Revolution," and he cautioned, in

---

407. For the *coup d'état*, see Sperber, *The European Revolutions, 1848-1851*, 238.
408. Metternich to Twiss, January 31, 1851, Bibliothèque nationale de France, Fol/ R.D./13810, 122-122v.
409. Twiss to Metternich, March 10, 1851, National Archives of the Czech Republic, Prague, RAM-AC/ 10/ 777, 42.
410. Baron de Syon, *Lettres de Beauséant* (Geneva, 1849).

particular, against the danger of taking liberalism in "small doses."[411] He particularly detested Pope Pius IX due to his flirtation with liberal ideas. In *L'ère des Césars*, published during the Second Republic, Romieu proposed the cure for the illness of liberalism: namely, "Caesarism," or the substitution of a lifelong monarch for constitutional government.[412] He would prove to be a strong supporter of Louis-Napoléon's *coup d'état* a year after his treatise was published.

Although himself a critic of liberal ideas, Twiss rejected these theorists of absolutism. "These writers," he argued, "seem to me to indulge in half-truths quite as much as their predecessors."[413] He argued, instead, for constitutional decorum: "A Republic may be an excellent form of government for people who are suitable for such a form—just as an aristocracy when the elements are aristocratical, or an absolute monarchy when such a government is needed. The blunder is to apply the wrong form to the wrong people. The great work for writers who profess to treat the science of politics" is to show to a community "what is the kind of government which is suitable to its political condition."[414] Naturally, he believed that constitutional monarchy was most suited to the English, while the further one travelled east, the more absolutism was appropriate. Importantly, he believed that there was a monarchical element in all government: namely, the executive, or the class he at times described as "mandarins," a class to which he belonged. "That the executive in every form," he noted, "is necessarily monarchical is a very important fact. Deliberation may be the work of one or several, but execution is necessarily the work of one."[415]

Republics were appropriate perhaps in America, and for the ancient Romans, but not for modern Europeans, and certainly not for the French, who struggled to establish a republic against their own selfish nature: "How is it that in certain countries there are efforts '*contra naturam*' whilst others pursue the natural tendency of their condition, and endeavour to perfect it? And if nations once get wrong in their ideas, what is the remedy?"[416] The Enlightenment ideal of perfectibility would be met by each people realising their own particular potential. In an account that was strongly reminiscent

---

411. *Revue des deux mondes*, vol. 6 (London, 1842), 561.

412. Auguste Romieu, *L'ère des Césars* 2nd ed. (Paris, 1850); *Revue des deux mondes*, vol. 7 (1850), 919. For Romieu, see Maurice Agulhon, *The Republican Experiment, 1848–1852*, trans. Janet Lloyd (Cambridge, 1983), 103.

413. Twiss to Metternich, March 10, 1851, National Archives of the Czech Republic, Prague, RAM-AC/ 10/ 777, 42.

414. Twiss to Metternich, March 10, 1851, National Archives of the Czech Republic, Prague, RAM-AC/ 10/ 777, 42-43.

415. Twiss to Metternich, March 10, 1851, National Archives of the Czech Republic, Prague, RAM-AC/ 10/ 777, 43.

416. Twiss to Metternich, May 8, 1851, National Archives of the Czech Republic, Prague, RAM-AC/ 10/ 777, 68.

of Alexis de Tocqueville's *Democracy in America* (which had been translated from French by Twiss's good friend Henry Reeve, who was himself a friend of Tocqueville), but no doubt reliant also on his own classical education, Twiss argued that republicanism rested upon a rejection of individualism and selfishness, a certain martial austerity, and sociability, none of which were to be found in Europe, and particularly not in France: "For instance, if a Frenchman can be led to imagine himself suited to be the citizen of a republic, and a republican form of government to be suited to the French people, when the characteristics of the individual Frenchman, of French Society, are utterly at variance with the homeliness and unselfishness of the true republican, his personal respect for his neighbour, his simple tastes, his pure morals, etc what shall undeceive him?"[417] The French had pursued a republic in 1848 as much as in 1789, therefore, because they had been deceived not only about their true nature but also about the purpose of doing so: "If on the other hand, the cry for a republic has only been a sham, set up against an existing monarch or his minister for a temporary purpose, they have probably embarked in Charon's boat [crossing the Styx to Hades] without stipulating that they shall be ferried back from Tartarus."[418]

France would have to find a new political path. The republic would fail, and the country would need to turn to an alternative, and real, political culture. As he had argued for both England and Austria, Twiss believed that this culture was to be found in sub-state institutions: "I believe the true political remedy is to be found in local institutions. They give employment to the active and ambitious. They are media of political education and they become in time the roots of the state system, and keep it from being swayed to and fro, or torn up."[419] He saw no opposition between the strength of the state and the flourishing of local politics and local corporations—indeed, this relationship underpinned his enthusiasm for federal systems such as Austria—but he insisted that such corporations should be under the control of the state. The French need only look to Belgium to see how a state could be maintained through its sub-state institutions: "I was talking with M. Van der Weyer [Sylvain Van der Weyer, Belgian plenipotentiary to Britain] the other day about his country, and he seemed to attribute its continued political existence as a state to its local institutions, the traditions of the Burgundian period, which resisted even Napoléon's strong will successfully."[420]

417. Twiss to Metternich, May 8, 1851, National Archives of the Czech Republic, Prague, RAM-AC/ 10/ 777, 68–69.
418. Twiss to Metternich, May 8, 1851, National Archives of the Czech Republic, Prague, RAM-AC/ 10/ 777, 69.
419. Twiss to Metternich, May 8, 1851, National Archives of the Czech Republic, Prague, RAM-AC/ 10/ 777, 69.
420. Twiss to Metternich, May 8, 1851, National Archives of the Czech Republic, Prague, RAM-AC/ 10/ 777, 69.

Such a culture could not flourish, however, without stability, and establishing the conditions for stability was the first task at hand: "The first political desideratum for France appears to be a settled form of government. It is not of so much importance that it shall be any one form, as that it should be settled, because until the principle of permanence triumphs over that of change, the best form risks being succeeded by the worst. Uncertainty is fatal to the continued existence of a state."[421] Following this logic, he effectively anticipated the *coup d'état* that would come within months, and he regarded that event as a necessity: "For this reason I think it best for France if the President's tenure of office should be renewed. Then we come to a President for life—then to a hereditary crown. The natural order would be the only safe one."[422] Louis-Napoléon's problem was that the constitution prohibited the re-election of the President.[423] When he seized power on December 2, replacing himself as President as a new emperor (although not named as such for another year), Twiss could barely restrain himself from declaring "I told you so!" He wrote of his frustration at having to "regard the events from afar" but also, as a consequence, of his intention to travel to France at the earliest moment and spend "*dix jours à Paris*" in order to observe.[424] He had been there only two months earlier and said, "I was well persuaded in October, in speaking with many French people in Paris [while staying at the Hôtel Meurice], that the social question would prevail over the political question." Again, therefore, he saw the struggle as one that was more concerned with class than "politics," as he understood that term: that is, a material struggle rather than a struggle over ideas. "Everybody," he reported, "waited for a forceful blow [*coup de force*], and many hoped for one, but where it would come from nobody knew."[425] Although he claimed that the crisis was "social" rather than "political," he nevertheless pointed to the inherent weaknesses in the constitution of the Second Republic, asking how the Council of State could deny the right to the Assembly to make law if sovereignty rested with the Assembly—"it was a silliness to suppose that the sovereign would recognise a superior." "*Voilà une impasse!*," he exclaimed, and of course the only means of breaking the impasse would be through a *coup d'état*: "How else to exit the situation other than through

---

421. Twiss to Metternich, June 6, 1851, National Archives of the Czech Republic, Prague, RAM-AC/ 10/ 777, 76.

422. Twiss to Metternich, June 6, 1851, National Archives of the Czech Republic, Prague, RAM-AC/ 10/ 777, 76.

423. For the *coup d'état*, see Agulhon, *The Republican Experiment, 1848–1852*, 138–165; Sperber, *The European Revolutions, 1848-1851*, 238.

424. Twiss to Metternich, December 19, 1851, National Archives of the Czech Republic, Prague, RAM-AC/ 10/ 777, 88.

425. Twiss to Metternich, December 19, 1851, National Archives of the Czech Republic, Prague, RAM-AC/ 10/ 777, 88.

the use of force?"[426] He was so fascinated with this political drama that, two months later, he again visited Paris to witness it firsthand. The visit confirmed his view that force had been necessary and showed that Twiss, for all his convictions on the rule of law, was as prepared as Metternich to countenance the logic of *raison d'état*: "I passed a fortnight at Paris and saw a great variety of leaders of political parties, and my conviction remained unchanged, that the *coup d'état* was under the circumstances a political necessity—it was the legitimate conclusion of another act of the revolutionary drama which France is content to exhibit to Europe."[427]

Louis-Napoléon's success gave Twiss several occasions on which to muse on the politics of necessity, which was justified by the priority of the needs of the state and a stable order, above all other political needs. He was ambivalent about Louis-Napoléon, admiring his cunning but condemning his "vulgarity." "The skill and address," he wrote, with which the coup "has been carried out led me to think that L.N. [Louis-Napoléon] himself, or some of his advisers, understand what they were about." He was not troubled by Louis-Napoléon's curtailment of the powers of the National Assembly: "Nor do I quarrel with the opinion of L.N. which he has maintained against every minister about him, that the Parliamentary system is not suited to France, certainly not to the France of today, possibly not to the France of the morrow, because the political organisation of the country has been carried out on monarchical principles, and the source of life is in the centre."[428] The new emperor's measures were justified by the need to maintain order: "It was the return of the 'Champion' of public order in a tournament against the giant of socialism."[429]

At the same time, Twiss was critical of Louis-Napoléon's vulgarity, particularly when he first came to power: "Since L.N. has come into power, my conviction increases that he has undertaken a task for which he is not suited" . . . he "has compromised his duty for his interest."[430] His attempt to undo measures enacted by Louis-Philippe and the Orléans regime was "one of the common blunders of vulgar minds." Notably, while it may have been "impolitic to allow Pretenders to the throne to possess large estates in France, the proceeding to divest them should have been otherwise regulated so as to have the appearance of a state measure,

---

426. Twiss to Metternich, December 19, 1851, National Archives of the Czech Republic, Prague, RAM-AC/ 10/ 777, 89.

427. Twiss to Metternich, March 3, 1852, National Archives of the Czech Republic, Prague, RAM-AC/ 10/ 778, 2.

428. Twiss to Metternich, March 3, 1852, National Archives of the Czech Republic, Prague, RAM-AC/ 10/ 778, 2–3.

429. Twiss to Metternich, October 19, 1852, National Archives of the Czech Republic, Prague, RAM-AC/ 10/ 778, 25.

430. Twiss to Metternich, March 3, 1852, National Archives of the Czech Republic, Prague, RAM-AC/ 10/ 778, 3.

than an act of personal vengeance."⁴³¹ He summarised Louis-Napoléon's character in such terms: "L.N. seems to me to be essentially a vulgar mind."⁴³²

At times, he grudgingly admired the emperor: "What of Napoléon III? 'The number of the Beast' in the Apocalypse!"⁴³³ He admired his Machiavellian qualities. It did not particularly trouble Louis-Napoléon that he did not "consult his ministers, to know their advice, but solely to clarify his own thoughts," while at the same time he could write admiringly, "But he walks step by step, looks everywhere, and knows how to seize his occasion."⁴³⁴ And he even found in Louis-Napoléon's reforms some ideas that reflected his own concern with local institutions: "Without doubt the head of state [L.N.] has qualities for that task [bringing order back] that could bring success. What he says is true, that liberty is a child of civil institutions."⁴³⁵ At this point, in 1853, Twiss was prepared to concede that Louis-Napoléon had proved to be a stabilising force in France, and therefore he judged his rule positively, despite the emperor's tendency to leave the rails: "At present we have strong governments . . . but we doubt the success of those governments because they employ physical force, but how can we regain moral strength after a physical conflict if not with physical force . . . For most people it is success which justifies the enterprise. The revolution succeeded in a manner for the moment . . . the order of government has succeeded similarly for the moment . . . and if I was the Director of the Grand Company of European Nations, I would keep L.N. in his part" despite the fact that he is an "engine-driver of a locomotive which has left the rails several times."⁴³⁶ He qualified this judgement, however, with the observation that "the remedy will be found in the duration of the order of things. It is the between-acts that comes to terminate." In the final act, as we shall see, he would change his view.

The Crimean War

The admiration that Twiss held for strong governments that employ force may be an unsurprising sentiment from a conservative after the 1848 revolutions, but it was not in step with the political climate in Britain in the 1850s, and

---

431. Twiss to Metternich, March 3, 1852, National Archives of the Czech Republic, Prague, RAM-AC/ 10/ 778, 3.

432. Twiss to Metternich, March 3, 1852, National Archives of the Czech Republic, Prague, RAM-AC/ 10/ 778, 12.

433. Twiss to Metternich, November 29, 1852, National Archives of the Czech Republic, Prague, RAM-AC/ 10/ 778, 30.

434. Twiss to Metternich, October 19, 1852, National Archives of the Czech Republic, Prague, RAM-AC/ 10/ 778, 26.

435. Twiss to Metternich, February 22, 1853, National Archives of the Czech Republic, Prague, RAM-AC/ 10/ 779, 3.

436. Twiss to Metternich, March 7, 1853, National Archives of the Czech Republic, Prague, RAM-AC/ 10/ 779, 12–13.

particularly not with British attitudes to European governments. The mood was against autocracy, and British policy was understood in terms of the need to protect liberalism and constitutional government.[437] Russia, in particular, came under suspicion, but the Austrian Empire was also not perceived warmly, and relations between Twiss and Metternich were placed under the strain. In a phrase that Metternich heavily underlined in red, Twiss wrote: "<u>I greatly regret that Austria and England . . . do not walk together.</u>"[438] At the same time that Twiss expressed the "hope that the alliance between Austria and England will be once again repaired," he placed much of the blame for the deterioration upon his own country: "The insular spirit is very susceptible."[439] A "deus ex machina" would be needed, he said, to bring the countries back together. A *deus ex machina* arrived within months: namely, the Crimean War.[440] Although it did not restore relations, it did bring Austria, which remained neutral in the conflict, closer to England than to Russia.[441] If the war had a rationale, it was to maintain the existing balance of powers; a cause in which Twiss had always enlisted, albeit in this instance, with growing doubts about the necessity of violence to achieve that end.

The war was provoked by the perception of the Ottoman Empire as the "sick man of Europe," an empire in the process of weakening and breaking up, raising the question of which of the great powers would move into the vacuum.[442] Russia, in particular, sought to spread its influence into the Balkans and used the pretext of protecting Orthodox Christians as the means of occupying Ottoman territory north of the Danube. The French and British sought to maintain the Ottoman Empire in its position, fearing that Russian influence could be extended south and effect trade to the East.[443] Although the Suez Canal had not yet been built, plans for a canal were already taking form. The Russians did not occupy Moldavia and Walachia until July 1853, but already in March it was apparent to Twiss and Metternich that war was brewing. Twiss certainly shared the perception that the Ottoman Empire was

---

437. Müller, *Britain and the German Question*, 159–163; Parry, *The Politics of Patriotism*, 214–215.

438. Twiss to Metternich, March 7, 1853, National Archives of the Czech Republic, Prague, RAM-AC/ 10/ 779, 13.

439. Twiss to Metternich, March 7, 1853, National Archives of the Czech Republic, Prague, RAM-AC/ 10/ 779, 8–9.

440. For background to the war, see Andrew Lambert, *The Crimean War: British Grand Strategy against Russia, 1853–1856*, 2nd ed. (London, 2011); Trudi Tate, *The Crimean War* (London, 2018), 13–48.

441. See Lambert, *The Crimean War*, 347–348, on Austrian neutrality as one of the four British aims in pursuing the war; and Deák, *Beyond Nationalism*, 43, on the divisions and tensions that the "blatant act of ingratitude" towards Russia caused within Austria.

442. Parry, *The Politics of Patriotism*, 211–219.

443. Robinson and Gallagher with Denny, *Africa and the Victorians*, 78–79.

failing, but he also shared the view that it must be maintained: "Turkey will be politically bankrupt, after having become commercially bankrupt," but "giving my opinion, I believe Turkey is still a political necessity for Europe."[444] A year later, during the war, he repeated this portrayal of a corrupt empire, but with even greater pessimism about the necessity of keeping it in place: "What will be the dénouement of the Gordian knot that we call the 'The Turkish Question'? I am not speaking of the situation of the day [the war] but of the destiny of the Tartar race who occupy the Golden Horn and who remain there simply because they are there. They are without roots, they dominate the trees which have roots, like a parasitical plant which we cannot uproot without uprooting the trees themselves."[445]

When the war had drawn to a close two years later, Metternich concurred: "Peace is made my dear Twiss. Is the pause equally assured? I have some scruples on that important subject. Two problems survive what the governments have stopped in a spirit of reason and wisdom, and those problems weigh upon the social body. One of the problems is a consequence of the irrefutable incapacity of states confessing Islamism to conduct themselves according to the moral rules [*règles morales*] of Chistianism."[446] Metternich believed that Ottoman power was a necessity with which European states must deal—a belief he had held since he unsuccessfully attempted to persuade Mahmud II to participate in the Congress of Vienna—but his understanding of Islam placed severe limits upon the participation of Muslim powers in the society of nations.[447] At this moment, he wrote again to Twiss on the question: "I am writing to you today about a brochure that has just appeared here. The author is a Serb and, given his origin, is not at all in favour of the Ottoman power. His work also does not have a character other than a glance cast over the anomalies that are the consequence of ideas that carry the desires of liberal reforms, not at all applicable to Muslim society, very good without any doubt for societies established upon the foundations which all Christian societies rest upon, but incompatible with the law, at the same time religious and political, upon which Islamism is governed. Please familiarise yourself with the work, written in the spirit of truth, it is worthy of respect."[448] Islam, there-

---

444. Twiss to Metternich, March 7, 1853, National Archives of the Czech Republic, Prague, RAM-AC/ 10/ 779, 15.

445. Twiss to Metternich, February 7, 1854, National Archives of the Czech Republic, Prague, RAM-AC/ 10/ 780, 5.

446. Metternich to Twiss, Vienna, April 20, 1856, Bibliothèque nationale de France, Fol/ R.D./13810, 134v.

447. On Metternich and the Ottomans at the Congress of Vienna, see Šedivý, *Metternich*, 41–43.

448. Metternich to Twiss, Vienna, April 7, 1856, Bibliothèque nationale de France, Fol/ R.D./13810, 129v–130v.

fore, was incapable of liberal reform.[449] From Metternich's perspective, this was not a particularly damning characteristic, but it nevertheless meant, he argued, that Muslim societies were governed by different laws from Christian societies, and he had stated many times that only Christianity provided the rules upon which a stable international order could be established. He was forced, therefore, to conclude that he could learn nothing from the Serbian author of this particular pamphlet: "I can frankly assure you that everything he presents as facts teaches nothing to me; I, who during a half century, dedicated myself to the duty of studying the Ottoman position and who the Sultan Mahmud [Mahmud II] believed to be a subject influenced by the spirit of the Prophet. It will be otherwise with respect to this publicist [the Serbian author], who is without doubt animated by excellent intentions but without care to understand what is Islamism."[450] Despite Metternich's satisfaction with the idea that he was moved by the Prophet, his and Twiss's scepticism of Muslim culture might lead one to conclude that Twiss would argue against the membership of Muslim societies in the society of nations. For Metternich, it was clear that the *ius publicum* which governed the Concert of Europe was the *ius publicum Europaeum*. He did not include Ottoman Europe within that system. If, however, it had been desirable to bring the Ottomans into the Concert of Europe, it would be necessary to reconcile their purported cultural incapacity to deal with the Christian European legal order with the reality of their power. This is a question which would become increasingly central to Twiss's thought over the coming decades, even while he held a similarly disdainful view of non-European societies. He argued that the Ottoman Empire's signing of the Treaty of Paris in 1856 was an important step in the expansion of international society beyond Western Europe to include what he described as "Oriental" nations. But the conundrum of how to reconcile legal equality with cultural inferiority persisted. This problem, with which Metternich had struggled since 1813, would remain central to Twiss's thought into the 1870s and '80s, when he believed he had arrived at a solution.

Twiss was also sceptical of the ideological claims used to justify the war, particularly the religious claims advanced by the Russians. After the ideological war of 1848, he was shocked to discover that religious war was still possible: "But what a curious thing," he observed. "After a struggle between order and anarchy, between belief and unbelief . . . we see the religions of the orient and the occident . . . fighting in the name of faith which teaches

---

449. On the hardening of European attitudes about Islam and reform over the course of the nineteenth century, even while Muslim elites continued in the pursuit of modernisation, see Aydin, *The Idea of the Muslim World*, 43–50, and on Metternich, 48.

450. Metternich to Twiss, Vienna, April 7, 1856, Bibliothèque nationale de France, Fol/R.D./13810, 130v.

universal peace."⁴⁵¹ Moreover, the particular kind of religious war in this instance recalled the Crusades. He wrote that "everybody here is for peace, but not for peace at any price," and if peace failed, "we return to the Crusades."⁴⁵² Six months later, he repeated his surprise, and emphasised his sense that such religious wars were more dangerous than the nationalist and class wars of 1848: "It is strange [*drôle*] to have a war of religion in the year 1853, after the events of 1848. It is yet another episode and almost more dangerous than one of irreligious anarchy."⁴⁵³ He would come to the view, however, that there were links between the two events.

As always, Twiss and Metternich employed several sources of information on the war, apart from the newspapers, including their political contacts, as well as other interested parties, such as the journalist Henry Reeve. Reeve wrote regularly for *The Times*, and he was close to many leading English and French intellectuals and politicians, including John Stuart Mill, François Guizot, and Alexis de Tocqueville, and in 1855, he became the editor of the *Edinburgh Review*.⁴⁵⁴ He was also a friend of Twiss and, as we have seen, one of his regular dining companions. In September 1853, just weeks before the Ottomans declared war upon Russia, Reeve travelled to Constantinople to examine the situation at close quarters. He was to travel through Vienna on his way home from Constantinople, and Twiss wrote to Metternich to tell him that he had given Reeve a letter of introduction in order that he might visit Metternich and provide him with the latest news on the brewing conflict.⁴⁵⁵ Importantly, Twiss noted, Reeve was a friend to Austria: "He is one of our most distinguished writers on foreign affairs, and has done great service to Austria in the Hungarian question . . . with a pen that influences public opinion in England more effectively than any other. He is a contributor to the Q.R . . . and although he looks at matters with a more English eye than I do myself, and with a view to English interests, yet he is very fair and just."⁴⁵⁶ Reeve also shared the generally pessimistic perception of the Ottoman Empire that

---

451. Twiss to Metternich, June 28, 1853, National Archives of the Czech Republic, Prague, RAM-AC/ 10/ 779, 17.

452. Twiss to Metternich, June 28, 1853, National Archives of the Czech Republic, Prague, RAM-AC/ 10/ 779, 18.

453. Twiss to Metternich, November 15, 1853, National Archives of the Czech Republic, Prague, RAM-AC/ 10/ 779, 35.

454. On the role of *The Times* in reporting on the war, and in mythologizing as well as presenting itself as the face of public opinion, see Tate, *The Crimean War*, 3–5.

455. "Had I been free I should have endeavoured to accompany a friend Mr Henry Reeve of Chester Square who will present this note to your Highness, on a visit to Constantinople, returning by way of Vienna": Twiss to Metternich, September 4, 1853, National Archives of the Czech Republic, Prague, RAM-AC/ 10/ 779, 25.

456. Twiss to Metternich, September 4, 1853, National Archives of the Czech Republic, Prague, RAM-AC/ 10/ 779, 26–27.

prevailed at the time.[457] Most importantly, however, Reeve would provide news of the latest developments: "As he is on his way home, and is likely to have observed many things carefully at Constantinople, he will be able to give your Highness some account of matters there."[458] Reeve duly arrived in Vienna and wrote to Metternich to request a meeting, while announcing that he had a letter of introduction from Twiss.[459] He wrote in his journal after the meeting: "Greatly gratified by a long conversation with Prince Metternich, who, at eighty-one, is the most extraordinary of living personages."[460] He visited Metternich again, in 1857, in his Schloss Johannisberg, on the Rhine. On that occasion, Metternich expressed his frustration at being unable to help Britain suppress the Indian Rebellion. "Nothing could be more friendly and amiable than his manner," Reeve wrote, and as they walked around the castle grounds "the remembrance of his celebrated conversations with Napoléon and all the great men of this age crossed my mind." On the opposite bank, "a crowd of tourists were come to see the view; but when they saw the old prince pacing up and down in front of his castle, their eyes turned from the Rhine and were riveted on him as if Charlemagne himself had stood before them."[461]

With well-informed sources such as Reeve, throughout the course of the war and during its build-up, Twiss and Metternich exchanged comments on the developments, although Metternich, as we shall see, was more circumspect. A month before the Russian occupation north of the Danube, Twiss wrote that tensions between Russia and the Ottomans had reached a point "neither of peace, nor of war necessarily, but an indefinite and abnormal state of things."[462] A week after the Ottomans declared war on the Russians, he regretted: "It is unfortunate that affairs have arrived at an impasse . . . There

---

457. "The Eastern question is one of which the importance will increase. H.R. [Henry Reeve] thinks Turkey cannot be maintained": Twiss to Metternich, September 4, 1853, National Archives of the Czech Republic, Prague, RAM-AC/ 10/ 779, 27–28.

458. Twiss to Metternich, September 4, 1853, National Archives of the Czech Republic, Prague, RAM-AC/ 10/ 779, 27–28.

459. Henry Reeve to Metternich, Vienne, October 28, 1853, National Archives of the Czech Republic, Prague, RAM-AC/ 10/ 779, 33.

460. Laughton, *Memoirs of the Life and Correspondence of Henry Reeve*, Vol. 1, 314–315.

461. Laughton, *Memoirs of the Life and Correspondence of Henry Reeve*, Vol. 1, 384. Several years later, in 1863, Reeve wrote a damning review of Alexander Kinglake's first two volumes in his eight-volume history of the Crimean War. He condemned Kinglake's antipathy for the French, and Louis-Napoléon in particular, regretting Kinglake's "feminine irritability" with an ally: [Henry Reeve], "Kinglake's *Invasion of Crimea*," *Edinburgh Review*, no. 240 (April 1863), 308. By this time, however, Twiss, and Metternich, if he had been alive, would have been more inclined to agree with Kinglake than Reeve on the character of Louis-Napoléon.

462. Twiss to Metternich, June 28, 1853, National Archives of the Czech Republic, Prague, RAM-AC/ 10/ 779, 24.

have been one or two mistakes in the handling of the matter."[463] As Ottoman forces crossed the Danube and attacked the Russians, Twiss commented that the "Russians have made the grave error of seizing possessions with the force of arms without having decided whether they wanted to fight a war."[464] In early 1854, with the British fleet stationed in the eastern Mediterranean, and Louis-Napoléon urging the British to join in an alliance against Russia, public opinion in England, particularly as expressed through the newspapers, was strongly in favour of a war to support British honour. With war, however, still not declared, Twiss exclaimed: "What confusion with the situation of the powers! If war does not explode, we shall need to add an appendix to Vattel in order to know the degrees of tension to which an 'intermediary state' can submit without war arriving."[465] Once Britain and France had entered the conflict, he reported, "At London everybody is happy with the progress of the enterprise," while at the same time: "I met Lord Granville [in Paris] the other day, and he told me that the French military have many doubts."[466] By January 1855, the lack of military success led to further doubts and a change of government in Britain.[467] Within two weeks, Aberdeen's government was succeeded by Palmerston, who took a harder line on the war. By April, however, such enthusiasm as there was for the war had faded: "The strategy excites no more. It is combat by canons! A kind of war of separation, where tactics are almost void."[468] This was the world's first taste of industrial warfare.[469] Twiss had kept a sceptical distance from the conflict, not declaring whether he sympathised more with the "forward party," led by Palmerston, who aggressively pursued the war, or the peace party, who counselled prudence.[470] The progress of the war, however, decided him: "The philosopher's stone that we must

---

463. Twiss to Metternich, October 23 4, 1853, National Archives of the Czech Republic, Prague, RAM-AC/ 10/ 779, 31.

464. Twiss to Metternich, November 15, 1853, National Archives of the Czech Republic, Prague, RAM-AC/ 10/ 779, 35–36.

465. Twiss to Metternich, February 7, 1854, National Archives of the Czech Republic, Prague, RAM-AC/ 10/ 780, 2.

466. Twiss to Metternich, October 1, 1854, National Archives of the Czech Republic, Prague, RAM-AC/ 10/ 780, 34.

467. "We speak of a change in the cabinet, which may well pass, due to a lack of military success, as the world does not appreciate diplomatic success other than by the outcome, which in this case has not yet developed": Twiss to Metternich, January 22, 1855, National Archives of the Czech Republic, Prague, RAM-AC/ 10/ 781, 2.

468. Twiss to Metternich, April 16, 1855, National Archives of the Czech Republic, Prague, RAM-AC/ 10/ 781, 6.

469. See Tate, *The Crimean War*, 123–124, on the Crimean War as a foretaste of the industrial war of the twentieth century and the shock of this new kind of war for contemporaries.

470. Parry, *The Politics of Patriotism*, 215.

find is that which will transform war into peace."⁴⁷¹ He was dismayed by the leadership: "The great question here at the moment, and elsewhere, is in what corner of the world we must search in order to find statesmen."⁴⁷² And as the war dragged on, he saw no improvement: "There is nothing new, except that the contrast between the canon blows in the orient and in the east of Europe is greater than ever."⁴⁷³

There were, however, consolations from the war, notably the closer relations between Austria and Britain. In 1853, as the Russians made their intentions towards the Ottoman Empire increasingly clear, France and Britain feared that the Austrians would side with the Russians, partly out of their sense of debt to the Russians in having helped overcome the 1848 revolution, but also because they assumed the Austrians would be seeking part of the spoils from the carve-up of Ottoman territory. The Concert of Europe, which had always relied upon Austria's role as arbiter, was no longer trusted and therefore no longer alive. After an evening at Countess Colloredo's in February 1853, Henry Reeve wrote in his journal, "It is astonishing how a dislike of the Austrians has filtered into every class of society."⁴⁷⁴ The Austrians, however, declared themselves neutral in the conflict, and as it progressed, they too began to fear Russian expansionism, and in contrast to Prussia, which remained strictly neutral, they moved increasingly close to the British.⁴⁷⁵ Twiss was greatly relieved: "Let me congratulate you on the excellent position which Austria has occupied on this Eastern question," although he was excessively optimistic about the revival of the Concert of Europe, claiming, "It has enabled her to resume her ancient duty of adjusting the equilibrium of power amongst the four states."⁴⁷⁶ In attempting to resume that role, Austria proposed negotiation, but even Twiss was forced to admit the failure of the diplomatic efforts. It was the Turkish rejection of the Vienna Note in 1853 that triggered the war, and when, in 1854, Austria had attempted again to negotiate peace, Britain and France rejected the effort. They now believed that the Concert of Europe aligned too closely with Austrian and Russian interests, and therefore "looked like the tool of autocratic Europe."⁴⁷⁷ In October 1854, Twiss

---

471. Twiss to Metternich, April 16, 1855, National Archives of the Czech Republic, Prague, RAM-AC/ 10/ 781, 5.

472. Twiss to Metternich, July 10, 1855, National Archives of the Czech Republic, Prague, RAM-AC/ 10/ 781, 9.

473. Twiss to Metternich, August 22, 1855, National Archives of the Czech Republic, Prague, RAM-AC/ 10/ 781, 12.

474. Laughton, *Memoirs of the Life and Correspondence of Henry Reeve*, Vol. 1, 287.

475. Müller, *Britain and the German Question*, 160; Parry, *The Politics of Patriotism*, 214–215.

476. Twiss to Metternich, September 4, 1853, National Archives of the Czech Republic, Prague, RAM-AC/ 10/ 779, 27.

477. Parry, *The Politics of Patriotism*, 214.

wrote of his disappointment at having "heard news" that Austria has spoken of a new "conference," but that the "Occidental powers don't want it."[478]

Twiss's initial interpretation of the conflict as a war of religion, or a crusade, began to give way to a more common perception that it shared some characteristics with the revolutions of 1848: that is, insofar as it was a struggle over political ideology rather than religion. For his contemporaries, this meant that the war was once again a struggle against autocratic government. Twiss had not come to that point, although he did see it as a struggle between the forces of order and disorder. In the second year of the war, he wrote: "I don't know where the flow of the war will take us. It is curious to see the West of Europe fall prey to the disorder of civil war in 1848, and then, voilà!, in 1854 the East of Europe falls prey to international war. We could almost believe that it is a natural cycle."[479] "The internal state of fever," he explained, "has passed but the second stage of the sickness is as grave."[480] The internal sickness was the civil wars, or intra-imperial wars, of 1848. The second stage of the sickness was the new war between empires, the inter-imperial war. Even broader forces were at work: "If I was to write the history of Europe since 1815, I would say that the period between the fall of the great Napoléon to 1848 was a great political parenthesis in the European drama, during which the people of Europe were allowed to take a rest before beginning the task of redressing the balance of national / political powers. I would call that epoch the period Metternich / Wellington, and I would start the new chapter with the words 'The touchstone of the value of that period of rest will be the duration of the wars for re-establishing the equilibrium of the European powers.'"[481] He was beginning to re-evaluate his understanding of the order created by the Congress of Vienna. It had been temporary, although he still believed that a new kind of "equilibrium" could be established. Nevertheless, change was now not simply inevitable but undeniable.

Metternich did not disagree, but he was more enigmatic and world-weary, and his letters on the war said little of the day-to-day details. He was sceptical of Russian intentions and claimed that, many years previously, when the Emperor Nicholas I had told him that Turkey was "*l'homme malade*," he had asked whether the Emperor was speaking "as his doctor or as his heir [*héritier*]."[482] "The world and its development [*allures*]," he announced pes-

478. Twiss to Metternich, October 1, 1854, National Archives of the Czech Republic, Prague, RAM-AC/ 10/ 780, 33.
479. Twiss to Metternich, June 12, 1854, National Archives of the Czech Republic, Prague, RAM-AC/ 10/ 780, 15.
480. Twiss to Metternich, June 12, 1854, National Archives of the Czech Republic, Prague, RAM-AC/ 10/ 780, 16.
481. Twiss to Metternich, June 12, 1854, National Archives of the Czech Republic, Prague, RAM-AC/ 10/ 780, 16.
482. Charles Greville, *A Journal of the Reign of Queen Victoria from 1852 to 1860*, Vol. 1 (London, 1887), 310.

simistically to Twiss, "are placed in a truly false direction."[483] He repeated his frequent advice: "For me not to misdirect you regarding what I think of this or that given situation, address your own thoughts and you will find the truth."[484] But he was also despairing: "The more I live the more I find I am reduced to understanding nothing, while others find I am comprehensible ... the first proposition I would make would be a revision of the language and an edition of a dictionary in which the meaning [*valeur*] of certain words would be clearly defined—such words as peace and war; caresses and snubs [*soufflets*]; abstention and neutrality—complete the list if you like."[485] The Concert of Europe had justified the suppression of liberty in the name of order, so Metternich's pessimism is unsurprising in the context in which order broke down. Twiss shared the sense that language had become corrupt, and in Metternich's last years, the two friends returned repeatedly to that theme. Twiss ironically suggested the need to revise the dictionaries, and Metternich agreed: "I finished the letter in which you made an appeal for the revision of dictionaries which would be in the interest of the social body."[486] The abuse of language, they believed, had made diplomacy impossible, but the confusion was deliberately pursued by interests—and they were thinking in particular of Napoléon III—who were seeking war rather than peace: "The confusion of languages is intolerable considering its consequences. For men to live in society, it is necessary that between them words have the same signification, that the 'yes,' as well, cannot become a 'non'; friendship to hate; mine to yours; etc. If you should ever find the need for another occupation as meritorious and dignified as the law, I suggest as something that would particularly claim my attention, the fixation and the clear and precise definition of the following words: alliance, engagement, treaty, of political bodies, intervention, not to mention plenty of other words which in today's situation are treated as sounds authorized to be interpreted and bad jokes. If you need a collaborator, count on my aid."[487]

As the Crimean War neared its conclusion, Metternich lamented that it had been "a deplorable struggle which cost the lives of half a million human beings ... in order to arrive at that which by other means could have been

483. Metternich to Twiss, February 16, 1854, National Archives of the Czech Republic, Prague, RAM-AC/ 10/ 780, 6.
484. Metternich to Twiss, February 16, 1854, National Archives of the Czech Republic, Prague, RAM-AC/ 10/ 780, 7.
485. Metternich to Twiss, February 16, 1854, National Archives of the Czech Republic, Prague, RAM-AC/ 10/ 780, 9.
486. Metternich to Twiss, Vienna, January 13, 1859, Bibliothèque nationale de France, Fol/ R.D./13810, 169.
487. Metternich to Twiss, Vienna, January 13, 1859, Bibliothèque nationale de France, Fol/ R.D./13810, 169v–170.

achieved by a softer [*plus douce*] route."⁴⁸⁸ Complementing his strong appetite for order, the Napoleonic Wars had left Metternich with the conviction that politics must be pursued through diplomacy rather than war. "It is not," he wrote, "with canons that civilisation progresses."⁴⁸⁹ When peace had arrived, he remained in doubt about its status depending upon whether its causes were, as he put it, "political" or "social": "The peace is made! . . . Is it political or is it social? I, who do not know at all how to play with words, I know only <u>political</u> interests which offer the material for peace treaties between nations. <u>Social</u> interests must be served by other routes."⁴⁹⁰

Twiss, on the other hand, was able to draw some lessons from the war. The first was that Europe, and the Austrian Empire in particular, had to open itself to the "East." The way in which to do that was through the Danube into the Black Sea, and yet that route had been blocked by international law. "There is a question," he wrote, "I would very much like to discuss with you—it is the Treaty of 1841."⁴⁹¹ The London Straits Treaty of 1841 blocked the Russian navy from passing out of the Black Sea into the Mediterranean and blocked the British and other navies from passing into the Black Sea, maintaining the balance of great powers, while making the Ottomans more dependent upon the British and French. The treaty, Twiss believed, had become an obstacle to the expansion of European influence to the East, but in maintaining that belief, he had to become bolder in disagreeing with Metternich: "You were decidedly <u>for</u> the treaty . . . while I am for and against: <u>For</u>, if the status quo can be maintained, <u>against</u>, if it means looking for a new starting point for a new order of things."⁴⁹² He had already concluded that the status quo of the Concert of Europe could not be maintained. He spelled out the implications: "There is no question that the capital of the Ottoman empire is protected by the treaty, but the result of the closure of the Bosphorus is that the Black Sea is not a European sea while great European questions find their resolution on the border [of the sea]." The consequence of the treaty, therefore, was to exclude European powers from the Black Sea, with the exception of Russia, even while their interests were affected by events in the region. He concluded, therefore, "There is a great political question for Austria. If the mouth of the Danube is open, and the river is declared to be European, which is to say that

---

488. Metternich to Twiss, Vienna, February 5, 1856, Bibliothèque nationale de France, Fol/ R.D./13810, 126v.

489. Metternich to Twiss, Vienna, April 7, 1856, Bibliothèque nationale de France, Fol/ R.D./13810, 129v.

490. Metternich to Twiss, Vienna, April 7, 1856, Bibliothèque nationale de France, Fol/ R.D./13810, 129-129v.

491. Twiss to Metternich, September 16, 1854, National Archives of the Czech Republic, Prague, RAM-AC/ 10/ 780, 34.

492. Twiss to Metternich, September 16, 1854, National Archives of the Czech Republic, Prague, RAM-AC/ 10/ 780, 34.

if the navigation of the Danube is subject to an Act of Congress, European politics will come to the East and Austria will not need to fear its orientation. In that case, if the Black Sea becomes a European sea, will it not be an advantage for Austria given the Slavic populations on the Danube?"[493] Here Twiss anticipated the outcome of the Treaty of Paris, two years later, which concluded the war: namely, the new treaty created freedom of commerce and navigation in the Danube subject to an international commission, while at the same time admitting the Ottoman Empire to the Concert of Europe, and therefore to the public law of Europe. This system of neutrality and free commerce would, according to Twiss, be a means whereby European powers could extend their influence beyond their boundaries. This is a theme to which he would return warmly throughout the rest of his career, and particularly in writing on the inclusion of "Oriental" states in the international community and the neutrality of the Suez Canal and Congo River. At the same time, when arguing for those extensions of influence through neutrality and the expansion of membership in international society, he would return to the 1856 Treaty of Paris as a key moment in that progress.

The second lesson that Twiss took from the Crimean War was an understanding that the nature of war itself was changing rapidly as a result of the impact of technology. To change war was to change the relations between powers. On the conclusion of peace in 1856, he wrote to Metternich: "Let me congratulate you on witnessing the restoration of peace. It has arrived sooner than anticipated. One thing seems to be proved, that it is more easy for great nations to exhaust themselves by war in a short time than it was, thanks to the invention of the steam engine, and although the sacrifice of life may be as great, yet it is accomplished in a shorter time, and Humanity benefits thereby."[494] He was not always positive about technology, having already lamented the "combat of canons" which had extinguished the strategic intelligence of the Napoleonic Wars, and also commenting during the war: "Here we are victimised every six hours by the electric telegraph which brings news from where nobody knows, and that news leaves everybody in a perfect uncertainty."[495] Although the war was shorter than it might have been in the past, the question

---

493. Twiss to Metternich, September 16, 1854, National Archives of the Czech Republic, Prague, RAM-AC/ 10/ 780, 35–36.

494. Twiss to Metternich, April 5, 1856, National Archives of the Czech Republic, Prague, RAM-AC/ 10/ 782, 3–4.

495. Twiss to Metternich, November 15, 1853, National Archives of the Czech Republic, Prague, RAM-AC/ 10/ 779, 35. By contrast, he complained during the Second Anglo-Sikh war about the tendency of the commander, General Hugh Gough, to use infantry rather than artillery, noting, "The poor Indian Army is thrown at the enemy by Lord Gough as if it was made up of canon balls and not living men": Twiss to Metternich, March 3 (second letter), 1849, National Archives of the Czech Republic, Prague, RAM-AC/ 10/ 775, 174.

remained: "Will the peace be durable?"[496] He answered optimistically: "I do not see any reason why it should not last if the order of things in France continues undisturbed. One thing is certain, that the military ardour of the French is not so intense as at the commencement of the nineteenth century. In England we do not seem to care much for war as for peace. We are accustomed to a chronic state of war at a distance, e.g., in India, and the war on the shores of the Black Sea was almost as remote as a war on the shores of the Persian Gulf."[497] France, or at least Napoléon III, recovered its ardour sooner than he hoped, and in India, also, war was coming on a scale that would surprise all.

Napoléon III and Italian Unification

Italian nationalism was not vanquished in 1849, even if the nationalist armies were, and by 1858, the Kingdom of Piedmont-Sardinia was once again pursuing its ambitions to create an Italian state through unification with Lombardy-Venetia, which the Austrian Empire had controlled by virtue of the Congress of Vienna in 1815. Napoléon III joined the Sardinian cause after they agreed to cede Nice and Savoy to France in exchange for its assistance. The alliance permitted Napoléon III to represent himself as an opponent of autocracy, embodied by the Austrian Empire. In Britain, conservatives once more noted the tie between nationalism and emancipation, and Liberals were torn between their opposition to Austrian autocracy and fear of Napoléon III's expansionism, while Radicals urged support for Italian nationalism.[498] The defensive treaty between Sardinia and France obliged the French to assist the Italians if they were attacked. It was necessary, therefore, for the Sardinians to provoke Austria into an attack, and they did this through a series of military manoeuvres on the Piedmontese border.

During the build-up of these tensions, the Austrian Emperor, Franz Joseph, hesitated to plunge the Empire into a war, despite the belligerence of his Foreign Minister, Count Ferdinand Buol-Schauenstein, and his generals. Metternich had already sent warnings to Buol about being goaded into war.[499] In April 1859, the Emperor turned to Metternich for counsel and visited him in his Vienna residence. Metternich warned Franz Joseph not to be led into war by provocation and, "for Heaven's sake," to "send no ultimatum to Italy." Franz Joseph responded, "It went out yesterday."[500] Partly in response to Metternich's advice, Franz Joseph sacked Buol, but the Austrians now

---

496. Twiss to Metternich, April 5, 1856, National Archives of the Czech Republic, Prague, RAM-AC/ 10/ 782, 3.

497. Twiss to Metternich, April 5, 1856, National Archives of the Czech Republic, Prague, RAM-AC/ 10/ 782, 5–6.

498. Parry, *The Politics of Patriotism*, 223–229; Finn, *After Chartism*, 203–206.

499. Palmer, *Metternich*, 337.

500. Cited in Palmer, *Metternich*, 337.

found themselves in a disastrous war—Napoléon III immediately dispatched 170,000 troops to Lombardy. With the war proceeding chaotically, Franz Joseph decided, in late May, personally to command the Austrian army, just as Napoléon was commanding the French.[501] He asked Metternich to draw up plans for a regency if he should die in battle.[502] News of Austria's defeat in the Battle of Magenta on June 4 caused Metternich to collapse, and a week later he died.[503]

Metternich and Twiss corresponded more frequently in the months prior to his death. They were stimulated by Napoléon III's treachery, by the desire to see a restoration of relations between Britain and Austria, and by the renewed dangers of nationalism, which promised the emancipation of both natural persons and the artificial person of the body politic, notably in Italian unification. As late as February, however, it was not obvious that a war was coming, although apparent that Napoléon III was seeking one. In relation to the French Emperor taking up Sardinia's cause, Twiss wrote ironically, "I think it very probable that one solution of the idea 'L'empire, c'est la paix' is intended to be given by Louis N. offering to settle everybody's quarrel. I confess that I am still rather mystified."[504] "With regard to this country," he observed, "it will follow its ancient policy. France is nearer, if anything, than it was at the early part of the century, and it is more formidable as a neighbour than it was, so that we dare not let it become more powerful, nor should we wish Germany to become weaker."[505] He even considered that there would be an advantage to relations between Austria and Britain if war should come, while referring euphemistically to the source of British antipathy to Austria: namely, that Britain was a constitutional monarchy, while Austria was autocratic: "England has been a good deal alienated from Austria as in peace-time there are very few bonds of sympathy between them—their institutions are widely divergent from one another, but in war-time there will be a common object of alarm."[506]

The previous August, France had celebrated the completion of a vast new naval base at Cherbourg, with Queen Victoria, Albert, and 100 members of parliament attending the event.[507] The press stoked the renewed fear of France as a maritime power and Louis-Napoléon as an expansionist, and Twiss believed

---

501. For the disastrous conduct of the war, see Deák, *Beyond Nationalism*, 47.
502. Palmer, *Metternich*, 338.
503. Palmer, *Metternich*, 339.
504. Twiss to Metternich, February 16, 1859, National Archives of the Czech Republic, Prague, RAM-AC/ 10/ 785, 2.
505. Twiss to Metternich, February 16, 1859, National Archives of the Czech Republic, Prague, RAM-AC/ 10/ 785, 3-4.
506. Twiss to Metternich, February 16, 1859, National Archives of the Czech Republic, Prague, RAM-AC/ 10/ 785, 4-5.
507. Parry, *The Politics of Patriotism*, 225.

that the fears were realised by his intervention in Italy: "France has followed Russia in her aim of becoming a maritime power. The maritime powers are the only powers that can give England any real cause for alarm ... What is its object? To give an *éclat* to the Sardinian marriage [the alliance of L.N. with Sardinia] or to save his own life from the poignards of the Italians? and if so, to deceive the hopes of the Italians?"[508] The particular poignard to which he referred was the failed assassination of Napoléon III a year previously by Italian nationalist Felice Orsini, which had the perverse consequence of pushing the French Emperor closer to the Sardinian cause.[509]

As in 1848 and 1849, the rise of nationalism led Twiss to contemplate the antidote, and he was led back to the conclusion he and Metternich had agreed upon on the former occasion: namely, that nationalism was an expression of excessive civic fervour, and it could therefore be tempered by providing alternative outlets for that energy, in particular local corporations such as the church or the city. The provision of such local and corporate government was a necessity for all empires: "What is wanted in Lombardy is ... a field of activity for local ambitions. That seems to be the necessary misfortune of provincial life. A weak nation formerly independent finds itself incorporated into a stronger nation, and it soon discovers that it has no vocation except to obey and be tranquil."[510] Metternich had, in fact, argued strongly for the autonomy of Lombardy-Venetia within the Empire in the years immediately following 1814, but he had failed to convince Francis I.[511] His reasoning at the time was that national sentiment needed, as Twiss argued, local means of expression. Twiss believed that the civic history of Italy made it particularly suited to this form of politics: "Can any field of action be given to the Italians in their towns? Their genius is <u>municipal</u>—it may be an Evil genius, but it is 'un esprit municipal.'"[512] It may be that the evil dimension to the Italians' municipal genius was its republican heritage. City republics within an empire remained the only vision Twiss could conjure for Italy. Unification seemed unimaginable and impossible: "The geographical configuration of Italy renders unity of any kind impossible."[513]

By April, Napoléon III's intentions were clear, but war was still not inevitable if the Austrians would not allow themselves to be provoked: "How the

---

508. Twiss to Metternich, February 16, 1859, National Archives of the Czech Republic, Prague, RAM-AC/ 10/ 785, 5–6.

509. Parry, *The Politics of Patriotism*, 224–225.

510. Twiss to Metternich, February 16, 1859, National Archives of the Czech Republic, Prague, RAM-AC/ 10/ 785, 7–8.

511. Haas, "Metternich and the Slavs," 127.

512. Twiss to Metternich, February 16, 1859, National Archives of the Czech Republic, Prague, RAM-AC/ 10/ 785, 11–12.

513. Twiss to Metternich, April 19, 1859, National Archives of the Czech Republic, Prague, RAM-AC/ 10/ 785, 21.

scene shifts and the spectators are deceived by the Great Actor!"[514] Twiss and Metternich resumed their roles as a conduit for the flow of information between the British and Austrian governments, with Twiss seeking information, for example, of the terms on which the Austrians took control over Lombardy in 1815: "I have told my friends here what nobody seems to have known, except Lord Aberdeen, that the Emperor Francis [Francis II] took charge of Lombardy at the earnest request of the Prince Regent. I have been asked if there is any published record of the fact but I am not aware of any. Is there anything in print on the subject? . . . people have forgotten that it was so planned."[515] The loss of memory was not confined to the matters of fact relating to the treaties of 1815; it was also felt in relation to understanding the reasons why the Congress of Vienna created a system balancing the great powers: "The traditions of the quadruple alliance are dying away . . . and a generation has grown up which never knew the state of things which the settlement of 1815 put an end to." Napoléon III's whole purpose was to destroy that system: "As to the condition of Europe at present, my own suspicion as to the Jeux Napoléon is that of vengeance for the disaster of 1815. He commenced by breaking up the old alliance [by pushing for the Crimean War] and compelled England to accompany him to Turkey. He now proposes to weaken Austria, which is the only offensive power of Germany which he needs to fear, and he will then try his last hand upon us, and after he has extinguished heretical England, he will ask the Pope to anoint him Emperor of the West! It is a grand scheme, which may well dazzle a fatalist, but to accomplish it, he must not allow himself to be led astray by secondary objects, and it is questionable whether the Sardinian marriage has not been a mistake. It would be curious if the Napoléon of Peace miscalculated his game through a like blunder to that which ruined the Napoléon of War."[516] The resurgence of nationalism and constitutionalism was to be understood in this context—they were the populist means by which Napoléon III could pursue his expansionist ambitions. It was indeed a grand scheme, but Twiss was not alone in such fears. He was articulating a broadly held view in England, as Jonathan Parry puts it, of "a standard French expansionist strategy by declaring sympathy for radical ideas: nationalism and the human brotherhood."[517] Part of Napoléon III's blunder, according to Twiss, however, may have been to forget that nationalism was a double-edged sword: "I hear that the feeling in North Germany is intense against the Italians and L.N. in

514. Twiss to Metternich, April 19, 1859, National Archives of the Czech Republic, Prague, RAM-AC/ 10/ 785, 14.

515. Twiss to Metternich, April 19, 1859, National Archives of the Czech Republic, Prague, RAM-AC/ 10/ 785, 14–15.

516. Twiss to Metternich, April 19, 1859, National Archives of the Czech Republic, Prague, RAM-AC/ 10/ 785, 15–19.

517. Parry, *The Politics of Patriotism*, 226.

setting up the Italian nationalities forgot that he was setting them up against the German nationalities."[518]

In April 1859, William Gladstone was member for Oxford and soon to join the ministry of the Palmerston government. He was a keen promoter of the Italians' independence and published an essay in the *Quarterly Review* in support of the cause. He did not forget the commitments undertaken in 1815: "We have a profound sense of the sacredness of treaty engagements and of the importance of maintaining the settlement at which Europe, after such terrible and prolonged convulsions arrived in 1815."[519] For Gladstone, however, a territorial title founded on a treaty, although a "good title," was not "absolute." It depended upon the fulfilment of the terms of the treaty, foremost of which, in this instance, was to treat the territory equally to other parts of the Empire and not to place it under "exceptional burdens."[520] By contrast, Gladstone doubted whether "in Christendom there be an instance corresponding with the Austrian power in Italy; an instance where a people glaringly inferior in refinement rule, and that by the medium of arbitrary will, without the check of free institutions, over a people much more advanced."[521] Gladstone also admitted the close tie between nationalism and emancipation, the tie that particularly worried Twiss, but which he saw as positive: "The thirst for national independence in Italy is inseparably associated with the hope of relief from political servitude."[522]

Twiss was scandalised by Gladstone's article, writing: "I beg to draw your attention to the article in the Q.R. which is said to be from the pen of Mr Gladstone. You are well aware of the weight which public opinion has upon any ministry in this country and how important it is that public opinion should have correct facts to study. I hold that Mr Gladstone's article is of a very mischievous tendency. He has studied the position of Austria in Italy through Sardinian glasses."[523] Gladstone's claims, he argued, regarding excessive Austrian taxation were based upon factual errors, or possibly falsehoods. Gladstone had suggested that one solution to the crisis would be to establish relations of "suzerainty" between the Italian provinces and Austria similar to that which "has long been established" between the "Ottoman Porte" and the European territories over which it was suzerain. Such an arrangement would require "a fixed pecuniary contribution" but would provide "an internal autonomy, practically complete, with their own native legislature, administration, and

---

518. Twiss to Metternich, May 4, 1859, National Archives of the Czech Republic, Prague, RAM-AC/ 10/ 785, 40.

519. [William Gladstone], "War in Italy", *Quarterly Review*, vol. 105 (1859), 551.

520. [Gladstone], "War in Italy," 551.

521. [Gladstone], "War in Italy," 549–550. See also Parry, *The Politics of Patriotism*, 223.

522. [Gladstone], "War in Italy," 549.

523. Twiss to Metternich, April 23, 1859, National Archives of the Czech Republic, Prague, RAM-AC/ 10/ 785, 22–23.

army."[524] Twiss responded "on p. 559 he has advanced a most extraordinary doctrine which I protest against as an international lawyer, and his proposal of an Austrian suzerainty is too ridiculous!"[525] Again, drawing upon Metternich's assistance to rebut such arguments, he wrote: "If there are any misstatements of facts I should like to be informed of them."[526]

The immediate task was to avoid a war between Austria and France that would play into Napoléon III's hands: "The real issue for England as for Austria is, what are the designs and plans of Louis-Napoléon."[527] By participating in Crimea, England had already pursued a war that had not been in its interests: "Under the pretence of an alliance he has dragged England after him through the dirt—Naples and Constantinople are instances."[528] It was now clear, in the conflict over Lombardy, that Napoléon III's strategy "<u>all this time</u> is to provoke Austria to commence offensive measures."[529] On the other hand, "The political object of Austria is to unmask Louis Napoléon or to compel him to disclose his real object to Europe."[530] Twiss had astutely analysed the strategic predicament, and he could foresee that Austria's error would be to initiate an attack because that would trigger the treaty France had made with Sardinia: "In the first place L.N. would only be justified in attacking Austria *chez elle* if he has a treaty offensive and defensive with Sardinia. He may attack the Austrians in Piedmont if he has only a defensive alliance."[531] He did not know that, just three days earlier, Metternich had had the conversation with the Emperor Franz Joseph in which he provided precisely the same advice, to which the Emperor responded that it was too late.

With the war commencing on April 29, Twiss wrote days later to declare that the battle of words was progressing well: "I am glad to say that I think the war has commenced under the most favourable auspices for Austria, and that public opinion in England is arranging itself against L.N. Everybody seems satisfied that he is not to be trusted and distrust puts an end to friendship and the conviction of having been deceived causes apprehension, and so hostility grows up ... I am

---

524. [Gladstone], "War in Italy," 559.

525. Twiss to Metternich, April 23, 1859, National Archives of the Czech Republic, Prague, RAM-AC/ 10/ 785, 25.

526. Twiss to Metternich, April 23, 1859, National Archives of the Czech Republic, Prague, RAM-AC/ 10/ 785, 25.

527. Twiss to Metternich, April 23, 1859, National Archives of the Czech Republic, Prague, RAM-AC/ 10/ 785, 26–27.

528. Twiss to Metternich, April 23, 1859, National Archives of the Czech Republic, Prague, RAM-AC/ 10/ 785, 26.

529. Twiss to Metternich, April 23, 1859, National Archives of the Czech Republic, Prague, RAM-AC/ 10/ 785, 27.

530. Twiss to Metternich, April 23, 1859, National Archives of the Czech Republic, Prague, RAM-AC/ 10/ 785, 29–30.

531. Twiss to Metternich, April 23, 1859, National Archives of the Czech Republic, Prague, RAM-AC/ 10/ 785, 30–31.

glad to say that I think the best part of the press will be against L.N. The Times has taken its line against him ... although it is a very difficult line to pursue in the present state of political parties."[532] Pursuing, once again, the question of shaping public opinion, he argued that throughout Europe it would be necessary to provide "accurate information": "It is extremely desirable, I think, that Western Europe, Germany as well as England, should have accurate information of what takes place between the armies. The old Napoléon by means of his bulletins falsified public opinion as to the real facts of many battles, and Europe had the idea that his course was always one of uninterrupted triumph. I believe that publicity at Vienna is now allowed through the Gazette in many matters which were formerly kept from public knowledge, but the education of the human race has advanced so much in the last forty years that it <u>will think</u> on what is going on around it, and the truth should if possible be accessible."[533] While Metternich had restricted the press when in power, Twiss believed that such restrictions could no longer succeed, given the advancement of enlightenment. The press needed to promote the "truth," or perhaps be used to manage public opinion, following the example of the first Napoléon, rather than be shut down.

Although the war did further heighten suspicion of Napoléon III in Britain, it also rekindled the feelings of injustice regarding the suppression of the Hungarian rebellion in 1849 and led to renewed support for Hungarian nationalism. In 1859, Kossuth was in Britain and declared, "All you do for Italy of course serves Hungary too indirectly."[534] At the same time, many members of the British parliament feared that an alliance between France and rebellious Italians and Hungarians could upset the European balance of power.[535] Twiss was aware of this risk—that the conflict could bring a revival of Hungarian nationalism—and wrote to Metternich, warning that Napoléon III "hopes to evoke the modern sentiment of nationalism in his aid. There is a point to which no doubt you have turned your attention and where there is some, <u>if not great</u>, cause for anxiety. I mean Hungary. One reason why Western Europe has looked upon Austria as no longer the great centre of equilibrium is that she believes that Hungary will fail her in her time of need."[536] Nationalism was, in his analysis, one of the causes for the breakdown of the Concert of Powers

---

532. Twiss to Metternich, May 4, 1859, National Archives of the Czech Republic, Prague, RAM-AC/ 10/ 785, 38–40.

533. Twiss to Metternich, May 4, 1859, National Archives of the Czech Republic, Prague, RAM-AC/ 10/ 785, 38–42.

534. Cited in Finn, *After Chartism*, 203. On the success of Kossuth's English tours, see Tibor Frank, "Marketing Hungary: Kossuth and the Politics of Propaganda," in László Péter, Martyn Rady, and Peter Sherwood, eds., *Lajos Kossuth Sent Word: Papers Delivered on the Occasion of the Bicentenary of Kossuth's Birth* (London, 2003), 221–250.

535. Szabad György, *Kossuth and the British "Balance of Power" Policy (1859–1861)* (Budapest, 1960).

536. Twiss to Metternich, May 4, 1859, National Archives of the Czech Republic, Prague, RAM-AC/ 10/ 785, 48–49.

because it destabilised the empires upon which that balance was based. His concern, however, was not abstract. Acting again as a conduit of information between Britain and Austria, Twiss continued: "I have had it brought to my attention from a most important quarter, and with a friendly view to aid Austria, that at Christmas it was stated at Constantinople by a person and from a source likely to be well informed that 'before midsummer's day there would be an insurrection in Hungary'—not a democratic insurrection but a national rising in the hope of regaining some of their local institutions."[537] It was also said that if the Emperor Franz Joseph would "only restore to the Hungarians some of their local institutions, they would follow him to a man against the French."[538] Twiss was told, "If you have any means of bringing this fact to the attention of those in high position in Austria it would be most desirable for their interests that this fact should be known." The use of local institutions as a vent for excessive political steam was precisely Twiss's own solution to the problems of nationalism, so it is unsurprising to find him endorsing the proposal enthusiastically: "There would not be any difficulty whatever in adjusting the system of central government with that of local administration and that Austria herself might find prodigious strength in the elements of her different nationalities which at times disquiet her."[539] The Emperor Franz Joseph, was, he argued, "a man of great character who could execute '*un coup d'esprit fort.*'" In addition to promoting the provision of information against strong Austrian censorship, Twiss was now also arguing for some liberalisation of the Austrian constitution. The advice was consistent with his arguments for over ten years that Metternich, and Austria, should at least seek to seem less autocratic, but while Metternich agreed with Twiss that Austria should not have been provoked into the war, it is unclear on this occasion whether he heeded the warning about Hungary or passed on the information.

Twiss's last letter to Metternich, on May 5, noted the progress of the war: "There is a telegram that the French have sailed for Naples. The Prince Consort [Albert] communicated it to the person who told me and, in telling it, added 'who could have thought it possible.'"[540] He merely added: "The English people have been living in a fool's paradise."[541] Metternich's last letter to Twiss was the last letter he wrote, and it was, according to his son, Richard, who edited his memoirs, "the last document to come from the plume of the

---

537. Twiss to Metternich, May 4, 1859, National Archives of the Czech Republic, Prague, RAM-AC/ 10/ 785, 49–50.

538. Twiss to Metternich, May 4, 1859, National Archives of the Czech Republic, Prague, RAM-AC/ 10/ 785, 50–51.

539. Twiss to Metternich, May 4, 1859, National Archives of the Czech Republic, Prague, RAM-AC/ 10/ 785, 53.

540. Twiss to Metternich, May 5, 1859, National Archives of the Czech Republic, Prague, RAM-AC/ 10/ 785, 75–76.

541. Twiss to Metternich, May 5, 1859, National Archives of the Czech Republic, Prague, RAM-AC/ 10/ 785, 76.

prince."542 It is the last letter in his memoirs, and it is the only letter to Twiss in the eight volumes of memoirs, but it was a fortunate inclusion because it was, in fact, unfinished—"*cette lettre est restée inachevée*"—and was never sent to Twiss, who would have remained unaware of its existence.543 The letter reflected Metternich's increasingly disoriented state: "I begin this letter without knowing the day on which it is sent."544 He nevertheless engaged with Twiss's letters of May 4 and 5: "I found in those [letters] that you sent to me on May 4 and 5 my own impressions of the grave situation in which Europe finds itself."545 The letter that follows reads like a valedictory, although many of Metternich's letters did. He began with a long preamble on how Twiss's "spirit follows a straight line" and, in that respect, was the same as Metternich's—an observation he had made several times over the years. While "you are English and I am German and Austrian, nothing prevents us from understanding each other." He then turned to the question of "the struggle." It was, he said, "a struggle to the death, [which] is engaged today between truth and lies, between law [*le droit*] and negation, and for conditions in which moral peace and material peace, with their natural consequences, order and liberty (the true and not the false), would be impossible."546 The "present situation," he continued, was not new. It was the "consequence of the revolution which today is seventy years since it revealed itself to me": namely, the French Revolution. During that whole time, Austria had been "attacked by her [France] in the foundation of its existence." Austria had "suffered without being discouraged" and after "twenty years of war" had prevailed in 1813. The victors then conducted themselves with "wisdom and moderation" which had been "without precedent in history."547 With "individualism beaten," Europe then "enjoyed the longest peace to be found in the annals of her history." But what could not be put aside was the "moral perturbation caused by the Revolution," which had become "chronic." The government of Austria, he argued, was not responsible for that condition because it found itself to be "politically isolated." "How then," he asked rhetorically, "are things placed today?" There was "no doubt about the response to the question." There had been a "notable change."

542. "Metternich au Dr Travers Twiss. Vienne, [no date] mai," *Mémoires de Metternich*, Vol. 8, 642, note.

543. "Metternich au Dr Travers Twiss. Vienne, [no date] mai," *Mémoires de Metternich*, Vol. 8, 642, note.

544. "Metternich au Dr Travers Twiss. Vienne, [no date] mai," *Mémoires de Metternich*, Vol. 8, 639.

545. "Metternich au Dr Travers Twiss. Vienne, [no date] mai," *Mémoires de Metternich*, Vol. 8, 639.

546. "Metternich au Dr Travers Twiss. Vienne, [no date] mai," *Mémoires de Metternich*, Vol. 8, 639–640.

547. "Metternich au Dr Travers Twiss. Vienne, [no date] mai," *Mémoires de Metternich*, Vol. 8, 640.

After having been "covered in fog and smoke," the situation had now become clear "to the sight of even the masses." The "spectres had assumed a form."[548] The "dice have been spilled from the horn." What "men of sense could not hide from" was the "incalculable harm that the ruin of the social order and its inevitable consequence—an era of complete anarchy which would present itself as a passage from an order of things destroyed to a new order of things—would have for the world." "Everything you have just read, my dear Twiss," he continued, "goes beyond the value of words. It is truth with the make-up [*fard*] removed," a claim to unadorned truth that he had made in one of his first letters to Twiss eleven years earlier.[549] The letter ends here, in mid-flow, and is characteristic of Metternich's writing in his last years—declining to address details, not even Twiss's portent of another Hungarian revolution, and confining himself to abstract observations about the betrayal of the Concert of Europe and a rather apocalyptic vision for the future which he was able to draw from his ability to divine truth that lay beyond language.

Global Revolution

The age of revolutions was not restricted to Europe; it was global, and in 1857, with the outbreak of war in India, Twiss made this observation himself: "What moral revolutions have traversed the world since the new year of 1848."[550] He engaged with those revolutions beyond the European stage and, in particular, in the British Empire, which was not spared the turbulence from which Britain itself was supposedly free.[551] The Admiralty Courts were the forum in which the everyday business of the law of nations was conducted, and as an Admiralty Advocate, Twiss provided opinions on relations between European and non-European powers on hundreds of occasions. He frequently complained to Metternich about the time-consuming nature of Admiralty business. In May 1849, he declared, "I am 'choked' with cases in the Ct of Admiralty, with ships putting their helms to starboard and larboard, that I must give up all idea of writing."[552] Moreover, as Queen's Advocate from 1867—the equivalent,

548. "Metternich au Dr Travers Twiss. Vienne, [no date] mai," *Mémoires de Metternich*, Vol. 8, 641.

549. "Metternich au Dr Travers Twiss. Vienne, [no date] mai," *Mémoires de Metternich*, Vol. 8, 641.

550. Twiss to Metternich, December 29, 1857, National Archives of the Czech Republic, Prague, RAM-AC/ 10/ 783, 15. For the age of revolutions in a global context, see Bayly, *The Birth of the Modern World*; David Armitage and Sanjay Subrahmanyam, eds., *The Age of Revolutions in Global Context* (Basingstoke, 2010).

551. Miles Taylor, "The 1848 Revolutions in the British Empire," *Past and Present*, vol. 166 (2000), 146–181.

552. Twiss to Metternich, April 23, 1849, National Archives of the Czech Republic, Prague, RAM-AC/ 10/ 775, 290. In February 1849, he apologised for not being able to visit Brighton on the coming Saturday because he would be "very much occupied until

that is, of an Attorney General for international law—he advised the government on a daily basis on matters touching the law of nations. More often than not, as one would expect in the government of a vast empire, those matters touched the interests of non-European nations. The fact that non-European sovereigns were frequently subjects within the Admiralty Courts, or central to problems to be considered by the Queen's Advocate, reflected an acknowledgement in practice, regardless of what some jurists maintained in theory, that those sovereigns belonged, at some level, to the society of nations.

From early in his career, Twiss was engaged in questions concerning India. In 1849, he dined at East India House with Horace Hayman Wilson, an Oxford colleague in the chair of Sanskrit and an employee of the East India Company, and F. H. Trithen, a former student of Wilson who had been appointed Professor of Modern Languages at Oxford two years previously, and had published a edition of the Sanskrit play *Mahaviracharita* the previous year.[553] The three men reported their "great satisfaction" with a "work" in East India House as "a specimen of oriental typography."[554] On such occasions, Twiss was always deepening his understanding of the empire. He frequently provided legal judgements for or about Indian sovereigns. In April 1863, he wrote an *Opinion* concerning the "Rajah of Mysore," Krishnaraja Wadiyar III. This *Opinion* may either have been commissioned directly by Krishnaraja Wadiyar or, more likely, was in response to a request from the newly established India Office. The *Opinion* addressed whether Krishnaraja Wadiyar could adopt a successor to his territories. The Wadiyar dynasty had ruled Mysore since the fourteenth century and passed through an inherited male line of succession. In the second half of the eighteenth century, the kingdom had fallen under the control of Hyder Ali and his son Tipu Sultan, who, through an expansionism which aggravated their neighbours, and through resistance to the East India Company, provoked the Anglo-Mysore wars. Those wars led to much of Mysore being broken up between the Nizam of Hyderabad, the Maratha Confederacy, and the East India Company, while the Wadiyars were restored to the remaining rump.[555] In 1831, the East India Company argued that Mysore was being badly governed and seized control of the administration, leaving Krishnaraja Wadiyar III with little power. A further threat to the Wadiyar dynasty arose from Krishnaraja Wadiyar not having a male heir and raising the danger

---

after Tuesday with Admiralty business in court": Twiss to Metternich, February 15, 1849, National Archives of the Czech Republic, Prague, RAM-AC/ 10/ 775, 125.

553. Francis Henry Trithen, ed., *The Mahá Vira Charita, or The History of Ráma: A Sanscrit Play by Bhatta Bhavabhúti* (London, 1848).

554. Twiss to Metternich, April 12, 1849, National Archives of the Czech Republic, Prague, RAM-AC/ 10/ 775, 257–258.

555. For background to the treaties arising from the Anglo-Mysore wars, see Robert Travers, "A British Empire by Treaty in Eighteenth Century India," in *Empire by Treaty*, ed. Saliha Belmessous (Oxford, 2015), 132–160.

that the British or the Nizam of Hyderbad could invoke the doctrine of lapse to entirely annex the state. In February 1863, Krishnaraja Wadiyar's son-in-law, Sardar Chikka Krishnaraj Urs, died, and several days later, his daughter gave birth to a boy. Only weeks later, Twiss was consulted on whether, according to the terms of the treaties which concluded the Anglo-Mysore wars and re-established the rule of the Wadiyars, Krishnaraja Wadiyar could name his grandson as the heir to his title. Twiss responded, "The territory ceded to the Rajah of Mysore, by the Treaty of Mysore, was ceded in absolute sovereignty descendible to his heirs."[556] The whole purpose of this treaty, and the Treaty of Seringapatam, he argued, was "settlement of the dominions" of the Tipu Sultan and the "effectual establishment" of the Maharajah, the Wadiyars, in the government of Mysore. Twiss was therefore "of [the] opinion that, as a Sovereign Prince, the Rajah of Mysore can adopt a successor to his dominions" and there was "nothing in the language of the treaties to prevent the exercise of such a right." He warned, however, that if the Maharajah died without naming a successor, his territories would revert to the Nizam of Hyderbad and to the British government, who had reinstalled the Wadiyars in Mysore. On April 25, Twiss further clarified his opinion, stating that the Maharajah could not establish his successor through a last will and testament but must do so by law and that, if he did so, he would effectively block any claims from the Nizam of Hyderbad upon Mysore.[557]

The complex treaty relations and lines of succession in India provided a number of occasions in which Twiss's expertise was employed. Again, in October 1864, the British government sought his opinion on the Nawabship of the Carnatic, in South India, which had become vacant in 1855 when the Nawab Ghouse Khan died. Azim Jah, the brother of Azam Jah, the eleventh Nawab, who preceded Ghouse Khan, claimed the title to the throne, but his claim was not approved by the British until 1867. Twiss's view may well have been critical to that recognition, because in his 1864 *Opinion*, he argued that, under the law of nations, the Carnatic Treaty of 1801 obliged the British East India Company, and its successor the British Raj, to respect the hereditary succession of the Nawabs of the Carnatic and to provide them with 20 per cent of the territory's revenue in exchange for their own assumption of authority and the remaining 80 per cent of revenue.[558]

Twiss also regularly provided opinions on jurisdiction and administration in areas within which Britain exercised extraterritorial power, including under the Ottoman capitulations. In a joint opinion, he advised the British government

556. Travers Twiss, "Ex parte: The Rajah of Mysore. 23rd of April, 1863," *Law Officer's Opinions, 1862–1886*, 8 vols., Harvard Law Library, MS 1110, Vol. 1, 9–10.

557. Travers Twiss, "Further Opinion on the Above. 25th April, 1863," *Law Officer's Opinions, 1862–1886*, Vol. 1, 10.

558. Travers Twiss, "In re the Nawaubship of the Carnatic: Opinion. October 15, 1864," *Law Officer's Opinions, 1862–1886*, Vol. 1, 42–44.

on whether British subjects in Turkey should take advantage of the Ottoman offer to allow the possession of real property in Turkey in exchange for the same subjects relinquishing their extraterritorial privileges—an offer already taken up by many French residents, but one that Twiss noted came at a high cost.[559] In a further joint opinion with three other law officers, he responded to the complaint by Ali Pasha Mubarak, a senior minister in the Egyptian government, while visiting London in 1868, that reform was needed in the judicial system in Egypt in cases concerning "natives and foreigners." Ali Pasha pointed out that in many cases, foreigners resident in Egypt withdrew themselves from the jurisdiction of the "native tribunals" and insisted upon being tried by their consuls. This was an abuse, as Twiss and his colleagues noted, of the principle in the law of nations that "*actor sequitur forum rei*": namely, that cases should be tried in the forum in which the grievance occurred. These abuses, moreover, were inconsistent with the "letter of the capitulations." The complaints of Ali Mubarak, therefore, "appear to us to be only too well founded," and the "usurped Consular jurisdiction" was "most galling and offensive."[560]

On questions regarding East Asian sovereigns, Twiss provided diverse opinions, including on the drafting of a treaty between Britain and the Rajah of Kedah, a dependency of Siam (and now a northern state of present-day Malaysia). This treaty outlined the obligations of the Rajah to protect British subjects from crime, specifically "gang robbery," "great personal violence," murder, arson, rape, and burglary.[561] He also provided opinions on jurisdiction in Japanese ports, the suppression of piracy in China, and the legality of Chinese stations imposing tax upon the opium trade.[562] Regarding Africa, he provided numerous opinions, including on the creation of a Vice-Admiralty Court in Zanzibar, as well as an admiring account of the ad hoc equity courts

---

559. Travers Twiss, "Turkey: Tenure of land by Foreigners in. 29 June, 1868," *Law Officer's Opinions, 1862–1886*, Vol. 2, 50.

560. Travers Twiss et al., "Egypt: Judicial System in, as to Alteration of, in Cases where Natives and Foreigners Are Concerned. 25th June, 1868," *Law Officer's Opinions, 1862–1886*, Vol. 2, 45–49. For the expansion of extra-territoriality in Egypt, see David Todd, "Beneath Sovereignty: Extraterritoriality and Imperial Internationalism in Nineteenth-Century Egypt," *Law and History Review*, vol. 36, no. 1 (February 2018), 105–137.

561. Travers Twiss et al., "Draft of Convention between Her Majesty and the Rajah of Queddah. 10 December, 1868," *Law Officer's Opinions, 1862–1886*, Vol. 2, 272–273.

562. Travers Twiss et al., "Japan: Vice-Admiralty Jurisdiction in Consular Courts in, 12th September 1868," *Law Officer's Opinions, 1862–1886*, Vol. 2, 180; Travers Twiss et al., "Regulations Drawn up by H.M's Minister in Japan on Opening of the Ports of Hiogo and Osaka, 29th February 1868," *Law Officer's Opinions, 1862–1886*, Vol. 3, 253–254; Travers Twiss et al., "As to Suppression of Piracy in the Chinese Seas, 28th August 1868," *Law Officer's Opinions, 1862–1886*, Vol. 2, 151; Travers Twiss et al., "As to Rendition to the Chinese Govt. of Pirates Captures by H.M's Cruizers, 12th September 1868," *Law Officer's Opinions, 1862–1886*, Vol. 2, 181; Travers Twiss et al., "As to the Establishment of Opium Tax Stations in the Vicinity of Hong Kong by Chinese Govt. 5th January, 1869," *Law Officer's Opinions, 1862–1886*, Vol. 2, 299.

that had been established between foreign traders and West African sovereigns.[563] In all these cases, he took seriously the notion of non-European sovereigns as actors in the law of nations.

Perhaps the most notable instance of Twiss's engagement with revolutions outside Europe was when he was employed in 1857 by the King of Awadh, the northern Indian state just beneath Nepal, to provide an opinion on the legality of the kingdom's annexation by the British East Indian Company in 1856. The East India Company had ruled much of India since the mid-eighteenth century through a system of indirect control, leaving local rulers in power but under Company domination through a system of unequal treaties. By the 1840s, the Company had grown impatient with that system, seeking direct British administration, and began a series of annexations of Indian states and cities. The last of those annexations was Awadh, which was a large state, approximately 400 kilometres from north to south and 200 east to west. It was a buffer between East India Company territories and Nepal, and was ruled by Nawabs, or kings, of Persian origin, from their capital at Lucknow. The seizure of Awadh on February 11, 1856, was a trigger for the 1857 Indian Rebellion—or the Indian Mutiny to the British, and the first Indian war of independence to some nationalists. The rebellion began amongst sepoys, or Indian soldiers, in the East India Company army, many of whom were concerned by the series of annexations and the potential loss, as a consequence of the suppression of local laws, of their own privileges. The rebellion spread rapidly throughout northern India and continued from May 1857 to July the following year. In that time, many thousands were killed on both sides, including many atrocities. The massacre of the British in Cawnpore (or Kanpur) and the siege of Lucknow hardened British attitudes, leading to reprisals after the war in which many more thousands of Indians were massacred.

On the eve of these events, just months prior to the rebellion, Wajid Ali Shah, the deposed King of Awadh, now in exile in Calcutta, resolved to appeal to British justice against the annexation of Awadh. Due to his own ill health, he sent to England his mother, the Queen Dowager or Queen Mother, as the English described her, his brother, his son, and a large retinue. The English press closely followed the procession of the Queen Dowager from Calcutta to Suez, through Egypt, and on to England, where the entourage arrived in August 1856.[564] While there, they made a petition to parliament, gained an

---

563. Travers Twiss et al., "Zanzibar: As to the Establishment of a Vice-Admiralty Court at. 30th September, 1869," *Law Officer's Opinions, 1862-1886*, Vol. 3, 35-38; Travers Twiss et al., "As to the Legality of Certain Courts of Equity Established beyond HM's Jurisdiction on the West Coast of Africa, August, 1870," *Law Officer's Opinions, 1862-1886*, Vol. 6, 337-339; Travers Twiss et al., "Extension of Jurisdiction in Certain Territory on the West Coast of Africa, 15th January 1872," *Law Officer's Opinions, 1862-1886*, Vol. 7, 423-424.

564. See, for example, *Worcestershire Chronicle*, August 13, 1856, 4; *Westmorland Gazette*, August 16, 1856, 3.

audience with the Queen, and requested, on behalf of Wajid Ali Shah, Travers Twiss's opinion on the standing of the annexation of Awadh in the law of nations. Twiss's response was consistent with his position on the revolutions of 1848: that is, his greatest concern was with respect for sovereignty and, in this case, sovereign agreements. He therefore found that the annexation was a violation of the law of nations. As always, he methodically recounted the history of the case. He explained that prior to 1798, the "Sovereigns of Oude [i.e., Awadh]" had made treaties of "equal alliance" with the East India government, but thereafter the treaties had been unequal: that is, they involved a degree of dependence of the Awadh sovereigns upon the East India Company government. The first of these later treaties in 1798 was one of "offensive and defensive alliance" on both sides, whereby the Awadh government agreed to a financial "subsidy" to the Company in return for "protection."[565] According to the terms of the second, in 1801, the East India Company provided a "territorial guaranty" in return for a large territorial cession.[566] In this treaty the "Sovereign of Oude" also engaged to establish a "system of administration" that would be "conducive to the prosperity of his subjects and be calculated to secure the lives and property of the inhabitants."[567] He undertook, that is, to provide the conditions for security and prosperity that were regarded, according to the law of nations, to be the responsibility of all sovereigns. The Treaty of 1837 pointed out, however, that the 1801 Treaty provided "no remedy for the neglect of that solemn and paramount obligation" to provide security and prosperity. The 1837 Treaty therefore stipulated that if "gross and systematic oppression should prevail within the Oude dominions," the British government reserved the right to appoint its own officers to administer the territory to the extent necessary to restore order at the expense of the Oude treasuries.[568] Article 8 of that treaty stipulated that if the Governor General of India should be compelled to resort to this measure, he would "endeavour, as far as possible, to maintain . . . the native institutions and forms of administration . . . so as to facilitate the restoration of those territories to the Sovereign of Oude when the proper period for such restoration should arrive."[569]

This article in the treaty was an obstacle to the policy of annexation, what was called "the doctrine of lapse," that had been pursued since the 1840s, because no such consideration to "native institutions" and administration was given under those annexations. The Governor General, James Broun-Ramsey, Lord Dalhousie, therefore insisted, when he annexed Awadh, that the Treaty of 1837 was "null and void" and that only the treaty of 1801 prevailed, which

---

565. Travers Twiss, *Case of His Majesty the King of Oude: Copy Opinion of Dr Twiss*, Bibliothèque nationale de France, Fol–NT-333, ff.1–2.
   566. Twiss, *Case of His Majesty the King of Oude*, ff.2–3.
   567. Twiss, *Case of His Majesty the King of Oude*, f.3
   568. Twiss, *Case of His Majesty the King of Oude*, f.4.
   569. Twiss, *Case of His Majesty the King of Oude*, ff.3–4.

contained no obstacles to annexation.[570] His grounds for that claim were that the Secret Committee of the Court of Directors of the East India Company had disallowed the treaty when they received it in 1838.[571] Twiss pointed out that this fact had not been transmitted either to the Court of Awadh or to British officers in India, who continued to refer to the provisions of the treaty between 1837 and the moment when the Governor General declared it null and void in 1855.[572] The question, therefore, was whether a treaty was valid when it had not been formally ratified but had been treated as valid by both parties to it. Twiss cited Grotius to point out that "if the Sovereign power is silent," as it had been in this case by failing to communicate its will, then certain acts performed by the executive government would provide "virtual ratification" if those acts "cannot be referred to any other source than the treaty." In this case, he argued that executive government on both sides had indeed behaved in ways that implied the validity of the treaty. He terminated his opinion with the following judgement on February 24, 1857: "I am constrained to come to the conclusion that the Governor-General of India, in Council, was not authorised by the Law of Nations to set aside the treaty of 1837 as inoperative, and to look exclusively to the treaty of 1801 as the instrument by which the mutual relations of the East India Company and the Rulers of Oude were regulated."[573] For Twiss, the concern was probably less the sovereignty of Awadh, which he noted had been forced into unequal alliances, and was therefore a dependent sovereign, but respect for sovereign agreements. He had argued in the case of Schleswig and Holstein that dependent states were virtually no sovereigns at all, although in consistently referring to the "Sovereign of Oude," he appeared to believe the degree of dependence of Awadh to be less than that for Schleswig and Holstein. The Dukes of Schleswig and Holstein, he argued, were not sovereigns during the periods in which the Duchies were dependent states of the empires of Denmark and Germany.[574] At the same time, dependant states were nevertheless subject to sovereign agreements, or treaties, and such agreements must be respected. Twiss's opinion was cited at great length in newspapers and, in one such article, John Davenport cited Vattel on the "sacred and inviolable" nature of treaties.[575] They were sacred, as Vattel argued, because they secured the "safety and repose" of nations, and all things that tended to the preservation of states were sacred, as it were, because self-preservation was the first law of nature. These were sentiments precisely in accord with Twiss's own views, so that it comes as no surprise that he found

570. Twiss, *Case of His Majesty the King of Oude*, f.5.
571. Twiss, *Case of His Majesty the King of Oude*, f.5.
572. Twiss, *Case of His Majesty the King of Oude*, ff.6–8.
573. Twiss, *Case of His Majesty the King of Oude*, fol. 10.
574. Twiss, *The Relations of the Duchies of Schleswig and Holstein*, 65–66.
575. *Morning Chronicle*, July 25, 1857, 3. See also *London Evening Standard*, May 13, 1858, 5.

in favour of the "King of Oude" and against the actions of the Company. That Twiss also ruled against a colonising company with sovereign pretensions is particularly striking, given the great efforts he made, later in life, to substantiate precisely such sovereign claims by a colonising company.

In addition to newspaper coverage critical of the annexation of Awadh, Twiss's opinion was also reproduced in a tract calling for the restitution of Awadh to the "family of Oude," written by Samuel Lucas, the anti-slavery campaigner and newspaper editor. Lucas also demanded reparation and an investigation into whether annexation was a benefit to commerce.[576] Such demands were not met, and the petition to the House of Commons did not succeed, but the East India Company was seen as responsible for the events that provoked the 1857 rebellion, including the annexation of Awadh. The government accordingly passed the Government of India Act in 1858, ending 250 years of Company activities and transferring its functions to the crown with the establishment of the British Raj.

Despite his own defence of Awadh, and the public use of that defence, Twiss maintained that Europeans were superior to the subject peoples of their empires, and he expressed those views, privately at least, in the context of the Indian war while writing to Metternich: "Another telegram has since arrived, and we may now with some reason expect that Lucknow will be saved. What an episode in the History of India the Mutiny of the Sepoys will form ... What a superiority of race the European has exhibited throughout this affair."[577] Towards the end of the conflict, he broadened these racial claims, which, in contrast to contemporary international lawyers such as James Lorimer, he generally did not explicitly state in his published treatises: "You will have rejoiced, I doubt not, at the steady progress our troops have been making in India. The superiority of the European branch of the human family is very striking for it must be in the race, seeing that the Orientals have traditions as old, or far older, than any in Europe."[578]

In fact, Twiss's celebration of the victory was not only private. The soldiers who resisted the Indian Rebellion were celebrated as heroes in England and were feted upon their return. Prominent amongst those celebrations was the annual Encaenia, or commemoration of founders at Oxford held in the Sheldonian Theatre, in which Doctorates of Civil Law were awarded to distinguished figures, which frequently meant to heroes of the Empire. The first

576. [Samuel Lucas], *Dacoitee in Excelcis* (London, 1859), 200. For Twiss's opinion, see 192–199.

577. Twiss to Metternich, October 14, 1857, National Archives of the Czech Republic, Prague, RAM-AC/ 10/ 782, 21.

578. Twiss to Metternich, December 29, 1857, National Archives of the Czech Republic, Prague, RAM-AC/ 10/ 783, 14–15. Aydin, in *The Idea of the Muslim World*, 38, argues that it is at precisely this moment that race begins to be employed as a consciousness that transcends loyalty to empires.

Encaenia to celebrate the heroes of the Indian Rebellion, as it was then called, was on Wednesday, June 16, 1858, just four days before the rebellion came to an end with the fall of Gwalior. On this occasion, Sir John Inglis was presented at the ceremony for the award of the DCL. Inglis had been responsible for the defence of the British garrison at Lucknow, taking over the command after the commanding officer, Sir Henry Lawrence, had died from a shell during the defence. The defence had captured the public imagination in Britain as several hundred British officers and soldiers, the vast majority of them Indian, had held out against several thousand sepoy rebels for 87 days. The man who presented Inglis for the honourary degree was the Regius Professor of Civil Law, Travers Twiss: "Dr Twiss, in the course of a Latin speech, dwelt upon the meritorious services of General Inglis and adverted to Lady Inglis [women had been portrayed as particular victims of the rebellion], Havelock and Outram [Major General Henry Havelock and Sir James Outram, who both relieved Lucknow], the mention of each being the signal for further applause."[579] Another report eulogised: "When General Inglis appeared, with the effects of indisposition still traceable upon his pallid features, thunders of applause burst from area and gallery, and for some time proceedings were utterly at a standstill."[580] A year later, in July 1859, with the rebellion fully concluded, the celebrations at the commemoration day continued. On this occasion, three of the "Indian heroes" were presented to the ceremony: namely, Sir John Lawrence, who had captured Delhi from the sepoys; Sir Archdale Wilson, who had commanded the British troops during the siege of Delhi after his superior died of cholera; and Brigadier Edward Greathead, who had also helped capture Delhi and led troops in Agra, Cawnpore, and Lucknow, while being responsible for punitive attacks on Indian villages. Travers Twiss performed his customary duty, presenting each of the DCL recipients "individually in an elegant Latin speech in which their public services, virtues, and good qualities were adverted to in glowing and eulogistic language."[581] The reception was "remarkable . . . and will long be remembered by those who witnessed it. The whole theatre rose—the doctors waved their caps like undergraduates—ladies clapped their small hands with all their might, the area was a sea of waving arms."

Such ceremonies were of central importance in the management of public opinion in Victorian Britain. Twiss, as we have seen, was highly aware of the need to monitor and manipulate public opinion, and while he used publishing to those ends, he would also have understood the importance of ceremony. Under pressure to remove itself from the lives of its citizens, the Victorian state was increasingly non-interventionist, while at the same time "civil

---

579. *Birmingham Daily Post*, June 18, 1858, 1.
580. *Essex Standard*, June 18, 1858, 3.
581. *Oxford Chronicle and Reading Gazette*, July 9, 1859, 2. See also *Oxford University and City Herald*, July 9, 1859, 11, 12.

society," as it has been described, enacted its own form of self-governance.[582] Public opinion was vital to such self-government, and the state took careful note of movements in public opinion. The government of public opinion was also to be found in other European states and domains, such as international law.[583] Importantly, to be governed by public opinion was not to submit to mob rule and passion.[584] It implied a departure from the Enlightenment rule of reason, but it was embedded in the history and culture of a nation. It was civilized, progressive, and middle class.

An example of state sensitivity to public opinion is found in the response to the Indian Rebellion. The Governor General of India, Charles Canning, had requested British soldiers to show clemency for those sepoys who were not directly involved in the killing. His policy caused outrage in some quarters in Britain and the Prime Minister, Lord Palmerston, refused to state his position on Canning publicly. Nevertheless, Lord Granville came to Canning's defence. Granville was between terms as Secretary of State for Foreign Affairs, and at this moment in 1857, he was the Lord President of the Council and a member of Cabinet. While Granville privately agreed with Canning's policy of clemency, his defence consisted of declaring in a public meeting on November 4, 1857, at Mansion House, a meeting which he later said was the most hostile he faced in his life, that Canning hadn't called for clemency at all.[585] We can understand better why he chose this line of defence—complete denial of the matter rather than explanation—when we examine Granville's private papers. There we find a large number of "confidential" police reports, sent from various London boroughs to Sir Richard Mayne, the head of the London Metropolitan Police, and also sent directly to Granville himself.[586] All the reports reveal the great public hostility to Canning's policy. According to the terms of the 1829 Police Act, the London Metropolitan Police were supposed to be concerned with the prevention of crime, although it has long been recognised that they played a political role, for example, in surveillance of the Chartists.[587] Nevertheless, even by those more political standards, the canvassing of public opinion on the policies of the Governor General of India reveals a remarkable collaboration between the supposedly impersonal authority and political interests. A report

---

582. Mandler, "Introduction," to Mandler, ed., *Liberty and Authority in Victorian Britain*, 18–21. See also Collini, *Public Moralists*, on the grounding of Victorian political thought in social values and customs.

583. Koskenniemi, *The Gentle Civilizer of Nations*, 15–16, 54–57.

584. Hilton, *A Mad, Bad, and Dangerous People*, 311.

585. For Canning and Granville, see Saul David, *The Indian Mutiny: 1857*; Jasper Ridley, *Lord Palmerston* (1970, Basingstoke).

586. For Mayne, see Philip Thurmond Smith, *Policing Victorian London: Political Policing, Public Order, and the London Metropolitan Police* (London, 1985), 35–38.

587. For "political policing," see Smith, *Policing Victorian London*, 5, and for the terms of the 1829 Act, 23–25.

on November 11, 1857, from a police officer in "B Division" states: "In reference to the policy of the Governor General of India in showing sympathy with the sepoys, I have heard very strong feelings expressed by persons of the middle classes capable of forming an opinion who strongly condemn it. I believe the general wish of the middle classes is that the mutineers should be severely dealt with."[588] A further report, on November 12, from "C Division" states: "The opinion of the middle classes in this division appears to be that the mutiny in India should be put down with a strong and vigorous hand," although this report added the qualification that "many people strongly condemn the mode in which some of the mutinous sepoys have been executed viz. blowing them from guns."[589] Such was the consensus amongst these reports, all made, as one put it, "after private and careful enquiries . . . with a view of ascertaining the general feeling."[590] Given this careful government pursuit of public opinion, events in which public sentiment were celebrated assumed great importance, and the Encaenia in which Twiss participated was one such event.

Twiss's efforts in support of the war did not, however, remain on the level of propaganda. Also amongst Granville's papers from 1857, when he was Lord President of the Council, is a letter from Twiss, written on August 28, 1857, three months after the outbreak of the Indian Rebellion and at its height. It is familiar in tone. Twiss begins, "I called in the hope of seeing you for a moment before I left London this morning," indicating the ease with which he was accustomed to access the highest officers in the government. In frustration, he then wrote: "I infer from your letter that HM Government is not likely to accept the offer. I ought to tell you that Count Taaffe was the person. He resigned his commission in the spring as he could not get an extension of leave of absence to come to England. He meant to offer his own services in command of the Regiment during the war without pay or appointment. He leaves England tomorrow for the Chateau of Ellischau near Silberberg Bohemia and I expect to join him at Dresden and pass a week with him in a very curious part of Bohemia. I believe from what I hear that the Hungarians would have equipped the Regiment."[591] It is implicit in this letter that Twiss had used his good offices to convey an offer from a Bohemian count to equip and lead a regiment to fight in the Indian war. It would appear to be a case of one empire helping another when faced with a nationalist crisis, and Twiss, who had been such a friend to the Austrian Empire when faced with their own nationalist crisis, was a natural person to transmit the offer. While this interpretation is undoubtedly valid, as far as it goes, the truth is more complex. Count Taaffe

---

588. Granville Papers, National Archives: PRO 30/29/23/10.

589. Granville Papers, National Archives: PRO 30/29/23/10.

590. Granville Papers, National Archives: PRO 30/29/23/10.

591. "Twiss to Granville," August 28, 1857, Granville Papers, National Archives, London, 30/29/23/10, 448.

was Charles Taaffe, son of Viscount Louis Taaffe, who had been the Austrian minister of justice during the 1848 Revolution. Although the Taaffes belonged to the Bohemian nobility, their origin was Irish. Francis Taaffe, 3rd Earl of Carlingford, born in Ballymote, County Sligo, was exiled in the 1650s in continental Europe with other Royalist forces during the English Civil War. While in exile, he entered the service of Ferdinand III, the Holy Roman Emperor, and his family settled in Bohemia. After the death of Viscount Louis Taaffe in 1855, his son Charles Taaffe, an officer in the Austrian army, claimed the moribund Irish title of his family, bringing the case to the House of Lords Committee for Privileges on July 28, 1857. The role of the Privileges Committee was to consider questions regarding parliamentary privilege, but it was also charged with judging disputed peerage claims. As such, it was the gatekeeper of the aristocracy. It examined cases in which people were attempting to transform their social status.

The lawyer who argued Count Taaffe's claim before the Lords was Travers Twiss.[592] Twiss was almost certainly recommended to the Taaffes by his friend Prince Metternich, now living alternately between Vienna and his estate. The Taaffes had been good friends to Metternich, and it was in Count Taaffe's house that Metternich and his family found refuge when they fled their own Vienna home through the garden gate during the riots of March 13, 1848.[593] Certainly Metternich was aware of Twiss acting for Taaffe. Twiss wrote to Metternich on August 11, 1857, to say his impending visit to Metternich's Schloss Johannisberg could be delayed by Taaffe's case: "I may be detained here by Viscount Taaffe's Peerage Case before the House of Lords."[594] More than a year earlier, Twiss was noting Taaffe's presence in London in his letters to Metternich.[595] Twiss succeeded in reinstating the Taaffe family's British title. His success reveals, once again, his expertise in cases dealing with the creation of new persons (or, perhaps in this case, the resurrection of old persons). The crown opposed the recognition of the Taaffe title in the case before the Lords, and arguing for the crown, the Attorney General declared that "aliens" could not make claims to English titles. In overcoming this argument, Twiss showed that persons seen as outsiders were not excluded from the processes of personification. This was a trope of invention he was able to employ both with his wife and in the creation of the Congo Free State. Amongst other measures, Twiss was rewarded, as we see from his letter, with a tour of Bohemia. Taaffe, for his part, attempted to show his gratitude by offering to help out the new empire, in which he was a

---

592. "Taaffe Peerage," *The Belfast Newsletter*, August 3, 1857, 2; "Taaffe Peerage," *Dublin Evening Post*, August 15, 1857, 3.

593. Palmer, *Metternich*, 212–213.

594. Twiss to Metternich, August 11, 1857, National Archives of the Czech Republic, Prague, RAM-AC/ 10/ 783, 5.

595. "Count Taaffe was at the Apthorpe's the other day": Twiss to Metternich, April 5, 1856, National Archives of the Czech Republic, Prague, RAM-AC/ 10/ 782, 8.

member of the nobility, by raising a regiment from another empire in which he was also a member of the nobility. A Bohemian regiment fighting for the British against the Sepoys in India might sound odd, and we might conclude that Granville and his fellow ministers declined the offer because it sounded odd to them too, but at this point, in August 1857, there was a strong sense in Twiss's letters to Metternich that the public perception, at least, of the war was that its outcome was still very much in the balance, and for that reason the offer from Taaffe and Twiss's role in it are not eccentric.

It would seem rather contradictory that Twiss was the person who declared, on the one hand, one of the most important acts leading to the Indian Rebellion, the annexation of Awadh, to have been illegal in the law of nations; on the other hand, he was the person responsible for eulogising the heroes of the war in one of the ceremonies of celebration and recognition, while at the same time he tried to raise a Hungarian regiment to fight in the war. It would not have been easy to distinguish between the unlawful acts of the empire, on the one hand, and the right of the Empire to defend itself, on the other. Just war could not be based upon unlawful acts, and despite the outpouring of patriotic feeling during the war, there was a significant level of discontent with India policy evident in the public protests at the annexations, as well as the Government of India Act. Some of this criticism, and Twiss's own thoughts on the war, are found in a letter he wrote to Metternich on July 20, 1857, shortly after the outbreak of the war. In that letter, he declared, "What great events are passing in the East."[596] The "difficult problem of political life," the problem of "centralization," which for Metternich and Twiss was the contest between the "unitary state," driven by nationalism, and empire, was "likely to be put to a severe trial" in the coming months. His thoughts turned to the challenges faced by the Roman Empire, which "advanced," he observed to Metternich, so long as it "protected all alike and maintained its military organization complete."[597] The preservation of subjects was the foremost obligation of sovereigns under the social contract thinking inherited from the seventeenth-century contract theorists, and it remained central in treatises on the law of nations, including Twiss's work, even while it was abandoned by positivists. It came before flourishing and happiness and all such objectives that had been added to the obligations of sovereigns by Enlightenment and utilitarian thinkers of the eighteenth and nineteenth centuries. On this central measure of preservation, or "protection of all alike," Twiss agreed with contemporary critics that the British Empire had fallen short: "We had overlooked both these conditions, upon which our Eastern Empire had grown up." In this criticism, we hear

---

596. Twiss to Metternich, July 20, 1857, National Archives of the Czech Republic, Prague, RAM-AC/ 10/ 783, 3.

597. Twiss to Metternich, July 20, 1857, National Archives of the Czech Republic, Prague, RAM-AC/ 10/ 783, 4.

an echo of his opinion on the Awadh case—the Empire had violated its own agreements. Nevertheless, his own critical distance from the events, which he perceived to be in the balance, was apparent in the dispassionate tone of his concluding remark to Metternich: "The result will be interesting, and before we meet, the impulse will have been given."[598] Metternich likewise believed the outcome to be in the balance, and he echoed Twiss's sense that European overseas empires were being mismanaged, in part because the Orient was a particularly difficult sphere to manage: "I wish for good news from India. I have many doubts about the outcome. We have played until present with oriental affairs. The veritable extreme."[599]

On another level, however, Twiss could accommodate the tensions in his positions on India because he was performing different offices, assuming different personae. This suppleness in personality, in being different people, which we all must perform to some degree or other—for example, one physical person may be mother, daughter, partner, professor, citizen, or member—is something at which Twiss was particularly adept. As his life progressed, he realised the creative potential of personality in both personal life and in international law. His life spanned a period in which the opportunities for performing different personae were expanding. Twiss, it is true, was opposed, ironically, to many of those changes. He was opposed to the Catholic Emancipation Act, particularly to the provisions that created the potential for new legal personalities for Catholic bishops. He was opposed to the Matrimonial Causes Act, which provided access to divorce for the middle classes. He was opposed to the revolutions of 1848, which sought to expand national personae as well as expanding the franchise and citizenship of natural persons. At the same time, Twiss was a very enthusiastic officeholder, and his opposition on many of these questions would not prevent him from seizing the expanding opportunities himself. Moreover, on other issues, he contributed to and even led the calls for new forms of personification, most importantly, as we shall see, on the question of who can be admitted to international society and, covertly, who could be admitted to Society.

598. Twiss to Metternich, July 20, 1857, National Archives of the Czech Republic, Prague, RAM-AC/ 10/ 783, 4.

599. Metternich to Twiss, Johannisberg, August 13, 1857, Bibliothèque nationale de France, Fol/ R.D./13810, 156v (postscript).

PART 3

Agnes Willoughby and Pharaïlde van Lynseele

Metamorphoses

In March 1872, Sir Travers Twiss, ennobled in 1867, and his wife, Lady Pharaïlde Twiss, were entangled in a libel trial in Southwark Police Court concerning her true identity. She was accused of having transformed herself from a London streetwalker into the daughter of a Dutch aristocrat serving in the Polish army, thus enabling her to be an appropriate spouse for Travers Twiss. During the trial, just across the Thames, at the Haymarket Theatre, a similar story of transformation had been running as a play during the previous three months. The play was *Pygmalion and Galatea*, written by William S. Gilbert, later one half of Gilbert and Sullivan, the composers of the comic operas. The play, one of several that Gilbert put on in the Haymarket Theatre, was his most successful play to date and provided the foundation for his later collaborations with Sullivan. It retells the well-known story from Ovid's *Metamorphoses* of the sculptor, Pygmalion, who falls in love with his statue, and such is the force of his love, the statue comes to life. For Ovid, this story exemplified his central concern in the *Metamorphoses* with transformation. The transformations in Ovid's poem were numerous—for example, the people of Corinth, Ovid said, had in earliest times sprung from fungus; Dionysius changed the three daughters of Minyas into bats; Athena, in a fit of jealousy, turned Arachne, the weaver, into a spider; and Zeus turned the Myrmidons of Aegina into humans from a colony of ants. Pygmalion, as Orpheus sings in Ovid's account of the story, was a Cypriot sculptor who resolved never to have anything to do with women after encountering the daughters of Propoetus, the Propoetides. These "foul" women were "said to have been the first to prostitute their

FIGURE 5. Ernest Normand, *Pygmalion and Galatea* (1881).*

* Atkinson Art Gallery, Southport, England

bodies," and, in punishment, Venus turned them to stone.[1] As a substitute, Pygmalion sculpted a statue of a woman who possessed "a beauty more perfect than that of any woman ever born. And with his own work he falls in love." He then began to doubt his own creation: "Often he lifts his hands to the work to try whether it be flesh or ivory; nor does he yet confess it to be ivory. He kisses it and thinks his kisses are returned; and speaks to it; grasps it and seems to feel his fingers sink into the limbs."[2] Finally, he lay in bed with the statue resting its head "on soft down pillows."[3] In recognition of Pygmalion's offerings at her altar, and of the depth of his love for the statue, Venus transformed her into flesh, and the two married.[4]

Ovid's *Metamorphoses* was revived by Renaissance artists, particularly through their concern with the notion that people can be the "makers and moulders of themselves," as Pico della Mirandola put it. In the succeeding centuries, the story of Pygmalion was recounted in numerous forms, operas, painting, and plays—for example, in Jean-Jacques Rousseau's *Pygmalion*—but it received its strongest reception in the nineteenth century. Victorians were fascinated with the Pygmalion myth to such a degree that they pathologized "statue-love" as a medical disorder.[5] The German psychiatrist Richard von Krafft-Ebing included a section on the "Violation of Statues" in his *Pschopathia Sexualis*, claiming, amongst other cases, that Clisophus of Selymbria "violated the statue of a goddess in the Temple of Samos, after having placed a piece of meat on a certain part."[6]

What fascinated Victorian readers of the Pygmalion myth was how a relationship between a man and a woman could transform the status of the woman, although such stories always transformed the man as well, raising the question of who was the sculptor and who the statue. In William Brough's 1867 burlesque version of the myth, *Pygmalion; or, The Statue Fair*, the sculptor Pygmalion creates a woman, a statue, as Brough tells us, an "unmistakable 'miss' made for sale."[7] Rather than spurning women because of his disgust with prostitution, as in Ovid's version of the story, Brough's Pygmalion prostitutes his statues at the same time that he scorns women. In vengeance, Venus

---

1. Ovid, *Metamorphoses, Books IX to XV*, trans. Frank Justus Miller, revised by G. P. Goold (Cambridge, Mass., 1916), Book X, 241–245.
2. Ovid, *Metamorphoses, Books IX to XV*, Book X, 250–258.
3. Ovid, *Metamorphoses, Books IX to XV*, Book X, 268.
4. Ovid, *Metamorphoses, Books IX to XV*, Book X, 275–295.
5. Alastair J. L. Blanchard, "Queer Desires and Classicizing Strategies of Resistance," in Kate Fisher and Rebecca Langlands, eds., *Sex, Knowledge, and Receptions of the Past* (Oxford, 2015), 31.
6. Richard von Krafft-Ebing, *Psychopathia Sexualis, with Especial Reference to Contrary Sexual Instinct*, trans. Charles Gilbert Craddock (London, 1894), 396. This example is discussed in Blanchard, "Queer Desires," 31.
7. William Brough, *Pygmalion; or, the Statue Fair* (London, 1867), 3.

uses Cupid's arrow to make Pygmalion fall in love with one of his statues, a woman for sale. Venus then brings the statue to life for Pygmalion but gives her no heart. The living statue is not a "Glad-stone," as Brough puns, suggesting she does not carry the possibility of transformation that was central both to the Pygmalion myth and to William Gladstone's ideas of improvement.[8] Unaware of Venus and Cupid's trick, Psyche happens upon the living statue and, out of pity, gives her emotions. The statue then falls in love with Pygmalion, and he finds himself marrying his would-be prostitute. In parallel stories, the King who is desperate to marry off his daughter, Princess Mandane, accepts her match with Pygmalion's apprentice, Cambyses, "who, with dreams beyond his station, ultimately attains a station beyond his dreams,"[9] and the King's general, Harpagus, is joined with Mopsa, a common maid. At the play's climax, Cupid summarised "The sculptor wouldn't love—he does so now. / The King who'd have a low-bred son in law / Has got the lowest one you ever saw / E'en the old soldier settles down in life / And takes the maid-of-all-work for his wife / Thus we've secured ... / The greatest happiness of the greatest number."[10] As Bentham put it, the greatest happiness of the greatest number "is the measure of right and wrong," and it is this measure, rather than social status, that permits the resolution of conflicts in the play through transformations of status.

In Gilbert's version, the story became a satire in which Pygmalion is already married, but the statue, Galatea, comes to life and falls in love with him. In contrast to Brough's burlesque version of the myth, however, Gilbert's Galatea discovers that the mortal world is corrupt and vulgar and decides to return to stone. Later versions of the story, such as George Bernard Shaw's *Pygmalion*, develop this tension between the liberating potential and the pitfalls of individual reinvention. In Shaw's case, those pitfalls are dramatized by using class to illustrate the dangers and limitations of transformation, so while Eliza Doolittle, the figure of Galatea, is able to become a simulacrum of a lady, she is unable entirely to escape her working-class origins.

Shaw spelled out what fascinated Victorians with the Pygmalion myth: namely, the possibility, and limits, of individuals undergoing metamorphoses of class and status. Such metamorphoses included the prostitutes who walked the Haymarket outside the Haymarket Theatre, as well as attending performances within, where Gilbert's *Pygmalion and Galatea* was performed.[11] As Roy Porter observed, "Prostitution flaunted itself in Victorian

8. Brough, *Pygmalion*, 23, for "Glad-stone."

9. Brough, *Pygmalion*, 3.

10. Brough, *Pygmalion*, 37. On Bentham's use of "the greatest happiness for the greatest number," see J. H. Burns, "Happiness and Utility: Jeremy Bentham's Equation," *Utilitas*, vol. 17, no. 1 (March 2005), 46–61.

11. For prostitutes in the Haymarket, see Henry Mayhew, *London Labour and the London Poor: Vol. 4: Those That Will Not Work* (London, 1862), 217.

London," with more than 2,800 brothels in 1859, some 80,000 prostitutes, and the streetwalkers outside the Bank of England standing in "rows like hackney coaches."[12] Prostitutes were subjects for transformation because they were elusive, both in terms of their moral standing, "neither moral nor irrevocably lost," and also because women moved rapidly, and relatively easily, in and out of prostitution.[13] The Haymarket and Regent Street were the heart of the nightlife in Victorian London, with many cafés, "brilliant coffee rooms lined with large mirrors," "wine vaults," "supper rooms," restaurants, theatres, dancing halls, commonly called "casinos," "Turkish divans," illuminated shops, with throngs of people of all classes crowding the streets, including beggars and nobility and, notoriously, numerous prostitutes in brothels in the lanes off these thoroughfares.[14] William Acton claimed he could count 300 prostitutes at any one moment walking the "*trottoir*" of the Haymarket, while, he complained, the "foreign" prostitutes, mainly Belgian and French, who typically congregated in Regent Street, particularly its lower half, including Twiss's future wife, only needed a passing shower as an excuse for "extravagantly raising their dresses."[15]

William Gladstone, the Prime Minister, was known for also walking the Haymarket in search of the same prostitutes, in order, so he said, to reclaim them from a life of vice, and described this duty "as the chief burden on my soul."[16] As he grew older, Gladstone turned increasingly towards ideas of self-improvement, and prostitutes, widely perceived as embodying the corruptions of industrial society, offered ideal material for his reforming zeal.[17] Some of the courtesans Gladstone formed attachments to, such as the notorious "pretty horse-breaker" Catherine Walters, certainly showed a remarkable ability to transform their own circumstances, albeit not in the manner Gladstone intended. Walters was a courtesan who, from the late 1850s, in her

12. Roy Porter, *London: A Social History* (London, 1994), 364. See also James Winter, *London's Teeming Streets: 1830–1914* (London, 1993), 110: "Nearly every visitor to nineteenth-century London recorded shock at seeing so many prostitutes in the open and carrying on their trade in such an aggressive fashion"; Chesney, *Victorian Underworld*, 363: "What is so striking is not just the number of prostitutes . . . but the blatancy with which they carried on their trade, even in the heart of fashionable London."

13. Poovey, *Making a Social Body*, 88–89. See also Walkowitz, *Prostitution and Victorian Society*, 13–31.

14. Mayhew, *London Labour and the London Poor: Vol. 4*, 357.

15. William Acton, *Prostitution, Considered in Its Moral, Social and Sanitary Aspects in London and Other Large Cities* (London, 1857), 112–113, and 109 for the concentration of Belgian and French prostitutes in the "lower half'" of Regent Street: that is, directly outside the Athenaeum, which Twiss frequented in the '40s and '50s when he was on the club's committee.

16. Cited in Walkowitz, *Prostitution and Victorian Society*, 32.

17. On prostitutes, corruption, and reform, see Poovey, *Making a Social Body*, 88–97. On the ambiguity of Gladstone's actions, see Koven, *Slumming*, 123.

THE HAYMARKET.—MIDNIGHT.

FIGURE 6. The Haymarket.*

teens, first worked the Haymarket and then rode horses in Hyde Park wearing a tight, waisted, riding habit. Horse-breakers were the prominent courtesans who rode in Rotten Row (a name corrupted from the medieval *route du roi*) in Hyde Park, in self-advertisement, and sometimes to advertise brothels to which they were attached, but also to promote the livery stables that lent them horses.[18] They captured the public imagination, drawing partly admiring, partly voyeuristic crowds, at the same time that they enraged the aristocratic women who also rode in the park. A letter by Irish satirist Matthew James Higgins in *The Times*, in June 1861, purportedly from seven "Belgravian" mothers, six aristocrats and one very rich, complained that "our dear girls are still at home," even after several seasons of "balls, bazaars, breakfasts, concerts . . . the Opera, Epsom, Ascot."[19] Their twenty-four girls were not, contrary to rumour, "all just alike . . . automatons put together for one object," and yet they could not marry because "what our simple-minded daughters call the 'pretty horsebreakers' occupy naughtily and temporarily where we should occupy *en permanence* . . . these bad rivals of our children are no longer kept

---

18. Sos Eltis, *Acts of Desire* (Oxford, 2013), 72–73; Chesney, *Victorian Underworld*, 377.
19. *The Times*, June 27, 1861, 6.
* Henry Mayhew, *London Labour and the London Poor*, Vol. 4 [London, 1862], 260

in the background, as things we know but, knowing, are to seem not to know." Prostitution, the letter was saying, was now openly present and acknowledged in middle-class, and aristocratic, society. At the same time, the satirical purpose of the letter echoed the figure of Edith Granger in Dickens's *Dombey and Son*, who had aristocratic blood but frankly acknowledged she was a commodity to be bought and sold in the marriage market.[20] "Shall we go," the letter from the Belgravian mothers concluded, "to the Bishops who are in town—to Convocation?" Higgins could not have known that the Vicar General, Travers Twiss, who summoned Convocation, was linked at precisely this moment with one of the horse-breakers. Even "the picture of the year," the letter finally lamented, "is a 'Pretty Horsebreaker.'"

Indeed, the image of the "pretty horse-breaker" became a topic of art and literature. William Brough, with Andrew Halliday, wrote a one-act satirical play, *The Pretty Horsebreaker*, which was first performed on July 15, 1861, little more than a month after the letter from the Belgravian mothers to *The Times* and expanding upon that letter's conceit.[21] The play portrayed a mother, Lady Creamy Stilton, with seven daughters, none of whom she could marry (recalling Jane Austen's *Pride and Prejudice*), while their "horse-breaker" country cousin, Bella Sunnyside, captures a propertied gentleman, Mr Upton Spout. Spout recognises Bella for a horse-breaker, declaring: "What young man of spirit and property would go out with ladies, when he can enjoy the society of a pretty horsebreaker, by stopping where he is."[22] Lady Stilton indignantly responds: "Your what—your pretty horsebreaker? I trust, sir, you will introduce nothing of the kind within this circle," but Spout persists with the description, while at the same time offering to marry Bella.[23] "Pretty horse-breakers" marrying aristocrats were, as we shall see, the subject of a particularly public sandal in 1861, the year this play was performed, in the case of Agnes Willoughby and William Windham. It is hardly surprising that Brough, who later wrote the 1867 version of *Pygmalion*, had the creative imagination to see the same transformative possibilities in the story of the horse-breaker as in his retelling of Ovid's myth.

The painting alluded to in Higgins's letter to *The Times*, "the picture of the year," was *The Shrew Tamed*, an 1861 work by Edwin Landseer. The image ostensibly represents the equestrienne Ann Gilbert practicing a technique learned from John Solomon Rarey, the celebrated American horse-whisperer, who had visited England two years previously to treat a troubled horse belonging to Queen Victoria. To great acclaim, he succeeded in calming the horse, lying down amongst its hooves. Travers Twiss, who became the

20. Nord, *Walking the Victorian Streets*, 87.
21. William Brough and Andrew Halliday, *The Pretty Horsebreaker* (London, 1861).
22. Brough and Halliday, *The Pretty Horsebreaker*, 14.
23. Brough and Halliday, *The Pretty Horsebreaker*, 17.

FIGURE 7. *The Shrew Tamed*, Edwin Landseer, 1861.*

"protector" of a least one celebrated horse-breaker, Agnes Willoughby, had in his library an 1859 copy of *J. S. Rarey's The Art of Taming Horses*, published the year in which he became involved with Willoughby.²⁴ Twiss had a direct interest in the question. He complained to Prince Metternich in 1849, for example, that he been "obliged to throw myself off a restive half-broken horse, that I was trying in a field near Barnet. I was fortunate in escaping, as I did, without any fractures but pain and fever today have perfectly incapacitated me."²⁵

Ann Gilbert's pose imitates Rarey's method, but Landseer's representation of her was immediately rumoured to be a likeness of another notable horsewoman and courtesan, Catherine Walters, Gladstone's friend, and the painting came to be known as "The Pretty Horsebreaker." The symbolism suggests that a gentleman may be easily seduced, or bewitched, by a woman of Catherine Walters's profession, although the editor of Rarey's book warned against "horse-whisperers" who worked like "wicked women, not endowed with any extraordinary external charms, who bewitch and betray the wisest men."²⁶ At the same time, *The Art of Taming Horses* declared that the models

---

24. *Catalogue of a Portion of the Miscellaneous Library of Sir Travers Twiss*, 45.

25. Twiss to Metternich, August 17, 1849, National Archives of the Czech Republic, Prague, RAM-AC/ 10/ 775, 365. Metternich congratulated him on returning to the saddle during a stay in Brighton: "I am charmed by what you are doing on your stay. You are following a homeopathic regime, you are healing through movement by horse—the injury you incurred is an accident of the species": Metternich to Twiss, Richmond, August 25, 1849, Bibliothèque nationale de France, Fol/ R.D./13810, 110. The following year, however, Twiss wrote of yet another "disaster in trying a new horse": Twiss to Metternich, February 15, 1850, National Archives of the Czech Republic, Prague, RAM-AC/ 10/ 776, 11.

26. J. S. Rarey's *The Art of Taming Horses* (London, 1859), 9.

* British Paintings, "(Sir) Edwin Henry Landseer—The Shrew Tamed," http:// goldenagepaintings.blogspot.com.au/2009/02/sir-edwin-henry-landseer-shrew-tamed .html

for women riders were to be found in Rotten Row: "The originals, few and far between, are to be found nine months a year daily in Rotten Row."[27]

Walters became self-employed and had a string of very eminent clients, including, for many years, the Marquess of Hartington, later the 8th Duke of Devonshire and leader of the Liberals and Liberal Unionists in parliament. She was a wealthy woman, moving in 1872 to 15 South Street, just off Park Lane (and around the corner from Travers Twiss), and possessing an income at times in the thousands of pounds. She was not the only courtesan to prosper. The journalist Henry Mayhew's *London Labour and the London Poor* reported that many respectable women had formerly been "prostitutes," just as many "prostitutes" had formerly been respectable women.[28] His report, as with much discussion about prostitution in mid-Victorian England, must be placed in the context of the Contagious Diseases Acts in the 1860s, which sought to control venereal disease and prostitutes, who were identified as the cause of the problem. Mayhew was himself partly voyeuristic upon the social life he reported. Bracebridge Hemyng, who wrote the section on prostitution in *London Labour and the London Poor*, was a young barrister when he worked for Mayhew and would later go on to a career writing popular novels.[29] Whether or not their observations about respectable women and prostitution were exaggerated, they underlined the anxiety, as a number of historians have observed, about contagion, both physical and moral contagion, between the classes. Moreover, their claims also revealed the reality of social mobility in Victorian society as well as anxiety and fascination about it. The interest was shared by Travers Twiss, who possessed a copy of the 1862 edition of *London Labour and the London Poor*.[30] Perceived as both victims and agents, prostitutes "crystalized pervasive concerns about determinism and free will."[31] The section on prostitution in *London Labour and the London Poor* began with the observation that "the liberty of the subject is very jealously guarded in England," with the implication being that prostitution flourished with growing individual liberty.[32] Indeed, the introduction of the Contagious Diseases Acts dismayed many women's rights activists, including Josephine Butler, who led the national association for repeal of the legislation.[33] The Acts were seen as a backward step when feminists were attempting to benefit from the extensions of the suffrage that had recently been granted to men, for example, in the

27. *J. S. Rarey's The Art of Taming Horses*, 118.
28. Mayhew, *London Labour and the London Poor: Vol. 4*, 242, on a curate's daughter who became a prostitute; for prostitutes marrying well, see 214, 219, 236. See also Nord, *Walking the Victorian Streets*, 10–11.
29. On Mayhew's voyeurism, see Walkowitz, *City of Dreadful Delight*, 20–21.
30. *Catalogue of a Portion of the Miscellaneous Library of Sir Travers Twiss*, 43.
31. Poovey, *Making a Social Body*, 88.
32. Mayhew, *London Labour and the London Poor: Vol. 4*, 210.
33. Walkowitz, *Prostitution and Victorian Society*, 103–105.

1867 Reform Act. The compulsory testing for disease of women who were suspected of prostitution was understood to be an infringement upon the liberty not only of those women, in particular, but of all women. A person's control over her or his body was fundamental to freedom. Prior to the Contagious Diseases Acts, as Harriet Martineau argued, "Every woman in the country had the same rights as men over her own person, and the law extended its protection over all alike."[34] The Acts removed that liberty. Florence Nightingale argued that women evading the Acts were, as Helen Rogers puts it, "affirming their constitutional liberties."[35] Prostitution, therefore, became a rallying point for women's rights through the second half of the century, and it focused that movement upon the power of the state, both in terms of the ways in which the state infringed upon women's rights and how it could also be a means to emancipation. Moreover, prostitution could even be perceived to provide opportunities for freedom. Writing under the *nom de plume* Justina, Nightingale argued that "clandestine prostitution" was a happy escape from the Acts.[36] Nightingale's perspective contrasted sharply with other works on prostitution, such as Honoré Antoine Frégier's *Des classes dangereuses de la population dans les grandes villes*, which categorized prostitution as either "public" or "clandestine."[37] Public prostitution, Frégier argued, was regulated by the authorities, and although it was undesirable, it was contained. Clandestine prostitution, on the other hand, he regarded as one of the greatest threats to public order because the women escaped all efforts to control them. Twiss may have been aware of Frégier's warnings regarding the dangers of prostitution because, along with his edition of Mayhew, he possessed a copy of *Des classes dangereuses de la population dans les grandes villes*.[38]

While prostitution sometimes inspired ideas of social transformation in the minds of Victorians and at times brought prosperity to the lives of courtesans such as Walters, it mainly inspired fear, dread, and condemnation and brought social exile and pariah status to anybody suspected of association with it. All prostitutes faced such dangers, particularly those of lower rank. Hemyng provided a taxonomy of London prostitution. At its summit were courtesans, or "seclusives," who lived in private houses and apartments and were divided into two classes: namely, "kept mistresses," with several lovers although pretending to have one, and who frequented the "higher classes of society"; and "prima donnas," who were not "kept" but had several men who visited them periodically and were to be found "where the fashionable congregate," including "in

34. Cited in Rogers, "Women and Liberty," 137.
35. Rogers, "Women and Liberty," 138. On the toleration of prostitution being associated with a free society, see also Winter, *London's Teeming Streets: 1830-1914*, 110-111.
36. Rogers, "Women and Liberty," 138.
37. Honoré Antoine Frégier, *Des classes dangereuses de la population dans les grandes villes, et des moyens de les rendre meilleures* (Paris, 1840), part 2, 153-191 is on prostitution.
38. *Catalogue of a Portion of the Miscellaneous Library of Sir Travers Twiss*, 5.

the parks, in boxes at the theatres, at concerts."[39] Mayhew's close collaborator John Binny, who also contributed to *London Labour and the London Poor*, deviated from Hemyng's account on the character of "kept mistresses" or "gay ladies," arguing that they were "as a rule faithful to the gentlemen who support them."[40] Those gentlemen, he controversially argued, included members of the House of Commons and the House of Lords, wealthy merchants, army officers, and "others in high life." Some courtesans, he reported, earned £800 a year and had a set of servants.[41] Such women would "ride in Rotten Row with a groom behind them, attend the theatres and operas and go to Brighton," as well as frequenting Holborn Casino, or the Casino de Venise, and the Argyle Rooms.

The Casino de Venise and the Argyle Rooms were dancing halls. William Acton marked the Casino de Venise out as different from other dancing halls in which the women were "lackadaisical" and the men "bored." The Casino de Venise contained a "brilliant ballroom, glittering with a myriad prisms" like a "a hall of diamonds in a fairy palace." The "habitués" danced in a "frenzy" to the polka—a recent fashion from the Austrian Empire—the quadrille and the waltz, sometimes to cacophonous music and dressed in beautiful evening clothes. Lawyers, officers, and members of parliament attended. While claiming not to be a habitué, Twiss was present at some large balls. One evening in 1849, he recounted: "I had intended to go to a large ball tonight, but at eleven o'clock it is so unnatural to make one's 'toilette de danse,' unless it happens every other night when it becomes second nature, that I prefer sitting down and writing a few lines on more interesting subjects."[42] According to Acton, one-third of the crowd at these balls were "prostitutes."[43] But rather than the women exhibiting "brutal manners and scandalous behaviour," Acton remarked upon their "radiant health and spirits" and judged many to be the social equals of their dancing partners. He thus lamented the "silly aspirations of society," which had prevented the matching of these pairs in "early and consistent" marriage and instead reduced the women to "mistresses and harlots." Binny, though, argued that the Casino de Venise was precisely where many respectable young women were seduced into prostitution.[44]

Continuing his taxonomy, Hemyng included "board lodgers," whose brothels provide board and lodging in return for a proportion of the money earned by the woman; "low lodging houses" or common brothels; streetwalkers, who

39. Hemyng, in Mayhew, *London Labour and the London Poor: Vol. 4*, 215, 217.
40. Binny, in Mayhew, *London Labour and the London Poor: Vol. 4*, 353–354.
41. Mayhew, *London Labour and the London Poor: Vol. 4*, 356.
42. Twiss to Metternich, May 31, 1849, National Archives of the Czech Republic, Prague, RAM-AC/ 10/ 775, 311.
43. Acton, *Prostitution*, 102. See also, e.g., Mayhew, *London Labour and the London Poor: Vol. 4*, 260.
44. Acton, *Prostitution*, 102; Binny, in Mayhew, *London Labour and the London Poor: Vol. 4*, 357.

worked particularly in the Haymarket and Regent Street; "sailors' women"; "soldiers' women" who were "very badly paid," on account of the low wages of soldiers, and amongst whom syphilis was said to be widely spread; "dollymops" or maids, "amateurs," who prostitute themselves for presents from soldiers; "thieves' women," who swindle men; "park women," using Hyde Park near Park Lane and Green Park, who were "degraded creatures, utterly lost to all sense of shame ... well known to give themselves up to disgusting practices, that are alone gratifying to men of morbid and diseased imaginations" and who did so for a few shillings; "clandestine prostitutes," who included "dollymops," "ladies of intrigue" who simply pursued their "libidinous desires," and "female operatives," or women employed in certain professions, such as dressmaking, who prostituted themselves "for money, or more frequently for their own gratification"; and finally "cohabitant prostitutes," who were women living with men out of wedlock.[45]

Mayhew, Hemyng, and Binny conceded that their attempts to categorize, and statistically analyse, prostitution were too neat. Many prostitutes crossed the boundaries of their taxonomy. There was mobility within the profession, so that some streetwalkers rose to become prominent courtesans, while onetime courtesans and "prima-donnas" were reduced to working in the parks at night. Moreover, Binny's account undermined the categorisation, as it showed that the same woman might work at one moment in a private apartment, while at other times, when business was quiet, she could try the dancing halls or even the Haymarket.[46] Others might become respectable through marriage, sometimes with an aristocrat. Such was the case with Valerie Susan Langdon, who worked in the Casino de Venise in the 1860s and '70s as a singer and also, it was said, as a prostitute. According to conflicting accounts, she met her husband, Sir Henry Meux, 3rd Baronet, either there or in Brighton. Meux possessed a vast fortune as proprietor of one the largest beer producers in London, and Valerie Meux commanded that fortune after her husband's death in 1900.

Agnes Willoughby

One courtesan who caused great scandal by marrying an aristocrat was Agnes Willoughby. Willoughby was also the first prostitute to be linked with Travers Twiss, and her story not only sheds light upon Twiss's subsequent scandal but also became entangled with it. Willoughby was one of the most notorious of the "pretty horse-breakers" in the 1860s. Few details of her early life were made public, even after she achieved notoriety, but accounts of her early years survive in the papers gathered by Field and Roscoe of Lincoln's Inn, for the

---

45. Hemyng in Mayhew, *London Labour and the London Poor: Vol. 4*, 220, 223, 213, 217, 233, 234.
46. Mayhew, *London Labour and the London Poor: Vol. 4*, 356–358.

petitioners in an insanity trial. She was born Agnes Ann Rogers, the daughter of William Rogers, who kept a beer shop "out of which he drank himself."[47] He then worked as a navvy on the railway, near Poole, Dorsetshire, before being "carried with his family," including his three daughters and his wife and her son by a previous marriage, into the Andover Workhouse in 1847. The 1840s were a period of failing crops and famine in which the workhouses were overflowing. Rogers died in the workhouse in 1848. At this time, Agnes Rogers was about 9 years old, and she remained in Andover Workhouse for another four or five years.[48]

Agnes Rogers had thus spent much her childhood living in one of the most notorious workhouses in Britain. It had been created as a direct consequence of the New Poor Law of 1834, which was guided by concerns about the idle poor and therefore established the principle that the conditions of the workhouse must be worse than those of the poorest labourer outside the workhouse. Andover quickly exemplified all that was worst about those laws. The workhouses separated families, rationed diets, and made uniforms compulsory. Following the legislation of 1834, construction of Andover Workhouse began in 1835. It was run effectively as a prison. Its Master, Colin McDougal, was responsible for a deeply corrupt regime. The diet was "below the basic minimum adopted in all the other workhouses," but even then, the Master appropriated the food that was meant for the inmates who, in turn, were driven to starvation.[49] Their main work was to crush bones for fertiliser. Inmates ate the marrow and fragments of flesh on the bones they were intended to crush. According to one inmate: "I was employed in the workhouse at bone-breaking the best part of my time . . . We looked out for the fresh bones; we used to tell the fresh bones by the look of them, and then we used to be like a parcel of dogs after them; some were not so particular about the bones being fresh as others; I like the fresh bones; I never touched one that was a little high; the marrow was as good as the meat, it was all covered over by bone, and no filth could get to it . . . sometimes I have had one that was stale and stunk, and I eat it even then; I eat it when it was stale and stinking because I was hungered, I suppose."[50] Children fought for the potato peelings thrown to the chickens.[51] In addition to starving the inmates, the Master and his 17-year-old son sexually abused the female inmates. One woman, known as Betty Duck, said that when the Master sexually propositioned her, "I considered myself, and I

---

47. *In Chancery: Observations: Windham vs Guibelei. Mr Bedwell. Field and Roscoe, Lincoln's Inn Fields*, Norfolk Record Office, WKC 4/30, 465×1, 2 of 2, fol. 1.

48. *In Lunacy: In the Matter of W. F. Windham, a Supposed Lunatic: Brief for the Petitioners. Mr Wm. Field. 36 Field and Roscoe, Lincoln's Inn Fields*, Norfolk Record Office, WKC 4/30, 465×4, 1 of 2, fol. 7.

49. Ian Anstruther, *The Scandal of the Andover Workhouse* (London, 1973), 132.

50. The Workhouse, "Andover, Hampshire," http://www.workhouses.org.uk/Andover/.

51. Anstruther, *The Scandal of the Andover Workhouse*, 133.

thought as the children were almost starved, and he said he'd give me some victuals and beer, that if he asked me again I would."[52] The conditions eventually became a scandal and, after an inquiry, a new Master was appointed the year that the Rogers family arrived. However, he also took to abusing sexually female inmates, and conditions were "if possible, worse than before."[53] From the age of 8 to 13, Agnes Rogers had the harshest of lives.

There is an account of her early life in the *Brief*, or notes, prepared by the Windham family solicitors, Field and Roscoe, for their barristers in William Windham's lunacy trial, and in another *Brief* for a separate trial in Chancery in which Windham's mother attempted to make a claim upon the estate. According to these accounts, at the age of 13, Agnes Rogers was sent by the workhouse authorities to fill the situation of nurserymaid in Weymouth, southwest from Andover.[54] Between the ages of 13 and 15, she began to walk from where she was employed in Weymouth to Dorchester, where the 3rd Light Dragoons were stationed and where, it was alleged, "she was a prostitute" to the regiment.[55] The *Brief* noted that: "She seems to have soon fallen into the paths of vice, for when in 1854 the 3rd Light Dragoons were stationed at Dorchester she was picked up on the Weymouth beach by a young officer of that regiment and she was in the habit for 2 or 3 months of walking over from Weymouth to Dorchester [11 km one way] to sleep with him."[56] Over time, "she was in all probability common to many other men of the regiment." According to one officer of the corps, she was "a little draggle tailed whore" to whom he threw his spare change.[57] After the 3rd Light Dragoons left Dorchester, Rogers became attached to a man named Willoughby, who had come to the country to shoot. He "kept" Rogers at Basingstoke, and at this time, she assumed the surname Willoughby.[58]

The use of false names was common amongst prostitutes, "a justifiable license," as a contemporary newspaper commented in the case of Willoughby,

---

52. Anstruther, *The Scandal of the Andover Workhouse*, 131.

53. Anstruther, *The Scandal of the Andover Workhouse*, 152.

54. *In Chancery: Observations: Windham vs Guibelei. Mr Bedwell. Field and Roscoe, Lincoln's Inn Fields*, Norfolk Records Office, WKC 4/30, 465×1, 2 of 2, fol. 2.

55. "[At] the age of 14 she appears to have begun the life she has since led. In the years 1853 & 1854 or about then she was a prostitute at Weymouth." *In Chancery: Observations: Windham vs Guibelei. Mr Bedwell. Field and Roscoe, Lincoln's Inn Fields*, Norfolk Records Office, WKC 4/30, 465×1, 2 of 2, fol. 2.

56. *In Lunacy: In the Matter of W. F. Windham, a Supposed Lunatic: Brief for the Petitioners. Mr Wm. Field. 36 Field and Roscoe, Lincoln's Inn Fields*, Norfolk Record Office, WKC 4/30, 465×4, 1 of 2, fol. 6.

57. *In Lunacy: In the Matter of W. F. Windham, a Supposed Lunatic: Brief for the Petitioners. Mr Wm. Field. 36 Field and Roscoe, Lincoln's Inn Fields*, Norfolk Record Office, WKC 4/30, 465×4, 1 of 2, fol. 7.

58. *In Lunacy: In the Matter of W. F. Windham, a Supposed Lunatic: Brief for the Petitioners. Mr Wm. Field. 36 Field and Roscoe, Lincoln's Inn Fields*, Norfolk Record Office, WKC 4/30, 465×4, 1 of 2, fol. 7.

"on the stage as well as in her own particular world"[59] *London Labour and the London Poor* similarly reported that prostitutes routinely assumed professional names. Writing about Paris, Mayhew and Hemyng observed that "most prostitutes pass under false names" even though the law, as William Acton noted, penalised the use of such names.[60] The better sort, they claimed in a list of thirty-four examples, took names such as Modeste, Olympia, and Artemisia, while the lower sort showed less refined taste, with names such as La Blonde, Brunette, Faux Cul, Belle Cuisse, La Boeuf, and Poil ras.[61] Personification, or the creation of a new person, was a practice as standard amongst prostitutes as it was amongst bishops and jurists. It assisted them in negotiating attempts by the state to control them, suppressing their liberties, as Harriet Martineau and Florence Nightingale argued, for example, through the Contagious Diseases Acts. The first of those acts was not passed until 1864, and by that time, Agnes Willoughby had ceased prostitution, but such measures reflected the broader identification of prostitution with vice and the consequent attempts to police prostitutes, particularly in port towns such as Weymouth.

When Willoughby travelled abroad, he employed a detective, "Mr Field," to watch over Agnes Rogers. This was most likely Charles Frederick Field, one of England's first private detectives, a friend of Dickens, and probably the inspiration for Inspector Bucket in *Bleak House*.[62] Field, who had a penchant for working in disguise, discovered her living "at a roadside public house, though she was now driving her own Brougham."[63] He also discovered that "she was receiving the visits of a Capt. Auriol [and Field] reported this to Willoughby and he at once got rid of her. Capt. Auriol's means do not appear to have been sufficient to support her and she accordingly removed to London bringing her family with her."[64] Here the story of Agnes Willoughby crossed that of Travers Twiss. The solicitors' notes state that "between 1854 and 1859 it is difficult to assign exact dates for her changes of circumstances," but that Mr Willoughby was her client during the first part of this period and Twiss in the latter part.[65]

59. "An Episode in High Life," *Western Daily Press*, December 7, 1861, 2.
60. Mayhew, *London Labour and the London Poor: Vol. 4*, 208; Acton, *Prostitution*, 106.
61. Mayhew, *London Labour and the London Poor: Vol. 4*, 208.
62. Not to be confused with the Field of the solicitors Field and Roscoe. Charles Field was also the subject of Dickens's essay "On Duty with Inspector Field": Philip Collins, *Dickens and Crime* (London, 1964), 204–207.
63. *In Lunacy: In the Matter of W. F. Windham, a Supposed Lunatic: Brief for the Petitioners. Mr Wm. Field. 36 Field and Roscoe, Lincoln's Inn Fields,* Norfolk Record Office, WKC 4/30, 465×4, 1 of 2, fol. 7. On Field's disguises, see Smith, *Policing Victorian London*, 70.
64. *In Lunacy: In the Matter of W. F. Windham, a Supposed Lunatic: Brief for the Petitioners. Mr Wm. Field. 36 Field and Roscoe, Lincoln's Inn Fields,* Norfolk Record Office, WKC 4/30, 465×4, 1 of 2, fol. 7.
65. *In Lunacy: In the Matter of W. F. Windham, a Supposed Lunatic: Brief for the Petitioners. Mr Wm. Field. 36 Field and Roscoe, Lincoln's Inn Fields,* Norfolk Record Office, WKC 4/30, 465×4, 1 of 2, fol. 7.

According to these notes, after Agnes Willoughby came to London, "probably her best friend was Dr Travers Twiss D.C.L. who took a house for her in St John's Wood and kept up an establishment for her there."[66] Twiss "kept" Willoughby, therefore, in the period from approximately 1856 or 1857 until 1859, when Metternich died. It is mildly surprising that Twiss would install Willoughby in St John's Wood, around the corner from his mother, brother, and sister (his father died in 1856).[67] Perhaps it was convenient to visit his courtesan and his mother on the same day. If that was case, the arrangement did not endure. The solicitors' report on Willoughby tells us that "a Mr Jack Garden of Rendlesham Hall Suffolk persuaded the lady to spend a night elsewhere and Dr Twiss got to know of it. He was very angry, went to the house and in her absence broke open her desk and took from it a bond he had given her to secure for her £200 a year."[68] Two hundred pounds a year was a substantial income; it was equivalent to a middle-class salary for a single man, although Agnes Willoughby had her family to think of. That Twiss could afford such a sum, in addition to the house in which Agnes lived, reflects his prosperity at this time. In any case, £200 was apparently not enough for Agnes Willoughby. She defended herself against Twiss's actions by using the law, or threatening to use it, a defence she used persistently throughout her life: "The woman threatened to indict him for stealing and the Dr compromised the matter and got rid of her by a payment of £2,000 down."

The payment of this large sum was not the last connection, however, between Twiss and Agnes Willoughby. Her shadow hung over him for the next twelve years, at least, although the information contained in the confidential solicitors' briefs was never made public. There are suggestions he may have become involved with her again, while she was with Garden and even after her marriage. Some twelve years later, Twiss was considered as a co-respondent in her divorce (which never transpired). To have been named in such a connection to such a person could have ruined him, as he well knew. He had almost been publicly linked to her as early as 1862. Bracebridge Hemyng described Willoughby in his chapter on prostitution in *London Labour and the London Poor*, although he did not name her: "The daughter of a labouring man, a beautiful girl, is kept by a gentleman in high position at St John's Wood at the

---

66. *In Lunacy: In the Matter of W. F. Windham, a Supposed Lunatic: Brief for the Petitioners. Mr Wm. Field. 36 Field and Roscoe, Lincoln's Inn Fields*, Norfolk Record Office, WKC 4/30, 465×4, 1 of 2, fols. 7–8.

67. Her house was in Blenheim Terrace, which ran perpendicular to, and almost crossing, Hamilton Terrace, in which Travers Twiss's family lived: *Commission de Lunatico Inquirendo: An Inquiry into the State of Mind of W. F. Windham, Esq.* (London, 1862), 196. On St John's Wood as an address for courtesans, see Chesney, *Victorian Underworld*, 402.

68. *In Lunacy: In the Matter of W. F. Windham, a Supposed Lunatic: Brief for the Petitioners. Mr Wm. Field. 36 Field and Roscoe, Lincoln's Inn Fields*, Norfolk Record Office, WKC 4/30, 465×4, 1 of 2, fol. 8.

rate of £800 a year. She has now received a lady's education, rides in Rotten Row, has a set of servants, moves in certain fashionable circles."⁶⁹ The gentleman in this account appears to be an amalgam of Garden and Twiss, but, even so, the description came uncomfortably close to identifying Twiss. It also suggests that Twiss's purchase of *London Labour and the London Poor* may not have been entirely disinterested.

Twiss's ties with Agnes Willoughby shaped how he conducted his own marriage. They also limited, so he claimed, how much he could pay his wife when she was first employed by him and may have shaped his wife's decisions about how to represent herself. It is important to understand the career of Agnes Willoughby in order to unravel the puzzle of Travers Twiss and Pharaïlde van Lynseele, the woman he married. It is possible to learn much about the context for Lynseele's life, and the choices she made, by understanding the life of a woman whose life was connected to hers and whose background was similar.⁷⁰

After she parted from Twiss, Agnes Willoughby stayed with Mr Garden for a short period, but they separated in 1859, at which time she purchased the licence for the Florence Tavern in Florence Street, Islington (a pub that remained open until 2013).⁷¹ At this inn, the hunting crowd met, and "she soon became notorious in Rotten Row and with Her Majesty's Stag Hounds." She leased two houses in St John's Wood and another in Paris.⁷² Willoughby had servants, a carriage, and footmen in livery. One newspaper account of Agnes Willoughby recognized that prostitution could offer a way out of the workhouse and destitution, illustrating her situation with a wry anecdote: "There is a story told somewhere of a parish doctor in a remote district coming up to London, and finding a girl, whom he had attended a short time before in a state of destitution, located in gilded apartments, attired in silks and jewels, and waited upon by powdered domestics. On manifesting his amazement and offering an interrogative exclamation, the Lady said 'La sir! Did you not know that I was ruined?'"⁷³

In 1859, Agnes Willoughby made the acquaintance of two men. The first was James Bowen May, a solicitor whom she met while hunting with the Queen's Stag Hounds.⁷⁴ Bowen May helped her with various legal problems

---

69. Bracebridge Hemyng, in Mayhew, *London Labour and the London Poor: Vol. 4*, 356.

70. Natalie Zemon Davis, "On the Lame," *American Historical Review*, vol. 93, no. 3 (June 1988), 572–603; Natalie Zemon Davis and Peter N. Miller, "About an Inventory: A Conversation between Natalie Zemon Davis and Peter N. Miller," https://www.youtube.com/watch?v=hwiR3dz4Wg8.

71. "Transfer of Licences," *The Era*, June 10, 1860, 7.

72. For the houses: *Commission de Lunatico Inquirendo: An Inquiry*, 156.

73. "The Windham Affair," *Westmoreland Gazette and Kendall Advertiser*, December 14, 1861, 8.

74. *In Chancery: Observations: Windham vs Guibelei. Mr Bedwell. Field and Roscoe, Lincoln's Inn Fields*, Norfolk Record Office, WKC 4/30, 465×1, 2 of 2, fol. 2.

and negotiated her marriage settlement. The second man was James Roberts, to whom Willoughby was probably introduced by Bowen May: "There is no doubt Mr Bowen-May has been for many years a friend of both the woman and Roberts although he tries to put a virtuous face upon it."[75] Roberts, or "Bawdy-House Roberts," was a brothel and gambling den owner, as well as a timber merchant.[76] According to a contemporary account, he "lived in a handsome house in Piccadilly, had a brougham, made a splendid appearance about town, and was a well-known man in certain circles."[77] Indeed, Roberts's house, according to the solicitors' notes, was "a place where the highest classes of prostitutes now and then live until Mr Roberts and their own exertions succeed in planting them on to some man of means and Mr Roberts then shares the plunder (or the swag)."[78] Roberts had an income of £5,000 per year.[79] He became Willoughby's lover. He also helped transform her into one of the "pretty horse-breakers," a phrase, one report commented, "the appropriateness of which we might well question . . . seeing as it indicates only an incident and not an essential attribute of their career."[80] She wore a scarlet riding habit in Rotten Row, where Twiss too rode.[81] Acutely aware of the equestrian association with prostitution, Roberts ran a horse in the Royal Hunt Steeplechases and named it Agnes Willoughby.[82] Despite the controversy surrounding the pretty horse-breakers, he advertised his trade at the steeplechase in the company of the gentry and aristocracy, including, in this instance, John Ponsonby, the 5th Earl of Bessborough and Master of the Buckhounds in Palmerston's government.

In 1860, Willoughby "renewed her intimacy" with Jack Garden. Now, according to some reports, he "allowed her the sum of £2,000 a year," although he was not her only client.[83] This was an extraordinary income, equal, as the report commented, to the most senior servants of the crown. Garden provided

75. *In Chancery: Observations: Windham vs Guibelei. Mr Bedwell. Field and Roscoe, Lincoln's Inn Fields*, Norfolk Record Office, WKC 4/30, 465×1, 2 of 2, fol. 3.
76. *Commission de Lunatico Inquirendo: An Inquiry*, 148.
77. *Commission de Lunatico Inquirendo: An Inquiry*, 7.
78. *In Chancery: Observations: Windham vs Guibelei. Mr Bedwell. Field and Roscoe, Lincoln's Inn Fields*, Norfolk Record Office, WKC 4/30, 465×1, 2 of 2, fol. 2.
79. *Commission de Lunatico Inquirendo: An Inquiry*, 160.
80. *The Westmoreland Gazette and Kendall Advertiser*, December 14, 1861, 8.
81. "An Episode in High Life," *Western Daily Press*, December 7, 1861, 2. For hunts, see *Commission de Lunatico Inquirendo: An Inquiry*, 155–156. For Twiss riding in the park, see Twiss to Metternich, May 31, 1850, National Archives of the Czech Republic, Prague, RAM-AC/ 10/ 776, 69.
82. "The Royal Hunt Steeplechases," *Windsor and Eton Express*, April 20, 1861, 4.
83. *Commission de Lunatico Inquirendo: An Inquiry*, 157–158. "The Windham Affair," *Westmoreland Gazette and Kendall Advertiser*, December 14, 1861, 8. Other reports place her income from Garden at £800, which was nevertheless substantial.

her with a house in Wigmore Street, Cavendish Square.[84] Willoughby opened a milliner's shop and ran it as a brothel, with herself and her two sisters working there. Neighbours complained: "The number of broughams that used to stop at the door began to make the house notorious and one of the inhabitants of Wigmore Street wrote to Mr Garden an anonymous letter and the consequence was the immediate shutting up of the shop."[85] Willoughby returned to walking the Burlington Arcade in Mayfair, a common parade for prostitutes where they could rent rooms by the hour above the outwardly respectable shops.[86] All classes could be found in the arcade. Travers Twiss was a visitor and may have met Willoughby there, although his own account was about coming upon the Emperor Napoléon III "next to me in the Burlington Arcade, carrying the baton of a Special Constable. He was paying homage to the law."[87] Certainly, police constables frequented the Arcade due largely to the problems of prostitution. Amongst the witness statements collected by Windham family solicitors, Police Constable Charles Brown testified later in 1861: "I know the person called Agnes Willoughby. I have seen her for the last 5 or 6 months walking as a prostitute in the Burlington Arcade of an afternoon."[88] Her return to streetwalking underlines that the careful distinctions made by contemporaries between the various classes of prostitutes were fluid.

By 1861, Agnes Willoughby was already well known to the public because of both the "pretty horse-breakers" controversy and the scandal surrounding prostitution more generally. During Ascot Week, between June 10 and 15, 1861, while riding on Rotten Row, she met a young man called William Frederick Windham.[89]

---

84. *In Lunacy: In the Matter of W. F. Windham, a Supposed Lunatic: Brief for the Petitioners. Mr Wm. Field. 36 Field and Roscoe, Lincoln's Inn Fields*, Norfolk Record Office, WKC 4/30, 465×4, 1 of 2, fol. 8.

85. *In Lunacy: In the Matter of W. F. Windham, a Supposed Lunatic: Brief for the Petitioners. Mr Wm. Field. 36 Field and Roscoe, Lincoln's Inn Fields*, Norfolk Record Office, WKC 4/30, 465×4, 1 of 2, fol. 8.

86. Chesney, *Victorian Underworld*, 400.

87. Twiss to Metternich, April 16, 1855, National Archives of the Czech Republic, Prague, RAM-AC/ 10/ 781, 5–6.

88. *In Lunacy: In the Matter of W. F. Windham, a Supposed Lunatic: Petitioners' Proofs. Mr Wm. Field. Field and Roscoe, Lincoln's Inn Fields*, Norfolk Record Office, WKC 4/30, 465×4, 1 of 2, fol. 35.

89. "During the Ascot Week . . . and the Ascot Week this year extended from about the 10th to the 15th of June, Mr Windham met probably on the ride in Rotten Row the woman known as Agnes Willoughby." The probable story seems to be that she met him on the ride and that she introduced him to her friend Mr James Roberts of no. 132 Piccadilly, at whose house Mr Windham used to meet and sleep with her. Some accounts mistakenly claim that they met at Ascot, rather than during Ascot week. For her meeting Windham at Ascot, see the case for the prosecution in the lunacy trial: *Commission de Lunatico Inquirendo: An Inquiry*, 7. For the meeting in Rotten Row, see the testimony of Mr David Llewellyn to the lunacy trial, (*Commission de Lunatico Inquirendo: An Inquiry*, 30), also reported in the

FIGURE 8. William Frederick Windham in the Windham family album, with Agnes Willoughby (now Windham) below.*

* Photographs of William Frederick Windham and Agnes Willoughby in "Private Copy: Windham Trial: Letters etc," Norfolk Record Office, MC 580/1, 780 × 1

Windham belonged to a prominent Norfolk aristocratic family that had produced government ministers and intellectuals for centuries. He was born on August 9, 1840. His father was William Howe Windham of Felbrigg Hall, and his mother was Lady Sophia Windham, the daughter of the Marquess of Bristol, of Ickworth House near Bury St Edmonds in Suffolk.[90] His parents married in 1835, and his father died on December 24, 1854, making Lady Sophia and his uncle (his father's brother), General Charles Ash Windham, the guardians of the 14-year-old William Frederick Windham.[91] William Windham was described by some as a high-spirited boy and by others as a "nasty dirty little beast."[92] In the year his father died, Windham, who had until this point been educated by tutors at home, was sent to Eton. He lasted two years there before his mother put him into the hands of a string of private tutors, with whom he travelled.[93] In 1857, General Windham filed a bill in Chancery to make the boy a ward of the court. He succeeded, and the suit which was to manage the Felbrigg estate until William came of age, at 21, was called *Windham vs Windham*.[94] A year after, in 1858, Lady Sophia left Felbrigg Hall to remarry. According to a report three years later: "The marriage was a concealed one on the part of Lady Sophia and on the occasion of it she gave a wrong description for her father Lord Bristol."[95] The solicitor's clerk who wrote those notes did not finish explaining how she described her new husband to her father, who died shortly after the marriage, but he was Theodore Maine Guibelei, a 24-year-old Italian singer (son of the opera singer Theodore Victor Guibelei) who had been her music tutor at Felbrigg. Upon her marriage, and consistent with her new legal personality, the suit at Chancery seeking government of the Felbrigg estate became *Windham vs Guibelei*.

Norfolk News, Eastern Counties Journal, and *Norwich, Yarmouth and Lynn Commercial Gazette,* December 28, 1861, 6.

90. William Howe Windham was born in 1802, Sophia Hervey in 1811.

91. *In Lunacy: In the Matter of W. F. Windham, a Supposed Lunatic: Brief for the Petitioners. Mr Wm. Field. 36 Field and Roscoe, Lincoln's Inn Fields,* Norfolk Record Office, WKC 4/30, 465×4, 1 of 2, fol. 2.

92. *In Lunacy: In the Matter of W. F. Windham, a Supposed Lunatic: Brief for the Petitioners. Mr Wm. Field. 36 Field and Roscoe, Lincoln's Inn Fields,* Norfolk Record Office, WKC 4/30, 465×4, 1 of 2, fol. 2.

93. *In Lunacy: In the Matter of W. F. Windham, a Supposed Lunatic: Brief for the Petitioners. Mr Wm. Field. 36 Field and Roscoe, Lincoln's Inn Fields,* Norfolk Record Office, WKC 4/30, 465×4, 1 of 2, fols. 2–4.

94. *In Lunacy: In the Matter of W. F. Windham, a Supposed Lunatic: Brief for the Petitioners. Mr Wm. Field. 36 Field and Roscoe, Lincoln's Inn Fields,* Norfolk Record Office, WKC 4/30, 465×4, 1 of 2, fols. 4–5.

95. *In Lunacy: In the Matter of W. F. Windham, a Supposed Lunatic: Brief for the Petitioners. Mr Wm. Field. 36 Field and Roscoe, Lincoln's Inn Fields,* Norfolk Record Office, WKC 4/30, 465×4, 1 of 2, fol. 2.

FIGURE 9. Felbrigg Hall, Norfolk, 1861.*

When he came of age, on August 9, 1861, two months after he met Willoughby, William Windham inherited Felbrigg Hall, the family estate in Norfolk, which included a vast park and forests and yielded an income of £3,100 per year.[96]

At the age of 28, he would come into further estates, bringing his income to £9,000 per year. From an early age, Windham was reputed to be "eccentric." He was obsessive about trains, which was normal enough for a child, but as a young man, his passion continued, and he was often to be found on train platforms, between Norwich and London, wearing a guard's uniform, opening and shutting carriage doors, carrying luggage for the passengers, blowing

---

96. *Commission de Lunatico Inquirendo: An Inquiry*, 3–4.

* Photograph of Felbrigg Hall, in "Private Copy: Windham Trial: Letters etc," Norfolk Record Office, MC 580/1, 780×1

the whistle, often at the wrong moments (once almost provoking an accident at the Cambridge station), and at times bribing the drivers to allow him to drive the engine.[97] He generally felt more comfortable with servants than with his own class, and he liked to wait at table and wash the dishes, tastes which his father indulged by giving him a footman's livery as a present.[98] As an adult, when he visited the Haymarket in London, he frequently impersonated a policeman and tried to move the prostitutes from the pavements. Both police and prostitutes tolerated and indulged him. Windham was sometimes found, on visiting other aristocratic houses, to be helping the servants clear the table after dinner rather than joining the guests. He was noted for hysterical, frequently inappropriate, and squeaky laughter.[99] He enjoyed singing, particularly what were described as "negro songs," such as "Old Bob Ridley" (he had a habit of calling everyone he met "Bob Ridley") and "We're All off to Dixie's Land," or "I Wish I Was in Dixie," a popular minstrel song that was a Confederate anthem during the American Civil War.[100] The war began in the year Windham met Agnes Willoughby, and the sheet music for the song survives in the Windham family papers.[101] The young man enjoyed pranks. When living in London, he would open the window in the dead of night and howl like a cat. He was inclined to use the Norfolk dialect, particularly when scolded.[102] He was often filthy from having carted coal or manure, and he had appalling table manners. Whether as a footman, a train guard, or a policeman, he had a passion for impersonating people below his station.

This behaviour could be taken, on the face of it, to be consistent with the Victorian practice known as "slumming," although in Windham's case he took it to extremes. Slumming was the term used to describe the fashion whereby middle- and upper-class Britons took to the streets and went into the workhouses and slums in order to see how the poor lived.[103] Many were motivated by philanthropic concerns; for others, slumming was a form of tourism. While

97. *In Lunacy: Re: Windham. Transcript of Proceedings*, Mon. Dec 11, 1861, "Mr Montagu Chambers, Counsel for the Petitioners," Norfolk Record Office, WKC 4/ 29/ 8/ fols. 65–67; see also *In Lunacy: Re: William Frederick Windham, a Supposed Lunatic: Affidavit of Dr Tuke. John and Chas. Cole, 36 Essex Street Strand*, Norfolk Record Office, WKC 4/30, 465×4, 2 of 2, fol. 4; *In Lunacy: Re: Windham: Transcript of Proceedings, 5th day, Testimony of Mrs Llewellyn*, Norfolk Record Office, WKC 4/ 29/ 11/ fol. 71.

98. *Commission de Lunatico Inquirendo: An Inquiry*, 4.

99. *Commission de Lunatico Inquirendo: An Inquiry*, 15, 21.

100. *In Lunacy: Re: Windham. Transcript of Proceedings*, Mon. Dec 11, 1861, "Mr Montagu Chambers, Counsel for the Petitioners," Norfolk Record Office, WKC 4/ 29/ 8/ fol. 80; *In Lunacy: Re: Windham: Transcript of Proceedings, 5th day, Testimony of Mrs Llewellyn*, Norfolk Records Office, WKC 4/ 29/1- 11, 464×7, 1 of 2, fol. 52 .

101. "Old Bob Ridley. No. 7 of the Buckley's Serenaders Songs. London, Metzler and Co.," Norfolk Record Office, WKC 4/ 30, 465×4, 1 of 2.

102. *Commission de Lunatico Inquirendo: An Inquiry*, 21.

103. See Koven, *Slumming*.

Windham's behaviour was outwardly similar, his motivations were different. He was driven by a desire to be the persons he imitated. He took that ambition to the point where eventually he lost all of his vast fortune and his estates, declaring bankruptcy. His last years were spent as a Norwich coachman, fulfilling his wish. Windham took advantage of social conventions which offered great scope for impersonation and reinvention. Like many of the prostitutes who impersonated aristocratic women, he also discovered the limits and penalties attached to crossing class boundaries.

From May to August 29, Windham lodged with Mr and Mrs Llewellyn, associates of his uncle, General Windham, in Duke St, Marylebone.[104] According to police at his trial, he spent much of his time associating with prostitutes in the Haymarket. Police Constable Charles Brown observed him "shouting about the Haymarket streets" and declared that "he often wanted to give girls into custody for being disorderly."[105] Sergeant Oliver, who patrolled the Haymarket, confirmed that he too had "frequently seen him in the night-houses of the Haymarket and its neighbourhood. He was generally in the company of prostitutes."[106]

Windham was not only interested in the women who walked the streets. According to his landlady, he systematically read *The Times* every morning over poached eggs and bacon (what he ate for breakfast became evidence of his insanity).[107] In a case of life imitating satire, over breakfast on the morning of Thursday, June 27, he alerted his guest, Mr Martin, a tenant farmer at Felbrigg Hall, and formerly its bailiff, to the letter from the Belgravian mothers in *The Times* regarding the difficulty of marrying their daughters.[108] Windham drew his attention to "articles and letters in *The Times*, about the pretty horsebreakers." Although Mr Martin could not recollect whether he had himself read "*A Mother of Seven Daughters* and *A Belgravian Mother*," he did recall Windham declaring, "I would rather marry a 'pretty horsebreaker' than I would a lady."[109]

By this point, Windham had already met Willoughby two weeks previously, which may have been the immediate cause of his reflection. He became obsessed with her. Receipts from Harry Emanuel, a jeweller in Hanover

---

104. *Commission de Lunatico Inquirendo: An Inquiry*, 31.

105. *In Lunacy: In the Matter of W. F. Windham, a Supposed Lunatic: Petitioners' Proofs. Mr Wm. Field. Field and Roscoe, 36 Lincoln's Inn Fields*, Norfolk Record Office, WKC 4/30, 465×4, 1 of 2, fols. 35.

106. *Commission de Lunatico Inquirendo: An Inquiry*, 52, 54, 180, 205. The police inspector, James Holden, testified he had often seen Windham in Haymarket "night-houses," and "I have seen him in night-houses with prostitutes and gentlemen," and "I generally saw him in the company of prostitutes": *Commission de Lunatico Inquirendo: An Inquiry*, 47–48.

107. *In Lunacy: Re: Windham: Transcript of Proceedings, 5th day, Testimony of Mrs Llewellyn*, Norfolk Records Office, WKC 4/ 29/1- 11, 464×7, 1 of 2, fols. 57–58.

108. *Commission de Lunatico Inquirendo: An Inquiry*, 163.

109. *Commission de Lunatico Inquirendo: An Inquiry*, 163, 196.

Square, Mayfair, which were kept by the family, show that, on June 29, he bought Agnes a "Fine Diamond Heart Locket" for £130 pounds, a "fine pearl necklace" for £76, and a "carbuncle and gold pin."[110] The salesman in the jewellers, Henry Dore, said that he knew Agnes Willoughby. She had previously visited "with another gentleman who had bought jewellery for her" (quite possibly Travers Twiss).[111] Windham's mother's second husband, Mr Guibelei, also saw him, in June, in Agnes Willoughby's box at the Lyceum Theatre, in Covent Garden: "I had been informed that she was extremely extravagant, and told him so." He further warned Windham that "she was living with another gentleman."[112] Guibelei was not the only person to warn Windham. Catherine Walters, or "Skittles" (whom William Gladstone frequently visited), knew Windham from Rotten Row and perhaps elsewhere, and had told him that he was involved with a dangerous woman. Windham's landlord, Mr Llewellyn, claimed that Windham had come home one day saying "he had had a jolly row with Skittles about Agnes Willoughby. He had had Skittles turned off Rotten Row, and had bullied her well on the ground." Questioned, he confirmed that "those were his words; he had let every body know who she was; he had taken the part of Agnes Willoughby."[113] Nevertheless, Catherine Walter's warning proved timely. By July, Agnes Willoughby had taken a new lover, the Italian opera singer Antonio Guiglini, who was the most successful tenor in London of the time.[114]

Willoughby became strongly attached to Guiglini. Her photos in the Windham family records show that she was posing for the same photographer (from Mayer Brothers), possibly at the same moment as the photo of Guiglini on his *carte de visite* in the collection of the Victoria and Albert Museum. Both cards show the photographer's name at the bottom, and Willoughby and Guiglini are standing on the same balcony, next to the same balustrade. The Victoria and Albert collection of the *cartes de visite* indicates that the scene is one which Mayer Brothers used regularly.

Learning of Agnes Willoughby's liason with Guiglini, Windham wrote her a distressed letter on July 27, pleading: "My own darling Agnes, I am very much vexed to hear that you have gone with this Mr Guidine [*sic*] down to

---

110. For Harry Emanuel, see John Culme, *The Directory of Gold & Silversmiths, Jewellers & Allied Traders, 1838-1914* (London, 1987); and the British Museum, "Harry Emanuel," https://www.britishmuseum.org/research/search_the_collection_database/term_details.aspx?bioId=87894.

111. Commission de Lunatico Inquirendo: An Inquiry, 62.

112. Commission de Lunatico Inquirendo: An Inquiry, 167. For her box, see "The Great Windham Lunacy Case," *The Sydney Morning Herald*, April 4, 1862, 3.

113. *In Lunacy: Re: Windham: Transcript of Proceedings, 5th day, Testimony of Mrs Llewellyn*, Norfolk Record Office, WKC 4/ 29/ 11 fol. 74.

114. For Guiglini's reputation: Charles Santley, *Student and Singer* (London, 1892), 69–70.

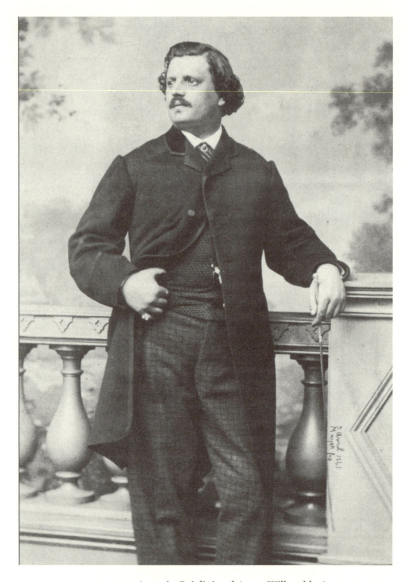

FIGURE 10. Antonio Guiglini and Agnes Willoughby.*

the country. I thought you were going (you told me) to visit your uncle and aunt and now I find that you have started off with this man, besides you never left town Thursday Evening but you went yesterday. Now Dear you know it is very unkind and heartless of you to deceive Willie ... I did think that Agnes loved me and would not go with anyone else instead of which I find out you

* For Guiglini: Victoria and Albert Museum, "Guy Little Theatrical Photograph," http://collections.vam.ac.uk/item/O188352/guy-little-theatrical-photograph-photograph-mayer-brothers/; for Agnes Willoughby: "Private Copy: Windham Trial: Letters etc," Norfolk Record Office, MC 580/1, 780×1

FIGURE 10. *(continued)*

have Agnes. I love you but darling you don't wish to break poor Willie's heart and make him wretched. Please dearest God bless you darling and believe me ever your true loving Willie."[115] It would not be surprising if Windham bore a grudge against Italian singers, having been abandoned, as he saw it, first by his mother for Guibelei and then by his lover (and, later, his wife), for Guiglini. Three days after this letter, on July 30, Windham wrote to say, "I received your telegram this morning at 2.00 o'clock," and he invited her to come to Felbrigg Hall. Willoughby was clearly not prepared to break from him or Guiglini. In this letter, Windham also made the remarkable declaration: "I consider myself engaged now to you," underlined in red by his family or their solicitors.[116] But the situation remained unclear, as he added: "My heart is too full of grief to write more: only pray do come if you love me, do Agnes."

According to an affidavit made by Willoughby's solicitor, Bowen May, he first met Windham with her on August 1, 1861, so it would appear that she responded to Windham's letter, and his declaration of engagement, by coming rapidly to London for a meeting to set in process a marriage settlement.[117] Windham explained to Bowen May that he intended to marry Willoughby, while Bowen May explained the necessity of a marriage settlement. Bowen May's account of that meeting is confirmed by a letter he wrote the same day to Chappell, Windham's solicitor, asking for a copy of *Windham vs Guibelei*: that is, a copy of the Chancery suit that governed the Felbrigg Estate.[118] Chappell responded to the request by pointing out that Windham was a ward of the court and that no claims could be made upon his estate.

A few days after Willoughby and Windham met Bowen May, she sent Windham her photograph, and on August 7, he replied to her to say, "I have sent you the Dog and some rabbits for your Uncle. I got your letter Darling quite safe. I cannot get my likeness here [at Felbrigg Hall] as there is no one who can do it. What short letters darling you write. Why don't you send longer ones. Goodbye my own darling . . . Willie Windham."[119] Willoughby had no uncle, but the invention of one explained her absences from London with

---

115. William Windham to Agnes Willoughby, July 27, 1861, *In Lunacy: In the Matter of W. F. Windham, a Supposed Lunatic: Exhibits to Affidavit of C. N. Cole. John and C. Cole, 36 Essex Street*, Norfolk Record Office, WKC 4/30, 465×4, 1 of 2, fol. 1.

116. William Windham to Agnes Willoughby, July 30, 1861, *In Lunacy: In the Matter of W. F. Windham, a Supposed Lunatic: Exhibits to Affidavit of C. N. Cole. John and C. Cole, 36 Essex Street*, Norfolk Record Office, WKC 4/30, 465×4, 1 of 2, fol. 2.

117. Affidavit of James Bowen May, *In Lunacy: In the Matter of W. F. Windham, a Supposed Lunatic: Affidavits Read before the Lords Justices by Respondent. Field and Roscoe, 36 Lincoln's Inn Fields*, Norfolk Record Office, WKC 4/30, 465×4, 1 of 2, fol. 2.

118. Bowen May to Chappell, August 1, 1861, *In Lunacy: Re: Windham. Notes for Cross Examination of Mr Bowen May. Field and Roscoe, 36 Lincoln's Inn Fields*, Norfolk Record Office, WKC 4/30, 465×4, 1 of 2.

119. William Windham to Agnes Willoughby, August 7, 1861, *In Lunacy: In the Matter of W. F. Windham, a Supposed Lunatic: Exhibits to Affidavit of C. N. Cole. John and C. Cole,*

Guiglini. The day before writing this letter, Windham had been in London visiting a Savile Row doctor, Henry Charles Johnson, who later stated in an affidavit: "I found him suffering from extensive ulceration about the genital organs. I prescribed for him. The sore was so large that I have no recollection of having said to him that he should refrain from having connection with the opposite sex. I considered it superfluous to caution him on such a matter for at the time I considered him physically incapable of having any such connection. / <u>The woman known as Agnes Willoughby called upon me 4 or 5 days before the marriage</u> and told me she was going to marry the said William Frederick Windham and she asked me if he was fit to marry. I knew the woman by sight and her character and I told her what was the complaint of Mr Windham and that he was most certainly not then in a marriageable condition."[120] Over two weeks after Windham's visit to Dr Johnson, on August 28, Willoughby wrote to Windham to say that the reason she could not see him was because she was being prevented, but that she had good news about his state of health: "Waiting answer. My Dear Willie, I think it very strange in not being allowed to see you after your wish. I must see you. Let the consequence be what it may for some particular business. Let me know all about seeing you. My doctor tells me you are not in danger so cheer up all will be well. From your ever affectionately, Agnes."[121] The chancre on Windham's penis would prove to be critical to his estate, and her declaration "Let the consequence be what it may" did not necessarily signify the equanimity that it implied.

Two days after he saw Dr Johnson, Windham wrote to her to complain: "All my relations seem so set against my marrying, but I have fully determined to marry whom I please . . . I cannot make out why <u>all my people</u> should be so much against visiting you and should tell me that nobody would visit you after I married you."[122] The timing of his complaint was important. The following day, August 9, was Windham's twenty-first birthday, the day he reached his majority and could, as he put it, marry whom he pleased. Now Willoughby could make legally binding contracts with him.

After Windham's letter complaining about his relatives, Willoughby sent a telegram to William also, to complain that she had been prevented from

---

36 Essex Street, Norfolk Record Office, WKC 4/30, 465×4, 1 of 2, fol. 2. This is the photograph above that remains in the family papers.

120. Affidavit of Henry Charles Johnson, *In Lunacy: In the Matter of W. F. Windham, a Supposed Lunatic: Brief: Affidavits in Support of Petition*. Field and Roscoe, 36 Lincoln's Inn Fields, Norfolk Record Office, WKC 4/30, 465×4, 1 of 2, fol. 30.

121. *In Lunacy: Re: Windham: Letter and Telegram from Agnes Willoughby to Windham of 28 August 1861*. Field and Roscoe, 36 Lincoln's Inn Fields, Norfolk Record Office, WKC 4/30, 465×4, 1 of 2.

122. William Windham to Agnes Willoughby, August 8, 1861, *In Lunacy: In the Matter of W. F. Windham, a Supposed Lunatic: Exhibits to Affidavit of C. N. Cole*. John and C. Cole, *36 Essex Street*, Norfolk Record Office, WKC 4/30, 465×4, 1 of 2, fol. 2.

visiting him at his London address: "Have been three times to see you but am not allowed on any account to come inside the house. Dr Babbington says you are not in danger. Do meet me as I have particular business to communicate to you. Send answer to Emanuels."[123] Harry Emanuel was the jeweller whom Willoughby frequented, and as this telegram reveals, he played an important professional role for her. Not only did he assist in facilitating a large part of her income—jewels—but he clearly also took this professional role seriously enough to provide other services—in this case, receiving communications from her clients, who would in turn, of course, provide business for Emanuel's. On August 13, Windham and Willoughby had returned to Emanuel's, and on this occasion, he purchased for her, according to the jeweller's receipts, "a very fine musical box" for £110, a "very fine diamond bracelet" for £210, and "a fine walnut wood dressing case" for £126, amongst a number of other items. In just one day's shopping, they had spent the annual incomes of many middle-class families. Finally, Windham had seemingly convinced Willoughby to break with Guiglini. Five days later, on August 18, he wrote to her to say: "My dearest little Agg, I received your nice letter this morning. I will tell you when I see you Tuesday morning what I think you had better do as regards Mr G. I don't think you ought to see him after you have written to him and told him that all is finished unless you see him with <u>Mr May</u> [underlined in red by petitioners] . . . when we arrive in London you shall meet me . . . and then we shall then go to <u>Mr May's</u> dearest together and see him."[124] The appointment with Willoughby's solicitor, Bowen May, was to make a marriage settlement. Windham wrote this on a Sunday, and the appointment with Bowen May was not until the Wednesday of the same week, the 20th. In the meantime, the following day, Monday, Windham's doctor, Doctor Buck from Norwich, visited him at home at Felbrigg and stated, "I examined his penis and found a large unhealthy sore thereon with a hardened base quite as big as a shilling."[125] He added, "I cautioned him over and over again not to have connection with any woman as he would not only endanger himself but most inevitably infect her." Doctor Buck returned the next day, Tuesday, the day that Windham promised in the letter above to talk to Willoughby about what to do about "Mr G." On arriving at Felbrigg, Buck found Willoughby and her entire family, her sisters, half-brother, and mother, in the dining room eating breakfast. Windham was sitting in a

---

123. *In Lunacy: Re: Windham: Letter and Telegram from Agnes Willoughby to Windham of 28 August 1861. Field and Roscoe, 36 Lincoln's Inn Fields*, Norfolk Record Office, WKC 4/30, 465×4, 1 of 2.

124. William Windham to Agnes Willoughby, August 18, 1861, *In Lunacy: In the Matter of W. F. Windham, a Supposed Lunatic: Exhibits to Affidavit of C. N. Cole. John and C. Cole, 36 Essex Street*, Norfolk Record Office, WKC 4/30, 465×4, 1 of 2, fol. 3.

125. *In Lunacy: Re: Windham: Proof of Mr H. J. Buck. Field and Roscoe, 36 Lincoln's Inn Fields*, Norfolk Record Office, WKC 4/30, 465×4, 1 of 2, fol. 2.

corner in a chair, and "A large organ was playing 'Pop Goes the Weasel,' a very popular song in the 1850s: 'Half a pound of tuppeny rice, half a pound of treacle. That's the way the money goes, pop goes the weasel.'"[126] Buck asked Willoughby if she wouldn't mind him consulting Windham alone, but she declined the request and told him to come the next day: "Her manner to me was very dictatorial."[127] The following day, Windham sent a letter dismissing him.

Willoughby and Windham were back in London the next day, Wednesday, and back at Emanuel's jewellers. On this occasion, they again spent extravagantly, including a "very fine pearl and brilliant bracelet" for £504 pounds, a "very fine 5 stone brilliant ring" for £120, and a "pair of very fine diamond earrings" for £105. Their most significant purchase, however, was one of the cheapest: namely, a "Solid Gold Wedding Ring" (underlined by the petitioners) for £1.10.6.

Also on this day, Wednesday, August 20, they visited Willoughby's solicitor, Bowen May, and he drew up the first part of a marriage settlement, promising that Windham would provide Willoughby with £14,000 of jewellery. There was still some work left to do at Emanuel's. Based upon the surviving receipts, they visited the shop again on numerous occasions.[128] They purchased hundreds of pieces, including numerous diamond and sapphire rings, necklaces, musical boxes, buttons, several horseshoes in ruby, diamond, and sapphire, watches, diamond bracelets and brooches, and ruby and diamond lockets. On October 11, the receipt showed purchases totalling £6,492.15:

The £14,000 gift, it would later emerge, was made in consideration of the claim that Windham had infected Willoughby with venereal disease.[129] In his affidavit, Dr Forbes Winslow stated, "It was said that he had a chancre as a large as a sixpence on his penis. He denied it. He, however, subsequently admitted that his wife had alleged that he had contaminated her and demanded compensation, and this compensation was jewellery to the value of £14,000."[130] Whether he had infected her or not is uncertain. One doctor at his lunacy trial thought he may have caught the disease as a schoolboy. He commented that the trains filled with boys from Eton to London were met by

---

126. *In Lunacy: Re: Windham: Proof of Mr H. J. Buck. Field and Roscoe, 36 Lincoln's Inn Fields*, Norfolk Record Office, WKC 4/30, 465×4, 1 of 2, fol. 3.

127. *In Lunacy: Re: Windham: Proof of Mr H. J. Buck. Field and Roscoe, 36 Lincoln's Inn Fields*, Norfolk Record Office, WKC 4/30, 465×4, 1 of 2, fol. 3.

128. August 21, 22, 23, 24, 26, 27, 29, 30, September 4, 9, 11, 23, 26, October 1, 7, 11, 14, 15, 16, 18, 19, 21, 22, 24, 28, and November 5.

129. P. E. Hansell—Norwich. *In Lunacy: Re: Windham: Report of Proceedings. Monday Dec.16, 1861*, Norfolk Record Office, WKC 4/29/8, 464×7, 1 of 2, fols. 94 and 107.

130. *In Lunacy: In the Matter of W. F. Windham, a Supposed Lunatic: Proofs of Dr Forbes Winslow, Dr Mayo, Dr Southey. Mr W. Field. Field and Roscoe, 36 Lincoln's Inn Fields*, Norfolk Record Office, WKC 4/30, 465×4, 1 of 2, fol. 2.

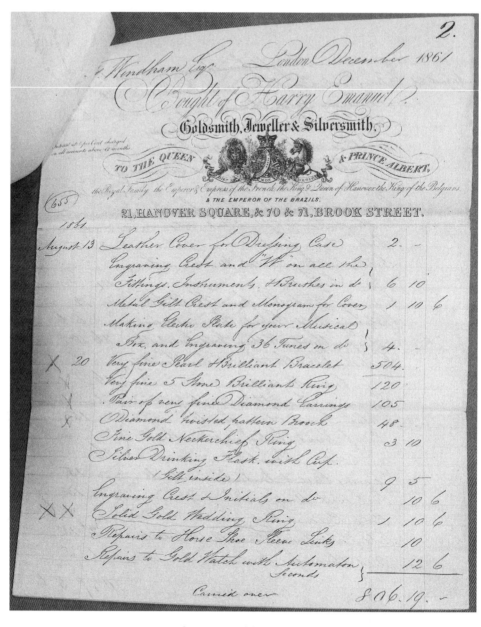

FIGURE 11. Receipt from Emanuel for wedding ring (underlined).*

* "W. F. Windham Esquire, London December 1861, bought off Harry Emanuel," Norfolk Records Office, WKC 4/ 30, 465×4, 1 of 2, fol. 2

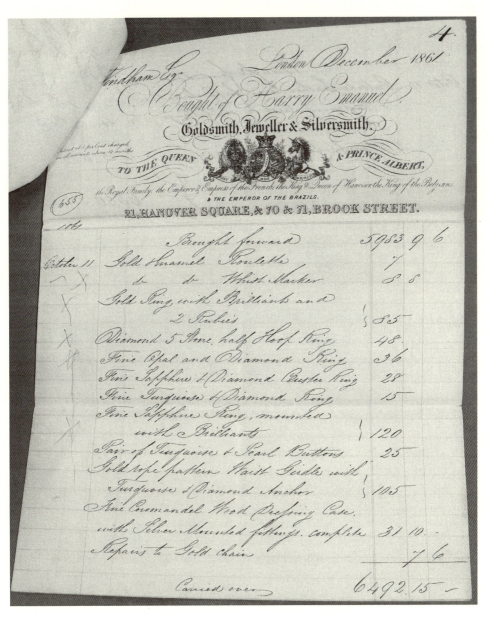

FIGURE 12. Receipt from Harry Emanuel.*

* "W. F. Windham Esquire, London December 1861, bought off Harry Emanuel," Norfolk Records Office, WKC 4/30, 465×4, 1 of 2, fol. 4

a "great number of women of the town," and Windham himself agreed it was only possible to "avoid" the "prostitutes" at Paddington if one was changing platforms.[131]

At the same trial, however, it was argued that the claims Windham was infected were concocted by Willoughby in order to extort more money from him. On March 8, 1862, Mr Bacon, one of the lawyers for the petitioners in Windham's lunacy trial, was invited to dine with Mr and Mrs Arden of Cavendish Square (around the corner from Agnes's Wigmore Street brothel). Bacon, perhaps bored by the dinner, or on the way to or from it, and finding no other writing material, scribbled some notes on the back of his invitation card. In those notes, he expressed his astonishment: "The whole story is so monstrous that but for the statements on both sides it would be incredible. 19 August— Buck finds him with chancre and swelled groin . . . Is there any evidence that the disease was communicated to Agnes? That W was made to believe that he had infected her is clear. The jewellery was obtained from him on that pretence. It is against the very instinct of any woman, still more of a woman of her profession, to permit any intercourse [in such circumstances]."[132] Whether or not Bacon was right, on August 21, the day after William signed the wedding settlement concerning the jewellery, the couple returned to Emanuel's again, making numerous purchases, including a "Gold Locket with Ruby and Diamond Double Horse Shoe <u>Engraving Agnes Windham from her husband September 16, 1861</u>" (the underlining on this receipt was again added at a later date by the petitioners' solicitors in the lunacy trial).[133] September 16 may have been the intended date for the marriage, but if that was the case, it occurred more rapidly than anticipated.

On August 26, Willoughby and Windham saw Bowen May again, and on the same day, a solicitor, Mr Jackson, wrote to the family solicitor in Norwich, Mr Hansell (who was responsible for preserving most of the materials surrounding the case over many years), and also to General Windham, to say that the entail on the Felbrigg estate had been barred, but he did not know by whom.[134] The General responded to Jackson, lamenting that "the accounts of my nephew are certainly as bad as anything can be . . . For my part I shall have nothing further to do with him," although, unfortunately for the General,

---

131. *Commission de Lunatico Inquirendo: An Inquiry*, 172.

132. *Mr and Mrs Arden Request the Pleasure of Mr Bacon's Company*, Norfolk Record Office, WKC 4/30, 465×4, 2 of 2.

133. "W. F. Windham Esquire, London December 1861, bought of Harry Emanuel," Norfolk Records Office, WKC 4/30, 465×4, 1 of 2, fol. 2.

134. "Mr Jackson to Mr Hansell, 26th August, 1861," *Letters to and from Jackson*, Norfolk Records Office, WKC 4/30, 465×4, 1 of 2, fol. 21; "Mr Jackson to General Windham," 26th August, 1861, *Letters to and from Jackson*, Norfolk Records Office, WKC 4/30, 465×4, 1 of 2, fol. 22.

nothing could have been further from the truth.[135] Hansell responded to Jackson in the same vein: "Every day he gets deeper into the mire ... it is a very sad case."[136]

Willoughby brought Windham to her solicitor, Mr Bowen May, on August 29 to sign the second part of the marriage settlement, a "disentailing deed" that would create a permanent income for Agnes. As a consequence, General Windham brought a motion to commit Bowen May before Windham's guardian, Vice Chancellor Wood, in the Chancery Court case *Windham vs Giubilei*, which governed both him and his estate. The grounds for the motion were that Bowen May and Rogers ("formerly known as Agnes Willoughby") induced Windham into a marriage contract when he was still in his "infancy" and without the sanction and knowledge of his guardian, the court, and Vice Chancellor Wood.[137] Bowen May claimed in the court that he warned Windham about Willoughby's character and tastes, telling him: "I think it right to tell you that the lady is a kept mistress and she is very extravagant."[138] Windham dismissed the warning, and negotiations then proceeded. According to Bowen May, Willoughby declared, "If I marry him I must have £1,000 a year settled." Windham protested that he hadn't sufficient income for that sum, and Bowen May proposed £600. Willoughby responded, "Do you think it is likely that I will give up £2,000 a year for such a settlement." Counsel for the petitioners in Windham's lunacy trial argued that Willoughby's claim to earn £2,000 a year was another ruse employed to drive a hard bargain with Windham.[139] The scepticism may have been justified, but there is no doubt that Agnes Willoughby had a considerable income before she met Windham, albeit without the long-term security that a marriage contract would provide. Bowen May confirmed that, prior to her marriage, "she was living with a gentleman who was reported to allow her £2,000 a year."[140] The gentleman was almost certainly Jack Garden, not Twiss.

The "disentailing deed," called *Windham vs Whidborne*, stated: "Whereas a marriage has been agreed upon and is intended to be shortly solemnized between the said William Frederick Windham and Agnes Ann Rogers and whereas upon the treaty for the said intended marriage it was agreed that

---

135. "General Windham to Mr Jackson," 27th August, 1861," *Letters to and from Jackson*, Norfolk Records Office, WKC 4/30, 465×4, 1 of 2, fol. 23.

136. "Mr Hansell to Mr Jackson, 27th August, 1861," *Letters to and from Jackson*, Norfolk Records Office, WKC 4/30, 465×4, 1 of 2, fol. 24.

137. *In Lunacy: Re: Windham: Notes for Cross Examination of Mr Bowen May*, Field and Roscoe, 36 Lincoln's Inn Road, Norfolk Record Office, WKC 4/30, 465×4, 1 of 2, fol. 1.

138. *Commission de Lunatico Inquirendo: An Inquiry*, 158.

139. *Commission de Lunatico Inquirendo: An Inquiry*, 196.

140. *In Lunacy: In the Matter of W. F. Windham, a Supposed Lunatic: Index to Affidavits Read before the Lords Justices by Respondents. Mr W. Field. Field and Roscoe, 36 Lincoln's Inn Fields*, Norfolk Record Office, WKC 4/30, 465×4, 1 of 2, fol. II.

the said William Frederick Windham should in manner hereinafter mentioned secure to the said Agnes Ann Rogers a perpetual yearly rent charge of eight hundred pounds to be increased to one thousand five hundred pounds as hereinafter mentioned by way of jointure and in bar of dower."[141] Whidborne, named as half of the suit in the deed, was Willoughby's doctor, and both he and her procurer of clients, Roberts, were named by the deed as the two new trustees of the Windham estate. The settlement provided for a continued income from the estate to William's mother, Lady Sophia, of £1,500 a year, while also guaranteeing that the £800 provided to Willoughby would increase to £1,500 in 1869. The deed stipulated that Willoughby's income was provided in perpetuity regardless of the circumstances of her marriage: that is, even if she separated or divorced.[142] In the event of her death, the deed stipulated income would revert to her sisters, provided that they take the name "Windham." The remaining annual income from rents of the estate would be for William Windham.

The same day, August 29, that Willoughby and Windham met with Bowen May and finalised the settlement, their wedding certificate was issued by the Doctors' Commons. It was witnessed as follows: "sworn before me T. H. Tristram. Surrogate."[143] This was Thomas Tristram, the man Twiss had pressured the Doctors' Commons six years previously to accept as their last member and who would remain a close friend of Twiss until the end of his life. Tristram signed as "surrogate" because he was not directly authorised to issue marriage licenses; he was the surrogate of the man who was, the Vicar General of the Province of Canterbury, who was, of course, Travers Twiss.[144] Twiss, therefore, was the man responsible for issuing his former courtesan, Agnes Willoughby's, marriage license, and he thereby participated in the act whereby she assumed a new legal personality, incorporated with William Windham.

The marriage ceremony took place on August 30 in St John's Wood. Willoughby spent the night before the wedding with Guiglini. Forbes Winslow, a prominent alienist—that is, a doctor concerned with the mind—asked Windham some months after about that night: "I referred to the fact that a Mr G

---

141. Indenture. Dated 29th August 1861. Windham v Whidborne. Settlement executed by W. F. Windham. *Mr W. Field. Field and Roscoe, 36 Lincoln's Inn Fields*, Norfolk Record Office, WKC 4/30, 465×4, 1 of 2, fol. 2.

142. Indenture. Dated 29th August 1861. Windham v Whidborne. Settlement executed by W. F. Windham. *Mr W. Field. Field and Roscoe, 36 Lincoln's Inn Fields*, Norfolk Record Office, WKC 4/30, 465×4, 1 of 2, fols. 3–5.

143. Wedding certificate for William Frederick Windham and Ann Agnes Rogers, 29 August 1861, Extracted from the Office of Faculties, Doctors' Commons, Norfolk Record Office, WKC 4/30, 465×2, 2 of 2.

144. For Twiss farming out licenses to grant marriage, see *South Eastern Gazette*, March 30, 1858, 5.

with whom his wife had been living previous to his marriage actually slept in the house where Mrs W was the night previous to his marriage. He admitted that such was the fact, said that he saw Mr G's boots at his bed room door but did not believe that Mr G actually slept in the same bed with his wife. He could not be impressed with the probability of such an occurance."[145] The following morning, the company who came to the church were small and were all gathered before the altar. Willoughby's doctor and the trustee of the Felbrigg estate, Dr Whidborne, "acted as father of the bride and gave her away."[146] A reception was then held in Agnes's St John's Wood house—the house that Travers Twiss had provided for her. Another alienist, Doctor Mayo, later asked Windham if it was appropriate to hold his wedding reception in the house of a man for whom she had previously been a prostitute. Windham, he said in his affidavit, "showed utter indifference to the imputation of marrying a woman out of the house of one who had kept her," and in a separate draft of his statement, he declared, "The great proof of his moral insanity is the fact of his taking his wife to marry her out of the house where she had been kept."[147] As Twiss thereby became part of the proof for the insanity of Windham, he would have been painfully aware of the cost of Willoughby's transformation into Mrs Windham. His relationship with Willoughby appeared to be an open secret, in some quarters, and given that Mayo ate regularly at Twiss's club, the Athenaeum, the two were likely to have known each other. Mayo wrote frequently to the club committee, on the back of his dinner bills, according to the custom, to complain bitterly about the punctuality of the service and the quality of the parmesan cheese, although he did praise the quality of the beef (his favourite dish with sherry).[148] Men dining at the club were inclined to gossip about the affairs of their fellow members.

Dr Whidborne reported that, at the wedding reception, Agnes Windham's mother and two sisters were present, along with the solicitor, Mr Bowen May, and several men who dressed like gentlemen but on closer inspection did not

---

145. *In Lunacy: In the Matter of W. F. Windham, a Supposed Lunatic: Proofs of Dr Forbes Winslow, Dr Mayo, Dr Southey. Mr W. Field. Field and Roscoe, 36 Lincoln's Inn Fields*, Norfolk Record Office, WKC 4/30, 465×4, 1 of 2, fol. 2.

146. *Commission de Lunatico Inquirendo: An Inquiry*, 157.

147. *In Lunacy: In the Matter of W. F. Windham, a Supposed Lunatic: Proofs of Dr Forbes Winslow, Dr Mayo, Dr Southey. Mr W. Field. Field and Roscoe, 36 Lincoln's Inn Fields*, Norfolk Record Office, WKC 4/30, 465×4, 1 of 2, fol. 4; *In Lunacy: In the Matter of W. F. Windham, a Supposed Lunatic: Proofs of Dr Forbes Winslow, Dr Mayo, Dr Southey. Mr W. Field. Field and Roscoe, 36 Lincoln's Inn Fields*, Norfolk Record Office, WKC 4/30, 465×1, 2 of 2, fols. 5–6.

148. See, for example, during a period when Twiss was frequently at the club and on the committee: Athenaeum: Marked Dinner Bills 1846–50, Dr Mayo, 26 February 1846; Athenaeum: Marked Dinner Bills 1846–50, Dr Mayo, 3 June 1848; Athenaeum: Marked Dinner Bills 1846–50, Dr Mayo, 24 June 1846; Athenaeum: Marked Dinner Bills 1846–50, Dr Mayo, 28 September 1849.

prove to be so.[149] After the wedding, Agnes Windham and William Windham went to Paris, taking her sisters and mother with them. They then returned to Felbrigg Hall. Agnes Windham immediately wrote, using the Felbrigg Hall letterhead, to William's uncle and former guardian, General Charles Ash Windham, asking him and his wife to dinner.[150] The General was at this time a close neighbour to Felbrigg, in Hanworth Hall, part of the Windham estate. He responded tersely to William Windham: "I have no intention of allowing my wife to associate with yours unless my impressions of the latter should be removed, and therefore shall not dine with you on Friday. / I have addressed you and not your wife as future proceedings will have to rest with you."[151] The exchange set the tone for the family relations over the following months and years. Sir William Foster of Norwich commented that the marriage "caused a strong feeling against him [William Windham] in the county."[152]

During September, Roberts too spent time living at Felbrigg, making an unsuccessful attempt to sell off the timber on the estate. He travelled on the night train up to Norwich with William and Agnes Windham. The train driver, Joseph Ford, testified that William Windham rode in the engine with him, while Roberts and Agnes Windham took over a compartment, laid boxes and cushions between the seats, drew the blinds, and asked the driver to lock them in for the night.[153] Ford observed, "Windham went up the platform at the stations calling out the names of the stations but not so much as usual—he must have seen the carriage with the blinds so drawn." At the end of September, Agnes and William stayed in Roberts's house in Piccadilly. In early October, Agnes left the house and went to Dublin, "where she stayed for some days with Guiglini (the singer)."[154] She returned to Felbrigg and, between October 11 and 18, William bought her another £5,419 of jewellery, although on this occasion Mr Emanuel travelled to Felbrigg Hall with a selection.[155] Nevertheless, she and William quarrelled. On one occasion, on returning to Felbrigg, Agnes Windham and William were caught in a violent storm, during which William

---

149. *Commission de Lunatico Inquirendo: An Inquiry*, 156–157.

150. "My Dear Genl, / It will give my husband and myself great pleasure if Mrs Windham and yourself will favour us with your company at Dinner at 7.00 o'clock on Friday next, Agnes Windham": Agnes Windham to General Windham, *In Lunacy: Re: Windham: From Windham to Uncle*, Norfolk Record Office, WKC 4/30, 465×2, 2 of 2.

151. General Windham to William Windham, September 19, 1861, *In Lunacy: Re: Windham: From Windham to Uncle*, Norfolk Record Office, WKC 4/30, 465×2, 2 of 2.

152. *Commission de Lunatico Inquirendo: An Inquiry*, 148.

153. *In Lunacy: In the Matter of W. F. Windham, a Supposed Lunatic: Proof of Joseph Ford. Mr W. Field. Field and Roscoe, 36 Lincoln's Inn Fields*, Norfolk Record Office, WKC 4/30, 465×4, 1 of 2.

154. *In Lunacy: In the Matter of W. F. Windham, a Supposed Lunatic: Brief for the Petitioners. Mr Wm. Field. 36 Field and Roscoe, Lincoln's Inn Fields*, Norfolk Record Office, WKC 4/30, 465×4, 1 of 2, fol. 11.

155. *Commission de Lunatico Inquirendo: An Inquiry*, 64, 172.

drove his carriage at great speed. The horses panicked, and Windham "got out and lashed them most unmercifully." She fled, chased by Windham, who then "dragged her along the road, she calling out for help and screaming." She was badly bruised.[156] She told the gardener, Ronald Robins, one Sunday morning to cut her some grapes because she was going away "and did not intend to return any more as she could not live with such a nasty beast as he had diseased her with a disease he had before marriage."[157] She now travelled to Glasgow and then Carlisle (where Guiglini was touring).[158] James Holden, "Inspector C Division" in the London Police Force, made an affidavit in which he said William accosted him on the night of October 30 in Stafford Street, in Mayfair, and lamented that "his mother had married a young man."[159] According to Holden, William Windham then "asked Brown [Charles Brown, a police constable] to arrest Agnes, who had run away with £14,000 of jewellery." He had tears "running down his cheeks," and "he caught hold of me by the shoulders and begged and prayed of me to do as he wanted."[160] Failing to prevail with the police officers, Windham caught the train to Glasgow and, on the way up, got out at every station and shouted the names of Agnes and Giuglini.[161]

Several days later, on November 5, William succeeded in tracking Agnes Windham to the Euston Hotel in London, where he wrote her a letter:

132 Piccadilly November 5th. Agnes, Since you seem so bent on getting a separation I suppose you will allow me to see you once more for the last time as I am going away for good and all. If you promise me however that you will live alone and not with any other man I will agree to these terms viz. . . . [a house, an allowance, horses and carriage, etc.; he does not seem to appreciate that she already has secured the income from the estate] . . . I will never break my word which I made to Heaven

---

156. *In Lunacy: In the Matter of W. F. Windham, a Supposed Lunatic: Proof of Gwynn. Mr W. Field. Field and Roscoe, 36 Lincoln's Inn Fields*, Norfolk Record Office, WKC 4/30, 465×4, 1 of 2.

157. *Affidavit of Ronald Robins of Aylmerton. In Lunacy: In the Matter of W. F. Windham, a Supposed Lunatic: Brief: Affidavits in Support of Petition: Mr W. Field. Field and Roscoe, 36 Lincoln's Inn Fields*, Norfolk Record Office, WKC 4/30, 465×4, 1 of 2, fol. 40.

158. *In Lunacy: In the Matter of W. F. Windham, a Supposed Lunatic: Brief for the Petitioners. Mr Wm. Field. 36 Field and Roscoe, Lincoln's Inn Fields*, Norfolk Record Office, WKC 4/30, 465×4, 1 of 2, fol. 11.

159. *In Lunacy: In the Matter of W. F. Windham, a Supposed Lunatic: Petitioners' Proofs. Mr Wm. Field. Field and Roscoe, Lincoln's Inn Fields*, Norfolk Record Office, WKC 4/30, 465×4, 1 of 2, fol. 37.

160. *In Lunacy: In the Matter of W. F. Windham, a Supposed Lunatic: Petitioners' Proofs. Mr Wm. Field. Field and Roscoe, Lincoln's Inn Fields*, Norfolk Record Office, WKC 4/30, 465×4, 1 of 2, fol. 37.

161. *In Lunacy: In the Matter of W. F. Windham, a Supposed Lunatic: Proof of Gwynn. Mr W. Field. Field and Roscoe, 36 Lincoln's Inn Fields*, Norfolk Record Office, WKC 4/30, 465×4, 1 of 2.

which was always to help you. I shall never loose [*sic*] of you as regards your interests though you have been cruel and unkind enough to leave me you are perhaps aware that I have been made acquainted with some of your goings on. You said you never knew any man save Mr Garden before you knew me. Do you not recollect poor young Campbell at Weymouth in the 3rd Light Dragoons. You ruined him and lived with him also I know that the reason you dislike Mr Roberts you slept with him at 11 Melton Place you also cohabited with Mr George Stone you went to Paris with him . . . My Uncle can prove on oath your history from your birth. You left my house and went to Dublin there you committed adultery with a foreigner [Guiglini]. Take care what you do about this getting a separation it is not as easy as you think <u>you have grossly deceived me into a marriage with you</u> [red underline by petitioners]. I thought you loved me. You turn round on me as I am afraid you have done on others after you have got all out of me you possibly could. I thought you were a good woman I find in you a heartless and Godless woman . . . In spite of your conduct I will be a friend to you while I live . . . From one who loves you still, namely William Windham. Mrs Windham. Euston Hotel, Euston Square.[162]

This was not, however, the end of their marriage.

The information about Agnes Windham that William had obtained from his uncle had been gathered as part of an extraordinarily thorough investigation by him into her background. William's uncle, General Charles Ash Windham, was a public figure by the year of William's marriage. In the Crimean War, he was the "Hero of the Redan" (where he led the victorious charge against orders), and he had also led British forces in the Indian Rebellion at Cawnpore and subsequently in the relief of Lucknow. Although initially publicly expressing frustration at William's marriage, the General was overheard by John Shoard, clerk to Frederick Chappell, Lady Sophia's solicitor, to say, "The marriage was the best thing that could happen for him [General Windham] the woman [Agnes Windham] had been tried by all the strongest backed fellows in London and they had not been able to knock a child out of her and Windham never could."[163] If Agnes Windham could not fall pregnant, as the General assumed, then his own children would inherit the Felbrigg estate.

The General soon changed his mind, however, possibly because he could see that there would be no estate left for his children to inherit if William

---

162. William Windham to Agnes Willoughby, November 5, 1861, *In Lunacy: In the Matter of W. F. Windham, a Supposed Lunatic: Exhibits to Affidavit of C. N. Cole. John and C. Cole, 36 Essex Street*, Norfolk Record Office, WKC 4/30, 465×4, 1 of 2, fol. 4.

163. *In Lunacy: Re: W. F. Windham, Affidavit of John Shoard*, Norfolk Record Office, WKC 4/30, 465×4, 2 of 2.

remained with Agnes Windham for long. By September, he began to collect evidence on her background, and in late October, he wrote to all family members to ask for their support in bringing a petition to the Lords Justices to find William to be insane and incapable of managing his property.[164] The General asked in his letter whether, at this stage, "you approve of his being placed (not in confinement) but under some restraint." Led by the General, fifteen family members, the entire family excepting William's mother, petitioned the Lords Justices to have William Windham tried in a Commission de Lunatico according to the Lunacy Act of 1845.[165] The main aim of the Lunacy Act had been to distinguish insanity from criminality and thus to treat people found to be insane as medical patients, although they would be deprived of their liberty in the same manner as criminals. On November 3, the Lords Justices established the Commission with the question whether "Mr W. F. Windham is lunatic or enjoying lucid intervals, so that he is sufficient for the governing of himself, his lands, manors, etc."[166] It was, of course, not uncommon for the families of men to have them tried for lunacy in order to gain control of their property, while women were often incarcerated to "get troublesome wives or daughters out of the way."[167]

Throughout October and continuing during the trial, the General busied himself with collecting evidence to prove William's insanity, employing a host of contacts and solicitors. One of the principal assumptions of the case was that the marriage with Agnes Windham demonstrated insanity, and that argument in turn depended upon the proof of her character. The General therefore devoted great energy to uncovering her story. He wrote to a Reverend Buckworth in Dorset, the county from which the Rogers family came, and on September 26, the Reverend responded: "I have obtained you the information you desired with regard to the present Mrs Windham, and I fear it will not be very satisfactory" before providing an account of her father and a list of her various

---

164. General Windham, 23 October 1861, *Re: Windham: Letters from Mr Chappell to Field and Roscoe*, Norfolk Record Office, WKC 4/30, 465×2, 2 of 2.

165. There is a short account of the trial in Wise, *Inconvenient People: Lunacy, Liberty and the Mad-Doctors in Victorian England* (Berkeley, 2012), 283–284. Otherwise, there are a number of popular accounts, including Donald MacAndrew, "Mr and Mrs Windham: A Mid-Victorian Melodrama from Real Life," in *The Saturday Book: Being the Eleventh Annual Appearance of This Renowned Repository of Curiosities and Looking-glass Past and Present*, ed. Leonard Russell (Watford, 1951), 191–210; R. W. Ketton-Cremer, "William Frederick Windham," in Ketton Cremer, *Felbrigg: The Story of a House* (London, 1962), 249–266. There are also some short online accounts. All the accounts are drawn from the (abridged) published record of the trial: *Commission de Lunatico Inquirendo: An Inquiry*.

166. *Commission de Lunatico Inquirendo: An Inquiry*, 198.

167. On the use of lunacy to deprive men of property, see Sarah Wise, *Inconvenient People*, and Knowles and Trowbridge, "Introduction," in Knowles and Trowbridge, eds., *Insanity*, 3–4; for "troublesome wives or daughters," see Elaine Showalter, *The Female Malady: Women, Madness, and English Culture, 1830–1980* (New York, 1985), 10.

clients.[168] The General, or his solicitors, even managed to obtain a firsthand account of Agnes Willoughby from one of her former clients, J. Preston, a former army officer. Writing to "My dear Drops," Preston remarked: "I heard from Batchelor at Doncaster [races] that Agnes had got well married and I hope that she will be steady and not make a fool of herself. You know nearly as much of her origin as I do, remembering her as a little slapper at Weymouth, she was then about 13 or 14, she said the former, but I fancy she was nearer 15 certainly not more."[169] By 1856, she was living with "Staunton of the equerries," who, the officer remarked with some astonishment, "showed me her portrait when we were going up in the Melbourne to Balaklava not knowing of course that I knew her, nor did I recognize it till seeing her in town a month afterwards." The next time he saw Agnes Willoughby, Preston observed, was "on my return from the East, April 1856, and I then met her in Sally Sutherland's the first night of my arrival and we cottoned but I found her too mercinary for me so did not patronize her much but still kept up the acquaintance." He insisted that she did not often work in Sally's brothel: "You belie her when you say she was a regular frequenter of Sally's. I don't think I ever saw her there three times. She flew at higher game. Also B. B. Williams (Shiny's father) could tell you a deal about A. So could Jack Gardiner, who she has been nominally kept by for a long time." Turning to her London life, he recalled, "She has kept a milliner's shop in Wimpole at Wigmore St. I forget which number I have not my old pocket book with the address in with me. No. 9 I think it was. But of course this was only as a cloak tho she told me (but then she was always such a liar) that it was worth 30 to 40 £ a week to her." He concluded: "You ask what was her style of life, whore certainly and had the character both amongst women and men of being a damned mercenary one, tho' I must say that when she found that it was not to be got from me she gave up running her rigs on me. Tho' when we first met in town she pretended bailiffs were in the house one afternoon and wanted me to pay £24.10.00 down and when I did seem to see it she began to laugh. I think I have told you all I know about her in a general way. I did pretty well at Doncaster..."[170]

Later, in January 1862, the General sent a letter to Robert Hassall Swaffield, a sheriff of Weymouth who had been "Chairman of the Board of Guardians of the Union," of the Weymouth Workhouse, when he had first encountered Agnes Rogers's mother. Swaffield recounted: "A woman by the name of Rogers applied for relief. I questioned her pretty closely as to the causes of her affliction when she informed me that a certain allowance she had depended on had been

---

168. Reverend Buckworth to General Windham, September 26, 1861, Norfolk Record Office, WKC 4/30, 465×2, 2 of 2.

169. J. Preston (from Pitcairlie in Fife) to Drops on October 29, 1861, Norfolk Record Office, WKC 4/30, 465×2, 2 of 2.

170. J. Preston to Drops, October 29, 1861, Norfolk Record Office, WKC 4/30, 465×2, 2 of 2; for Sally's brothel, see Chesney, *Victorian Underworld*, 364.

stopped and that she was totally destitute. The payment she depended upon came from a gentleman who had shamefully abused and violated her daughter when 13 years of age."[171] This letter reveals that the Rogers family were not free of the workhouse after Agnes Rogers left Andover at the age of 13. It also suggests that she was prostituted by her mother in order to provide an income for the family. Swaffield said he investigated the claim against the gentleman, who proved to be a magistrate, named as "Mr Turtor," and, upon finding it to be true, attempted to take proceedings against him, but Turtor had paid for the family's removal from Weymouth.[172] The General wrote on the back of this letter, for the benefit of his solicitors, "Agnes Rogers was for a considerable period under the protection of old Turtor, a man more than sixty years of age. This was with the knowledge and connivance of her mother. They were a most profligate and abandoned family."[173] After the General gathered this evidence, Agnes and William Windham were called to an interview in his solicitors' office, Field and Roscoe, where she was "reminded" by General Windham of her past. On hearing the stories from Weymouth, "She winced palpably."[174]

The General and his solicitors also had both William and Agnes Windham spied upon by detectives, solicitors' clerks, and employees. William's estate manager, Peatfield, at Felbrigg wrote to the General on an almost daily basis, promising "I shall continually send you account of him . . . I forward with this the Acct Bk for your inspection."[175] The General's solicitors had Agnes followed and obtained reports on her activities with Guiglini: One undated letter, from "Nemo" [i.e., Nobody—also a mysterious character in Charles Dickens's *Bleak House*, published ten years earlier], reported: "Friday. It may be of some use to you to be informed that Mrs Windham (*soi-disant*) Agnes Willoughby called at a House Agents in the neighbourhood of Edgware Road and treated with the agent for the purchase of a furnished house near the Regent Park. She was then at the Euston Hotel and accompanied by a gentleman in a Hansom Cab. This gentleman she said was her secretary Mr Guibelei who was to be referred to in her absence as she was going into the Country. From another source I am informed that Mrs Windham and Mr Guibelei have been acquainted intimately for a length of time. If you require further details, an advertisement

---

171. Robert Hassall Swaffield to General Windham, January 12, 1862, Norfolk Record Office, WKC 4/30, 465×2, 2 of 2.

172. Robert Hassall Swaffield to General Windham, January 12, 1862, Norfolk Record Office, WKC 4/30, 465×2, 2 of 2.

173. Robert Hassall Swaffield to General Windham, January 12, 1862, Norfolk Record Office, WKC 4/30, 465×2, 2 of 2, verso.

174. *In Lunacy: In the Matter of W. F. Windham, a Supposed Lunatic: Brief for the Petitioners. Mr Wm. Field. 36 Field and Roscoe, Lincoln's Inn Fields*, Norfolk Record Office, WKC 4/30, 465×4, 1 of 2, fol. 7.

175. Peatfield to General Windham, December 16, 1861, *Re: Windham. From Mr Peatfield*, Norfolk Record Office, WKC 4/30, 465×2, 2 of 2.

in the Morning [Post?] intimating where Nemo can call, time and place to be inserted."¹⁷⁶ When Field, the General's London solicitor, sent this letter to Hansell, his Norwich solicitor, he added that William was "locked up in" Roberts's house, while "the last is that Agnes has gone off to Italy with Guiglini."¹⁷⁷

All of this activity on the part of the General and his solicitors did not pass unnoticed. Henry Francis Wood, the clerk in the Field and Roscoe office, who said he had been "engaged in collecting evidence respecting the life of Agnes Windham previous to her marriage," remarked that her defence against his claim that she had been "a prostitute for many years and was one at the date of her marriage" was that she "had never professed to be a virtuous woman."¹⁷⁸ Her candour protected her from the charge of having married Windham under false pretences. Roberts, on the other hand, responded more aggressively to the investigation into his own activities. Writing to the General on October 16, 1861, under his coat of arms and motto "Valor et Lux," Roberts declared: "Sir, I am led to understand that you are maliciously circulating reports having reference to myself and I warn you to abstain from so doing. I have certainly come into contact with Mr W. F. Windham whose estate you are so desirous of possessing, and I am also aware that you intend placing him in a lunatic asylum. I can only bear testimony to the fact that I have seldom met a man of his age so shrewd upon his own affairs. I have my own affairs to attend to but I warn you in your anxiety to get hold of what you will never possess not to stoop to the desperate means of vilifying those who will be found a match for you with whatever weapons you choose to play. I have strongly recommended him to indict you and I shall then be prepared to bring forth the little peccadilloes of yourself as put forth in the Times a few years back and which perhaps you might not like reissued. Yours most faithfully, J. Roberts."¹⁷⁹

Roberts did not invent the story of the General's "peccadilloes." As a young officer, the General had been reported in *The Times*, seventeen years previously, to have exposed himself to a 15-year-old girl in Regent's Park.¹⁸⁰ Five

---

176. Undated letter from "Nemo," *Re: Windham: Letters to General Windham*, Norfolk Record Office, WKC 4/30, 465×2, 2 of 2.

177. Field to Hansell, November 2, 1861, *Re: Windham: Letters to General Windham*, Norfolk Record Office, WKC 4/30, 465×2, 2 of 2.

178. Affidavit of Henry Francis Wood of 36 Lincoln's Inn Fields, *In Chancery. Windham v Guibelei, Draft Notice of Motion for Committal, Field and Roscoe, 36 Lincoln's Inn Fields*, Norfolk Record Office, WKC 4/30, 465×1, 2 of 2, fol. 3. According to Wood, "I was present again at the meeting [in the office of Field and Roscoe] in which again she stated she had never professed to be a virtuous woman before she married WFW."

179. Roberts to General Windham, October 16, 1861, *Re: Windham: From Mr Peatfield*, Norfolk Record Office, WKC 4/30, 465×2, 2 of 2.

180. On September 9, 1844, a "gentleman living upon his fortune" was presented to Bow Street Police Court after having spent the night in Bridewell Prison and after having refused the previous day to give his name "for his appearance the next sessions to answer the charge of having indecently exposed himself to a girl of 15 in St James Park." After the

weeks after Roberts sent this letter, the General's solicitor, Field, wrote to his Norwich solicitor about preparations for the prosecution of Windham and his associates. Field instructed Hansell to pursue "the woman" and Bowen-May and to leave Roberts for a later moment.[181] Nevertheless, two months after Field's letter, the General received a letter from Roberts's solicitor, Bowen May, announcing proceedings against him for "gross scandal" for "attributing to the gentleman [Roberts] an indictable offence, namely 'keeping brothels' whereby he has been immensely injured in reputation and pocket."[182] The proceedings were a form of blackmail. Bowen May sent a letter the next day asking for an immediate reply and whether the General would provide "proper tribute for the frightful injury you have inflicted upon my client," in which case the charges would be dropped.[183] Other threats received by the General included a poison-pen letter that he tore up (judging from its state in the family papers): "Sh. You vilaine impostaire assassin for youre unhappy brother's son, take care if you will to enjoy what you already have. The English true patriots shall give good lesson's [sic] for your vilaine plots of titled blackguards. We have already your own addresses. Take care vilains."[184] The writer of this letter raised the interesting possibility that it was the General, and not Agnes Windham, who was the "impostaire." With its language of "true patriots" and attack upon "titled blackguards," the author also associates her cause with Radical, or possibly even Chartist, politics, which were spurred by resurgent nationalism in the late 1850s and early '60s, when this note was written.[185] Her personal transformation transpired in the context of broader poltical movements for liberty.

As Roberts's letter to the General reveals, he, and undoubtedly William and Agnes Windham, knew by the middle of October 1861 that the family was planning to have William judged insane. As a consequence, William Windham consulted his own solicitor, Cole, regarding his defence. By this point, he and Agnes Windham had separated. Nevertheless, just a day after he wrote the letter to her acknowledging their separation, he arrived at the Euston Hotel to find her dining with Cole. The proprietor of the hotel, Mr Wheeler, swore on affidavit that William "made disturbances in my house with his shouting and excitement and with his hammering at his wife's bedroom door to gain

---

night in prison, he "gave the name of Charles Windham, and stated that he was an officer in the army," *The Times*, September 9, 1844, 7.

181. Field to Hansell, November 25, 1861, *Re: Windham: Letters to General Windham*, Norfolk Record Office, WKC 4/30, 465×2, 2 of 2.

182. Bowen May to General Windham, February 5, 1862, Norfolk Record Office, WKC 4/30, 465×2, 2 of 2.

183. Bowen May to General Windham, February 6, 1862, Norfolk Record Office, WKC 4/30, 465×2, 2 of 2.

184. Anonymous to General Windham, December 13, 1861. *Re: Windham: Letters from Mr Chappell to Field and Roscoe*, Norfolk Record Office, WKC 4/30, 465×2, 2 of 2.

185. Finn, *After Chartism*, 188–225.

admission." The solicitor's clerk added in the margin of the affidavit: "The said W.F.W . . . found his said wife dining with Mr Cole herself. She had then drunk a good deal and was far gone in intoxication." Wheeler said he "endeavoured to make him [William] understand the impropriety I had witnessed in his Wife's conduct since she came to my house and I have pointed out to him that she seemed to loath him and would not allow him to go into her bedroom but I failed to make any impression on him. I do not believe he has the slightest feeling of jealousy and I believe that whatever she did, however gross it might be, would not make the least difference in his infatuation for her."[186] In the papers of the Windham family's Norfolk solicitor, Hansell, the letters from William to Agnes Windham accompany Cole's affidavit, suggesting that they were probably preserved because she handed them over to Cole.[187] Cole was incensed to learn of Wheeler's affidavit, which implied that he was sleeping with his client's wife, and he exchanged a series of letters with the General's solicitors, Field and Roscoe, endeavouring to have his name deleted from the document. Finally, "On the 7th of November a meeting took place . . . The object of the latter was to make some arrangement so as to keep the matter from becoming public."[188] Cole succeeded, and his partner, Charles Nicholas Cole, wrote to Field on November 11 to say, "I am glad to hear that you are willing to strike out the offensive passage" and that "General Windham will not serve his case by pressing that line of proceeding."[189] Cole's success in suppressing public mention of any other than a professional connection between him and his client's wife is consistent with the protection of a number of men who had been connected with Agnes Windham, including Travers Twiss, during William Windham's trial. Their names were never uttered. William Windham nevertheless dismissed the Coles as his solicitors. Charles Cole made his own determination regarding Windham's mental health, stating: "Windham is not mad, but he is a downright idiotic ass."[190]

186. *Affidavit of Mr Wheeler of the Euston Hotel, Euston Road: In Lunacy: In the Matter of William Frederick Windham, a Supposed Lunatic, Field and Roscoe, 36 Lincoln's Inn Fields, for Hansell*, Norwich, Norfolk Record Office, WKC 4/30, 465×2, 2 of 2, fols. 1–2.

187. *Exhibits to Affidavit of C. N. Cole, In Lunacy: In the Matter of William Frederick Windham, a Supposed Lunatic, Field and Roscoe, 36 Lincoln's Inn Fields, for Hansell*, Norwich, Norfolk Record Office, WKC 4/30, 465×4, 1 of 2, fols. 1–4.

188. *In Lunacy: In the Matter of W. F. Windham, a Supposed Lunatic: Brief for the Petitioners. Mr Wm. Field. 36 Field and Roscoe, Lincoln's Inn Fields*, Norfolk Record Office, WKC 4/30, 465×4, 1 of 2, fol. 12; For the implication that Cole was sleeping with Agnes, see also Field to Hansell, November 9, 1861, *Re: Windham: Letters to General Windham*, Norfolk Record Office, WKC 4/30, 465×2, 2 of 2.

189. Cole to Field, November 12, 1861, *Re: Windham: Letters to General Windham*, Norfolk Record Office, WKC 4/30, 465×2, 2 of 2. C. H. Cole should not be confused with H. W. Cole, who represented William Windham.

190. *Re: Windham: Coles' Proof. Mr Field*, Norfolk Record Office, WKC 4/30, 465×4, 1 of 2.

The Lords Justices granted the petition to have Windham tried for lunacy. The first issue that the petitioners brought to court was the claim that the marriage of Agnes and William Windham had been in contempt of court because, even if it had been concluded after he came of age, it had been plotted while he was still a minor and therefore made against the jurisdiction of the Court of Chancery, which managed the Windham estate until his majority. The Lords Justices, however, instructed the petitioners that this claim could not be heard in the case concerning lunacy and that, rather, it properly belonged to the suit *Windham vs Guibelei*, which had been established to bring the estate to Chancery. The General and his family accordingly brought a separate action for contempt of court, on November 26, 1861, against Agnes Windham and her lawyer, Bowen May, under the suit of *Windham vs Guibelei*.[191] The stakes, if she and her solicitor lost this case, were high. The action called for them to be found "guilty of a contempt and stand committed to the Queen's prison." For this reason, she disappeared. The case was delayed because she could not have the writ served upon her.[192] When it was finally heard, the judge gave Bowen May a "tremendous trouncing" but conceded that he "had not sufficient evidence to commit him," so that the outcome was that the marriage was found to be legitimate.[193]

While *Windham vs Guibelei* was being heard, the financial toll of the extraordinary efforts to seize the Felbrigg estate was mounting. The General's London solicitors, Field and Roscoe, wrote to Hansell, his Norfolk solicitor: "We must have some money for all this. Can't you let us have a cheque for £300 or £400 or where shall we get it?"[194] Preparations for the case had been exhaustive. Hundreds of pages of notes were made for the cross-examination of witnesses. Questions for William included: "Does he think his wife an honest woman?" "Why does not his mother help him?" "Has he any jealousy about his wife?" "Has he received returned letters from the dead letter office written from Felbrigg by her to Guiglini?" "Why have the Country Gentlemen refused to visit him? And how has he lost his position in the county?" "Did he understand that the Annuity given to his wife was a perpetual one?"[195]

---

191. *In Chancery: Windham v Guibelei: Notice of Motion for Committal. Field and Roscoe, 36 Lincoln's Inn Fields*, Norfolk Record Office, WKC 4/30, 465×4, 1 of 2, fol. 1 verso.

192. Field to Hansell, November 27, 1861, *Re: Windham: Letters to General Windham*, Norfolk Record Office, WKC 4/30, 465×2, 2 of 2: "Re: Windham. We have received the anonymous letters. We are having a great hunt after the woman (who is keeping out of the way)."

193. Field to Hansell, December 4, 1861, *Re: Windham: Letters to General Windham*, Norfolk Record Office, WKC 4/30, 465×2, 2 of 2.

194. Field to Hansell, November 27, 1861, *Re: Windham: Letters to General Windham*, Norfolk Record Office, WKC 4/30, 465×2, 2 of 2.

195. *In Lunacy: Re: Windham: Notes for Examination of W. F. Windham. Mr W. Field. Field and Roscoe, 36 Lincoln's Inn Fields*, Norfolk Record Office, WKC 4/30, 465×4, 1 of 2, fol. 1 verso.

The solicitors' clerks wrote character profiles for each witness and investigated their backgrounds, looking for weaknesses in witnesses for the defence. One thumbnail sketch for a Norwich innkeeper, Mr Snowling, reads: "Innkeeper Norwich. / Has been promised a farm . . . He is continually with Windham. / Roberts went there. / It is a regular nest of the fellows in this case. / Debauchery"; while another for a Mr Stubbs, a character witness for William, states: "Ginger Stubbs. / Broke on the [Epsom 1859] Derby when Abizard lost and Thormanby won. / Keeps a woman Mrs Ginger in Queen Street. / A noted Billiard player. / The foreman of the Jury (Sir George Armitage) knows him."[196] Based upon months of investigations, the clerks also wrote an exhaustive background brief for the benefit of Chambers, the barrister for the petitioners. It was in this brief that Twiss was named as Agnes's "best friend" and protector when she came to London. Such meticulous presentation was expensive. Even the lawyers worried about the costs. Field wrote to Hansell on November 28: "We shall have to give Mr Chambers [the barrister] 50 guineas a day. The General wishes us to have Barstow as a junior. Will I take Bedwell into court as well? I am afraid of the cost. / Further evidence of course we must look up: We expect you will hunt all you can."[197]

Peter Hansell, the Norwich solicitor, devoted years to the case, and it appears to have become an obsession beyond his professional practice. He collected all the papers, letters, affidavits, newspaper clippings, notebooks, and court transcripts and even produced a scrapbook devoted to the Windham case, which extended for many years after the formal proceedings had concluded. The Master of Lunacy, Warren, wrote to him after the case had concluded, thanking him for a copy of the trial transcript.[198] The lunacy trial itself, one of many trials surrounding the case, would run for thirty-three days, from December 16, with 140 witnesses being called.[199] Although it fell well short in duration of that of the Chancery case *Jarndyce and Jarndyce* in Dickens's *Bleak House*, it would have a similar impact upon the litigants. Of the central participants, all except Agnes Windham were financially ruined.

The proceedings commenced in the Court of the Exchequer. The stakes were William Windham's liberty over both his person and his property. The Master of Lunacy, or judge, for the Commission, Samuel Warren, pointed out that a person could be tried for lunacy whether or not "the party is absolutely insane." He repeatedly stated that the case was a matter of "personal

---

196. *In Lunacy: Re: Windham: Notes for Cross Examination of Respondents' Witnesses, Mr W. Field. Field and Roscoe, 36 Lincoln's Inn Fields*, Norfolk Record Office, WKC 4/30, 465×4, 1 of 2.

197. Field to Hansell, November 28, 1861, *Re: Windham: Letters to General Windham*, Norfolk Record Office, WKC 4/30, 465×2, 2 of 2.

198. Office of the Masters in Lunacy to Peter Hansell, March 20, 1862, *Re: Windham: Letters to General Windham*, Norfolk Record Office, WKC 4/30, 465×2, 2 of 2.

199. *Commission de Lunatico Inquirendo: An Inquiry*, 198.

liberty and property," that the "liberty of the subject" was at issue, and that the case was one about whether a man could be "left at perfect liberty."[200] He instructed the jury that it was possible that "the party is unable to act with any proper and provident discretion, and is liable to be robbed by anyone, under that imbecility of mind, which is not strictly insanity; but, as to the mischief it produces, calling for as much protection as actual insanity."[201] In Windham's case, it was felt that he would probably not be incarcerated in an asylum if found to be insane, but would be placed under protection.[202] His defence counsel, accordingly, argued "he ought not to be deprived of his liberty," while counsel for his mother declared that the trial was one of "personal freedom and personal independence."[203]

The evidence presented at the trial prompted a lengthy discussion with counsel about the presence of women in the room, and it was agreed that they should be barred. More than once, proceedings had to be halted while women were removed from the court.[204] Repeatedly throughout the trial, the Master of Lunacy, and some counsel, warned witnesses against stating the names of men associated with Agnes Windham.[205] Having read the background briefs, counsel for the petitioners knew that Twiss had been her "best friend." They were aware of how explosive that revelation made in court would have been. Mr Field, for example, warned a witness in cross-examination: "Tell us what he has told you on different occasions about Agnes Willoughby but you need not mention any gentleman's name in connection with her."[206] Here the Master interjected: "Be sure you do not mention any names, for it would be very unsatisfactory." Although such cautions were not uncommon, it did not hurt Twiss's cause that Warren came from the same town of Wrexham in North Wales and was born two years prior to Twiss.[207] Agnes Windham's other

200. P. E. Hansell—Norwich. *In Lunacy: Re: Windham: Report of Proceedings. Monday Dec. 16, 1861*, Norfolk Record Office, WKC 4/29/8, 464×7, 1 of 2, fols. 8, 10, and 13.
201. *Commission de Lunatico Inquirendo: An Inquiry*, 199.
202. *Commission de Lunatico Inquirendo: An Inquiry*, 199.
203. *Commission de Lunatico Inquirendo: An Inquiry*, 183, 174.
204. P. E. Hansell—Norwich, *In Lunacy: Re: Windham: Report of Proceedings. 5th day*, Norfolk Record Office, WKC 4/29/11, 464×7, 1 of 2, fols. 106–107; P. E. Hansell—Norwich, *In Lunacy: Re: Windham: Report of Proceedings, Monday Dec. 16, 1861*, Norfolk Record Office, WKC 4/29/8, 464×7, 1 of 2, fol. 16.
205. See, for example, P. E. Hansell—Norwich, *In Lunacy: Re: Windham: Report of Proceedings. Monday Dec. 16, 1861*, Norfolk Record Office, WKC 4/29/8, 464×7, 1 of 2, fol. 87.
206. P. E. Hansell—Norwich, *In Lunacy: Re: Windham: Report of Proceedings. 6th day*, Norfolk Record Office, WKC 4/29/12, 464×7, 1 of 2, fol. 75.
207. Moreover, in 1853, Warren was awarded a Doctorate of Civil Law at Oxford (a fact we learn from his obituary, which Hansell pasted into the scrapbook on the case fifteen years later, in 1877): "The Late Mr Samuel Warren", in "P. E. Hansell Norwich, Solicitor for the Petitioners, Private Copy. Windham Trial. Letters etc," Norfolk Record Office, MC 580/1, 780×1. This was three years before Twiss, as Regius Professor of Civil Law,

London protectors, Jack Garden and Roberts, were mentioned in the trial, as was Guiglini, and they were also mentioned in the publicity surrounding the trial, particularly in the newspapers. The trial went into minute detail concerning William and Agnes Windham's lives, and yet, remarkably, Twiss was never mentioned. Perhaps his colleagues in the Inns of Court were doing their best to protect him. Another possibility is that he paid for the silence. Field and Roscoe's notes say that Twiss "got rid of her [Agnes] by a payment of £2,000 down," but he told his wife just a few months later that he had "great losses during the last year" and that, at the moment the lunacy trial was looming, he had paid out £8,000 to Willoughby on November 3, 1859, "besides property she had taken from Park Lane."[208] The sum was equivalent to his annual salary. Later testimony raised the possibility that Twiss's connection with Agnes Windham did not end in 1859.

The two most important witnesses at Windham's trial were the doctors appointed by the Commission to judge his sanity, although the Master of Lunacy, who had qualified as a doctor, advised the jury on how to hear expert medical testimony. He warned: "Regard them solely as witnesses not as judges," and added "do not adopt their mere ipse dixit, however eminent or respectable they may be."[209] The appointed doctors, Forbes Winslow and Thomas Mayo, were leading experts in mental disorders. They also represented two very different, and opposed, approaches to the science.[210] Mayo adhered to the doctrine that psychological disorders were moral. In his *Elements of the Pathology of the Human Mind*, he argued, "The moral causes and preventives of insanity are to be looked for among the passive conditions of the mind."[211] It was not, he added, to the "love or power or riches or of praise that insanity can be directly traced." Rather it was "the regretfulness, the despondency, the timidity, the anxiousness" of the mind that led to a loss of the "power of the will" over the thoughts. His views were consistent with an eighteenth-century tradition of treating insanity through "moral management."[212] Winslow, on the other hand, has been described as the "great pioneer of psychological medicine."[213]

---

presented the awards of DCL; nevertheless, it could only have brought Twiss and Warren's circles closer together.

208. *Glasgow Daily Herald*, March 6, 1872, 5.

209. For Warren's education, see "The Late Mr Samuel Warren," in "P. E. Hansell, Norwich, Solicitor for the Petitioners, Private Copy. Windham Trial. Letters etc," Norfolk Record Office, MC 580/1, 780×1; P. E. Hansell—Norwich, *In Lunacy: Re: Windham: Report of Proceedings, Monday Dec. 16, 1861*, Norfolk Record Office, WKC 4/29/8, 464×7, 1 of 2, fol. 11.

210. Finkel, *Insanity on Trial*, 59–62.

211. Thomas Mayo, *Elements of the Pathology of the Human Mind* (London, 1838), 19–20.

212. On moral management, see Porter, *Madness*, 103.

213. Walkowitz, *City of Dreadful Delight*, 173; see also Wise, *Inconvenient People*, 282. He was the father of psychologist Lyttelton Forbes Winslow, who would later pursue Georgina Weldon and who also came into Twiss's story.

He was the most extreme Victorian exponent of the idea that mental disease is physiological, rather than moral, and this enabled him to persuade the law to accept the plea of insanity.[214] However, he believed that neither moral philosophy nor, for that matter, law were necessary in the judgement of sanity.[215] For Winslow, the sanity of a person could be entirely judged from her or his behaviour rather than from her or his statements. A trial in law, as far he was concerned, was not necessary to make a judgement about a person's sanity. Winslow's medicine thus made a robust challenge to the jurisdiction of law, a dispute in which the law prevailed. For Mayo, on the other hand, the moral character of a person was as much a guide to her or his sanity as behaviour.

In his testimony, Forbes Winslow stated his doctrine that the actions, and not the conversation or statements, of a person are key to establishing lunacy. The insane are cunning, he explained, so what they say must be discounted in a judgement about their soundness of mind. They must be judged by their actions.[216] Nothing Windham could say could alter Winslow's judgements, while his actions were damning. He argued that Windham being present while his wife slept with other men was evidence of his being "drunk, drugged, or insane."[217] Similarly, an indication of Windham's "unsound mind" was his "insensibility to the impropriety of living with a person like Roberts," indicating a "paralysis of the moral sense."[218] Moreover, Windham had "said he was fully aware that she [Agnes] had been kept by several men." Winslow added, "He mentioned only one name, but it was a distinguished one."[219] Twiss was the only distinguished person associated with Agnes Willoughby prior to William Windham. He succeeded in remaining in the shadows in this case, while at the same time being a constant presence.

According to Winslow, Windham having "no apparent sense of shame" indicated a paralysis of moral sense. That paralysis was also demonstrated by his marriage to Agnes Willoughby. He would not "understand that it was an act of indecency" to marry such a woman, particularly when she was "living with a paramour up to the night before her marriage."[220] The implications for anyone of Windham's class—including Twiss, who married such a woman—was that they were in danger of being judged insane. Forbes Winslow

---

214. Finkel, *Insanity on Trial*; Walkowitz, *City of Dreadful Delight*, 173.
215. Finkel, *Insanity on Trial*.
216. *Commission de Lunatico Inquirendo: An Inquiry*, 72.
217. *Commission de Lunatico Inquirendo: An Inquiry*, 69.
218. *Commission de Lunatico Inquirendo: An Inquiry*, 71.
219. *Commission de Lunatico Inquirendo: An Inquiry*, 64.
220. *Commission de Lunatico Inquirendo: An Inquiry*, 64; *In Lunacy: In the Matter of W. F. Windham, a Supposed Lunatic: Proofs of Dr Forbes Winslow, Dr Mayo, Dr Southey. Mr W. Field. Field and Roscoe, 36 Lincoln's Inn Fields*, Norfolk Record Office, WKC 4/30, 465×4, 1 of 2, fol. 2.

concluded that Windham was in a "degree of mental imbecility."[221] The Master of Lunacy, Samuel Warren, then warned him about making legal judgements, citing a judge, Baron Alderson, in a case some years previously who had instructed a medical witness: "If you can give us the results of your scientific knowledge upon this point we shall be glad to hear it, but while I am sitting on this bench I shall not permit any medical witness to usurp the functions of both judge and jury."[222] Warren's position was clear in the struggle between law and medicine about jurisdiction over lunacy.[223]

Unfortunately for Windham, Dr Mayo, who was opposed to Winslow in the understanding of their science, was nevertheless in complete agreement with him that Windham was of "unsound mind." Mayo provided an opinion on Windham for the petitioners' barrister, Chambers. He predictably seized the opportunity to denigrate Winslow: "I have read Dr Winslow's evidence—it must be used carefully—for a great deal of it proves eccentricity only. I think none of it of any importance."[224] In contrast to Winslow, he based his judgements largely upon Windham's moral character, and he told Chambers to cross-examine him on that point in the witness stand: "I wish to be drawn out as much as possible as to his moral conduct. This is the great point."[225] Mayo had "suggested to Windham that it was a gross consideratn on his part to say that he had enjoyed his wife before his marriage, when he intended to marry, simply to blind people as he said—I think the idea as worse a one as could cross the human mind." He concluded "His conversatn as to his wife shows moral depravity . . . The great proof of his moral insanity is the fact of his taking his wife to marry her out of the house where she had been kept."[226] It was Twiss who had "kept" her in that house. Like Forbes Winslow, Mayo warned that no credence could be given to anything Windham said in his own defence, when interviewed, because he had "all the cunning of a half-witted man."[227] While counsel for Windham pointed out that he had expressed regret over his actions, that he had resolved to institute proceedings to divorce his wife, and

---

221. *Commission de Lunatico Inquirendo: An Inquiry*, 68.
222. *Commission de Lunatico Inquirendo: An Inquiry*, 71.
223. For the tension between law and medicine, see Porter, *Madness*, 154–155.
224. *In Lunacy: In the Matter of W. F. Windham, a Supposed Lunatic: Proofs of Dr Forbes Winslow, Dr Mayo, Dr Southey. Mr W. Field. Field and Roscoe, 36 Lincoln's Inn Fields*, Norfolk Record Office, WKC 4/30, 465×4, 1 of 2, fol. 5.
225. *In Lunacy: In the Matter of W. F. Windham, a Supposed Lunatic: Proofs of Dr Forbes Winslow, Dr Mayo, Dr Southey. Mr W. Field. Field and Roscoe, 36 Lincoln's Inn Fields*, Norfolk Record Office, WKC 4/30, 465×4, 1 of 2, fol. 6.
226. *In Lunacy: In the Matter of W. F. Windham, a Supposed Lunatic: Proofs of Dr Forbes Winslow, Dr Mayo, Dr Southey. Mr W. Field. Field and Roscoe, 36 Lincoln's Inn Fields*, Norfolk Record Office, WKC 4/30, 465×4, 1 of 2, fols. 5–6.
227. *In Lunacy: In the Matter of W. F. Windham, a Supposed Lunatic: Proofs of Dr Forbes Winslow, Dr Mayo, Dr Southey. Mr W. Field. Field and Roscoe, 36 Lincoln's Inn Fields*, Norfolk Record Office, WKC 4/30, 465×4, 1 of 2, fol. 4.

that he had also distanced himself from Roberts since the trial started, nevertheless Mayo argued that such actions were also mere cunning.[228] Windham, he argued, did good things because of his fear of being punished, not because he understood the difference between good and bad.[229] Dr Buck, from Norwich, agreed that Windham suffered from "moral insanity": "By moral insanity I imply a state of mind evidenced by recklessness, cruelty, inordinate vanity, falsehood, gluttony, obscenity and gross immorality."[230] It did not help Windham's cause that during the trial he was reported to have blacked his face on Christmas night at Felbrigg Hall and had sung "negro" songs.[231] Nor did it help that he was associating with prostitutes in the Haymarket again during the trial.[232]

Apart from the doctors, the two key witnesses for the petitioners were Mrs and Mr Llewellyn, with whom Windham had lived in Duke Street in Marylebone, London, in the six months prior to his marriage, by arrangement through General Windham. In their affidavit, and under cross-examination, the Llewellyns testified to Windham's erratic and "insane" behaviour. He ate twelve eggs for breakfast, he ran about the house naked and exposed himself to servants, he called everybody "Old Bob Ridley," except for Mrs Llewellyn herself, whom he called "you old Hag" and "you old Bitch," and Agnes Willoughby, whom he called a "Jack-Whore."[233] He came in Willoughby's carriage black with dirt after riding in the engine on the Eastern Counties Railway.[234] Mr Llewellyn confessed that he gave Windham "a few lashes" with a horse whip when his behaviour was too unruly but said that "he took it very good temperedly."[235] The testimony of both Llewellyns during the trial raised concerns that they, and other witnesses, had been suborned by General Windham.[236]

William Windham's barristers, Sir Hugh Cairns and Mr John Karslake, cross-examined Mrs Pritchard and Henry Shapis, the Llewellyns' servants, who claimed that their employers had attempted to force them to provide

---

228. *Commission de Lunatico Inquirendo: An Inquiry*, 155.

229. *Commission de Lunatico Inquirendo: An Inquiry*, 73.

230. *In Lunacy: Re: Windham: Proof of Dr H. J. Buck. Mr W. Field. Field and Roscoe, 36 Lincoln's Inn Fields*, Norfolk Record Office, WKC 4/30, 465×4, 1 of 2, fol. 1.

231. *Commission de Lunatico Inquirendo: An Inquiry*, 182.

232. *Commission de Lunatico Inquirendo: An Inquiry*, 182, 201.

233. P. E. Hansell—Norwich, *In Lunacy: Re: Windham: Report of Proceedings. 5th day*, Norfolk Record Office, WKC 4/29/11, 464×7, 1 of 2, fol. 57, fol. 52, fol. 66, and fols. 90-99; P. E. Hansell—Norwich, *In Lunacy: Re: Windham: Report of Proceedings. 6th day*, Norfolk Record Office, WKC 4/29/12, 464×7, 1 of 2, fol. 123.

234. P. E. Hansell—Norwich, *In Lunacy: Re: Windham: Report of Proceedings. 5th day*, Norfolk Record Office, WKC 4/29/11, 464×7, 1 of 2, fol. 71.

235. P. E. Hansell—Norwich, *In Lunacy: Re: Windham: Report of Proceedings. 6th day*, Norfolk Record Office, WKC 4/29/12, 464×7, 1 of 2, fol. 132.

236. P. E. Hansell—Norwich, *In Lunacy: Re: Windham: Report of Proceedings. 5th day*, Norfolk Record Office, WKC 4/29/11, 464×7, 1 of 2, fol. 131 and fol. 142.

false testimony, because they wished to serve the General.[237] Pritchard stated that the Llewellyns were "sucking the poor boy dry."[238] Eliza Dignam, Mrs Llewellyn's sister, who lived in her house while Windham lodged there, then stood and claimed that her sister's testimony was lies paid for by the General. Mrs Llewellyn's brother, a beggar, likewise claimed that his older sister had tried to buy his testimony.[239] Moreover, in an extraordinary turn, Eliza Dignam, who had testified that she was virtually destitute, stated that her sister had taken her to visit James Roberts, the brothel owner for whom Agnes Willoughby worked. The possibility was thus raised that it was the General's servants, the Llewellyns, in whose care he had placed William Windham, who had introduced him to Roberts and so created the link to Agnes Willoughby.[240] Mrs Llewellyn responded to these claims by arguing that her sister had indeed become acquainted with Roberts, and that she had been to his house three times with Eliza.[241] She said that she had enrolled her sister in a school to train as a governess but that she had left it and gone to Roberts. She lamented, "He has got hold of my sister for a bad purpose."[242] Under questioning from Agnes Windham's counsel, Mr Llewellyn then implied that Mrs Llewellyn's sister had, in fact, been working as a courtesan for some time previously to her meeting Roberts.[243] In the notes made by the petitioners on each witness, a clerk at Field and Roscoe recorded that Eliza Dignam had "met Roberts at Cremorne [Cremorne Gardens, in Chelsea, pleasure gardens that were a popular promenade for prostitutes]—he asked her to go and call upon him and she afterwards went and had champagne at Roberts's house. Is now living at no 14 Charwood St Pimlico. A gentleman of the name of Col Sidmore pays for her rooms and goes and sits with her for hours."[244] In other words, Dignam had herself, like Willoughby, become part of Roberts's extensive prostitution network.

Further complicating matters, Mr Llewellyn had thrown Eliza Dignam out of his house after finding her in bed with Windham. All was not, however, as it seemed. Karslake implied that Mr Llewellyn's anger was due to the fact that his sister-in-law had been his lover. Mr Chambers, the petitioners' barrister,

---

237. *Commission de Lunatico Inquirendo: An Inquiry*, 136–139.
238. *Commission de Lunatico Inquirendo: An Inquiry*, 137.
239. *Commission de Lunatico Inquirendo: An Inquiry*, 142.
240. *Commission de Lunatico Inquirendo: An Inquiry*, 141.
241. P. E. Hansell—Norwich, *In Lunacy: Re: Windham: Report of Proceedings. 6th day*, Norfolk Record Office, WKC 4/29/12, 464×7, 1 of 2, fols. 31–35.
242. P. E. Hansell—Norwich, *In Lunacy: Re: Windham: Report of Proceedings. 6th day*, Norfolk Record Office, WKC 4/29/12, 464×7, 1 of 2, fol. 30.
243. *Commission de Lunatico Inquirendo: An Inquiry*, 38.
244. "Eliza Sophia Dignam," *Notes for Cross Examination of Respondents' Witnesses. In Lunacy: Re: Windham*, Norfolk Record Office, WKC 4/30, 465×1, 2 of 2.

responded, "Good God! You cannot mean to put that."[245] The petitioners' own papers, however, included a letter written by Eliza, imploring her brother-in-law to allow her to return to his house: "My trouble at the time was great indeed. I was mad. Make an excuse for a lunatic I was then. I ask you now to forgive poor little Eliza ... did I not love you from a child. Yes Llewellyn you can never I shold think quite forget your little sweetheart as you used to call me ... let us be as good friends as ever, do love."[246] Upon finding Eliza Dignam walking the Burlington Arcade (also used by Willoughby), and concluding "she was walking there for the purposes of prostitution," Llewellyn assaulted his brother-in-law, who, he assumed, was pimping her "at a little distance."[247] Mrs Llewellyn wrote to her sister about her "world of sorrow" and described her husband as a "heartless wretched coward."[248] Under cross-examination, she would only say of her sister: "She had done me a grievous wrong which I cannot mention here."[249] Questions also arose about Mrs Llewellyn's relations with the General. He spent much time with her alone, and it appeared she was his mistress prior to her marriage to Llewellyn, who was the General's former butler.

The controversies surrounding the Llewellyns undermined their testimony, particularly as Eliza Dignam declared that her sister and the General had attempted to suborn her. Moreover, a series of doctors, including Dr Gwynn, who had known Windham since he was a boy, contradicted Forbes Winslow and Mayo, declaring him to be eccentric rather than insane.[250] One, Dr Thomas Harrington Tuke, was the son of Edward Tuke, the founder of a Quaker asylum which emphasised the moral treatment of patients.[251] Tuke observed that Windham was sane, albeit that "the <u>real</u> or <u>pretended aversion</u> and peevishness shown to him by his wife seemed to me to have increased

---

245. P. E. Hansell—Norwich, *In Lunacy: Re: Windham: Report of Proceedings. 5th day*, Norfolk Record Office, WKC 4/29/11, 464×7, 1 of 2, fol. 149.

246. "Eliza Sophia Dignam," *In Lunacy: Re: Windham: Notes on Witnesses*, Norfolk Record Office, WKC 4/30, 465×1, 2 of 2, fol. 3.

247. "Conway Dignam," *Notes for Cross Examination of Respondents' Witnesses. In Lunacy: Re: Windham*, Norfolk Record Office, WKC 4/30, 465×4, 1 of 2, fol. 3.

248. P. E. Hansell—Norwich, *In Lunacy: Re: Windham: Report of Proceedings. 5th day*, Norfolk Record Office, WKC 4/29/11, 464×7, 1 of 2, fol. 146.

249. P. E. Hansell—Norwich, *In Lunacy: Re: Windham: Report of Proceedings. 5th day*, Norfolk Record Office, WKC 4/29/11, 464×7, 1 of 2, fol. 147.

250. *In Lunacy: Re: Wm. Frederick Windham, a Supposed Lunatic. Affidavit of Dr Gwynn. John and Charles Cole, 36 Essex Street, Strand*, Norfolk Record Office, WKC 4/30, 465×4, 2 of 2; *In Lunacy: Re: Wm. Frederick Windham, a Supposed Lunatic. Affidavit of Dr Babington. John and Charles Cole, 36 Essex Street, Strand*, Norfolk Record Office, WKC 4/30, 465×4, 2 of 2.

251. For the Tukes, see Porter, *Madness*, 104–105; Rebecca Wynter, "'Horrible dens of deception': Thomas Bakewell, Thomas Mulock and anti-asylum sentiments, c.1815–60," in Knowles and Trowbridge, eds., *Insanity and the Lunatic Asylum in the Nineteenth Century*, 14; Wise, *Inconvenient People*, 247–248.

rather than diminished his passion for her . . . his wife is remarkably handsome and though equally young evidently <u>possessing very great experience and knowledge of the world</u>."[252] After eighteen days, the trial turned to the testimony of the domestic servants who had worked in the houses and hotels where Windham lived. These were the people with whom he preferred to spend his time, and they testified that, as Jane Morris, a chambermaid, claimed, he "always behaved like a gentleman." James Reynolds, a wagoner, said that he had never seen Windham do anything that suggested "he was not right in his mind."[253] His tutor thought him sane, even though he didn't take to Ovid—he was apparently more interested in transforming his own life than in reading about transformation.[254] Anne Thurston, a servant at Felbrigg, said he "was just like other young men," while the butler, James Knowles, declared him to be "very kind" to the servants but nevertheless of "sound mind."[255] Numerous other witnesses confirmed these impressions.[256]

In his concluding speech, Sir John Coleridge, counsel for Agnes Windham, deplored the hypocrisy of the petitioners and of the society that would sanctimoniously condemn the sins of others as lunacy without reflection on their own moral standing. (Later, as Attorney General, Coleridge would condemn in the same terms the man who revealed that Lady Travers Twiss had been a prostitute). "I would rather," he said of William and Agnes Windham, "be the Magdalens who washed her Divine Master's feet with her tears and wiped them with the hairs of her head than the self-complacent Pharisee who condemned the woman because she was a sinner."[257] Coleridge complained of the "obloquy and invective, insult and reproach that has been heaped upon Mrs Windham."[258] He pointed out that the whole case had been about the scandal of marrying a prostitute, rather than a mere question of sanity: "Mrs Windham, her character, her marriage, her settlement, her whole life up to the present moment, have been the chief weapons of attack upon her husband's sanity." In another person, Windham's behaviour would not have led to a lunacy trial: "Mr Windham was neither the first nor the last, neither the youngest nor the oldest, neither the wisest nor the most foolish person who had been captivated by Agnes Willoughby." He observed that many of the mothers and the grandmothers of the aristocracy might be discovered to have a similar background to Agnes Willoughby. However,

---

252. *In Lunacy: Re: Wm. Frederick Windham, a Supposed Lunatic. Affidavit of Dr Tuke. John and Charles Cole, 36 Essex Street, Strand*, Norfolk Record Office, WKC 4/30, 465×4, 2 of 2, fol. 2.

253. *Commission de Lunatico Inquirendo: An Inquiry*, 121.

254. *Commission de Lunatico Inquirendo: An Inquiry*, 140.

255. *Commission de Lunatico Inquirendo: An Inquiry*, 122.

256. *Commission de Lunatico Inquirendo: An Inquiry*, 122–136.

257. Russell of Killowen, Right Hon. Lord, "The Late Lord Chief Justice of England: Some Reminiscences," *The North American Review*, vo. 159, no. 454 (September 1894), 258.

258. *Commission de Lunatico Inquirendo: An Inquiry*, 183.

the marriage of a man of Windham's standing to a prostitute, and the transformations of status it entailed, carried the great risk of condemnation by the law and the state, and could endanger his very liberty. "The object of the petitioners," declared Coleridge, "is to get rid of the marriage with Agnes Willoughby."[259] "The marriage" had been "treated as the crowning act of his insanity." Coleridge's sentiments were increasingly echoed in newspaper reports during the trial, with the *Morning Star*, for example, asking (in newspaper cuttings collected by Hansell): "Is foolish love—if this calf-feeling can be called love—an evidence of insanity? If so, what a large proportion of mankind shall we not condemn as witless ... Antony, who lost the world to a wanton, and was content so to lose it, is not usually reckoned to have been mad."[260] The jury found Windham to be sane, but the cost of the trial proved to be immense. *Punch* quipped: "Windham is sane: but England must be cracked / To bear such process as hath fixed the fact."[261] The reputations of the doctors who had testified against Windham were also damaged, Winslow in particular. Charles Dickens's journal *All the Year Round* (the successor to *Household Words*) declared: "The jury of laymen of the world came to a decision contrary to Dr Winslow's. What confidence does this give us in a mad-doctor's accuracy of opinion concerning the sanity of any one of us?"[262]

The question immediately rose as to who would pay outstanding costs in excess of £20,000. The Windham family exchanged letters in which its members distanced themselves from the General and declared they had never understood that joining the petition implied accepting the costs.[263] William Windham brought a suit in Chancery, arguing that the family should pay all the costs in the trial, given that they had initiated the proceedings, but the judge, Lord Justice Knight Bruce, found that he must pay his own costs because the family had "bona fide" concerns regarding his behaviour. In making the judgement, Bruce observed that fifteen jurors were for dismissing the charge but seven for him being insane.[264]

259. *Commission de Lunatico Inquirendo: An Inquiry*, 184.
260. *Morning Star and Dial*, December 6, 1861, 4, in Windham Family Papers, Norfolk Record Office, WKC 4/31, 465×5.
261. Cited in Ketton-Cremer, *Felbrigg*, 261.
262. Cited in Wise, *Inconvenient People*, 284.
263. Field to Hansell, February 20, 1862, *Re: Windham: Letters to General Windham*, Norfolk Record Office, WKC 4/30, 465×2, 2 of 2. Field and Roscoe to Lucas and Boyle, January 31, 1862, *Re: Windham*, Norfolk Record Office, WKC 4/30, 465×4, 1 of 2. This letter was to Lord Alfred Hervey's solicitor, saying that there was at least £10,000 to pay in costs and that they would welcome ideas on how to pay it. The reply from Hervey states that "the expenses must be a serious matter" for the General: that is, rejecting the claim. Field's response showed that the conflict was deepening: "Your letter rather troubles me because it would lead to the belief that I was wrong in writing"—Field to Hervey, February 3, 1862, *Re: Windham*, Norfolk Record Office, WKC 4/30, 465×4, 1 of 2.
264. "The Windham Case: Mr W. F. Windham's Application for Costs Refused, Wednesday, April 23, 1862," Norfolk Record Office, WKC 4/30, 465×3, 1 of 2; "The Question

Eight months after the trial, on October 29, 1862, Windham brought a suit for divorce to the new Court for Divorce and Matrimonial Causes, created by the Matrimonial Causes Act four years previously, and presided over by Judge Creswell Creswell. He named Antonio Giuglini as co-respondent. He stated that his wife had "committed adultery" with Giuglini, and that, in September and October of that same year, "on diverse occasions" his wife, Agnes Ann Windham, had committed adultery with "diverse persons" at 32 Oxendon Street, just off the Haymarket, and again with "divers persons" at 23 Trevor Square in Knightsbridge, implying that she had returned to prostitution.[265] In response, Giuglini denied, first, that he had committed adultery with Agnes Windham and, second, that "if he did," then "William Frederick Windham connived at the said adultery."[266] Agnes Windham likewise swore that she had not committed adultery with Giuglini or the "divers persons" mentioned in the petition, and that "if she did," William Windham had "connived" at both the adultery with Giuglini and with the "diverse persons." Moreover, she declared, if she did commit adultery with diverse persons as alleged, it was only up to September 29, and it was only because he "treated her with cruelty" and "wilful neglect and misconduct conduced to the said adultery."[267] In March 1863, William Windham presented the court with a denial of these charges.[268] In subsequent affidavits, Agnes Windham accused him of infecting her with syphilis, while he responded that, if it was true that he was infected with syphilis, she had "knowledge of the fact and consented to connubial intercourse."[269]

At this moment, in 1863, Giuglini was at the height of his popularity, playing in the opera *Faust*, in the title role as the aging scholar, Faust, who is transformed, in an Ovid-like manner, into a handsome young man through the power of his pact with the Devil. Shortly after he played in this role, Agnes Windham left him and returned to her husband. The divorce proceedings

---

of Costs in the Windham Case," *Daily Telegraph*, April 24, 1862, 5, in Windham Family Papers, Norfolk Record Office, WKC 4/31, 465×5.

265. In Her Majesty's Court for Divorce and Matrimonial Causes, October 28, 1862, Windham v Windham and Guiglini, National Archives, London, C16/226/ Part 1.

266. Statement of Respondent and Co-respondent, In Her Majesty's Court for Divorce and Matrimonial Causes, December 16, 1862, Windham v Windham and Guiglini, National Archives, London, C16/226/ Part 1.

267. Statement of Respondent and Co-respondent, In Her Majesty's Court for Divorce and Matrimonial Causes, December 16, 1862, Windham v Windham and Guiglini, National Archives, London, C16/226/ Part 1.

268. The Petitioner William Frederick Windham in reply to the answer of the Co-respondent Antonio Guiglini, In Her Majesty's Court for Divorce and Matrimonial Causes, March 6, 1862, Windham v Windham and Guiglini, National Archives, London, C16/226/ Part 1.

269. The petitioner William Frederick Windham, in reply to the answer of the co-respondent Antonio Guiglini, In Her Majesty's Court for Divorce and Matrimonial Causes, March 6, 1862, Windham v Windham and Guiglini, National Archives, London, C16/226/ Part 1.

were halted. In July, the Court of Divorce and Matrimonial Causes dismissed the petition for divorce, and the irritated Judge Cresswell ordered William Windham to pay costs for both respondent and co-respondent. Giuglini lost his mind in the following months, was committed to Chiswick Asylum, and died two years later at the age of 40.

William Windham bought a coaching business in Norwich, and on May 9, 1863, the Norwich Argus advertised his Express Coach running from Norwich to Cromer.[270] Shortly after, in the autumn of 1863, Agnes Windham became pregnant. William Windham's financial position was now dire. The family estimated his debts at £80,000. On November 26, 1863, he sold £20,000 of this debt to the trustees of his estates—that is, to his wife—in exchange for which the trustees received the Felbrigg estates themselves as well as a life interest in the neighbouring Hanworth Hall and its estates, where the General resided.[271] Agnes Windham, therefore, became the owner of General Windham's home. She agreed, at the same time, to provide William with an annuity of £500, considerably less than the annuity he had once provided her, but with a condition that it would cease if he was declared bankrupt.[272] The *Norwich Argus* wrote of the "Lucretia . . . who ate up a young heir alive one night and lunched upon his guardian in the morning."[273] Felbrigg itself was sold, but, on Agnes Windham's death, the Hanworth Hall estate and its £5,000 to £6,000 annual rents would revert to William or to his heir. If he had no child, the heir would be General Windham or his children.[274] At this time, one newspaper wrote of "that womanly constellation of delicacy, virtue, pride and honour—Agnes Windham," but it soon gave up the sarcasm, describing her as having "a life black with every species of wickedness and unilluminated by a single virtue."[275]

On February 8, 1864, William Windham had declared bankruptcy, losing his annuity, and the *Norwich Argus* advertised the Cromer to Norwich Express, with Henry Bingham as its proprietor and W. F. Windham as the coachman.[276] Windham now lived in a room rented in a Norwich hotel and was completely absorbed into the coach driver's world. When Sir Francis

270. "The Express Coach," *The Norwich Argus*, May 9, 1863, in "Private Copy: Windham Trial: Letters etc," Norfolk Record Office, MC 580/1, 780×1.

271. Notice of Indenture of Trust and Settlement, November 26, 1863, in "Private Copy: Windham Trial: Letters etc," Norfolk Record Office, MC 580/1, 780×1.

272. "Not Over Yet," undated and unattributed newspaper cutting, in "Private Copy: Windham Trial: Letters etc," Norfolk Record Office, MC 580/1, 780×1.

273. "Condonation," *The Norwich Argus*, May 9, 1863, in "Private Copy: Windham Trial: Letters etc," Norfolk Record Office, MC 580/1, 780×1.

274. "Death of Mr W. F. Windham," *Norfolk News*, February 3, 1866, in "Private Copy: Windham Trial: Letters etc," Norfolk Record Office, MC 580/1, 780×1.

275. "Not Over Yet," undated and unattributed newspaper cutting, in "Private Copy: Windham Trial: Letters etc," Norfolk Record Office, MC 580/1, 780×1.

276. "April 27, 1864" and "Cromer and Norwich: The Original Day Coach," in "Private Copy Windham Trial. Letters etc," Norfolk Record Office, MC 580/1, 780×1.

Burnard, who would later become the editor of *Punch*, was a passenger in Windham's coach, he recognised the man who had been at the centre of so much controversy. Burnard remarked that, while reminiscing about Eton, Windham "played the gentleman" for a moment, but then assumed a different persona. He threw "refinement to the winds, exchanged course chaff with the passers-by, laughed with the guard, used the most outlandish expressions, whipped up his team, and took us up to the inn in fine style, when ... with a true coachman-like touch of his hat and in broad country-tongued dialect, he said, 'Good-day, sir.'"[277] In an account of Windham's bankruptcy, *The Lancet* lamented that Forbes Winslow had not been heeded and satirised the calls for "liberty of the subject" during his insanity trial, observing that the consequence of such liberty had been his ruin. The *Daily Telegraph* retorted that fools should be allowed to ruin themselves at the hands of "harlots" and swindlers; if not, what kind of asylum would hold all the fools of England? "We protested, therefore, against a precedent which would have been dangerous to society and civil liberty." It added: "Ten thousand more times precious than all the estates of Norfolk is the principle of individual liberty." The problem, according to the *Daily Telegraph*, were the lawyers who fed off such disputes: "There is a tribe of special harpies who have grown fat with his blood, and bloated upon his ruin; these ought to be denounced—the pettifoggers we mean—the backstreet attorneys."[278] Hansell, the family lawyer, was so assiduous at collecting all the materials that related to the case that he even carefully stored this report so damning of his own profession, but, as a Norfolk solicitor, he may well have agreed with the assessment of London barristers. Despite all such protests, Windham had pursued his social transformation. He had succeeded in traversing the social spectrum, albeit in the opposite direction to his wife, refashioning himself from a landed aristocrat into a coachman. His story underlined the potential for exploiting social conventions as a means to person reinvention and served as a reminder that doing so could take a person in more than one direction.

By April 1864, William and Agnes Windham were reunited and, on April 19, she gave birth to a son, Frederick Howe Lindsay Bacon Windham, who was now the heir to the Hanworth Estate and its rents. Unsurprisingly, the General and even the newspapers questioned the legitimacy of the child, and according to some reports, so did William. The *Norwich Argus* sneered, under the title "The Heir of Hanworth:" "Mr W. F. Windham has been presented with a son. We understand that the reputed father is so enraptured with his son that a lawsuit is already on the *topis* as to its legitimacy."[279] By

277. Cited in Ketton-Cremer, *Felbrigg*, 265.

278. *Daily Telegraph*, April 30, 1864, 5, in Windham Family Papers, Norfolk Record Office, WKC 4/31, 465×5.

279. "The Heir of Hanworth," *The Norwich Argus*, April 23, 1864, in "Private Copy: Windham Trial: Letters etc," Norfolk Record Office, MC 580/1, 780×1.

July, they had separated again. Having failed to prove the child illegitimate, the General sought to become his guardian, arguing that his mother was unfit.[280] Agnes Windham succeeded, however, in convincing Vice Chancellor William Wood, one of the Lords Justice, who had been the guardian of her husband, William Windham, that along with "a medical gentleman of repute," she could be her son's guardian. William Wood was not particularly sympathetic to Agnes Windham's cause. In a letter to the General, he described the marriage of William and Agnes as "disastrous."[281] Nevertheless, he judged that Agnes Windham, along with "a medical gentleman of repute," would be the guardians of her and William Windham's son.[282]

The General brought a new suit, *Smith vs Windham*, forcing Agnes Windham to pay William's creditors £2,000 and to pay the annuity of £500 a year.[283] At the same time, she insured his life for £12,000.[284] The annuity never had to be paid because on February 2, 1866, at the age of 26, Windham was "taken with a severe fit of sickness" and died "rather suddenly" in his Norwich hotel room.[285] It was "supposed that he ruptured some internal vessel." The remaining interest in the Hanworth Estate was inherited by his son. Neither the General nor any other member of the Windham family came to the funeral, nor did Agnes Windham. Her medical advisor, Dr Gibon, and her sister, formerly Thirza Rogers, now "Mademoiselle La Fuente" (she had married a Spaniard in Paris in 1863), were present.[286] The General and Agnes Windham, however, wrote separately to the *Daily Telegraph*, on February 10, a week after William Windham's death. The General complained that the verdict of the jury in the lunacy trial was responsible for his nephew's death. Agnes Windham disputed an earlier report in the paper that she had only been prepared to pay her husband an annuity after having been forced to do

---

280. "Master Windham," *The Leader*, October 30, 1869, in "Private Copy: Windham Trial: Letters etc," Norfolk Record Office, MC 580/1, 780×1.

281. "William Wood to General Windham, January 31, 1862," in "Private Copy: Windham Trial: Letters etc," Norfolk Record Office, MC 580/1, 780×1.

282. "Master Windham," *The Leader*, October 30, 1869, in "Private Copy: Windham Trial: Letters etc," Norfolk Record Office, MC 580/1, 780×1.

283. "Death of Mr W. F. Windham," *Norfolk News*, February 3, 1866, in "Private Copy: Windham Trial: Letters etc," Norfolk Record Office, MC 580/1, 780×1.

284. "Death of Mr W. F. Windham," *Norfolk News*, February 3, 1866, in "Private Copy: Windham Trial: Letters etc," Norfolk Record Office, MC 580/1, 780×1.

285. "Death of Mr W. F. Windham," *The Times*, February 3, 1866, in "Private Copy: Windham Trial: Letters etc," Norfolk Record Office, MC 580/1, 780×1; "Death of Mr W. F. Windham," *Norfolk News*, February 3, 1866, in "Private Copy: Windham Trial: Letters etc," Norfolk Record Office, MC 580/1, 780×1.

286. "The Funeral of Mr W. F. Windham, Feburary 10, 1866," unattributed newspaper cutting, in "Private Copy: Windham Trial: Letters etc," Norfolk Record Office, MC 580/1, 780×1 for Thirza, "Announcement of the Marriage of Thirza Rogers," in "Private Copy: Windham Trial: Letters etc," Norfolk Record Office, MC 580/1, 780×1.

FIGURE 13. Hanworth Hall, where Agnes Windham-Walker lived with her second husband.*

so by the General. She protested that the annuity was "an entirely voluntary act on my part." She also took the opportunity to add, in response to a claim by the General, that "if my late husband falsely swore that my boy was not his son, it was by advice and at the instigation of members of the legal profession."[287]

Agnes Windham kept a firm grip on all her estates, partly through a constant presence in the courts. In the years immediately following William Windham's death, she maintained a public profile. In 1868, for example, the newspapers reported that Agnes Windham was again in the courts because a telegraphic company was suing her for the balance of the cost of a telegram, £4,7s, to Cuba, which read: "Tell Silvio he must come in a month or give me up. Reasons—answer."[288] The judge found for the plaintiffs. There were reports of various other liaisons, but in 1869 she married George Walker, the agent of Hanworth Hall. In the same year, Hanworth Hall became her and her son's property, as it would have been for William if he had not lost the estate. Its rents were now over £10,000 a year.[289] She, her 5-year-old son, Master Frederick, and Walker moved into the Hall, enacting a transformation to respectability. General Windham, the former resident, resumed his military career in Canada.

On October 7, 1869, Agnes Windham-Walker sent the following invitation to her neighbours and tenants: "Frederick Howe L.B. Windham desires through his mother and guardians to request the pleasure of the attendance of

287. "'To the Editor of the Daily Telegraph, Ann Agnes Windham," in "Private Copy: Windham Trial: Letters etc," Norfolk Record Office, MC 580/1, 780×1, and "On Two Letters in *The Telegraph*," *Norwich Argus*, Feburary 17, 1866, in "Private Copy: Windham Trial: Letters etc," Norfolk Record Office, MC 580/1, 780×1.

288. "Mrs Agnes Windham and 'Silvio,'" October 19, 1868, unattributed newspaper cutting, in "Private Copy: Windham Trial: Letters etc," Norfolk Record Office, MC 580/1, 780×1.

289. "Master Windham," *The Leader*, October 30, 1869, in "Private Copy: Windham Trial: Letters etc," Norfolk Record Office, MC 580/1, 780×1.

* Stephen Richards, "Hanworth Hall, Hanworth," https://www.geograph.org.uk/photo/3396996

FIGURE 14. Frederick Howe Lindsay Bacon Windham at the age of 5.*

all his Neighbours, Friends, and Tenantry on the 20th instant to celebrate his taking possession of his estates."[290]

Nine hundred people dined for lunch, and 120 for dinner. Agnes Windham-Walker's well-publicised background did not spoil their appetite. She had fought

---

290. "'Master Windham,' *The Leader*, October 30, 1869, in "Private Copy: Windham Trial: Letters etc," Norfolk Record Office, MC 580/1, 780×1.

* Photograph of Frederick Howe Lindsay Bacon Windham, in "Private Copy. Windham Trial. Letters etc," Norfolk Record Office, MC 580/1, 780×1

her way to material prosperity through a relentless use of the law and the courts, but she also understood that social status was performed through symbolic acts. At Frederick's feast: "The paternity of the Windham family was illustrated by the pictures on the wall, interspersed with arms, banners and flags." One banner bore the inscription: "Long Live the Youthful Heir." The child's health was toasted by the Reverend Veitch, of Hanworth, who said it "had fallen to his lot to bring into Christ's Church the mother of the infant, and he had presented her to the Lord Bishop of London [Twiss was Chancellor of Bishop Jackson's diocese] for confirmation."[291] Confirmation brought a person into a new relationship with Christ, and some Anglicans would take a confirmation name, a new persona, signifying that new relationship. The process of assuming a new persona was familiar to Windham-Walker, who had used various names to create new identities in the past. The church offered its own path of transformation through redemption. She made a speech of thanks in which she reserved her strongest gratitude for Reverend Veitch, to whom she owed "that spirit of Christian humility and grace to which I was a stranger before I knew him."

In further acts symbolic of her transformation, Agnes devoted herself to charity. The scrapbook on the Windham case made by Peter Hansell, the family lawyer, was kept into the 1880s, twenty years after the lunacy trial. One cutting is of a letter sent to a newspaper, making a plea for support of the British Free School in Boulogne, where "if it had not been for the timely assistance rendered by Mrs Windham-Walker—to whose many kind deeds I referred last week ... the school must some time ago have been closed."[292] Nevertheless, Mrs Windham-Walker could never be free of her background nor from the cynicism of others. Another newspaper cutting in the same scrapbook refers to Mrs Windham-Walker's son, Frederick, who is "about attaining his majority." The report must therefore date to approximately the early 1880s.[293] This article declares that Mrs Windham-Walker of Hanworth Hall "will soon be adopted as the patron-saint of Boulogne, in such esteem is she held there."[294] A report in the local journal of Boulogne, *La Colonne*, praised a party which the former resident of Andover Workhouse had just given, "as usual each year," for 105 poor people of Boulogne. *La Colonne* then turned to Frederick, who was "the

---

291. "Master Windham," *The Leader*, October 30, 1869, in "Private Copy: Windham Trial: Letters etc," Norfolk Record Office, MC 580/1, 780×1.

292. "From the Belfry," unattributed newspaper cutting, in "Private Copy: Windham Trial: Letters etc," Norfolk Record Office, MC 580/1, 780×1.

293. "Mrs Windham-Walker," unattributed newspaper cutting, in "Private Copy: Windham Trial: Letters etc," Norfolk Record Office, MC 580/1, 780×1; "June 11, 1886. Windham-Batt," unattributed newspaper cutting, in "Private Copy: Windham Trial: Letters etc," Norfolk Record Office, MC 580/1, 780×1; the scrapbook also contains a short notice of her son's marriage in 1886.

294. "Mrs Windham-Walker," unattributed newspaper cutting, in "Private Copy: Windham Trial: Letters etc," Norfolk Record Office, MC 580/1, 780×1.

direct descendent of the Lords Windham who are so illustrious in the magistracy of England . . . and the grand-nephew of the famous General Windham the hero of the attack on the Redan, who fought side by side with the French in Crimea." While the son was currently "making a tour round the world," he would, on his return, follow his mother's virtuous example and "only have to learn the good that his mother has done during the last three years she has resided in our town." The article added to this last quote from *La Colonne* the laconic observation: "And *La Colonne* doesn't appear to be a satirical journal either." Twenty years after the lunacy trial, and more than ten years after her very public redemption by Christ and Reverend Veitch, such cynicism marked the limits to her re-invention from a courtesan to a lady of the manor.

Agnes Rogers's success in transforming her material circumstances and the creation of a number of new personae for herself (Agnes Willoughby, Agnes Windham, Agnes Windham-Walker), and her child, came at a cost. She was notorious and was never able to relinquish her past, albeit that she managed to remove herself as far as possible from the Andover Workhouse. While Windham pursued his own transformation into a coachman, public opinion judged him to have been a victim. He was almost judged insane, and his efforts cost him his life. The warning to anyone who contemplated making a similar connection to that made between William and Agnes Windham could not have been starker. Twiss had good reasons to follow the Windham trial closely, particularly as he played an unnamed but important role in the story. The great risks incurred by people who behaved as William and Agnes Windham had were readily apparent, and yet Twiss was himself to marry a prostitute little more than six months after Windham's lunacy trial. For her part, Pharaïlde van Lynseele, who married Twiss, learned about Agnes Willoughby from Twiss himself. Lynseele, like Agnes Willoughby, was prepared to risk notoriety in exchange for advancement, or "improvement." After Twiss's near miss in the Windham case, he might have avoided any other suggestion of scandal in future, or at least for some years. Being named as co-respondent, and therefore as Agnes Windham's "protector," in the Windham divorce proceedings would almost certainly have ruined the man who was responsible for issuing marriage licenses in the Province of Canterbury. He was responsible for prosecuting such abusers of convention as his Oxford colleague, Reverend James Bonwell—a case he judged in 1859, the same year he became Agnes Willoughby's "best friend." But Twiss was not deterred by any of these circumstances. Not to be deterred by all that had transpired in the case of William Windham and Agnes Willoughby, in which Twiss himself was so deeply implicated, was perhaps reckless, but it was also to demonstrate an extraordinary faith in the powers of invention, and an extraordinary confidence on the part of Lynseele and Twiss in their mastery of those powers.

For Twiss's public thoughts on the autonomy of persons and the possibilities of personal transformation, we need only look to his published work. On

June 12, 1861, during Ascot Week, the week in which Willoughby and Windham met, Twiss was busy in Oxford writing the preface to a work deeply concerned with precisely these questions. This work was his *The Law of Nations Considered as Independent Political Communities*, his most important contribution to the theory of international law, in which the persons whose autonomy he examined were states. He accepted the view which, as he pointed out, was derived from Grotius, Pufendorf, and Hobbes, that a state was a "Moral Person," which, he argued, citing Vattel, has "a will peculiar to itself, and is susceptible of obligations and rights."[295] The society of nations, according to this reasoning, consists of "*so many free persons* living together in a State of Nature." Within states, Twiss pointed out, individuals did not enjoy liberty "fully and absolutely," because they had made a "partial surrender" of their freedom to the sovereign in exchange for their security and the perfection of their being.[296] By contrast, in the society of nations, states enjoy the liberty common to persons in the state of nature, what he described, citing Wolff, as "perfect liberty and independence, of which they cannot be deprived without their own consent."[297] This freedom included the "cardinal" right to self-preservation. A fundamental means of self-preservation was the right of a state to "territorial aggrandisement" and the "enlargement of its dominions," including the incorporation of new "Provinces" by their consent or "occupation of vacant territory to which no other Nation can lay claim." In taking this expansionist course, the state is "pursuing the legitimate object of its Being."[298] Such a view was common in the history of the law of nations. Grotius had written in the opening of his work *De Indiis*, or *Commentary on the Law of Prize and Booty*, that the expansion of the Dutch state through trade (although not, he argued, through occupation) was fundamental to its survival in its struggle with the Habsburg Empire.[299] From the sixteenth century, European writers on politics had declared that the pursuit of greatness was fundamental to the preservation of states. Twiss cited eminent American diplomat Henry Wheaton to this end, arguing that a state may "increase its national dominions, wealth, population, and power by all innocent and lawful means."[300]

It is essential to ask to what degree this image of the autonomous and acquisitive person of the state was a model for the natural individuals who were Twiss's contemporaries. At the same time, we might ask to what degree the image of the autonomous rights-bearing individual was a model for the understanding of the expanding state.[301] There are strong affinities between

295. Twiss, *The Law of Nations* (1861), 6.
296. Twiss, *The Law of Nations* (1861), 6.
297. Twiss, *The Law of Nations* (1861), 6.
298. Twiss, *The Law of Nations* (1861), 144, 146, 147.
299. Hugo Grotius, *Commentary on the Law of Prize and Booty*, ed. Martine Julia van Ittersum (Indianapolis, 2006), 10.
300. Twiss, *The Law of Nations* (1861), 147.
301. A question posed by Richard Tuck: Tuck, *The Rights of War and Peace*, 14–15, 234.

the behaviour of the state, described by Twiss, and the behaviour of his friend, Agnes Willoughby, who also exploited every opportunity to increase her wealth, dominions, and power. That she was able to do so, and that she believed she should do so, was encouraged by the contemporary discourse upon the self-improvement of the individual, as well as of individual rights, enabled by law, discourses which she exploited in full.

Neither the state in which Agnes Willoughby prospered, however, nor the society of states described by Twiss were characterised by an entire absence of constraints. One of the most important of those constraints was who gets to count as a "person" and therefore as a member of the society enjoying the benefit of the full range of rights belonging to its members. Clearly, as a woman, and as a poor person, Agnes Willoughby was denied many of the privileges, particularly legal privileges, available to wealthy males in the society in which she held limited membership. Nevertheless, she consistently used the law and the courts to achieve her ends, beginning with her threats against Twiss. At the same time, she was able to make up for some of the inequality in the law for women by employing legal circumventions, such as trusts, which had been developed over hundreds of years, in part precisely in order to address the problem of maintaining the wealth of women.[302] Some of these barriers to the property of women would also be addressed in subsequent years in the Married Women's Property Acts of 1870 and 1882.[303] Agnes Willoughby was also able to exploit the extra-legal discourses of self-improvement to justify her growing wealth and autonomy.

The society of states described by Twiss also imposed constraints upon membership or personhood. Only nations, Twiss emphasised, could be members of the society of states. Individuals and private associations, as we saw in his work on the Oregon Territory, had no standing in that society. This did not mean that the society of nations was entirely static. In his 1861 *Law of Nations*, he admitted that there were processes whereby communities may enter and leave the society of nations—for example, he argued, when the states under the Holy Roman Empire assumed the power to manage their own external affairs as a consequence of signing the Treaty of Westphalia.[304] On the other hand, states could leave the society of nations—for example, when the city-states of Geneva and Neuchatel, where Vattel was born, joined the Swiss Confederation.[305] Twiss emphasised, however, that these were extremely gradual and organic processes. Nation-states were not born overnight. Personhood could take centuries to achieve, and radical transformation was out of the question.

302. F. W. Maitland, "Trust and Corporation," in *The Collected Papers of F. W. Maitland*, ed. H.A.L. Fisher, Vol. 3 (Cambridge, 1911), 321-404.

303. Holcombe, *Wives and Property*; Shanley, *Feminism, Marriage, and the Law in Victorian England*.

304. Twiss, *The Law of Nations* (1861), 9.

305. Twiss, *The Law of Nations* (1861), 10.

Both these questions—the constraints upon the autonomy of the natural person and the constraints upon the autonomy of the moral person—were to be challenges for Twiss in the years ahead. In both cases, he sought to circumvent those constraints, through argument and through misrepresentation. The question arises again, therefore, of the degree to which the loosening of constraints upon natural persons and moral persons were informed by each other. The question arises whether, for Twiss, the natural person in the civil state was modelled upon the "perfect liberty and independence." of the moral person in the society of nations. At the same time, we must question whether he saw the potential of self-improving individuals as models for artificial persons who could pretend to personhood in the society of nations. He would deal with the second question in the context of making claims to international personhood for a private corporation that would stake its claim to statehood through "territorial aggrandisement." In the case of his thinking about moral persons, or the state, Twiss would take his ideas to another level in the 1870s and '80s, and he would elaborate his argument then in a revised second edition of *The Law of Nations*, as well as in extensive engagement with King Leopold's plans for the Congo, but in the case of natural persons, he first showed signs of a new way of thinking in the context of his marriage to a prostitute in the months immediately after the Windham marriage.

Pharaïlde van Lynseele

In 1859, Twiss met Pharaïlde van Lynseele. Her own version of her early life, when in court in 1872, was that she was the daughter of a Dutch nobleman who had performed military service in Poland and had then travelled to Java, where he subsequently died. Her mother, she said, had also died shortly after her birth. This story was a fabrication. She was born on October 9, 1834, in Kortrijk, in the Flemish northwest of Belgium. Her parents were Pierre Denis van Lynseele, an illiterate carpenter, aged 28, and Barbe Thérèse Vanderschoore, a peasant farmer's daughter.[306] Her birth certificate was witnessed by

---

306. "'Courtrai 1834 the 10th of October Birth certificate of Pharaïlde Rosalie Van Lynseele,' Rijksarchief, Kortrijk, Burgerlijke stand, Vlaanderen, Geboorten 1834, 624 (State Archives, Kortrijk, Civil Service, West Flanders, Births 1834, 624): *L'an mil huit cent trente quatre, le dix octobre à dix heures du matin, par-devant nous Reynaert Beernaert, Echevin , officier délégué de l'état civil de la ville de Courtrai province de la Flandre occidentale, est comparu Pierre Denis Van Lynseele, âgé de vingt-huit ans charpentier né à Aelbeke domicilié à Courtrai hameau 'de Walle,' lequel nous a présenté un enfant de sexe feminin né hier à huit heures et demie du soir, de lui déclarant, et de Barbe Thérèse Van der Schoore son épouse, et auquel il a declaré vouloir donner les prénoms de Pharaïlde Rosalie; les dites déclarations et présentation faites en présence d'Augustin Van der Schoore, âgé de cinquante-cinq ans, cultivateur , domicilié à Belleghem et de Jean Barbe, âgé de vingt-sept*

her maternal grandfather, Augustin Vanderschoore, and a cattle dealer, Jean Barbe, but because Jean Barbe was also illiterate, the certificate was signed by Augustin Vandershoore and the magistrate who issued the certificate, Reynaert Beernaert. No details of her early life survive, in contrast to Agnes Willoughby.

By the late 1850s, Pharaïlde van Lynseele was working as a prostitute in London. The city attracted large numbers of French and Belgian prostitutes, many of whom were drawn into rapidly growing urban areas from rural poverty, just as women such as Agnes Willoughby had been.[307] In London, Lynseele adopted a new name, Marie Gelas, and a new persona, as was customary for women in the sex trade. She worked in Regent Street, where, in its lower half, according to Acton's contemporary account, the Belgian prostitutes congregated, and it is likely that there she met Twiss.[308] Acton complained that, whereas English prostitutes "of any grade" believed that it was "bad taste" to solicit, the "foreign" prostitutes of lower Regent street "proclaimed" their "craft" "*à haute voix*," such that the street was full of "noisy, soliciting, gesticulating prostitutes." This was not the purpose for which Regent Street had been intended. It was designed and constructed by John Nash, earlier in the century, to demarcate the upper classes of Mayfair from the working classes of Soho, and it was intended that the street should be a space for fashionable and tasteful commerce, with grocers and butchers' shops excluded.[309] The classes, however, could not be kept apart. Acton cited a case that came before the Marlborough Street Magistrate in 1855 and was reported in the *Globe*. The newspaper recounted that "several of the inhabitants of Regent Street" complained to the magistrate that "the lower part of Regent-street, in particular, was infested all day long by throngs of French and Belgian prostitutes, whose immodest and audacious behaviour had a serious effect on the business of the street."[310] The magistrate sympathised but stated that he must discharge the five prostitutes brought before him because they had only been charged with "walking about publicly." It was necessary, he argued, not to "bring up a few for judgement" but to take a more systemic approach to the problem. It was precisely in the lower of half of Regent Street, right at the bottom of the street, where the Athenaeum was and still is located. The case reported in the *Globe*

---

ans Marchand de bestiaux domicilié à Courtrai et après lecture faite du présent acte, le père et le second témoin ont déclaré ne pas savoir écrire, le premier témoin a signé avec nous. A Van der Schoore, Reynaert Beernaert."

307. Acton, *Prostitution*, 112–113. For the broader phenomenon of migration from rual poverty: Walkowitz, *Prostitution and Victorian Society*, 15.

308. Acton, *Prostitution*, 109.

309. Christopher Hibbert, Ben Weinreb, John Keay, and Julia Keay, "Regent Street," *The London Encyclopaedia*, 3rd ed. (London, 2010); Winter, *London's Teeming Streets*, 18.

310. "Marlborough-Street," *The Globe*, December 28, 1855, 4.

described the scene on the street in one of the years in which Twiss was on the club's governing committee. He met Pharaïlde van Lynseele just a few years later, possibly while leaving the club and walking through the "throngs" of prostitutes on his way back to his house in Park Lane.

In addition to working in Regent Street, Lynseele worked from a brothel at 46 Half Moon Street, in Mayfair.[311] William Thomas Stead, the pioneer of the "New Journalism," described the Half Moon Street brothels in a series of articles he wrote in 1885 as part of his campaign against child prostitution. Stead had befriended Josephine Butler and joined her fight to repeal the Contagious Diseases Act. He published "The Maiden Tribute of Modern Babylon" in the *Pall Mall Gazette*, which he edited. The articles helped propel the Criminal Law Amendment Act (1885), raising the age of consent for girls from 13 to 16.[312] The Half Moon Street establishments were known, he said, for initiating 14- and 15-year-old girls into the business by tying their arms and legs to four-poster beds while the client "effected his purpose."[313] To prove his point, Stead bought 13-year-old Eliza Armstrong, the daughter of a chimney sweep, from her mother for £5. He had her examined by a midwife to prove she was a virgin; she was then drugged and taken to a brothel, where she was kept in a room prepared for Stead's arrival. Stead drank a bottle of champagne, and after Eliza screamed in fright at his appearance in the room, he left and had Eliza adopted. His demonstration backfired. He was prosecuted for abduction by the barrister Harry Poland (who had fifteen years earlier acted in the case for libel on behalf of Pharaïlde Twiss and her husband, Travers), and he spent three months in Holloway Prison.[314] Nevertheless, he inspired George Bernard Shaw, who had worked as a journalist for the *Pall Mall Gazette* in the 1880s, at the time of Armstrong case, while Stead was editor. When the newsagent W. H. Smith refused to sell issues of the *Gazette* carrying Stead's sensational revelations, Shaw offered his services to his editor selling the paper on the street.[315]

Years later, however, in his version of the Pygmalion myth, Shaw satirized the philanthropist Stead's disregard for Eliza Armstrong's well-being merely in order to prove a point. Shaw's *Pygmalion* recounted the story of the transformation of Eliza Doolittle into a lady. Like Armstrong, Doolittle was a chimney

---

311. "The Charge of Libel upon Sir Travers and Lady Twiss," *The Daily News*, March 6, 1872, 5.

312. For a detailed examination of Stead, see Walkowitz, *City of Dreadful Delight*, 81–134.

313. William Thomas Stead, "The Maiden Tribute of Modern Babylon," in Stephen Donovan and Matthew Rubery, eds., *Secret Commissions: An Anthology of Victorian Investigative Journalism* (Ontario, 2012), 184.

314. For Poland's account of his role, see Ernest Bowen-Rowlands, *Seventy-Two Years at the Bar* (London, 1924), 208–211.

315. Walkowitz, *City of Dreadful Delight*, 81.

sweep's daughter. Professor Higgins's insensitivity to Doolittle, including his offer to buy her from her father, recounted Stead's own brutality. Like Shakespeare's Caliban, Eliza cursed the gift of polite speech. Reformers had attached their hopes to the Armstrong case, which inspired feminists to champion the cause of "endangered" girls, fallen women, and working class women generally, while, at the same time, they expressed "repugnance and ambivalence" towards "unrepentant prostitutes."[316] The consequences of these efforts were, as Judith Walkowitz argues, contradictory and mixed in terms of reform, at least from a twenty-first-century perspective, leading to the imposition of disciplinary regimes on working-class women (pushing them, for example, into servitude so as to save them from vice) and laws controlling homosexuality, but stimulating new "possibilities of thought" amongst middle-class women.[317] The possibilities of reform similarly produced mixed results for Pharaïlde van Lynseele.

Lynseele worked beyond Half Moon Street and Regent Street. She frequented Holborn Casino, the Argyll Rooms, the Turkish Divans, the theatres, including the Adelphi, and Cremorne Gardens, all of which were popular with prostitutes. Lying between the Thames and the King's Road in Chelsea, Cremorne Gardens opened in 1845 and were hugely popular with the public. The Gardens included a dancing platform, a lake, illuminations, fireworks, a burlesque theatre, a circus, an orchestra, and hot air balloons. At night, as William Acton recounted, they were also a haven for hundreds of prostitutes and equal numbers of "men of the upper and middle class."[318]

Between 1859 and 1862, Pharaïlde van Lynseele lived at a number of addresses, beginning with 12 Upper Berkeley Street, just northwest of Hyde Park. She moved to 11 South Street (now South Terrace), in Thurloe Square, South Kensington, on Saturday October 1, 1859, and in October 1861, she moved to Neville Terrace, Brompton. The census of 1861 reveals that the residents of 11 South Street were Marie Pharaïlde Gelas, "widow," aged 26, from Belgium, Thérèse van[illegible], "servant," aged 55, from France, and Pierre Denis, "boarder," age 54, from France, whose profession was given as "carpenter."[319] Pharaïlde Van Lysneele was living under her professional persona, in a house with her parents, whose names were adjusted from those appearing on her birth certificate. Her father used his first two names only, and claimed to be French rather than Belgian, but correctly described his trade as a carpenter. These facts were confirmed by the testimony of a jeweller, Denis Faure, who Lynseele later conceded had done work for her. As

316. Walkowitz, *City of Dreadful Delight*, 133.
317. Walkowitz, *City of Dreadful Delight*, 134.
318. Acton, *Prostitution*, 16–17.
319. "Marie Pharaïlde Gelas," in *Census Returns of England and Wales, 1861*, National Archives, London, Class: RG 9; Piece: 21; Folio: 42; Page: 28; GSU roll: 542558.

in the case of Agnes Willoughby, a close relationship with a jeweller, as well as a lawyer, was one means that courtesans used to accumulate their wealth. Faure, of 15 Lamb's Conduit Street, declared at the Bow Street Police court on July 14, 1871: "During all the time that the said Marie Gelas resided in South Street and Neville Terrace aforesaid, her father and mother and brother lived and resided with her . . . The real and proper name of the said Marie Gelas was Pharaïlde Vanlynseele."[320] In the 1861 census, Faure described himself as a "goldsmith and jeweller" who was 30 years old.[321] His address at that time was 161 Frith Street in Soho, where he was a lodger in the house of Thérèse Lemond from Liege, in Belgium. Lemond described herself as a "dressmaker," itself a profession frequently given as a cover for prostitution and brothels. Soho, at this time, was a notorious area for crime and prostitution. Faure had been the dining companion of Lynseele and a solicitor named Alexander Chaffers.

According to Alexander Chaffers's testimony, which is surprisingly but not entirely reliable, he first met Pharaïlde van Lynseele "between nine and ten o'clock in the evening, and accompanied her to her lodgings in Upper Berkeley Street, where I remained with her a couple of hours, and gave her a sovereign [i.e., one pound]."[322] Chaffers was the fulcrum around which both Lynseele's and Travers Twiss's lives turned. He haunted them for the next thirty years. At first, he performed a role for Lynseele similar to that played by the disreputable solicitor Bowen May for Agnes Willoughby. He was born, according to the information he provided to the 1871 census, in 1823.[323] He practiced as a solicitor at 43 Bedford Row, next to Gray's Inn, between 1845 and 1863. He was disinherited by his father in 1865 due to "circumstances" which were not specified, and he unsuccessfully challenged his exclusion from his father's will. By the late 1860s, he was too poor to pay for his practicing certificate as a solicitor. He was declared bankrupt in 1868, and his poverty is certainly one reason he turned to blackmailing Travers Twiss. Chaffers was a serial litigator. Indeed, he was such a vexatious litigator that he inspired the Vexatious Litigation Act in 1896, and he was the first person in England to be declared "habitually vexatious" and to therefore lose the right to bring cases to court without judicial permission.[324] As an expert litigator, Chaffers was involved in some of the most notorious Victorian legal cases, including Georgina Weldon's celebrated defence in her lunacy trial.

---

320. Alexander Chaffers, *The Twiss Libel Case* (London, 1873), 14.

321. "Denis Faure," in *Census Returns of England and Wales, 1861*, National Archives, London, Class: RG 9; Piece: 174; Folio: 74; Page: 23; GSU roll: 542586.

322. "Extraordinary Charges of Libel," *Bermondsey and Rotherhithe Advertiser*, March 9, 1872.

323. "Alexander Chaffers," in *Census Returns of England and Wales, 1871*, National Archives, London, Class: RG10; Piece: 651; Folio: 41; Page: 13; GSU roll: 818940.

324. Michael Taggart, "Alexander Chaffers and the Genesis of the Vexatious Actions Act 1896," *Cambridge Law Journal*, vol. 63, no. 3 (2004), 656.

Although she had been born into a gentry family, Georgina Weldon's ambition was to pursue a career on the stage, but her father and husband prevented her. She devoted herself to amateur peformances and filled her house in Bloomsbury with orphans, in an effort to create a National Training School in music, while also developing a passion for spiritualism.[325] Her husband was devoted to his mistress and separated from his wife, providing an income of £1,000 per year, but in 1878, he enlisted the aid of psychiatrist Lyttleton Forbes Winslow to have Georgina Weldon committed to an asylum. Winslow was the son of the doctor who had pronounced William Windham to be of unsound mind in 1862. He had led a campaign against spiritualism, which was perceived as a threat to the materialistic basis of medicine.[326] With another doctor, they provided the two medical signatures that were necessary to have Weldon admitted to an asylum.[327]

Weldon, however, suspected their intentions. Her spiritualist friend, Louisa Lowe, who had herself been incarcerated in an asylum, wrote that nothing "was easier than to get a sane person into a lunatic asylum."[328] Weldon fled to Lowe's house and then brought her case before a magistrate in Bow Street Police Court, who called the attempt to incarcerate her an "unjustifiable design upon her liberty."[329] The magistrate also pointed out, however, that a man and woman who were married were one person in the law, so a married woman could not bring any action in law by herself. She had no legal personality apart from her husband. This situation changed, however, in 1880, with the Married Woman's Property Act, which, as well as allowing women to hold property separately from their husbands, also allowed them a separate legal personality.[330] This second emancipation was a necessary complement to the first: that is, to hold property, a person must be able to defend that property in law. Legal personality also allowed women to pursue issues in law apart from property, and in Weldon's case, this meant that, during the 1880s, she was able to launch a series of successful lawsuits against her husband and the doctors who had signed the lunacy certification. Revelling in her legal standing, and also having limited means, she represented herself in court. She brought more

---

325. For Weldon, see Walkowitz, *City of Dreadful Delight*, 171–189; Wise, *Inconvenient People*, 325–374. For an unsympathetic popular account, Brian Thompson, *The Disastrous Mrs Weldon* (New York, 2000). For Weldon's writings: Roy Porter, Helen Nicholson, and Bridgett Bennett, *Women, Madness and Spiritualism: Vol. 1: Georgina Weldon and Louisa Lowe* (London, 2003).

326. Walkowitz, *City of Dreadful Delight*, 173–174.

327. Walkowitz, *City of Dreadful Delight*, 174. On the requirement of two signatures, see Lyttleton S. Winslow, *Manual of Lunacy: A Handbook Relating to the Legal Care and Treatment of the Insane* (Cambridge, 1874), 154.

328. Walkowitz, *City of Dreadful Delight*, 179.

329. Walkowitz, *City of Dreadful Delight*, 180.

330. Holcombe, *Wives and Property*; Shanley, *Feminism, Marriage, and the Law in Victorian England*.

than 100 further cases, many concerned with her musical career, as the courts became a tool with which to pursue her transformation from a daughter of the gentry into a soprano of the theatre, all of which could be justified, as one judge remarked, in terms of "liberty of the subject."[331]

Weldon did receive some legal training. Her tutor in law was another serial litigant, Alexander Chaffers, who helped draft her pleadings and strategy in an office near Lincoln's Inn.[332] One account argues that Chaffers also represented Weldon in court "until prevented from doing so."[333] Weldon's case was another example of Victorian society creating the conditions in which a subject could pursue a new persona, and in which law reform even allowed the creation of new legal persons, at the same time that rigid conventions punished such transformations. Lunacy law was once again an instrument with which to punish those who challenged convention. Weldon—like Agnes Willoughby or, in his own way, William Windham—could be seen to have triumphed over convention, and she is celebrated by some historians in those terms, but her triumph was nevertheless achieved at a cost.

While Chaffers challenged conventions in Weldon's case, he was not always on the side of emancipation, creativity, or license in conflicts over convention, and certainly not in the case of Pharaïlde van Lynseele. In fact, he claimed, albeit disingenuously, to be outraged by Lynseele's flouting of convention. After their first meeting, Chaffers "subsequently visited the said Marie Gelas [Lynseele] very frequently, and constantly passed the whole night with her."[334] On August 18, 1859, Lynseele allegedly came to his office and told him that she had seen Travers Twiss, and they "had not come to terms."[335] This was the first mention of Twiss in Lynseele's story, and according to Chaffers's statutory declaration, it was the first time he had heard about the connection between them. Twiss could have met Lynseele in Regent Street outside the Athenaeum, but it could have been at Café de Venise or Cremorne Gardens.

All parties in the subsequent dispute over the identity of Lynseele agreed that Chaffers had known Travers Twiss's brother Richard, who also could have been the conduit for Lynseele meeting Travers Twiss. Richard Twiss and Chaffers possibly became acquainted through them both working as London solicitors in the Inns of Court. Chaffers claimed that on August 1, 1859, more than two weeks before he heard from Lynseele about Travers Twiss, he had introduced her to Richard Twiss at Cremorne Gardens. Richard was in the company

---

331. Walkowitz, *City of Dreadful Delight*, 184.

332. Taggart, "Alexander Chaffers," 663.

333. "Alexander Chaffers," in Frederic Boase, *Modern English Biography*, Vol. 4, 1908, 628. See also Taggart, "Alexander Chaffers," 663, n.40.

334. *Bermondsey and Rotherhithe Advertiser*, March 9, 1872.

335. "The Charge of Libel upon Sir Travers and Lady Twiss," *The Daily News*, March 6, 1872, 5.

of Charlotte Toms, a mutual acquaintance of Lynseele and Chaffers.[336] Chaffers claimed he sometimes dined with Lynseele, Richard Twiss, and another mutual acquaintance called Charlotte Parre, and the four went to a ball at Brown's Concert-room and took a private box at the opera in Covent Garden.[337] Lynseele spent afternoons with Travers Twiss in her South Street house and then attended the opera with Chaffers in the evening. They saw Verdi's *Rigoletto*, a story, adapted from Victor Hugo's *Le Roi s'amuse*, of a Duke and a jester's daughter, Gilda, who fall in love, leading to the tragic death of Gilda.[338]

Lynseele's statement that she and Twiss "had not come to terms" implies that a relationship existed between them prior to August 18, 1859. They soon did come to terms. In his statutory declaration, Chaffers stated that "on the 27th of August, 1859, the said Marie Gelas informed me that the said Travers Twiss had agreed to keep her as his mistress, and allow her £5 a week."[339] Cross-examining Lynseele in court, Chaffers stated that, on August 24, she told him, "Dr Twiss had agreed to keep you [Lynseele] and allow you £20 a month, and that he could not allow you any more as he had had great losses during the year."[340] Within the week, on August 30, Lynseele took a lease on a new house in South Street, although she did not move there until October. Chaffers continued to visit her and sometimes, he said—for example, on September 3 and September 17, 1859—spent the night with her after Twiss had left. Twiss, at this moment, had only very recently broken with Agnes Willoughby, and on November 3, Lynseele told Chaffers that Willoughby had cost Twiss £8,000.[341] Through the remainder of 1859 and in 1860 and 1861, Lynseele divided her time between Twiss and Chaffers. Lynseele and Twiss travelled together on the continent, and when they separated, Chaffers toured with Lynseele, in Belgium, visiting Kortrijk, her birthplace, and including a tour of the Rhine in September 1861. On Wednesday, November 27, 1861, Chaffers dined with Lynseele in London and told her that she would marry Twiss.[342]

There was nothing unusual in a Victorian gentleman such as Twiss taking a mistress, nor was there anything unusual in such a man taking a prostitute

---

336. "The Charge of Libel upon Sir Travers and Lady Twiss," *The Daily News*, March 6, 1872, 5.

337. "The Charge of Libel upon Sir Travers and Lady Twiss," *The Daily News*, March 6, 1872, 5–6.

338. "The Charge of Libel upon Sir Travers and Lady Twiss," *The Daily News*, March 6, 1872, 6.

339. *Bermondsey and Rotherhithe Advertiser*, March 9, 1872.

340. "The Charge of Libel upon Sir Travers and Lady Twiss," *The Daily News*, March 6, 1872, 5.

341. "The Charge of Libel upon Sir Travers and Lady Twiss," *The Daily News*, March 6, 1872, 5.

342. "The Charge of Libel upon Sir Travers and Lady Twiss," *The Daily News*, March 6, 1872, 6

as a mistress, and according to the broad Victorian understanding of prostitution, any woman who was a mistress was almost by definition a prostitute.[343] Nevertheless, under the name Marie Gelas, Pharaïlde van Lynseele practiced a kind of prostitution that exceeded cohabitation. She was, according to Chaffers, one of the most notorious women of her profession, a "heroine of the demi-monde," the "inmate of a score of London dens," including Holborn Casino and the brothel in Half Moon Street.[344] That Twiss would take such a woman as his mistress was not remarkable. It might be more unusual if he had not. After all, reports of the Casino de Venise and Cremorne Gardens noted that they were not only full of prostitutes but also teeming with gentlemen.

What was unusual, although not, as we have seen, unprecedented, in Twiss's and Pharaïlde van Lynseele's case, was that, in 1862, they married. They did not publicly acknowledge either that Lynseele had worked as a prostitute nor that she was from a peasant family. This fact separated the marriage of Twiss and Lynseele from that between Agnes Rogers (or Willoughby) and William Windham. It would appear that they hoped to save themselves from the ignominy brought upon the Windhams by a more thorough transformation, one in which the person of Lynseele was transformed beyond the change in legal and material status. The marriage necessarily rested upon the invention of a new persona for Lynseele as the daughter of a Dutch nobleman who had been an officer in the Polish army and had disappeared in Southeast Asia. This fiction was necessary for her to be accepted in Twiss's social circles. Nevertheless, such a fiction carried great risks, and the question we must ask is why Lysnseele was prepared to endure public scorn and humiliation if her past was revealed after her marriage? The explanation, in her case, would appear to be that, as for Agnes Willoughby, the prospects for a transformation of status, notably abandoning the numerous difficulties and humiliations of a life of prostitution, as well as the potential for material advancement, outweighed the risks attached to public shame. Willoughby, however, made little effort to conceal her past, and the connection between Agnes Rogers and Agnes Willoughby was quickly revealed. She paid a price as an outcast in polite society even decades after she made her fortune. Lynseele, by contrast, invented an entirely new persona, and she rose to the creative challenge of doing so. She based that persona upon the name on her Belgian birth certificate, in order to protect herself. She also went to great lengths to invent Marie Gelas as a person completely separate from Lynseele, apart from a moment in the 1861 census in which she gave her name as Marie Pharaïlde Gelas.

Why Twiss was prepared to risk his fortune and career for such a marriage is another matter. We might ask the same of William Windham, although

---

343. Walkowitz, *Prostitution and Victorian Society*, 14–15.
344. Chaffers, *The Twiss Libel Case*, 2; "A Pitiless Persecutor," *Chicago Daily Tribune*, May 27, 1882, 3.

Windham's fortune did not depend upon his reputation. His estates would have been secure if he had not chosen to give them away or if he was not found to be a lunatic. Ignominy was certainly a price Windham had to pay, but it was not the same as ignominy *and* material ruin, although Windham was seemingly little bothered by either. His ambitions were very different to those of Twiss. For Twiss, however, the holder of so many public offices, including those that were authoritative over marriage law in two-thirds of England, it is difficult to calculate why he would marry a prostitute, particularly when he had seen, at uncomfortably close quarters, how such a marriage could lead to ruin. One answer may be a kind of sexual obsession of the kind from which Windham himself was said to suffer, and which he avowed, but such an obsession, it might be thought, could be satisfied by the arrangement that Twiss had already established to "keep" Lynseele as his mistress, as could any affective attachment. Part of the explanation appears to be that, in the conduct of his marriage, Twiss demonstrated a belief that social personae and status were more flexible than he had maintained at the time of the 1848 revolutions. From his and Lynseele's actions, we can see that, like Agnes Willoughby—and William Windham, in his own way—Twiss had come to the view that social personae are subject to invention, and he, as much as Lynseele, sought the creative challenge of that tranformation.

The key question is the circumstances in which he developed that greater flexibility, a radical flexibility, in understanding the creation of new persons. One factor that we know impacted his life from the 1850s was his very close familiarity with prostitutes, such as Willoughby and Lynseele, for whom radical reinvention was an art of survival and a means potentially to flourish. The creation of new personae was essential to his work as an ecclesiastical lawyer. It was his task, for example, to make new legal personalities for bishops. But the radical potential in the creation of new persons in a manner that broke convention—the transformation of a woman from a prostitute to, as he would put it, a "lady of blood" in Society—was something new for Twiss. The germ for that idea could be found in his own close observation of precisely such transformations performed by Willoughby, Catherine Walters, and Lynseele's own transformation into Marie Gelas prior to becoming Pharaïlde Twiss. This is an important point because it underlies a broader radicalisation in Twiss's thinking about the creation of persons, particularly the creation of the person of the state, that became apparent in the years after his marriage and, in particular, in the creation of the Congo Free State. There were certainly limits to this flexibility in the creation of persons. Twiss did not believe that a woman from Lynseele's background could be publicly acknowledged as his wife, nor, clearly, did Lynseele herself, but he did believe that she could be transformed by adopting a different persona. Such creations required ritual and symbolic performances. Similarly, Pharaïlde van Lynseele understood that the creation of new personae—for example, her performance as Marie Gelas—was necessary in order to succeed in the world of London prostitution. Both Lynseele and Twiss understood that ritual and symbolic performances would be necessary for her to become Pharaïlde Twiss.

In March 1862, Lynseele travelled to Dresden with four promissory notes from Twiss for £500 each. She was to remain there "until August when the said Travers Twiss was to join her, and be then married."[345] Lynseele and Twiss had by this time resolved upon the new persona for Lynseele. She would be the daughter of a Dutch aristocrat who had served in the "Polish army" and had then been exiled in the Kingdom of Saxony, which partly explained the choice of Dresden as a place to be married. At this time, Saxony was still nine years from becoming part of the German Empire in 1871. Marie Pharaïlde Twiss said she was born in 1840, so she was to be six years younger than Lynseele. She was not sure where she was born. Her mother had died when she was a very young child. She never knew her mother and could not, in court, say where her mother was from, what her name was, nor when she died nor where she was buried—although Twiss later claimed that she was an Austrian noblewoman, an abbess. Pharaïlde's father, Major-General Raoul Felix van Lynseele, had been an officer in the Polish army. Unable to look after his child, he left her first in a school in Krakow, between 1846 and 1848, and then in the care of family friends, Madame and Monsieur Jastreuski, who lived in Brussels. She took a governess, Marie Gelas, who travelled to England with her in 1859 and let a house in South Street where Pharaïlde also stayed. Madame Gelas and Madame Jastreuski had subsequently died. Leaving the service of Poland, Raoul Felix van Lynseele travelled to Java, although Pharaïlde could not say "whether he was a Major-General in the King of Holland's service." He died in 1864, two years after the marriage of Pharaïlde, and left her no property. She met Twiss through her guardians, the Jastreuskis, whom he visited in Brussels, and also through mutual friends, the Andersons, who lived in Hamilton Terrace near Travers Twiss's mother, but both had died in 1865.[346] Lynseele also explained in court that her confirmation name was Marie, which is why she was known as Marie rather than Pharaïlde.[347] It was a common practice for Catholics, and for some Anglicans, to take a new name in the ceremony of confirmation, usually as a child, whereby they were able to receive the Eucharist, the personification of Christ. The confirmation name was thus a new persona who enters a new relationship with Christ. It was not only lawyers who were able to think of physical persons or things holding multiple personalities.

345. "Extraordinary Charges of Libel," *Bermondsey and Rotherhithe Advertiser*, March 9, 1872, 1.

346. The above account is from "The Charge of Libel upon Sir Travers and Lady Twiss," *The Daily News*, March 6, 1872, 5; "Extraordinary Charges of Libel," *Bermondsey and Rotherhithe Advertiser*, March 9, 1872, 1; and "The Travers Twiss Case," *New Zealand Herald*, May 22, 1872, 3.

347. "The Travers Twiss Case," *New Zealand Herald*, May 22, 1872, 3.

Having established a new personality in March 1862, not for the first time in her life, Lynseele left for Dresden. According to Chaffers, she travelled first to Ostend, where she met Chaffers and travelled with him to Brussels on March 29. In May, they were in Berlin, a fact Lynseele and Chaffers agreed upon.[348] In August, Lynseele was in Dresden for the marriage, which was to take place in the chapel of the British Legation. During these months, Twiss was in London, busy performing his numerous offices. On Thursday, August 21, in his role as Vicar General, he prorogued the Convocation of the Province of Canterbury, in the Jerusalem Chamber of Westminster.[349] It is not stated in the reports whether the Archbishop, John Sumner, was present, but it is not likely. He had been ill since May the previous year, and he died two weeks after Convocation, on September 6, after fourteen years in the office of Archbishop.[350] Twiss may have calculated the timing of his marriage in anticipation of Sumner's imminent death. Certainly, the two events were very closely aligned. Whether or not Twiss took Sumner's last days into his calculations, he travelled to Dresden shortly after Convocation. It was not his first visit to Dresden—he had visited there a number of times over the previous ten years.[351] He was married there to Pharaïlde van Lynseele on August 29.

Lynseele and Twiss chose Dresden for their marriage because, according to her new persona, she was supposed to be from a family that sought refuge in Saxony, and her family could therefore be present at her wedding, although there was no clear story on any living relations, and none signed the marriage certificate. More importantly, Dresden was far removed from the inquisitive eyes of London Society. Twiss and Lynseele could marry there in perfect respectability, without questions regarding her origins or family. There could be no reports, as there had been in the case of the Windham marriage, of people who attended dressed like gentlemen, or ladies, but only having the appearance of being so. Dresden was also convenient because the British legation there had an Anglican chapel. It was one of the few places in Europe in which English subjects could marry according to the rites of the church that it was Twiss's job to uphold.

348. "The Extraordinary Libel Case," *South London Press*, March 9, 1872, 12.

349. "The Convocation of the Prelates and Clergy," *Chelmsford Chronicle*, August 22, 1862, 2. See also "Domestic Times," *Hereford Times*, August 30, 1862, 11; "Convocation," *North Devon Journal*, September 4, 1862, 6.

350. "John Sumner," *Oxford Dictionary of National Biography* (Oxford, 2019).

351. Twiss to Metternich, August 20, 1850, National Archives of the Czech Republic, Prague, RAM-AC/ 10/ 776, 76; Twiss to Metternich, September 9, 1852, National Archives of the Czech Republic, Prague, RAM-AC/ 10/ 778, 22; Twiss to Metternich, September 19, 1855, National Archives of the Czech Republic, Prague, RAM-AC/ 10/ 781, 19; Twiss to Metternich, December 29, 1856, National Archives of the Czech Republic, Prague, RAM-AC/ 10/ 782, 31.

Moreover, the chaplains of central and northern European Anglican churches, including Dresden, were appointed by the Bishop of London. Given, therefore, that Twiss was the Chancellor of the Diocese of London from July 1858, the Chaplain in Dresden was a person necessarily dependent upon his own good offices. As Chancellor of the Diocese and judge of its consistory court, Twiss was required to have an expertise on foreign marriages and chaplaincies abroad. The Bishop of London frequently called upon that expertise. In 1862, for example, just a few months after Twiss's marriage, controversy arose because of protests from the Chaplain of Bonn, who was also under the jurisdiction of the Diocese of London, concerning the fees levied upon certificates of births, deaths, and marriages, and also upon the proofs concerning those rituals. The Chaplain to the English community in Bonn, James Anderson, wrote to Bishop Tait raising these concerns. On the back of this letter, Tait scrawled, possibly to his own Chaplain, William Henry Fremantle, or to John Shephard, the registrar of the diocese, "Ask Twiss what he thinks."[352] On November 11, 1862, John Shephard wrote to the Chaplain in Bonn, James Anderson, saying that the diocese insisted in the case of births, deaths and marriages upon the "verification [of certificates] by a Public Notary under his Hand and Official Seal."[353] He added, "This verification does not (as you seem to assume) arise from any doubt of you being 'what you profess to be' but to protect the public from any spurious or false copies . . . and also to give them a more authentic and legal character when produced." Fremantle, Tait's Chaplain, then wrote to Twiss to say that Shephard's letter seemed "reasonable" to the Bishop, but that "he would be glad to have your opinion" because it was a matter that affected all British chaplaincies.[354] As if to underline that point, Fremantle added: "I do not know whether you have yet returned. I have not had an opportunity of congratulating you on your marriage," indicating he realised that Twiss had himself just married several weeks previously in the Dresden chapel. Twiss responded with a letter directly to Tait, acknowledging that it "may be worthy of consideration" that in *lex fori* cases of marriage—that is, in cases in which the marriage takes place under another jurisdiction—"whether some attempt might not be made to secure legal evidence to be preserved in England through the presence of a Notary Public on occasion of such marriages being solmenized." Such was already the case, he pointed out, for marriages "celebrated in an English church or chapel."[355] Implicitly, he was

---

352. James Anderson to A. C. Tait, November 6, 1862, Lambeth Palace Library, Tait Papers, Official Letters London, Continental Chaplaincies, A-B 409, f.338 verso.

353. John Shephard to James Anderson, November 11, 1862, Lambeth Palace Library, Tait Papers, Official Letters London, Continental Chaplaincies, A-B 409, f.347.

354. Fremantle to Twiss, November 14, 1862, Lambeth Palace Library, Tait Papers, Official Letters London, Continental Chaplaincies, A-B 409, ff.349–349 verso.

355. Twiss to A. C. Tait, December 22, 1862, Lambeth Palace Library, Tait Papers, Official Letters London, Continental Chaplaincies, A-B 409, f.355.

recognising that the proofs required in *lex fori* marriages, or marriages overseas, were not as rigorous as those used in England.

Here was one of the reasons that Twiss and Lynseele had chosen to marry in an English chapel overseas only months before he gave his view on the legal status of such marriages. Why they chose Dresden, amongst the various possible locations in Europe, including Bonn, related to the particular state of that chaplaincy. Indeed, the question of who held the chaplaincy of Dresden had been highly controversial since 1857 and was resolved only days after Twiss took his office as Chancellor of the Diocese on July 17, 1858. Twiss and Lynseele's knowledge of that dispute would have influenced their decision in choosing Dresden for their marriage and, therefore, Saxony as her origin. In 1857, the position of chaplain to the English chapel in Dresden became vacant. Problems arose, however, when the English residents of that city elected two men, Henry Dale and George Gardiner, through two separate processes, to the vacant chaplaincy. As Gardiner himself wrote, the "two several parties claim to have each legitimately elected a chaplain."[356] The two elections were produced by a division within the congregation regarding the kind of church they wished. This was a division that reflected conflict in England between the church reformers and the Oxford Movement, which sought closer ties with the Catholic Church. Dale was the reformers' candidate, and he was elected by a large majority of the parishioners but without a due regard for process. Gardiner was a high church candidate elected through the correct process but with only a handful of votes. Both parties insisted upon the legitimacy of their chaplain. The dispute would have been unremarkable if it hadn't become extremely heated, with accusations of slander and foul play, raising concerns in the Foreign Office about damage to Britain's reputation in Saxony. Gardiner wrote of "embarrassing and painful circumstances, of no ordinary kind."[357] Mr Forbes, Dale's representative, wrote to the Foreign Office complaining of the "tiresome and ungentlemanlike dispute."[358] The Foreign Office wrote repeatedly to Bishop Tait regarding the "parties who have brought so much scandal upon the English Church at Dresden."[359]

The Earl of Clarendon, the Secretary of State for Foreign Affairs, pointed out that Tait had power over the appointment of a new chaplain insofar as only he, with the assistance of the Chancellor of the Diocese (soon to be

---

356. Gardiner to A. C. Tait, December 19, 1857, Lambeth Palace Library, Tait Papers, Official Letters London, Continental Chaplaincies, D 412, f.163.

357. Gardiner to A. C. Tait, December 19, 1857, Lambeth Palace Library, Tait Papers, Official Letters London, Continental Chaplaincies, D 412, f.163.

358. Forbes to Malmesbury, July 16, 1858, Lambeth Palace Library, Tait Papers, Official Letters London, Continental Chaplaincies, D 412, f.436.

359. Hammond to A. C. Tait, January 8, 1858, Lambeth Palace Library, Tait Papers, Official Letters London, Continental Chaplaincies, D 412, f.188 verso.

Travers Twiss), could issue a new license to that chaplain.[360] He did not wish, however, simply to impose a solution, and doubts were raised about his ability to do so. Dale wrote to him, declaring: "I had, however, the confident opinion of one of our most eminent English lawyers that however much such dissensions were to be regretted and whichever party might be to blame for them, it was not a case to be ruled in any degree by English law or custom but simply a dispute ... in which the wishes of the majority must be absolutely decisive."[361] The Colonial Church and School Society wrote to Tait to portray the conflict in terms of establishing a "constitutional system in the regulation of their Church affairs" for "all the members of the Church of England abroad."[362] Tait accordingly instructed both candidates to withdraw so that new elections could be held.[363] Dale was successful in those elections, and Mr Forbes wrote to Clarendon on July 16 that "the Reverend Henry Dale received yesterday the Bishop of London's license," while at the same time taking the opportunity to gloat over the "low set" who had opposed Dale.[364] The following day, July 17, Twiss was installed as Chancellor of the Diocese of London. Given his own bitter opposition to the Oxford Movement, Twiss would have surely taken satisfaction in observing the defeat of one of their acolytes. One of his first official duties was to congratulate the new Chaplain of Dresden upon his appointment, the same man who would perform his marriage a little more than three years later.

In those intervening three years, there were a number of occasions on which Twiss was in contact with the Chaplain of Dresden, occasions which underlined the dependence of the Chaplain upon the goodwill of the Diocese of London and its officers. In the weeks after Twiss's appointment as Chancellor, the reverberations over the appointment of the Dresden Chaplain continued to be felt, and the Diocese reassured the Foreign Office that the matter was settled.[365] In October 1858, Dale corresponded with the Bishop and the Dio-

---

360. Clarendon to A. C. Tait, January 12, 1858, Lambeth Palace Library, Tait Papers, Official Letters London, Continental Chaplaincies, D 412, f.191.

361. Dale to A. C. Tait, March 18, 1858, Lambeth Palace Library, Tait Papers, Official Letters London, Continental Chaplaincies, D 412, ff.214–214 verso.

362. Colonial Church and School Society to A. C. Tait, March 17, 1858, Lambeth Palace Library, Tait Papers, Official Letters London, Continental Chaplaincies, D 412, f.211.

363. Colonial Church and School Society to A. C. Tait, February 15, 1858, Lambeth Palace Library, Tait Papers, Official Letters London, Continental Chaplaincies, D 412, f.198; Gardiner to Pargiter, February 12, 1858, Lambeth Palace Library, Tait Papers, Official Letters London, Continental Chaplaincies, D 412, f.202 verso.

364. Forbes to Clarendon, July 16, 1858, Lambeth Palace Library, Tait Papers, Official Letters London, Continental Chaplaincies, D 412, f.436.

365. Forbes to Clarendon, July 16, 1858, Lambeth Palace Library, Tait Papers, Official Letters London, Continental Chaplaincies, D 412, f.436; Malmsbury to A. C. Tait, July 31, 1858, Lambeth Palace Library, Tait Papers, Official Letters London, Continental Chaplaincies, D 412, f.436.

cese about the appointment of offices, particularly of a churchwarden, within his community and emphasised his conformity with correct procedures.[366] By November 1860, he wrote to Tait to ask leave to be absent from Dresden for a year from the summer of 1861 due to the ill health of his family.[367] On the back of this letter, Tait wrote, for other officers of the diocese, that he had no objections to Dale's absence if a suitable substitute was found.[368] Dale returned to his post in the summer of 1862, just prior to Twiss's marriage, and he left it conclusively a year later, in 1863.[369]

When Twiss and Lynseele arrived in Dresden for their marriage, therefore, the chaplaincy had been in turmoil for some years before, and the chaplain had only just returned to duty after a year's absence. To understand why Lynseele and Twiss chose to marry in the English chapel in Dresden, we cannot ignore the controversy that swirled around that chapel during the years immediately prior to the marriage. We must consider the debt that Dale would have to Twiss, and his dependent relations with Twiss, and the very great distractions that Dale would have experienced in the years prior to the marriage, his absence in the preceding year, and his departure shortly after. The Dresden chaplaincy was precarious like no other in Europe, and Twiss and Lynseele chose their location to be married accordingly. Henry Dale found himself in the situation of performing the marriage ceremony of one his superiors, to whom he owed the continued enjoyment of his position. He was a man who was not likely to ask difficult questions of Travers Twiss or of his spouse: questions, for example, about whether she was who she said she was. These questions, according to Twiss in his letter regarding Bonn, were not systematically asked in foreign chaplaincies other than at the prerogative of the Chaplain. He was acutely conscious that the current state of the law for overseas marriages was not rigorous in requiring such proofs.

There was, however, yet another crucial difference between marrying in the Anglican chapel in Bonn and that in Dresden which related to inconsistencies in the law concerning overseas marriages. In 1849, the British Consular Marriage Act was passed in an effort to raise the standards of overseas marriages, particularly concerning the identity of the people marrying. The Act demanded that the people who proposed to marry must live in the area of the consular chapel for a minimum period of one month prior to the marriage, so that the chaplain could get to know them and judge whether they were fit to

366. Dale to A. C. Tait, July 26, 1858, Lambeth Palace Library, Tait Papers, Official Letters London, Continental Chaplaincies, D 412, f.442.

367. Dale to A. C. Tait, November 24, 1860, Lambeth Palace Library, Tait Papers, Official Letters London, 1858, Oct–Dec, 111, f.1.

368. Dale to A. C. Tait, November 24, 1860, Lambeth Palace Library, Tait Papers, Official Letters London, 1858, Oct–Dec, 111, f.2 verso.

369. Petition from Dresden congregation to A. C. Tait, January 8, 1863, Lambeth Palace Library, Tait Papers, Official Letters London, Continental Chaplaincies, D–F 413, f.36.

be married and whether they were who they said they were. A second requirement under the Act were banns. The marriage must be publicly proclaimed prior to the event in order to give other people the opportunity to raise questions regarding its legitimacy. These rules were rigorously followed in consular marriages in Europe, but they were not applied in the case of the marriage of Twiss and Lynseele. While Pharaïlde arrived in Dresden in advance, Twiss did not live in Dresden prior to his marriage—he only arrived days prior to it—nor was their marriage publicly proclaimed. They had good reasons to avoid such measures. The reason they were not obliged to conform to the rules of the Consular Marriage Act became clear from a Royal Commission on the Laws of Marriage concluded in 1868. As evidence to the Commission showed, the 1849 Consular Marriage Act contained a loophole; it did not mention embassies or legations. In the hierarchy of nineteenth-century diplomacy, embassies were only established between the great powers of Europe. Legations were sent to lesser powers, such as Belgium and, in this case, Saxony. Consulates were established in places where numbers of foreign nationals lived but outside the relations between the powers. Most marriages overseas were held in consulates, but marriages in embassies did occur if the ambassador or plenipotentiary minister, in the case of a legation, gave permission. Such marriages, the Royal Commission found, were conducted in a legal gray area and did not involve the usual requirements for residency, proclamation, or proofs. By invoking the extraterritorial status of an embassy, they could make some claim to having been conducted according to the laws of England if they were performed by a chaplain of the Church of England. By marrying in a legation, Twiss knew that he was exempt from the requirements of the Consular Marriage Act, which would have applied if he had, for example, have chosen to marry in the Anglican Chapel in Bonn (Berlin, not Bonn, was the location for the British Embassy to the Kingdom of Prussia).

Twiss knew these things simply because he was a marriage lawyer but, specifically, because, in 1867 and 1868, he sat on the Royal Commission into Marriage Laws and helped write its report—once again underlining the great respect in which his knowledge on the subject was held, a knowledge he put to both professional and personal use.[370] The object of the Commission was to inquire into and report on the state of the "various laws now in force" with respect to "the constitution and proof of the contract of marriage" across the various jurisdictions of Britain. It was also charged with examining the state of the laws, and proofs of marriage with respect to marriages of British subjects conducted in the colonies and "Marriages of British Subjects in Foreign Countries," such as Twiss's own marriage.[371] These were subjects upon which

---

370. *Report of the Royal Commission on the Laws of Marriage, Presented to Both Houses of Parliament by Command of Her Majesty* (London, 1868).

371. *Report of the Royal Commission on the Laws of Marriage*, 5.

Twiss had advised the Bishop of London and the Archbishop of Canterbury for many years. The Commission was comprised of fourteen members, including John Inglis, the Justice Clerk of Scotland; Thomas O'Hagan from the Court of Common Pleas in Ireland; Roundell Palmer, the Attorney General who, twenty years later as Lord Chancellor, would work with Twiss on the Berlin Conference; Sir Hugh Cairns, who had been William Windham's barrister in his lunacy trial (and so probably would not have been aware of the connection between Twiss and Agnes Willoughby that was made in the notes of General Windham's solicitors) and would become Lord Chancellor later in 1868; and William Page Wood, the English Vice Chancellor of the Chancery Court, who had been William Windham's guardian and became Lord Chancellor in Gladstone's first government of 1868.[372] Only one year previous to this Commission, in 1866, William Wood had granted Agnes Windham guardianship over her son, William. The chair of the Commission was Frederick Thesiger, Lord Chelmsford, who was the Lord Chancellor until 1868 in the Earl of Derby's government (to be replaced by Hugh Cairns). Despite the eminence of the Commission's members, Twiss's voice was prominent during the lengthy examinations of witnesses conducted over the two years of its sittings.

The recommendation of the Commission was to establish uniformity of the laws regarding marriage across the various jurisdictions of Britain, including England, Scotland, and Ireland, as well as overseas. Much in the recommendations of the Commission was in step with the spirit of the times, removing barriers of class, gender, and religion in marriage, at least in theory. Thus, the stated *Principles of a Sound Marriage Law* included first that it should "embrace a maximum of simplicity" because it affects "every class" and "almost every person, the most humble and illiterate as well as the most exalted and learned."[373] It should also be such as "every woman can understand by study." For differences of religion, the *Principles* recommended that the "state should be absolutely impartial and indifferent, as between the members of different religious denominations." This indifference of the state was to extend to Quakers and Jews, and even to those people who wished to marry "without any religious ceremony," so that the report recommended that marriage "in the office and presence" of a "district registrar" should be "incorporated into the future marriage law of the United Kingdom."[374] In all these recommendations, the spirit of liberality was in accord with Twiss's own marriage, both because he married a woman of humble background, and because she was a Catholic by birth. The only recommendation in the *Principles* which jarred with the Twisses' marriage was that whereby the State "should discourage and place obstacles in the way of sudden and clandestine marriages," albeit that that clause was

---

372. *Report of the Royal Commission on the Laws of Marriage*, iii.
373. *Report of the Royal Commission on the Laws of Marriage*, xxv.
374. *Report of the Royal Commission on the Laws of Marriage*, xxxviii.

made more with the idea of elopement in mind, and the so-called "irregular" Scottish marriages (for example, without a clergyman), than an invention on the scale of the Twiss marriage.

One of the important questions that came before the commissioners was the marriage of British subjects overseas. During the period in which the Commission received submissions and held hearings, problems regarding overseas marriages occupied much of their time. Overseas marriages were within Twiss's expertise, particularly as Chancellor of the Diocese of London, and in the examination of witnesses his voice was, along with that of the Commission's chair, Lord Chelmsford, most prominent amongst those of the other commissioners. One of the persons interviewed, the Reverend Robert Walter Stewart, British Chaplain at Leghorn (Livorno) in Italy, made a plea for uniformity between the marriages held in consulates and embassies. Stewart pointed out that the Marriages Confirmation Act of 1823 required consulates to demand that both persons who would marry, whether both or only one of them was a British subject, to be resident for a month in the area of the consulate prior to marriage, and that a public declaration of the marriage should be made. At the same time, he pointed out, embassies and legations made no such requirements for marriage, and he concluded: "It would be very desirable that marriages at the embassy be put on the same footing as marriages performed as the consulates, that there should be the same proclamation and terms of residence. If there is to be a proclamation at the consulate, and a residence of a month, there should be the same thing with regard to marriages performed at the embassy."[375] Stewart also pointed out that the reason consulates required residency and proclamation, or banns, for marriages was "in order to inquire into the character of those who were to be married, but it is perfectly useless as long as the usage of marriage at the embassy remains as at present." His point was that anybody of doubtful character could circumvent the requirement by going to an embassy, instead of the consulate, because embassies, he argued, were not mentioned in the legislation: "I am not aware whether there is any Act of parliament which sanctions marriages at embassies. At present a man has nothing to do but call on the ambassador, if he can get access to him, or on the secretary of the legation the day before, saying he wishes to be married the next day, and he is married without any further difficulty ... (Mr Dunlop.) And no residence or proclamation is required?—No. According to this act [for consulates] there is residence and proclamation; in the case of marriage at the embassy there is no proclamation and no residence required."[376]

Listening to this evidence, Twiss who had married in a legation, in the same legal gray area as an embassy, tried to get Stewart to acknowledge that

---

375. *Report of the Royal Commission on the Laws of Marriage*, 88.
376. *Report of the Royal Commission on the Laws of Marriage*, 88.

couples of mixed nationality, one British and one local, who married in embassies would nevertheless be subject to the laws of the country in which they married, if not to British law. Stewart pushed back: "280 (Dr Twiss.) This Act applies to parties one of whom may be a subject of the country where the marriage is solemnized?—[Stewart] Yes. / 281 [Twiss:] In the case of marriages in ambassadors' chapels they will not marry without notice or without compliance with the law of the country to which one of the parties is subject?— . . . [Stewart] I am not aware of any case of that sort and I know of no legal provision for it, such as is contained in the consular Act. I wish to bring out now the contrast between what British subjects have to submit to under this consular Act and the privilege which they have at the embassy. I think marriages at both places should be put on the same footing."[377]

For Stewart, putting marriages conducted in embassies and consulates on the same footing meant bringing the same residency and proclamation requirements to bear on embassies because he believed those requirements were important checks against fraud. He had shown that a situation effectively existed where marriages conducted at embassies and legations were of very doubtful status in both British law and in the law of local authorities, so that, he argued, the authorities had dealt with that problem until present by turning a blind eye to the irregularities. The law regulating marriage in embassies and legations, he argued, was at best consuetudinal: that is, a customary law.[378] Lord Chelmsford agreed: "It is not a pleasant state of things, is it, that the marriage should merely be winked at, because if it was brought into question it might be invalidated on the ground of its being contrary to the law?" Chelmsford, probably without realising it, was implicitly putting Twiss's own marriage into question insofar as it had been conducted in this legal vaccum. Rather, however, than doing as Stewart suggested and introducing residency and proclamation requirements for embassies and legations, the Royal Commission recommended the inverse: that is, they recommended that those requirements be dropped from consular marriages, and in so doing, they brought the law into agreement with the marriage of one of the commissioners himself, Travers Twiss. In the section of their report entitled "Marriage of British Subjects in Foreign Countries," the commissioners wrote that such marriages are legal when conducted "by a Minister of the Church of England in the chapel or house of any British Ambassador," thus removing any doubts created by the failure to mention embassies in the existing legislation and retrospectively validating Twiss's marriage. They acknowledged that the Marriages Confirmation Act of 1823 had worked very well for overseas marriages, but that it nevertheless created difficulties: "A great difficulty in the way of many persons arises from the regulation that both parties must have dwelt within

---

377. *Report of the Royal Commission on the Laws of Marriage*, 88.
378. *Report of the Royal Commission on the Laws of Marriage*, 88.

the district of the Consul, before whom the marriage is to be solemnized, not less than one calendar month before notice can be given of their intention to intermarry . . . It happens, however, not unfrequently that one of the parties intending to contract marriage is resident in England, or in another consular district, and cannot afford to leave his occupation for so long a time . . . It appears to us that this regulation causes great inconvenience to individuals without any corresponding advantage to the public, and that it would be sufficient if the party only, who gives notice to the Consul, should be required to be resident in the consular district for a calendar month next preceding the giving of the notice. We recommend that the Act should be amended in this particular."[379] Given that that aspect of the Commission's report touched on Twiss's particular expertise, and that he had been prominent amongst the commissioners when this question was discussed in its sittings (just as John Inglis, the Justice Clerk of Scotland, had been prominent in discussion of the "irregular" Scottish marriages), he had a strong voice in the report's recommendations on overseas marriages.

The House of Commons duly debated the Commission's recommendations on consular marriages on June 26, 1868, and the House of Lords adopted them in passing the Consular Marriage Act of 1868, on July 14.[380] Whereas Twiss's marriage had exploited a loophole—namely, the absence of legations and embassies in the legislation regarding residence and proclamation—that exception now became the rule for all marriages overseas (until the 1848 and 1849 British Consular Marriage Acts were repealed by the Foreign Marriage Act of 1892). In the process, the Commission made marriage law more liberal, in the sense that it was less subject to regulation and state surveillance. That liberal reform was made in the image of the marriage of one of the commissioners himself.

Twiss was not only able to exploit a world that was increasingly concerned with the removal of constraints, what contemporaries and Twiss himself called a more liberal world; he was also able to help remove those constraints and thus make his world more in the image of himself and his wife. We might conclude that this was a case where reform was inspired not by ideas themselves but by the opportunism of an individual. There would be some truth in such an interpretation of the new marriage act, but it is too simple. At the same time that Twiss was helping to make law in the image of his own marriage, and doing so opportunistically, we must also remember that his own marriage and the reinvention of his wife as a Dutch and Austrian noblewoman and member of London Society, were not mere opportunism; they were themselves inspired by ideas of personal transformation and improvement that were prevalent at

---

379. *Report of the Royal Commission on the Laws of Marriage*, lii.
380. *House of Lords Hansard*, July 14, 1868, Vol. 193, c.1158.

this time. Ideas were driven by opportunism, but opportunism was not devoid of the motivating force of ideas.

In choosing Dresden to marry, Twiss and Lynseele were exploiting *lex fori* jurisdiction: that is, they exploited the fact that the law in Dresden was Saxon and their marriage fell between two jurisdictions. English law did not apply in Dresden, and although the English legation building there, which was closely tied to the chapel, could claim limited extraterritorial jurisdiction, the chapel could not. The Church of England nevertheless recognised the validity of certificates of birth, death, and marriage made before their overseas chaplains. This recognition did not fall far short of the limited jurisdiction that Pope Pius had claimed, in 1850, in England in *Universalis Ecclesiae*, to which Twiss had so strongly objected in his *The Letters Apostolic of the Pope Pius IX Considered with Reference to the Law of England and the Law of Europe*. As Twiss understood from that earlier conflict, the quasi-extraterritorial nature of his marriage placed it in a fluid legal space which assisted Lynseele in the fluidity of her own persona.

The certificate of Twiss and Lynseele's marriage states that the ceremony was performed on August 29, 1862, between "Travers Twiss, Bachelor residing in London" and "Pharaïlde Rosalinde Van Lynseele, Spinster residing in Courtray [i.e., Kortrijk]" and conducted "according to the rites of the Church of England."[381] It is not entirely clear why Lynseele gave her real birthplace, in Kortrijk—or Courtrai, for Walloons—as her current residence. The marriage took place not in the chapel but in the "House of Her Britannic Majesty's Minister Plenipotentiary at Dresden," presumably in the expectation that this might create a stronger case for British extraterritorial jurisdiction. The service was performed by "Henry Dale, British Chaplain at Dresden," who duly signed the certificate. Three witnesses signed beneath Dale; two were residents of Dresden, and the third was "Charles Townshend Barnard, Her Majesty's Chargé d'affaires." The second page of the certificate is an oath signed by Twiss and Lynseele that there was "no lawful cause of impediment" to their marriage arising from "consanguinity"—that is, from a blood connection—nor from previous marriages, nor "otherwise howsoever." The cause of "otherwise howsoever" might include using a false persona, but Lynseele was careful to use the name she was born with when she married, as had Anne Rogers, who did not use "Willoughby" on her marriage certificate, thus avoiding the risk of a possible future annulment of the marriage on the grounds of using a false identity. The false aspect to Lynseele's persona came from who she said she was, not from the name she used at the time of her wedding (albeit that she had lived under the name Marie Gelas for some years previously). The oath and

---

381. Certificate of marriage between Travers Twiss and Pharaïlde Rosalinde Van Lynseele, August 29, 1862, National Archives, London, *General Register Office: Miscellaneous Foreign Marriage Returns;* Class: RG 34; Piece: 1, ff.220–221.

the marriage certificate were both printed forms used for overseas marriages, with blanks for names, location, dates, and other details to be filled by hand. The printed statement included "it is proposed to solemnize the said intended marriage, as British subjects, in the Chapel, or House," but this phrase was adjusted by hand to "it is proposed to solemnize the said intended marriage, as *one of the parties being a* British subject, in the Chapel, or House."[382] The fact that one party was not British further weakened the contract. This oath was then sworn before Barnard and witnessed by Dale. No member of Twiss's or Lynseele's families witnessed these documents. There is no suggestion of any friends or family being present. A small announcement appeared in some newspapers a week later on September 6: "Twiss-Van Lynseele-Aug.29, at the British Legation, Dresden, by the Rev. H. Dale, British Chaplain at Dresden, Travers Twiss, Esq., Q.C., to Mademoiselle Van Lynseele, only daughter of Major General van Lynseele."[383] Although short, the announcement nevertheless was careful to establish Lynseele's pedigree, and the Dutch origin of the Major General explained the Flemish name van Lynseele. No other details on the marriage are extant. The event was very discreet.

Having performed the legal ritual, Lynseele and Twiss immediately began the work of introducing, in a very controlled manner, the idea and symbols of the orphaned daughter of a noble Dutch, Polish, and Austrian family into their discourse with influential persons in London Society. Two days after the wedding, while still at Dresden, Twiss wrote to Austen Henry Layard, the celebrated archaeologist and Orientalist. Layard had excavated the ancient Assyrian cities of Nimrud and Ninevah in the 1840s and '50s and discovered the library of Ashurbanipal, which included, amongst its thousands of tablets, the *Epic of Gilgamesh*. Twiss had known Layard since the 1840s, when they were both members of the Royal Geographic Society and of the Athenaeum.[384] In 1861, Layard became Under-Secretary for Foreign Affairs, and in August 1862, at the moment of his marriage, Twiss was seeking a position as Admiralty Advocate, which gave him a reason to court Layard. He began his message by noting that he had received no despatch in Dresden from the Foreign Office courier. He appeared to anticipate, therefore, some news on the position as Admiralty Advocate. He then noted that he would go to Vienna by the end of the week. He suggested that there Layard should "send me a line" and explain how a person in the Foreign Office would "speak with me on the subject" without stating what that subject was.[385] "Otherwise," he observed, "I would

---

382. Certificate of marriage between Travers Twiss and Pharaïlde Rosalinde Van Lynseele, fol. 221.

383. *Bell's Weekly Messenger*, September 6, 1862, 8.

384. Twiss was elected to the Athenaeum in 1845, Layard in 1848.

385. Twiss to Layard, August 31, 1862, British Library, Layard Papers, Add. MS 38988, fol. 288.

hesitate to ask him any questions."386 He did not want to act precipitously in relation to the position, as he had been perceived to do in the past (when, for example, seeking to be candidate for the seat of Oxford). The letter shifted suddenly to the matter of his marriage. "I took advantage," he announced, "of the hospitality of the British legation to marry a young lady of Dutch family Mademoiselle van Lynseele daughter of Major General V. Lynseele. But I narrowly escaped finding no clergyman, as Rev. Mr Dale a self supported chaplain only returned by the same train which brought me. I am rather surprised that there is no Foreign Office chaplain here, as it seems to be a more eligible post for such a person, and as there is no Consul here no consular marriages can take place. The legation is therefore the only place of refuge for the votaries of Hymen."387 The aim of this letter was to make the event of the marriage seem almost accidental when, in fact, it had been carefully planned. Lynseele had been in Dresden for some time. Twiss knew Dale's movements because of his position as Chancellor of the Diocese of London and his correspondence on Dale. Similarly, as Chancellor of the Diocese, as well as an international lawyer, he would have no reason to be surprised that Britain had a legation rather than a consulate in Dresden, which is precisely why he prearranged to meet Lynseele there. At the same time, the letter added an element to Lynseele's new persona that helped explain her name. Frequently, Twiss referred to her as the daughter of an officer from the Polish army, but in this letter, he mentioned, for the first time, that Major General van Lynseele was originally Dutch—a Dutch officer fighting in the Galician, or Austrian Polish, army.

Having already gone to great lengths to make their marriage as discreet as possible, Twiss and Lynseele were blessed with good fortune, or possibly a combination of fortune and design, when the Archbishop of Canterbury, one of Twiss's main employers, died in the week after the marriage. Any public attention their marriage may have attracted was buried under the publicity surrounding the Archbishop's death and preparations for his funeral. Just days after his wedding, Twiss was back in England as one of the "chief mourners" at Sumner's funeral, which was held privately on Friday, September 12, at St Mary's Church in Addington Village, south of London, where the nineteenth-century archbishops resided in Addington Palace (while using Lambeth Palace for public purposes).388 On November 26, Twiss was present, in his role as Vicar General of the Province of Canterbury, for the swearing in of the new Archbishop, Charles Longley, at St Mary-le Bow's Church, Cheapside (the church of the Court of Arches and Doctors' Commons), and again for his

---

386. Twiss to Layard, August 31, 1862, British Library, Layard Papers, Add. MS 38988, fol. 288 verso.

387. Twiss to Layard, August 31, 1862, British Library, Layard Papers, Add. MS 38988, fols. 288 verso–289.

388. *Bell's Weekly Messenger*, September 13, 1862, 2.

"enthronization" at Canterbury Cathedral on December 21, on which occasion Twiss read the new Archbishop's mandate.[389] In reading Longley's mandate, Twiss participated in the creation of a new artificial person. The See of Canterbury is a corporation sole, a legal person, and its bishop, the Archbishop of Canterbury, personifies that corporation, just as all bishops personify their churches. Twiss's role in creating the new legal person of the archbishop again underlined the fact that the creation and proofs of personae were central to his everyday work. In Longley's enthronization, Twiss was involved in both the legal and ritual aspects of making the new person of the archbishop. He appreciated that both elements were essential to the making of new persons, and having already attended to the making of the new legal person of his wife through the marriage ceremony in Dresden, he and Pharaïlde Twiss would now pursue the ritual and symbolic elements in her transformation.

In September, Twiss added an important new office to his already impressive collection of offices. On August 14, 1862, the Queen's Advocate General, Sir John Harding, resigned. The Queen's Advocate General performed the function of Attorney General in civil law for the government. He was consulted by government on Admiralty matters in particular and so played the role of a foreign policy advisor. Roundell Palmer, who was Solicitor General from 1861 to 1863 in Palmerston's government, remarked vexedly that when a British ship, *The Prince of Wales*, was wrecked and plundered on the Brazilian coast, "reprisals were taken on the advice of Sir Robert Phillimore only" (Phillimore being at that time the Queen's Advocate General), while Palmer was completely bypassed.[390] This was the position that Tait had first mooted for Twiss in 1852, only for him to be passed over. It was, as one newspaper put it, a "valuable piece of patronage."[391] Following Harding's resignation, many newspapers reported that Twiss had indeed been successful in gaining the post. [392] In fact, despite the rumours, it went to his rival Robert Phillimore, only a year younger than Twiss and the only civil lawyer in England as eminent as Twiss himself. As Archbishop Sumner's Vicar General, Twiss had been the judge of the Ecclesiastical Court which in 1856 condemned George Denison, Phillimore's brother-in-law, for heresy as a consequence of having taken an insufficiently figurative view of personification in the case of the Eucharist (Denison was then acquitted, a year later, on a technicality). Twiss, we know from his own marriage, could take an extremely figurative and elastic view of personification. Phillimore, who saw the Church of England as part of

---

389. *The Times*, November 27, 1862, 5; *The Times*, December 13, 1862, 9.

390. Roundell Palmer, Earl of Selborne, *Memorials: Family and Personal 1766–1865* (London, 1896), 2 vols., Vol. 2, 377–381.

391. *Manchester Courier and Lancashire General Advertiser*, August 16, 1862, 4.

392. See, for example, *Northern Whig*, August 15, 1862, 3: "Dr Travers Twiss Is Spoken of as the New Queen's Advocate." See also *Oxford University and City Herald*, August 16, 1862, 13.

the Catholic Church, had appeared in that trial as the defence lawyer for his brother-in-law.[393] Judging by the fact that Tait had written ten years earlier to his wife, in 1852, that Twiss was in a "state of anxiety" in anticipation of the government awarding the office, his disappointment on missing out for the second time ten years later must have been all the stronger. He eventually succeeded in being elevated to Advocate General in 1867, when Phillimore was appointed Dean of the Court of Arches.

Twiss's consolation prize in September 1862 was to be made government Advocate in the Admiralty Court, the position that Phillimore had to resign in order to become Queen's Advocate, and which Twiss had been negotiating with Layard in late August. This was, nevertheless, a significant addition to his prestige and income just weeks after his marriage, and he thanked those who helped him in gaining the position. On September 11, he wrote from Vienna to Henry Petty-Fitzmaurice, the Marquess of Lansdowne, "to thank you very sincerely for your kindness in writing to the Duke of Somerset. I am forwarding his answer to me. I had a letter from the Lord Chancellor [Richard Bethel, Baron Westbury] intimating his expectation that I should be appointed Admiralty Advocate."[394] The Duke of Somerset, Edward Seymour, was 1st Lord of the Admiralty and so had an influence over who the government chose as Admiralty Advocate. Twiss then turned to the political economy of Bohemia, where he had visited Metternich over the past ten years in summer, while insinuating his new marital status and his wife into the discussion: "I have been paying a visit with my wife, a daughter of Major General van Lynseele, in Bohemia where I have an opportunity of seeing how a large proprietor is able to manage his property. There are no farmers in our sense of the word." He expanded at length on the political economy of Bohemia while mentioning that he and Pharaïlde Twiss had been staying at Count Taaffe's "chateau" in Ellischau, or Schloss Ellischau. Having, as we have seen successfully reinvented the Taaffe family as British aristocrats in 1857, Twiss was now calling upon their debt to him by presenting his new wife for their acceptance, while letting the Marquess of Lansdowne know that he had done so. He also mentioned, "I paid Count Rechberg a visit yesterday." He was referring to Johann Bernhard, Count von Rechberg und Rothenlöwen, who had been a protégé of Metternich and whom Metternich, as late as 1859, just before his death, had succeeded through his influence in installing as the Austrian Foreign Minister.[395] Rechberg had had a career as a diplomat, but Twiss met him when he accompanied Metternich in exile in England, and it was almost certainly due

---

393. For Phillimore's defence of his brother-in-law, see "Robert Phillimore," *Oxford Dictionary of National Biography* (Oxford, 2019). Twiss and Phillimore appear, despite their rivalries, to have always remained on friendly terms; we have already seen that Twiss proposed Phillimore as a member of the Athenaeum three years later.

394. Twiss to Lansdowne, September 11, 1862, British Library, Add. MS. 88906/ 10/ 22.

395. Palmer, *Metternich*, 338.

to Twiss's close relationship with Metternich that he was now able to visit the Austrian Foreign Minister. Twiss reported that Rechberg "thinks the Austrian Empire is gradually improving—that the people have more confidence—and there are certainly appearances of comfort and wealth." He concluded his letter to Lansdowne with the observation: "I hope to be in England about the 23rd or 24th of Sept. Yours very truly, Travers Twiss."

This careful management of the news regarding his marriage is consistent with Lynseele and Twiss choreographing the event, but what is baffling in this instance are the dates. English newspapers reported Twiss's presence at Archbishop Sumner's funeral on September 12, and yet this letter from Vienna to Petty-Fitzmaurice is dated September 11, while forecasting his return on September 23. The question of his presence at the funeral is beyond doubt; it appeared in numerous newspaper reports. The funeral was a small, "comparatively private" affair, not a state occasion, and Twiss was named amongst the chief mourners in a released statement.[396] The date of September 11 at the top of the letter cannot be correct, nor can the dates on which Twiss claimed he would return to England. The letter was not what it appeared to be. This dissembling should not surprise, given that the letter contained another important falsehood: introducing Pharaïlde Twiss as the daughter of Major General van Lynseele. It is not entirely clear, however, why Twiss would want to present himself to an English aristocrat as being on vacation in Bohemia when he was in fact attending the widely publicised Archbishop's funeral. The letter reinforced Twiss's credentials as Admiralty Advocate, for which Petty-Fitzmaurice had recommended him, because it showed his ease of access to the aristocracy of Europe and, in particular, to the Foreign Minister of a major power. Whether the meeting with Count Rechberg actually took place must be questioned, along with the rest of the letter's contents, including Twiss's claim to be in Vienna when he was in London. But that claim contained a risk of discovery, and one must ask why Twiss was prepared to take such risks. While his and Lynseele's pursuit of her metamorphosis into Pharaïlde Twiss, daughter of a Dutch nobleman, was conducted in a way that minimized the possibility of discovery, they were unable to remove such risks altogether and were sometimes driven by their success to take bold steps, albeit that in this case there is no evidence that Twiss's deception was ever discovered. What he hoped to gain by it is a matter of conjecture, but it may be that he had certain objectives planned for his trip with Pharaïlde Twiss, and when those aims were cut short by the Archbishop's death, he was forced to improvise.

The great challenge for Pharaïlde and Travers Twiss after their marriage was, having tested the waters with Layard, the Marquess of Lansdowne, and the Taaffes, to introduce Pharaïlde Twiss to London Society and to have her

---

396. *Carlisle Patriot*, September 13, 1862, 4; *Cambridge Chronicle and Journal*, September 13, 1862, 6.

accepted as the orphaned daughter of minor Dutch and Austrian nobility. The copy in their library of Sarah Ellis's 1843 *The Wives of England: Their Relative Duties, Domestic Influence and Social Obligations* provided a model for the kind of behaviour expected of a new wife to a man of Travers Twiss's status.[397] Ellis ran a school for the moral education of young women and published a series of works on that subject. Above all, Ellis advised, a new wife should seek reason and truth before happiness because the pursuit of happiness too often ended in disappointment: "Let us hope only to be happy ourselves, so long as we make others happy."[398] Utilitarians often cautioned that the pursuit of happiness should be understood in a broad rather than a crude sense. Nevertheless, in Ellis's account, women were clearly an accessory to this central aim of Victorian political economy. They were an accessory to men. She declared, "Those who argue for perfect equality" of men and women knew little of that "higher philosophy," namely the Bible, which showed the natures of men and women were different.[399] A woman, once she married a man, had "voluntarily placed herself in such a position that she must necessarily be his inferior."[400] Ellis's chapter on the first year of married life warned the new wife of the disappointment of everyday life that followed courtship, as well as the dangers of a husband's family and the necessary superiority of a husband to a wife. In a Machiavellian vein, she advised, "Look at things as they really are and not as they might be."[401] This "common sense" attitude to marriage meant that the new couple should avoid an appearance of wealth and status that did not fit their means, albeit that "this very act of assuming a certain position, and this very dread of falling back, is what the whole world is striving about at this very hour."[402] With these words, she dismissed the contemporary obsession with improvement. False appearances, she warned, were "sufficient to poison the fountain of domestic concord at its source."[403] "Deception" was an "evil" which always "draws after it a long train of falsehood."[404] This was particularly apposite advice for the Twisses, although it did not come close to anticipating the magnitude of their own concern with appearance.

Ellis's tips may well have helped prepare Pharaïlde Twiss for London Society, but in order to meet that challenge, she had to perform certain rituals that were appropriate to the new person she had become. Twiss was well known in London's demi-monde, but he also moved in elevated circles, and he and

397. *Catalogue of a Portion of the Miscellaneous Llibrary of Sir Travers Twiss*, 47.
398. Sarah Ellis, *The Wives of England: Their Relative Duties, Domestic Influence and Social Obligations* (London, 1843), 69.
399. Ellis, *The Wives of England*, 72.
400. Ellis, *The Wives of England*, 79.
401. Ellis, *The Wives of England*, 55.
402. Ellis, *The Wives of England*, 54.
403. Ellis, *The Wives of England*, 55.
404. Ellis, *The Wives of England*, 57.

Pharaïlde Twiss now sought to have her introduced to those circles. She was first presented at dinner parties, including parties in their house in Park Lane. The most important indicator, however, of the acceptance of a woman at the highest level of Society was to be presented at court. Travers and Pharaïlde Twiss therefore began the complex arrangements to have her presented to Queen Victoria at Buckingham Palace. This presentation would seal her transformation from a Regent Street prostitute to a member of London Society. It would also trigger the downfall of the Twisses.

To qualify for presentation at court, a woman had to be a daughter of the aristocracy, the gentry, or wealthy members of Society, she had to be of good moral character, and she had to be presented by another woman, usually her mother, who had herself been previously presented at court.[405] These debutants were usually young women who were being presented to Society as eligible wives, but married women, such as Pharaïlde Twiss, were also permitted to be presented if they were young. The presentation itself observed strict rules of etiquette, as described by Lady Colin Campbell in her Victorian manual *Etiquette of Good Society*. The person presenting a young woman was first obliged to deliver in advance her name on a card to the office of the Lord Chamberlain, the senior officer of the Royal Household. If that person was deemed suitable by the Lord Chamberlain and the Queen, permission was given to proceed. The dress of the woman was tightly regulated. It was to be white, with a train of not more than two yards, and was to conform to numerous other specifications. She was obliged to wear two ostrich feathers in her hair if she was unmarried and three if she was married. She would attend Buckingham Palace on the day of the Queen's Drawing Room and, carrying her train, wait her turn to be brought to the Throne Room. On entering the room, she would let down her train, which, as Campbell put it, "is instantly spread out by the lords-in-waiting with their wands."[406] When she entered, she must perform a deep curtsey and then kiss the hand of the Queen, or receive a kiss, in the case of the aristocracy.

Lady Campbell was herself presented to court in the 1870s some years after Pharaïlde Twiss, but the conventions of presentation remained largely static throughout Victoria's reign. Lady Campbell, or Gertrude Campbell, had been born Gertrude Elizabeth Blood in 1857, and her parents were wealthy Irish landowners. Her *Etiquette of Good Society* described a world which was as closed as the European society of states: that is, a club in which new members could only be introduced by existing members: "the life," as she conceded in her preface, "of comparatively few people."[407] Nevertheless, the closed nature of that world was more of an ambition than a reality. William Makepeace

---

405. Lady Colin Campbell, *Etiquette of Good Society*, rev. ed. (London, 1893), 206–208.
406. Campbell, *Etiquette*, 207.
407. Campbell, *Etiquette*, iv.

Thackeray satirised those pretensions when his far-from-virtuous heroine Becky Sharp, in *Vanity Fair,* contrived to be presented at court. Campbell herself was familiar with some of the trials suffered by women such as Pharaïlde Twiss and Agnes Willoughby. She met Lord Colin Campbell, the son of the Duke of Argyll on holiday in Scotland in 1880, and became engaged to him within days. His parents were not happy with the prospective marriage because of her undistinguished family. Her own father, on the other hand, was unhappy with the marriage because Campbell was said to suffer from the "loathsome disease": that is, from syphilis, although he was assured by his future son-in-law that was not the case and the couple married in July 1881.[408] Lord Campbell initially insisted upon separate lodging from his new wife, but by November 1881, she had contracted venereal disease from him, as Agnes Windham had claimed to have done from her own husband. Gertrude Campbell successfully applied for a judicial separation in 1884 on the grounds of having been infected by her husband, but she unsuccessfully sued for divorce in 1886.[409] She then proceeded to reinvent herself as a prolific and successful writer, writing on numerous questions, including etiquette, with a chapter on marriage (covering topics such as the interview with the prospective father-in-law), which she must have done with a painful awareness of the elasticity of the conventions which she described.

That very same elasticity offered opportunities for people such as the Twisses. In presenting Pharaïlde Twiss to court, the first challenge was to find a woman who could make the presentation. While the young woman's mother usually performed that role, Pharaïlde Twiss's mother, while living in London according to the 1861 census, was in no position to do so and was not, according to her new persona, her mother at all—her fictional mother was dead. Pharaïlde Twiss, however, had not been on equal terms in the past with any of the women in London Society who were now needed to present her to court. Travers Twiss's mother, Fanny, was probably eligible to present Pharaïlde at court if she had herself been presented when a young woman. In 1863, however, she was an old woman, and she died in October, so she may have already been ill when Travers and Pharaïlde Twiss determined to proceed with the presentation early in that year.

On Monday, May 18, *The Times* and the *Morning Post* announced that, the previous Saturday, the Princess of Wales had held a Drawing Room at St James's Palace on behalf of the Queen (who was still in mourning for Prince Albert, who had died less than eighteen months earlier). The court, the newspapers announced, "was attended by 2,000 of the nobility and gentry" and included numerous members of foreign nobility, diplomats, and ambassadors,

---

408. *The Colin Campbell Divorce Case with Portraits* (1886), 2.
409. "Campbell [*née* Blood], Gertrude Elizabeth [Lady Colin Campbell]," *Oxford Dictionary of National Biography* (Oxford, 2019).

with many of the notables with whom Twiss worked and dined, such as the Countess d'Apponyi, Viscount Palmerston, and the newly installed Archbishop of Canterbury. The proceedings included 500 "presentations of ladies." In the list of women presented to the Princess of Wales, frequently by their mothers but also by women of the nobility and gentry, was "Mrs Travers Twiss by Lady Alcock."[410] Lady Alcock was perfect for the role. Like the Dresden location for the wedding, Lucy Alcock satisfied the formal requirements for the presentation but was at the same time an outsider. She had been born Lucy Windsor, in 1814, the daughter of a missionary, and married the Reverend John Samuel Lowder in 1840, with whom she had five children. Following the first of the Opium Wars, Britain established a treaty port at Shanghai in 1843, and the first church was built there in 1847. From early 1848, Lowder became the first Chaplain of that church, although he drowned while bathing less than two years later.[411] A subscription was immediately held to provide support for his widow and five children, and 15,000 Spanish silver dollars were raised (Spanish silver dollars from Mexico were used in the treaty ports).

In 1846, the year before Lucy Lowder arrived in Shanghai, the British diplomat Rutherford Alcock was transferred to the consulate there. He and his wife, Henrietta Alcock, became close friends with Lucy and John Lowder prior to John Lowder's death. During this period, Alcock established the municipal regulations for the British community as well as negotiating the international settlement whereby the city was shared between the various occupying powers.[412] In 1853, Henrietta Alcock died, and Rutherford became free to marry again, although, in 1858, he was appointed the British consul general in Japan, where he insisted upon the opening of treaty ports as negotiated under the treaty of Edo, made in the same year. Japan had only very recently, since 1854, been forced to open its ports as a consequence of the unequal treaties made with the European powers and the United States. The treaties were strongly resented in Japan, and a large number of *rōnin*, or masterless samurai, who were not controlled by the government, attacked the British legation in 1861, killing twelve members of the bodyguard. The 150 attackers were eventually repulsed, as Alcock tells the story in his 1863 *The Capital of the Tycoon*, by Alcock and five of his staff, "five Europeans," including "Mr Lowder," the son of his friend from Shanghai.[413] "There is probably not in all the annals of our diplomacy," Alcock declared, "an example of such a bloodthirsty and deliberate

---

410. *The Times*, May 18, 1863, 5; *Morning Post*, May 18, 1863, 2.

411. "Melancholy Death of the Rev. John Lowder," *Taunton Courier, and Western Advertiser*, January 16, 1850, 8.

412. "Alcock, Sir (John) Rutherford," *Oxford Dictionary of National Biography* (Oxford, 2019).

413. Rutherford Alcock, *The Capital of the Tycoon: A Narrative of Three Years Residence in Japan*, 2 vols. (New York, 1863), Vol. 2, 143–158.

plot to massacre a whole legation."[414] Constant attacks on the European and American legations led to the Japanese government and treaty powers agreeing that diplomatic missions should be sent to Europe and the United States to negotiate over the terms of the treaties. The Japanese mission to Europe was prepared in 1861, consisting of thirty-five members.[415] Alcock resolved to follow them in order to facilitate negotiations in London, while, at the same time, seeking a period of leave. He returned to Britain, in March 1862, and was knighted (he became Knight Commander of the Bath) on his arrival.[416] He also, at this time, married Lucy Lowder in Brussels on July 8, 1862.[417]

Pharaïlde van Lynseele had travelled through Brussels in March on her way to marrying Travers Twiss in August in Dresden, so she may have met the Alcocks in Brussels. Travers Twiss and Rutherford Alcock were certainly well acquainted before Lady Alcock presented Pharaïlde Twiss to the Princess of Wales on May 16, 1863. Two months before, at 10:00 a.m. on Saturday, March 28, Alcock had been awarded an honorary Doctorate of Civil Law in the Convocation ceremony at the University of Oxford. Although DCLs were supposed to be awarded by the University Orator, who was at this time Richard Michel, the person who awarded the degree to Alcock and gave the oration praising his eminence and achievements was the Regius Professor of Civil Law, Travers Twiss, although this was not the only occasion on which Twiss apparently stood in for Michel.[418] The records of the Hebdomadal Council, the governing body of the University, maintained a high degree of confidentiality regarding the decision-making process behind honorary degrees; however, the minutes show that, on March 9, 1863, Alcock was nominated by the Warden of All Souls, Francis Knyvett Leighton, who would later become the University's Vice Chancellor.[419] The reasons for the proposal are not recorded, although Alcock's heroic deeds in the service of empire were typical qualifications. Leighton may well have been acting on the suggestion of a member of the University who was not on the Council, such as Twiss. A ballot was held, on March 16, in which the proposal was approved, and on March 23, the Council

414. Alcock, *The Capital of the Tycoon*, 158.

415. Alcock, *The Capital of the Tycoon*, 323.

416. Alexander Michie, *The Englishman in China during the Victorian Era: As Illustrated in the Career of Sir Rutherford Alcock, K.C.B, D.C.L.*, 2 vols. (London, 1900), Vol. 2, 70.

417. Michie, *The Englishman in China*, 73; "Rutherford Alcock and Lucy Lowder, Marriage Affidavit," National Archives, London; General Register Office: Foreign Registers and Returns; Class: RG 33; Piece 6, fol. 9.

418. The *Morning Post*, June 20, 1863, 5, reports that during the Grand Commemoration of the previous week, it had been Twiss who gave the oration and presented the candidates for the DCL "in his capacity of Regius Professor of Civil Law." For the roles of Orator and Regius Professor of Civil Law in the award of DCLs, see L. H. Dudley Buxton and Strickland Gibson, *Oxford University Ceremonies* (Oxford, 1935), 90–91.

419. Minutes of the Hebdomadal Council, Oxford University Archives, Bodleian Library, Oxford HC 1/2/1, fols. 396–398.

ordered the conferral of the degree. The register of Convocation recorded the award and the fact that it was made by Twiss.[420]

Twiss earned Alcock's gratitude, which he expressed by sharing his expertise in Japanese culture. He had set up the Japanese section of the Great Exhibition, which began in May 1862 and was visited by the Japanese diplomatic delegation, who had succeeded in gaining delays in the opening of its ports. He wrote a number of works on the Japanese language and culture, including the 1861 *Elements of Japanese Grammar, for the Use of Beginners*. When Twiss was obliged, by financial ruin, to sell his library ten years later, the catalogue included eighty works in Japanese and on Japan, many of which he is likely to have received from Alcock, and the *Vocabulary* in the list was probably Alcock's own work.[421]

Alcock had also contributed to the Chinese section of the Crystal Palace exhibition in 1851. Twiss was initially an enthusiast for the exhibition, writing that it "rises up as it were by magic, enclosing under its glass room the largest elm trees in Hyde Park."[422] He was not, however, "in the interior" of the Crystal Palace at the time of the opening on May 1, "which I regret, as it seems to have been more of a reality than great ceremonials generally are." The observation is noteworthy from a person for whom the performance of ceremonies was a central part of professional life. He was sensitive to the need for ceremonial fictions to appear as realities. Perhaps precisely because he routinely performed ceremonials such as the swearing in of bishops and the Oxford Encaenia, he was particulary conscious of the ritualistic, and rhetorical, nature of ceremony. He exploited that sensibility in order to participate in the creation of his wife's persona.[423]

---

420. Oxford University Archives, Bodleian Library, Oxford, NEP/subtus/Reg Bu, fol. 305. Unfortunately, the record of the speech does not survive, although it was widely reported in the newspapers: *Hampshire Advertiser*, March 28, 1863, 3; *Hampshire Advertiser*, April 4, 1863, 2; *Oxford Times*, April 4, 1863, 5; *Oxford Journal*, April 4, 1863, 5.

421. *Catalogue of a Portion of the Miscellaneous Library of Sir Travers Twiss*.

422. Twiss to Metternich, December 28, 1850, National Archives of the Czech Republic, Prague, RAM-AC/ 10/ 776, 116. When the exhibition opened, he observed, "The living tide rolled onwards to the Park from all parts of this great metropolis for 3 or 4 hours without intermission": Twiss to Metternich, May 8, 1851, National Archives of the Czech Republic, Prague, RAM-AC/ 10/ 777, 67.

423. By June, Twiss had tired of the exhibition, declaring: "The English people are undergoing a curious process of dissipation, mental rather than bodily, in the Crystal Palace. It has really put a stop to all serious business—no books are sold—no goods are bought—no laws can be made by the legislative body": Twiss to Metternich, June 6, 1851, National Archives of the Czech Republic, Prague, RAM-AC/ 10/ 777, 77. He said that only the hatters were making a good trade: "The Hatters are said to be making a good thing of the influx of strangers—never were so many hats sold." But he concluded, "I shall be glad to see the building removed from the Park." When the building was removed, it was taken to Sydenham and reconstructed with the surounding gardens containing dinosaur sculptures, designed under the direction of the biologist Richard Owen, whom Twiss may have known

Twiss had other ties with Alcock, notably through the Athenaeum: Alcock became a member in 1846, the year after Twiss.[424] Although that is the year that Alcock also left for China, he sometimes returned to London, such as in 1851, and probably met Twiss through Admiralty work. The ties lasted decades, although they were tested by the scandal. More than twenty years after his marriage, when Twiss wrote to justify the transformation of a private corporation into a state, he held out the North Borneo Company as a precedent for what was to many unthinkable in international law. The North Borneo Company, he argued, had performed all the functions of a state, while being autonomous from the crown. Alcock was the chairman of the Company at that time and the man who had been a driving force behind its creation.[425]

Above all, the ties between Twisses and the Alcocks were most evident in the presentation of Pharaïlde Twiss to court by Lucy Alcock just weeks after Travers Twiss had, in a Latin oration, publicly praised Rutherford Alcock's accomplishments in Japan and China and awarded him the DCL. Pharaïlde Twiss could not have found a woman better suited for presenting her to court. Although she possessed the necessary social status, Lucy Alcock had been living for years in China and would leave Britain again with her new husband to live in Japan from 1864. She was therefore not in a position to have known Pharaïlde Twiss prior to 1862 nor in a position to follow the progress of her protégé in the years after she was presented to court. The careful choreographing of both the marriage and the rituals around the introduction of Pharaïlde to Society succeeded in creating the new personage of Pharaïlde Twiss, daughter of Dutch and Austrian aristocrats, wife of an eminent jurist, member of London Society. It was, however, the very sign of Pharaïlde Twiss's arrival as a member of London Society, her presentation at court, that triggered her and Travers Twiss's downfall.

The several years after their marriage passed relatively quietly for the Twisses, and the invention of Pharaïlde Twiss proved to be as successful as could be hoped. Twiss's professional career progressed smoothly. While Twiss was sitting on the Royal Commission on Marriage Law, Phillimore was appointed, in 1867, to the High Court of the Admiralty and also as Dean of

---

from the Athenaeum. Twiss's enthusiasm was renewed, and he wrote to Metternich: "I would have liked that you could have seen the garden of the Crystal Palace at Sydenham. It will be a grand ouvre of 'landscape gardening,' and almost all a reality. For example, there are paleontologique monsters ... the mastodon, the deionthinium, the plesiosaure, etc etc etc": Twiss to Metternich, June 26, 1854, National Archives of the Czech Republic, Prague, RAM-AC/ 10/ 780, 11.

424. "Rutherford Alcock," Athenaeum. Candidates Book, 1833-40, Mem/1/1/5, July 6, 1838, 1720.

425. Michie, *The Englishman in China*, 486. For Alcock in the North Borneo Company, see Press, *Rogue Empires*, 81–82.

the Court of Arches, and he resigned as Queen's Advocate. Twiss, at last, was appointed to the position of Queen's Advocate in August 1867, and on November 4, he received, at Windsor Castle, the knighthood that came with it.[426] The Twisses were now Sir Travers and Lady Pharaïlde. Their creation of a new persona had seemingly evaded the pitfalls encountered by Agnes Willoughby and William Windham. The only uncertainty on their horizon was Alexander Chaffers. Less than two weeks after Lucy Alcock presented Pharaïlde Twiss to Court at St James' Palace, on May 16, 1863, Travers Twiss wrote to Alexander Chaffers, his wife's former client, inviting him to dinner at the Twisses' Park Lane home on May 29 (Arthur Cook, the clerk to Twiss's solicitors, Barnes and Bernard, confirmed, when the invitation was produced by Chaffers in his libel trial, that it was written in Twiss's hand).[427] Chaffers claimed that he was invited to dinner again on a number of occasions in 1863, including June 5 and July 15, and although Pharaïlde Twiss denied this in court, Chaffers produced another undated dinner invitation written in Travers Twiss's hand.[428] He also claimed that, on June 9, Pharaïlde Twiss spent "two or three hours" with him in his office.[429] It is perhaps unsurprising that, having toured the continent with Chaffers prior to her marriage, Pharaïlde Twiss would invite him to dinner. Chaffers was also a friend of Richard Twiss, presumably because both were lawyers in the Inns of Court, but also, according to Chaffers, because they spent time together at Cremorne Gardens, where Pharaïlde Twiss first met Richard in the company of another woman, Charlotte Parre.[430] Travers Twiss may well have been happy to have his brother's friend to dinner. It is clear, however, that, in 1864, the Twisses began to distance themselves from Chaffers. The cause for their estrangement was that Chaffers had already begun to blackmail the Twisses by saying he would reveal Pharaïlde Twiss's background.

By the mid-1860s, Chaffers's financial situation was increasingly desperate. He had been disinherited by his father, and his finances would remain precarious for the rest of his life, much of which he spent in St Pancras workhouse.[431] In 1864, Chaffers wrote to Pharaïlde Twiss, demanding £150 for past

---

426. *Western Daily Press*, August 20, 1867, 2; *Yorkshire Post and Leeds Intelligencer*, November 6, 1867, 3; *Alnwick Mercury*, November 16, 1867, 6.

427. "The Charge of Libel upon Sir Travers and Lady Twiss," *Daily News*, March 13, 1863, 2.

428. "The Charge of Libel upon Sir Travers and Lady Twiss," *Daily News*, March 6, 1872, 5.

429. "The Charge of Libel upon Sir Travers and Lady Twiss," *Daily News*, March 6, 1872, 5.

430. "The Charge of Libel upon Sir Travers and Lady Twiss," *Daily News*, March 6, 1872, 5.

431. "Donne v Chaffers," *The Times*, November 29, 1867, 9; "Chaffers, A.," *The Times*, July 22, 1868, 6. See also Taggart, "Alexander Chaffers and the Genesis of the Vexatious Actions Act 1896," 657.

services he had performed for her as her solicitor.[432] Twiss's lawyers described these as "sham" demands—that is, as covers for blackmail—although in the case of Agnes Willoughby and her solicitor, James Bowen May, the services of a solicitor were essential for successful courtesans. Pharaïlde Twiss responded to Chaffers in this instance by paying him £50, for which he gave "an acknowledgement in full of all demands."[433] In 1865, the year he was disinherited, Chaffers began writing to Travers Twiss, claiming he had been snubbed by his wife. The claim to have been injured was a screen behind which to hide blackmail attempts. It should be stressed, however, that Chaffers's thirty-year pursuit of Travers and Pharaïlde Twiss was motivated by more than his financial problems. He tormented them well beyond the hope of any material gain and appeared to be driven by his own sense of justice, as well as by a growing sense of spite. Twiss responded anxiously to Chaffers's initial claims to have been snubbed (and his letter was later presented in court):

> January 9. Dear Sir, I am surprised to find that you still feel annoyed by a matter of such very unimportant signification, after your receipt of my letter of the 27th ult., which I had considered sufficient to set your anxiety at rest. But as you still seemed unable to account for my wife twice passing you in her carriage "without," as you say, "taking the slightest notice of you," you will permit me to state, as your complaint involves a question of social etiquette, that the rule which I have always understood to be received in society, and which my father, whom you well know to have been "a gentleman of the old school," always impressed on me, is for a gentleman who meets a lady of his acquaintance, passing in her carriage along the streets, to bow to her in the first instance, and for the lady to return the salutation. I have always observed this rule myself, and have impressed on my wife always to observe it. She was at the time, and still is, under the impression that you passed on your way on both occasions when you met her in the carriage without bowing to her. Faithfully yours, Travers Twiss.[434]

This letter reveals Twiss's careful attention to etiquette and formality. It further reveals Pharaïlde Twiss's transformed status and circumstances. She moved about London in her carriage and behaved in a manner consistent with the "rules," as Twiss puts it, of "society." The letter also implies that Chaffers knew not only Twiss's brother, Richard, but also his father. Given that Richard lived in the family home, it is possible that Chaffers visited the St John's Wood address while Robert Twiss was still alive, prior to 1856.

432. "Extraordinary Charges of Libel," *Morning Post*, March 1, 1872, 3.
433. "Extraordinary Charges of Libel," *Morning Post*, March 1, 1872, 3.
434. "The Charge of Libel upon Sir Travers and Lady Twiss," *Daily News*, March 13, 1872, 2.

Twiss did not succeed in placating Chaffers or in diverting his attempts at blackmail, and on May 27, 1865, he wrote again: "Dear Sir, I am very glad you have written to me, and I am happy to assure you that you are in error in that there can be any serious intention to slight you. Nobody can regret more than myself that there should be a quarrel between you and my brother, who used to be such friends, and who may be from time to time brought into contact professionally. You may be assured that I should not wish any member of my family to espouse my brother's quarrel by slighting you. Yours very faithfully, Travers Twiss".[435] Twiss still did not succeed in putting Chaffers off and, on July 31, 1865, Chaffers changed his tack, this time bringing an action in court against Travers and Pharaïlde Twiss for £121 for legal work he claimed to have performed for Pharaïlde van Lynseele between 1858 and 1862, as well as charging Twiss with slander.[436] Again, these appear to be sham claims made to extort money, and this time it worked. The hearing of a charge of slander would have brought the whole story of the Twisses' marriage into court. Twiss's solicitors settled the claim for £75, although they claimed that they paid this sum "without the knowledge of Lady Twiss or Sir Travers," thereby protecting their clients from any suggestion of being susceptible to blackmail.[437] Over the next two years, Chaffers brought a number of other actions against Twiss and "Marie Gelas" for "work done," but they were unsuccessful.[438]

In 1867, Chaffers said that he had heard of Twiss's knighthood and appointment to the position of Queen's Advocate, and he had heard, also, that Twiss planned, as a consequence of his advancement, to present his wife again at court. Chaffers claimed that he could not allow a woman of Lady Twiss's background and character to be presented to the Queen. He also had a new pretext for blackmail, although he always denied the charge of blackmail. He had by now realised that the Twisses were more susceptible to having their fashioning of Pharaïlde Twiss as a Lady of the Court revealed than they were to claims of services rendered in the past. On December 23, 1867, Chaffers wrote to Twiss from Bedford Row, close to the Inns of Court. He demanded to know "whether it is your intention to have Lady Travers Twiss presented [at court]?"[439] He could not, he said, "allow such a public scandal and such an unpardonable insult to her Majesty to be a second time perpetrated without making the Lord Chamberlain [who managed the Royal Household] acquainted with the facts." He added that if he did not receive a denial from Sir Travers of any intention to

---

435. "The Charge of Libel upon Sir Travers and Lady Twiss," *Daily News*, March 13, 1872, 2.

436. "The Charge of Libel upon Sir Travers and Lady Twiss," *Daily News*, March 13, 1872, 2.

437. "Extraordinary Charges of Libel," *Morning Post*, March 1, 3.

438. "The Charge of Libel upon Sir Travers and Lady Twiss," *Daily News*, March 13, 1872, 2.

439. Alexander Chaffers, *The Twiss Libel Case*, 3.

again present Lady Twiss to Court, he would "lay before the Lord Chamberlain a statement of the facts."

Receiving no response from Twiss, Chaffers wrote again on January 9, 1868, threatening that if he received no assurances—including, presumably, financial assurances—within one week, he would write to the Lord Chamberlain. Still, he received no response, and on February 1, he wrote to Lady Twiss, this time in French, saying that he had written two letters to her husband in which he "explained" that if they had the "audacity" to present her again to Her Majesty the Queen, he would be obliged to tell the Lord Chamberlain "all the facts because I could not permit for a second time such a great scandal."[440] He warned, "I do not know whether you have told your husband all the truth but now he must know all." It is uncertain what "all the truth" might mean, given that Twiss was aware that his wife was a prostitute when they first met, having kept her initially at £20 a week, but it corresponds with similar statements Twiss would make himself in years to come about other, unnamed, scandals involving his wife. Chaffers continued this letter by saying that he knew that Lady Twiss had always said that she would "deny everything," but that she should know that he had many witnesses to her true identity, including her parents, "everyone at Berlin," and "the woman, tenant of Half Moon Street, living in that well-known house [i.e., the brothel] close to Piccadilly." He concluded by saying that he regretted the necessity of these measures, but that he had not forgotten the injuries she had done him, for which he would soon take action against her and her husband. He finally apologised for the faults in his French but noted that he had not "at present a little woman from Courtrai as a teacher, and it shows."[441] Still receiving no response, Chaffers wrote to Travers Twiss again, on February 6. Although the Twisses had not responded to Chaffers, Pharaïlde Twiss had not been presented to court again, which Chaffers claimed would be his reason for having to take further action. Nevertheless, he now took his cause beyond the Twisses, and in doing so, he began to lose any power of blackmail he could have over them. Once his claims about Pharaïlde Twiss were made public, his pursuit of the Twisses was no longer financial but vengeful.

On April 17, 1868, Chaffers wrote to Sir Rutherford Alcock in Japan. Alcock had indeed returned to Japan, with Lucy Alcock, as Consul General in 1864, but, by 1868, they had moved to Peking (now Beijing), so it is not certain that Alcock received the letter. In it, Chaffers asked whether Lucy Alcock had "satisfied herself as to Mrs Twiss being a fit and proper person" prior to presenting her to St James's Court. He wondered whether the Alcocks had made any inquiries upon the subject and warned that their correspondence may be "laid

---

440. Chaffers, *The Twiss Libel Case*, 4.
441. Chaffers, *The Twiss Libel Case*, 4.

before the Lord Chamberlain."⁴⁴² On May 19, 1868, Chaffers wrote again to Lady Twiss, telling her he had written to Rutherford Alcock and saying that he would send his response (which never came), along with a "statement of the facts," to the Lord Chamberlain. He said he would also send the same statement and correspondence to the Archbishop of Canterbury, the Lord Chancellor, the Attorney General, and the Chancellor of the University of Oxford—that is, to Travers Twiss's employers.⁴⁴³ Despite these threats, Chaffers said that, at this point in mid-1868, he took no further steps because Lady Twiss had still not been presented for a second time at court five years after her first presentation.

In 1869, the Twisses called Chaffers's bluff and continued with their invention of Lady Travers Twiss by attending court. The fact that they did so indicates how important her presence at court was to her reinvention. On Wednesday, March 10, Lady Twiss once again attended a Queen's Drawing Room, and this time the Queen herself was present. Having already been formally presented at court, Lady Twiss appears in the list of attendees, as one of the "Ladies," following the Duchesses, Marchionesses, Earls, Viscounts, Viscountesses, and Lords, but preceding the "Honourables," the "Messieurs," and the "Mesdames."⁴⁴⁴ Travers Twiss was not in the list of attendees. Chaffers saw the report on the Queen's Drawing Room in *The Times* and, true to his word, wrote to the Lord Chamberlain, John Townshend, on March 16, 1869. His letter was simple, announcing that Lady Twiss "was not a fit and proper person" to have been present at the Queen's Drawing Room held on the previous Wednesday. This fact, he said, was well known to her husband, "her Majesty's Advocate General," and could be proved by testimony. The Lord Chamberlain's comptroller, Spencer Ponsonby, remembered more as a cricketer than a public servant, replied to Chaffers two days later, asking if he was "prepared to furnish proofs."⁴⁴⁵ Chaffers responded with his claims about the true identity of Lady Twiss. She had, he said, lived under the name Marie Gelas and lived in South Street, Brompton, while being kept by Travers Twiss "as his mistress and living under his protection." She had also been "an habituée at a well-known establishment in a street leading out of Piccadilly [i.e., the brothel in Half Moon Street]." He said he had "several witnesses" who could corroborate these facts, and he believed that, if questioned, Sir Travers Twiss would confirm them. Ponsonby wrote to Chaffers, saying that the Lord Chamberlain had made inquiries about his claims without being able to establish their truth and asked if Chaffers had any objection to his name being used in his further

442. Chaffers, *The Twiss Libel Case*, 4.
443. Chaffers, *The Twiss Libel Case*, 5.
444. "The Queen's Drawing Room," *London Evening Standard*, March 11, 1869, 3.
445. Chaffers, *The Twiss Libel Case*, 5.

inquires.[446] Chaffers replied, consenting and suggesting the Lord Chamberlian write to Twiss, asking him "the status in society of the family of Lady Twiss" and also if and where Lady Twiss had resided in England prior to her marriage. He also suggested that the Lord Chamberlain, who had permitted the presentation of Pharaïlde Twiss to court on the recommendation of Lady Alcock, should write to the Alcocks to "know what acquaintance Lady Alcock had with Lady Twiss prior to Lady Alcock becoming sponsor for Lady Twiss's presentation at Court."[447] If Chaffers knew that Twiss had presented Rutherford Alcock for the DCL at Oxford and that Lady's Alcock's presentation of Pharaïlde Twiss at court was the quid pro quo, he was not saying so.

Ponsonby responded to Chaffers, telling him that the Lord Chamberlain had informed Twiss about the "charge" that Chaffers had made against him and his wife. If the accusations were untrue, Chaffers was now guilty of having libelled the Twisses, but it would be another three years before the charge of libel was brought to court. The following month, Ponsonby again wrote to Chaffers to tell him that the Lord Chamberlain had made inquiries "as to the accusations," that Twiss had made a "distinct denial" of their truth, and that it was not his intention to "take any further steps in the matter."[448] Chaffers replied by asking for a copy of Twiss's denial and demanding precisely which accusations Twiss had denied. He declared that he could not "lie under the imputation of having made a false accusation" and said he would take "steps by which the matter may be judicially inquired into."[449] Ponsonby answered simply that the Lord Chamberlain declined to "give you the information you require."

Chaffers changed his approach and wrote to the Queen's private secretary, Charles Grey. He outlined his entire correspondence with the Lord Chamberlain's office, and advised that the matter would be brought before the House of Commons, presumably by Chaffers's member of parliament (although this never happened). He also asked for Grey to make inquiries, and repeated, "I cannot submit to lie under the imputation of having made a false accusation," which the Lord Chamberlain's refusal to pursue the matter "fixes upon me."[450] On May 23, 1869, Grey replied that he could not have anything to do with a matter that lay entirely in the province of the Lord Chamberlain and sent his reply and Chaffers's letter to his office.

Chaffers took no further action until he read in *The Times*, almost two years later, on March 6, 1871, that Sir Travers and Lady Twiss had been present at a reception given at the Foreign Office by Lord Granville, the Secretary

---

446. Chaffers, *The Twiss Libel Case*, 6.
447. Chaffers, *The Twiss Libel Case*, 7.
448. Chaffers, *The Twiss Libel Case*, 7.
449. Chaffers, *The Twiss Libel Case*, 8.
450. Chaffers, *The Twiss Libel Case*, 9.

of State for Foreign Affairs. The company at this banquet were led by a large contingent of nobility, including the Prince and Princess of Wales, Prince and Princess Teck, the Prince and Princess of Saxe Weimer, and numerous dukes and earls, as well as the ambassadors of most of the major powers and many lesser ones.[451] Sir Travers and Lady Twiss were in their midst, and Chaffers was newly enraged. He now wrote to Granville. Twiss had worked with Granville over many years. He had written to Granville, as we have seen, in 1857, conveying the offer from the Bohemian count Charles Taaffe, to equip and command a regiment to help supress the Indian Rebellion.[452] More than twenty-five years later, Granville, as Secretary of State for Foreign Affairs once again, would use Twiss's expertise at the 1884–1885 Berlin Conference (despite the scandal that still clung to Twiss). Chaffers, however, in 1871, wrote to Granville to reveal another dimension to Twiss. He informed him that Twiss had "kept" his wife "as his mistress" prior to his marriage, that she had at that time lived under the name of Madame Gelas, that she was a "habituée" of the "well known" Half Moon Street brothel, and that all these facts could be proven by several witnesses. He pointed out that this woman had been presented at court by Lady Alcock and that, despite his attempts to bring the matter to the attention of the Lord Chamberlain, no action had been taken. He added that he had himself "frequently paid my sovereign and partaken of her hospitality *mensae et thori* [from table and bed]."[453] Implicating himself in the scandal was a new step and reflected a growing desperation. His stated logic was that he was prepared to expose his own dishonour in order to preserve the public honour. Nevertheless, Granville ignored his letter.

Relentless, Chaffers turned back to Twiss, writing to him, on March 13, 1871, to tell him about all that he had attempted, and failed, with the Lord Chamberlain, the Alcocks, and Granville. He said that "one of us" was guilty of "direct and wilful falsehood" and that, because he could not live under "such an imputation," he would now seek to have the matter brought before a tribunal and would also write to the Archbishop of Canterbury and the Lord Chamberlain.[454] Deciding that he had to take further steps in order to provoke a more public dispute, Chaffers made a statutory declaration at Bow Street Police Court on April 4, 1871, stating:

> I, Alexander Chaffers, of 89, York Road, Lambeth, in the County of Surrey, gentleman, do solemnly and sincerely declare as follows—1. I have been for several years past acquainted with Sir Travers Twiss, Bart., of 19 Park Lane, in the county of Middlesex, Queen's Advocate, and Dame

---

451. "The Extraordinary Charge of Libel," *The Times*, March 6, 1871, 10.
452. "Twiss to Granville," August 28, 1857, Granville Papers, National Archives, London, 30/29/23/10, 447–450.
453. Chaffers, *The Twiss Libel Case*, 10.
454. Chaffers, *The Twiss Libel Case*, 11.

Pharaïlde, his wife. 2. The said Travers Twiss was married to Pharaïlde Vanlynseele in August, 1862, at Dresden, in the Kingdom of Saxony. 3. The said Pharaïlde Vanlynseele is a native of Belgium and resided in London for several years previous to 1862, and always went under the name of Maria Gelas. In April, 1859, the said Maria Gelas was living in lodgings at 12 Upper Berkeley Street, Connaught Square, and continued to reside there until the month of September, 1859, when she removed, and took a house in South Street, Thurloe Square. In 1860 the said Maria Gelas took a house in Neville Terrace, Brompton, where she resided until March, 1862. 4. My first acquaintance with the said Maria Gelas was on Friday, 15th of April, 1859, when I spoke to her in Regent Street between nine and ten o'clock in the evening, and accompanied her to her lodgings in Upper Berkeley Street, where I remained with her a couple of hours and gave her a sovereign. 5. I subsequently visited the said Maria Gelas very frequently, and constantly passed the whole night with her. 6. In the summer of 1859, I frequently saw the said Maria Gelas at Cremorne Gardens, sometimes alone and sometimes in company with another foreign prostitute. 7. On the 18th of August, 1859, the said Maria Gelas informed me of her intimacy with the said Travers Twiss, and on the 27th of August, 1859, the said Maria Gelas informed me that the said Travers Twiss had agreed to keep her as his mistress and allow her £5 a week. 8. I have frequently seen the said Maria Gelas at the Argyll Rooms, different music halls in the Haymarket, and at the Holborn Casino. On one occasion, I saw the said Maria Gelas dancing at the Holborn Casino with her hair all hanging down, and further so misconducting herself that the master of the ceremonies was obliged to speak to her. 9. The said Travers Twiss regularly visited her (the said Maria Gelas) and kept her as his mistress from August, 1859, to March, 1862. In March, 1862, the said Travers Twiss sent the said Maria Gelas to Dresden, where it was arranged she was to remain until the following August, when the said Travers Twiss was to join and be then married. 10. Previous to the said Maria Gelas leaving London in March, 1862, the said Travers Twiss gave her four promissory notes for £500 each. And I make this solemn declaration, conscientiously believing the same to be true, and by virtue of the provisions of an act made and provided. Declared at the Police Court Bow Street, in the county of Middlesex, this 4th day of April, 1871, A. Chaffers. L. Vaughan, one of the magistrates of the police courts of the metropolis.[455]

Just as Chaffers paid careful attention to the various addresses at which Maria Gelas resided, thereby highlighting her improving fortunes, it is notable

---

[455]. "Extraordinary Charges of Libel," *The Standard*, March 1, 1972, 6.

that his own address, given in the opening of the declaration, reflects his own declining fortunes. Whereas his earlier letters had been written from addresses in the Inns of Court, he now gave York Road, Lambeth, as his residence, between Lambeth Palace and the rapidly growing Waterloo Station. Much of this area on the south bank of the Thames, with the exception of the Archbishop's palace, had been marshland until the early nineteenth century, and it was then developed for markets, as well as the railway. The journalist George Augustus Sala, who contributed to Dickens's *Household Words* (to which Twiss subscribed), was a close observer of Lambeth. Writing of one street in particular, "The Cut," Sala declared in 1859: "It is simply Low. It is sordid, squalid, and, the truth must out, disreputable . . . there is mingled with the poverty, a flaunting, idle, vagabond, beggarly-fine don't care a centishness."[456] Of Bow Street Police Court, where Chaffers made his declaration, Sala wrote that there "hangs an indefinable but pervading miasma of meanness and squalor. A settled mildew seems to infect the walls and ceiling."[457]

Apart from the environment in which Chaffers made his declaration, we see from its content that he was prepared to ruin his reputation (he could not descend much further materially, although he would take the next step down into the workhouse) in order to ruin Sir Travers and Lady Pharaïlde Twiss. He portrayed Lynseele as the lowest class of prostitute, having discovered her in Regent Street, where the Belgian prostitutes concentrated. He also connected her with all the popular haunts in which gentlemen met prostitutes, the Haymarket music halls, Cremorne Gardens, Holborn Casino, and the Argyll Rooms. According to the dates he provided, his own relations with Maria Gelas, or Pharaïlde van Lynseele, overlapped with those between herself and Twiss. One of the striking aspects of Chaffers's testimony is the speed with which Twiss went from having met Lynseele to agreeing to keep her as his mistress—a mere nine days.

On the same day, April 4, that Chaffers made this statutory declaration, he sent copies of it to Viscount Castlerosse, the Vice Chamberlain of Her Majesty's Household.[458] The Viscount was deputy to the Lord Chamberlain and responsible for communication between the sovereign and the House of Commons. The letter recounted all the details of Chaffers's unsuccessful pursuit of the Twisses over the preceding years and claimed that the Viscount needed the facts before him when two members of the House of Commons would (so Chaffers said) question him on the subject.[459] Castlerosse, however, replied to Chaffers to say he had sent his correspondence to the Lord

---

456. George Augustus Sala, *Twice Round the Clock; or the Hours of the Day and Night in London* (London, 1859), 274.
457. Sala, *Twice Round the Clock*, 120.
458. Chaffers, *The Twiss Libel Case*, 12.
459. "The Travers Twiss Case," *New Zealand Herald*, May 22, 1872, 3.

Chamberlain, whom Chaffers had already unsuccessfully attempted to alert to the case. Nevertheless, Chaffers wrote to Ponsonby once again to ask if the Lord Chamberlain would do anything to investigate the allegations. Ponsonby replied, on April 25, that the Lord Chamberlain had communicated the statutory declaration to Twiss and that he had no intention to take "further steps in the matter."[460] Clearly disturbed, Twiss now took an important new step: he wrote to his good friend, mentor, and professional collaborator of many years, Archibald Tait.

When Twiss had married in Dresden in 1862, Tait had been the Bishop of London and, in the same year, when Archbishop Sumner had died, Charles Longley was created as the new person of the Archbishop through the ceremony performed in part by Twiss. Longley only lasted six years, however, and, when he died, Tait was nominated the new Archbishop of Canterbury in November 1868. This meant that Tait vacated his position as Bishop of London. His replacement was John Jackson, Bishop of Lincoln. In St Paul's Cathedral, in late January 1869, Jackson was confirmed as the new Bishop in a ceremony in which Travers Twiss officiated. After "various schedules were read and signed," Jackson "knelt down before the Vicar General [Twiss], and took the usual oaths. Sir Travers Twiss then declared a definitive sentence, and this act ipso facto filled the diocese of London and vacated the diocese of Lincoln."[461] Twiss, as always, was the master in the creation of new persons, and in the case of new bishops, his mere words performed the acts to transform a man from being one person to another.

One week later, with Tait freed from the diocese of London, he was "enthroned with great state," as *The Times* reported, in a ceremony in which Twiss again, as Vicar General of the Province of Canterbury, officiated alongside his former protégé from University College, Arthur Stanley, the Dean of Westminster. Three thousand worshippers attended the ceremony of enthronement at Canterbury Cathedral. The bishops and clergy entered the thronged cathedral in all-white surplices in the middle of which were "the scarlet gowns of the Vicar-General (Sir Travers Twiss)" who carried the mandate for the Archbishop.[462] The Archbishop-elect then entered the cathedral and took his seat on the throne, at which point "the Vicar General [Twiss] presented to the Archdeacon the mandate of enthronement," which the Archdeacon read, completing the enthronement.

The three men, two standing next to the throne, the other sitting on it, had been close friends for over thirty years and were now at the centre of this ceremony performed with "great state." Twiss, as we saw, had helped Arthur Stanley to a fellowship in 1839, while Stanley, like Twiss, had been a

460. Chaffers, *The Twiss Libel Case*, 13.
461. *Stamford Mercury*, February 5, 1869, 6.
462. *The Times*, February 5, 1869, 10.

long-standing friend of Tait. Stanley wrote to Tait, addressing him affectionately by his nickname as "my Dear Belvedere," while Tait addressed Stanley as "My Dear Child."[463] These men had come together at Oxford to meet the challenge of the Tractarians—a challenge, as they saw it, not only to the Church of England but to the sovereignty of the state. The fact that, thirty years later, they held a number of the most powerful offices in the church reflects their determination to stymie the Oxford Movement within the institution of the church. If we are to believe the supporters of the Oxford Movement, writing a generation later, the purpose of Twiss, Tait, and Stanley was also to stymie an understanding of society in which the creation of new corporate persons could occur outside the control of the state.[464] A liberal society, according to these critics, would allow such artificial persons, and indeed all persons, to flourish virtually unrestricted alongside, rather than underneath, the state. According to this view, Twiss, Tait, and Stanley were reactionaries seeking to maintain a hegemony of the state and the established church over all aspects of life. Such a portrait would not have been inaccurate for Twiss in the 1840s, but we know that, by the 1850s, he had come to a different understanding of the elasticity of society. Nevertheless, he sought to maintain that new outlook beneath an exterior of conservatism, including the collective triumph of the three friends from Oxford in the ceremony of the enthronement.

The three of them now stood around the throne in Canterbury Cathedral while Twiss delivered the mandate creating Tait as the new person of the Archbishop. After the service, a select group of guests were invited for lunch in the cathedral library to celebrate the event. The three men retired to the lunch with their wives, and although *The Times* does not specify, this would have meant Tait with Catherine Tait, daughter of William Spooner, Archdeacon of Coventry; Stanley with Lady Augusta Stanley, daughter of Thomas Bruce, the seventh Earl of Elgin (the man who removed the Elgin Marbles), a lady-in-waiting to Queen Victoria and sister of Lord Elgin, Viceroy of India and the man who ordered the destruction of the Old Summer Palace in Beijing; and Twiss with Pharaïlde Twiss, who was the daughter of Pierre Denis van Lynseele and Thérèse Vanderschoore, peasants of Courtrai, but who had been re-created as the daughter of Count van Lynseele, a major general in the Dutch and Polish armies.

This was the comfortable and powerful world that Chaffers, with his obsession and fury, now descended upon. Once Twiss received word from the Lord Chamberlain, on April 25, 1871, that Chaffers had made the statutory declaration, he decided that he must inform Tait, whom Chaffers had already threatened to contact. On April 27, he wrote to Tait to warn him that he could receive a slanderous letter from Chaffers, "an unprincipled scoundrel," regarding him

---

463. Davidson and Benham, *Life of Archibald Campbell Tait*, Vol. 1, 93.
464. Laski, *Studies in the Problem of Sovereignty*.

and his wife.[465] Within two weeks, on May 8, Twiss received another letter from Chaffers, saying that he was not surprised that Lady Twiss should "deny the charges made against her," but that he was astonished by Sir Travers's "audacity" in denying that he had kept her as his mistress "for some years."[466] A month later, on June 10, Twiss wrote to Tait again, setting out the story of the "most wicked libel" in more detail.[467] Chaffers, receiving no responses from his letters, sought new material. On July 14, 1871, the jeweller Denis Faure made a further statutory declaration at Bow Street Police Court regarding Lady Twiss, stating, "The real and proper name of the said Maria Gelas was Pharaïlde Vanlynseele." Faure declared that he was "well acquainted with Marie Gelas" in 1859 and 1860 and gave her addresses in South Street Brompton and Neville Terrace Brompton. He stated also that her mother, father, and brother lived with her.[468] On July 17, Chaffers sent Faure's declaration to the Lord Chamberlain's office, along with a copy of the Twisses' marriage certificate. The following day, he sent his own statutory declaration of April 4 to Lord Granville, to Rutherford Alcock, and to Twiss's solicitors, Barnes and Bernard.[469] Infuriatingly, for Chaffers, he did not receive responses from these efforts, and Twiss and Lynseele did not, as he expected, sue him for libel, despite the very public nature of the humiliation. The Twisses were apparently concerned about the evidence Chaffers could present in court to prove Lady Twiss was indeed the woman he claimed her to be. Owing to the lack of any "acknowledgement," as Chaffers put it, from any of the parties, the matter was quiet for a few months while he waited for his next opportunity.

That opportunity involved Baroness Angela Burdett-Coutts, the daughter of Sir Francis Burdett and Sophia Coutts, from the Coutts banking family. In 1837, as a young woman (born in 1814), Burdett-Coutts inherited her grandfather Thomas Coutts's fortune and became the wealthiest woman in Britain. She devoted her fortune to philanthropy. One of her earliest projects was the creation in 1847 of a home for the redemption of prostitutes, Urania Cottage, in which she collaborated with Charles Dickens.[470] Burdett-Coutts also pursued a number of projects with the church, including the creation of colonial bishoprics, which required the legal expertise of Travers Twiss.[471] In the

---

465. Twiss to A. C. Tait, 27 April 1871, Lambeth Palace Library, Tait Papers, Tait 176 ff. 348–349.

466. Chaffers, *The Twiss Libel Case*, 13.

467. Twiss to A. C. Tait, June 10, 1871, Lambeth Palace Library, Tait Papers, Tait 176, ff.350–351.

468. Chaffers, *The Twiss Libel Case*, 14.

469. Chaffers, *The Twiss Libel Case*, 14

470. "Coutts, Angela Georgina Burdett-, suo jure Baroness Burdett-Coutts (1814–1906)," *Oxford Dictionary of National Biography* (Oxford, 2019).

471. Memorandum of a Convention, undated, Lambeth Palace Library, Papers of Baroness Burdett-Coutts, MS 1381, ff.161–163.

FIGURE 15. Columbia Market in 1869.*

1860s, Burdett-Coutts bought land in the East of London. She demolished the slums there and built, for £170,000, the Columbia Market, named after British Columbia, where she had recently established a new bishopric, with Twiss's aid.

Her idea was that the market would increase the supply of food to the poorest area of London. The structure, as *The Times* observed, was perhaps more fit for a cathedral or a university. In any case, it did not flourish as a market because the majority of sellers preferred outdoor markets. At this time, on advice from Dickens, she also built Columbia Dwellings nearby, in an attempt to provide housing for the poor. Owing to the failure of the market, Burdett-Coutts decided to transfer the titles to the buildings in trust to the Corporation of London in the hope that it might find a better use for them (they would later be demolished). To negotiate this transfer, she once again employed Twiss.[472]

On October 16, 1871, Chaffers wrote to Twiss's solicitors to say that he had noticed that the Corporation of London planned a celebration of "the transfer of Columbia market" and that it would be inviting Baroness Burdett Coutts and the Twisses to that celebration. Chaffers wrote that he objected to Lady Twiss as a proper person to be a guest of the Corporation. He had originally argued that Lady Twiss was an inappropriate person to be presented at court; he had now expanded his fabricated indignation to include the city. He promised that he would send the Lord Mayor a copy of his statutory declaration, as well as sending a copy to Burdett-Coutts. True to his word, three days later, he sent Burdett-Coutts, who took an active interest in the improvement of the lives of prostitutes, his statutory declaration that Lady Twiss had herself been a prostitute.[473] At the same time, he sent a copy of the declaration to Mr Bontems, the chairman of the London Corporation's Markets Committee. Twiss

---

472. "Columbia Market," *The Times*, September 15, 1871, 9.
473. Chaffers, *The Twiss Libel Case*, 15.
* *The Illustrated London News*, May 1, 1869, 440; accessed through Archive.org

nevertheless attended the ceremony to mark the handover, on November 4, although Lady Twiss was not mentioned (as Twiss's letters written in the following days reveal, she was in Belgium), and he was thanked warmly in the speeches for having conducted the transfer. *The Times* reported, "The transfer had been previously negotiated on behalf of the Baroness by three gentlemen of consideration and standing, in whom she had complete confidence, at the head of whom was Sir Travers Twiss," and Mr Bontems, the chair of the Markets Committee, was particularly concerned to "offer the thanks of the committee to their friend Sir Travers Twiss."[474] Given that Bontems and Burdett-Coutts had both received Chaffers's statutory declaration in the previous two weeks, their public statements of complete confidence in Twiss were timely.

In private, however, the tone was different. Within days of the ceremony for Columbia Market, perhaps further provoked by the public statements of support for Twiss, on November 9, Chaffers sent copies of his statutory declaration to Archbishop Tait, to his friend Dr Tristram in the Doctors' Commons, and also to his other employers and persons of influence, the Bishops of London (John Jackson), Lincoln, Hereford, and St David's, as well as the Archbishop of York, the Earl of Harrowby (Dudley Ryder), known as a stalwart defender of the Church of England, and the Home Secretary, the Right Honourable H. A. Bruce.[475] Twiss had refrained from prosecuting until this point, but now Tait left him no choice, no doubt concerned about the reputation of the church, which had been damaged by other scandals in recent years. The day after he received Chaffers's letter, Archbishop Tait wrote to Twiss to say that he had at last received the letter Twiss had warned him about and that so had the Lord Chamberlain, thus revealing that he had been in discussions with the Lord Chamberlain about the matter. Tait instructed Twiss: "I think under the circumstances you have no course open to you, but to prosecute the man for libel."[476] His reference to the Lord Chamberlain implied that they had come to this view jointly. He now instructed Twiss to do precisely what Chaffers wanted, to pursue a public trial, and what Twiss had clearly wished to avoid. The only other option for Twiss was recorded by his close friend, Goldwin Smith, in his *Reminiscences*, where he said that, at this juncture, "a prudent friend" of Twiss "offered to take the blackmailer out of the way by finding him constant employment abroad. But they determined to go into court."[477] Twiss apparently decided that even Australia was not far enough away for Alexander Chaffers and that a sentence of hard labour for criminal libel was his best chance of silencing him.

---

474. *The Times*, November 4, 1871, 12.

475. Chaffers, *The Twiss Libel Case*, 15. For Chaffers's letter to Tristram, see "The Charge of Libel upon Sir Travers and Lady Twiss," *Daily News*, March 13, 1872, 2.

476. Tait to Twiss, November 10, 1871, Lambeth Palace Library, Tait Papers, 176, f.352.

477. Smith, *Reminiscences*, 86.

Finally cornered by Chaffers, Twiss had no choice but to respond to Tait by return of post, on November 11, agreeing that he must prosecute the "calumnies."[478] The same day, he wrote to the Bishop of London, John Jackson, the man who employed him as Chancellor of the Diocese of London, warning Jackson that he may "possibly have received a letter from A. Chaffers" which contained "a libel of myself and Lady T."[479] Twiss used his letter to portray Chaffers as a bankrupt and a blackmailer: "He is a bankrupt who has been persecuting me for some time with false actions for debt and libel." "He has been twice bankrupt in 1866 and 1868. After his bankruptcy he could not bring any more actions so he took to writing slanderous letters."[480] With a "view to extorting money from me," Twiss claimed, "he has put his libel into circulation." "Lady T," Twiss announced, "will return from Belgium this week," at which point he would be "under the necessity of prosecuting him criminally," as she was the principal subject of the alleged libel.[481] At the top of this letter, Jackson scrawled: "Twiss: The man I believe to be a little mad but thoroughly indignant," giving some insight into private perceptions of Twiss but also suggesting that at this point Jackson, at least, was prepared to give him the benefit of the doubt.[482]

A month later, on December 28, Twiss wrote to Jackson again, this time at greater length, giving some outline of his and Lady Twiss's defence: "I must trespass on your kindness to assist me in punishing that infamous man who signs himself 'A Chaffers.'"[483] By referring to Chaffers in this way, Twiss put in question who Chaffers claimed to be, thereby diverting attention from whether Lady Twiss was the person she claimed to be. He told Jackson that he would need an affidavit from him confirming that he had received the defamatory letter from Chaffers in order for the Twisses to proceed against Chaffers in a criminal case for libel. Twiss explained: "I could have proceeded against him some time ago by civil action for damages but it would have been a practical absurdity from which I recoiled, as the man has been twice bankrupt, is living in a small backroom on the Surrey side of Waterloo Bridge where he keeps himself alive by copying law papers and has been reported to me by one who saw him lately in the streets as having barely shoes and clothes fit to be worn.

---

478. Twiss to Tait, November 11, 1871, Lambeth Palace Library, Tait Papers, 176, ff. 353–354.

479. Twiss to Jackson, November 11, 1871, Lambeth Palace Library, Jackson Papers, 33, f.140.

480. Twiss to Jackson, November 11, 1871, Lambeth Palace Library, Jackson Papers, 33, ff.140v–141r.

481. Twiss to Jackson, November 11, 1871, Lambeth Palace Library, Jackson Papers, 33, f.141v.

482. Twiss to Jackson, November 11, 1871, Lambeth Palace Library, Jackson Papers, 33, f.140.

483. Twiss to Jackson, December 28, 1871, Lambeth Palace Library, Jackson Papers, 33, f.142.

By sending his declaration to yourself and the other bishops with whom I am officially connected, he has I hope brought himself within the reach of the criminal law and Sir John Karslake will apply on the first or second day of next term for a criminal information against him but for this purpose."[484] Chaffers was as poor as Twiss claimed. The census of the same year showed that Chaffers was one of two lodgers living with a family of six, the Painter family, at 89 York Road, Lambeth.[485]

Twiss plausibly argued that, given Chaffers was so poor, a civil suit against him for defamation would not have led to the award of any recoverable damages, albeit that for the Twisses the important issue in a trial would be the truth of the claims, not compensation. By the terms of the Libel Act of 1843, criminal cases for libel, on the other hand, could only be pursued in instances of serious harm which disturbed the public peace. Most libel cases were brought as civil torts: that is, for damages. Criminal libel was an unusual charge that had its origins in seventeenth-century sedition laws. By the terms of the same Act, a defence in such cases had to prove that the allegedly defamatory statements were made for the public good. It was not sufficient that a statement, if damaging to another person, could be shown to be true; it also had to have a public benefit. Chaffers, a solicitor, knew the law and anticipated his defence, from his constant repetition that the presentation of Lady Twiss to the Queen and to the Corporation of London was damaging to the public good. Given that the public-good defence was not needed in the common law tort for libel, it is clear that Chaffers anticipated that he could be prosecuted under the criminal law. Moreover, the 1843 Act permitted, for the first time, a defence against the charge of criminal libel by the proof that the claims made were true. This allowed Chaffers to prove his innocence by demonstrating that Lady Twiss had indeed been a prostitute and had been Travers Twiss's mistress. The stakes, however, were high, as the punishment for criminal libel was imprisonment and hard labour. Twiss also revealed in this passage from the letter to Jackson that his barrister was Sir John Karslake, who had defended William Windham against the charge of lunacy for having married a prostitute who happened to have been Travers Twiss's previous mistress. The legal world was small and interconnected.

Having explained to Jackson why he had taken so long to prosecute Chaffers, Twiss moved on to the details of preparations for the trial. He complained that "it could be a year before it could be tried, such is the state of the criminal law," and this observation led him to the difficulty of finding witnesses: "One of my most important witnesses whom he [Chaffers] attempted to secure to his

---

484. Twiss to Jackson, December 28, 1871, Lambeth Palace Library, Jackson Papers, 33, ff.143–144.

485. *Census Returns of England and Wales, 1871*, National Archives, London, Class: RG10, Piece: 651; Folio: 41; 13; GSU roll: 818940.

side by a bribe of £150 some time back is dying of cancer but we shall obtain his affidavit. Other witnesses will have to be brought over from Belgium who will prove that Lady T was not in England at the times specified in 1859. I may have to bring over witnesses from Germany, but so many persons are dead or dispersed that it is not easy to find some who would have been available at an earlier period [i.e., who would have been available if Lady Twiss had been libelled ten years earlier]." This would become a familiar refrain in the Twisses' case: namely, all the people connected to Lady Twiss in the past were dead or had disappeared. "We shall see," he concluded, "what the Law of England is worth in such matters."[486]

While preparing his case, Twiss continued with his usual engagements. On the day before he sent this letter to Bishop Jackson, he attended an annual dinner in support of "schools for the orphan and necessitous children of commercial travellers."[487] He said in his speech to the dinner that he was present on behalf of Baroness Burdett-Coutts. His supporters clearly still wished to make a public display of confidence in him, even if, like Tait, they urged him to bring the matter to a conclusion. Frustrated, as always, and unaware that Twiss was at last building a case for criminal libel against him, Chaffers wrote to Tait on January 2, 1872, asking why he had not responded to his statutory declaration, pointing out that if his allegations were true, Twiss would not be "a fit person to hold the appointment of Vicar-General of the Province of Canterbury," and threatening that if he continued to receive no response, he would bring the matter to the attention of "Convocation"—that is, to the church council upon which both Twiss and Tait sat.[488]

On January 11, 1872, Twiss wrote again to Jackson, thanking him for forwarding Chaffers's letters—the first task in a libel trial was to prove publication of the libel, so the collection of this evidence was important. He then observed, "The man is full of expedients, it is a pity he cannot turn them to a better purpose," a comment that revealed a grudging and justified admiration for Chaffers's legal inventiveness. Twiss turned to the legal problems of the case, noting, "Our law is very peculiar. If he had any means to warrant my bringing a civil action, we should be on equal terms—but in regard to criminal proceedings, if I should proceed by information, he will bring in an affidavit, to which I shall not be allowed to answer, if by indictment, we cannot cross-examine him."[489] This observation, in the first instance, ignored the fact that Twiss had previously explained that he had deliberately shunned making a civil case for libel against Chaffers. The matter of whether the action was

486. Twiss to Jackson, December 28, 1871, Lambeth Palace Library, Jackson Papers, 33, f.142–146.
487. *The Times*, December 28, 1871, 3.
488. Chaffers, *The Twiss Libel Case*, 15.
489. Twiss to Jackson, January 11, 1872, Lambeth Palace Library, Jackson Papers, 33, ff.148–49.

brought by "information" or "indictment" was a very old one in English law which concerned whether the case was brought by the court or the prosecution, but in either case, it reflected Twiss's anxiety that the details of the case would be publicly aired and not refuted. He said he would send Jackson the affidavits when they were ready, and the Bishop would then "understand what a dangerous man he is to grapple with." "The trial," he gloomily concluded, "is a practical absurdity."[490]

A week later, Twiss wrote to Tait that he should not be surprised to receive another letter from Chaffers, as he had received "credible information that he is concocting more slanders against me." He promised Tait that, when he received the affidavits Twiss had collected regarding Chaffers, he would see "what a wicked and dangerous man he is."[491] He said he had employed a detective to "ascertain if he has any confederates," but lamented that "the misfortune is that he requires no legal aid, and is an adept at the game which he is playing." He also announced that he had decided to proceed against Chaffers through an indictment. The previous day, Twiss wrote an almost identical letter to Jackson, showing that he was carefully managing the views of his employers. "The police," Twiss observed, "have their eye upon him to ascertain if he has any confederates." He concluded, "He is a more dangerous man than Tichborne as he knows too well the use of words and how to steer within an inch of the law and does not require the assistance of a lawyer. I have determined to indict him but it will be a very long business and very troublesome."[492]

The difference between the two letters was the reference to Tichborne. Twiss was not the only person to notice parallels between his own troubles and the Tichborne case, which was on the front pages of the newspapers in the early months of 1872, alongside Twiss's own case when it came to trial. Many of the participants in the two cases made connections and comparisons between them, including Twiss himself in this instance, Chaffers, the newspaper reports, and, as we shall see, a barrister in the Tichborne case. Each of these participants seized upon different aspects of the two cases to compare, but underlying them all was a strong common element in the two trials: namely, both were cases which centred upon the invention of a person, and that invented person, in both cases, was alleged to be false. For Twiss, Tichborne was dangerous because he impersonated a member of the aristocracy, thereby raising the radical possibility that aristocracy was a matter of performance and ritual rather than "blood," as he put it. Of course, privately, this is precisely the understanding that Lynseele and Twiss had reached.

490. Twiss to Jackson, January 11, 1872, Lambeth Palace Library, Jackson Papers, 33, ff.148–149.
491. Twiss to Tait, January 19, 1872, Lambeth Palace Library, Tait Papers, 184, ff.70–71.
492. Twiss to Jackson, January 18, 1872, Lambeth Palace Library, Jackson Papers, 33, ff.150–151.

The Tichborne case arose when Roger Tichborne, the heir to the Tichborne baronetcy, was lost in a shipwreck in 1854.[493] In 1866, a butcher living by the name of Thomas Castro, from Wagga Wagga, in New South Wales, came forward, claiming to be the lost heir. The mother of Roger Tichborne identified Castro as her son, albeit that he had rougher manners and speech, including having lost the ability to speak French, compared with the man who had been lost. The rest of the family, aside from the mother, contested the claim of the Wagga Wagga butcher, known as the Tichborne Claimant. Nevertheless, the Claimant succeeded in gaining control over the estate. As in the Windham case, the issue for many family members was the estate. By May 1871, in financial trouble, the Claimant forced his own claims to court in a civil case. The case ran through into the early months of 1872 and was at the forefront of public attention when the Twiss case became public. Both cases captured the Victorian fascination with the metamorphoses of persons from one status to another. Twiss invoked Tichborne to support his claim that Chaffers was not all that he seemed, although most observers would make the connection between Lady Twiss and Tichborne.

On January 24, Twiss wrote to Tait with more information regarding the further slanders Chaffers had been "concocting." He had noticed that one of Chaffers's letters to Tait contained a reference to a second statutory declaration, and he had just discovered that this was the declaration of Faure claiming that Pharaïlde van Lynseele and Maria Gelas were one and the same person.[494] Twiss declared that Chaffers had only gained this declaration because he had fooled Faure into believing that he was the solicitor for Lady Twiss, and he reported that Faure had now signed an affidavit to that effect (although not retracting the claim that Gelas and Lynseele were the same person). He spoke of his "unwillingness, as your lordship's Vicar General, to allow such a matter to be made public. This is the key to his persistent annoyance." Twiss was right that making the matter public was the key to Chaffers's motives, but he could not persuade Tait that a trial should be avoided without telling Tait that Chaffers's claims were true. To do that would have led to Twiss resigning his offices. He had to pin his hopes on having Chaffers condemned, and so he concluded that "although great scandal may be caused by publicity I have your Grace's sanction to prosecute him criminally." Great scandal was certainly an important fear, not simply because it would tarnish Twiss but because, given that he was a holder of so many high offices in the church, it would tarnish the church itself. On February 3, Robert Gregory, a Canon at St Paul's Cathedral, wrote to Jackson to tell him that the morning's post had brought a letter, which he enclosed, from A. Chaffers. He said he had "never heard of Chaffers or the contents before" and that he needed advice on how to proceed. His

---

493. For the Tichborne case, see McWilliam, *The Tichborne Claimant*.
494. Twiss to Tait, January 24, 1872, Lambeth Palace Library, Tait Papers, 184, ff.72–77.

immediate thought was that, given "Sir Travers Twiss's high official position in the Diocese," it might be possible to "limit the scandal, if the document can be suppressed."[495] Chaffers was determined, however, that the scandal should not be limited, and on February 12, still not aware of the case being built against him, he sent a letter outlining the history of his attempts to bring out the truth regarding Lady Twiss, and a copy of his statutory declaration, to Francis Hart Dyke, the Queen's Proctor: that is, the solicitor representing the crown in the Court of Probate and Divorce, and one of Twiss's colleagues for the past thirty years.[496] Chaffers added at the bottom of this letter to Dyke that it was his intention to publish the letter and to send copies of it to the daily papers so that there was no possibility that his claims could continue to be ignored.

On February 5, Twiss wrote to Tait with news on progress in the preparations for the trial. There were, he said, "technical difficulties" because, for a libel to be successful, there must be proof of publication and that the publication, in the case of letters, occurred either where the letters were posted or where they were received. The proof of posting was provided by the stamped envelopes, but with the exception of Twiss's friend, Dr Tristram, all the people who had received Chaffers's letters had dispensed with the envelopes.[497] In order to explain the long time it was taking to bring charges against Chaffers, Twiss explained to Tait that Chaffers had written to his solicitors threatening to send his charges to Convocation, and so for the solicitors, "It was thought better to delay the summons that he [Chaffers] might not be able to say that I moved at last in order to shut his mouth." Even Twiss himself acknowledged with the comment "at last" that he had taken a very long time to respond to Chaffers's provocations. He proceeded in this letter to observe that "Lady T. will return from Brussells tomorrow," indicating that she had been in Belgium for the second time in as many months. She may have been visiting family, but the next statement in the letter gives a more likely indication of what she had been doing: namely, gathering witnesses for her defence: "We shall bring three or four witnesses from Brussels, her guardian the Comte de Zerambe [Jastreuski] amongst them, who will prove she was in Belgium during the whole of 1859 when the man details his orgies."[498] The three or four witnesses did not materialise but the purported guardian did, and it remains a mystery who he actually was or where Pharaïlde Twiss found him—Chaffers's guess was that Count de Zerambe was an actor. Twiss's final observation in the letter appealed to Tait's values as well as giving an indication of the toll that Chaffers's persecution was beginning to have upon him: "His game is to sow discord between man and

---

495. Gregory to Jackson, February 3, 1872, Lambeth Palace Library, Jackson Papers, 33, f.152.
496. Chaffers, *The Twiss Libel Case*, 16.
497. Twiss to Tait, February 5, 1872, Lambeth Palace Library, Tait Papers, 184, ff.78–79.
498. Twiss to Tait, February 5, 1872, Lambeth Palace Library, Tait Papers, 184, ff.79r–v.

wife. He has destroyed, I believe, the happiness of several families ... Punishment may be slow but it will, I hope, be sure. You may imagine what difficulty I have in attending to such a matter having my hand and head full of business of a public nature, and in the presence of such an adversary it will be safe to make no mistake in our proceedings ... he is utterly reckless of consequences."[499] In yet another letter written to Tait the same day, Twiss returned Chaffers's correspondence with Tait and promised, "As soon as he has had his chance of petitioning the Convocation he will be summonsed."[500]

The summonses duly appeared two weeks later. On February 22, 1872, Twiss obtained four summonses against Chaffers at the Southwark Police Court: that is, in the police district in which Chaffers lived, covering Lambeth, and in which the alleged libels were published through having been posted. Chaffers was summonsed to appear at the court on February 29, charged, first, with "having on the 16th October, 1871, unlawfully threatened to publish a certain libel upon the said Sir Travers Twiss and Lady Twiss, his wife, with the intent to extort then and thereby money from the said Travers Twiss."[501] This was the occasion on which Chaffers had written to Twiss's solicitors, threatening that he would take further action if Sir Travers and Lady Twiss attended the celebrations for Baroness Burdett Coutts handing over Columbia Markets to the London Corporation. Second, Chaffers was charged with "having on the 9th November, 1871, unlawfully and maliciously written and published a false, scandalous, malicious, and defamatory libel, containing divers false, scandalous and malicious matters and things of and concerning the said Sir Travers Twiss and Lady Twiss, his wife."[502] This charge concerned the letters that Chaffers had sent on the same day to numerous Bishops, Dr Tristram, and the Archbishop. The third and fourth charges were that Chaffers had "on the 12th February, 1872, unlawfully threatened to publish a certain libel upon the said Sir Travers Twiss and Lady Twiss, his wife, with intent then and thereby to extort money" and had "unlawfully and maliciously written and published a false, scandalous, malicious, and defamatory libel."[503] These charges concerned the letter he sent to the Queen's Proctor, F. H. Dyke, and the threat contained in that letter to send its details to the daily papers. In a separate summons, made mysteriously at the same moment, Chaffers was charged with having falsely accused a Mr Henry Williams of having entered into a bigamous marriage.[504]

A week after Twiss obtained the summonses, he wrote to Bishop Jackson to say that Chaffers would appear in Southwark Police Court the next

499. Twiss to Tait, February 5, 1872, Lambeth Palace Library, Tait Papers, 184, f.79v.
500. Twiss to Tait, February 5 (second letter), 1872, Lambeth Palace Library, Tait Papers, 184, ff.80–81.
501. Chaffers, *The Twiss Libel Case*, 16.
502. Chaffers, *The Twiss Libel Case*, 16.
503. Chaffers, *The Twiss Libel Case*, 17.
504. "The Second Charge against Chaffers," *The South London Press*, March 16, 1872.

day. "The man," he declared, "is the incarnation of evil and I hope we shall be able to send him to prison for some time."[505] Chaffers appeared before Magistrate Benson at Southwark Police Court on Thursday, February 29, 1872. It was Chaffers who was supposed to be on trial, but the proceedings were rapidly transformed into a trial of Lady Twiss, largely because the 1843 Libel Act allowed Chaffers to call witnesses, including Lady Twiss herself, in order to prove that his claims were true. The Twisses were represented by Harry Poland, one of the most eminent barristers of his time (prosecuting, amongst many famous cases, William Stead, who had revealed the nature of the Half Moon Street brothels in which Lady Twiss herself had worked).[506] Chaffers represented himself. He had no money to employ a barrister, but he also clearly relished the opportunity of cross-examining the witnesses himself, particularly Lady Twiss. No transcripts were made of Police Court trials in this period. Only the records of some cases in the superior courts were kept, but such was the interest in the case that the newspapers, particularly *The Times*, carried detailed, and sometime verbatim, reports on the proceedings.

On the first day, Poland made a two-hour speech opening the prosecution in which he detailed the history of the marriage between Travers Twiss and Pharaïlde van Lynseele, including the place in which they married and the presentation of Lady Twiss at court.[507] He represented Chaffers as a man who had done some minor legal work for Lady Twiss prior to her marriage. He recounted the claims made against them by Chaffers over the past several years, and he presented the statutory declaration made by Chaffers. Having outlined the case, Poland turned to the first witness for the prosecution: namely, Thomas Tristram, a man who had been Twiss's student when he studied civil law at Oxford in the 1850s, when Twiss was Regius Professor, and who owed his subsequent career in the Doctors' Commons and in the law, and a sizable fortune, to Twiss. Tristram testified that he had known Pharaïlde van Lynseele prior to her marriage to Twiss when he had met her father, General van Lynseele.[508] He recounted having received Chaffers's letter and having taken it to Twiss. Francis Dyke was then called, and he testified that he had known, and worked with, Sir Travers for thirty years, that he had known his wife since their marriage, that she was "a lady in every sense of the word," and that they had been "on very intimate terms."[509] He then recounted having received Chaffers's letter a fortnight previously and said he took it immediately to Twiss. Chaffers then asked Dyke whether, if his allegations regarding the

---

505. Twiss to Jackson, February 28, 1872, Lambeth Palace Library, Jackson Papers, 33, ff.154–155.

506. For Poland's reminiscences of the Twiss trial, and of Stead, see Bowen-Rowlands, *Seventy-Two Years at the Bar*, 128–130, 208–210.

507. "Extraordinary Charges of Libel," *Morning Post*, March 1, 1872, 3.

508. "Extraordinary Charges of Libel," *Morning Post*, March 1, 1872, 3.

509. "Extraordinary Charges of Libel," *Morning Post*, March 1, 1872, 3.

Twisses were true, Sir Travers would be a "a proper person" to hold the offices of Vicar General and Queen's Advocate. Dyke said he would not be, but that there was "no truth in the declaration and the letters." The magistrate then adjourned the case.

Poland insisted that Chaffers should put up "substantial bail," and Mr Benson, the magistrate, agreed, asking him for £200. Chaffers could not provide such sureties, and he was therefore removed to nearby Horsemonger Lane Gaol in Southwark until the next hearing. The principal prison of Surrey, Horsemonger Lane Gaol had achieved notoriety as a place of public execution, a practice that continued until just shortly before Chaffers arrived there.[510] Dickens had written, famously, of one particular instance, the dual public hanging of husband and wife murderers Marie and Frederick Manning. Dickens described, in *The Times*, the "scene of horror and demoralization as was enacted this morning outside Horsemonger Lane Gaol." Of the vast crowd, he wrote: "When the two miserable creatures who attracted all this ghastly sight about them were turned quivering into the air, there was no more emotion, no more pity, no more thought that two immortal souls had gone to judgement, no more restraint in any of the previous obscenities, than if the name of Christ had never been heard in this world, and there were no belief among men but that they perished like the beasts."[511] When Chaffers was imprisoned, albeit temporarily, in this gaol, Twiss wrote triumphantly to Tait with the news and remarked upon the "wonderful weakness" of Chaffers in court "compared with the strength of his pen."[512] "We go on tomorrow," he added as a postscript, "and shall demolish him."

Chaffers had to remain longer in Horsemonger Lane Gaol than anticipated because on Friday, March 1, the second day of the trial, Harry Poland, to the great irritation of the magistrate, Mr Benson, was summonsed to Bow Street Police Court to prosecute Arthur O'Connor, the Irish man who had two days previously allegedly made an attempt upon the life of the Queen (albeit with no ball in his pistol).[513] The Twiss case resumed the next day, Saturday, March 2. Lady Twiss was the first witness called by Harry Poland and "in a slightly foreign accent" gave her name as Pharaïlde Rosalind Twiss.[514] She stated that she was a Catholic and received Marie as her confirmation name. She then testified that she was married in Dresden in 1862 "in the presence of my guardian, John Oliphant, the wife of the King's Chapelmaster and other friends" and the Chaplain, Henry Dale (Oliphant's signature is not on the wedding certificate. It

---

510. Newgate was the most famous location for executions: Chesney, *Victorian Underworld*, 356.

511. Charles Dickens, "To the Editor of The Times," *The Times*, November 14, 1849, 4. On Manning's execution, see also Chesney, *Victorian Underworld*, 362.

512. Twiss to Tait, February 29, 1872, Lambeth Palace Library, Tait Papers, 184, ff.82–83.

513. "The Libel upon the Queen's Advocate and Lady Twiss," *London Evening Standard*, March 2, 1872, 6.

514. "Extraordinary Charge of Libel," *The Times*, March 4, 1872, 11.

is signed by Dale and Charles Barnard, the *chargé d'affaires*). Lady Twiss said her "other guardian" was "Count Felix Zerambe Jastreuski who was in the court." Her father was a Major General of the Polish Army and had been a friend of Count Jastreuski. The two friends "had fought together in the Polish wars, and were exiled from Poland."[515] Count Jastreuski and his wife raised her when her father left her with them in Brussels at the age of 6 in 1846. After two years, she had been sent to a boarding school. Her father left to serve in the "East Indies." At an unspecified date, Pharaïlde van Lynseele returned to her guardians' house in Brussels, and there they employed a governess for her. The name of the governess was Maria Gelas, but "she is now dead." Madame Gelas had given her lessons up to 1859, after which point she received music lessons from Monsieur Desmarets, who was present in court. Chaffers accused Desmarets of being Lady Twiss's lover, who visited her regularly while Travers Twiss was overseas on business. He later wrote that the collapse of the libel case had occurred "by the few questions I put to her soi-disant music-master, Monsr. Desmares."[516]

This account gave new detail on Count van Lynseele. Poland had been partitioned in the eighteenth century between Prussian, Russian, and Austrian territories, and remained in that state until 1918. If by the Polish wars, Pharaïlde Twiss and Jastreuski were referring to the Polish war against Russia in 1830 and '31—a war that came to be seen as a struggle for Polish national liberation—the possibility of exile could make sense because the Russian army suppressed the rebellion, but the chronology of Count van Lynseele giving his daughter to Jastreuski in 1846 did not fit. If he and Count Jastreuski had been forced into exile in the mid-1840s after serving in the "Polish army," the description raised the possibility that her father had served in the Galician uprising of 1846, which was mainly concentrated in the Free City of Krakow, and had fought against rather than with the Austrian Polish army. If they had fought with the victorious Austrian Polish army, they would not have needed to flee into exile. This was the uprising that Metternich had suppressed while annexing Kraków in breach of the Treaty of Vienna—a contradiction of aims that Metternich and Twiss, as we have seen, spent some time attempting to justify. It was unlikely, although not impossible, that a Dutch general would have found himself fighting with the small and disorganised Galician forces. The fictional aspect of both nationalist struggles, however, was significant, as they would place Twiss in sympathy with one of the nationalist uprisings that flowed into the revolutions of 1848 that he had so strongly opposed, at least until Metternich's death. Along with his new embrace of personal metamorphosis from the moment he met Lynseele, he also seemed newly prepared to symbolically align himself with national metamorphosis and a more radical approach to the creation of artificial persons.

515. "Extraordinary Charge of Libel," *The Times*, March 4, 1872, 11.
516. Chaffers, *The Twiss Libel Case*, 19.

Continuing her testimony under examination from Harry Poland, Lady Twiss said that she had an English maid called Louisa Thomas between 1858 and 1862. While in Brussels, she became friends with an English woman, Mrs Anderson, and in September 1859, she came to England to stay with Mr and Mrs Anderson, who lived at 63 Hamilton Terrace, the same street in which Travers Twiss's mother, brother, and sister lived. While on this visit, she met Mrs Twiss, who was a friend of the Andersons, and she then stayed a week with Mrs Twiss. She met Travers Twiss when he attended a party at his mother's house. At the same time, Maria Gelas, who was no longer in Pharaïlde van Lynseele's employment, came to London to seek work as a governess, and she asked Lynseele to come and live with her. She agreed to do so, and in November 1859, she went to live in Maria Gelas's home in South Street, Brompton, where she remained until Easter 1860 before returning to Brussels. Over the next two years, she moved between Brussels and Maria Gelas's house in South Street, accompanied on one occasion by "Madame Dennay," who nursed her through an illness. During this period, she attended a dinner at Travers Twiss's Park Lane house in the company of her guardians, the Jastreuskis, Mr and Mrs Anderson, and Dr Tristram. In March 1861, her father returned from Java to Brussels, but then he left for Vienna and then went back again to Java in July. In November 1861, Madame Gelas moved to Neville Terrace, and Lynseele stayed with her until February 1862, when she returned once again to Brussels. During this period, Madame Gelas had become "very ill." Harry Poland then asked Lady Twiss whether, during this period, she had made the acquaintance of the jeweller Denis Faure, who had made the statutory declaration that she was one and the same person as Maria Gelas. Lady Twiss responded: "Yes. He was a jeweller. I saw him in the house of Madame Gelas in South Street . . . I knew nothing of him, as he was no friend of mine."[517] Twiss proposed to her in Brussels in 1861 and her father, who was back in Java, consented to the marriage, however: "He died in Java in 1864. Madame Jastreuski died in 1870. Madame Gelas and Dennay are also dead . . . Mr and Mrs Anderson died in 1865." Mrs Twiss, who had been a real person, was also dead. Lady Twiss's evidence was, accordingly, difficult to prove either true or false because few witnesses survived. She then made the incontestable statement, almost as a lament, that after her marriage: "When we arrived in London I was introduced to my husband's friends and to society. I visited the Archbishop of Canterbury, the Bishop of London, Dr Tristram, Mr F. H. Dyke and other families of distinction."[518] She was recalling the proofs of her reinvention and her admission to Society.

Harry Poland now asked Lady Twiss how she came to know Alexander Chaffers. She replied that in November 1859, she had been ill in bed, and

---

517. "Extraordinary Charge of Libel," *The Times*, March 4, 1872, 11.
518. "Extraordinary Charge of Libel," *The Times*, March 4, 1872, 11.

Madame Gelas had taken her to the office of Chaffers, who "was her solicitor," to make a will. The next time she saw him, she said, was in 1863, when she and her husband were walking in Regent's Park and Chaffers "congratulated me on my marriage" and she introduced him to Travers. Poland then asked her if it was true that she met Chaffers "in Regent Street in 1859," to which she replied "No." The questioning continued:

POLAND: "I have to ask you a very serious question, and one I hardly like to ask a Lady. Was there every any improper intimacy between you and the defendant?"
LADY TWISS: "(Indignantly.) Certainly not."
POLAND: "Did he ever give you a sovereign as the wages of guilt?"
LADY TWISS: "No. Oh! no. Why ask me that?"
POLAND: "Did he ever pass the whole night with you?"
LADY TWISS: "No."
POLAND: "Have you ever been at the Argyll Rooms, Holborn Casino, or any of the music halls about the Haymarket?"
LADY TWISS: "No, never."
POLAND: "Were you ever spoken to in any place of amusement about having misconducted yourself in such a manner as having called the attention of the master of ceremonies."
LADY TWISS: "No, never."
POLAND: "Were you ever reprimanded by the master of the ceremonies in any place of amusement?"
LADY TWISS: "No, never."
POLAND: "Were you ever at Cremorne before your marriage?"
LADY TWISS: "No. I went there to a day fete in 1865 with Captain Marsden and Lieutenant Marsden, sons of my husband's sister, and we returned home together to dinner."
POLAND: "Is it true that in 1859 you informed the defendant that you were intimate with Dr Twiss, and that he agreed to keep you and allow you £5 a week."
LADY TWISS: "No, it is false."
POLAND: "Did you ever give the defendant any such information."
LADY TWISS: "No, never."
POLAND: "Did any improper intimacy take place between you and your husband before marriage."
LADY TWISS: "No."[519]

Poland then asked Lady Twiss about Chaffers's demands for money. She conceded that he dined once with the Twisses at Park Lane but that he was never invited again after he made the claim for £150. She recounted the history of

[519]. "Extraordinary Charge of Libel," *The Times*, March 4, 1872, 11.

his subsequent "vilifications" of her character and said that after he sent his statutory declaration to the Lord Chamberlain: "We communicated with the Lord Chamberlain, and he expressed his satisfaction at the explanation, and I am still entitled to go to Court."[520] This statement ended Poland's examination of Lady Twiss, while once again underlining how important the presentation at court was to the metamorphosis of Pharaïlde van Lynseele into Lady Travers Twiss.

Chaffers, conducting his own defence, now began his cross-examination of Lady Twiss as a prosecution witness. He first asked her "to sit more round [facing him], as he could not hear her distinctly, and he particularly wanted her to hear him."[521] He then began his examination:

CHAFFERS: "Were you not born at Courtrai?"
LADY TWISS: "No, I was not."
CHAFFERS: "Would it not surprise you to hear that you were born there?"
LADY TWISS: "I don't know exactly where I was born, but I went to Brussels when I was very young."
CHAFFERS: "Have we not been intimate some years?"
LADY TWISS: "No."
CHAFFERS: "Did you not go with me to Courtrai in September, 1860, and did we not have a bedroom, No. 15, overlooking the Grand Plaz."
LADY TWISS: "No, never. How can you say so?"

Chaffers continued with a minute examination about all the places and people he and Pharaïlde van Lynseele had visited during their stay in Belgium, including meals, coffees together, events attended, and games of cards they played. At one point, Lady Twiss exclaimed: "Why do you ask such questions? I am a foreigner, and you told me the newspapers won't believe a foreigner. You wicked man!" Harry Poland, her barrister, intervened and "begged her ladyship to be calm" and answer the questions, but again when Chaffers asked her, "Did we not sleep at No. 41 bedroom at the Hotel Royal on the Platz [in Ghent], second floor, on the 12th of September, 1860" [after, in fact, Lynseele was being "kept" by Twiss], she once again exclaimed, "No, you wicked man! You have ruined all your family yourself, and now you seek to ruin me."[522] The magistrate intervened and said it was time to conclude the day's proceedings. He asked Chaffers if his cross-examination would take much longer. Chaffers replied that he had "hardly commenced. It would last some hours yet and he had some very important questions to ask Lady Twiss."[523] He was accordingly

---

520. "Extraordinary Charge of Libel," *The Times*, March 4, 1872, 11.
521. "Extraordinary Charge of Libel," *The Times*, March 4, 1872, 11.
522. "Extraordinary Charge of Libel," *The Times*, March 4, 1872, 11.
523. "Extraordinary Charge of Libel," *The Times*, March 4, 1872, 11.

removed to Horsemonger Lane Gaol, where, this being a Saturday, he had to remain until the following Tuesday before his next opportunity to question Lady Twiss.

On Tuesday, March 5, the case resumed in Southwark Police Court. The court was now "crowded by persons anxious to hear the evidence."[524] By this time, almost all the newspapers in Britain were carrying detailed reports of the proceedings. Lady Twiss was sworn, and the magistrate, Mr Benson, reminded her where the cross-examination had ended the previous Saturday. Chaffers resumed his questions, asking first her age, to which she replied, "Thirty-two," although it was, in fact, thirty-seven. He then asked Lady Twiss about the Andersons, where she first met them, when they died, and whether their only daughter survived, to which she responded that she didn't know. He asked about the addresses at which Maria Gelas lived, although he stated that he didn't know that Maria Gelas had given her name in the 1861 census as Marie Pharaïlde Gelas—that is, with Lynseele's first two names—of 11 South Street, aged 26. He asked her whether he met her, Lynseele, on July 7, 1859, in Cremorne Gardens and then went "home to sleep with you all night," which Lady Twiss denied. Harry Poland interjected at this point to say "these insulting questions were not at all professional" and that "it was, in fact, a system of torture."[525] Mr Benson responded that he would prevent torture, if he could, but he could not stop the questions. It was, he said, "a unique case, and he could not exclude evidence," although he urged Chaffers not to recount "every day in the year." Chaffers turned to the brothel at 46 Half Moon Street, asking Lady Twiss about her time there, which was once again denied, as was her knowledge of the landlady there. He asked about their visits to the Argyll Rooms, the Burlington Arcade, Cremorne Gardens, the Crystal Palace, and the Turkish Divan, as well as numerous other nights they spent together. On the night of May 6, 1859, he asked: "Did not another woman come and sleep in the same bed with us?"[526] He then introduced Travers Twiss into the story, asking whether she had not "spent the evening" with Twiss on September 3, 1859, before Chaffers himself arrived at midnight to spend the rest of the night with her.[527] Now, he said, Twiss "agreed to keep you," and aided by Twiss's £20 a month, she moved to South Street. Benson, frustrated by the detailed questions, which received repeated denials, told Chaffers that he may have a diary but that Lady Twiss could not be expected to remember events ten years previously. Chaffers responded that he would produce witnesses to corroborate his claims.

---

524. "Extraordinary Charge of Libel," *The Times*, March 6, 1872, 11.

525. "Extraordinary Charge of Libel," *The Times*, March 6, 1872, 11.

526. "Extraordinary Charge of Libel," *The Times*, March 6, 1872, 11; "The Charge of Libel upon Sir Travers and Lady Twiss," *The Daily News*, March 6, 1872, 5.

527. "Extraordinary Charge of Libel," *The Times*, March 6, 1872, 11.

Chaffers next asked Lady Twiss whether, on November 3, 1859, "did you not tell me that Dr Twiss's last mistress, Agnes Willoughby, had cost him £8,000, besides property she had taken from Park Lane."[528] Lady Twiss responded "no," of course, but this was the first public mention of any connection between Travers Twiss and Agnes Willoughby. It is difficult to understand how Chaffers could have learned of their connection, thirteen years later, without originally having heard it from Pharaïlde van Lynseele, although it could be possible that it was rumoured in the Inns of Court after the Windham trial or that he heard it from his friend Richard Twiss. The claim that Agnes Willoughby had taken property from Twiss's Park Lane house was new—it had not been mentioned in the lawyers' notes in the Windham trial—and the great sum Chaffers claimed Twiss paid to Willoughby was greater than the £2,000 stated ten years earlier.

Asking Lady Twiss how they first met, she answered that they had been introduced by Madame Gelas. "Had she known me long?" Chaffers playfully asked. Lady Twiss said that they had only met on that one occasion in order to make a will, but that the will had subsequently been destroyed. She said that she did not know that his office at Bedford Row had a sitting room and a bedroom. Chaffers asked her: "Has any improper intimacy taken place between us there?" She denied this and denied also having been arrested on July 2, 1860, and placed in Abraham Sloman's sponging house at 4 Cursitor Street, off Chancery Lane.[529] Sponging houses were detention houses for debtors, who were held there until they could pay their debt; if they couldn't, they were sent to a debtors' prison. Charles Dickens's father had also been put in Sloman's house in Cursitor Street. Charles had to pay to get him out, and his experiences of the humiliations of debt inspired his commentaries on the subject in *David Copperfield* and *Sketches by Boz*.[530] Lady Twiss denied that she had "lodged a sum of money with the sheriff's office and got out the same evening," she denied that she had been imprisoned in Sloman's, and she denied that she spent the whole day in Chaffers's office on July 4, 1860, preparing affidavits to get her money out of court.[531] Later in the cross-examination, she said that it had been Madame Gelas, and not herself, who had been locked up in Sloman's.

Chaffers turned to the period after Lady Twiss's marriage. He now claimed something further: that he continued his sexual liaison with Pharaïlde Twiss

---

528. "Extraordinary Charge of Libel," *The Times*, March 6, 1872, 11.

529. "Extraordinary Charge of Libel," *The Times*, March 6, 1872, 11.

530. Montagu Williams, the barrister and writer, described Sloman's, in his *Round London*, through the eyes of a friend who was taken there, and declared to Williams: "Slowman's, the sponging house in Cursitor Street, Chancery Lane. Ah, my dear fellow, you've never seen a sponging house! Ye gods! What a place! I had an apartment they were pleased to call a bedroom to myself certainly, but if I wanted to breath the air, I had to do so in a cage in the back garden—iron bars all around and about the size of the beast receptacles at the Zoo": Montagu Williams, *Round London: Down East and Up West* (London, 1892), 131.

531. "Extraordinary Charge of Libel," *The Times*, March 6, 1872, 11.

after her marriage. He asked if she had not come to see him on November 13, 1862, "and stop several hours." On December 4, they had lunched together, and on December 11, "did you not come and stay with me till half past 4." On that day, he claimed, they also quarrelled, "and you said you would not come again," but she came again on January 11, 1863. To all these questions she replied with a simple "no." He raised the matter of Monsieur Pierre Denis and "Madame Denis," who had lived with Madame Gelas. He asked if he and Pharaïlde Twiss had not lunched with Pierre Denis on January 17, 1863, and she said "no." He asked if she knew Pierre Denis, and Lady Twiss responded, "I know M. Deny who was husband to the housekeeper to Madame Gelas. M. Deny did not live in South Street."[532] Actually, as we know from the 1861 census, Pierre Denis, aged 54, did live in South Street, along with Marie Pharaïlde Gelas, 26, and Thérèse Van[illegible], who was surely the Thérèse Barbe Vanderschoore who was stated to be the mother of Pharaïlde Rosalie van Lynseele on her birth certificate, along with the father, Pierre Denis van Lynseele. Chaffers accordingly asked Lady Twiss, "Will you positively swear that Madame and M. Deny were not your father and mother M. and Madame Van Lynseele," and she replied firmly, "I positively swear they were not." He then gave numerous dates throughout April, May, June, July, October, and November 1863 when Pharaïlde Twiss came to his office, including June 9, "when you stayed two or three hours." Again, she denied all. She agreed he had dined once with her and her husband in Park Lane, but not on the other occasions he claimed. She denied that her brother was Edmond Constant and that Chaffers had done legal work for him, at Pharaïlde Twiss's request, in order to establish a public house.

Chaffers went back over various aspects of Pharaïlde Twiss's story, and then the questioning turned to her father, who had gone to Java, where he died. The magistrate, Mr Benson, intervened to ask: "Did you receive letters from him [Major General van Lynseele]?" Lady Twiss responded: "He always corresponded with my guardians . . . I don't know what was his employment at Java. I don't know if he was a Major-General in the King of Holland's service . . . I did not see the letter announcing his death." Chaffers asked the name of her mother, to which she replied: "I don't know; I never heard. I don't know how soon after I was born she died. I don't know where she was buried or when she died. I don't know whether Dr Travers Twiss knew her."[533] "Did you not," Chaffers asked, "used to call me 'Bébé' in South Street, and Sir Travers Twiss 'Bonhomme.'" "No, never" she replied. "Did you not speak to me in indecent French language while you were in South Street?" "No, I did not." "Did you not smash my hat in South Street in a passion?" "No, I did not."[534] Lady

532. "Extraordinary Charge of Libel," *The Times*, March 6, 1872, 11.
533. "Extraordinary Charge of Libel," *The Times*, March 6, 1872, 11.
534. "Extraordinary Charge of Libel," *The Times*, March 6, 1872, 11; "The Extraordinary Libel Case," *South London Press*, March 9, 1872, 12.

Twiss denied having more than twice met the jeweller, Faure, who swore she was Maria Gelas. Chaffers asked her if they had gone to the Adelphi Theatre on December 2, 1859, to see *Dead Heart*, a dramatization of the fall of the Bastille. The *London Illustrated News* from that year confirms that the Watts Phillips play *Dead Heart* was playing at the Adelphi in December 1859. Lady Twiss responded, as always, that they did not.

Chaffers continued: "Did you not tell me on the 15th of December [1859], when we dined at 11, South Street, there was something the matter with your mouth and lip you thought was venereal, and you asked me to send you my doctor?" "No, never," she replied. On December 28, he said, Lynseele wrote him a "furious letter." The implication was that she believed it was Chaffers who had given her venereal disease. His doctor's name, he informed Harry Poland, was Straube of Moorgate Street, and he called on Pharaïlde van Lynseele on January 2, 1860. Poland insisted upon seeing the letter Chaffers claimed Lynseele had written, but Chaffers responded with a question to the witness: "Did you not," he asked, "call at my office in Bedford Row, and throw all the letters into the fire." On January 5, he said, they went to the jeweller, Widdowson's in the Strand, and chose a bracelet worth £26. This behaviour mirrored precisely the occasion upon which Agnes Willoughby insisted upon compensation from William Windham for giving her venereal disease. The payment in jewellery, which could be used to preserve wealth, was the same, although the sums were less. In a further parallel, Lady Twiss declared: "No, I did not go to Meyers, the Photographer in Regent Street." She repeated: "I did not go to Meyers and have my portrait taken."[535] Mayer Brothers were the photographers who took Agnes Willoughby's photograph, and also that of her lover Giuglini, as *cartes de visite*. While the photographs were used by members of Society as calling cards, they were also used by courtesans for professional purposes. We have already seen General Windham's correspondent, the army officer Preston, remembering that "Staunton of the equerries" showed him Willoughby's "portrait when we were going up in the Melbourne to Balaklava." In this instance, Chaffers responded that he would summons Mayer.

Chaffers proceeded with numerous detailed questions about events, such as Lynseele persuading him to dye his hair; that she "got in a passion and smashed my white hat" on August 12, 1861; their attendance with Richard Twiss and another prostitute in a private box at the opera (provided for Lynseele by the Italian tenor Pietro Neri Beraldi); their many engagements throughout the course of 1861; and Lynseele's constant passing between himself and Twiss: "On the 15th of June, did I not dine with you and Marie Weiss, and I left you at 10, because Dr Twiss was coming to take you to Cremorne?"—"No, I did not go to Cremorne and join you there."[536] The magistrate asked if Marie Weiss,

---

535. "Extraordinary Charge of Libel," *The Times*, March 6, 1872, 11.
536. "Extraordinary Charge of Libel," *The Times*, March 6, 1872, 11.

who Chaffers said had at the time been staying with Lynseele, was now "to be found," and Chaffers responded that she could be but that "her name is assumed," implying that she was a prostitute and also alluding to the routine manner in which new personae were created in the milieu of prostitution.

After a brief adjournment at 5:00 o'clock in the afternoon, Chaffers announced to the magistrate that he wished to summons Archbishop Tait and the Lord Chamberlain or their representatives in order that they may deny that he ever tried to extort money from them. The magistrate replied that their written assurances would suffice, but the mention of the Archbishop's name in such a case was precisely what the church wished to avoid. The involvement of the Vicar General of the Province of Canterbury and the Chancellor of the Diocese of London was sufficiently grave. Chaffers then returned to Lady Twiss and now questioned her about a trip he said she made to Belgium in August 1861. According to Chaffers, he joined her in Courtrai and met her aunts and other relatives. On September 22, he claimed, she met Twiss at Antwerp and then travelled with him on the Rhine. She then rejoined Chaffers in Belgium, he said, but at this point, the magistrate again objected that he was going through the year "day by day." Chaffers therefore moved on to her return to London in October and November 1861, and his prediction to her, on November 27, that "Dr Travers Twiss would marry you." Coming to 1862, having asked Lady Twiss whether she recalled having met a long list of people, Chaffers asked whether on "Wednesday, 10th of March, did you not throw a teacup at my head?" She agreed that she left England in March, in preparation for her impending marriage in Dresden, but denied that she again met Chaffers in Belgium on March 29. The magistrate intervened and asked if she met Chaffers in Berlin, and she responded: "Yes. We dined at the Hotel du Rhin at Berlin, when the defendant came up to me at the door of the hotel and asked me if I were not Madame Van Lynseele. I said 'Yes,' and that was all that passed. I only spoke to him for a minute or two. That was in May,—I think the middle of May. I was with Countess Petrouski and three other ladies." Chaffers replied, "Did you not stay with me at Berlin and stay with me several days?" He asked had they not gone to the opera together in Berlin and had they not then travelled together to Dresden, where she would soon marry. He then asked if she had not told Richard Twiss that, at this time, Chaffers had "misappropriated" a "large sum of money" that belonged to her. This was presumably the promissory notes that Twiss had sent with her to Dresden, and it marks the beginning of Chaffers's blackmail. It may also have been the source of the subsequent falling out between Richard Twiss and Chaffers. At the end of the day, now 8:00 p.m., Harry Poland re-examined Lady Twiss about her testimony, and she replied: "There was never any misconduct or familiarity between me and the defendant. All the questions he has put to me are a tissue of falsehoods."[537]

---

537. "Extraordinary Charge of Libel," *The Times*, March 6, 1872, 11.

Chaffers spent two further nights in Horsemonger Lane Gaol before the next hearing on Thursday, March 7. The examination of Lady Twiss having been concluded, the next witness was a man called Count Felix Jastreuski, or sometimes Zareuski. If, as subsequently proved to be the case, Pharaïlde van Lynseele had not been the orphaned daughter of a Major General in the Polish army, but was rather born into and brought up by a Belgian peasant family, then Count Jastreuski, who claimed to have raised her, was to some degree an invention himself. He was, accordingly, another person created in order to support the invention of Lady Twiss herself. Chaffers, perceiving this fact, later complained of the perjuries committed by "that buffoon, calling himself Count Jevstrenski—a title I suspect conferred by himself."[538]

Cross-examined by Mr Collins, Harry Poland's assistant, Jastreuski, as *The Times* spelled his name, introduced himself through an interpreter provided by the court: "I am of a family of counts" and had lived in Brussels since 1833. His business, he said, was the manufacture of pianofortes.[539] His wife had died two years previously. He had served in the Polish army with his cousin, Count Felix R. van Lynseele, who was from the family of Count Zareuski. Count van Lynseele left his 6-year-old girl with Jastreuski and his wife in 1846, and she "was like a child of our own." Count van Lynseele had then gone to Java on business that was not entirely clear. In 1850, he had returned to Brussels and, according to Jastreuski, had arrived there with Travers Twiss. Mr Collins, the barrister for the prosecution, asked Zareuski whether Twiss and Count van Lynseele had come from Vienna: "Do you know whether they came from Vienna together?"—[Zareuski:] "Yes. They came together from Vienna. After a short stay at Brussels, Count van Lynseele returned to Java."[540] It was true that Twiss had been in Brussels in 1850. Melanie Metternich described his visit in her diary.[541] We also know that, prior to 1851, Prince Metternich had warned Twiss not to travel to Vienna or into the Austrian Empire at all, judging that it was still too dangerous. Metternich himself returned there in June 1851 (initially to Schloss Johannisberg and later in the summer to Vienna), when Twiss visited. It is unlikely, therefore, that Twiss travelled between Vienna and Brussels in 1850.

Continuing his testimony, Zareuski claimed that his wife employed Madame Gelas as a governess and she was a widow (a very young widow, according to the 1861 census). He knew the Anderson family and the story of how Pharaïlde van Lynseele came to know them. He had visited the mother of Travers Twiss on one of his trips to London. When Pharaïlde had become sick

---

538. Chaffers, *The Twiss Libel Case*, 20.
539. "The Extraordinary Charge of Libel," *The Times*, March 8, 1872, 11.
540. "The Extraordinary Charge of Libel," *The Times*, March 8, 1872, 11.
541. *Mémoires, documents, et écrits divers laissés par le Prince de Metternich*, 8 vols. (Paris, 1884), Vol. 8, 77.

while staying with Madame Gelas, he had sent Madame Deny ("Denis" in the 1861 census—the name Pharaïlde's father used in England) to look after her. Having said that Pharaïlde was in Belgium in the spring of 1861, Jastreuski claimed that when her father returned from Java in the spring of the same year, his daughter was in London. The magistrate interjected: "That is inconsistent with what you say. You say in the spring the father came from Java" to Blankenberghe. Mr Collins prompted Jastreuski to correct his narrative, and he duly remembered that "we were all" in Blankenburg (the Saxon resort town).[542] After six weeks, Count van Lynseele returned to Java in 1861 and was never seen again. Jastreuski knew nothing of Pharaïlde's mother other than having been told that she was an Austrian noblewoman. He denied that Monsieur and Madame "Deny" were the mother and father of Pharaïlde van Lynseele. Chaffers asked if Jastreuski sent Pharaïlde money while she was staying with Madame Gelas, and he replied that he had sent her £30 a month. There was no trace of those payments, however, he said, because the money had been sent as bank notes that he obtained from money changers in Brussels rather than as transfers through a bank.

With Jastreuski's shaky account concluded, the magistrate made a short speech, in which he confessed, "I have experienced the greatest pain and distress" from witnessing the "unspeakable agony to Lady Twiss and her friends" that the proceedings were inflicting. He said he had considered whether it was possible to "restrain a cross-examination which places so foul a page in the report in the newspapers," but he had concluded that he was obliged by the Libel Act of 1843 to allow witnesses for the defence to be cross-examined.[543] He then adjourned the case for the day but announced that the proceedings would move the next day from the Southwark Police Court to the more comfortable surroundings of the Sessions House on Newington Causeway.

On Friday, March 8, Chaffers appeared for the sixth time, this time in the Sessions House next door to Horsemonger Lane Gaol, and once again, the case attracted a large crowd, having "excited considerable interest."[544] The proceedings began with a debate between Harry Poland, Chaffers, and Benson about whether Lady Twiss should be recalled to answer new claims raised in the course of the cross-examinations. Poland wanted her called at the end of the trial, but Chaffers objected that she should not be given the opportunity to respond to all the witnesses, and he prevailed. Lady Twiss was recalled. Poland began by asking if she had ever been arrested and placed in a sponging house or prison, as a result of a charge brought by "Rebecca Clements," and whether she had had Chaffers's help in preparing affidavits to recover her money. She denied this claim but agreed that something of the kind happened to Madame

---

542. "The Extraordinary Charge of Libel," *The Times*, March 8, 1872, 11.
543. "The Extraordinary Charge of Libel," *The Times*, March 8, 1872, 11.
544. "The Extraordinary Charge of Libel," *The Times*, March 9, 1872, 11.

Gelas, adding: "I only have very little recollection about the matter. I have only the slightest idea that the thing happened." Poland then introduced a new claim regarding Pharaïlde van Lynseele: namely, that her portrait had been commissioned by her guardians, the "Jastrebskis" (as the name was now spelled in *The Times*), and painted by her drawing master, Monsieur Guillaime, in Brussels in 1859. Lady Twiss confirmed this was true. At Dresden, she said, she had stayed with a Professor Peschel. Madame Gelas had consulted a Doctor Straube. Lady Twiss identified two letters sent to her in May 1862, in Dresden, by a Maid of Honour to Queen Marie of Saxony.[545] Lady Twiss stepped down. The Twisses's strategy was clear: that is, they understood that at any moment Chaffers could present witnesses who might, for example, say that she had been in the sponging house or visited Doctor Straube regarding venereal disease, but these acts would be placed upon the personage of Marie Gelas rather than Lynseele.

Louisa Harrison, who was said to have been Pharaïlde van Lynseele's maid, was the next witness called by Poland for the prosecution. She confirmed the details of Lady Twiss's version of her comings and goings from London between 1859 and 1862. She agreed that she had married Edmond Constant, who, she said, had merely been a servant in Madame Gelas's service and was not, as Alexander Chaffers claimed, Lady Twiss's brother. If, of course, Madame Gelas was Pharaïlde van Lynseele and Constant was her brother, then Louisa Harrison, who claimed to have been her maid, was in fact her sister-in-law. Harrison and Constant, after marrying, had taken the lease on the Royal Oak beer shop on Blackfriars Road in August 1863. Harrison agreed that Madame Denis (Pharaïlde's mother in reality) worked as a servant in Madame Gelas's house in South Street, but denied that Madame Denis's husband lived there with her—this point is contradicted by the 1861 census. She claimed that Alexander Chaffers stayed in her beer shop for a week in 1864. During this time, she said that he at one point told her she could earn £150 by supporting his claims about the true identity of Pharaïlde Twiss. She claimed that Chaffers said: "Dr Twiss would rather pay any sum of money than come before a Judge, or before society, as it would look very bad against her." Poland pressed: "Was anything said as to Dr Twiss being Vicar-General?—Yes. He said as Dr Twiss was holding such a position as Vicar General, it would look very bad against him." Thus Lady Twiss's sister-in-law reinvented herself as her former maid in order to present the evidence that Chaffers's defamations were conducted for the purpose of extortion. Her husband, Edmond Constant, had died in 1865 and so could not be brought to witness, and she had remarried Richard Harrison, a greengrocer on the High Street in Hounslow, in 1870. Chaffers then cross-examined Louisa Harrison but without shaking her testimony (she was a better witness than Count Jastreuski). He asked her if

---

545. "The Extraordinary Charge of Libel," *The Times*, March 9, 1872, 11.

anybody had witnessed the conversation she alledged took place between her and him, and she replied, "No." She finally denied that Lady Twiss had "given or promised me money or clothes."[546]

The prosecution next called Mrs Rose Reuter, who had known Dr Straube, who had treated Madame Gelas. Dr Straube had died, she said, in 1868. Mr Benson called for Lady Twiss to be returned to the court so Mrs Reuter could look at her to state whether she resembled Madame Gelas. When Lady Twiss was, Mrs Reuter exclaimed, "Oh! decidedly not." She then protested to the court, "I beg to say I know none of the parties in this case. I saw a lady's name outraged, and I felt bound to come forward."[547] Chaffers, to Mr Benson's surprise, said he had no questions at all to ask the witness. Reuter was followed by Edmond André Guillaume, a painter from Brussels, who said he had given Pharaïlde van Lynseele drawing lessons two or three times a week in 1859 and 1860. Guillaume said his portrait of Lady Twiss was still hanging in the house of Count "Jastrebaki." Harry Poland declared that this evidence should dispose of the "ghastly story" that Lady Twiss had been working as a prostitute in London in those years. Mr Benson responded, "No evidence on this point must be considered *de trop*."[548] Again, Chaffers declined to ask the witness any questions.

As if to show that no evidence was too much, Mr Paul Des Mares took the stand and told Mr Poland that he was a music teacher in Brussels and that he had been Pharaïlde van Lynseele's music teacher in 1859 and 1860. He was also acquainted with Madame Gelas at the time, and she was not the same woman and of a different appearance: "She was a small woman with a southern appearance." Chaffers now posed questions. The witness denied that he was staying at the house of Travers Twiss. He said there was another Monsieur Des Mares who lived in Brussels who was a relation of his, "but he declined to state the relationship." Chaffers pressed, and he still refused. Mr Benson communicated with the witness on the matter and stated that it was a question of "pedigree" and that Mr Chaffers should not open up sores that had no bearing on the matter. Des Mares said that Chaffers was confusing him with his relative because he had lived in the same house for four years.[549] Chaffers did not reveal the mystery behind this witness's identity, but again witnesses for the Twisses were clearly not who they claimed to be.

The final witness for the day was Mr Arthur Cook, managing clerk to Barnes and Bernard, the Twisses' solicitors, called by Harry Poland in order to recount the various actions Chaffers had brought against Travers and Pharaïlde Twiss between 1864 and 1871, which he claimed were shams to extort money. These writs included Chaffers's bill of costs for having performed the work of

---

546. "The Extraordinary Charge of Libel," *The Times*, March 9, 1872, 11.
547. "The Extraordinary Charge of Libel," *The Times*, March 9, 1872, 11.
548. "The Extraordinary Charge of Libel," *The Times*, March 9, 1872, 11.
549. "The Extraordinary Charge of Libel," *The Times*, March 9, 1872, 11.

purchasing a beer shop on Blackfriars Road for Edmond Constant, "the brother of the defendant Pharaïlde," and his wife Louisa.[550] If true, this claim helped explain why Louisa Harrison testified on behalf of Lady Twiss (apart from family loyalty)—she had been, and possibly still was, financially dependent upon her. That dependence underlined a common dimension of prostitution—seen also in Willoughby's case—it was a family business, often involving parents and siblings. The writ also sought damages for a slander uttered by Pharaïlde Twiss to Richard Twiss, against Alexander Chaffers, in 1865. Richard Twiss subsequently "circulated such slander in all directions." Richard Twiss, stated the writ, "has absconded, and cannot now be found." The writ stated that he had been "advertised for in the Standard" but to no avail.[551] The *London Evening Standard* of December 20, 1870, contained the following announcement: "RICHARD TWISS—Any one FURNISHING the ADDRESS of RICHARD TWISS late of 12 Gray's Inn Square, Solicitor, to Mr Baker, solicitor, 69 Chancery Lane, will be REWARDED for their trouble."[552] Richard Twiss had indeed disappeared. If he had been called as a witness at the trial, he would have either been obliged to state his knowledge of Pharaïlde van Lynseele prior to her marriage or to have perjured himself. The witnesses who had been brought from Belgium, on the other hand, Jastreuski, Des Mares, and Guillaume, were in no danger of being convicted of perjury after they returned to Belgium. Neither Richard Twiss nor Travers Twiss were called as witnesses in the trial. As the proceedings of this day drew to a close, Chaffers pressed Harry Poland on precisely this question, asking if he intended to call Sir Travers. Poland stated that Twiss would "give evidence at the trial in the event of a committal." Twiss knew that matters would be grave enough if they lost their case, but they would be even worse, in that event, if he lost the ability to practice as a lawyer as a consequence of having perjured himself. He would later write about his fear of perjury. This being Friday, March 8, the case was adjourned till the following Tuesday, March 12. Chaffers faced another four nights in Horsemonger Lane Gaol before he could resume his examination.

When, on Tuesday, March 12, proceedings resumed in the Sessions House, Newington, the court was once again "crowded during the day."[553] Arthur Cook, the clerk from Barnes and Bernard, was recalled. He stated that since the previous Friday, the solicitors had been served with a notice from Alexander Chaffers to produce the documents relating to the action he had taken against the Twisses in the previous year, in particular the bills of costs he had made against them. Cook accordingly produced Chaffers's bills of costs against Maria Gelas for work done in releasing her from the sponging house. He also produced a bill

---

550. "The Extraordinary Charge of Libel," *The Times*, March 9, 1872, 11.
551. "The Extraordinary Charge of Libel," *The Times*, March 9, 1872, 11.
552. *London Evening Standard*, December 20, 1870, 1.
553. "The Extraordinary Charge of Libel," *The Times*, March 13, 1872, 11.

for work done in securing the lease on 11 South Street, where Maria Gelas had lived. Harry Poland explained that "the documents had, with other papers, been found among the property of Madame Gelas which she left on relinquishing the house in Neville Terrace, Brompton." He did not explain why the Twisses' solicitors, Barnes and Bernard, would have anything to do with papers left by Maria Gelas, and Magistrate Benson immediately declared that "he thought the prosecution ought to give some account of where the bills of costs produced by the witness [Arthur Cook, the clerk] came from." Poland replied merely that it was "sufficient to prove that they bore the handwriting of the defendant." While Poland sought to prove that the actions brought by Chaffers had been against Maria Gelas rather than Pharaïlde Twiss, or Pharaïlde van Lynseele, in doing so he had exposed an unexplained link between the Twisses' solicitors and Maria Gelas. Mr Benson pointed out that "the only question was one of identity": namely, whether Maria Gelas and Pharaïlde van Lynseele were the same person. Chaffers, for his part, pointed out that the bills of costs all stated the name of Maria Gelas as "M. P. Gelas," with the "P" standing for Pharaïlde which, as we know from the 1861 census, was a correct deduction.[554]

Responding to further questioning from Chaffers, Arthur Cook said, "He did not know that his employers [Barnes and Bernard] had, on Sir Travers Twiss's behalf, been concerned in action brought against him by Agnes Willoughby, afterwards Mrs Windham."[555] This was the second time in the trial that Chaffers made a public link between Agnes Willoughby and Travers Twiss, and again with new information on what passed between them: namely, that Willoughby followed through on her threats to take legal action against Twiss and that he had been forced to defend himself. If Chaffers could establish a link with Willoughby through his cross-examination of Cook, it would assist him in justifying the claim in his statutory declaration that Twiss had led an "immoral life" prior to his marriage and this was one of the grounds for the accusation of libel. Poland, however, immediately sought to stop Chaffers from making any further statements of this kind, and so objected to the line of questioning on Agnes Willoughby as a "breach of privilege": that is, in order to encourage open and honest testimony, the court protected statements made in court from defamation laws so long as they were relevant to a case. That protection could not be abused. Mr Benson supported Poland's objection, saying Chaffers had "no right" to put questions about Twiss and Willoughby, as they had "no reference to the matter at issue."[556] The full story, therefore, of Twiss as Willoughby's first "protector" when she came to London was not revealed.

Arthur Cook was replaced on the witness stand by Edward Dax, a clerk in the office of the Exchequer which was responsible for questions concerning

---

554. "The Extraordinary Charge of Libel," *The Times*, March 13, 1872, 11.
555. "The Extraordinary Charge of Libel," *The Times*, March 13, 1872, 11.
556. "The Extraordinary Charge of Libel," *The Times*, March 13, 1872, 11.

debts. Dax produced Rebecca Clements's affidavit on July 2, 1860, that Maria Gelas was about to quit England, escaping her debts, thus enabling her arrest and imprisonment in a sponging house. He also produced the affidavits, prepared by Chaffers, which led to the release of Gelas and which stated that Maria Gelas had no intention of leaving. These statements were signed by her "servants" Edmond Constant and Pierre Denis (that is, in reality, by her brother and father). They noted, amongst other matters, that Gelas had just rented, for two years, two of her rooms in South Street to the Italian opera singer "Signor Neri Baraldi." Pietro Neri Baraldi was not of the same standing as Antonio Giuglini, Willoughby's lover, who Sir Charles Santley, the great English baritone, remembered as "the hero" whenever "music was the subject of conversation."[557] Nevertheless, he played at the Lyceum and Covent Garden. Lynseele shared, with Willoughby, a taste for the company of Italian opera singers. From her private box at opera in Covent Garden, she could have watched him play the Duke of Mantua in *Rigoletto*.

The final witness for the day, Mrs Harper of Islington, testified that she knew Madame Gelas because she and her husband had let her their house in Neville Terrace, Brompton. Madame Gelas, she said, was not the same person as Lady Twiss because Gelas was "rather taller and more slender" than Lady Twiss. This did not clarify matters greatly for the prosecution, as Des Mares, the music teacher, had testified that Gelas was a shorter woman of stouter appearance. The difficulty was greater when, prior to the adjournment, a representative from the Sherriff's Office of Middlesex stated that the officer who had arrested Maria Gelas nine years previously was now dead and so could not be called upon to state whether Lady Twiss was the same person.[558] Poland requested an adjournment for the day because he stated that the prosecution "now wished to bring other testimony." Benson agreed to the adjournment but added that he expected the following day would conclude the case for the prosecution, allowing Alexander Chaffers to bring his own case for his defence and to call all the witnesses he had promised would be called—hitherto he had been restricted to cross-examining the witnesses for the prosecution—as well as to present all the documents he had promised would be presented, including the birth certificate of Lady Twiss.

The hearing was to resume on Wednesday, March 13. On that day, the Sessions House at Newington was once again "densely crowded" at midday, the appointed time the proceedings were due to recommence, and the case "excited very great interest, as it has all along done."[559] There was eager anticipation of Chaffers's defence. The court was informed, however, that proceedings were delayed because Harry Poland was in consultation with the Twisses' solicitors.

---

557. Santley, *Student and Singer*, 76.
558. "The Extraordinary Charge of Libel," *The Times*, March 13, 1872, 11.
559. "The Extraordinary Charge of Libel," *The Times*, March 14, 1872, 11.

Half an hour late, Poland and Mr Barnes, the solicitor, entered the court and took their seats. Poland then addressed the magistrate and told him that "since I was here yesterday Lady Twiss has determined not to appear again in court, and she has, I am informed, left London." Poland concluded that he was "reluctantly compelled to abandon this prosecution, as it would be idle to proceed without her evidence." His instructions, and those of Barnes and Burnard, he said, had been withdrawn by the Twisses. He observed that this development was "painful and annoying to me and to this gentleman who instructs me" and apologized for wasting the time of the court. The announcement, as *The Times* reported, caused "much excitement and surprise." Mr Benson told Poland he had "put the Court in some difficulty," pointing out that "one of the most serious charges that can be made against a man" had been withdrawn when the prosecution was almost complete. He declared, however, "I have no option but to say that the defendant, who has been charged with crimes of the deepest dye, must be discharged." But Benson was not finished. He now turned to Chaffers and said: "This exceedingly un-looked-for termination of the proceedings against you leave me with no choice but to give you the benefit of all that feeling of want of confidence in their case which has induced the prosecutors to announce their intention of appearing here no more. I do not remember in the history of any Criminal Court a result so demoralising as I am the afraid the result of this trial may be to those who look at it superficially or hastily. I fear that to the vulgar, uneducated mind your escape today may convey an impression that a libel, though malicious, is justifiable if it is true. I only hope that everybody who sees you walk forth a free man today will consider well the subject and not come to that conclusion." In addition to venting his spleen, Benson was reminding his audience that, in the law of libel, the truth of a statement was not a sufficient justification for defamation. There must also be a public benefit in the publication of the libel for it to be justified, and, of course, Chaffers had claimed that there was a public benefit in this case as a woman of Lady Twiss's character should not be presented at court, or to the Corporation of London for that matter. Nor was it in the public interest that a man of Twiss's standing, in the offices he held, should be married to such a woman.

While condemning Chaffers by saying the truth of his claims were insufficient justification for their publication, the magistrate acknowledged that there was truth in his accusations regarding the Twisses. Benson continued his monologue: "With regard to what you said of the conduct of that woman—that unfortunate woman, whose courage, after having been brave for a few days, has failed her, who has shrunk from meeting the frightful charges which, perhaps, some former connexion with or knowledge of her in early days has enabled you to make—she has gone. But you, for your conduct in this case, making it necessary that steps should be taken against you, and for your behaviour in your defence, will possibly for the rest of your life be an object of contempt to all honest and well thinking men."⁵⁶⁰ This last remark, *The Times* reported, "elicited considerable applause in court." Benson, however, was not finished: "I have nothing more to say to you except to warn you not to imagine you may further persecute these unfortunate people,—the husband wrapped in distress and shame through some weakness in his wife's evidence which may have been concealed from him, and the woman shrinking from the fearful publicity consequent upon again facing a court of justice and submitting to the ordeal to which you subject her." Benson's point was that his was a court of first instance, and if he found Chaffers guilty of libel, he was obliged to submit him to trial in a higher court, in which case Lady Twiss would have again been cross-examined. He was wrong, however, that Chaffers could not further persecute the Twisses. Chaffers would pursue them into their old age, and beyond the grave, even when he was himself in the workhouse. Benson futilely reiterated: "I warn you not to renew or repeat the frightful tyranny which some knowledge you may have enables you to exercise over her. Above all things, let me warn you not to think you will be acquitted by the verdict of any civilized society of the gross misconduct of which you have been guilty because there may be some vestige of truth in the assertions you have made."⁵⁶¹

This should have been an end of Chaffers's incarceration, but it was not because he was also being held on the charge of having defamed Mr Henry Williams by virtue of having accused him of bigamy. That case was also to be prosecuted by Harry Poland, although it was brought by different solicitors. Poland told Mr Benson that the parties to that second case were not present because the sudden implosion of the Twiss case had been unexpected. Benson therefore remanded Chaffers until the next day, March 14, when the charge by Williams would be heard. The following day, however, after Chaffers had spent another night in Horesemonger Lane Gaol, he arrived at Southwark Police Court to hear from the clerk of the court that the prosecution solicitors, Norris and Son, had withdrawn their brief from Harry Poland because Mr Williams did not intend to proceed with his charge.⁵⁶² Benson, once again the magistrate, said that he had nothing to add in addition to what he had stated the previous day about Chaffers's character. This was a "frightful instance," he said, of the "terrorism" that could be exercised by an "adept in libel" when a second charge could be "as suddenly withdrawn as was the first." Chaffers, who had a night to think about Benson's tirade of the previous day, stated that "not having heard my case, you ought not to have made any observations." He was then discharged and left the court on Thursday, March 14. The following year, in his own account of the trial, Chaffers commented "why because the prosecution led by Sir Travers Twiss had collapsed

---

560. "The Extraordinary Charge of Libel," *The Times*, March 14, 1872, 11.
561. "The Extraordinary Charge of Libel," *The Times*, March 14, 1872, 11.
562. "The Second Charge against Chaffers," *The South London Press*, March 16, 1872.

the other prosecution by Mr Williams should not be proceeded with I am at a loss to imagine." Henry Williams and the Twisses were not connected "in the slightest way," and it was difficult to explain other than as part of an elaborate web woven to save Lady Twiss.[563]

Two days after the collapse of the libel trial, on Friday, March 15, Twiss wrote to Tait, holding out the hope of another indictment of Chaffers and a new trial, and also offering an explanation for why they had abandoned the previous case: "I am going to hear a consultation tomorrow with Sergeant Ballantyne whether I can indict Chaffers at the Old Bailey for libel with good chance of success. Lady Twiss did not fear Chaffers's evidence, as not one of his witnesses could say that she was Madame Gelas, and the others would have denied it, she had made some false statements in her evidence and Chaffers had summoned a witness to contradict her. She was anxious to go into Court and explain, but she was in such an excited state that she would only have made matters worse and Chaffers might have claimed that she should be committed for perjury. I would not therefore let her get in the witness box. She is of a highly excitable temperament and under momentary excitement makes no distinction between what exists in fact and what exists in imagination. Such is the explanation of what appeared to be a strange conclusion of an eventful drama."[564] His letter reveals that, as the trial progressed, imprisonment for perjury became a danger equal to the scandal itself, and, indeed, Chaffers subsequently pursued her on that basis. He later wrote of his astonishment that Twiss did not take the stand as a witness in his own trial, but the fear of perjuring himself was probably one restraint. Twiss did not specify what false statements Lady Twiss had made, and he was not ready to concede that she had lived under the persona of Maria Gelas. Instead, he was turning to Serjeant William Ballantine, the serjeant-at-law, who had just concluded the civil case in which he had represented the Tichborne Claimant in his effort to prove that he was the true Roger Tichborne.[565] It was a prudent choice. The parallel between Lady Twiss and the Tichborne Claimant's metamorphoses were evident, as was Ballantine's expertise and experience in such matters. Tait was cautious in response: "My dear Twiss, I had your letter yesterday. I do most earnestly trust that you may be able to clear yourself in this dreadful matter. Fully remembering as I do the kindness I have received from you ever since my early days in Oxford, I shall rejoice as much as any of your many friends who have received kindness at your hands if this wretched cloud is dispelled."[566] Behind Tait's nostalgia was a justifiable pessimism. Despite the

---

563. Chaffers, *The Twiss Libel Case*, 18.
564. Twiss to Tait, March 15, 1872, Lambeth Palace Library, Tait Papers, 184, ff.84–85v.
565. William Ballantine, *Some Experiences of a Barrister's Life* (New York, 1883), 430–441.
566. Twiss to Tait, March 17, 1872, Lambeth Palace Library, Tait Papers, 184, f.86.

outward expression of sympathy, he made his thoughts plain in the entry to his personal diary of the same day, March 17: "The astonishing and dreadful exposure and collapse in the Police Court respecting Twiss and Lady Twiss has filled us all with horror."[567] That private sense of horror was a more reliable indicator of the Twisses' future social prospects than the publicly expressed kindness.

Whatever new action Twiss had been contemplating against Chaffers at the Old Bailey did not materialize. Lady Twiss had already fled London for Switzerland, partly, no doubt, in the need to escape the publicity and scandal aroused by the case, but probably also to put herself beyond the law should Chaffers pursue her for defamation or perjury—fears that would later prove to be warranted. On the Monday morning, Twiss wrote again to Tait: "Will you kindly let me know your wishes as I have failed in my process against Mr Chaffers and my wife will become insane, if she is not so already, if I were to submit her to another examination. If you think it will be a proper step on my part to resign my office of Vicar General, let me kindly know your wishes."[568] Tait did not hesitate to accept Twiss's resignation: "I apprehend from your letter this day received that the hopes expressed in your letter of the 15th have failed and that you find yourself unable to go into court to vindicate your character. I need not tell you that this fills me with the greatest regret. I should indeed have rejoiced had you been able to clear yourself, but as matters stand at present I have nothing left me but to accept your resignation of the office of Vicar General."[569] Tait reminded Twiss that it was not just Lady Twiss's character that had been called into question, but Twiss himself. Twiss replied with a short note to Tait resigning as Vicar General of the Province of Canterbury and expressing his thanks for the kindness Tait had shown him over many years. He similarly wrote to Bishop Jackson, explaining that his proceedings against Chaffers had failed and offering his resignation.[570] Jackson accepted, and Twiss sent his formal resignation as Chancellor of the Diocese of London on March 19.[571] At the same time, he resigned all his other church offices, including his positions as Chancellor of the Dioceses of Lincoln and Hereford. He requested the Prime Minister, William Gladstone, to submit to the Queen his resignation as Queen's Advocate, the position which had gained his knighthood. This should have been a victory for Chaffers, yet, relentless as always, he

---

567. A. C. Tait, Personal Diary, March 17, 1872, Lambeth Palace Library, Tait Papers, 48, f.94.

568. Twiss to Tait, March 18, 1872, Lambeth Palace Library, Tait Papers, 184, ff.87–88.

569. Tait to Twiss, March 18, 1872, Lambeth Palace Library, Tait Papers, 184, f.89.

570. Twiss to Jackson, March 18, 1872, Lambeth Palace Library, Jackson Papers, 33, f.156.

571. Twiss to Jackson, March 19, 1872, Lambeth Palace Library, Jackson Papers, 33, f.157.

complained that Twiss, despite the fact that his career was in tatters, remained a Queen's Counsel and a bencher of Lincoln's Inn.[572]

Not everyone lacked sympathy. The Twiss trial was, according to reports, the "town-talk for a fortnight" in London, in March 1872.[573] The day after the trial collapsed, the *Daily News* observed, "The abrupt withdrawal on the part of the prosecution shrouds the whole affair in the most bewildering mystery," but it then quickly asserted that "this strange decision" had set free "a man who has earned the contempt of his fellow creatures by his cowardly conduct, and which is only too likely to bring down on an unhappy woman the most cruel suspicions of which a woman can be the object." "Whether or not the allegations against Lady Twiss are true," the journal lamented, "it is impossible to regard without much commiseration the spectacle of a woman being mercilessly dragged before the public." It concluded, "The elements of a wild and bitter tragedy are contained in such portions of this story as have come to light."[574] *The Times* joined in the condemnation of Chaffers and even criticized the magistrate in the case, Mr Benson, for some of his remarks concerning Lady Twiss, although it agreed that there was a danger the trial could encourag a belief that libel was justified merely because it was true. The newspaper remarked that Lady and Sir Travers Twiss "have a claim on our pity."[575] The editorial complained, "It is not long since Mrs Radcliffe has been subjected to a moral torture hardly less severe by the detestable falsehoods of the claimant in the TICHBORNE case." The reference here was to Roger Tichborne's cousin, Katherine Doughty, who became Katherine Radcliffe on her marriage. Radcliffe was one of the members of the Tichborne family who declared that the claimant was an imposter. In retaliation, the claimant stated in court that this was because he had seduced Katherine Radcliffe.[576] Radcliffe was then obliged to take the witness stand in order to deny the claim. "Even upon the assumption of her [Lady Twiss's] guilt," the paper continued, "her assailant merits the condemnation of every generous mind."

The paper finally called for an end to the use of statutory declarations for the purposes of vilification and defamation. On precisely this question, it had published a letter, three days previously, inspired by the Twiss case. The letter was written by Twiss's old adversary, George Bowyer, who in 1850 had defended Pope Pious IX's *Universalis Ecclesiae*, which re-established the

---

572. Chaffers, *The Twiss Libel Case*, 3.

573. *The Annual Register: A Review of Public Events at Home and Abroad for the Year 1872* (London, 1873), 14–16.

574. *Daily News*, March 14, 1872, 2.

575. "The Startling and Wholly Unexpected Issue of the Libel Case," *The Times*, March 14, 1872, 9. For a review of sympathetic opinion towards the Twisses, see "Epitome of Opinion in the Morning Journals: The Twiss Libel Case," *Pall Mall Gazette*, March 14, 1872, 2.

576. McWilliam, *The Tichborne Claimant*, 50.

Catholic hierarchy in England. Twiss vehemently attacked Bowyer in his *Letters Apostolic of the Pope Pius IX*, and Bowyer had responded with *Observations on the Arguments of Dr Twiss respecting the New Catholic Hierarchy*. More than twenty years later, he wrote to *The Times*, while the trial was still in progress, to defend Twiss against Chaffers and to condemn the misuse of statutory declarations. "What do we see in this case?" Bowyer asked. "A man respected and esteemed by all who know him" driven into court with his wife and "stigmatized by disgraceful charges" merely because a man can go before a magistrate and make a statutory declaration. It was only because Twiss had the "moral courage" and had not submitted to blackmail that the abuse had been revealed. How many more cases remained silent? "If I were still in parliament," he concluded, "I would take it in hand."[577] Indeed, in the parliament, on March 15, William Keppel, Viscount Bury, asked, in the context of the "late proceedings, which had more or less given great personal pain to the persons connected with them, and had been the cause of general regret," whether Sir John Coleridge, the Attorney General "was willing to introduce such amendment of the law as would render statutory declarations less liable to abuse." Coleridge, the representative of Agnes Willoughby in the Windham trial, responded that it was not because "there had been found one scoundrel to abuse the legal process" that the law on statutory declarations, which was found to work in "hundreds and thousands of other cases" of attorneys going about their business, should be changed.[578] Chaffers observed that, in the House of Commons, "the Attorney General did me the honour of calling me a scoundrel," but noted that in the Tichborne trial Coleridge had asked the British public to "suspend their judgement until they heard both sides of the question." Coleridge represented the Tichborne family against the claimant during the civil trial of the Tichborne case, declaring that the claimant was "comparable to Martin Guerre and the other great imposters of history."[579] Indeed, the story of Martin Guerre, a story in which Arnauld de Tilh temporarily succeeded in assuming not only the identity but the life of Martin Guerre, completely reinventing himself, had great resonance with cases of Victorian metamorphoses, including that of Pharalide van Lynseele.[580]

Coleridge had, in fact, encountered Chaffers prior to his speech in the House of Commons on statutory declarations. Almost ten years earlier, as opposing counsel, he had described Chaffers as "scandalous and vexatious" in a case where Chaffers pursued the return of papers from a trustee when the papers had already been returned to him, possibly in order to secure costs.[581]

---

577. George Bowyer, "Statutory Declarations," *The Times*, March 11, 1872, 5.
578. *House of Commons Hansard*, March 15, 1872, Vol. 210, cc.30–33.
579. Chaffers, *The Twiss Libel Case*, 21; McWilliam, *The Tichborne Claimant*, 51.
580. For the story of Martin Guerre, see Davis, *The Return of Martin Guerre*.
581. Taggart, "Alexander Chaffers," 658.

The Times, in an article reprinted from the *Law Magazine and Review* (one of the journals in which Twiss published), criticized Coleridge's defence of the law of statutory declarations in the House of Commons, arguing that in the Twiss case, Chaffers was not going about his business as an attorney.[582]

Not all newspapers were sympathetic with the Twisses. Many used sympathy as a means of arousing prurient interest. Some revelled in the scandal. On March 13, *Trewman's Exeter Flying Post* reported, "The Tichborne sensation has exploded ... But the Twiss case is replacing it in the newspapers and replacing it with 'charming fitness.'"[583] Delighted, the newspaper declared: "This case is the smartest, naughtiest—ugliest piece of scandal that we have had on hand for many a long day." The author was quick to state, "It is an atrocious libel, I believe, from beginning to end." With this caveat aside, the article indulged in the possibilities of the case: "There is generally something in the misfortunes of our best friends which is not altogether unpleasant to us. This to many people is particularly pleasant; for it is a novelty of the highest piquancy to hear an attorney standing up in a police-court and talking about the amours of the Vicar-General of the Province of Canterbury—of the days when he kept Agnes Willoughby, one of the *élite* of her class, as Sir John Coleridge once affectionately described her, and lost £8,000 or £10,000 by her."[584] The connection between Twiss and Willoughby had now not only been made publicly in court, and been reported in *The Times*, but had become material for the amusement of gossip columnists, and this was before the case had yet collapsed. The author proceeded to describe "his secret negotiations with a Polish adventuress whom he picks up with an attorney at Cremorne, and marries for the sake of economy, making £5,000 by the transaction—and of the lady's liaisons with her old paramours, of her surreptitious visits to Cremorne, and of the thousand other things of this kind which it makes one's blood tingle to read of in the newspapers." One of the salient aspects of this account is that it revealed, as in the Windham case, that what was published in newspapers and elsewhere had been sanitised when compared with what had transpired in the court or in the solicitors' briefs. This article was only prepared to hint at aspects of the Twiss libel which had been implicit from the published account—such as Lady Twiss maintaining her "old paramours" after she had met Twiss—but were left unstated.

The salacious account in *Trewman's Exeter Flying Post* finally concluded that "these Tichborne and Twiss cases" had put the business of the parliament in the shade, such was the public fascination with them. The Tichborne civil case had run from May 10, 1871, to March 6, 1872, while the Twiss libel case began on February 29, 1872, and concluded on March 13, 1872. While accounts

582. "Statutory Declarations," *The Times*, April 1, 1872, 9.
583. "London and Paris Gossip," *Trewman's Exeter Flying Post*, March 13, 1872, 8.
584. "London and Paris Gossip," *Trewman's Exeter Flying Post*, March 13, 1872, 8.

of the Twiss trial had made connections with the Tichborne case, when the Tichborne claimant was put to a criminal trial, beginning in April 1873, the comparisons were reversed: now, participants in the Tichborne trial drew upon the Twiss case. The Tichborne claimant dispensed with William Ballantine as his advocate and employed Edward Kenealy, a talented but eccentric Irish barrister. During the course of the trial, Kenealy sought to discredit Lady Radcliffe, and he did so by comparing her with Pharaïlde Twiss. His account illustrates the public perception of Pharaïlde Twiss after the collapse of the libel trial. Kenealy appealed to the jury to consider more carefully Katherine Radcliffe "before you put undoubted faith in what she says." He then turned to the Twiss case: "Gentlemen, we are living in the days of Lady Twiss. Her history has passed before our eyes and that ought to make us cautious before we give implicit belief to what ladies of a certain kind swear. How many French witnesses did Lady Twiss call? Everybody, of course, feels for that unhappy woman, but there is a fact you cannot shut your eyes to. A person occupying by right of her husband a high, social position comes forward and gives false evidence supported by false witnesses. She did not dare to face the ordeal to which she would have finally been subjected."[585] The judge, Alexander Cockburn, who was the Lord Chief Justice, was in no mood to hear Kenealy's views on the Twiss case, as he felt the trial was already taking too long, and he responded: "You assume that which, as I am aware, is not true, that a class of French witness examined in this case are in the same category as the class of French witness examined in Lady Twiss's case." The jury, he said, should not be influenced by the credibility of the witnesses called in the Twiss case. Kenealy's claim that the Twisses presented "false evidence supported by false witnesses" is indicative of public perception, but the Lord Chief Justice's dismissal of the quality of the witnesses in the Twiss trial was damning. Despite public expressions of sympathy, Lady Twiss and Sir Travers had been publicly discredited. It was widely accepted that witnesses such as Jastreuski, Edmond André Guillaume, Pharaïlde van Lynseele's drawing teacher, Monsieur Des Mares, and her music teacher, Guilla, were performing roles, albeit to a degree that is difficult to establish. All were adopting personae in order to save the persona of Lady Twiss. Dr Tristram, who owed so much to Twiss, from his days as a student to his professional appointment, may have met somebody he believed to be General van Lynseele, or he may have been lying to protect his mentor. In either case, the trial had been an elaborate hoax.

Kenealy's conduct in the Tichborne trial was so abusive that he was disbenched and disbarred from legal practice. In his multi-volume vindication of his actions, he asked why it was that he had merely asked about the credibility of Lady Radcliffe as a witness and had been disbarred, whereas Travers Twiss

---

585. Edward Kenealy, *The Trial at Bar of Sir Roger C. D. Tichborne* (London, 1877), Vol. 3, 356.

had presented false witnesses and was allowed to continue to practice at the Bar. He proceeded to re-publish the newspaper accounts of the Twiss trial to prove his point. Kenealy said he asked this question "with no feeling whatever against Sir Travers Twiss (for whom we are sorry)," but while Kenealy "did nothing but his duty to Tichborne as Counsel and Advocate, and for this he was disbenched, disbarred, and ruined. Dr Twiss, knowingly or unknowingly, produced false witnesses in a Court of Justice, and for this he was never in the least interfered with by his Benchers, but still practices his profession and retains his rank of Q.C., as if nothing had happened."[586] Alexander Chaffers had asked the precisely same question about Twiss's continued legal standing.

While Chaffers had succeeded in greatly damaging both Lady Twiss and Sir Travers Twiss, he had also inflicted enormous damage upon himself, and he did so in a calculated way. He knew what the consequences of his testimony would be for his own reputation. When, in 1873, he self-published his own account of the case, he conceded, "It was not pleasant to expose my own immorality," but he had been obliged to do so, he argued, in order to save himself from conviction.[587] He did not say that he had forced the circumstances in which he was obliged to defend himself. He declared, "I do not say with Mawworm—'I like to be despised'; but I do say that . . . I care little for the censure or the sneers of a public whose ideas of justice are to condemn one without a hearing."[588] Chaffers, however, was not completely insensitive to censure. He did not appreciate being called a scoundrel by the Attorney General, and on October 1, 1872, he wrote to the Home Secretary to object to the manner in which Magistrate Benson had addressed him at the conclusion of the Twiss trial. He said it was a duty of any person to inform the Lord Chamberlain of "an outrage upon society, and such a gross insult to her Majesty" as had been performed by "a foreign adventuress" who had lived "a grossly and openly immoral life." In that case, he declared, "a magistrate has no right to condemn, or make severe observations upon, the conduct of any person" who brings such a scandal to light without giving that person an opportunity "of being heard in his own defence." "The effect of Mr Benson's observations," he said, "has been of the most fearful consequence to me, and they have, in fact, utterly ruined me, besides causing me the greatest annoyance, and subjecting me to the grossest insults and even threats of personal violence."[589]

The consequences of the trial for the Twisses were even graver. In the days after its conclusion, Sir Travers and Lady Twiss fled London for Switzerland. From Basle, Sir Travers wrote to Bishop Jackson to say that he had left London

---

586. Kenealy, *The Trial at Bar*, 240.

587. Chaffers, *The Twiss Libel Case*, 19.

588. Chaffers, *The Twiss Libel Case*, 1. Mawworm was a villain in Isaac Bickerstaffe's 1769 play *The Hypocrite*.

589. Chaffers, *The Twiss Libel Case*, 22–23.

"about three weeks ago," immediately after his resignations.[590] He said he had been "quite broken down in mind and body." The proceedings against Chaffers had been stopped because his wife had made a statement "with regard to her intimacy in 1859 with a lady, who was afterwards one of her best friends and who is now dead, which a member of the lady's family impugned, and was determined to come into court, and to declare it to be false and I was thus placed in a position of greater embarrassment than that which Mr Chaffers' original libel had given rise to. I had no option but to discontinue the proceedings." It was not from fear of Chaffers's witnesses, he said, that they abandoned the case. He was confident that those witnesses would distinguish between Lady Twiss and Madame Gelas, but "I could not allow in the presence of such an adversary my wife to be charged with perjury." "I was always aware," he added, "that perjury would be one of the rocks" upon which the case could be "shipwrecked," particularly when Chaffers, "the criminal," was allowed to cross-examine his wife. His cross-examination was a "stain upon our civilization" which would never have been allowed in a "continental tribunal." Chaffers, Twiss observed, "was aware that my wife had a family secret, which he had not been allowed to penetrate, but of which he could take advantage, namely that her mother was an Austrian lady of rank who retired early in life into a convent of which she became Abbess and whose name could not be disclosed, and with this object he suggested she was a person of low origin." The illegitimate daughter of an Austrian abbess and a Dutch count—Pharaïlde and Travers Twiss were once again busy creating a new persona.

On the point of leaving London, Lady Twiss, "half-distracted" by the case, had received a letter from Dr Hermann Zumpe, "the Attorney General of the King of Saxony," in whose house near Dresden they had been married (although this is not quite accurate; they had been married from the house of the Plenipotentiary Minister, Charles Townshend Barnard). Dr Zumpe wrote that "*il y a ici des hommes de la plus haute considération qui répondent de votre honneur*" ("here there are men of the highest standing who will answer for your honour") and that she should seek company amongst people who "*apprécient vos vertus malgré les petits nuages qui les obscurent*" ("appreciate your virtues despite the little clouds which obscure them"). Once again, Twiss was trying to maintain his wife's persona with the testimony of others, as one would expect a lawyer to do. He observed that when he left London he "hardly contemplated being able ever again to resume active work, and I had almost determined to renounce my country the laws of which allowed such a terrible wrong to be perpetrated."[591] He announced, however, that he had become

---

590. Twiss to Jackson, April 13, 1872, Lambeth Palace Library, Jackson Papers, 33, ff.159–161.

591. Twiss to Jackson, April 13, 1872, Lambeth Palace Library, Jackson Papers, 33, ff.159–161.

resigned to his misfortune and looked forward to being able to resume his "profession after a good holiday." They had taken an apartment on the bank of the Rhine, looking upon the old town of Basle, with a "most picturesque" view. He had just written to the Archbishop, he said, "almost my first letter." His wife, he concluded, "begs to unite with me in best wishes, and hopes Mr Jackson is gaining strength steadily." In a postscript, he added that he was pleased to learn of his friend, Dr Tristram's, "appointment": that is, his appointment as the new Chancellor of the Diocese of London, replacing Twiss. Tristram was a man "of sound judgement and right feeling."

The letter to Jackson attempted to establish a plausible story with which Twiss, and his friends, could live and work in the future. The letter to Archbishop Tait, to which he referred, went further. It repeated, almost verbatim, most of what was stated in the letter to Jackson, but it added a plea for employment and income.[592] Twiss repeated that he had experienced a kind of nervous breakdown: "I felt myself compelled to leave London by the consciousness that my mind would have given way under the weight of the calamities, which have so suddenly overtaken me if I had remained there. In fact I was hardly responsible for my actions when I left, so completely were the nerves of my brain disordered."[593] Twiss, however, never wrote a letter without a purpose. Just weeks after the calamities of the trial, he was looking for some kind of redemption and some hope of a professional future: "The disturbance however has proved to be functional, and I am gradually regaining my powers of mind and memory, and I have hopes now still to be useful and able to support myself by my own exertions, as I have hitherto done since I took my degree of B.A. at Oxford. My career since that time has, I hope, not been without some benefit to my country and my fellow beings, and I may sincerely say that the interests of 'Self' have been the last object which I had in view, and it is from this disregard of my own interests that my future will be full of gloom, if my assumption of active life in some humbler department at home or abroad should be made impossible by the inflection of any mark of the Queen's displeasure." Tait's patronage was key to his future in England, although he knew that he was only fit, at best, for some "humbler" office than he was accustomed to, even an office abroad. He hoped that Tait may also have the influence to overcome the opposition of the Royal Household to any future office.

Continuing this long letter, he then observed that the proceedings against Chaffers had been stopped "by the fact that my wife had made certain statements during her examination with respect to her acquaintance in 1859 with a lady now dead, who was afterwards one of her best friends, the truth of

---

592. Although the letter is undated, it is clear from the letter to Jackson that it was written on April 12 or 13, and was addressed also from Basle.

593. Twiss to Tait, [no date: April 1872], Lambeth Palace Library, Tait Papers 184, ff.92–93.

which statements some members of the lady's family impugned, and as they were determined to come forward and declare my wife's statements to be false, the case could not proceed." The almost verbatim repetition suggests a story well-rehearsed and planned over the previous weeks. It is not clear to whom Twiss was referring, but this was a new explanation for why the trial failed. He repeated that he had been "reliably informed" that some of Chaffers's witnesses could distinguish Lady Twiss from Maria Gelas and said that they had not, therefore, abandoned their case out of fear of his witnesses. Rather, he said, the "case was stopped" due to "different considerations, which have been more embarrassing to me than the original libel." He does not say what could be more embarrassing than the original libel, but it may be the possibility of perjury that he raised with Bishop Jackson. In any case, it is clear that Twiss had decided upon a defence in which he knew he could no longer deny everything, so he chose to concede some faults in order to obscure the truth. Importantly, however, he was placing all the burden of falsehood upon his wife and deflecting it from himself. Amongst other things, he appeared to hope that such a strategy gave him the best chances of returning to some kind of public office, however humble.

Twiss then turned to the public reception of the trial and its aftermath, aware that the trial had brought out not only speculation as to Pharaïlde Twiss's past but also the stories about Twiss and Agnes Willoughby: "I am aware that my absence from London has left the field open to Mr Chaffers and I am informed that a variety of stories against me are in circulation without anybody authorised to contradict them. These stories must either originate with Mr Chaffers or are the gossip of society, and I know of no remedy for them. The cross-examination alone to which my wife was exposed, the toleration of which was a stain upon our civilisation, such as no tribunal of no other country would have permitted, was enough to blight the character and destroy the happiness of any woman." When Lady Twiss left London, she was, he said, "driven wild by the misery of her false position," but she was greatly encouraged by a letter sent by Dr Herman Zumpe, from Dresden, and he quoted the same lines he sent to Jackson. Her education and manners, he said, had satisfied all those who knew her, "although the name of my wife's mother cannot for many reasons be disclosed, and the secret of her birth must always remain a mystery. I am well advised that she was an Austrian lady of rank and that my wife is a lady by blood."[594] Oddly, he did not employ the story about her being the daughter of an Austrian abbess, although that may be because the letter to Tait was written before the letter to Jackson and the story had not yet taken shape. He lamented, "For ten years she has lived before the world in London without reproach," and indeed they had almost succeeded in their creation

---

594. Twiss to Tait, [no date: April 1872], Lambeth Palace Library, Tait Papers 184, f.93r.

of the daughter of a Dutch nobleman who lived in Poland to whom now was added a mysterious Austrian lady of rank.

Hoping to have satisfied doubts about his wife, Twiss returned to the question of his own future, which he only hinted at when writing to Jackson. One difficulty he said was "as to what course I ought to adopt as regards the Lord Chamberlain." Twiss reminded Tait that "Your Grace had conferred with him [the Lord Chamberlain] before I commenced proceedings against Mr Chaffers," so that it was the Lord Chamberlain and Tait who had been responsible for the disaster of the trial. He said that, during the many years he had been persecuted by Chaffers, he had "refused to buy him off," although the payments he made in sham proceedings for "legal work done" looked very much like hush money. In growing desperation, he wrote: "Circumstances however not foreseen by me occurred to stay the proceedings, and the moment that I found that I could not clean up the difficulty of my wife's position I placed at once in your Grace's hands the resignation of my office of Vicar General and requested Mr Gladstone to submit to the Queen the resignation of my office of Queen's Advocate. In fact I did all which I could to relieve the Church and the State of any obloquy which might attach to them from my official relations to them." While stressing that his actions had been honourable, he also underlined the fact that the scandal brought by his marriage had been an unwanted scandal for the church and also for the state. Nevertheless, Twiss now turned to the matter of his income: "But in giving up my offices I have given up the income which has been the support of my family and of many who depended upon me, and I am anxious that no additional mark of the Queen's displeasure should be inflicted upon me, which could lead the world to believe the libel to be true, and destroy my future chances of usefulness in some humbler department of life." There are no records or mentions of Pharaïlde and Travers Twiss having children, so the family to whom Twiss refers as dependent is possibly that of his sister (his brother had disappeared) and also Pharaïlde Twiss's family. Importantly, as a man who had always relied upon his wits for his income, having little in terms of inherited fortune, he was conscious that the scandal spelled financial ruin. He therefore concluded this long letter by begging Tait to "communicate" with the Lord Chamberlain and "submit my case to the gracious consideration of the Queen."

Tait, responding to the strong bonds of friendship, agreed to Twiss's request and wrote to the Lord Chamberlain, even enclosing Twiss's letter. The Royal Household, however, was unsentimental, and the Lord Chamberlain, Earl Sydney, responded in a letter to Tait to say that the case had been "fully considered" and, rather than offering Twiss a position of some humble kind, as requested, he had "decided that Lady Twiss's Presentation at Court should be 'cancelled.'"[595] Cancellation of a presentation at court was a very rare act and

---

595. Lord Chamberlain to Tait, April 15, 1872, Lambeth Palace Library, Tait Papers 184, ff.94–95.

a deep humiliation. Moreover, the presentation at court was one of the acts that had been central to the invention of Pharaïlde Twiss as a "lady by blood," as Twiss put it, and its cancellation would, as he feared, make it difficult to continue to present her as such. It annulled her social personality. No similar action, Earl Sydney continued, would be taken towards Sir Travers because "there does not appear to be any direct evidence to show that he was cognisant of Lady Twiss's alleged character when she was presented at Court." The emphasis placed upon the question of direct evidence indicates the suspicions raised by circumstantial evidence and, as a consequence, the degree to which Twiss's own ingenuity was a matter of speculation. He had come close to having official action taken against him by the Royal Household, presumably including the cancellation of his knighthood. The Lord Chancellor had taken his view of the matter after having "submitted the matter to Her Majesty for consideration." He finally asked if "Your Grace would be kind enough to consider this communication as regards Lady Twiss as private for the present until I can take the necessary official steps." Sir Travers, he added, had written a "very similar letter to that which Your Grace enclosed" directly to the Lord Chancellor's office. The official steps to be taken against Lady Twiss included an announcement, four days after Sydney wrote to Tait, in *The London Gazette*, the official record of the state: "Lord Chamberlain's Office, April 18, 1872, Notice is hereby given that, the Presentation at Court of Lady Twiss has been cancelled."[596] That notice was then reported in all the daily newspapers.

With new offices barred, the Twisses' financial situation became dire. Within weeks of the Lord Chamberlain's response, in May 1872, they let their house in Park Lane. At the same time, they put what were reported in the newspapers to be the "costly contents" up for auction. The wine cellar alone was expected to raise a considerable sum: "As Sir Travers was known to possess some rare vintages, a lively competition is anticipated." It was also reported that Twiss's friends, "who sympathize with him in the great calamity that has befallen him, are getting up a subscription on his behalf, except that it is being done in a very quiet and unostentatious manner," apart from the fact that it was announced in the daily newspapers. "Some handsome amounts," this report continued, "will be forthcoming from among the members of the Athenaeum Club, to which he belongs, and from which there is not, I understand, any desire to exclude him, although it is improbable that he will care to go there again."[597] Twiss's supposed sense of shame in this report was not exaggerated. He declined the charity of his friends. His good friend from University College, Goldwin Smith, with whom he had

---

596. *The London Gazette*, April 18, 1872, 1.
597. "Sir Travers Twiss," *The Dundee Courier and Argus*, May 6, 1872, 2. See also *Shields Gazette and Daily Telegraph*, May 15, 1872, 2.

drunk a bottle of Metternich's wine before his marriage, said he saw Twiss "some years after his fall," and yet, even at this remove, when Smith crossed the Strand to shake his hand, Twiss had "dived into the crowd."[598] He was, according to Smith, "a ruined man." When University College celebrated its millennium on June 19, 1872, Twiss should have been at the heart of the celebrations. Instead, he was absent from the feast attended by the Chancellor of the Exchequer and 120 other distinguished guests. The toast to the College was made by another of Twiss's old friends, Arthur Stanley, now Dean of Westminster, whom Twiss had contrived to have admitted as a fellow thirty-three years earlier. In his speech, Stanley reminisced on his first years in the College, saying he had been "taken in by this college, through the kindness of one who is not and could not be here today, but whom I cannot fail to recall with grateful remembrance."[599] Even uttering Twiss's name, at a joyful occasion, had become awkward.

Of Pharaïlde Twiss there is less information, although the little that survives for later years, as we shall see, is vital. By October 1872, Chaffers had begun his pursuit of her for perjury. On Wednesday, October 16, Chaffers appeared in the Southwark Police Court once again, but this time seeking warrants or summonses for perjury against Pharaïlde Twiss and Louisa Harrison (her purported former maid) for having stated in the same court, and at the Sessions House, that "Lady Twiss was not Madame Gelas." Chaffers called two witnesses by subpoena, but they could not, *The Times* reported, give any "positive" evidence. The magistrate, again, was Mr Benson, and he "declined to accede" to Chaffers's proposition. Chaffers "left the court in rather an angry mood." Chaffers, however, told a different story, although "not a word" of his version "appeared in any newspaper."[600] He was, he said, proceeding to examine one of his witnesses when the magistrate intervened and told the witness that he was not obliged to give evidence "unless he chose." The witness then immediately left court.[601] Chaffers wrote to the Home Secretary to object to the behaviour of Magistrate Benson, asking whether it was a "new thing for a magistrate to throw obstacles in the way of a prosecutor proving the commission of such a fearful crime as perjury."[602] Mr Benson, he said, had told him in a "furious passion" that his subpoenas were "improperly issued," so Chaffers enclosed them for the inspection of the Home Secretary. He also wanted to call attention to the "want of punctuality" of Mr Benson, who never took his seat before 11:20 in the morning, whereas all the Equity Court judges took their

---

598. Smith, *Reminiscences*, 87.
599. "The Millenary of University College," *The Guardian*, June 19, 1872. I would like to thank Robin Darwhall-Smith for pointing out this occasion and the significance of Stanley's words.
600. Chaffers, *The Twiss Libel Case*, 22.
601. Chaffers, *The Twiss Libel Case*, 21.
602. Chaffers, *The Twiss Libel Case*, 23.

seats just after 10:00.[603] Chaffers's complaints fell upon deaf ears, and his pursuit of Lady Twiss was for some time postponed.

By the following year, the Twisses appear to have exhausted the money they had raised from the sale of the contents of their home because they put their library up for auction. The "Miscellenaeous Library of Sir Travers Twiss, removed from Park Lane," included many thousands of volumes, on display in the auction rooms of Patrick and Simpson at 47 Leicester Square. The library had been painstakingly collected over decades and included gems such as the first edition of Richard Hakluyt's 1589 *Principal Navigations*, as well as numerous sixteenth-, seventeenth-, and eighteenth-century works on law, politics, history, and literature.[604]

The humiliation for Pharaïlde and Travers Twiss reached a climax when they became the inspiration for a three-volume novel published by Joseph Hatton in 1874, under the title *Clytie: A Novel of Modern Life*.[605] Hatton began the story with the sentence: "Two men loved her."[606] In the novel, the characters Clytie, the daughter of a musician, and her aristocratic husband, Tom Mayfield, have their lives shattered by a blackmailer, Philip Ransford, who uses a statutory declaration to reveal his knowledge of a time in Clytie's past when she worked in the theatre, and during which she was almost trapped into prostitution. As a consequence, Clytie is excluded from the Queen's Drawing Room, and the couple sue Ransford for libel. *Clytie* was not even a good novel, displaying "Hatton's florid melodrama at its crudest," but in choosing the character Clytie from Ovid, Hatton recognised the manner in which the story of Pharaïlde van Lynseele's transformation into Lady Travers Twiss captured the Victorian concern with metamorphoses.[607] In Ovid's *Metamorphoses*, Clytie was a water nymph who fell in love with the sun god, Helios. She destroyed her rival for his love, but this turned Helios against her. With "her love turned to madness," while lying on a rock staring at him for nine days, she transformed into a flowering plant, the turnsole, and "though roots hold her fast, she turns ever towards the sun and, though changed herself, preserves her love unchanged."[608] It is not entirely clear why Hatton chose the figure of Clytie for the story of the Twisses, but some aspects of Ovid's account resonated, notably Venus condemning Helios, who brought light to all corners and saw "all things first." He had shed light on the "shame of Venus and Mars," so Venus

603. Chaffers, *The Twiss Libel Case*, 24.
604. *Catalogue of a Portion of the Miscellaneous Library of Sir Travers Twiss*.
605. Joseph Hatton, *Clytie: A Novel of Modern Life*, 3 vols. (London, 1874).
606. Hatton, *Clytie*, Vol. 1, 1.
607. John Sutherland, "Joseph Hatton," in *The Stanford Companion to Victorian Literature* (Stanford, 1989), 284.
608. Ovid, *Metamorphoses, Volume I: Books I to VIII*, translated by Frank Justus Miller. Revised by G. P. Goold, (Cambridge, Mass, 1916), Book IV, 259, 268–269.

sought vengeance, causing him to suffer from the vexations of love.[609] If it was not bad enough to have the story dramatized in a novel, the novel was adapted to the stage and performed at the Ampitheatre in Liverpool, in 1875, and in the Olympic Theatre, in Drury Lane, London, in 1876.

The journal *Athenaeum*, which "loathed Hatton," reviewed *Clytie* as "an utterly worthless book."[610] Too much of the novel consisted of a "young man . . . made to deliver long speeches to a plaster bust." The first and third volumes were merely "introduction and conclusion to the second, in which all the interest, such as it is, is concentrated." "We say advisedly such as it is," the reviewer continued, because "our readers will know what to expect when we tell them that this interest is made to depend on an almost literal reproduction of the details of an excessively nasty trial for slander, which disgusted all decent people two or three years ago." The disgust concerning Chaffers's trial might have been supposed to rest primarily on his conduct, but this was not the reviewer's meaning. Rather, he argued that if a reader wanted to discover Hatton's virtues as a moralist, he or she would be obliged to "renew his or her memory of the circumstances of the trial to which we have alluded." Such circumstances meant that "we can hardly recommend the book to any one who has no taste for the unsavoury." Indeed, so distasteful was the trial that "We wonder whether any ladies will read it, and, if so, they will own to having done so. If they do, it will be a curious instance of the conventional propriety which thinks it no harm to read in a novel that which it would be ashamed to avow acquaintance so long as it had only appeared in a police report."[611] Not only Chaffers, but the Twisses also, were enshrouded in this "unsavoury" air, and even knowledge of their circumstances was shameful and potentially harmful.

The Times was no kinder to Hatton, albeit a little more to the Twisses. It noted that it was only the notoriety of their tribulations that had given the novel any success, so that when "a whisper got about that the story was not quite what such stories should be, the book found its way into most country boxes from libraries, yet it is not in the least worth reading." *The Times* also complained of the "eternal bust and the weary soliloquies," as well as the "inanity of the story." "But the most offensive part of the book," it concluded, "is a long trial, given in all its disgusting minuteness, and almost copied verbatim from the law reports of a year or two ago. If even the idea of persecuting a rich woman and driving her to madness and flight were original, it would hardly be a pleasing subject for a novel." Despite sympathy, however, it was impossible for the Twisses to return to Society.[612]

---

609. Ovid, *Metamorphoses, Books I to VIII*, Book IV, 170–195.
610. Sutherland, "Joseph Hatton," 284.
611. "Novels of the Week," *The Athenaeum*, June 27, 1874, 861.
612. "Recent Novels," *The Times*, August 21, 1874, 12.

PART 4

King Leopold and the Congo

Revival through International Law

From these ashes, it may not be thought that Twiss who, in 1872, was 63 years old, could revive his career or his fortunes. But he did so through two measures: first, by pursuing a life in international law; second, and against what we might expect, by pursuing the insights he had gained into the creation of new persons, in both his professional and personal life, and bringing it to his understanding of the state. In 1849, Twiss had written to Metternich: "I have always considered the life of the individual man to represent the life of nations." He now set about bringing that insight to life. He took his understanding of the metamorphosis of the life of the individual man, or woman, and brought it to the understanding of the state. Twiss had seen the potential for the transformation and creation of persons in his daily legal practice. He had been responsible for the creation of the new person, or corporation, of bishops and archbishops. He had judged the interpretation of the creation of the body of Christ from the host. These were all conventional processes of metamorphoses, condoned and institutionalised by law. In the pursuit of his marriage, however, we see that Twiss and Pharaïlde van Lynseele took the idea of metamorphosis further. They were aware of contemporaries, such as Twiss's former lover, Agnes Willoughby, who sought to reinvent themselves, albeit at the cost of some notoriety. Twiss and Lysnseele improved upon such metamorphosis with a more thorough transformation of the person of Pharaïlde van Lynseele as an entirely new person, not merely in circumstances, but also in birth and "blood," as Twiss put it. In many ways, this expanded idea of the potential for individual transformation was consistent with contemporary ideas of improvement.

This more radical or, to use Twiss's word, "liberal," interpretation of metamorphosis, as something that could go beyond existing conventions and law, is a perspective that Twiss would now develop in his approach to international

[392]

law and, specifically, in the creation of the person of the state. When Twiss said in 1849, "I have always considered the life of the individual man to represent the life of nations" he added the caveat "to a certain extent, although nations do not grow like men equally fast in point of time."[1] By the 1870s and 1880s, Twiss began to develop an idea of a state that could, in fact, grow faster than natural persons and could do so by virtue of the metamorphosis of the person of a private corporation into the person of the state. The notion that private individuals and associations can exercise sovereign power, and thereby become states, was a position to which he had been implacably opposed when he had written on the Oregon boundary dispute in the 1840s. Now he was expanding the insights he had gained from the metamorphoses of natural persons from one status, and one form, to another, to the question of international law and international relations. Hersch Lauterpacht observed that international law developed largely through analogies taken from private law (and Twiss understood this point in his own innovations—for example, in applying the private law concept of *territorium nullius* to the occupation of territory by states).[2] We may say further that international law developed through analogies based upon the understanding that states are persons. The expanded Victorian understanding of the possibilities for personal transformation were an inspiration to international lawyers in their notion of the person of the state.

To appreciate that it was radical to say that private individuals, or associations, can exercise sovereign power, and thereby hold a place in the society of nations, it is necessary first to understand the conventional position on membership in the society of nations in the nineteenth century: namely, membership was restricted to sovereign states. In the seventeenth century, writers on the law of nations had permitted a certain degree of latitude on exactly who could act in the society of nations. Hugo Grotius, while committed to developing a theory of relations between sovereign states, nevertheless left room for actors who were not sovereigns to act in that space. When he addressed the justice of the Dutch captain Jacob van Heemskerk capturing the Portuguese ship the *Santa Caterina*, he emphasised that Heemskerk was acting under direction from the Dutch state, but he also made it clear that Heemskerk's actions, and those of the Dutch East India Company, or Vereenigde Oost-Indische Compagnie, which was at that moment being formed, would have been justifiable by the necessity of preserving his own life. Such latitude was necessary in a world of weak European states in which much of the work of imperial expansion, particularly in the case of the Dutch, and the English, was

---

1. Travers Twiss to Prince Metternich, February 6, 1849, National Archives of the Czech Republic, Prague, , RAM-AC/ 10/ 775, 103.

2. Hersch Lauterpacht, *Private Law Sources and Analogies of International Law*. For Twiss on *territorium nullius*, see Fitzmaurice, *Sovereignty, Property, and Empire*, 278.

outsourced to corporations, or chartered companies. Indeed, the expansion of English, and subsequently British, Dutch, and French imperium was placed largely in the hands of corporations such as the English East India Company, established in 1600, and the Dutch East India Company, the Virginia Company, the New England Company, the Massachusetts Bay Company, the Providence Island Company, the Compagnie de la Nouvelle-France, the North Africa Company, the Compagnie des Indes Orientales, and the Hudson's Bay Company. Nevertheless, while many of those companies acted in ways and places that were far removed from the sovereigns that had created them, and although they performed many, and sometimes almost all, of the functions of the state, they always acted in the name of those sovereigns, even if their actions had sometimes to be retrospectively sanctioned. As European states gained in power, moreover, during the course of the eighteenth century, they became increasingly jealous of the exercise of sovereignty, and they reigned in the powers of the chartered companies. The Dutch East India Company, for example, declined over the course of the eighteenth century, becoming defunct in 1799, while the English East India Company had its powers progressively curtailed from the late eighteenth century and was disestablished following the Indian Rebellion in 1857 (which it had provoked). The conventional position of eighteenth- and nineteenth-century international law was that only states were actors in international society. This position, as we have seen, was clearly stated by Emer de Vattel in the build-up to the Seven Years War. We have also seen that Twiss cited Vattel approvingly on precisely that principle when rejecting the right of private individuals to claim that they could establish a new state in California after having crossed the Rocky Mountains. By the early twentieth century, this orthodoxy was broken. It had become common for various kinds of artificial persons—including associations such as the Red Cross and sub-state societies—to claim a status in international society. Looking back over this change, in 1944, Hersch Lauterpacht observed, "I suppose that twenty-five or thirty years ago every respectable writer on international law had little hesitation in stressing emphatically that States only, and no one else, were the subjects of international law. I doubt whether this is to-day the pre-eminently respectable doctrine."[3]

Twiss's argument for the international standing of Leopold's "private association" (to use Twiss's term), the idea that this corporation could be an actor in international society, made in 1884 and 1885, was therefore precocious, to say the least. He was advancing an idea that was widely regarded by his legal peers and by statesmen, as quite simply "heretical." It was certainly unprecedented.

---

3. Lauterpacht in the discussion following Vladimir R. Idelson, "The Law of Nations and the Individual," *Transactions of the Grotius Society* 30 (1944), 66, cited in Natasha Wheatley, "Spectral Legal Personality in Interwar International Law: On Ways of not Being a State," *Law and History Review*, vol. 35, no. 3 (August 2017), 755.

Corporations and other non-state artificial persons had exercised power in international space, but at least since the eighteenth century, they had done so with the sanction of the sovereigns that created them and licensed their actions, even if that was sometimes retrospectively. What Twiss was proposing was radical and new, but it was not the first time he had supported a radical transformation of a person providing that person with access to a new society. He had changed his views on the flexibility of social membership in mid-century, although he had never wished to seem like a radical, nor had Pharaïlde van Lynseele (in contrast to Agnes Willoughby, who, like Alexander Chaffers, sometimes seemed indifferent to social condemnation, or at least resigned to it). They therefore cloaked the radical transformation of Lynseele in the conservatism of the time, presenting her as always having belonged to Society as a "lady by blood." Twiss, similarly, argued that the transformation of the International African Association was nothing new, appealing, as we shall see, to medieval precedents. Moreover, he and Pharaïlde van Lynseele had gone through an elaborate set of proofs in order to make the metamorphosis from prostitute to "lady by blood." Similarly, it would not be possible merely to assert that a private association could become a state. Such a claim, as we shall see, could cause outrage. To succeed, Twiss knew, it would again be necessary, in addition to making a discursive case, to perform an elaborate set of institutional proofs in the transformation of a private corporate person, in this instance the International Africa Association, into a state, the Congo Free State, and he undertook many of these proofs on Leopold's behalf.

Prior to achieving this transformation, Twiss had first to re-create himself as an international lawyer above all else. He had held many offices and roles over the course of his career. He began primarily as an Oxford don, but by the late 1840s, he was foremost an ecclesiastical lawyer, which was the main source of his income. Even the Regius Professorship of Civil Law produced little, as Twiss complained, in terms of income. He had also published on political economy, and held the Drummond Chair of Political Economy, as well as publishing on international law, for which he held the chair at King's College, London. He had published, in the year of his marriage, 1862, an important work of international law, and he practiced the law of nations through his position as Queen's Advocate in the Admiralty Courts prior to having to resign that post. Nevertheless, international law was a branch of his broader civil law and ecclesiastical law career and did not provide him with any equivalent income to that maintained by the Vicar General of the Province of Canterbury, nor that as Chancellor in the Dioceses of London, Hereford, Suffolk, and Lincoln. For English international jurists, prior to, and even for some years after, the Matrimonial Causes Act of 1857, international law was a second string to their bows. When, however, Twiss lost the offices essential to his income and he was denied new offices, he had to find a new way in which to maintain himself and what he described as his "family." He maintained his practice as a lawyer, and in that capacity, he continued to act, for example, as a trustee and in conveyancing properties in the counties of Denbighshire and Flint in Wales, notably for the Cefn Park estate in Wrexham, where his family still had standing.[4] He continued to work as a barrister (he had not been disbarred, despite the protests of Chaffers), and he kept rooms in Inns of Court, at 3 Paper Buildings, Temple. Remaining highly conscious of the importance of appearances, he had a new *carte de visite* of himself as a barrister made for his new practice.

This card was probably made after the scandal of Twiss's marriage because, depending upon various account of the company, Maull & Co. were operative between 1873 and 1878.[5] It is clear from Twiss's letters in the 1870s and '80s that all these efforts, however, did not bring him the income he needed. To survive, he turned to international law, no longer as a branch off his main occupation but as his principal occupation. In this respect, his life follows the fortunes of the rise of international law as a profession in the nineteenth century.[6]

Until the mid-nineteenth century, international law, and the law of nations, was recognised as a system of conventions existing between states, and it was written about by civil lawyers who were usually concerned with the law more generally or by diplomats who were involved in the practice of governing the relations between states. In mid-century, international law began to be perceived as a discipline which could have its own professional practitioners. The creation of the Professorship of the Law of Nations at King's College, London,

---

4. Conveyance of Land in the Parish of Llanfair in the County of Denbigh, 5 October, 1877, Denbighshire Archives, Ruthin, Wales, DD/WY/347; Sir Travers Twiss Knight and the Honble E. Kenyon to United School District Board, Conveyance of a Parcel of Land, 18 December, 1876, Denbighshire Archives, DD/CD/1; Edward Williams Esq to Sir Travers Twiss and the Honourable Edward Kenyon, Conveyance of Abenbury Lodge, 23 October 1884, Denbighshire Archives, Bdl 18, Box 3; Miss Jane Preston and others to Sir Travers Twiss and the Honourable Edward Kenyon, Reconveyance, 13th February 1878, DD/CP/887. Twiss's involvement in the affairs of Denbighshire was long standing: "Messers Oswald, Bunbury, and Rainey to Dr Travers Twiss and the Honourable Edward Kenyon, Reconveyance of the Cefn Estate, 24th of June, 1859, Denbighshire Archives, Box 2 Bdl 4"; and it continued through to the last years before his death: J. B. Davies-Cooke and others to Sir Travers Twiss and Capt. Kendall, Conveyance, 13 November, 1895, Denbighshire Archives, Bdl 27, Box 4.

5. The photographer, Henry Maull, was active between 1856 and 1908, but his businesses employed different names and that which is marked on Twiss's *carte de visite* was used between 1873 and 1878, according to the Royal Society collection of Maull photographs. *The Encyclopaedia of Nineteenth Century Photography* (New York, 2008), 905, claims that "Maul & Co." began in 1865.

6. For the professionalization and institutionalisation of international law in the second half of the nineteenth century, see Koskenniemi, *The Gentle Civilizer of Nations*. For the English contours of that shift, see Lobban, "English Approaches to International Law in the Nineteenth Century," 65–90.

first held by Twiss, the Chichele Professorship of International Law at Oxford in 1859, and the Whewell Professorship of International Law at Cambridge in 1868 reflected that professionalization. Similar developments took place throughout Europe and America. In 1873, the year after Twiss's life was shattered by the libel trial, a group of European jurists, led by the jurists Gustave Moynier and Gustave Rolin-Jaequemyns, established a new congress of international law, the Institut de droit international.[7] The Swiss Moynier was the co-founder of the International Committee for Relief to the Wounded, which later became the International Red Cross, while Rolin-Jaequemyns, a Belgian jurist, had, in 1868, been a co-founder of the first journal devoted to international law, the *Revue de droit international et de législation comparée*, another marker of the creation and professionalization of the discpline. Motivated by what they regarded as the uncivilized manner in which the Franco-Prussian War had been fought two years earlier, these men brought a group of leading European jurists together in Ghent, in September 1873, to establish the Institut, which was committed to the scientific analysis of the laws of nations, and thus hoped that a civilizing influence would arise from that study. At the same time, American jurist David Dudley Field led a proposal for a similar but more ambitious organisation, the Association for the Reform and Codification of the Law of Nations, which first met in October 1873, in Brussels. Twiss was absent from the conversations that led to the creation of these organisations, and from their first meetings, because he was deeply consumed by his own affairs while the Franco-Prussian War raged in 1871, and he continued to be so until 1873, but, from 1874, he engaged with both organisations and would use them to promote his new ideas for membership in international society, amongst other things.[8]

The principal means Twiss used to maintain himself and his family over the next twenty years was through publishing on the law of nations. In 1871, while he was still Queen's Advocate in the Admiralty Courts, Twiss edited the first volume of the *Black Book of the Admiralty*, in a series of four volumes that would be published until 1876. The Advocate General was a natural choice to edit the *Black Book of Admiralty* because it was the record of medieval judgements on the laws of the sea that were the foundation for Admiralty law and for much of the law of nations. This work had been commissioned by the Master of the Rolls, as part of a series of *Chronicles and Memorials of Great Britain and Ireland During the Middle Ages*, which was financed by the Treasury and paid Twiss over £300 for each volume. In 1871, £307 was a small fraction of his income, but by the time the second volume was published in 1873, he

---

7. The best account for the foundation of the Institut de droit international is Koskenniemi, *The Gentle Civilizer of Nations*, ch. 1.

8. For Twiss joining the Institut de droit international in 1874, see *Annuaire de l'Institut de droit international* (1880), 77.

FIGURE 16. Travers Twiss, *Carte de visite*, Maull & Co.*

had no regular income, and the £307 he was paid would have been welcome.[9] Volumes three and four, for which he was paid £399 and £373, respectively, were further important additions to his means. The sales were more modest. With 750 copies printed for each volume, by 1876 the first volume had only

9. *Returns of All the Record Publication Relating to England and Wales Published since the Year 1866*, House of Commons Parliamentary Papers, 1877, 8.

* Travers Twiss *carte de visite*, by Maull & Co., Harvard University, Law School Library, Historical and Special Collections, Art 00.1885 F

FIGURE 16. (*continued*)

sold 226 copies, at £10 each (money returned to the Treasury), with 108 given away and the rest in storage. Income was earned by commissions rather than sales.

Twiss accompanied the four volumes with lengthy introductions and copious notes on the texts. He explained in the first two volumes that the *Black Book of the Admiralty* was the collection of conventions applied by medieval customary courts, such as the court of the coastal town of Ipswich, which sat daily to "administer justice between men of various nations" who had been brought together by the "spirit of commerce."[10] The conventions applied by these courts were taken from the merchants and mariners of Spain and France, who "brought with them many traditions of maritime law" developed in the Mediterranean.[11] Those conventions included texts such as the Rolls of Oléron, the island off the French Atlantic coast, in which Eleanor of Aquitaine had promulgated laws of the sea based upon the Rhodian Laws of the Mediterranean after her return from the Second Crusade. These laws were "not identical with the Law of imperial Rome" but were derived from it, albeit with many modifications. Oléron, and its laws, had entered English legal tradition when Aquitaine became under English sovereignty when Eleanor married Henry II of England in 1152. As Twiss pointed out, the conventions of the sea were also carried by mariners along the Atlantic coasts.

Twiss represented himself as a kind of Savigny of the sea. As we have seen, his *Epitome of Niebuhr*, published forty years earlier, had been a homage to Friedrich Carl von Savigny's historical method and to Savigny's recognition that the text Barthold Niebuhr discovered in Verona was the lost manuscript of the *Institutes of Gaius*, one of the most important texts of Roman law. For Twiss, as for Savigny, the practice of jurisprudence must be founded upon its theory, and, therefore, the theory had to be founded upon a careful historical reconstruction of the evolution of legal texts and their relation to the societies which produced them. Savigny applied those principles to the civil law, with its foundation in Roman law, as Twiss now sought to apply them to the law of nations. Moreover, he too claimed credit for unearthing foundational legal texts. He had been working on the Black Book since at least 1867, when he wrote a series of letters to Frederic Madden, the Keeper of Manuscripts at the British Museum on the subject. Those letters reveal that Twiss was busy working between the British Museum, the Bodleian in Oxford, and the Public Record office, comparing various manuscripts concerning medieval Admiralty law with what was known of the *Black Book*. In the correspondence, he attempted to establish "the antiquity of the Admiralty" through various methods, including dating oaths and tracing conventions back to the reigns of Edward I and Edward III, as well as Henry II.[12] He also dismissed late-eighteenth- and early-nineteenth-century legal scholar Alexander Luders's claim that a certain manuscript in the Bodleian was the *Black Book*.[13] When he published

---

10. Travers Twiss, *Monumenta Juridica: The Black Book of the Admiralty* (London, 1873), Vol. 2, viii.

11. Twiss, *Black Book of the Admiralty*, Vol. 2, ix.

12. Travers Twiss to Frederic Madden, July 10, July 17, July 22, August 8, 1867, British Library, Egerton MSS, 2848, Sir F. Madden Correspondence, vol. xii, 1863–1870, 239–252 verso.

13. Travers Twiss to Frederic Madden, July 17, 1867, British Library, Egerton MSS, 2848, Sir F. Madden Correspondence, vol. xii, 1863–1870, 241 verso.

the first volume of the *Black Book of the Admiralty*, Twiss pointed out that the original texts had been lost since the eighteenth century. He was forced to rely on accounts of the *Black Book* to identify the texts with which it was constituted and then to search for those texts in England and across Europe to bring the original compilation back together—this was the methodology he revealed in his letters to Madden and in the first two published volumes. In Volume 3 of the *Black Book*, Twiss triumphantly announced: "The Black Book of the Admiralty, which has been lost sight of for more than half a century, has very recently come to light."[14] It had been "discovered accidentally at the bottom of a chest" which had belonged to a former registrar of the Admiralty Court. It had only been found because "the circumstance of the Editor [that is, Twiss] having made public the contents of the missing Black Book happily led to the recognition of the volume, which was beneath a mass of unimportant legal papers and might otherwise which have escaped examination." Twiss had played Savigny to the (unnamed) discoverer's Niebhur. It was indeed an important discovery, and its publication in the third and fourth volumes of his edition of the *Black Book* enabled him to compare the texts he had correctly calculated had comprised the original compilation with those of the original. John Westlake, who would later be appointed to the Whewell Chair of International Law at Cambridge, praised the editions, saying that they had "for the first time made it possible to obtain a clear and connected view, of the general nature and growth of the Admiralty law," while, at the same time, he credited Twiss with having, through his investigations, "provoked" the discovery of the original manuscript of the *Black Book*.[15]

For Twiss, the *Black Book of the Admiralty* was an ancient constitution of the sea, and thus of the law of nations. It was a foundation for the liberty and civilisation of the present day and of international society. It was a compilation of medieval conventions that were a "nursery of that spirit of liberty and equal justice" which was administered not only in municipal law but also in relations with strangers.

That ancient constitution of the law of nations was all the more important, he argued in the fourth volume of the *Black Book*, at a time when jurisdiction over Admiralty matters was being brought under common law courts. Here he was reflecting the concern amongst Admiralty lawyers and judges that the absorption of the High Court of the Admiralty in 1875 into the Probate, Divorce, and Admiralty Division of the High Court would lead to a loss of autonomy in Admiralty law. England, Twiss declared, "has embarked upon a grave experiment in jurisprudence" and had effectively made every county court an Admiralty Court, with the House of Lords as the supreme court of

---

14. Twiss, *Black Book of the Admiralty*, Vol. 3 (London, 1874), vii.

15. John Westlake, "The Black Book of the Admiralty," *The Academy: A Weekly Review of Literature, Science, and Art*, vol. 5 (January 17, 1874), 54–55.

appeal rather than the Queen in Council.[16] He worried that English judges, "trained in the exclusive study" of English municipal law, would struggle as judges of "maritime causes." The fear would prove to be unfounded. Admiralty kept its separate jurisdiction within the new division, but, fearing the triumph of municipal law, which he had already seen transpire in the law of marriage, Twiss hoped that the *Black Book of the Admiralty* would provide the county judges and the House of Lords with the conventions necessary to make decisions that were consistent with the law of nations. He warned that "innovations upon the common law of the sea are of dangerous precedent," and imposition, by any country, of "its own municipal law upon foreign shipping" could be reciprocated by other nations and would "alienate nations from one another." The implications were clear. A failure to observe the conventions of the sea would "foment international dissensions," while an understanding of them would promote "the general peace of the civilized world."[17] Twiss's ambition for his edition of the *Black Book of the Admiralty* was therefore driven by the contemporary rise of hopes for greater international peace based upon a better understanding of the law of nations at the same time that he saw it responding to the challenge to that peace posed by jurisdictional changes in England.

Buoyed in part by his work on the *Black Book*, in 1874, Twiss approached Tait again for his assistance in gaining office. In that year, Montague Bernard, the first Chichele Professor of International Law, had resigned his position. The Chichele Professorships were created by All Souls College as part of the University reforms from the report of the Commission of 1854. They were elected by a panel that included the Lord Chancellor of Britain, the Secretary of State for Foreign Affairs, a representative of the Probate, Divorce, and Admiralty Courts, and "the Visitor" of All Souls College. The Visitor's job, amongst other things, was to interpret the College statutes in instances of disputes. All Souls had been founded by Henry Chichele, a fifteenth-century Archbishop of Canterbury, and by convention, the Visitors to the College were the Archbishops of Canterbury. When, in 1874, All Souls established the committee to appoint a new Chichele Professor of International Law, Archbishop Tait was, as Visitor, one of the electors on the committee. Twiss was certainly very familiar with the Archbishop's role as Visitor of the College. When archbishops were asked to resolve questions regarding the College statutes, they frequently turned to their closest legal advisors—that, is to the Vicar General of the Province of Canterbury, who had, for twenty years prior to 1872, been Travers Twiss. In 1861, for example, three junior fellows of All Souls College objected to the criteria that the College Warden and fellows used to elect new fellows. The Warden and fellows followed the ordinances set down by the Oxford Commissioners in 1854. Those ordinances stated that the qualifications of candidates

---

16. Twiss, *Black Book of the Admiralty*, Vol. 4 (London, 1876), cxxxii.
17. Twiss, *Black Book of the Admiralty*, Vol. 4, cxxxiv.

should be tested by examination and that the Warden and fellows should then elect the candidate who, after the examination, "shall appear to them to be of the greatest merit and most fit to be a Fellow of the College." This last clause the Warden and fellows took as giving them some latitude to investigate the character and morals of the candidates through private discussions. The three junior fellows of the College who objected to this process argued that the election should be entirely based upon the examination results: that is, upon an intellectual qualification. The case was brought to the College Visitor, John Sumner, who was the Archbishop of Canterbury. Sumner established a hearing for the complaint in March 1861, which was judged, or "assessed," by Travers Twiss and Lord Wensleydale. The case for the junior fellows was argued by John Coleridge, who in the following year would represent Agnes Windham in the Windham lunacy trial, and the case for the Warden and fellows was argued by Hugh Cairns, who would represent William Windham in his lunacy trial.[18] In their judgement on the case, Twiss and Wensleydale favoured the interpretation of the statutes by the Warden and fellows. They argued that the choice of the candidate who was "most fit" was comparative and not based solely upon intellectual merit. The decision must, therefore, entail a judgement of morals and character, and that judgement should be made privately and in consultation. Their report concluded: "After ascertaining the intellectual qualifications of the candidates, their fitness to be Fellows of the College must be investigated . . . as to their morals and character."[19]

Twelve years later, in 1874, seeking to be appointed to the Chichele Professorship of International Law and Diplomacy, Twiss wrote to Tait who, as Visitor at All Souls, was a member of the committee that would choose Bernard's replacement. Twiss's letter was both a job application and a statement of the current state of the study of international law. He began the letter by reminding Tait of their long-standing relationship: "Under the circumstances of the close official relations which have existed between Your Grace and myself for many years, I venture to think that it will not be contrary to my duty to address a few lines to Your Grace on the subject of the Chichele Professorship at Oxford, in order that Your Grace may be fully aware of my motives for seeking to fill that office."[20] Having also announced his candidacy for the post, Twiss explained his recovery from his breakdown after the scandal: "When I left England in 1872 I hardly expected my life would be prolonged for many months, but the bracing air of Switzerland coupled with perfect rest from hard work restored me to health and mental rigour much sooner than I could reasonably have hoped for." He informed Tait of his work on the *Black Book of*

---

18. *Oxford University and City Herald*, March 16, 1861, 11.

19. *Oxford Journal*, March 16, 1861.

20. Twiss to Tait, July 7, 1874, Lambeth Palace Library, Tait Papers, Personal Letters 1874, 93, ff.69–70.

the Admiralty and its importance to international law: "Immediately after my return to England I resumed at once a work, upon which I was engaged under the direction of the Master of the Rolls before I left England and I published a volume in the course of last year. I have since completed another volume which is now passing through the Press. Both these volumes contain the text of interesting medieval M.S.S hitherto unpublished on subjects of International Maritime Law. I have found however that the labour of collecting such materials and the supervision of their publication is very trying to the eyesight, and as the work of printing is necessarily very slow, I have also found that such works do not give me full occupation."[21] It is apparent here that Twiss had returned to England after his escape to Switzerland, although it was not clear at this point where Lady Twiss was residing. His letter was addressed to Tait from his room in the Inns of Court, 3 Paper Buildings, Temple. As publishing was not providing him a full occupation, nor, although he does not state it, the income to which he was accustomed, Twiss now turned to his vision for the Chichele Professorship: "Meanwhile in travelling on the continent for the purpose of examining M.S.S and of conferring with writers of authority on subjects of International Law, which has always been my favourite pursuit, I have met with great encouragement from them to undertake a more complete work on the Law of Nations. I have also good reason to think that the circumstances in which Europe is placed at present are very favourable to the advancement of the scientific study of the rules of international conduct, which ought to be regarded by Statesmen as binding on all civilised nations; whilst at the same time there are crude notions afloat in this respect, the proper antidote for which is to be [brought?] for in an enlarged teaching and in a more systematic exposition of the established rules and of the principles upon which they are founded. Those rules, I need hardly say to Your Grace, are not merely commended from acceptance of the practice of nations, but by their intrinsic equity and convenience, and although they may require in some cases to be applied with still more equality than heretofore to adjust them to the altered conditions of international life, the principles upon which they rest require only to be explained in order that they should find favour with all reasonable minds." The creation, in only the previous year, of international institutes for the "scientific study" of international law had, for Twiss, heralded the moment at which great jurists could, through "systematic exposition," explain the principles which govern the conduct of "civilized" states, and he was one such jurist. All he required was a platform, the Chichele Professorship, in order to bring this vision to reality: "Under these circumstances an opportunity has presented itself at Oxford which would enable me to explain with authority those principles, and will restore me to a life of Academic usefulness which I

---

21. Twiss to Tait, July 7, 1874, Lambeth Palace Library, Tait Papers, Personal Letters 1874, 93, f.69.

should never have quitted from choice, unless I had felt that duty called me to the metropolis to take a more active part in life. With what advantage to my country I have endeavoured to fulfil that duty it is for others to say, but Your Grace will bear me witness that I have never spared myself nor allowed any self-consideration to influence my conduct. I am anxious all the remaining years of life, which may be spared to me, to continue to the utmost of my power to the welfare of my country, and it is in the humble conviction that I can do it good service as a teacher of International Law that I have submitted my name to Your Grace as one of the Electors to the Chichele Professorship, as a candidate for that office."[22] Twiss's former abandonment of Oxford, he explained, had been necessary in order for him to serve his country, which he would do best now as a teacher. He concluded this letter with a revealing offer: "I may add that I shall reside in Oxford, if I should be elected in accordance with whatever may be the requirement of the Professorship, alone and independent of all family ties." Celibacy was still a requirement for Oxford fellowships at this time, but there was growing pressure for professionalization of the universities. A report from a new commission into the universities, published in the year Twiss wrote this letter, led to the Universities of Oxford and Cambridge Act of 1877, which allowed colleges to admit married fellows. Given that celibacy was a requirement at the time Twiss wrote, it is difficult to know exactly what he meant by saying he would be "alone and independent of all family ties," but it seems he envisioned separate arrangements for Lady Twiss if Tait, and the committee, believed she would be a barrier to his appointment. As it transpired, however, Twiss did not abandon his wife for some years to come.

Twiss's application to Tait was audacious, given that Twiss had himself ruled that fellowships at All Souls College, of which the Chichele Professorship was necessarily one, should be based upon "morals and character" as well as intellectual qualifications. Tait was clearly of the same view, for he responded to Twiss accordingly on July 16, 1874: "My dear Twiss, You may rest assured that your claims for the Chichele Professorship will be thoroughly considered but I fear there will be little probability of your success. No one of your old friends can feel more than I do for what has befallen you, but it would be wrong to say that I think myself, that the difficulty in the way of your appointment could with propriety be set aside. Most heartily do I trust that in some way an opportunity may occur to enable you to recover yourself from the painful position in which you have been for the last two years."[23] Whereas two years earlier, Tait had written to the Lord Chamberlain to test the waters for

---

22. Twiss to Tait, July 7, 1874, Lambeth Palace Library, Tait Papers, Personal Letters 1874, 93, ff.70-71.

23. Tait to Twiss, July 16, 1874, Lambeth Palace Library, Tait Papers, Personal Letters 1874, 93, f.71.

Twiss, now he wrote that he would himself pose an obstacle to the return of Twiss to any office. Twiss, it appears, was putting his friends in a difficult position, forcing them to declare themselves against him. It must by now have been obvious, even to him, that he could not return to public office, in England at least. His income would have to continue to come from publishing, but as he told Tait, publishing did not occupy him enough—we might also understand that it did not earn enough.

Indeed, his editions for the Master of the Rolls were increasingly less successful. He followed the *Black Book of the Admiralty* with an edition of Henry of Bracton's *De Legibus et Consuetudinibus Angliae* in six volumes between 1878 and 1883. Bracton's medieval compilation of laws drew no hard distinction between Roman and civil law, on the one hand, and the common law of England, on the other, although the degree to which the latter is indebted to each tradition is moot.[24] For this reason, Twiss, as a civil lawyer, was potentially an appropriate editor. Nevertheless, Frederic Maitland, the eminent legal historian, dismissed his effort as "six volumes of rubbish," and subsequent judgements concur: "The translation contains errors which are sometimes dangerous because they are plausible, and are sometimes so obvious that they could hardly mislead anyone with an elementary knowledge of the law in Bracton's time, or even of Latin."[25] As we shall see, a subsequent edition of Glanvill that Twiss also produced for the Master of the Rolls excited even greater condemnation. He needed an occupation that was something more than publishing, although publishing would prove to be the means to that new role. When Tait's letter of 1874 made it clear that all offices in England were barred to Twiss, he threw himself not only into the study of international law but also into participation in the newly created institutions for the advancement of international law. He turned from national to international service and the search for international roles.

The Standing of "Oriental Nations" in International Society

Twiss had established a reputation as one of the outstanding international lawyers of his generation, a reputation built on his early work on the Oregon Territory, his Professorship in International Law at King's College, his Regius Professorship of Civil Law at Oxford, as well as upon his position in the Admiralty Courts as Queen's Advocate, upon his *Law of Nations* in two volumes,

---

24. For a persuasive account of the proximity between the traditions, see Tamar Herzog, *A Short History of European Law* (Cambridge, Mass, 2018).

25. Maitland, cited in C.H.S. Fifoot, *Frederic William Maitland: A Life* (Cambridge, Mass., 1971), 62. Percy Henry Winfield, *The Chief Sources of English Legal History* (Cambridge, Mass., 1925), 258.

one on peace and one on war, and more recently his work on the *Black Book of the Admiralty*. In the 1870s, he consolidated that reputation with publication of a series of articles in law journals, including the *Law Magazine and Review*, the *Revue de droit international*, and the *Annuaire de l'Institut de droit international*. With this standing, he was elected as a member of the Institut de droit international at its August and September meeting in Geneva in 1874, which he attended. He immediately set about involving himself in its affairs, and one of his first duties was to address himself to the question of the applicability of the law of nations to non-European nations, a question put to the Institut by David Dudley Field. In 1874, Field, an American law reformer who was deeply committed to the codification of law, presented the Institut with a memorandum in which he posed the question of whether, and in what conditions, the "unwritten" European law of nations was applicable to "Oriental nations."[26] By "unwritten," Field meant the fundamental principles. He explained that, during a recent voyage around the world, he had had the opportunity to observe the law of nations in practice. He discovered that non-European countries that had not been submitted to Christian powers found themselves in an "abnormal" condition from the point of view of international law. What we call the "law of nations" was just, he said, an "assemblage of juridical rules" which Christianity had made to sanction Christian peoples and from whose authority "the greatest part of the world escapes." He conceded that this European "international law" was not completely unknown outside Europe and that it was invoked, for example, in relations between China and Japan. Nevertheless, he pointed out that the international relations that prevailed between non-European nations were very different from those between Christian states. The law of nations in the Ottoman Empire, in Asia, with the exception of Siberia and "Hindustan," in all of Africa, with the exception of Liberia (a colony of freed United States slaves), to the degree that it was recognised, was practiced with many exceptions and modifications.[27]

In general, Field observed, it could be said that the law of nations, as it was understood in the Christian world, had not reached the rest of the world in its fullest expression (*plénitude*).[28] The reason for this, he argued, was evident. This system of law was developed in Europe with the purpose of aiding commerce and community between nations. By contrast, non-Christian nations were isolationist, uninterested in community with the rest of the world. A consequence of this contrast was that when people came from Europe and

26. David Dudley Field, "De la possibilité d'appliquer le droit international européen aux nations Orientales," *Revue de droit international et de législation comparée*, vol. 7 (1875), 659.

27. Field, "De la possibilité d'appliquer le droit international européen aux nations Orientales," 659.

28. Field, "De la possibilité d'appliquer le droit international européen aux nations Orientales," 662.

America to live in these non-Christian nations, they were obliged to live apart and to conduct their commerce apart. In other words, this difference necessitated the creation of extra-territorial enclaves. This separation also necessitated those enclaves creating their own laws and conditions of security. Turning back to the question of the applicability of the European law of nations to "Oriental nations," he argued that the fact it had not been adopted more generally was "purely historic." This was a system of rights born in Europe, applied in Europe, and fashioned for Europe, before any considerable relations existed with countries outside Europe.[29] The important differences were not religious but more generally cultural. They were not differences of civilisation, the civilized and "non-civilized." Is it possible, he asked in reference to China, to call a country that had a regular system of government for thousands of years uncivilized?[30] The question of the applicability of the law of nations cannot, he argued, be answered by the matter of civilisation. It was necessary, therefore, that Oriental nations enjoy all the privileges and duties of the law of nations, including those of sovereignty, equality, perpetuity, territory, and property. At the same time, as long as the legal institutions and practices of those countries remained repugnant to Europeans, it was necessary that Europeans carry their extra-territorial powers with them when resident there. While visiting China, Field declared, he had witnessed firsthand legal practices in which witnesses were tortured if they refused to admit to crimes, in which there was no legal representation, in which women did not possess the same rights that they enjoyed in European and American nations. It would be "revolting," he concluded, to submit "our own" citizens to such justice.[31] The way forward, until such time as "Oriental nations" had "assimilated" to Occidental norms, would be to submit all legal questions involving European and American nationals in Oriental nations to mixed tribunals which followed European standards but were presided over by both consuls and an "indigenous judge."[32] It was in the interests of "humanity" and "civilization" that "Oriental nations" be "as quickly as possible submitted to the empire of international law."[33] This would mean, he noted in a subsequent statement of this ambition, that they would be admitted to the enjoyment of all the "rights" and all the "duties" "determined by international law."[34]

---

29. Field, "De la possibilité d'appliquer le droit international européen aux nations Orientales," 665

30. Field, "De la possibilité d'appliquer le droit international européen aux nations Orientales," 664.

31. Field, "De la possibilité d'appliquer le droit international européen aux nations Orientales," 667.

32. *Annuaire de l'Institut de droit international* (1878), 131.

33. Field, "De la possibilité d'appliquer le droit international européen aux nations Orientales," 667.

34. *Annuaire de l'Institut de droit international* (1878), 131.

In their meeting at The Hague in August 1875, the members of the Institut decided to establish a commission to examine the question put by Dudley Field's memorandum on "Oriental nations." They formulated the question of that commission as: "In what conditions and to what point are the customary laws of Europe applicable to Oriental nations?"[35] The meeting agreed that seven of its members would examine this question, including Dudley Field, and that the committee would be chaired by Travers Twiss, who would write the report. Twiss insisted that a questionnaire regarding the issues should be printed and sent to "competent persons" in "various countries."[36] The questions were as follows: Question 1: "Is there between the ideas and beliefs of the nationals of oriental countries, on the one hand, and those of Christian nations, on the other hand, touching their obligations, in relation to foreign peoples and individuals, a difference that is so radical that it makes it impossible to contemplate admitting oriental nations to the general community of international law?" Question 2: "Are the notions of oriental nations regarding the observation of the stipulations of treaties fundamentally different from those of Christian nations on the same subject?" Question 3: "Do you think it is necessary for Christian governments to accord special protection to missionaries manifested in direct interventions?" This question was qualified by "two generally accepted propositions": namely, that "Christian nations do not have the right to impose upon non-Christian nations their religion and civilization"; and that subjects of non-Christian powers do not remove themselves from subjection to the government and laws of their country by virtue of having embraced Christianity. The first clause revealed that concern about the universality of the principles underlying the law of nations motivated jurists to reject any suggestion that it was a projection of European religion. The law of nations had been developed during and following the wars of religion in Europe and had, as a consequence, always been presented as a system of values that were independent of religion. Grotius had famously boasted that his laws of nations, based upon the principle of self-preservation, would work even if there was no God. The first proposition shows a similar desire for the law of nations to be free of cultural prejudice arising from the civilizing mission. This second clause, that the Christianity of certain subjects of non-Christian powers did not remove them from the duty of subjection to those powers, was likely to have been motivated by the Russian intervention into the Ottoman Empire to supposedly protect Christian subjects (this was a point that Joseph Hornung, a professor of the history of law at Lausanne, who was on Twiss's committee on the status of "Oriental" nations, was concerned about).[37]

---

35. *Annuaire de l'Institut de droit international*, vol. 1 (1877), 9, 37.
36. *Annuaire de l'Institut de droit international*, vol. 1 (1877), 140–141.
37. For Hornung, see Fitzmaurice, "Scepticism of the Civilizing Mission in International Law," 373–376.

Question 4 was: "Does the conduct of Christian missionaries in the country of which you have a special knowledge provide an occasion or pretext for hostile sentiments towards Christian countries?" Question 5: "Does the social state of Oriental peoples, notably in Persia, Egypt, China, Turkey, and Japan etc, justify the maintenance of consular jurisdiction or other exceptional jurisdiction with the forms of protection that accompany capitulations? In what ways and in what measure could those jurisdictions be modified?" Question 6: "Is the right of jurisdiction that European countries exercise in the Orient accompanied by a duty to organise courts, consular or otherwise, in a way that will guarantee good and impartial justice?"[38]

In the 1877 meeting of the Institut at Zurich, Twiss reported that he had received some "interesting" answers to his questionnaire, including from "Persia," China, and Egypt, but that the inquiry remained incomplete.[39] The commission was therefore prolonged. He finally presented his report to the meeting of the Institut at Ghent in 1879.[40] He noted that he had received few responses to his questionnaire because of confidentiality. He commented that questioning retired diplomats was useless because of the speed with which "Oriental" nations were changing, so their advice would be outdated. It was necessary to distinguish, he added, between different degrees of civilisation amongst the non-European nations.[41] Some, such as China, Japan, and Turkey, were civilized and recognized the law of nations; others were cannibals or pagans with little civility. For the first two questions, he obtained information on the "ideas and beliefs of Oriental nations" from "European experts" and "even from Asian diplomats accredited to European courts." From those sources, he had "been assured" that: 1. The difference between Oriental ideas and beliefs and "ours" is not so great that it is impossible to contemplate admitting "them" to the community of international law; 2. That "the ideas or beliefs of Oriental peoples concerning the observation of treaties are not fundamentally different from those of Christian peoples." There are differences between countries, such as China and Japan, in their ability to respond quickly to diplomatic issues, but their understanding of their treaty obligations is nevertheless the same. On questions 3 to 6, he found evidence that missionaries had been the cause for hostility to Christian powers.[42] On extraterritorial jurisdiction, he found that "the time has not arrived when European nations can dispense with the forms of protection" which they had obtained by virtue of capitulations, but, he added, "we demand with reason" an improvement in those systems of justice.

38. "Questionnaire," *Annuaire de l'Institut de droit international*, vol. 1 (1880), 298–299.
39. *Annuaire de l'Institut de droit international* (1878), 131.
40. *Annuaire de l'Institut de droit international*, vol. 2 (1880), 314.
41. "Rapport," *Annuaire de l'Institut de droit international*, vol. 1 (1880), 301.
42. "Rapport," *Annuaire de l'Institut de droit international*, vol. 1 (1880), 304.

To Twiss's report, Hornung, who had been in the commission, added a dissenting report. Hornung declared that he could not "prevent himself from making a remark prejudicial to the question."[43] "As much," he observed, "as we wanted to occupy ourselves with Oriental nations, we are always doing so from our own interests and our own point of view." We think only, he argued, about "our commerce, our nationals and coreligionists." The "question of the Orient is just a pretext for certain powers who wish to expand." In "our rapport with the non-European world we only see our own interests." The "opium affair" and the "even greater brutality with which Russia had expelled the peoples of the Caucasus region were sufficient to prove the inferiority of civilized states. They forced China to open her ports: was that in the interest of China?" "Everything that happens in Egypt" was "uniquely for the profit" of Europeans.[44] "And with the question with which we are now concerned," he concluded, "we are only addressing 'the interests of our nationals.'" Hornung's vision was paternalistic. He argued that "intelligent peoples" should only use their strength to aid the "weak."[45] But it was more than merely paternalistic. He looked forward to the creation of the "world state" that had been "dreamed of by Kant" which could not be realised until civilized humanity looked to a greater moral purpose than its own interests or those of its nationals or coreligionists.[46] Hornung promised to expand further upon this question in a forthcoming article in the *Revue de droit international*, which duly appeared as a series of papers on "*Civilisés et barbares.*"[47]

Twiss's report was, therefore, sandwiched by the sharply contrasting views of two members of his committee. Hornung, on the one hand, rejected the question posed by the committee and argued that they should address themselves to what duties European states owed "Oriental" states, and the Scot James Lorimer, on the other, supported one of the most radically racial interpretations of the law of nations amongst nineteenth-century jurists. Lorimer distinguished between progressive Europeans and non-progressive races, which were everybody else. He observed that the great question facing the future of international law was whether "the entire subjection of these [non-progressive] races" would be necessary, or whether it was possible there would be "the gradual development of some oriental form of political organisation hitherto unknown to the history of politics."[48] He was pessimistic about this second possibility, particularly insofar as the "Mahommedan" races were

43. "Rapport," *Annuaire de l'Institut de droit international*, vol. 1 (1880), 305.
44. "Rapport," *Annuaire de l'Institut de droit international*, vol. 1 (1880), 305.
45. "Rapport," *Annuaire de l'Institut de droit international*, vol. 1 (1880), 306.
46. "Rapport," *Annuaire de l'Institut de droit international*, vol. 1 (1880), 307.
47. For Hornung's "*Civilisés et barbares,*" see Fitzmaurice, "Scepticism of the Civilizing Mission."
48. Lorimer, *The Institutes of the Law of Nations*, Vol. 1, 100. For Lorimer, see Jennifer Pitts, "Boundaries of Victorian International Law," in *Victorian Visions of Global Order*,

concerned. "The Turks, as a race," he wrote, "are probably incapable of the political development which would render their adoption of constitutional government possible."[49] The Koran "stood between" Muslim countries and the "world without," "unless we are all to become Mahometans."[50]

Twiss steered a course between Lorimer and Hornung. He agreed with Lorimer that there was a hierarchy within the society of nations, but in contrast to Lorimer, he placed a large number of "Oriental" nations in the top level of that hierarchy. He agreed with Hornung on the equality of many non-European peoples, and he similarly rejected the civilizing mission as a basis for the law of nations. Twiss was not, however, like Hornung, a sceptic of empire. He insisted upon equality in order to extend extra-territorial rule and to impose upon non-European states an international jurisdiction which guaranteed the navigation and commerce of European states. He made clear his impatience with the anti-imperial views of jurists such as Hornung in a commentary he provided upon his own report on the status of "Oriental nations" in international law. That commentary was outlined in a letter he wrote to Sir Austen Henry Layard in 1880, the same year in which the *Annuaire* published his report. Twiss had known Layard, as we have seen, since the 1840s, when Layard had achieved fame as the archaeologist of Ninevah, and he had dealt with him when Layard was Under-Secretary for Foreign Affairs in the 1860s. In 1877, Prime Minister Disraeli appointed Layard as the British ambassador to Constantinople against the background of the 1877–1878 Russo-Turkish war, in which Russia claimed to be intervening in the Ottoman Empire in order to protect its Christian subjects from massacres perpetrated by the Ottomans.[51] It was precisely such interventions in the name of co-religionists to which Hornung had objected in his dissenting report to the Institut and which had been condemned by the Institut more generally as against the principles of the law of nations. William Gladstone, in Britain, had used the conflict in the Ottoman Empire to attack the Disraeli government, and he argued in his 1876 pamphlet *Bulgarian Horrors and the Question of the East* that outside powers should intervene to support Christians in the empire.[52] Layard strongly opposed Gladstone's perspective but eventually found himself in opposition, also, to the Sultan, Abdul Hamid II, who suspected the British of being complicit in the diminution of Ottoman power after the Berlin Congress of 1878. In 1880, Layard wrote a pessimistic and overheated dispatch regarding the state of the Ottoman Empire which was

---

ed. Duncan Bell (Cambridge, 2007), 67–88; and Jennifer Pitts, *Boundaries of the International: Law and Empire* (Cambridge, 2018), 171–173.

49. Lorimer, *Institutes*, Vol. 1, 123.

50. Lorimer, *Institutes*, Vol. 1, 123–124.

51. Jonathan Parry, "Sir Austen Henry Layard," in the *Oxford Dictionary of National Biography* (Oxford, 2004–2019).

52. William Gladstone, *Bulgarian Horrors and the Question of the East* (London, 1876).

published by Gladstone, who had returned to government in April of that year. Layard was then recalled from Constantinople, and he retired to Venice, where he moved into a palazzo, the Ca' Cappello, on the Grand Canal (now known as Ca' Cappello Layard), where Twiss wrote to him in September 1880. Layard's position as ambassador to Constantinople brought him to Twiss's attention when he was writing his report on "Oriental nations" in international law. In a candid statement of his views, Twiss wrote to Layard that he was enclosing a copy of his "memoir" on "jurisdiction in the Levant, which I have had to study as Rapporteur for the Institut de droit international."[53] Twiss says that he discovered "on enquiring at the Foreign Office that your address is at Venice." "I hardly venture," he noted frivolously, "that Ca. Capello means Casa Capello." He then turned to his subject: "Now I must beg pardon, when you are immersed in the study of Great Matters of Colour, for recalling your attention to a subject which is perhaps ... marked by you as of no colour, or black, in your memory." "The modern attempt," Twiss observed, "to wash the blackamoor white is after all only a new Crusade." For Twiss, therefore, cosmopolitan arguments were merely an attempt to impose European culture upon non-Europeans. He argued, instead, that Europeans and "the Blackamoor" were "oil and vinegar," albeit that some regarded them as "indivisible." When the work of integrating Europeans and non-Europeans "is accomplished who shall sup on the salad? which the French do and seem inclined to do." He concluded by extending his sympathy for what he believed was Layard's rough treatment by Gladstone: "Hoping you are well after all the ill requited labour of your post further East." From this letter, it is apparent that Twiss's arguments for the equality of "Oriental nations" did not prevent him from employing a racialized perspective upon international relations, although it is also evident that his racialized perspective did not prevent, and indeed encouraged, his arguments for equality.

We have seen that Twiss had discussed the problem of the status of "Oriental nations," particularly the Ottoman Empire, with Metternich twenty years earlier, at the time of the Crimean War. Metternich, in turn had addressed the same question in 1813 and 1814 when he attempted to bring the Ottomans into the Concert of Europe. Twiss had agreed with Metternich upon the difficulty of squaring the circle of the cultural incommensurability of non-European societies with a European system of "international" law, on the one hand, and the reality of the power of those societies, on the other hand, in relations between states. Twiss's conception of that problem in the last decades of the century, therefore, was consistent with Metternich's own formulation over seventy years previously. Metternich, however, combined his conviction that Ottoman power must be acknowledged with a deep pessimism about the

---

53. "Travers Twiss to Austen Henry Layard," British Library, Layard Papers: Additional MS. 39034, 170r–171v.

ability of Muslim cultures to adapt to European notions of law (it had not occurred to him that another course was possible). Twiss shared his pessimism, but he believed he had found a solution to the conundrum.

While Twiss's idea for international jurisdiction over non-European nations was evident in his report to the Institut de droit international, it was stated more clearly in a series of articles and pamphlets he published in the *Law and Magazine Review* while preparing that report, particularly in the articles on the "Applicability of the European Law of Nations to African Slave States," in 1876, and in the address he gave to the seventh annual conference of Dudley Field's Association for the Reform and Codification of the Law of Nations held in the Guildhall of the City of London in 1879, entitled: "On International Conventions for the Maintenance of Sea Lights," which the Association published as a pamphlet in the same year.[54] In "Applicability of the European Law of Nations to African Slave States," published the year after the Institut de droit international established the commission charged with examining the position of "Oriental nations" in international law, Twiss pointed out that the countries which the Institut had "chiefly in view" for that question were Turkey, Egypt, Persia, China, and Japan. They had not foreseen, he observed, that "the first difficulty in the way of the Mahommedan races being admitted to a full participation in the European Concert of Public Law would arise in respect of the Arab States on the East Coast of South Africa."[55] The context for this remark was the crisis over what were known as the Fugitive Slave Circulars issued by the Admiralty under instruction from the British government in 1875 and 1876.

It was a relatively common occurrence that slaves in ports visited by British naval vessels would swim to the ships and take refuge on them, claiming protection under British law. British naval vessels claimed extra-territorial powers when in the territorial waters of non-British states, and because slavery was not recognized in British law, it had been common for British ships to protect escaping slaves and put them down in another port where they would be free. In the 1860s and '70s, this policy came under increasing pressure, particularly after the opening of the Suez Canal in 1869, which brought British ships travelling to India and Australia through the ports of slave-owning societies in the Red Sea, the Persian Gulf, and the Gulf of Oman, and on the East Coast of Africa. Benjamin Disraeli's government was concerned that the protection of slaves by warships when visiting the ports of foreign governments would antagonize the people and governments of friendly powers. Enslaved pearl divers in the Persian Gulf, for example, could take refuge on British

---

54. Travers Twiss, *On International Conventions for the Maintenance of Sea Lights* (London, 1879).

55. Travers Twiss, "Applicability of the European Law of Nations to African Slave States," *Law Magazine and Review* (May 1876), 409.

ships, bringing the viability of their masters' enterprises into peril.[56] Extraterritoriality, argued a government report, should not be allowed "to set aside the law" of another country.[57] In fact, that is precisely what extra-territoriality was intended to do, but this was one of many instances of contradiction and difficulty to which the idea of extra-territoriality gave rise. The policy of the government, and the Admiralty instructions issued in the Fugitive Slave Circulars, was intended to guarantee stability in areas of British interest abroad, in what has been described as its informal empire, but it succeeded in reviving anti-slavery interests at home.

Twiss, however, wrote to protest the Fugitive Slave Circulars out of motives other than anti-slavery. For Twiss, at the heart of the crisis, which dominated political debate in Britain in late 1875 and in 1876, was the question which the Institut de droit international had commissioned him to report upon: namely, what was the status of "Oriental nations" in international law? In contrast to some anti-slavery advocates, Twiss did not point to the institution of slavery as evidence of the inequality of certain non-European states in the society of nations.[58] As we have seen, he argued in his 1861 *Law of Nations* that the 1856 Treaty of Paris was a "formal act of reception" whereby the Ottoman Empire was admitted to the "Fellowship of European Nations."[59] He repeated this claim in his article on the African "Slave States," adding that, even prior to the 1856 treaty, the "Ottoman Porte" had, from a "Christian point of view," been "received as a Peer into the European Parliament of States" when its ambassadors were admitted into the courts of "Two Great European Powers," as well as through treaties that it had made with European states since the sixteenth-century treaty with the French.[60] Nevertheless, he argued, recent years had seen a "growing desire on the part of the Mussulman Races to place themselves on the same platform of Public Law with the Christian Races of Europe." He asked, therefore, to what degree "Mahommedan Governments" were subject to the rules of international law—a subject in which he was deeply engrossed, given his work on the commission for the Institut. He observed that William Scott, Lord Stowell, in whose footsteps he had in many ways followed since his days at University College, had addressed the same question in 1800 in the Admiralty Prize Court. Stowell had argued that it would be "extremely hard" on persons who lived in the Kingdom of Morocco if they were held to be "bound by all the rules of the Law of Nations as it is practised amongst

---

56. William Mulligan, "The Fugitive Slave Circulars, 1875–1876," *Journal of Imperial and Commonwealth History*, vol. 37, no. 2 (2009), 188.

57. Mulligan, "The Fugitive Slave Circulars," 187.

58. On anti-slavery activists' perceptions of slave states, see Mulligan, "The Fugitive Slave Circulars," 193.

59. Twiss, *The Law of Nations* (1861), 105.

60. Twiss, "Applicability," 410.

European States."⁶¹ The European law of nations, he said, was a "pretty artificial system" which was unfamiliar to Moroccans and so should not be applied "in its full rigour." They could, however, be expected to be familiar with conventions that were "universal" and "simple"—in this instance, the observance of a blockade in war—and could be held to such an "elementary principle."⁶²

Twiss took two principles from Stowell's judgement. First, that European nations could not "extract" from "African nations a strict compliance" with European international norms. Second, that European nations could require African nations to observe "European usages" where those usages were in accordance with "natural right and where the African Nations cannot be ignorant of them." Any other basis for deepening relations between European and African nations would lead to a "humiliation" of the African nations and a "degradation" of the Europeans. Centuries of treaties between Europeans and Africans, he added, had supplied African nations with a "knowledge of European Usages."⁶³ He then declared that a further principle must govern relations between European and African nations: namely, that if African nations were to have the "benefit" of "European usages of international intercourse," they must also "submit to the inconvenience of them."⁶⁴ To this end, he cited the maxim *"Qui sentit beneficium sentire debet et onus"*: that is, whoever has the benefit of something must also accept the burden. As an example, he said that an African nation could not "claim from a European Nation the recognition of its right to the free navigation of the High Seas" without conceding the same right to European nations as well as committing to the restraint of piracy.⁶⁵

Now, reasoned Twiss, "a good deal has been said" about the "Fugitive Slave Circulars" and the "personal *status* of the African slave." The slave, he said, reminding his audience that he was an expert on the subject of making persons, has "properly speaking, no *personal status*. The slave, in fact, has no *personality*."⁶⁶ The slave was a "thing, a chattel," who, like an ox or an ass, was the property of his master. When "he" escapes slavery, on the other hand, he "becomes once more a man."⁶⁷ Slavery, he pointed out, was a "local institution" and a "local law" to which slaves were "accidentally subject." The "Mahommedan Powers" had accordingly accepted, through numerous treaties, that it was a "rule of the Common Law of nations" that if a slave "escaped beyond the jurisdiction of the law, in virtue of which he is a slave," he becomes once more a man. These treaties, Twiss argued, were something to which African nations

61. Twiss, "Applicability," 411.
62. Twiss, "Applicability," 412.
63. Twiss, "Applicability," 412.
64. Twiss, "Applicability," 413.
65. Twiss, "Applicability," 413.
66. Twiss, "Applicability," 415.
67. Twiss, "Applicability," 416.

were bound "if they wish to be admitted within the pale of the European State-System."[68] The provisions of the treaties were "based on the recognition" of a *"jus commune gentium"* (a common law of nations) which was "applicable equally to African as to European States" and upon which "a young bud of positive law" was growing upon an "old stock of natural right." Here Twiss was making the quite remarkable claim for equality between European states and the Muslim states of Africa in international law. The reason he was doing so, however, was not because, like Hornung, he was a Kantian cosmopolitan or some other kind of opponent of empire.

Twiss proceeded in this article to go into a detailed account of the treaties that had for centuries past been established between Muslim African nations and European states. In these treaties—for example, those between Britain and Morocco, or Denmark and Tunis—he found the recognition of two principles: first, that if a slave escapes beyond the "jurisdiction of the law in virtue of which he is a slave," the state under whose jurisdiction he places himself is entitled to protect him; and, second, that a slave has placed "himself" in the jurisdiction of another state when he has escaped on board "one of its public Ships of War."[69] The plea of "comity" between nations, which the Disraeli government had used to justify the return of slaves to their masters in the hope of not antagonizing foreign powers, was, he said, "out of place." Comity was no ground for why the "Free Nations of Europe should submit to abandon the exercise of their rights of Sovereignty within their own Public Ships of War under conditions, in which they have hitherto persistently maintained those rights in their intercourse with the Slave States of Africa."[70] If Britain were to abandon the practice of protecting fugitive slaves, it would place itself in conflict with its "sister Christian states."[71] And yet, the Lord Chancellor, Hugh Cairns (who had represented William Windham in his lunacy case), addressing the House of Lords, had "expressed a difficulty" in "accepting the doctrine of the extraterritoriality of a British ship of war in the sense . . . that she carries with her the juridical attributes of British soil, wherever she goes."[72] The Lord Chancellor, Twiss argued, had been misled by the fact that "the term 'Extraterritoriality' is a metaphor" and that it did not signify the same thing in the case of a ship of war and an ambassador's house. The creation of resident embassies was, he observed, a recent development in international relations, and the "doctrine of the immunity of the Ambassador's house from the local law was an innovation" from a generally accepted principle that the laws of a nation bind all people within that territory.[73] On the other

68. Twiss, "Applicability," 417.
69. Twiss, "Applicability," 418.
70. Twiss, "Applicability," 421.
71. Twiss, "Applicability," 428.
72. Twiss, "Applicability," 430.
73. Twiss, "Applicability," 435.

hand, the doctrine that the sea within three miles of a coast is part of that country's territory employed the idea of "territory" as a metaphor in order to explain empire over the sea. When we speak of the extraterritoriality of ships of war in territorial waters, we "array metaphor against metaphor." Territorial waters were the more misleading of the two metaphors, because nations do not have the same absolute right to determine law in the waters that border their territory as they do when persons traverse their territory.[74] The extraterritoriality of ships therefore trumped territorial waters. Returning, therefore, to the "position of European Public Ships of War in the so-called territorial waters of African Slave States," Twiss reached the "ready answer" that if the African states "are desirous to live under a Common Law with the European Nations," they must concede the extraterritorial powers of European ships of war.[75] Pointing to the maritime nature of Britain's empire, he concluded, "No nation is more interested" than Britain in maintaining the "authority of *international usage* in all matters which regard the navigation of the High Seas."[76]

In this article, Twiss asserted the equality of African nations in international law in order to argue for their obligations in maintaining principles of extraterritoriality, which, he claimed, had been recognised by centuries of practice. Those powers of extraterritoriality, not least the extraterritoriality of gunboats, were precisely the means by which European nations were, from the mid-nineteenth century, once more expanding their empires across the globe, in Asia, Africa, and the Pacific and, closer to Europe, in the Ottoman Empire. More important, however, than the claim to portable extraterritoriality was the broader notion that these African states had obligations under the law of nations. Twiss further developed this idea of the equality of non-European states in international law and their corresponding obligations in his 1879 pamphlet *On International Conventions for the Maintenance of Sea Lights*, which he had delivered to the Association for the Reform and Codification of the Law of Nations in London. He began this article by pointing out that, for all nations that were "members of the European family," there was a "primary duty on the part of each nation to light up its coasts to passing vessels" in order to meet their larger commitment to freedom of the seas.[77] He pointed out, however, that "hardly anything" had been said of this duty by writers on international law. Nevertheless, he observed, the question of lighthouses was all the more urgent since the invention of steamships, "the great maritime discovery of the present century."[78] He proceeded to provide a detailed history

---

74. Twiss, "Applicability," 436.
75. Twiss, "Applicability," 436.
76. Twiss, "Applicability," 437.
77. Twiss, *Sea Lights*, 3.
78. Twiss, *Sea Lights*, 3.

of lighthouses, from ancient times to the present, in order to demonstrate that "the modern lighthouse is an institution capable in certain cases of producing such great international benefit, that its erection and maintenance may well deserve the co-operative action of civilized states."[79] Here, therefore, was a duty, alongside the provision of channel markers and actions against piracy, that lay upon all states that wished to participate in the society of nations, and he articulated it in precisely those terms: that is, as "the international duty of states to light up their sea-coasts."[80]

Having established this duty that lay upon members of the society of nations, Twiss turned to examining in what ways it was incumbent upon non-European states. Repeating the claims he made in previous publications and in the Institut commission on the place of "Oriental nations" in international law, he declared that "Asiatic and African states" had "recently been admitted into the European concert of public law."[81] The Ottoman Empire, he observed, had "farmed out" its lighthouse-keeping duties to a French company.[82] The 1858 Treaty of Tientsin, which ended the Opium Wars, obliged China to provide sea lights and placed the "administration of the maritime customs . . . entirely under the direction of European officers."[83] In 1866, Japan had signed a common tariff convention, which guaranteed the provision of navigational aids that were then provided by British engineers at a cost of over £1 million.[84] These agreements had all sanctioned European commerce. The "two great civilised nations of the far East" had "acceded effectively to the established practice of the nations of the Western world."[85] In other words, for Twiss, the admission of these "Oriental nations" into the law of nations brought with it duties which they were obliged to perform, such as the provision of lighthouses, and also sanctioned their submission to an international regime, where necessary, in order to meet those obligations.

There were other countries, however, with which "Europe has been brought into contact under a system of trade" but which did not have the means to "meet the expenditure" necessary to "light up their coasts." Moreover there were "some countries" in which no civilized government exists."[86] "How", he asked, "shall we provide for the safe navigation of the steamship along coasts, and amidst islands which are not under the sovereignty of any civilized power".[87] He enumerated the various sites on the eastern side of

79. Twiss, *Sea Lights*, 9.
80. Twiss, *Sea Lights*, 12.
81. Twiss, *Sea Lights*, 13.
82. Twiss, *Sea Lights*, 14.
83. Twiss, *Sea Lights*, 14.
84. Twiss, *Sea Lights*, 14-15.
85. Twiss, *Sea Lights*, 15.
86. Twiss, *Sea Lights*, 15.
87. Twiss, *Sea Lights*, 16.

the Suez Canal which required lighthouses but were not under the control of any power who would provide them, including in the Gulf of Aden, islands in the Indian Ocean, the Arafura Sea and Torres Straits, north of Australia, and the east coast of Africa, including the coast of Somalia. Many of these places, according to Twiss, were under systems of government but unable to provide navigational aids. The "Somali Arabs," for example, were the "lords of the soil" but were not a people who could be treated with.[88] What was necessary in such countries, or in countries with "no civilized government," was a system of "international lighthouses" protected, if necessary, by "a fort" and "a strong garrison of soldiers."[89] He held out, as an example of international cooperation to create such lighthouses, the 1865 Cape Spartel Convention, in which the Sultan of Morocco handed the administration of the lighthouse on Cape Spartel, above the Straits of Gibralta, to a concert of European and American powers. "Why should we not hope," he asked, "to see the day arrive when INTERNATIONAL LIGHTHOUSES shall be amongst the trophies of peace, which the civilization of Europe shall set up amidst the islands of the far East?"[90] He concluded by observing, "We are in the present day only on the threshold of the East African question." Indeed, in 1879, when he wrote, European powers were turning their attention to Africa as a new field for colonization, in part because advances in medicine enabled the settlement of tropical latitudes and because steam power enabled the navigation of fast-flowing rivers that had previously been impenetrable. "If the civilization of Europe is to penetrate into the heart of Africa from the east," Twiss concluded, "the first great step will be to secure to the European mariner a safe approach to its shores, and this may be materially furnished by an international concert."[91]

In this article, Twiss clarified two developing streams of his thought in the 1870s and '80s. First, he argued for the equality of many non-European nations in international society and international law. He did so because he viewed membership in society as something that comes with both rights and duties. He understood that granting membership to non-European governments, such as the Turks, Chinese, Japanese, or even the "Slave-states" of Africa, meant that Europeans could demand that those governments meet certain standards of behaviour, and, if they failed to do so, they could be held to account and have certain "duties" imposed upon them—for example, in the imposition of extraterritoriality by foreign powers. This idea of the equality of "Oriental nations" can be contrasted with common representations of nineteenth-century perceptions of the equality of nations in international law. It is frequently argued that in order to extend their empires,

---

88. Twiss, *Sea Lights*, 17.
89. Twiss, *Sea Lights*, 17.
90. Twiss, *Sea Lights*, 24.
91. Twiss, *Sea Lights*, 24.

Europeans developed a system of international law which assumed a fundamental inequality between European and non-European powers, and this enabled them to impose their sovereignty upon the non-European world. There is no question that such a characterisation holds true for certain jurists, such as James Lorimer, who developed highly racialized and hierarchical theories of international law. But that vision of inequality was just one amongst a number understandings of the relations between Europeans and non-Europeans in international law. Some jurists, such as Hornung, argued for the equality of certain non-European nations in international law in order to restrain European imperialism, even if they did so in the context of a paternalistic view. Highly influential voices, such as Dudley Field and Twiss, argued for the equality of non-European nations precisely in order to extend European and American empires, or "informal empires." Historians have perhaps also been deaf to these arguments because they were based upon the idea of duties. Knowing that Europeans used international law as an instrument of expansion, we have tended to assume that an argument for expansion must be based upon dominance, and dominance must be based upon inequality, and most probably, from a twenty-first-century perspective, inequality in the possession of rights. The arguments Twiss made for the dominance of Europeans, however, were based upon the assumption of equality and the duties that equality brought with it. Failure to meet those duties led to accountability and the extension of sovereignty over the recalcitrant powers. Twiss's argument for the equality of "Oriental nations" in the society of nations were consistent with broader movements for the expansion of the franchise, for example, in the Reform Act of 1867 which extended the vote to working-class men. Just as male subjects of the state were increasingly granted political standing and women were granted legal personality through the Married Women's Property Acts, Twiss also endorsed a broader franchise for the subjects of international society. Instead, however, of basing that franchise upon rights, or negative liberty, as was the case with the 1867 Reform Act, he based it upon both rights and duties.[92]

The second stream of thought that Twiss developed in these articles and reports of the '70s and '80s was the matter of internationalisation or, more precisely, the international jurisdiction over certain territories, practices, or technologies. International jurisdiction, too, would be fundamental to the projection of European sovereignty upon the non-European world. In countries which fell short of membership in the law of nations, Twiss recommended that European powers collectively impose an international order which would allow the creation of conditions in which, for example, commerce could flourish and certain people—for example, slaves and indentured workers—would

---

92. For the centrality of negative liberty to the 1867 Reform Act, see Philip Harling, "The Powers of the Victorian State," in Mandler, ed., *Liberty and Authority in Victorian Britain*, 33.

be protected. Twiss published prolifically during the '70s and '80s, and many of his articles and presentations to the Institut and to the Association for the Reform and Codification of the Law of Nations stressed the importance of international jurisdiction as a solution to problems. Some of these articles dealt with the increasing incidence of collisions at sea due to the invention of steamships.[93] While the existing Admiralty courts of the various European and American powers exercised civil jurisdiction in the case of collisions, they had no powers to make criminal convictions. Several accidents in international waters in the 1870s led to the loss of hundreds of lives and created pressure for a criminal code of the sea that could punish negligent captains and crews.[94] Twiss addressed these concerns with articles in which he argued for an "International Court" which would be based upon the model of Consular Courts: that is, the courts used to exercise extraterritorial jurisdictions. The Consular Courts established mixed tribunals for cases of conflicts between locals and expatriates in which the consul of the occupying power would sit in judgement with a local judge. Twiss argued that a similar system could be used for criminal cases in international waters, with a judge from the admiralty court in the country closest to the conflict presiding over the case with a consul from the country of the ship of the more remote country, sitting with "one legal and two nautical assessors."[95] Any other system, he argued, would place British subjects in the obnoxious circumstance of being judged entirely by the standards of other nations. Internationalism was a matter of national interest.

Twiss examined the possibilities for other kinds of international regime; for example, in a paper given to the Association for the Reform and Codification of the Law of Nations, he questioned whether submarine telegraph cables should be recognised as "neutral" or possessing an "international" character and therefore be immune to hostile acts.[96] In an 1875 article in the *Revue de droit international*, he argued that the recently opened Suez Canal should be declared a neutral zone, protected from belligerent acts against the Ottoman Empire. He recalled that his old friend Prince Metternich had advised the Pasha of Egypt, Muhammed Ali, in the 1840s, that his plans for a canal should be placed in the context of neutrality.[97] Metternich argued that the

---

93. Travers Twiss, "Collisions at Sea: A Scheme of International Tribunals," *Law Magazine and Review* (November 1878), 1–15; Travers Twiss, "The Criminal Jurisdiction of the Admiralty of England: The Case of the *Franconia*," *Law Magazine and Review* (February 1877), 145–177; Travers Twiss, "Collisions at Sea," *Albany Law Journal* (October 12, 1878), 287–288.

94. *London Evening Standard*, September 14, 1878, 5.

95. Twiss, "Collisions at Sea: A Scheme of International Tribunals," 10.

96. Twiss, "The International Protection of Submarine Telegraph Cables," *Association for the Reform and Codification of the Law of Nations*, 98–105.

97. Travers Twiss, "La neutralisation du Canal de Suez," *Revue de droit international et de législation comparée*, vol. 7 (1875), 682.

London Straits Convention of 1841, which barred warships from the Dardanelles, should be a model for the Suez Canal. Twiss agreed and added also that the Suez Canal should be governed along the lines of the convention agreed at the Treaty of Paris, in 1856, setting up an international commission to guarantee freedom of commerce and navigation on the Danube River.[98] We have already seen in his correspondence with Metternich that Twiss believed that the neutrality of the Danube would be a means to provide Western European powers with access into the Black Sea, and to the East more generally: that is, as means of expansion. Twiss similarly saw agreements for free navigation and commerce as a means of further extending British power. The Suez Canal, which the British saw as a threat to its control over the seas, he now presented as an opportunity for strengthening its Eastern dominions and commerce. Indeed, as we have seen, fifteen years earlier he had written to Gladstone, who had also thought about the neutrality of the Suez Canal, expressing his enthusiasm for the idea and offering to share his correspondence with Metternich on the subject.[99]

Twiss and King Leopold

Twiss's interest in the possibilities of international jurisdiction and neutrality became for him another means, alongside the argument for the equality of "Oriental nations" in the law of nations, for the extension of European power over the non-European world or, as he saw it, the extension of international jurisdiction over the non-European world. He thought most deeply about this possibility in the context of the expanding interest in Africa amongst European nations in the 1870s and '80s. On August 21, 1879, Twiss sent his article on lighthouses to the Chief of Cabinet, Baron Paul de Borchgrave d'Altena, to King Leopold II, of Belgium. Alongside many European states, Leopold had been developing an interest in Africa throughout the 1870s. Since the 1860s, he had eagerly sought the creation of Belgian overseas territories, but he was frustrated by the refusal of the Belgian government to support his proposals. The government was nervous about the impact that Belgian expansionism might have upon the neutral status of Belgium, which had, under the Treaty of London in 1839, been a condition of its creation. Leopold resolved to pursue his interests in Africa independently of the Belgian government and under the guise of internationalism, humanitarianism, and anti-slavery efforts.

In 1876, Leopold organised and hosted a conference in the Royal Palace at Brussels that brought together geographers, explorers, military men, and businessmen from all the major European powers and from the United

---

98. Twiss, "La neutralisation du Canal de Suez," 692.
99. "Twiss to Gladstone," November 5, 1861: British Library, Gladstone Papers, Additional MS. 44397, fols. 170–171.

States, including Twiss's friend Rutherford Alcock, who had retired from diplomatic service to become the President of the Royal Geographical Society. Also amongst the attendees were Baron von Richtofen, President of the Geographical Society in Berlin, the Orientalist Sir Henry Rawlinson, anti-slavery activists such as Thomas Fowell Buxton, businessmen such as William MacKinnon from the British India Line, and famous explorers, including Victor de Compiègne and Gustav Nachtigal, although not including Henry Stanley, who was, at that moment, in Africa exploring Lake Victoria.[100] In his letter of invitation, Leopold wrote that "Belgium, a central and neutral state," was an excellent location for such a conference. He added: "I have not been guided by egotistic views. No, gentlemen; if Belgium is small, she is happy and satisfied with her lot."[101] This statement reflected the Belgian government's disinterest in colonization, but it hid Leopold's purpose and his preparedness to act as a private individual, if necessary, rather than through the Belgian state.

Leopold claimed that the aim of the conference was to establish an organisation "to plant definitely the standard of civilisation on the soil of Central Africa."[102] He gave some indication of what was to come with the claim: "I should be happy that Brussels should become in some way the headquarters of this civilising movement."[103] The conference agreed to work towards establishing posts in Africa for its further study and exploration, and it discussed which African territories needed further exploration. Leopold proposed the creation of an international commission to carry forward the work of exploring and "civilizing" Africa, and the conference duly endorsed the "common international plan."[104] That international commission would be composed of national committees which would inform it of progress towards its goals in each member nation. The conference agreed to create this Association and also agreed with the proposal from Sir Henry Bartle Frere (who would prove to be a disastrous administrator in South Africa) that Leopold be made its President for the first year.[105] Leopold also provided space in Brussels for the headquarters of the new organisation, and in 1878, the International African Association was formerly created in London.[106] The various national committees were established and attracted members and subscriptions to aid in the work of civilizing Africa.

100. Robert Stanley Thompson, *Fondation de l'État indépendant du Congo* (Brussells, 1933), 42; Hochschild, *King Leopold's Ghost*, 43–44.
101. Henry Wellington Wack, *The Story of the Congo Free State* (New York, 1905), 9.
102. Wack, *The Story of the Congo Free State*, 10.
103. Wack, *The Story of the Congo Free State*, 9–10.
104. Thompson, *Fondation de l'État indépendant du Congo*, 46; Wack, *The Story of the Congo Free State*, 11–12.
105. Thompson, *Fondation de l'État indépendant du Congo*, 46; Wack, *The Story of the Congo Free State*, 12.
106. Thompson, *Fondation de l'État indépendant du Congo*, 35.

In July, 1877, Rutherford Alcock wrote to *The Times* to express the great sympathy that the Royal Geographical Society had with the aims of the International African Association, but to explain that the British committee, the African Exploration Fund, was obliged to be remain autonomous from the Association because the Geographical Society was unable, by the terms of its constitution, to belong to a political movement.[107] At the same time, Alcock announced a public meeting to be held in two days' time in the Egyptian Hall of Mansion House to raise funds for the further exploration of Africa and the suppression of the slave trade. The meeting was attended by, amongst others, Thomas Fowell Buxton and Verney Lovett Cameron, who had been the first European, two years earlier, to traverse Africa from East to West. In his address to the meeting, Alcock declared that in no age had "progress been so manifest" as in the "advancement of civilization" through "African discoveries." He also stressed that "this country should find new markets to take its produce, and Africa opened up a wide field to them."[108]

Although he was an active member of the Royal Geographical Society, not to mention a close friend of Alcock, Twiss ignored their desire to act separately from Leopold and their fear, as Henry Stanley put it, of "trammelling themselves with engagements of an international nature."[109] Twiss was strongly interested in engagements of an international nature, particularly since he had been barred from national engagements. He wrote, in 1879, to Leopold's Chief of Cabinet, Borchgrave, to say that he had enclosed two copies of his article on "International Conventions on the Maintenance of Sea Lights," published in that year, which had "an immediate bearing on the attempt to civilize Africa from the East Coast in which his Majesty is taking so noble a lead, and in which I am desirous to cooperate in a very humble manner by suggesting an international concert to light up the seaway along the East African Coast."[110] In 1877, Henry Stanley had continued his explorations from Tanzania, in Africa's east, west to the Lualaba River, which he followed to where it joined the Congo, and following that, he descended through the Congo Basin to the mouth of the Congo on the west coast of the continent.[111] To great acclaim in Europe, he thereby proved that the Lualaba and the Congo were part of one vast river system extending through the centre of Africa and open to the Atlantic. Twiss had in mind such explorations of the continent from the east, but when news of Stanley's explorations reached Leopold in September 1877,

---

107. Rutherford Alcock, "African Exploration," *The Times*, July 17, 1877, 10.

108. Rutherford Alcock, "African Exploration," *The Times*, July 20, 1877, 11.

109. Henry Stanley, *The Congo and the Founding of Its Free State*, 2 vols. (London, 1885), Vol. 1, 36.

110. Twiss to Borchgrave, August 21, 1879, Archives du Palais Royal, Brussels, *Commandements du Roi*, A96/CD4XI/22.

111. Jesse Siddall Reeves, *The International Beginnings of the Congo Free State* (Baltimore, 1894), 19; Hochshild, *King Leopold's Ghost*, 46.

he moved his focus to the Congo and to the means of exploring it from the west. The Congo River had, prior to this time, proved impossible to explore beyond its lower reaches, both because it flowed too fast for sailing vessels and because, 155 kilometres from its mouth, it was broken by a long stretch of massive falls. Leopold, however, approached Stanley as soon as he set foot back in Europe, convincing the explorer to work for him. Together, they developed a plan to establish trading posts in the Congo Basin through bypassing the falls, initially by foot and then by rail (which was planned even at this early stage), and bringing steamships to the Upper Congo.[112] After a series of meetings with Stanley in 1878, Leopold created a new company, the Comité d'Etudes du Haut Congo, which would move his attention to the Congo and leave the International African Association as an empty public front but a useful diversion.

When, almost a year later, he sent his article on "sea lights" to Leopold, Twiss was clearly out of step with Leopold's latest plans, although that is not surprising because, during the late 1870s, Leopold financed three separate expeditions attempting to reach the Congo from the east, and he was still publicly talking about advancing the civilisation of Africa generally and not saying that he had resolved to carve out one vast region for himself.[113] Nevertheless, Twiss's gesture revealed two important aspects of his future relationship with Leopold. First, he showed that he was eager to make himself useful in Leopold's plans to "civilize" Africa, and also that he wished to take a role in international affairs that went beyond publishing on questions of international law. Second, while the east coast of Africa was of diminishing interest for Leopold, Twiss's article identified the internationalisation of African territory that was not under effective sovereignty as a means of imposing European rule, and this question would prove to be key to his future contributions and to Leopold's success in seizing a large part of Congo Basin as his own fiefdom.

As early as 1877, Leopold wrote to an aide: "I'm sure if I quite openly charged Stanley with the task of taking possession in my name of some part of Africa, the English would stop me. If I ask their advice, they'll stop me just the same. So I think I'll just give Stanley some job of exploration which would offend no one, and will give us the bases and headquarters which we can take over later on."[114] The words proved to be remarkably prescient. In August 1879, after careful preparations, Stanley returned to the Congo with Leopold's funding, approaching this time from the Atlantic. He established a station at Vivi on the Lower Congo and then set about constructing a wagon path to bypass 80 kilometres of rapids that separated the Lower from the Upper Congo River. Throughout 1880 and early 1881, using African labourers,

---

112. Stanley, *The Congo and the Founding of Its Free State*, Vol. 1, 21.
113. Hochschild, *King Leopold's Ghost*, 66.
114. Quoted in Hochschild, *King Leopold's Ghost*, 58.

Stanley cut the road from Vivi through to the Upper Congo. He used wagons to carry steamboats up that road and launched the *Royal* on the Upper Congo on February 21, 1881.[115] Throughout 1881 and 1882, Stanley used his steamboats to explore the Congo and to settle new stations, including "Léopoldville" (now Kinshasa) on "Stanley Pool" (now Pool Malebo) in honour, as Stanley put it, "of the munificent and Royal Founder of the 'Association Internationale du Congo.'"[116]

Leopold had created the new corporation to which Stanley referred, the International Association of the Congo, in November 1879. It had been deliberately named in order to cause confusion with the philanthropic International African Association. Leopold wrote to an aid: "Care must be taken not to let it be obvious that the Association of the Congo and the African Association are two different things."[117] This new organisation was a single shareholder corporation, with Leopold the shareholder. In contrast to the International African Association, its objective was to carve out a territory in the Congo Basin through the creation of stations and commerce, and, crucially, through making treaties with native rulers which ceded sovereignty to the corporation. According to Stanley, and Leopold, the chiefs of the Congo Basin were sovereigns of their territories, and it was their possession of that political authority that enabled them to cede the very same sovereignty to the International Association of the Congo—once again, equality in the law of nations could be used to deprive a non-European people of their power.[118]

This, however, was wishful thinking. Europeans did not admit the possibility that sovereign power could be ceded to organisations that did not hold sovereignty, and many did not accept the idea that sub-Saharan African peoples possessed sovereignty. Nor, for that matter, did they accept that private organisations, such as Leopold's Association, had any standing in international society or international law. In 1884, the notion that a non-state corporation could go about the business of claiming title to territory and overseas possession for itself, without the sanction of a state, was simply preposterous as far the law of nations was concerned. Twiss, it will be recalled, had made precisely that point in rejecting the possibility that free settlers crossing the Rocky Mountains in the early nineteenth century could establish their own commonwealths or states outside the license of any sovereign. Moreover, over the course of the nineteenth century, states progressively diminished the power of corporations to do the work of empire and colonisation. In the first half of the century, both the South Australia Company, established in 1835, and the New Zealand Company, established in 1837, were created not simply with the intention of

---

115. Stanley, *The Congo and the Founding of Its Free State*, Vol. 1, 240.
116. Stanley, *The Congo and the Founding of Its Free State*, Vol. 1, 386.
117. Quoted in Hochschild, *King Leopold's Ghost*, 65.
118. Stanley, *The Congo and the Founding of Its Free State*, Vol. 2, 378-381.

colonizing but also with a vision for a new kind of civil society. The legacy of the seventeenth-century chartered companies, which fashioned themselves as company-commonwealths, was still present. Many corporations continued to behave as semi-autonomous political societies, despite the efforts of sovereigns to rein them in, but the mood was nevertheless against the corporate sovereign. Following the 1857 Indian Rebellion, which had been provoked by continuing land grabs by the East India Company, the British government shut the Company down, removing from it all governing responsibilities and moving to a system of direct administration over India. The dis-establishment of the East India Company marked the nadir in the sovereign ambitions of overseas trading corporations, and it was said that their time had passed. In the 1870s and '80s, however, overseas trading companies were again established to do the work of expanding imperium, and Leopold's International Association of the Congo was the most radical expression of that resurgence.[119] Unlike other colonising companies, it had no licence from a state and therefore no conventional means by which it could acquire territory. The International Association's position can be usefully contrasted with that of Pierre Savorgnan de Brazza, who, on the other side of the Congo River from Stanley, was similarly collecting signatures to supposed treaties of cession, which, as far as Europeans were concerned, did constitute a transfer of sovereignty because Brazza was working under the authority of the French state.

Merely stating that the International Association of the Congo could acquire sovereignty was not enough, because, for the Company to survive and realise its pretensions to acquire sovereignty, it had to be recognised by other sovereign powers. The young French geographer and diplomat Louis Delavaud stated the conventional position on the status of private associations in international society in an article in the *Revue de géographie* in March 1883, which reflected on the rival claims of Brazza and the International Association of the Congo. "It is a principle of law," Delavaud began, "that only states can exercise sovereign rights, that no private companies can have them."[120] "Amongst sovereign rights," he continued, "the most important is the possession of territory," which includes, he noted, "the right of annexation." This right, he observed, "belongs solely to states: it can be exercised by those who are mandated by the state," and it can be used to "ratify acts after they have occurred." "It can therefore," he declared, "be exercised by Monsieur Brazza, and it cannot be exercised by Mr Stanley, who is the agent of a commercial company." In international law, this declaration by Delavaud was entirely conventional, and it highlighted the great obstacle facing Leopold if he was to realise his ambition of creating a state in the Congo through the actions of his

---

119. Press, in *Rogue Empires*, examines some of these ventures.

120. Louis Delavaud, "La France et le Portugal au Congo," *Revue de géographie* (March 1883), 224.

private company and without the mandate of Belgium or any other state. Devalaud argued, moreover, that the area of the Congo occupied by Brazza was "*sans maître*," whereas the territory occupied by Stanley was already under the sovereignty of Portugal, which had had a presence in the Lower Congo since the fifteenth century, with the Kingdom of Kongo in that region being a "vassal" of Portugal since the sixteenth century.[121] Stanley, he pointed out, could only acquire sovereignty if he had been granted the right of annexation by a sovereign and then used that right to wage a war of conquest against the Portuguese claims. To put it another way, Devalaud noted that, if Stanley was "mandated by a state," then he had committed acts of war against Portugal. But this was impossible, he concluded, and could only be the consequence of a misunderstanding. The creation of the International Association of the Congo had only been made possible by the English, who had deliberately impeded the civilizing efforts of other powers in the region, particularly the Portuguese. Nevertheless, "that private company does not have the right to behave like a sovereign state."[122]

For the International Association of the Congo to be admitted to the society of nations, the franchise for membership in that society had to be radically revised. Twiss would successfully prosecute that argument. Until this point—for example, in the 1877 meeting that had established the International African Association—Leopold had relied heavily upon the advice of geographers, explorers, military men, and businessmen, in order to pursue his designs. Once, however, he had overcome the logistical obstacles, he realised that the possibility of establishing a new state in the Congo would depend upon the success of diplomatic and legal argument. He began now, therefore, to rely upon the services of jurists and political economists, usually members of the Institut de droit international, including the German jurist Egide Arntz who lived in Brussels, Émile de Laveleye, the Belgian political economist, who was a founder of the *Institut*, and the Swiss jurist and founder of the International Red Cross, Gustave Moynier, but the lawyer who was able to overcome opposition to recognition of Leopold's corporation as member of the society of nations would prove to be Travers Twiss. Twiss made a series of arguments which would be necessary to the creation of a new state with Leopold as its sovereign. First, he argued that the Congo should be internationalised, thereby preventing rival European states, and particularly the French, from extending their own claims in the region. Second, he argued that a private association could have a standing in international society, thereby making it possible for the International Association for the Congo to make treaties with native sovereigns in which they ceded to it sovereign power. Third, he argued that private associations could be transformed into states.

---

121. Delavaud, "La France et le Portugal au Congo," 225.
122. Delavaud, "La France et le Portugal au Congo," 226.

For the first claim, that the Congo should be internationalised, Twiss published a series of articles through the course of 1883 and 1884 which built upon his previous publications of the 1870s on international jurisdiction. His first article on the Congo, "*La libre navigation du Congo*," was finished on July 24, 1883, and was written in Brussels, where he was clearly in consultation with Leopold and his staff.[123] This article gave a detailed account of the geography of the Congo River, one of the "four great rivers of Africa," and its neighbouring territories, as well as a history of European, and particularly Portuguese, involvement in the region. Portugal was becoming increasingly alarmed at the meddling of other European powers in a region to which they made claims based upon historical discovery, even if they backed those claims with very limited activity. They pushed their concerns increasingly through negotiations with Britain, beginning in 1882, to establish a treaty which would divide sovereignty over the central West African coast with control north of the Congo going to Britain and south of the Congo to Portugal.[124]

Twiss observed that the subjects of a number of European powers had established factories in the Lower Congo, but that a state of virtual anarchy existed on the river due to the absence of any preponderant authority. He said he sympathised "with all my heart" with the "humanitarian idea" expressed by his colleagues from the Institut de droit international, Emile de Laveleye and Gustave Moynier, when they proposed the "neutralisation" of the Lower Congo.[125] Their proposal was intended to reduce the potential for conflict in the region which arose from the growing number of competing powers. He pointed out, however, that the word neutralisation, in its application to territorial waters, had a "sole sense": namely, "in international conventions it interdicted the entrance of all armed ships for all states that signed the convention." Unfortunately, he observed, the banks of the Congo were inhabited not only by the subjects of various European powers but also by many native pirates, who constantly troubled the commerce of the Europeans, not hesitating to kill those who resisted.[126] There was no question that Leopold wanted the goods, that he hoped to develop in the Middle and Upper Congo (at this time he was interested in ivory, but his attention would soon turn to rubber), to be protected by his own armed steamboats when they descended into the Lower Congo to be brought to European markets. Twiss proposed, instead, to "*internationaliser le Congo*," as had been the case with the Danube after the Crimean War.[127] Here, the idea of internationalisation that he had been

123. Travers Twiss, "La libre navigation du Congo," *Revue de droit international et de législation comparée*, 15, 1883, 437–444.
124. See Crowe, *The Berlin West African Conference*, 17.
125. Twiss, "La libre navigation du Congo," 440.
126. Twiss, "La libre navigation du Congo," 440–441.
127. Twiss, "La libre navigation du Congo," 442. Engelhardt, "La question du Danube," *Revue de droit International et de législation comparée*, 1882. For the Danube as a

exploring as a tool of European expansion in articles throughout the 1870s became an instrument for expanding the power of the International Association for the Congo. More recently, he had been examing those ideas in relation to the Suez.[128] Internationalizing the Congo would, in particular, allow the navigation of armed vessels and prevent the Portuguese from imposing their sovereignty over the river. At the same time, Twiss proposed a regime of *"désintéressement"* for the Middle and Upper Congo which would allow, he said, the stations established there to flourish. In this instance, he apparently had in mind an international accord that could block any attempt by the French to expand their claims to sovereignty in the Congo Basin under the treaties made by Brazza.

Prior to the publication of the first of Twiss's articles titled *"La libre navigation du Congo"* in July 1883, the head of Leopold's cabinet, Jules Devaux, wrote to Laveleye, on April 20, to say, "His Majesty finds that the idea of Sir T. Twiss to internationalise the lower Congo very good."[129] This was a blow for Laveleye's own plan for neutralisation.[130] Devaux added that Leopold also liked very much Twiss's project of *"désintéressement"* for the Middle and Upper Congo, but that he believed France would not consent to it. The striking aspect of Devaux's letter is that Leopold and his ministers knew the details of Twiss's first publication on the free navigation of the Congo three months before it was published. Their knowledge points to the depth of his collaboration with Leopold, which he had himself sought four years previously with his letter to Borchgrave. In the intervening four years, Twiss and Leopold's ministers had coordinated their efforts to justify occupation of the Congo, leading to the series of publications by Twiss in 1883 and 1884.

---

precedent for the neutralisation of the Congo, see Crowe, *The Berlin West African Conference*, 133; Engelhardt, "Le droit fluvial conventionnel," *Revue de droit international et de législation comparée*, Vol. 16 (May 1884), 360; Engelhardt, "Du principe de neutralité dans son application aux fleuves internationaux et aux canaux maritimes," *Revue de droit international et de législation comparée* (1886), 159–167.

128. Twiss, "De la sécurité de la navigation dans le canal de Suez," *Revue de droit international et de législation comparée* (November 1882), 572–582; Twiss, "Le canal maritime de Suez et la commission internationale de Paris," *Revue de droit international et de législation comparée*, Vol. 17 (1885), 615–630.

129. Devaux to Laveleye, April 20, 1883, Archives du Palais Royal, Brussels, *Commandements du Roi*, A136/43. Laveleye's role in promoting Leopold's colonial ambitions is discussed in Jan Vandersmissen, *Koningen van de wereld: Leopold II en de aardrijkskundige beweging* (Leuven, 2009); and Jan Vandersmissen, "The King's Most Eloquent Campaigner: Emile de Laveleye, Leopold II, and the Creation of the Congo Free State," *Journal of Belgian History*, vol. 41 (2011), 1–2, 7–57.

130. Cf. Vandersmissen, "The King's Most Eloquent Campaigner," 35–36, claims that the letter was arguing that Twiss supported Laveleye's idea of neutralising the Congo, albeit that Twiss was actually arguing that neutrality would lead to anarchy (as Vandersmissen concedes).

On August 16, 1883, Twiss completed a pamphlet in London with the title *An International Protectorate of the Congo River*. This pamphlet was published later in August and then republished in November in the *Law Magazine and Review*.[131] In this work, Twiss further expanded upon his argument for the internationalisation of the Congo, pointing out that the Portuguese had failed to exercise sovereignty in the Lower Congo, where, in consequence, anarchy prevailed. He pointed out again that Laveleye's proposal for the neutralisation of the river would prevent armed vessels from patrolling it and only encourage the "piratical tribes" at its mouth.[132] He ridiculed Portuguese pretentions to sovereignty over most of the Lower Congo based upon "priority of discovery four centuries ago."[133] The situation in the Upper and Middle Congo, Twiss noted, was even more uncertain, with merchants who visited the area unable to know to whom they owed obedience and "to what magistrates they shall be responsible."[134] Nevertheless, while attacking the sovereignty of Portugal, he also challenged French claims, arguing that Brazza had only established "usufruct" through his treaties, not sovereignty.[135] Clearly, while he claimed that he was only concerned with the creation of sovereign authority over the territory, he was carefully excluding all Leopold's rivals. Recalling his analysis of "Oriental sovereignty" in his series of articles in the 1870s, Twiss then declared, "The time has now arrived when Europe may feel called upon to engraft the same principles of public law upon the institutions of a sister continent."[136] Accordingly, he was prepared to recognise that the "native races" of the Congo possessed sovereignty, albeit not of the same order as found in Europe: "The organisation of the native races on the banks of the Congo is still *tribal*, and *territorial* Sovereignty in the sense in which it has superseded *personal* Sovereignty in Europe, is still unknown. Personal Sovereignty, however, is recognised by the European traders on the Congo." Although he did not yet state it, the implication was that these native feudal lords were able to cede their personal sovereignty to the International Association of the Congo, which, as territorial sovereign, would effectively become a state.

On August 28, 1883, Lord Selborne, Roundell Palmer, who was the Lord Chancellor of Britain, sent to Lord Granville, the Secretary of State for Foreign Affairs, a copy of Twiss's *International Protectorate of the Congo River*. Twiss, as we have seen, had worked closely with Granville during the 1857 Indian Rebellion, when Granville was Lord President of the council. Even several years before that, Twiss had written sympathetically of Granville's

---

131. "An International Protectorate of the Congo River," *Law Magazine and Review*, 250 (1883), 1–20.
132. Travers Twiss, *An International Protectorate of the Congo River* (London, 1883), 11.
133. Twiss, *An International Protectorate*, 14.
134. Twiss, *An International Protectorate*, 19.
135. Twiss, *An International Protectorate*, 18.
136. Twiss, *An International Protectorate*, 17.

brief months as Secretary of State for Foreign Affairs, comparing his time in the office favourably with his predecessor, Palmerston: "Ld. P [Lord Palmerston] was one of those pilots who seem to wish to steer amidst rocks and shores . . . I believe that Ld Gr [Granville] meant to sail otherwise."[137] Selborne had known Twiss since 1839, when they acted together to liberalise access to fellowships at University College, and Twiss described him as "an Oxford friend."[138] They worked many times together over the following forty-four years, including when both had been members of the 1867 Royal Commission into Marriage Laws. Twiss had sent his tract on the Congo to Selborne before it was published. As Selborne wrote to Granville: "This is an interesting Paper by Sir Travers Twiss. It is not yet published as it is to be delivered by him at the Institut de droit international."[139] The context for Twiss's act in sending the unpublished text to Selborne is crucial to its meaning. Granville's office, at this moment, was deep in the vexed, and ultimately doomed, negotiations with Portugal over a treaty for mutual recognition of claims in West Africa. Eager to sabotage the agreement, Twiss therefore used his friendship with Selborne to provide the British side of the negotiations with a treatise which belittled the Portuguese claims and therefore made it clear that any concessions Britain made were to be cheaply granted. It would appear that he succeeded, as Selborne pointed out to Granville that Twiss's tract "advocates the scheme which you may remember that I also suggested as a *mezzo termine* [middle ground or compromise]."[140]

On September 4, 1883, thirty members of the Institut de droit international, including Twiss, held their annual meeting in a hotel in Munich.[141] One of the questions on their agenda was the situation of the Congo in international law. On the first day of the conference, Gustave Moynier circulated a letter he had written in July supporting Laveleye's proposition for neutrality, but he noted that Twiss had subsequently "contradicted" that proposal for "internationalisation" in his "*La libre navigation du Congo*," which was also circulated. Moynier then read a new memoir he had written on the subject in which he spoke of the great "anxiety" that the race for the Congo could produce conflict between a number of European states.[142] He therefore declared

---

137. Twiss to Metternich, March 3, 1852, National Archives of the Czech Republic, Prague, RAM-AC/ 10/ 778, 14.

138. Twiss to Metternich, March 23, 1851, National Archives of the Czech Republic, Prague, RAM-AC/ 10/ 777, 52.

139. Selborne to Granville, August 28, 1883, National Archives, London, FO 84/ 1807/ 70.

140. Selborne to Granville, August 28, 1883, National Archives, London, FO 84/ 1807/ 70 verso. For the copy of Twiss, *An International Protectorate*, circulating in the Foreign Office, see National Archives, London, FO 84/ 1807/ 72–83.

141. *Annuaire de l'Institut de droit international* (1885), 13–14.

142. *Annuaire de l'Institut de droit international* (1885), 252.

that when he had supported Laveleye's proposal for neutrality, in his letter of the previous July, he had made a mistake.[143] On the other hand, he declared, he was not convinced that Twiss's idea of "internationalizing" was much better, and he could not see a reason for different regimes, internationalisation, and disinterestedness governing the Lower and Upper Congo. Moynier proposed an international commission which would guarantee free navigation and commerce on the river and would empower an armed force to impose the interests of its signatories.[144] Alphonse Rivier then read a letter to the meeting that Laveleye, who was absent from the meeting, had written the day before in response to Moynier's proposals. In this letter, Laveleye agreed with Moynier on the importance of free navigation of the river but said that he had come to the view (no doubt under pressure from Leopold) that Twiss's proposal was the means to guarantee that outcome: "I have come, for my part, completely to the idea recommended by Sir Travers Twiss for a protocol of disinterestedness."[145]

The question was then turned over to open debate at the conference. Moynier proposed that a commission be established to consider the question in greater depth. The Italian jurist Augusto Pierantoni, one of the founders of the Institut, objected to the idea that anybody from a country with a vested interest in the Congo could take part in that commission. Leopold Freiher Von Neumann, professor of law at Vienna, desired to hear some contrary views and noted that the Institut was not created to set forth "utopian" ideas but should remain a practical character. He accordingly noted that Moynier's propositions would founder on all the objections to neutrality already raised by Twiss.[146] Alphonse Rivier suggested that a commission with five members would best deal with the status of the Congo. Egide Arntz declared that he could not agree with all of Moynier's propositions, and that "neutralization is a term too vague," but that the Institut should address themselves to how the Congo could be a zone of free navigation. Rivier responded that a commission should be established on that question with five members: Twiss, Arntz, Moynier, French jurist Louis Renault, and German professor H. von Marquardsen. Pierantoni's objection to vested interests was entirely ignored, and despite further resistance from him, the commission that would debate the status of the Congo in international law was formed with three of Leopold's closest legal advisors amongst its five members.[147] Three days later, Egide Arntz presented to the conference the report of the commission, which simply concluded that the Institut should inform the major powers that they supported the proposition that freedom of navigation should be "applied" to

---

143. *Annuaire de l'Institut de droit international* (1885), 253.
144. *Annuaire de l'Institut de droit international* (1885), 273.
145. *Annuaire de l'Institut de droit international* (1885), 274.
146. *Annuaire de l'Institut de droit international* (1885), 275.
147. *Annuaire de l'Institut de droit international* (1885), 278.

the Congo River.¹⁴⁸ For Twiss, this would imply that an international rather than a neutral regime be imposed, but the commission did not clarify that question. Their recommendation, however, that the powers should apply freedom of navigation on the Congo was debated at the Berlin Conference the following year and led to the creation of an International Commission of the Congo River empowered to enforce freedom of navigation. The proposal for that Commission, however, proved to be a mere stalking horse for Leopold's greater ambitions of sovereignty for the International Association which would render it redundant.¹⁴⁹

In his second article in the *Revue de droit international* on the free navigation of the Congo River, published in November 1883, Twiss suggested that the Congo was like a young tropical plant, whose seed had not yet begun to develop, but which could "suddenly take unexpected proportions."¹⁵⁰ New states, presumably, could grow faster in tropical conditions than they could in Europe. In this article, Twiss focused on the status of Leopold's International Association of the Congo, which, in accord with Leopold's policy of mystification, he called the International African Association.¹⁵¹ The International Association, he argued, had concluded treaties with the "sovereign chiefs of the country." Already here was a remarkable claim in international law—namely, that a private company could make treaties of cession with sovereign authorities, and Twiss turned immediately to that question. He observed that the arrival of the French at Stanley Pool had put Stanley in the position of making his own sovereign claims, so that Brazza's arrival had "aroused the question of whether the representative of an association that does not have the political character of a state, can, through the cession on the part of a sovereign of the country, acquire and exercise the sovereignty of a territory."¹⁵² Such a practice, he added, would have to be considered in terms of the "unwritten law of nations" because, at least in this instance, it was to occur outside Europe and therefore outside the European law of nations.¹⁵³ Twiss had already laid the groundwork, in articles written during the 1870s, for arguing that non-European nations could have a standing in a universal, unwritten law of nations. While such a broad understanding of the law of nations was needed to admit the possibility of private associations assuming sovereign powers, he was also anxious to point out that his proposal had a number of precedents

---

148. *Annuaire de l'Institut de droit international* (1885), 278.
149. See the discussion in Crowe, *The Berlin West African Conference*, 128–135, of the International Commission of the Congo, as distinct from the Association.
150. Travers Twiss, "La libre navigation du Congo. Deuxième article," *Revue de droit international et de législation comparée*, vol. 15 (1883), 547.
151. Twiss, "La libre navigation du Congo. Deuxième article," 549.
152. Twiss, "La libre navigation du Congo. Deuxième article," 550.
153. Twiss, "La libre navigation du Congo. Deuxième article," 550.

in the European customary law of nations.[154] It was necessary, he insisted, to "refute the assertion put about by certain publicists that only states can exercise the rights of sovereignty."[155] The Teutonic Knights, initially a chivalric order and a "charitable association" rather than a sovereign power, had taken upon themselves the role of civilizing the Prussian and Baltic peoples. In doing so, they "acquired the sovereignty of a barbarian country," which established a "grand analogie" with the "action of the International African Association."[156] Here he also explicitly acknowledged the important role for analogy in developing principles of international law.

The Teutonic Knights, argued Twiss, were not the only medieval order to acquire sovereignty in such a way. Even more famous, he pointed out, were the Order of Knights of the Hospital of St John of Jerusalem, a charitable association which, upon leaving Jerusalem at the beginning of the fourteenth century, established themselves in Rhodes, over which they established sovereignty, and after that in Malta, where they again "obtained territorial sovereignty" from Charles V.[157] These two examples he cited "in order to show that, according to the customary law of Europe, associations that are not organised as states can, nevertheless, exercise sovereign rights."[158] His ground here was weak. It was problematic to compare sovereignty in medieval times, an epoch in which sovereignty was fragmented, with the conventions that surrounded sovereignty in a system of modern states that claimed to monopolise sovereign authority. He conceded as much and stated that because both examples were medieval, and belonged to an epoch in which Christianity was propagated "at the point of a sword," it would be preferable also to cite examples from the "commercial epoch" which began with the discoveries of Christopher Columbus.[159] In this context, he cited Louis Delavaud's declaration: "It is a principle of law that only states can exercise sovereign rights, that no private companies can do so."[160] Delavaud's claim was "too absolute," Twiss argued, because "historical facts contradict it." Amongst the members of the United States of America, at least four had been "private associations which had established territorial sovereignty before they received a charter of incorporation from the crown of England."[161] "Everybody knows," he continued, "that a trading company acquired, through treaties with the indigenous people, the sovereignty of the English Indies." An "identical Dutch company" had done the same in "Java and the Molluqas." Should there, he asked, be a different law applying in Africa

---

154. Twiss, "La libre navigation du Congo. Deuxième article," 550.
155. Twiss, "La libre navigation du Congo. Deuxième article," 550.
156. Twiss, "La libre navigation du Congo. Deuxième article," 551.
157. Twiss, "La libre navigation du Congo. Deuxième article," 552.
158. Twiss, "La libre navigation du Congo. Deuxième article," 552.
159. Twiss, "La libre navigation du Congo. Deuxième article," 552.
160. Twiss, "La libre navigation du Congo. Deuxième article," 553.
161. Twiss, "La libre navigation du Congo. Deuxième article," 553.

from that which had prevailed in America? Here he was quite audaciously contradicting the arguments he had made in the 1840s against the claims to establish sovereignty by "private associations" (as he described them) of people in the Oregon Territory. It should come as no surprise that he might change his views over a forty-year period. Circumstances, too, had changed. The disingenuous aspect to his altered position, however, lies both in the fact that he made no reference to his earlier position (even though the work on the Oregon Territory remained an important text in international law) and also in the fact that both statements on the status were made as statements of theory, not as a lawyer arguing a brief for a client. He did not declare his collaboration with Leopold in the articles on the free navigation of the Congo.

Conscious that some people would argue that the age of chartered companies had passed, Twiss asked whether such ideas were perhaps outdated, belonging to another epoch.[162] Following the demise of the East India Company, an event with which he himself had been engaged through his legal opinion for the King of Awadh, and the extension of direct crown control over India, the possibility arose that all colonising activities would come under crown control and the age of expansion through companies had ceased. This was not, however, the case. The new imperialism of the 1870s and '80s saw a return to the use of companies as a means of expansion, and he pointed this out. There was, he said, a very recent example of a private company acquiring sovereign rights. This was the British North Borneo Company, which had acquired "territorial sovereignty" in Borneo by virtue of their delegation from the "chiefs of that country."[163] Twiss, undoubtedly, was well informed on the activities of the North Borneo Chartered Company because its chairman, from 1882, was his old friend Sir Rutherford Alcock, to whom he had presented the DCL at Oxford and whose wife had presented Lady Twiss to the court.

There was an important difference, however, between Alcock's NBCC, and almost all chartered companies, and the International Association of Congo, and this difference was something that Twiss was attempting to obscure. It was the fact that the NBCC was empowered by the British crown to accept cessions of sovereignty from the "indigenous chiefs," as Twiss put it, of Borneo on behalf of the crown, whereas Leopold's company had no such licence granted from the Belgian government or any other government. Leopold's company was claiming that indigenous chiefs were ceding sovereignty to it through treaties and yet it possessed no sovereignty or standing in the society of nations, nor was it licensed by any sovereign power (in this sense, it was not establishing a colony because it represented no colonising power). Twiss treated the cessions made to the NBCC, or to the chartered companies that established American colonies, as if they were the same as those made by the

162. Twiss, "La libre navigation du Congo. Deuxième article," 553.
163. Twiss, "La libre navigation du Congo. Deuxième article," 553–554.

International African Association. He did not hesitate, therefore, to proceed with the following claim: "It is therefore evident that the difficulties that the establishment of stations, by the International African Association, on the Upper Congo, can meet from the European powers will not come from being in contradiction with a principle of the law of nations by virtue of which only states can exercise sovereign rights."[164] Rather, he argued, the problems would arise from Portugal's "pretensions," on the basis of prior discovery, whereby they attempted to deny the claim that indigenous chiefs could cede sovereign rights without Portugal's consent. Certainly, France, he pointed out, had ignored Portugal's claims insofar as they had licensed the activities of Brazza in the Upper Congo.[165]

Returning to the question of the right of private companies to receive the cession of sovereign rights, he declared that there was no difference between the right of "Asian chiefs" to cede their sovereignty to private companies, referring to the NBCC, and the right of Africans to do the same.[166] "Why," he asked, "would it be forbidden for an indigenous chief to cede his territory to an international European company which, according to the law of nations, is perfectly capable of accepting and exercising such sovereignty."[167] "Coming back to our sheep" [*nos moutons*], he continued—that is, to the publicists who had argued that only a state could exercise sovereign rights—did they not know that the free cities of the Holy Roman Empire were not subjects of the emperor but vassals of the empire? The fact that those cities had exercised sovereignty did not, however, resolve the problem of whether a private company could, but his point, throughout his articles on this question, appeared to be to obscure and confuse the question, and thereby prevail in the creation of a new sovereign personality through an entirely new means. As in the case of the creation of the new person of Lady Twiss, direct acknowledgement of the limitations of that person as a candidate for membership in a restricted society would only fail, so the means of expanding the membership of that society required some resort to obfuscation, along with, as we shall see, and as was the case for Lady Twiss, broader legal argument and proofs and the use of the rituals and symbols of membership.

Why not, Twiss continued, establish a system of free cities, like those of the Holy Roman Empire, on the banks of the Upper Congo, along with an international protectorate on the Lower Congo.[168] The only thing standing in the way of such a system, he added, was Portugal. At the same time, he argued, Portugal was "impotent" to establish its own sovereignty over Congo.[169] It had

164. Twiss, "La libre navigation du Congo. Deuxième article," 554.
165. Twiss, "La libre navigation du Congo. Deuxième article," 555.
166. Twiss, "La libre navigation du Congo. Deuxième article," 555.
167. Twiss, "La libre navigation du Congo. Deuxième article," 555.
168. Twiss, "La libre navigation du Congo. Deuxième article," 558.
169. Twiss, "La libre navigation du Congo. Deuxième article," 561.

failed to occupy the banks of the Lower Congo and left them in the power of "indigenous tribes," who, as pirates, were "enemies of the human race"—this was a standard characterisation of pirates in the law of nations since at least the seventeenth century.[170] Nevertheless, he observed, when the Institut de droit international requested that the Portuguese government provide evidence supporting its claims to sovereignty over the Congo, they responded by citing the case of the capture of the German merchant vessel the *Hero* by the French in the mouth of the Congo in December 1870, during the Franco-Prussian war.[171] Upon a protest by the Portuguese to this capture in their sovereign waters, the French governor of Gabon, where the boat had been taken, returned it to the Congo and released it. Twiss contested this account, arguing that the governor of Gabon had released the ship of his own accord and not due to a Portuguese protest. Nevertheless, he was not satisfied with his own response. He finished this article on November 21, but two weeks earlier, on November 7, he had written a letter to Louis Renault, the Professor of International Law at Paris, with whom he had joined in the Commission on free navigation of the Congo in the Institut conference in Munich two months earlier. In this letter, Twiss asked for more details on the case of the *Hero*. Renault responded on December 5, 1883, writing from the French Archives Diplomatiques, and apologised for having not responded sooner to Twiss's letter of November 7.[172] He said he had been engrossed in finding material with which to answer Twiss's inquiry.

Renault's response was too late for the article completed on November 21, but Twiss was not prepared to leave the fate of the Portuguese claims to open debate, particularly given that Renault brought new information to light. According to Renault, the Commanding Admiral of the French South Atlantic station had instructed the captain of the *Loiret*, which had captured the *Hero*, that "the pretensions of the Portuguese over the Congo are unsupportable. It is difficult to admit that they can claim neutrality over a coast upon which they have neither an agent nor a canon."[173] At the same time, the admiral explained that he had commanded the *Hero* to be released in accordance with the instructions he had received for the conduct of the war, whereby all merchant vessels, even those of the enemy, were to be treated as neutral. The *Hero* was released, therefore, not due to French recognition of Portuguese sovereignty but simply because of a broader commitment to the manner in which the Franco-Prussian war was to be conducted. Twiss immediately forwarded Renault's letter to Sir Edward Hertslet, who was the English archivist of the

170. Twiss, "La libre navigation du Congo. Deuxième article," 563.
171. Twiss, "La libre navigation du Congo. Deuxième article," 559.
172. Louis Renault to Twiss, December 5, 1883, National Archives, London, FO 84/1808/326.
173. Louis Renault to Twiss, December 5, 1883, National Archives, London, FO 84/1808/327.

Foreign Office and a trusted advisor to the government on treaties.[174] Hertslet, in turn, forwarded the letter to the parliamentary Under-Secretary for Foreign Affairs, Lord Edmund Fitzmaurice, who was negotiating the treaty with the Portuguese.[175] Twiss's strategy of direct intervention, as we shall see, had the desired effect.

Leopold was so impressed with Twiss's second article on the free navigation of the Congo that he immediately sent a copy to the Belgian Foreign Minister, citing it as proof that there should be no conflict with the Portuguese.[176] By this time, Leopold had long relinquished hope of the Belgian government participating in his planned colony, and he seemingly relished the idea of establishing his own personal state, but he nevertheless sought to placate the government about the implications of his plans, particularly given fears about him endangering Belgium's neutrality, and particularly in relation to possible conflict with Portuguese claims to the Congo. At the same time, in Leopold's papers we find that his ministers and advisors compiled extracts from treatises on international law, including from Johann Kaspar Bluntschli, Auguste-Wilhelm Heffter, and William Beach Lawrence, on the question of how new states could be created. They cited Bluntschli, for example, on the principle that "a new state has the right to enter into the international association of states, and to be recognised by other powers, <u>when its existence is beyond doubt and is assured</u>."[177] The emphasis was added by the person who transcribed this passage. It underlined the central problem for Leopold. These extracts ignored passages from the same texts which denied the right of private associations to have any standing in international society. Bluntschli, for example, a few paragraphs prior to the passage, declared that individual persons, nations not organised as states, political parties, and private associations, while all possessing the right to be protected by states, were not "international persons in the true sense of the word."[178]

Twiss caused controversy around the world with his very public promotion of the idea that a private association could take a place in international society and that it could even receive concessions of sovereignty from sovereign powers in international society (remembering that he had also argued that African

---

174. R. A Jones, "Hertslett, Sir Edward," in *Oxford Dictionary of National Biography* (Oxford, 2019).

175. Hertslet to Fitzmaurice, December 10, 1883, National Archives, London, FO 84/1808/326.

176. Leopold II to Minister of Foreign Affairs, 19 December 1883, Ministère des Affaires Etrangères, Brussels, Correspondance et documents Afrique, Association Internationale du Congo, 2, 1883, 106.

177. Extracts from works of international law (no date), Archives du Palais Royal, Brussels, *Commandements du Roi*, A136/58.

178. Johann Kaspar Bluntschli, *Le droit international codifié* (Paris, 1874), 67–68, paragraphs 23–25.

nations could be sovereign members of international society). Newspapers in Europe, including Germany, Belgium, and Portugal, and in the United States, commented with various degrees of surprise at Twiss's proposals, which placed the unfolding events in Africa, and particularly in the Congo, in a new light.

Even in the British Foreign Office there was scepticism of Twiss's support for the claims of the International Association. On January 4, Edward Hertslet, the Foreign Office expert on treaties, wrote a memo on the subject of "Belgian Contracts with African Chiefs on the Congo."[179] He began by declaring that the "contracts" could be regarded "in no other light than as treaties." He then argued that the fact that those treaties were made without the authority of the Belgian king, as the head of the Belgian state, meant that "they would appear to be entirely illegal," with no binding effect upon any party or nation unless the king chose to ratify them "with the consent of the chambers": that is, with the consent of the Belgian parliament. Belgian subjects "on their own responsibility," he continued, had "no more right to enter into treaty stipulations, relating to cessions of territory or protection, with African states, under the name of 'Contracts' or any other name, than they would have to enter into similar engagements with any civilized state." This was not only a point of international law, he argued, but also confirmed by the Belgian constitution. Hertslet's position on the so-called treaties that so-called "Belgians" were making in the Congo was conventional insofar as it entirely rejected the notion that such agreements could have any status in international law if they were not supported by sovereign authority on both sides, and while he was confident that "African states" could possess such authority, he dismissed the idea that Leopold's agents held an equivalent standing.

Following this January 4 declaration, which was intended as a guide to the British government in its negotiations with Portugal, Hertslet read Twiss's second article on free navigation of the Congo River, and on January 16, 1884, he wrote a further, and longer, memo for circulation in the Foreign Office under the title *Private Treaties with African Chiefs*.[180] He commenced: "Sir Travers Twiss has recently written an article in the 'Revue de Droit international' in which he maintains that the treaties conducted by the Belgian Association in the Congo are perfectly legal." He added, "I hesitate, therefore, to offer an opinion against so high an authority." He did not hesitate, despite this partly ironic observation, for long. The "question of the cession of sovereignty," he observed, had been "introduced into the Belgian contracts." He thought two warnings should be observed about such cessions. First, the "Treaty of Waitangi of 5 Feb. 1840 [it was actually February 6] by which New Zealand was

---

179. Edward Hertslet, Belgian Contacts with African Chiefs on the Congo, January 4, 1884, National Archives, London, FO 84/ 1808/ 236–237.

180. Edward Hertslet, Private Treaties with African Chiefs, January 16, 1884, FO 84, 1808, 238–243.

ceded to this country" had given rise to disputes over the "ownership of land" which had "never been settled to this day." Second, while he did not dispute the right of "African chiefs" to "part with their territory," he again contested the right of individuals, including British subjects, to "accept such territory on their own account, and to act as if they possessed sovereign rights over it." At the bottom of this memo, a commentary on Hertslet's arguments was added in another hand, with a signature that is unclear. This person again signalled a certain wariness about arguing with Twiss but went further: "I would not venture to enter the lists [i.e., to issue a challenge] with Sir Travers Twiss—but he uses certain hackneyed arguments of the advocates of the Belgian Association and so raises a suspicion that he is one of the many who have received a brief from the King."[181] This suspicion was well founded, although we do not know exactly how well the King rewarded Twiss's labours. Leopold kept detailed account books for the Congo, detailing provisions, personnel, and arms sent to Africa and the amounts they cost, but Twiss's name does not appear in those accounts, nor do the great majority of advisors and agents he employed in Europe and around the world.[182] Nevertheless, despite the uncertainty surrounding Twiss's financial relationship with Leopold, his interestedness on the question of the Congo was now well known at least within the Foreign Office. The commentator on Hertslet's memo continued to point out that Twiss treated Leopold's various Congo organisations, the International Association and the Comité d'Études du Haut-Congo, as "companies" whereas the King, "though repeatedly urged," had "declined to form a company." "Consequently," the author observed, "no one clearly knows what is tangible in them—who is the head or who is responsible?"[183] Leopold had, in fact, formed a single-shareholder company, the International Association of the Congo, but as the author rightly perceived, all his other organisations were smoke screens for the activities of that company. The concern here, the author argued, was what would happen to the treaties of cession if these associations collapsed—who would be regarded as possessing sovereignty in the Congo? Underneath this author's commentary on Hertslet's memo, Julian Pauncefote, the Permanent Under-Secretary of the Foreign Office, added yet another commentary in which he too declared: "Though the chiefs may have relinquished their sovereignty over it [their territory], such sovereignty is not transferred to the British subjects who have bought it, as no private person or association can exercise sovereign rights except as the agent of a recognised sovereign and on his behalf, as in the case of the British Borneo Co who are mandatories of

---

181. Foreign Office Memo, January 16, 1884, National Archives, London, FO 84, 1808, 241v.

182. See Royal Palace archive account book: Indicateur, 1863–1898, Archives du Palais Royal, Brussels, D.1.c.

183. Foreign Office Memo, January 16, 1884, National Archives, London, FO 84, 1808, 242.

the Sultans of Sula and Borneo." Pauncefote turned Twiss's example of Borneo against him, pointing out the important difference between the Borneo Company and the International Association. At this point, in January 1884, it seemed the legal opinion in the Foreign Office against the sovereign claims of the International Association was insurmountable and that Twiss's arguments could never prevail against such orthodox views. The rigidity of that opinion in January makes it all the more extraordinary that, by December of the same year, the same office would agree to recognise the Association as a sovereign state and solicit Twiss to write the treaty recognising that new state.

Unsurprisingly, there was an outraged response to Twiss's articles in Portugal. An article in the newspaper *La Correspondencia de Portugal*, in January 1884, declared that Twiss was employed in the "glorification" of the work of the International African Association and the Comité d'Études du Haut-Congo.[184] Twiss, the article observed, "attempts to prove, with examples drawn from history, that a private society can exercise sovereign power." The author declared that Twiss could be left to "fantasise" about an international protectorate on the Lower Congo and a system of free cities on the Upper Congo. The purpose of the article was merely to correct Twiss's "errors of fact" upon which he based his argument. Twiss had claimed that France, Holland, and Britain contested Portuguese sovereignty over the Congo, but, the author observed, France had generally recognised Portuguese authority in the region, as had Holland. Twiss's article on the free navigation of the Congo ended with the most "flagrant contradictions," whereby, having argued that no European maritime power admitted the Portuguese pretensions to sovereignty on the African coast between 8 degrees and 5 degrees latitude south, he then declared that Portugal had failed to civilise the banks of the Congo, despite the fact that its sovereign pretensions had never been challenged by another European power.[185] He also made "comical" geographical errors, undermining his challenge to the Portuguese mission to "civilize and occupy."

This article was sufficiently concerning for the Belgian legation in Portugal that they sent it to Walthère Frère-Orban, the Belgian Minister for Foreign Affairs and former Prime Minister.[186] The Belgian government, while remaining aloof from Leopold's designs, kept a close eye on them. It had refused to participate in Leopold's proposal because of the potential threat to Belgium's

184. "O Congo e a 'Revista de Direito Internacional,'" *La correspondencia de Portugal*, Ministere des Affaires Etrangères, Brussels, Correspondance et documents Afrique, Association Internationale du Congo, 3, 1884, 3–5.

185. "O Congo e a 'Revista de Direito Internacional,'" *La Correspondencia de Portugal*, Ministère des Affaires Etrangères, Brussels, Correspondance et documents Afrique, Association Internationale du Congo, 3, 1884, 3–5.

186. Belgian Legation to Walthère Frère-Orban, Lisbon, January 7, 1884, Ministère des Affaires Etrangères, Brussels, Correspondance et documents Afrique, Association Internationale du Congo, 3, 1884, 3.

neutrality that would arise from engaging in competitions to colonise Africa. Increased tension with Portugal was accordingly unwelcome. In response to such fears, a forty-four-page tract was published anonymously in Brussels in 1884 which made it clear that Leopold's intentions were no secret and that Twiss's efforts were not at all disinterested.[187] The title of this tract was *Sir Travers Twiss et le Congo*, casting Twiss as the central figure in the drama that was being played out over the future of the Congo. It presented a point-by-point refutation of Twiss's legal pronouncements on the question. The author accused Leopold of seeking a colonial empire for Belgium. According to the author, if Belgium acquired a colonial empire, it would lose its neutrality. "Who would believe," the author stormed, that anybody would wish to spend millions civilising central Africa out of a "simple love of humanity." "What ambitious project," he continued, "is hidden under this peaceful flag?" In any case, the author argued, a neutral but colonial Belgium was a contradiction and was politically imprudent, not to say dangerous.[188]

The author then directly attacked Twiss: "It is to give sovereign rights to this commercial Association that Sir Travers, stirring the ashes of the past, has had to reach as far as the middle ages in order to find the model of a sovereign civilising institution . . . One must have the grand personality of Sir Travers Twiss to not see in that proposition a challenge against good sense."[189] Becoming even more heated, the author declared: "We will not trust inept friends, the example invoked further of the sovereign order of Saint John of Jerusalem, better known under the name of the order of the Knights of Malta, is even more unhappy. Moreover, what are we doing almost at the dawn of the twentieth century, invoking the old European customary law and why search examples from the night of the past which modern law has for a long time repudiated."[190] In conclusion, the author argued that to recognise "as a rule of international law the right of a private association to exercise sovereignty would be a monstrous juridical heresy. Facts have sometimes conferred certain privileges upon associations, but to demand today the recognition of absolute

---

187. It is often argued that, prior to the Berlin Conference, nobody suspected Leopold's intention to turn the International Association into a colonial state. See, for example, Casper Sylvest, "'Our Passion for Legality': International Law and Imperialism in Late-Nineteenth-Century Britain," *Review of International Studies*, vol. 34, no. 3 (2008), 411: "In some ways, the most arresting part of the story . . . lies in Leopold's success in convincing nearly everyone of his peaceful, philanthropic intentions"; and 415: "Twiss was, of course, only one (and not the most important) among the moralists fooled by Leopold. But it is not only his naïvety which is representative." See also Koskenniemi, *The Gentle Civilizer of Nations*, 157–165. This also seems to be the position of earlier scholarship. See, for example, Reeves, *The International Beginnings of the Congo Free State*, 71, and also, to some degree, Crowe, *The Berlin West-African Conference*.

188. Anon., *Sir Travers Twiss et le Congo*, 5–6.

189. Anon., *Sir Travers Twiss et le Congo*, 39.

190. Anon., *Sir Travers Twiss et le Congo*, 40.

rights, without them even being exercised in fact, as is the case in the Congo, this would seem to us to leave the path of serious juridical debate."[191] It was no surprise that this author declared Twiss's claim that a private association could exercise sovereignty to be a monstrous judicial heresy, suggesting he had left the path of serious juridical debate. Those sentiments indicate the degree to which Twiss faced almost insurmountable opposition in the legal and diplomatic community to the transformation of the personality of the International Association of the Congo. He had succeeded in the past, however, in bringing a person forbidden from a particular society into full membership in that society, and he would do so again.

In April 1884, Twiss published a second edition of his most important work on international law, the *Law of Nations Considered as Independent Political Communities: On the Rights and Duties of Nations in Time of Peace*. In the first edition, published in 1861, this treatise had followed his earlier work of 1846 on the Oregon Territory by insisting that all questions in international law were matters that belonged to "nations." There was no room in this vision for private individuals or associations acting in the society of nations. Where "individuals" did appear in this account was insofar as the law of nations, he pointed out, was derived by analogy from the "Law of Nature in regard to primitive acquisition" of property: that is, the Roman law that things which belonged to nobody could be possessed by the first person to take them was the basis of the law of occupation in the law of nations, but it was restricted only to nations.[192] Such an understanding of occupation did not fit with Twiss's arguments in favour of the rights of International Association of the Congo (or the International African Association, as he called it), to accept cessions of sovereignty from African peoples, nor did it fit with his argument that that Association could be transformed into a state. He therefore republished the treatise with a new preface that was devoted almost entirely to his arguments regarding the Association and, specifically, to the idea that "private associations" could "accept cessions of territory with full rights of dominion from the native chiefs of Africa" which could "in due course of time" achieve "recognition of such settlements as independent States."[193] Chartered companies which had accepted such cessions were "too numerous to mention," although chartered companies, as Twiss knew, had license from their sovereigns to acquire territories, and so they were the agents of sovereigns in the society of nations, not mere private individuals. He moved to surer ground when he gave the example of the American Colonisation Society, which had established the colony of Liberia—here, at last, was an example of a private association that had established a colony within living memory, and he mentioned the fact

---

191. Anon., *Sir Travers Twiss et le Congo*, 40.
192. Twiss, *The Law of Nations* (1861), 160–163.
193. Twiss, *The Law of Nations* (1884), x.

that he made the acquaintance of Liberia's first President, Joseph Roberts, at a dinner in the house of the French diplomat and one-time Minister of Foreign Affairs Édouard Drouyn de Lhuys, in Paris.[194] The case of Liberia, Twiss declared, showed that "the judicial difficulty, which has been suggested to be in the way of private associations forming settlements in Africa, and acquiring for their settlements full rights of dominion—the right of Empire over the territory ceded to them—is without foundation."[195]

He then turned to observe that this question had "recently become one of practical interest" in regard to settlements established "on the banks of the Upper Congo, by a philanthropic association" operating under "the title L'Association Africaine Internationale."[196] This Association was distinguished from previous settlements, such as Liberia, by the fact that it would be open "freely to the commerce of all the world," while at the same time welcoming "any stranger" who agreed to obey its laws.[197] The Association, according to Twiss, would establish a free state that epitomized the free trade and liberal thought that was flourishing in the last quarter of the century, particularly in Gladstone's England. It was a state that would realise many of the emancipatory ambitions of the times, including new concerns about ending slavery (of course, in reality, the Congo Free State would rapidly descend into a dystopian nightmare which only ever payed lip service to these goals that Leopold exploited to realise his own ambitions). The climate of enfranchisement and emancipation which this new state embodied included Twiss's radical arguments about expanding the franchise for membership in the society of nations. Nevertheless, he insisted that the principles that would allow the International Association to accept cessions of sovereignty in the Congo were not new. Rather, he argued, jurists limited the acquisition of new territories in international law to sovereigns because they misunderstood the history of the law on the matter. Roman law, he argued, did not distinguish various kinds of dominium as did the writings of the "Feudalists," or medieval post-Glossators. While the Romans spoke only of dominium as "ownership," the Feudalists distinguished *dominium supremum*, or the right of empire, from *dominium directum*, which signified vassalage. More recently, he argued, *dominium supremum* had been replaced by *dominium eminens*, which signified the sovereignty of the prince. He then claimed that international lawyers restricted the occupation of territory to being a matter for "Sovereign Princes or associations chartered by them" but that there was no reason for such a restriction because rights of *dominium eminens* could be acquired "private associations" and did not have to be limited to sovereign princes. Twiss's contemporaries did not restrict the claim that the

---

194. Twiss, *The Law of Nations* (1884), xii.
195. Twiss, *The Law of Nations* (1884), xii–xiii.
196. Twiss, *The Law of Nations* (1884), xiii.
197. Twiss, *The Law of Nations* (1884), xiv.

acquisition of territory should be restricted to sovereign princes; they understood that right to belong to the state more generally. Nevertheless, these arguments succeeded, once again, in obscuring the issue.

Certainly, the new edition of Twiss's *Law of Nations* pleased Leopold. Twiss signed the preface to this new edition on April 16, 1884, yet two months earlier, he sent a draft of the new text to Leopold. Leopold's cabinet secretary replied to Twiss, on February 21, that the King had received the work.[198] The draft of the secretary's letter in response to Twiss shows deletions and additions made in Leopold's hand, with careful attention to the terms in which Twiss should be flattered: "You know, Monsieur, the great value that His Majesty attaches to your opinions so clear and the sincere regard which he holds for you how much the King values your work and you know the sentiments as one of that His Majesty holds for you. Also the King he was charmed to receive this publication of such an eminent jurist whose name has such authority amongst statesmen enjoys such a great and legitimate authority and I am charged with expresssing all the gratitude of the King for the kind attention you have paid to him in sending your masterful work." This letter shows the value that Leopold placed on Twiss's services as well as his desire that Twiss should feel appreciated. At the same time, through his editing, Leopold avoided emphasising the esteem that Twiss's work was held in amongst statesmen, choosing instead to celebrate his more abstract "great and legitimate authority," possibly because he was trying to evade a cynical construction of his motives. The letter also reveals that Twiss was redrafting his major work on the law of nations in consultation with the King and his cabinet.

Diplomatic Negotiations

Leopold employed Twiss's standing amongst statesmen in the weeks between this letter and the appearance of the new edition of his *Law of Nations*. The first major breakthrough in gaining recognition of the international legal personality of the International Association of the Congo was when its flag was recognised, on April 22, 1884, by the United States as that of a friendly power. Twiss's arguments proved to be crucial to that recognition, although American diplomat Henry Sanford was the person who took Leopold's case to the US Secretary of State, Frederick Frelinghuysen. Sanford had been American ambassador to Belgium until 1869, and in 1876, he had been the delegate from the American Geographical Society to Leopold's conference. Leopold then employed him as his envoy in the United States, working to gain recognition of the International Association. As early as December 1882, Sanford raised the question of recognition of a flag for the International Association in

---

198. Borchgrave(?) to Twiss, February 21, 1884, Cabinet du Roi, Archives du Palais Royal, Brussels, *Commandements du Roi*, A136/18.

a letter to Frelinghuysen, putting it in the context of French and Portuguese ambitions and the danger of US merchants being shut out of the region, as well, of course, as the more noble humanitarian aims of Leopold's enterprise compared to the venal nature of the other powers.[199] Disingenuously, and like most of Leopold's helpers, Sanford stressed his own disinterestedness, declaring, "I am writing on behalf of no one, only as an American citizen desirous to see his country participate in its full share of the important results of what is now going on in Africa."[200] Sanford succeeded rapidly in gaining support from both Frelinghuysen and President Chester Arthur, who, in a message to Congress, praised the work of the International African Association (not knowing that organisation was moribund and Leopold now worked through his International Association of the Congo). The Association, Arthur said, had obtained "large tracts of land" through cession, it "offers freedom of commerce and prohibits the slave trade," and it had established a "nuclei of states... under one flag."[201] The United States, he said, could not be "indifferent" to this work and may have to "cooperate with other commercial Powers in promoting the rights of trade and residence in the Kongo Valley."

Despite the support of the President and Secretary of State, Leopold's plans continued to meet opposition and scepticism in the United States. Writing to Sanford, Leopold's henchman and President of the Committee for the Study of the Upper Congo, Maximilien Strauch, on December 24, 1883, told him he could find help in combatting the objections of certain Americans with an article that had just been published in the *Law Magazine and Review* in November: namely, a "remarkable article ['An International Protectorate of the Congo River'] of the eminent English jurisconsult, Sir Travers Twiss."[202] This article, Strauch argued, demonstrated "the sovereign rights that the International Association has acquired in the Congo in the territories in which the indigenous chiefs have abandoned such rights." In order to bring Twiss's *International Protectorate* to a larger audience, his article was then republished on January 21, 1884, a few weeks after Strauch's letter to Sanford, in the largest distribution newspaper in the United States, the *New York Herald*. Always watchful of the progress of Leopold's plans, the Belgian Legation in the United States forwarded the article in the *Herald* to the Belgian Foreign Ministry, noting the newspaper's "appreciation" of Twiss's "study."[203] The *Herald* had funded Henry Stanley's first expeditions in Africa in search of David

---

199. François Bontinck, *Aux origines de l'État Indépendant du Congo. Documents tirés d'archives américaines* (Louvain, 1966), 114–116.

200. Bontinck, *Aux origines de l'État Indépendant du Congo*, 115.

201. Bontinck, *Aux origines de l'État Indépendant du Congo*, 144.

202. Bontinck, *Aux origines de l'État Indépendant du Congo*, 148.

203. Belgian Legation in US to Belgian Foreign Ministry, 21 January, 1884, Ministère des Affaires Étrangères, Brussels, Correspondance et documents Afrique, Association Internationale du Congo, 3, 1884, 106,12. See also 17 February, 1884, Ministère des Affaires

Livingston, and it was now engaged in promoting his ventures for Leopold in the Congo, as well as the claims of the International Association.

In a commentary accompanying Twiss's article, the newspaper observed, "The topic on which Sir Travers Twiss writes is of timely interest to American readers. The recognized standing of the writer as a jurist will command attention for what he has to say and give weight to his views."[204] The newspaper argued that the "untold wealth" of the Congo was "of special interest" to "Americans" because it had been "opened to the commerce of the world" by American "enterprise and capital." Three weeks later, on February 16, the *Herald* published a further article, "Sovereignty Beyond Question," based upon an audience their correspondent gained with King Leopold. A subsection of this article was devoted to the matter of "How Individuals May Become Sovereign," in which the author effectively summarised Twiss's own contributions to the issue. Individuals could become sovereigns in one of two ways: either, by "creating themselves a state"—for example, if they "should establish themselves upon a desert island or upon territory not occupied by another State." Such had been the argument in the Oregon Territory which Twiss had so strenuously opposed. The second case was "succeeding to a sovereign," and such cases could include the cession of sovereign powers to individuals or associations. Here the newspaper used the example Twiss furnished in his second article on the Free Navigation of the Congo: namely, the creation of the North Borneo Chartered Company, chaired by Rutherford Alcock. The article stressed, moreover, that the creation of a new state did not require recognition from other states: "New sovereigns, at the head of which are individuals or associations acting under concessions from chiefs of savage tribes, exist independently, in their own right and of their own force, without requiring the recognition of other states."[205] The claim was in contrast with the United States' own Declaration of Independence, made as much for external as internal consumption, but the defiant tone belied the desperate efforts to gain precisely such recognition that were underfoot.[206]

The powerful public campaign orchestrated for the recognition of the International Association of the Congo as a state, at the heart of which lay Twiss's own claims, culminated on March 26, 1884, with the publication of

---

Étrangères, Brussels, Correspondance et documents Afrique, Association Internationale du Congo, 3, 1884, 106, 26.

204. Belgian Legation in US to Belgian Foreign Ministry, 21 January, 1884, Ministère des Affaires Étrangères, Brussels, Correspondance et documents Afrique, Association Internationale du Congo, 3, 1884, 106, 12.

205. Travers Twiss, "The Congo Question," January 21, 1884, *New York Herald*, in Ministère des Affaires Étrangères, Brussels, Correspondance et documents Afrique, Association Internationale du Congo, 3, 1884, 106, 12.

206. On the external audience for the American Declaration of Independence, see David Armitage, *The Declaration of Independence: A Global History* (Cambridge, Mass., 2007).

the report on the Congo from the Senate Committee on Foreign Relations, chaired by Senator John Tyler Morgan. That report recommended that legislation recognising the flag of the International Association as that of a friendly power should be passed through the Senate, and on April 10, the Senate voted to recognise the flag and to adopt the report's recommendations.[207] The report argued that the interest of the United States in Africa was "exceptional" because of the large population of people of African origin in America.[208] It pointed out that the colony of Liberia had been established in order, as it claimed, to provide a home for slaves released under "violation of the slave trade laws." Moreover, it observed that the colony had been established by a private philanthropic association, with no assistance from any state, thereby establishing "a recognised precedent in favor of the right of untitled individuals to found states in the interests of civilization in barbarous countries."[209] A similar venture had unfolded in the Congo, according to the report, whereby civilisation and commerce were being promoted by the International African Association for the benefit of African people. There was "no historical record" of such a "rapid and general assembling of separate and independent rulers under a banner," that is, under the flag of the Association. The Association had made nearly 100 treaties in which "powers were not ceded to a new and usurping sovereignty seeking to destroy existing governments, but are delegated to a common agent for the common welfare."[210] The "Free States of the Congo," the report declared, guaranteed "civilization, order, peace, and security to the persons and property of all who visit the Congo country, as well as to its inhabitants."[211] It is, the report concluded, "our duty to recognize" the "sovereign power" of the "Free States."[212] The International Association possessed sovereignty "*de jure*" if the "local governments" had the right to make

---

207. Bontinck, *Aux origines de l'État Indépendant du Congo*, 196.

208. Such interests were not likely to be positive. Twenty years later, Henry Wellington Wack, the author of *The Story of the Congo Free State*, sent a copy of his work to Henry S. W. West, of Baltimore, containing a letter declaring, "It is the belief of the writer that the American people will, with their expanding problem of the Negro at home, find it sociologically and commercially, perhaps even politically, desirable to interest themselves in the phases which the native life of Africa is fast assuming under the colonial methods pursued by the British, Germans, French, Portuguese, and Belgians": Henry Wellington Wack to Henry S. W. West, November 16, 1905, author's copy.

209. *Occupation of the Congo Country in Africa*, United States Senate, 48th Congress, 1st session, Report 393 (March 26, 1884), 1, in Ministère des Affaires Étrangères, Brussels, Correspondance et documents Afrique, Association Internationale du Congo, 3, 1884, 106, 54.

210. *Occupation of the Congo Country in Africa*, United States Senate, 2.

211. *Occupation of the Congo Country in Africa*, United States Senate, 3.

212. *Occupation of the Congo Country in Africa*, United States Senate, 3.

concessions of sovereign power to it, and it possessed sovereignty "*de facto*" to the degree that it had entered into "treaty relations" with "native tribes."[213]

In support of these arguments, the Report of the Senate Foreign Affairs Committee appended a number of documents. The documents included the correspondence of Frelinghusen and Morgan, as well as of the American Chamber of Commerce. They also included the first treaty made by the Association, the Treaty of Vivi. But foremost amongst the evidence cited by the report in favour of recognition were the legal opinions of Egide Arntz and Twiss. Arntz was a Prussian-born jurist who held a post in law at the University of Brussels and worked for Leopold. He was Secretary-General of the Institut de droit international, and in 1883 and 1884, he published, along with Twiss, a number of articles justifying occupation of the Congo by the International Association and challenging the claims of Portugal to the same territories. The Senate report introduced Twiss and Arntz's publications with the observation that "the able and exhaustive statement of the eminent English jurist, Sir Travers Twiss, and of Professor Arntz . . . leave no doubt upon the question of the legal capacity of the African International Association, in view of the law of nations, to accept any powers belonging to these native chiefs and governments."[214] The "practical question" which Twiss and Arntz had answered was "Can independent chiefs of savage tribes cede to private citizens (persons) the whole or part of their states." This was indeed the question that Twiss had answered affirmatively: namely, can a sovereign people cede its sovereignty to a private person or private association? When he had addressed the question of the Oregon Territory in the 1840s, the issue he refuted was merely whether private persons or associations had a standing in the law of nations. While now reversing his position on that question, he was taking the further step of arguing that sovereigns could cede their powers to such private individuals in relation to whom Vattel had observed, in the passage cited by Twiss, the claims to hold a place in the society of nations were "ridiculous."

The first two treatises appended in the Senate report were Twiss's 1883 *An International Protectorate of the Congo River* and his 1883 "*La libre navigation du Congo*," translated into English. These were followed by Arntz's 1884 *De la cession des droits de souveraineté par des chefs de tribus sauvages*, which was also translated. Arntz began his treatise by posing the central question: "Can independent chiefs of savage tribes cede to private citizens the whole or part of their states, with the sovereign rights that pertain to them?"[215] He began by acknowledging the doctrine of occupation in international law: namely, that

---

213. *Occupation of the Congo Country in Africa*, United States Senate, 3.

214. *Occupation of the Congo Country in Africa*, United States Senate, 6.

215. Egide Arntz, "Can Independent Chiefs of Savage Tribes Cede to Private Citizens the Whole or Part of their States?" in *Occupation of the Congo Country in Africa*, United States Senate, 30.

land which belonged to nobody, or "without a master," could be possessed by the first person, or state, to seize it. He then noted, "Savage tribes, although living in very imperfect communities," could no longer be regarded as subject to such a doctrine.[216] Their territories could no longer be "regarded to-day as things without a master, and belonging to the first occupier. He then cited a number of nineteenth-century jurists, including Kluber and Heffter, who confirmed this point and attacked the "propaganda" of the civilising mission.[217] He concluded, "Communities of non-civilized tribes, forming according to the law of nations, as today admitted, independent States, the first logical consequence that follows is that these states cannot be acquired by reason of occupation by other states."[218] It was only possible, therefore, for such territories to be acquired through the cession of sovereignty. The key question for Leopold's Association, then, was "Can a cession be made to a private citizen?"[219]

In answering this question, Arntz referred his readers directly to Twiss: "We are happy to abridge this part of our work by referring to the article 'The Free Navigation of the Congo' published by our eminent colleague of the Institute, Sir Travers Twiss." Arntz then summarised Twiss's arguments on the question, including an analysis of Twiss's historical examples of private association that had acquired sovereignty from the Knights of Jerusalem and William Penn through to the contemporary British North Borneo Company. Summarising the dispute between Twiss and Delavaud, Arntz asked "in virtue of what principle of international law is it sought to be shown that one who is a private citizen today cannot become a sovereign tomorrow, and be in possession of the plenitude of sovereignty? Such a principle does not exist."[220] Arntz argued, disingenuously, that the question on which he was delivering his opinion was a "novel one": "It has not been foreseen or treated in works of international law."[221] "Many authors," he argued, "treat a question which touches upon this one, but which differs from it a good deal. They ask if an individual can make in his own name an act of occupation newly discovered without a master." Such authors had rightly replied negatively to this question, he continued, because the individuals in question were "navigators" who

216. Arntz, "Can Independent Chiefs of Savage Tribes . . . ," in *Occupation of the Congo Country in Africa*, United States Senate, 31.
217. Arntz, "Can Independent Chiefs of Savage Tribes . . . ," in *Occupation of the Congo Country in Africa*, United States Senate, 32.
218. Arntz, "Can Independent Chiefs of Savage Tribes . . . ," in *Occupation of the Congo Country in Africa*, United States Senate, 32.
219. Arntz, "Can Independent Chiefs of Savage Tribes . . . ," in *Occupation of the Congo Country in Africa*, United States Senate, 33.
220. Arntz, "Can Independent Chiefs of Savage Tribes . . . ," in *Occupation of the Congo Country in Africa*, United States Senate, 33.
221. Arntz, "Can Independent Chiefs of Savage Tribes . . . ," in *Occupation of the Congo Country in Africa*, United States Senate, 34.

discover new territories "in a public ship, often public officers or individuals commissioned by their own governments—agents of the government—and they cannot occupy in their own name." His argument here was, again, artful. There was little controversy about whether individuals who were agents of their governments could claim territory in their own names—to do so would have been to act outside both the law of nations and the instructions of their own governments. Moreover, the question of whether individuals could acquire sovereign rights on their own had been treated in international law, including by Twiss in his extensive treatise on the Oregon Territory. On the other hand, many of the examples cited by Arntz and Twiss of private individuals or associations who had acquired sovereign title were in fact taken from cases where those individuals were precisely agents of government and had not been acquiring such titles for themselves but for their states, even if, in some cases, there had been delays in governments recognising such acquisitions, even retrospectively. Such was the case with most of the many examples of the English colonies established in America that Twiss and Arntz cited, as it was with the North Borneo Company.

What both Twiss and Arntz were succeeding in doing was to create so much haze about the question of the acquisition of sovereign rights by private associations that they made it possible for that question to be admitted to serious debate. In doing so, they were in step with Leopold's policy, more generally, of pursuing the true nature and aims of his venture in the Congo behind a fog of claims regarding humanitarianism, anti-slavery actions, and a multiplicity of organisations which hid his actions. Unsurprisingly, Leopold kept copies of Twiss's and Arntz's pamphlets in his own files, as well as the proceedings of the Senate Committee (as did the Belgian Foreign Ministry).[222] Recognition of the sovereign status of the International Association of the Congo was a triumph in his progress to creating an internationally accepted state. In his own 1885 account of the triumph of the Congo Free State, Henry Stanley cited the Senate Committee report (which Leopold had personally presented to him) and the opinions of Twiss and Arntz as the legal accompaniment to his own explorations.[223] In 1884, however, there was still much work to do in progressing from recognition of the International Association as a state by one power to recognition by all the powers.

News of the United States' recognition was more cautiously received by European powers. On May 6, 1884, the conservative German newspaper

222. M. E. Arntz, *De la cession des droits de souveraineté par des chefs des tribus sauvages* (Brussels, 1884), in Archives du Palais Royal, Brussels, *Commandements du Roi*, A136; Belgian Legation, United States, to Minister of Foreign Affairs, Brussels, 3 April, 1884, Ministère des Affaires Étrangères, Brussels, Correspondance et documents Afrique, Association Internationale du Congo, 3, 1884, 106, 54.

223. Stanley, *The Congo*, Vol. 2, 380. For Leopold's presentation of the report to Stanley, see Bontinck, *Aux origines de l'État Indépendant du Congo*, 216.

Norddeutsche Allgemeine Zeitung responded sceptically to news of the United States' recognition of the flag of the International Association of the Congo as that of a friendly power, but it cast Twiss as a central figure in that event. The Belgian legation to Berlin sent this article to the Belgian Foreign Minister, noting the excitement caused in Berlin by the American recognition and, in particular, by the arguments of "certain notable geographers and jurisconsults notably Travers Twiss and Arntz which were included in the report of the US Senate Committee."[224] *Norddeutsche Allgemeine Zeitung* pointed out that the recognition of the International Association by the United States would now "bring to the attention of a great many people" a subject which had only previously occupied "historians and jurisconsults" who were concerned with the "question of the formation of states."[225] Foremost amongst those figures, the newspaper observed, were the English jurist, Sir Travers Twiss, and the Belgian Egide Arntz, whose treatises on the question of the formation of states had been included in the report of the Senate Committee for Foreign Affairs, which had recommended the recognition of the International Association. The article then cited the precedents that Twiss had given as proofs that private associations could be recognised as sovereign powers: namely, the "formation of the state of Liberia, whose territory was acquired by some Americans"; "the foundation of the colony of Pennsylvania"; and the medieval Teutonic Knights. "The two savants," Twiss and Arntz, the article continued, "both agree that independent chiefs of savage races could legitimately cede, totally or partially, to private persons, their territories along with the rights of sovereignty attached to them."[226] "But what," asked the article, "is the International African Society?" Its formation, although public, did nothing to clarify the question. The creation of the Committee for the Study of the Upper Congo in 1878 further muddied the matter. The two organisations shared the same flag and the same membership, and yet their statutes were unknown. "One point completely obscure," the author continued, was "what is the position in law of the society."[227] The Society had made "over a hundred treaties with negro chiefs." Some of those treaties ceded "territory and property," others ceded sovereignty, yet others placed the chiefs under the "protection" of the

224. Belgian Legation, Berlin, to Minister of Foreign Affairs, Brussels, 6 May 1884, Ministère des Affaires Étrangères, Brussels, Correspondance et documents Afrique, Association Internationale du Congo, 3, 1884, 106.

225. "Politischer Tagesbericht," *Norddeutsche Allgemeine Zeitung*, May 6, 1884, 1, in Ministère des Affaires Étrangères, Brussels, Correspondance et documents Afrique, Association Internationale du Congo, 3, 1884, 106.

226. "Politischer Tagesbericht," *Norddeutsche Allgemeine Zeitung*, May 6, 1884, translation into French by the Belgian Legation, Berlin, Annexe B du rapport du 7 Mai: Minister of Foreign Affairs, Brussels, May 6, 1884, Ministère des Affaires Étrangères, Brussels, Correspondance et documents Afrique, Association Internationale du Congo, 3, 1884, 106.

227. Belgian Legation, Berlin, Annexe B du rapport du 7 Mai.

society, and some were agreements only to free trade and the construction of routes. Some treaties, the article went on, had been concluded with agents of the International African Association, others with the Society for the Study of the Upper Congo. "Who," the author asked, "has acquired the rights stipulated in the treaties and who can exercise them?" The Teutonic Knights, the article concluded, had "long swords," and it asked whether this new entity in the Congo would be strong enough to defend itself against its neighbours. All these questions revealed the degree of scepticism that Leopold's venture, and Twiss's arguments, still faced, even after American recognition. The questions also reflected the confusion about the identities of the International Association of the Congo, the Society for the Study of the Upper Congo, and the International African Association, which Leopold had deliberately sown.

On May 8, 1884, Twiss responded to criticisms of his arguments supporting Leopold's claim in the Congo with a third installment of his *"La libre navigation du Congo"* in the *Revue de droit international et de législation comparée*, this time signed "Londres" not Bruxelles. In particular, in this article, he responded to the anonymous author of *Sir Travers Twiss et le Congo*. Twiss accused the author of being Portuguese, an "avocat du Portugal," and therefore merely defending Portugal's claims upon the Congo. While the tract attacking Twiss was anonymous, it was published in Brussels, and the author identified himself on the title page as "a member of the Royal Geographical Society of Antwerp," while at the same time declaring throughout the tract that "our country [*patrie*] finds its happiness in neutrality" and "our beloved homeland [*patrie*]" has "higher aspirations" than to be "dependent upon a vast colonial empire."[228] Given this strong statement of patriotism, the author was either Belgian, as he claimed, or a very duplicitous Portuguese, as Twiss would have it, although it is clear that scepticism of Leopold's ambitions was not isolated to Portugal.

Twiss began this article by lamenting that, despite his own efforts, "Unfortunately, we continue to find publicists who persist in denying the capacity of private associations to acquire . . . rights which imply the exercise of sovereignty," such that he felt compelled to respond.[229] One of these writers, the anonymous author of *Sir Travers Twiss et le Congo*, had even gone so far as to declare that "supporting that a private association can acquire the right to exercise sovereignty in an uncivilized country was, on my part, a monstrous heresy." Twiss then pointed out that rather than trying to appeal to a dark medieval past, the Knights of Malta still existed as a sovereign order. Instead, however, of continuing to draw attention to his medieval examples, he quickly turned to a detailed history of the creation of Liberia, a contemporary example

228. Anon., *Sir Travers Twiss et le Congo*, 5–6.
229. Travers Twiss, "La libre navigation du Congo. Troisième article," *Revue de droit international et de législation comparée*, vol. 16 (1884), 237.

of a private association that created a state in Africa and therefore a far stronger precedent for the claims of the International Association of the Congo. Nevertheless, even Twiss conceded that Liberia's path from a colony established by the American Colonization Society in 1821 with the aim of "repatriating" freed slaves to Africa, through its own Declaration of Independence in 1847, to recognition from the United States in 1862, had taken over forty years, while Leopold's Association was attempting a similar recognition in the space of six years. An important difference, however, he argued, between the aims of the American Colonization Society's colony in Liberia and the International Association's territories in the Congo was that Liberia had imposed customs and tariffs at its borders, whereas trade to the Congo was free. The very purpose of the International Association, he argued, was to guarantee such free trade, including the free movement of labour.[230] Such claims, while entirely fictitious and contrary to the extraordinarily secretive control Leopold exercised over the Congo, were intended to meet British and American concerns that the creation of the new state should provide opportunities to their own companies.

"The serpent in the grass," he continued, was that we thought the "anonymous publicist" had wanted "a serious juridical discussion" of the "capacity of the International African Association to acquire sovereign right by concession of the indigenous chiefs of the Upper Congo," but, he observed, according to that author "those chiefs do not have sovereign rights to concede."[231] Here we see the importance of Twiss's essays in the 1870s which argued precisely that "Oriental nations," and even African nations, had a standing in the society of nations, and those arguments were now paying dividends which, given that he sent his work on lighthouses to Leopold's secretary in 1878, were not accidental. His anonymous "Portuguese" attacker, according to Twiss, denied the right of the Congo chiefs to cede sovereignty because Portugal had established sovereignty over the territory by right of discovery of the Congo River 400 years earlier. This argument, Twiss reasoned, assumed that territories were accessory to rivers.[232] He responded that he had "combatted that doctrine forty years ago, in treating the question of the Oregon," when he had shown that rivers are accessory to territories, rather than the other way around. He did not mention, of course, that one of the central claims of his treatise on the Oregon Territory was that individuals and private associations crossing the Rocky Mountains had no standing in the society of nations and no rights of sovereignty, and that their claims were "rash and ridiculous" as against those of sovereign nations. On the other hand, Twiss returned to the point that the anonymous publicist had argued that the "uncivilized tribes" of the Upper

230. Twiss, "La libre navigation du Congo. Troisième article," 243.
231. Twiss, "La libre navigation du Congo. Troisième article," 243.
232. Twiss, "La libre navigation du Congo. Troisième article," 244.

Congo "do not have the capacity to exercise the rights of free peoples." "That is a discourse," he lamented, "a bit harsh, which offends the humanitarian sentiment of our epoch."[233] As he had shown in his articles of the 1870s, Twiss understood that emancipation, the granting of rights to free peoples, was a means of establishing dependence.

In May 1884, shortly after the US Senate had recognized the International Association as a state in April, Leopold had asked Egide Arntz to begin work on drafting a constitution for the new state. By July, however, Arntz had fallen seriously ill and had made little progress.[234] He died on August 23.[235] Leopold then decided to put his trust in Twiss to draft the constitution of the new state, and he agreed to perform the service.[236] At the same time, Leopold did not want news of the drafting of the constitution to become public, presumably because he did not want the powers to conclude that he had pre-empted their approval. Stanley had returned from Africa to England in 1884 and was so excited by the diplomatic and legal progress that he began to talk openly not only about the impending recognition of the state but also about its constitution. His loose talk prompted Leopold to instruct the attaché to his cabinet, Comte de Lalaing, to order Stanley to be quiet. Lalaing wrote to Stanley: "The Association is actively engaged in working out the Constitution of the new independent State but no decision has yet been come to, and until this is done, the Association intends to avoid all public discussion of the details of that Constitution."[237] The implications of Lalaing's letter for Twiss are also clear. He was now deeply engaged in the secretive and duplicitous manoeuvres Leopold employed to pursue his ambitions, manoeuvres which were only revealed to his most trusted advisors, and which had as their aim the creation of a new person in international society. To engage in secret and duplicitous manoeuvres to create a new person was nothing new for Twiss. Leopold had found the right person for the job.

By July and August 1884, when Twiss was given the job of drafting a constitution for Leopold's proposed state, negotiations between Britain and Portugal over the treaty dividing central West Africa between them had, after two years, become increasingly difficult. Although the treaty had been signed, Lord Edmund Fitzmaurice, the parliamentary Under-Secretary for Foreign

---

233. Twiss, "La libre navigation du Congo. Troisième article," 244. Writing as late as 1919, Arthur Keith sceptically argued, "It is still more doubtful . . . whether the signatories [to the Congo treaties] had the right to undertake the obligations which they did . . . it still remained to be seen whether the Powers would accept the validity of the claim to sovereign rights by the Association," Arthur Berriedale Keith, *The Belgian Congo and the Berlin Act* (Oxford, 1919), 49.

234. For Arntz's illness, see *Biographie Coloniale* Belge (Brussels, 1948), Vol. 1, 33.

235. Bontinck, *Aux origines de l'État Indépendant du Congo*, 218.

236. Bontinck, *Aux origines de l'État Indépendant du Congo*, 218.

237. Bontinck, *Aux origines de l'État Indépendant du Congo*, 218.

Affairs, was not confident that it would be ratified by parliament. The French and Germans also indicated that they would refuse to recognise it. Confidence in the treaty was further undermined by news that the Portuguese were, at the same time, secretly engaged in discussions with France about the possibility of another treaty. Even within the Foreign Office, confidence in the treaty was low, to a large degree due to the efforts of Twiss. Sir Julian Pauncefote, the Permanent Under-Secretary of the Foreign Office, wrote, on July 21, to the strongest supporter of the treaty in the Office, Thomas Villiers Lister, the Assistant Under-Secretary responsible for Africa, to say, "Lister, we must be very careful about what we write to Berlin [regarding the status of the Congo]. First, as regards the case of the 'Hero,' Sir Travers Twiss has shown from French official documents that there never was a recognition of Portuguese sovereignty in the Banana Waters."[238] Pauncefote had obtained a copy of the letter from Renault that Twiss had forwarded to the Foreign Office a year earlier. Lister, who was pro-Portuguese, responded stubbornly, "As regards (1). I have before me Sir Travers Twiss's papers. He referred only to the point whether France had in releasing the Hero admitted that she did so because the ship was captured in Portuguese waters . . . Sir T. Twiss does not deal with the German view."[239] Twiss had succeeded in sowing doubt, but the question remained unresolved.

The Berlin Conference of 1884 and 1885

The German view, as Lister put it, and also a view shared in France, was increasing concern that Britain was moving to seize control over the region, at the same time that they were aggressively expanding their influence throughout Africa. German Chancellor Otto von Bismarck's perceptions of British over-reach were formed, in particular, by his anger over Germany's claims to the port and adjoining territory known as Angra Pequena in South West Africa.[240] German commercial interests, led by the trader Adolf Lüderitz, had established a port there in 1883 and had requested protection from Bismarck.[241] He, in turn, asked the British Foreign Office if they had any claims over the territory, albeit not revealing his own interest. The Foreign Office initially failed to respond to his inquiry and then made claims based upon contiguity with the Cape Colony, but, significantly for the coming conference at Berlin, not based upon any kind of occupation. Lord Granville, the Foreign Secretary, had badly mismanaged this affair, succeeding in provoking Germany over a territory which was of no importance to Britain.

238. Pauncefote to Lister, July 12, 1884, National Archives, London, FO 84, 1812, 90–92.
239. On Lister's pro-Portuguese sympathies, see Crowe, *The Berlin West African Conference*, 88.
240. Robinson and Gallagher with Denny, *Africa and the Victorians*, 173.
241. Crowe, *The Berlin West African Conference*, 37–41.

Bismarck persuaded the French that the only way to cut off these perceived British ambitions was to call a conference of all the powers, including Turkey, in Berlin in order to agree on the principles upon which Africa could be divided and upon which European expansion might be conducted more generally.[242] Bismarck believed that the only restraint upon British expansionism would be an agreed system of international rules regarding occupation of territory and freedom of trade and navigation.[243] The French government agreed upon the necessity of that system, even if they were nervous about the restraints it could impose upon their own ambitions. Over the course of August 1884, Bismarck and the French ambassador to the German Empire, Baron Alphonse Chodron de Courcel, negotiated three issues, or three "bases," which the conference of all the powers in Berlin would debate. Those bases were: 1. Freedom of commerce in the basin and mouths of the Congo; 2. The question of the application to the Congo and the Niger of the principles adopted by the Congress of Vienna, with a view to rendering inviolable the liberty of navigation on several international rivers; 3. The definition of formalities to be observed in order that occupation on the coasts of Africa shall be effective.[244]

These were the formal matters for discussion at the conference, but the Berlin Conference, from November 1884 through February 1885, also determined another, equally important matter that was not on its formal agenda: namely, the sovereign status of the vast region known as the Congo. The day after the United States had recognised the flag of the International Association of the Congo as that of a friendly power, on April 22, 1884, the French government had also recognised their flag, but that act was kept secret at the time. French recognition of the Association as a sovereign power was motivated by fear of the Anglo-Portuguese treaty, which, at that moment, was still alive. Leopold negotiated the French recognition of the Association at a possible cost. The French insisted that a clause be included in the treaty which stated that if the Association was forced to sell its territories, France would have the first option to purchase them. The European powers widely expected that the International Association would not endure. Leopold, on the other hand, had no intention of relinquishing any territories in the Congo, so his concession to France cost him nothing in reality. He gained a great deal, however, because

---

242. For accounts of the Berlin Conference and the events leading up to it, see Crowe, *The Berlin West African Conference*; Robinson and Gallagher with Denny, *Africa and the Victorians*, 172–177; William Roger Louis, "The Berlin Conference and the (Non-) Partition of Africa," in Louis, *Ends of British Imperialism: The Scramble for Empire, Suez and Decolonization*. Accounts from closer to the events include Reeves, *The International Beginnings of the Congo Free State*; Edmond Fitzmaurice, *The Life of Granville George Leveson Gower*, 2nd ed., Vol. 2 (New York, 1905), 337–378; Keith, *The Belgian Congo and the Berlin Act*.

243. Crowe, *The Berlin West African Conference*, 64–66.

244. Crowe, *The Berlin West African Conference*, 67.

it was now in the interest of every other European power that was anxious about the expansion of French empire to help ensure that the ambitions of the International Association were realized.[245] All the European powers were gradually brought to recognition of Leopold's International Association, out of fear that it was better that a minnow be granted such a vast territory than one of their own number. During the course of the Berlin Conference, the powers accordingly signed treaties recognising the International Association as a sovereign state, but in order to do so, they first had to overcome their objections to a private organisation with no license from a sovereign state having, in the first instance, signed treaties with indigenous sovereigns ceding their territory and, second, being elevated itself into the society of nations.

Germany and France invited twelve further powers—Austria-Hungary, Belgium, Denmark, Italy, The Netherlands, Portugal, Russia, Spain, Sweden, Norway, Turkey, and the United States—as well as themselves, to the Berlin Conference. In addition to their own ambassadors, the delegation of each state included experts in geography, law, and commerce, and some unofficial delegates also attended, as well as others who were not even on the lists of unofficial delegates, such as George Taubman-Goldie, who had interests in the Niger.[246] There was no delegation from the International Association because it was not a state and, by convention, could have no seat at an international table. Leopold's agents were present, however, in a number of other delegations, particularly though the inclusion of Sanford and Stanley in the American delegation and Twiss in the British delegation.

It appears that Twiss came to be invited because he had made himself indispensable to any legal discussion of the status of the Congo, even within the Foreign Office. On November 12, 1884, in the days before the Conference opened, the chief British negotiator, Ambassador Edmund Malet, wrote to Granville, the Secretary of State for Foreign Affairs, to say: "I have been requested by the German Government to send in the names of the British Plenipotentiaries and Delegates to the Conference. Having heard incidentally that Sir Travers Twiss and a geographer are to be associated with me, I beg your Lordship to inform me on the point before I send in the list."[247] On the back of Malet's telegram, Granville wrote: "The British Ambassador is the only 'Plenipotentiary.' The others are Delegates to assist him and the Official Delegates are Mr Meade, Mr Anderson, Mr Crowe and Mr Hemming. In addition to these Sir Travers Twiss has been requested to proceed to Berlin to place his services at the disposal of the Embassy in case advice on questions of Intl Law should be required. Mr Bolton has also been requested

---

245. Crowe, *The Berlin West African Conference*, 80–84.
246. On the "mysterious" Goldie, see Crowe, *The Berlin West African Conference*, 100.
247. Telegram from Malet to Granville, November 12, 1884, Berlin, National Archives, London, FO 84/1814, 310.

to proceed to Berlin to advise the Embassy on geographical questions, but neither Sir T. Twiss nor Mr Bolton should be put on the Official List of Delegates. G." While Twiss had been included, he was not an official delegate. It is not clear why he was not granted official recognition; it may have been because he held no government office, although it had not been forgotten, neither in Britain nor Europe, that he had been denied any further official offices due to his marriage scandal. Percy Anderson was chief of the African department of the Foreign Office. Robert Meade was an Assistant Under-Secretary in the Colonial Office, where A.W.L Hemming was also Principal Clerk. Joseph Archer Crowe had been on the Danube Commission and attended as a "commercial attaché." Four British merchants also accompanied the delegation.[248]

Two days after receiving this telegram from Malet, Granville wrote Twiss a letter of introduction to be returned to Malet: "Sir, This letter will be delivered to you by Sir Travers Twiss, who proceeds to Berlin to-morrow at my request in order to place his services at the disposal of Your Excellency in advising upon any questions of International Law as such may arise during the sittings of the Conference in the affairs of the Congo. Sir Travers Twiss is well acquainted with the subject and his great experience as a jurist especially on questions of International Law qualify him in a high degree for the duties which will devolve upon him. I have no doubt therefore that you will derive great assistance from his counsel on such points as you may have to refer to him. G."[249] Indeed, Granville's introduction understated Twiss's usefulness. He proved to be indispensable to Malet and to the Foreign Office during the Conference. He was a key figure in the negotiation of all three bases. Above all, he enabled recognition of the Congo Free State, not only through the force of his arguments but through acting as an instrument in the provision of information, chairing of committees, and drafting of key treaties and the Congo constitution. He recognized that the creation of a new person required both the idea of that person and certain ritual performances of personality, and he was crucial to both. This was a point he had appreciated from the ritual creation of new bishops and archbishops, as much as from the ritual creation of the new person of Mrs Travers Twiss. The transformation of the International Association resembled that of Pharaïlde van Lynseele in the degree to which it exceeded the conventions on such performances, taking newly liberal ideas of personal transformation to their extreme.

The first session of the Berlin Conference was held on November 15, 1884. The Conference would consist of ten sessions lasting until February 26, 1885, although, as Sybil Crowe observes, most of the work done in the Conference

---

248. For all these figures, see Edmond Fitzmaurice, *Life of Granville*, Vol. 2, 374–375; and Crowe, *The Berlin West African Conference*, 99–100.

249. Granville to Malet, November 14, 1884 National Archives, London, FO 84/1814, 348.

was not during the sessions but in the various committees and sub-committees conducted on the side, and of these, the committee to determine the third basis, the rules on occupation, was chaired, as we shall see, by Twiss.[250] The first two weeks, from November 15 to December 1, were concerned with the "first basis": that is, with freedom of commerce in the Congo basin. December meetings were concerned with the second basis: namely, freedom of navigation on the Congo and Niger. The Conference adjourned over Christmas and resumed on January 7 with discussion of the third basis, rules governing occupation, which took it until the end of January. The Conference continued to the end of February to allow territorial negotiations to continue. Territorial negotiations between the International Association, France, and Portugal were also held outside the Conference but, on Bismarck's insistence, continued throughout its sitting.[251] The General Act of the Conference concerned the three bases, but it also included a declaration on suppressing the slave trade in West Africa, and it appended the treaties recognising the International Association as a state.

Twiss arrived at the Conference three days after it started, on November 18, and the following day, Malet wrote to Lord Granville: "I have the honour to report that Sir Travers Twiss arrived here last evening."[252] Twiss had relatively little to do with negotiating the first basis, although, in these first weeks of the Conference, he was active in discussions over the suppression of the slave trade in the Congo. The Committee of the British and Foreign Anti-Slavery Society wrote to Earl Granville, the Foreign Secretary, on November 21, to suggest that the Berlin Conference was an opportune moment at which to reform international law on the slave trade by assimilating it to the law of piracy, as had been proposed at the Congress of Vienna in 1815. The committee noted that the legal work for this proposal might be left in the hands of Travers Twiss, "who they understand is now at Berlin."[253] In addition to placing responsibility in Twiss's hands, this letter made it clear that it was public knowledge that Twiss was present in Berlin. Three days later, Malet wrote to Granville to say that Bismarck was opposed to the declaration on the slave trade at the Conference and wished for one more "anodyne its wording."[254] Suppression of the slave trade made a good justification for extending European sovereignty over Africa, but it did not make for good business. Granville responded the following day: "Consult Twiss and report his views. We are

250. Crowe, *The Berlin West African Conference*, 101.

251. Crowe, *The Berlin West African Conference*, 102.

252. Malet to Lord Granville, November 19, 1884, National Archives, London, FO 84/1815, 86.

253. Secretary of the British and Foreign Anti-Slavery Society to Earl Granville 21 November, 1884, National Archives, London, FO 84/ 1815/142.

254. Malet to Granville, 24 November, 1884, National Archives, London, FO 84, 1815, 237r.

unable at present to appreciate difficulty raised and think our proposal should stand subject to modification if necessary after discussion in Conference."[255] Twiss wrote in haste to Pauncefote on December 3 to say that he had been visited by "Herr von Frantzius" of the German Foreign Office, who told him that Bismarck's concern with the slave trade declaration was that, if slavery was declared a crime, legislation would be necessary to sanction that crime. The unstated question was who would pass such legislation and who would enforce it when the issue was international. Twiss suggested instead that it was "desirable" to "cut off the supply of the overseas slave trade by suppressing the slave markets and the passage of the cargo along the high road of the Congo Basin." He believed that "we might obtain the Prince's acceptance of a Declaration to this extent": namely, that trade in slaves is forbidden by the law of nations and that signatory powers should suppress that trade "as much as possible."[256] Pauncefote circulated a memo in the Foreign Office in response to Twiss's letter, observing: "This letter from Sir T. Twiss ... seems to show that my suspicion was well founded and that Prince Bismarck wants only a moral declaration and not a legal one."[257] On December 6, Malet revealed that Twiss had been allowed to negotiate the declaration on slavery with the German Foreign Office. He wrote to Granville that the matter had been "finally settled between Sir Travers Twiss and Herr Frantzius, the gentleman appointed by the Chancellor to discuss the question."[258] They agreed upon the text: "According to the established principles of international law the traffic of negroes, and the commerce which furnishes negroes to the traffic, is forbidden and it is the duty of all nations to suppress these as much as possible." Malet added: "I cannot get the Prince to support more than this. The great point gained is that the slave gangs are brought within the operation of the law of nations. May I accept this text and propose it?" Despite Pauncefote's scepticism, Twiss's wording on the suppression of slavery became precisely that employed in the new *Projet de déclaration* on the commerce in slaves, stating that slavery was forbidden and that all nations should suppress it as much as possible.[259]

The implications of this declaration for Leopold's International Association of the Congo were profound because it concerned the trade in slaves in the Congo Basin. By this time, most powers at the Conference were coming to recognise the Association either as the sovereign power over that territory or as the future sovereign power. Twiss was effectively negotiating, therefore,

255. Granville to Malet, 24 November, 1884, National Archives, London, FO 84, 1815, 237v.

256. Twiss to Pauncefote, December 3, 1884, National Archives, London, FO 84/ 1816/ 205–206.

257. Pauncefote, Memo, [no date], National Archives, London, FO 84, 1816, 208, 12, 84.

258. Malet to Granville, December 6, 1884, National Archives, London, FO 84, 1816, 280–281.

259. Projet de déclaration, National Archives, London, FO 84, 1817, 308v.

the terms to which Leopold was to be held on the question of slavery. On December 16, Malet wrote to Granville, underlining the degree to which the Association and slavery were identified in the Congo: "International Association: Colonel Strauch and I have signed the Declarations and the Convention. The French text translated by the Colonel was examined and found to be correct by Sir Travers Twiss, on whose advice also I have accepted the word 'suppress' instead of 'abolish' before the word 'slavery.'"[260] Strauch was attending the Conference as an unofficial delegate and one of Leopold's key organisers in advancing the claims of the International Association. Leopold effectively had two of his key advisors on each side of a negotiation over the responsibilities of the International Association. Crucially, Twiss had succeeded in greatly reducing the stringency of the declaration on slavery, by committing the International Association only to its suppression, rather than its abolition.[261] While he had, in his later years, come to accept a broader understanding of the social mobility of natural persons in Europe, and while he also argued that African peoples should be enfranchised (so that they could cede their sovereignty), he evidently did not fully extend that expanded view of freedom to enslaved peoples. He had, of course, supported the extraterritoriality of British ships of war which assisted fugitive slaves, but his concern in that instance was probably more with sustaining extraterritoriality than with assisting slaves. Whether, in 1884, he knew that he was furnishing tools that would help free the Congo Free State effectively to enslave millions is uncertain, but it is hard to see any other purpose for which one might want to water down a pledge to abolish slavery.

Hopes for the Conference in the Foreign Office were low in some quarters. The pro-Portuguese Assistant Under-Secretary, T. V. Lister, commented on Bismarck's opening speech and protocol with the observation: "Bismarck's speech is extremely vague & leaves it doubtful whether the Conference is to do more than register a few platitudes about freedom of commerce and navigation."[262] He added, "I do not see how claim of Portugal to the Lower Congo can be contested." Granville responded on the same note: "Logically no but practically I think it will be." Even while the powers were supposed to be focused upon the questions of freedom of commerce which constituted the agenda of the Conference, they were worrying about who would win sovereignty over the Congo.

By December 1, thoughts had turned to the negotiation over free navigation of the Congo and Niger rivers, and Bismarck threatened to make trouble

---

260. Malet to Granville, December 16, 1884, National Archives, London, FO 84, 1817, 303.

261. Malet to Granville, December 16, 1884, National Archives, London, FO 84, 1817, 310.

262. Lister, Memo on Protocol, Nov 17, 1884, National Archives, London, FO 84, 1815, 19–20.

for Britain over the Niger if it did not recognize the International Association as a state.[263] In fact, over the next four weeks, Twiss became indispensable. From Malet's telegrams, it is clear that Granville instructed the delegation to use Twiss's services: "Your excellency considered that time would be saved if we were to take advantage of Sir Travers Twiss's presence here."[264] Malet promised the Foreign Office that "Sir T. Twiss will be consulted" during the negotiations.[265] Accordingly, Twiss prepared "for communication, and the foreign office, a draft neutrality declaration which might be made applicable to the Niger as well as the Congo."[266] Twiss, Malet observed, "is strongly of the opinion that the clause [on neutrality of the rivers] should bear the form of a separate declaratory act." Twiss was concerned that the treaties on the neutrality of the rivers should be kept separate from acts concerning freedom of navigation of those rivers because any outbreak of conflict would render the treaties void and could therefore imperil the acts if they were part of them. On this question, Malet cited Twiss's *Oregon Territory*.[267] Twiss submitted his draft neutrality declaration the same day, and Malet sent a copy by telegram to the Foreign Office.[268] His declaration expressed the free trade ambitions of the Conference, so that the signatories would agree to "facilitate and develop commercial relations between their respective states and the countries comprised in the basin of the Congo/Niger." He also stipulated that freedom of navigation should be extended to the merchant vessels of all powers at times of war.[269] Here again, Twiss was actively engaging in endorsing and implementing the liberal ideology of the moment—understood in terms of free trade and navigation—as well as projecting it, through law and positive agreements, into new parts of the globe. The memos passing between the Foreign Office and Berlin over the following weeks frequently included the clause "consult Twiss," and he offered his view on matters including the French position on the neutrality of the rivers, neutrality during war, and the carrying of coal during war.[270] His proposals consistently met the approval of Malet and Granville.

263. See Crowe, *The Berlin West African Conference*, 147.
264. Malet to Granville, December 3, 1884, National Archives, London, FO 84, 1816, 190.
265. Telegram from Malet, December 2, 1884, National Archives, London, FO 84, 1816, 126.
266. Malet to Granville, December 3, 1884, National Archives, London, FO 84, 1816, 190.
267. Malet to Granville, December 3, 1884, National Archives, London, FO 84, 1816, 190v.
268. Malet to Granville, December 3, 1884, National Archives, London, FO 84, 1816, 185.
269. Malet to Granville, December 3, 1884, National Archives, London, FO 84, 1816, 185. See also Malet to Foreign Office, December 1, National Archives, London, FO 84, 1816, 113, in which Twiss suggested an addition to the convention on the Niger guaranteeing protection of all foreign merchants, which, he said, was merely to assume the responsibilities of "territorial sovereignty."
270. See, for example, Granville to Malet, December 16, 1884, National Archives, London, FO 84, 1817, 295; Memorandum on the neutrality of rivers during war, no date, National Archives, London, FO 84, 1816, 199; Malet, December 5, 1884, National Archives, London, FO 84, 1816, 249–251; Malet to Granville, December 10, 1884, no.208, National

The Conference adjourned for Christmas, and it resumed on January 7 to discuss the third basis on the rules of occupation. Twiss was now even more deeply involved in the deliberations. He was appointed by the Conference to chair the committee established to draft the rules. He also directed the British position on occupation. This role was crucial for Leopold because it transpired that the negotiations over the rules of occupation became a proxy for the terms upon which the claims to sovereignty in the Congo by the International Association could be accepted. The double nature of the negotiations was apparent in an opinion on the legal aspects of the third basis that the Solicitors General at the Royal Courts of Justice provided for Lord Granville on January 7, the day the Conference resumed. The solicitors noted "that Your Lordship would be glad to be informed whether we concurred in the views expressed by Sir Travers Twiss, and if so whether we had any further suggestions to make for the assistance of Your Lordship in framing Instructions to Her Majesty's Ambassador at Berlin on the subject."[271] They then proceeded to situate the question to be determined by the third basis: "The recognized modes of acquiring new territory are (1) conquest (2) cession and (3) occupancy or settlement. We apprehend that it is only to the latter of these modes of acquisition that the third basis, proposed in Baron Plessen's [the German chargé d'affaires in London] despatch, is intended to apply." While the laws of occupation remained a very important justification for colonization, however, Leopold had not pursued title to the Congo through occupation so much as by numerous treaties of cession made with the native rulers (Brazza had pursued similar methods for the French).[272] Although Leopold's claims were not officially on the table at Berlin, the participants were negotiating recognition of the Association on the sidelines. The Solicitors General therefore continued: "Supposing it [the third basis] to apply also to the acquisition of territory by cession . . . the importance of requiring that a cession of territory should be recognized as acquired by a Sovereign power only applies when the cession has been made to a recognized and authorized agent of such Power, would not be great if a cession of sovereign rights to individuals is still to be recognized. For it would be impossible to prohibit individuals who had attained such sovereign rights from afterwards ceding their rights to the Sovereign power whose subjects they were. We have hitherto, as in the case of the Borneo Company for example, recognized as valid the transfer of sovereign rights to individual subjects of our own. We gather too, that we have acknowledged the acquisition of

---

Archives, London, FO 84, 1817, 26v; Malet to Granville, December 10, 1884, no.209, National Archives, London, FO 84, 1817, 29; Malet, December 11, National Archives, London, FO 84, 1817, 71.

271. Solicitors General to Granville, January 7, 1885, National Archives, London, FO 84, 1819, 105–113.

272. See Fitzmaurice, *Sovereignty, Property, and Empire*, 271–301, on the meshing of occupation and treaty in *territorium nullius*.

such rights by the International Association, and we presume that it would not be consistent with our policy in this respect to deny the right to obtain future cessions of the same description."[273] This statement represented a significant shift in international law on the question and a substantial concession to the position that Twiss had argued for Leopold over the previous years. The Solicitors General were prepared to acknowledge that individuals could acquire sovereignty through cessions, even if they were not officially authorized agents of a sovereign power, if they subsequently transferred those sovereign rights to the state to which they were subject. Moreover, the Solicitors General used the example of Borneo, which Twiss had himself cited in order to make this claim.

Nevertheless, while important, this concession did not do all that Leopold required because the International Association was not going to transfer the sovereign rights it had acquired to a state. Rather, it wished to use those cessions in order to transform itself into a state. The law officers then observed that recognition of sovereignty nevertheless leads to further problems, particularly the size of the territory that should be recognized: "The real difficulty arises with reference to the extent of territory around and beyond that actually occupied, to which the assumption of sovereignty may extend, and which can be regarded as appurtenant to the territory so occupied. This is obviously a matter of cardinal importance. / We concur with Sir Travers Twiss in the view that the general principle is, that if a nation has made a settlement it has a right to assume sovereignty over all the adjacent vacant territory, which is necessary to the integrity and security of the settlement."[274] Here Twiss had laid the groundwork for the recognition of what would be a vast territory claimed by the International Association of the Congo on the basis of contiguity with its several stations along the Congo River.

As with the second basis, Twiss's views were sought on every step of the negotiation over the third basis. Bismarck had succeeded in gaining French support for the Conference because of their mutual distrust of Britain's vast and disordered empire. They were concerned that Britain used a wide spectrum of legal arguments and categories in order to justify different kinds of authority dubiously made over a great variety of territories. The purpose of the Conference was to submit the business of establishing empires to a legal order and code—and thereby restrict the ongoing expansion and growing power of Britain—and the third basis on occupation was at the heart of that desire.[275] Specifically, the aim of the Conference was to ensure that the principle of effective occupation—the idea that when a territory is claimed it must be fully and

---

273. Solicitors General to Granville, January 7, 1885, National Archives, London, FO 84, 1819, 105-113.7.

274. Solicitors General to Granville, January 7, 1885, National Archives, London, FO 84, 1819, 105-113.

275. Crowe, *The Berlin West African Conference*, 176-186.

properly governed and inhabited—which had long been recognized in international law, was accepted by agreement amongst the powers and would thereby pass from a principle with roots in Roman and natural law into the positive law of nations. The powers negotiated over a *"Projet de déclaration,"* which stated the desire for a *"doctrine uniforme relativement aux occupations,"* whereby a territory would become the property of one of the powers when it was subjected, first, to a notification of occupation, followed by a "jurisdiction sufficient for peace to be observed, [and] respect for the rights acquired."[276] For Britain, the negotiation over the third basis was divided between the outlook of Granville, who, as Secretary of State for Foreign Affairs, was anxious not to further alienate France and Germany, particularly after his mishandling of the Angra Pequana conflict, and Selborne, who, as the highest law officer of the crown, realized that the subjection of all types of imperial possessions to the universal measure of effective occupation would lead either to a great increase in Britain's administrative responsibilities in territories over which it held a loose authority, or would otherwise lead to the delegitimization of many of those possessions.[277] Selborne, accordingly, monitored the negotiations closely, and Twiss could be seen to side with his old colleague in the advice he gave to Malet and the Foreign Office.

When the *Projet de déclaration* was circulated on the first day of the Conference, Twiss immediately objected to the inclusion in its first clause—the clause regarding the need for notification—of a term suggesting that occupation had to be effective. On the second day of negotiations, Julian Pauncefote accordingly wrote to Clement Hill in the Africa Department of the Foreign Office: "I agree with Twiss as to omission in first paragraph . . . we should insist on more time for consideration."[278] The day after that, he circulated a memo on the third basis, commenting: "As regards the first paragraph we are all agreed as to the omission suggested by Sir Travers Twiss of the words *'ou de le reconnoitre effectif ou,'*" and he concluded with instructions to Malet to accept Twiss's terms.[279] The same day, January 9, Twiss wrote a long letter to Pauncefote outlining his concerns about the third basis; the Foreign Office notes on the back of this letter record that a copy was sent to the Lord Chancellor, Selborne. In this letter, Twiss sought to prevent Granville from failing again to appreciate the significance of the stakes involved in diplomacy over colonization in Africa. He wrote: "Dear Sir Julian, The 'Projet de déclaration' has been circulated and I presume that the text of it has been forwarded to

276. *Projet de déclaration*, January 7, 1885, National Archives, London, FO 84, 1819, 125.

277. Crowe, *The Berlin West African Conference*, 176–186.

278. Pauncefote to C. S. Hill Esq, January 8, 1885, National Archives, London, FO 84, 1819, 142.

279. Pauncefote memo, January 9, 1885, National Archives, London, FO 84, 1819, 158–159.

Lord Granville. I think it is of importance that his attention should at once be directed to the meaning of the term 'occupation.'"[280] Twiss's tone then became even more directing: "It will be within his Lordship's memory that the first dispute between the United States and Great Britain in respect of what is known as the Clayton-Bulwer Treaty arose upon the meaning of the term 'occupy.' Great Britain used the word in the sense of 'taking possession,' whilst the United States maintained that it properly meant holding/keeping possession. I was requested by Mr Addington to draw up a paper on the subject."[281]

The Clayton-Bulwer Treaty was negotiated in 1850 due to tensions between the United States and Britain over plans to build the Nicaragua Canal, subsequently made redundant by the Panama Canal.[282] Both powers were concerned that any occupation by the other in Central America would establish sovereignty over a territory through which both desired freely to pursue their trade. Henry Addington, to whom Twiss refers, was Pauncefote's predecessor as Permanent Under-Secretary for Foreign Affairs, while Granville had been engaged in questions raised by the Treaty in 1851, during his first of three periods as Foreign Secretary. Twiss succeeded here in reminding Pauncefote, and all else who read this letter, of his mastery, based in experience, of Britain's international legal relations. He was, moreover, reminding that audience that the Clayton-Bulwer Treaty had foundered upon a failure to agree on the meaning of "occupy," with the United States insisting, consistent with the Monroe Doctrine, that all present and future British occupations in Central America should be abandoned, and Britain committing only to make no further occupations in addition to those possessions they already held in Honduras, the Bay Islands, and on the Mosquito Coast.

Twiss then made his closeness to Selborne's position on the Berlin Conference explicit: "Now Lord Chancellor Selborne has very justly pointed out the distinction between annexations and protectorates, where he says that 'annexation is the direct assumption of territorial sovereignty, while Protectorate is the recognition of the right of the Aborigine or other actual inhabitants to their own country with no further assumption of territorial rights that is necessary to maintain the paramount authority and discharge the duties of the protecting power.'"[283] He clarified what was at stake in the Conference: "A substantial distinction would thus appear to exist between territory taken possession of and territory taken under protection." While Bismarck was striving

280. Twiss to Pauncefote, January 9, 1885, National Archives, London, FO 84, 1819, 187–190 verso.

281. Twiss to Pauncefote, January 9, 1885, National Archives, London, FO 84, 1819, 187–190 verso.

282. G. F. Hickson, "Palmerston and the Clayton-Bulwer Treaty," *Cambridge Historical Journal*, vol. 3, no. 3 (1931), 295–303.

283. Twiss to Pauncefote, January 9, 1885, National Archives, London, FO 84, 1819, 187–190 verso.

to eradicate the British distinctions between various kinds of authority over imperial territories, Twiss was alerting the Foreign Office that the German proposal for the third basis would support Bismarck in that effort. For Bismarck, as Twiss put it: "Protection is regarded as veiled sovereignty carrying with it the same paramount rights as avowed sovereignty." The danger in the "*Projet*" for the third basis, as Twiss argued, was that Britain would be obliged to treat all its possessions equally: "I am rather disposed to think that if the Powers accept the terminology of the Projet they will in fact ignore the distinction drawn by the Lord Chancellor and will affirm that a Protecting Power has the same rights and obligations as regards territory as a Sovereign Power."[284] Returning to the Clayton-Bulwer Treaty, he concluded: "Bearing in mind then the interesting difficulties which have arisen between the United States and Great Britain by reason of the disputed interpretation of the term occupy in the Clayton-Bulwer Treaty, I have thought it advisable to direct Lord Granville's attention to the ambiguous meaning of the term in the 'Projet.'"

Finally, Twiss used the letter to draw attention to the condition regarding notification in the *Projet* on effective occupation. The *Projet* stated that notification by a power of its act of occupation should be made a condition of international recognition of new sovereign territories held by European powers. Twiss objected: "Now notification as I understand correctly its object is for the benefit of Foreign Nations so they may be aware of the altered national character of a territory and its people, but according to the 'Projet' its intention would appear to be to declare the occupation to be effective however slight might be the formalities observed in taking possession and however unsubstantial may be the act of possession itself. In other words, the 'Projet' would declare notification, if not objected to, to be a criterion of effective occupation which would be a step backward rather than a step forward."[285] His point would appear to be that, while notification might be an important step in making new occupations of territory, it should not itself become a condition of effective occupation, particularly if notification was taken to be the most important act in establishing sovereignty. His advice on this point was consistent with conventions in the law of nations since the early seventeenth century at least. Grotius too had observed that a thing had to be actually taken with the hands in order to become the possession of somebody.

This letter largely defined the British position on the third basis. Pauncefote wrote a telegram immediately to Hill in the Foreign Office: "Since messenger left have received important letter from Twiss which you will get today by early post[. C]opy should go to Chancellor today and instructions to Berlin

---

284. Twiss to Pauncefote, January 9, 1885, National Archives, London, FO 84, 1819, 187–190 verso.

285. Twiss to Pauncefote, January 9, 1885, National Archives, London, FO 84, 1819, 187–190 verso.

suspended until you receive Twiss's letter and instructions."²⁸⁶ He followed this with a letter the same day to Hill in which he, Pauncefote, unwittingly made it clear he had completely misunderstood the nature of Twiss's arguments: "Dear Hill, This is a most important letter from Twiss. Please send a copy today to the Lord Chancellor. The instructions to Malet (if sent off today as I think they might be) should be limited to the 1st Paragraph and should add that instructions will follow as to the second the difficulty being that no distinction is made between Protectorates and Occupations . . . We shall incur great odium and suspicion in apparently rejecting all obligations flowing from Protectorates, and I agree with Twiss's remarks in this letter—I think it might be useful to accept the obligations in Para 2 as attached to Protectorates in Africa. Please send a messenger down to the Lord Chancellor with these observations. I see in the Paper that Lord Granville is away. I am writing in great haste to have the Early Post. Truly yours, J. Pauncefote."²⁸⁷ In a "Note by L.C." written the following day, addressed to no particular person but clearly for circulation in the Foreign Office and now in the Foreign Office papers, Selborne immediately responded, making it clear that Pauncefote had misunderstood the importance of Twiss's letter: "I do not construe Sir Travers Twiss's letter of the 9th of January, (so far as relates to the subject of Protectorates), as Sir Julian Pauncefote appears to. Sir Travers Twiss expresses his agreement with the distinction, as I had stated it, between the nature of an annexation, and the nature of a Protectorate. He justly observes that this distinction is disregarded in the 'Project,' as now framed; and that, if the Powers accept the terminology of the Project, they will, in fact, ignore it, and will affirm that a Protecting Power has the same rights and obligations, as regards foreigners, as a Sovereign Power. . . . [another paragraph] . . . To myself, it appears to be eminently undesirable to lay down a principle, the inevitable effect will be, to turn every Protectorate into an Annexation. I think that in many cases, (e.g., our present Protectorate, whether so called or not, in Afghanistan . . .) this would be in the last degree inexpedient and would also be unjust towards the actual rulers and inhabitants of the Protected country . . ."²⁸⁸ Twiss and Selborne were effectively dictating the British position on effective occupation at the Berlin Conference, while both the Secretary of State for Foreign Affairs and the Permanent Under-Secretary in the Foreign Office fell into line, but only after two weeks of resistance and negotiation.

On January 15, Malet wrote to Granville that the Commission, on the third basis, had agreed to delete the words Twiss had recommended to be omitted

286. Pauncefote to Hill, January 10, 1885, National Archives, London, FO 84, 1819, 185-186.

287. Pauncefote to Hill, Stourfield, Christchurch Hants. [i.e., Pauncefote's home], December 10, 1884, National Archives, London, FO 84, 1819, 191-193.

288. "Note by L.C.," January 11, 1885, National Archives, London, FO 84, 1819, 202-203v.

from the *Projet*—"either to recognize as effective or." The idea that notifications of occupation should specify boundaries remained, but "Sir Travers Twiss whom I have consulted does not consider it important to insist on the amendment being carried."[289] Nevertheless, the following day, Malet even succeeded in supressing the question of boundaries, so that "the result of the two days discussion is that both amendments proposed by Her Majesty's Government have been accepted."[290] There remained, however, "considerable difficulty," according to Malet, on the question of having protectorates and occupation treated separately, and he concluded gloomily: "It will be impossible to obtain further concessions [regarding the wording of protectorates] as I am not supported by any other Power."[291] The following day, he explained to Granville that Bismarck insisted upon the same obligations for protectorates as for occupations; otherwise, states could simply declare protectorates in order to exclude other European powers and yet take no responsibility for those territories.[292] At the same time, he noted the concern that the wording for the unoccupied parts of West Africa could be applied to all colonial possessions around the globe.

On January 19, Malet wrote to Granville that, in light of the stalemate at the Conference over the wording of the third basis, the powers had agreed to establish a "Sub Committee of the West African Conference" which had "met on Saturday the 17th instant to agree upon the ultimate wording of the Third Basis. Sir Travers Twiss was in the chair."[293] How Twiss had managed to get himself elevated into this position is not explained, but presumably his eminence amongst the international lawyers at the Conference was a factor, and Bismarck, who was working hard to achieve recognition of the International Association of the Congo, may well have been aware of Twiss's work for Leopold. Malet reported that the wording Twiss's committee agreed upon was as follows:—"in the same manner the Signatory Powers recognize the obligation to establish and to maintain in the territories under their protectorate an authority sufficient 'pour faire observer la paix,' render justice, respect private rights and, the case occurring, liberty of commerce and of transit under the conditions in which they may have been established."[294] "Sir Travers Twiss,"

---

289. Malet to Granville, January 15, 1885, National Archives, London, FO 84, 1819, 259–261.

290. Malet to Granville, January 16, 1885, National Archives, London, FO 84, 1820, 12–13.

291. Malet to Granville, January 16, 1885, National Archives, London, FO 84, 1820, 12–13.

292. Malet to Granville, January 17, 1885, National Archives, London, FO 84, 1820, 30–31.

293. Malet to Granville, January 19, 1885, National Archives, London, FO 84, 1820, 58 (60–61 is a transcription of this telegram).

294. Malet to Granville, January 19, 1885, National Archives, London, FO 84, 1820, 58.

Malet added, "has authorized me to state that this wording is, in his opinion, one which may properly be accepted by Her Majesty's Government." He added that "should your Lordship concur with Sir Travers in this opinion," it would be prudent to agree as quickly as possible in order to stop "groundless suspicions" on the part of the other powers in the event of a delay. Granville wrote on the back of the memo that Malet should be informed that "we cannot give him a reply until after the meeting of the Cabinet tomorrow."[295]

Over the following days, Malet continued to telegraph Granville, informing him that his colonial advisors in Berlin had told him that they "think that the two paragraphs approved by Sir Travers Twiss might be accepted but they prefer the former" wording, in which obligations would be imposed upon protectorates because they feared a "rupture" in the talks for which Britain would be held responsible.[296] By January 23, Selborne had lost patience with Malet and wrote to Pauncefote backing Twiss's judgement over Malet's "colonial advisors." He argued that Malet placed "the smooth working of the conference [above] all other considerations connected with the question at issue."[297] He repeated that the principles agreed could not be applied to other protectorates, and that Britain's position was different to that of the other powers: "There is no substantial obstacle, in their case, to their treating the distinction between Protectorate and Annexation as purely nominal; so that by Protectorate they mean (as Sir Travers Twiss said) Annexation, under another name. But it is otherwise with us." And he again repeated: "I cannot think that on this subject the views of the 'Colonial advisers' of Sir E. Malet at Berlin ought to have any preponderating weight." In Twiss's analysis, the Germans regarded protectorates as impersonations of something other than what they were, while, in the British view, the impersonated authority was real. Pauncefote was so concerned by Selborne's letter that he took it to the Home Secretary, Sir William Harcourt, who, as he reported to Granville, "adhered very strongly to the opinion that we should accept the obligations which the other powers desire to see attached to Protectorates."[298]

Selborne and Twiss may well have lost this battle had Bismarck not himself reversed his position and agreed to allow all mention of protectorates to be

---

295. Malet to Granville, January 19, 1885, National Archives, London, FO 84, 1820, 58.

296. Malet to Granville, January 21, 1885, National Archives, London, FO 84, 1820, 115; Malet to Granville, January 21 and 22, 1885, National Archives, London, FO 84, 1820, 42; Malet to Granville, January 22, 1885, National Archives, London, FO 84, 1820, 147–149. My account here differs from Crowe, in *The Berlin West African Conference*, 188, who places Twiss in the same camp with Malet's colonial advisors, although that interpretation does not appear to be supported by the correspondence, nor was it shared by Selborne.

297. Selborne to Pauncefote, January 23, 1885, National Archives, London, FO 84, 1820, 161–163.

298. Harcourt to Granville, January 23, 1885, National Archives, London, FO 84, 1820, 158–160.

excluded from the final act of the Conference regarding occupation.[299] Malet pointed out, gratefully, that Britain had always understood it had been invited to a conference on occupation, not protectorates.[300] Why Bismarck changed his position is not clear, but it may have been because he had already prevailed by this point in getting his way on the most important question to be decided at the Conference, albeit one not on the official agenda: namely, the matter of who exercised sovereignty over the Congo. The wording agreed upon for the third basis was, as Malet observed, "the original amendment of the Declaration on the Third Basis, proposed by me for the omission of all mention of Protectorates from the paragraph defining the obligations of Powers in case of future occupations." It was, that is, the amendment formulated by Twiss, and it now passed into the Act of the Conference and so into positive international law. The paragraph now read: "The Signatory Powers acknowledge the obligation to assure—'assumer'—in the territories occupied by them on the coasts of the African continent, the existence of an authority sufficient to cause acquired rights to be respected, and, the case arising, liberty of commerce, and of transit, under the conditions which shall have been stipulated."[301] Britain could thereby continue to distinguish between the various levels of occupation it engaged in, from settler societies, which were understood to establish both sovereignty and property over territories, through to "protection," which controlled the external relations of territories while leaving internal arrangements relatively untouched.[302] Even in such nebulous terms, these requirements for occupation in this declaration were nevertheless a fiction in terms of their application to the Congo Free State. It was therefore particularly ironic, and fitting, that it should have been composed by Twiss, who had also written the constitution of that state. When the Protocols and General Act of the Berlin Conference were presented to the British parliament in March 1885, Twiss was mentioned a number of times as having contributed to the debates in Berlin, but his role in having shaped the second and third bases, in particular, was buried.[303]

299. Malet to Granville, January 28, 1885, National Archives, London, FO 84, 1820, 203–205.

300. Malet to Granville, January 29, 1885, National Archives, London, FO 84, 1820, 221–224: a long letter from Malet to Granville relating the series of conversations with Bismarck leading to the omission of the words regarding protectorates in the third basis.

301. Malet to Granville, January 28, 1885, National Archives, London, FO 84, 1820, 203–205. See also the *Rapport de la commission chargée d'examiner le projet de Déclaration relative aux occupations nouvelles sur la côte d'Afrique*, at January 31, 1885, National Archives, London, FO 84/ 1820/ 233–238, especially p. 6 of that report.

302. See Fitzmaurice, *Sovereignty, Property, and Empire* for the distinction between the occupation of sovereignty and the occupation of property.

303. Protocols and General Act of the West African Conference, March 1885 (London), 103, 143, 147.

The Congo Free State

The most important matter determined at the Berlin Conference was the item that was not on the official agenda: that is, recognition of the International Association of the Congo as able to make treaties ceding sovereignty and, by extension, as the sovereign power over the Congo Basin. This was also the matter in which Twiss played the greatest role. We have seen that the United States had already recognised the Association as a sovereign power earlier in the year of the Conference. France and Germany had followed suit by the time the Conference had started, with the French expecting that the failure of the International Association would lead to their own sovereignty over the territory. For Bismarck, recognition of the Association by the other powers was one of his main objectives for the Conference, thereby preventing any other major power from carving out a vast part of Africa for themselves.

In the months between the US recognition and the start of the Conference, Britain was the most important power that needed to be convinced of the claims of the International Association, but their acquiescence was complicated by their negotiations with Portugal over that country's own claims to sovereignty on the West Coast of Africa. Twiss, as we have seen, did his best to discredit the Portuguese pretensions. At the same time that the Foreign Office continued negotiations with Portugal on a treaty regarding West Africa, Bismarck brought pressure to bear directly on Granville for the matter to be determined outside those negotiations. On August 7, the British Ambassador in Berlin, Lord Ampthill, wrote to Granville to say that he had been visited that afternoon by the German ambassador, Count Georg Munster, who "said he had instructions to speak to me on the question of the Congo." The German ambassador's message was that Bismarck understood the British sought "perfect freedom of commerce and navigation" in the Congo and that Germany was also "prepared to negotiate on that basis."[304] Bismarck warned, however, that "it would be a pity" if Britain's negotiations with Portugal "were to run the risk of the advantages" which would be obtained from a "full interchange of views." Munster then observed, "Prince Bismarck thought it might be desirable to include the International Association in any arrangement that might be made," adding that it was not desirable by ignoring the Association "to throw it too much into the hands of France." Ampthill responded that Bismarck's proposals required "very careful consideration," particularly given that the "international status of the Association was doubtful." Britain knew, he noted, that the Association had "promised the reversion of all their acquisitions to France" should they fail. Britain also knew that the Association had "been concluding a series of agreements with native chiefs giving to the Association, and therefore

---

304. Ampthill to Granville, August 7, 1884, National Archives, London, FO 84, 1812, 206–209.

in a possible eventuality to France, the exclusive right of regulating trade and transit through the territories of those chiefs." Ampthill carefully avoided refering to those "agreements" in the terms used by the Association: namely, as "treaties" ceding sovereignty. He concluded his conversation with Munster by conceding only that Britain would be prepared to discuss the matter further.

At the same time that Bismarck was applying pressure on Britain to recognise the International Association, Portugal was attacking the Association's claims in continuing discussions with the Foreign Office. On August 9, the British Ambassador in Lisbon, George Petre, wrote to Granville to say that the Portuguese Foreign Minister, José Vicente Barbosa du Bocage (a noted zoologist, particularly of Africa), had sent him the treaties that the International Association had been signing in the Congo, along with the Portuguese protests to those treaties, all of which Petre enclosed in his letter. Revealing his own scepticism on the issue, Petre noted that the Congo "chiefs" had "made a gift of their sovereign rights to the Belgian Association in exchange for some trifling presents, including a case containing 12 bottles of gin."[305] In reference to the treaties being made by several of the rival powers in the region, he observed: "What may be the relative value of these rival treaties and conventions it is not for me to say, but it is clear that there is not much difficulty in obtaining them."

The full pretensions of the International Association were also made clear in the treaties. Each one stated that the particular African signatory "had ceded to the International Association of the Congo its rights of sovereignty to all the territories under its authority and including all dependant villages and lands hereafter cited."[306] A treaty made by Henry Stanley on April 19, 1884, in the Haut Congo, was included in these papers and contained a clause to make it absolutely clear what was at stake: "It is agreed between the above parties that the term 'cession of territory' does not mean the purchase of soil by the association, but the purchase of the suzerainty by the association and its just acknowledgement by the undersigned chiefs."[307] Portugal reacted furiously to these claims. They sent a ship's captain, Guilherme Augusto de Brito Capelo (later the governor of Angola), to the trading village of Boma, about 80 kilometres up the Congo River, to spy on the activities of the Association. From Boma, he wrote on June 2, 1884, directly to the British officer Sir Francis de Winton, who acted as the representative of the International Association in the Lower Congo. Capelo stated his surprise at finding that the Association had been concluding treaties with African chiefs claiming to cede sovereignty. "I will come straight to the point," Capelo declared, "to demonstrate to you the nullity of these pseudo-treaties made according to the so-called

---

305. Petre to Granville, August 9, 1884, National Archives, London, FO 84, 1812, 219–220.

306. "Traité," National Archives, London, FO 84, 1812, 221.

307. "Traité," National Archives, London, FO 84, 1812, 221v–222.

THE INTERIOR OF VIVI STATION. (*From a photograph.*)   [*To face page* 153, *Vol. I.*

FIGURE 17. Contemporary engraving of the station of Vivi in the Congo Free State (1887).*

principles of the law of nations. The International Association of the Congo cannot be considered a recognised and legally constituted political entity that can appropriate sovereign rights in a country."[308] Having thus stated the very substantial, and well known, legal and political obstacle Leopold's Association had to overcome in order to make sovereign treaties, let alone become a state, Capelo went on to outline Portugal's own sovereign claims to the Congo. He concluded by threatening that "measures would be taken, even the most energetic" in order sustain Portugal's rights to the Congo.

Capelo received an immediate reply, on June 4, from Leopold's agents, Henry Stanley and Francis de Winton, both resident at Vivi, the Association station approximately 65 kilometres farther up the Congo River from Boma, on the opposite bank of the river from Matadi, and the furthest navigable point prior to Stanley Falls. They first pointed out that the treaty between Britain and Portugal recognising Portuguese sovereignty on the west coast of Africa had not been ratified by the British parliament. In response to the observation that the Association could not be regarded as a "political entity," they argued

---

308. Guilherme Augusto de Brito Capelo to Sir Francis de Winton, National Archives, London, FO 84, 1812, 225v.

* In Henry Stanley, *The Congo and the Founding of Its Free State*, 2 vols. [London, 1885], Vol. 1, 153 [facing].

that they had been "constrained by the native chiefs to enter into political arrangements with them" so as to impose order upon the Congo. There "being no government in the country they, of necessity, had to create one."³⁰⁹ They were aware of the debate over "sovereign rights, and whether individuals can obtain such rights from native chiefs who own undisputed territories." And they were satisfied that "these rights are very fully discussed by jurisconsults who have made the subject of international law a special study." The particular jurists Stanley and Winton had in mind were Twiss and Arntz. They proceeded to give Twiss's example of the treaties concluded in North Borneo as an example of a company being ceded sovereign rights and they then cited a paragraph from Arntz's pamphlet on the matter of whether "independent chiefs or savage tribes [can] cede to any private individual." They noted Capelo's threat to use force to support Portuguese rights and responded that they would reply in kind, if need be. One of the remarkable aspects of this exchange is that international law was being used as the ground of dispute in a confrontation far up the Congo River. This was an area that Joseph Conrad passed through six years later, spending two weeks in Matadi, and that he used as material for his *Heart of Darkness*.³¹⁰ More specifically, the exchange between Capelo, Stanley, and Winton revealed the degree to which international law, and Twiss in particular, were key elements in the case of the Association for statehood, and it reveals that the question of the status of "a private individual," namely, the International Association, in international society was key to the authority of Leopold's agents in the Congo itself, just as those agents were fully aware of how contentious that claim was in international law.

Many of the Portuguese concerns about the Association were shared by the British Foreign Office. Lister wrote to Granville, on August 4, raising concerns about Francis de Winton, particularly noting that the Portuguese "Govt. have a very faire right to complain that an English officer is allowed to annex full sovereignty on behalf of a filibustering Co. territory which HMG [Her Majesty's Government] had asked by the signature of the Congo Treaty to belong to Portugal."³¹¹ Lister asked: "Did he [de Winton] receive permission from the W.O [War Office?] to join the African Association in the pay of the King of the Belgians? Was the F.O. consulted?" The representation of the Association as a filibustering company—that is, as an unauthorised military expedition—revealed that there was still great resistance to their recognition as a sovereign state.

---

309. Francis de Winton and Henry Stanley to Capelo, National Archives, London, FO 84, 1812, 226v–228.

310. Joseph Conrad, *Diary*, in Conrad, *Heart of Darkness* ed. Paul B. Armstrong (New York, 2006), 253.

311. Lister to Granville, August 21, 1884, National Archives, London, FO 84, 1812, 283–284.

It was soon clear both that the International Association had pretensions to more than filibustering and that de Winton was not the only Briton working for Leopold. On November 6, days before the Berlin Conference convened, Pauncefote circulated within the Foreign Office the draft constitution of the new state into which the International Association would be formed. His memo stated, "Sir Travers Twiss has handed me for Lord Granville's information this copy of the Draft Constitution of the new state by the King of the Belgians under the name of 'L'Afrique Equatoriale.'"[312] On the back of this memo, he wrote: "Keep copy and return original to Sir T. Twiss with compliments and thanks." Knowing by this point that he had been included in the British delegation to Berlin, Twiss had decided to share his inside knowledge of Leopold's plans, probably with Leopold's consent and with a view to advancing those plans.

The first article of the constitution stated that the territories of the Congo had been "acquired by the International African Association by cession from the indigenous chiefs" and that those territories "constitute an independent state under the highest authority of His Majesty King Leopold II."[313] The constitution embodied the sovereign recognition that the Association had already received from important powers, but it was also a useful tool in presenting as a fait accompli the claims that an association could receive cessions of sovereignty and be transformed into a state, although much more argumentation would be necessary for that view to prevail in Britain. It would be another two weeks before Lister would reveal that Twiss was, in fact, the author of the constitution and not just the agent by which it was presented to the British government. Nevertheless, the presence of the constitution concentrated minds in the Foreign Office upon the need to negotiate the status of the International Association.

On November 15, 1884, the day the Berlin Conference started, Granville wrote to Malet to explain the position of the British government on the status of the International Association of the Congo. He observed, "The question of the status of the African International Association is one which will probably be incidentally discussed at the Conference," so he would explain "the views of H.M.G. [Her Majesty's Government] on that subject."[314] He began sceptically: "In the opinion of H.M.G. the association under existing circumstances does not present the conditions which constitute a State." At this point, Pauncefote wrote in the margin to the draft of this letter: "N.B. It has not even the

312. Julian Pauncefote, Memo, November 6, 1884, National Archives, London, FO 84, 1814, 222.

313. *Projet. La constitution de l'Etat—L'Afrique Equatoriale*, FO 84, 1814, 220–221. For another annotated copy of the constitution, see *Projet. La constitution de l'Etat—L'Afrique Equatoriale*, National Archives, London, FO 84, 1815, 80–81.

314. Granville to Malet, November 15, 1884, National Archives, London, FO 84, 1814, 373–376.

status of a Corporation or 'Societé Anonyme.'"³¹⁵ By this Pauncefote meant that the Association was not a joint stock corporation, and this was true. It was a corporation, and therefore possessed legal personhood, but Leopold was the only shareholder. Granville continued more optimistically, however, to state that the Association "no doubt possesses elements out of which a State may be created. Its constitution is at present unknown and has probably no existence except on paper; but there is no reason why it should not become a reality. / The Association is still in its infancy; but having regard to the noble aims of its founder and to the liberal and enlightened principles which it is understood to advocate, H.M.G. will watch with great interest & sympathy its efforts to develop itself into a new State. / If these efforts should result in the establishment of a political organisation possessing a regular government & those constituent elements which, according to recognised principles of Public Law, are as indispensable to the existence of a State, H.M.G. will gladly unite with other governments in recognising its rights to claim a place in the family of nations."³¹⁶ The reference to the uncertain state of the Association's constitution was probably to the fact that Twiss's version of it was a draft and to the fact that his paper version had not been ratified by any political body. The requirement for "political organisation possessing a regular government" was a bar too high for the Association. For this reason, Granville concluded, ominously for the hopes of Leopold and Bismarck: "Such a result must necessarily be the task of time. No community can struggle at once into political existence and a considerable period must elapse before the promoters of this great enterprise could be expected to afford adequate protection to foreigners or to provide sufficiently for the exercise of civil and criminal jurisdiction over them. / Therefore until those conditions can be satisfied, H.M.G. are of opinion that the regime of Consular Jurisdiction should be allowed to continue in the territories of the Association, without prejudice to its right of dominion therein."³¹⁷ The British government had come a long way merely by conceding that a "private individual" could receive cessions of sovereignty and, in time, establish a state, but they were not prepared, at this point, to concede that such a flimsy organisation could, in such a short time, realise its pretensions to statehood without the backing of any sovereign authority. Nevertheless, recognition of consular jurisdiction was a long way short of Leopold's ambition to establish a vast personal state. Granville ended his letter by making what was the seemingly unobjectionable statement that the British would "cooperate in its [the Association's] endeavours to promote the work of civilisation

---

315. Pauncefote, note on Granville to Malet, November 15, 1884, National Archives, London, FO 84, 1814, 373.

316. Granville to Malet, November 15, 1884, National Archives, London, FO 84, 1814, 373–376.

317. Granville to Malet, November 15, 1884, National Archives, London, FO 84, 1814, 373–376.

in those regions on the great principles of religious liberty and the freedom of commerce and navigation."

Such seemingly formulaic sentiments were, however, objectionable to Thomas Lister, the pro-Portuguese Assistant Under-Secretary, who wrote the following day to Pauncefote (who had helped Granville draft his letter), to say: "Pauncefote: I think your compliments to the Association at the end of this despatch go rather too far. The only evidence I have ever seen of its endeavours to promote freedom of commerce and navigation are the treaties it has made with the chiefs by which it secures to itself an absolute monopoly to the exclusion even of the Agents of all other traders. I would suggest in the last paragraph the word 'its' should be altered to all, thus—'to cooperate in all endeavours to . . .' T.V.L."[318] Lister's judgements of Leopold's cynicism proved, with hindsight, to be accurate. Roger Casement and Edward Morel were not the first observers to see through Leopold's liberal and humanitarian rhetoric, although sceptics, as Pauncefote's reponse to Lister in the margins of his note revealed, were at this time few. As Pauncefote put it: "I cannot say I concur in the proposed alteration—the passage concerned does no harm as it stands and nobody doubts the aim which the King of the Belgians has had in view."[319] Pauncefote was wrong. Not only his assistant, Lister, but, as we have seen, also the Portuguese and Twiss's anonymous Belgian attacker, as well as geographers (such as the Frenchman Louis Delavaud), jurists, and the German press, were all concerned, as early as 1884, about the transformation of a private association into a state, as well as about the activities of that association in the Congo.

All such concerns were about to be trumped. Bismarck accentuated the pressure upon the British. Malet wrote to Granville on November 19, the day Twiss arrived at the Conference, to say that Bismarck had informed him that it was "of advantage" to assist the Association "to become a state" and that, as soon as Leopold wished, he, Bismarck, would give the "same measure" of recognition to the Association as the United States had. Malet added that Bismarck would be "be very glad if Her Majesty's Government could do the same."[320] At the Foreign Office, Lister still led resistance against the claims of the Association. He argued that it was one thing to assist the Association to become a state and "another to recognise it as being one." He pointed out that a new state should have "a clear idea of its boundaries," as well as proof of its claims to its territories, that it should "explain its constitution" and give assurance of the freedoms of its subjects.[321] Pauncefote concurred in this view,

---

318. Lister to Pauncefote, November 16?, 1884, National Archives, London, FO 84, 1814, 378–379.

319. Pauncefote note on Lister to Pauncefote, November 16?, 1884, National Archives, London, FO 84, 1814, 378–379.

320. Malet to Granville, November 19, 1884, National Archives, London, FO 84, 1815, 82.

321. Lister to Malet, November 19, 1884, National Archives, London, FO 84, 1815, 75–76.

noting ironically that Germany, the United States and France appeared to be "in possession of information" regarding the Association that was not available to Britain or the other powers.[322] He suggested that Malet pursue "some middle course" with Bismarck whereby "the Association might be recognised not as an actual State, but as a State in course of formation."[323] He added, "It wd be a new feature in the practice of Nations, but I do not see any great objections to it under all the circs." Under his signature, Pauncefote added an afterthought: "Twiss shares our views as expressed in our instructions to Malet and it wd be well if Malet were to consult him as to the possibility of a middle course."[324] Pauncefote appeared here not to appreciate the degree to which Twiss had backed Leopold's ambitions. Twiss's views on the ability of the Association to have a standing in international society, and to receive cessions of sovereignty, were well known. He may have disguised from the British government his views on the standing of the Association as a state in order that he could participate in the British delegation to the Conference. At this point, while Twiss had given the constitution of the pretended state to the Foreign Office, it was not yet acknowledged to be his work.

The following day, November 21, Malet wrote to Granville to say, "I am informed by Sir Travers Twiss that a clause has been inserted in the Treaty recently signed between the German Government and the International Association to the effect that the Association will not cede any of its territories to a Power which does not undertake at the same time to accept all its obligations with regard to freedom of trade on the Congo. I have to add that Sir Travers Twiss tells me that he has not personally seen the Treaty."[325] Germany had recognised the International Association as a state on November 8, a week before the Berlin Conference started, but Bismarck concealed this act from the British, even while he urged them to their own act of recognition. Twiss's advice to Malet about the treaty was the first time that the British government learned that the German government had recognized the Association as a state. The fact that the government was unable to obtain such information itself, and the fact of German concealment, were a cause of embarrassment but, at the same time, they underlined Twiss's pivotal role in negotiating the status of the Association and his value as a broker of information. He was expert in the artifice necessary to the creation of new legal persons, and his leaking of information on this occasion was calibrated to advance not only his own position but also

322. Pauncefote to Malet, November 20, 1884, National Archives, London, FO 84, 1815, 77–79.

323. Pauncefote to Malet, November 20, 1884, National Archives, London, FO 84, 1815, 77–79.

324. Pauncefote to Malet, November 20, 1884, National Archives, London, FO 84, 1815, 78v.

325. Malet to Granville, November 21, 1884, National Archives, London, FO 84, 1815, 132; Crowe, *The Berlin West African Conference*, 144.

that of the statehood of the Association. It presented the cautious officeholders of the British government with a fait accompli and with a far more limited range of options. Those limits quickly became apparent.

News of the German recognition travelled quickly, and on the day after Malet learned from Twiss about the treaty, a member of parliament asked Granville whether it was true that Germany and France, as well as the United States, had "formally recognized the Congo Free State" and whether the British government would do likewise.[326] Granville responded that he was aware of the acts of recognition, but that the matter of the British position was "so closely connected" to the proceedings of the Conference that the honourable member would understand that "a pledge of secrecy" regarding those proceedings prevented any reply to the question.

On November 23, Lister wrote to Granville concerning Twiss's constitution for the new state: "I enclose the Draft Constitn [constitution] of the Congo Assocn. It is to be remarked that Leopold II does not style himself Roi des Belges. This is probably intentional and seems to imply a fear that the Belgian Govt. or Parliament may object to their becoming an African Monarch."[327] On this point, Lister was correct: Leopold's new state in Africa was not a colonial state. It was not supported by Belgium. It was an autonomous, self-creating state, an anomaly and a legal and political innovation, and consciousness of that fact was exerting pressure on the Foreign Office. Lister's memo continued: "It is a point for consideration whether the constitution should not be promulgated and submitted to foreign powers before the Assocn can be recognised as a State. It is I imagine the constitution wch makes the State wch the powers may recognise." Here Lister indicated that, despite German recognition of the new Congo state, the British government was still insisting that some kind of legal and political process had to be performed before the existence of that state became a fact in the international community. Lister's point that the constitution makes the state underlined the crucial role played by Twiss. He also now revealed the fact that it was Twiss who played this role. Below Lister's note, Granville wrote: "Should anything be written to Malet upon this?" Lister then wrote beneath that query: "The constitution is I believe the work of Sir T. Twiss & except the question of jurisdn [jurisdiction] over foreigners I see nothing in it to remark upon. It is a highly coloured sketch of a Bureaucratic Utopia. T.V.L."[328] Implicit in Lister's response was that it was not necessary to alert Malet to the nature of the constitution because he was being advised by the man who wrote it. His attitude to Leopold's claims remained

---

326. Reply of Granville in Parliament, Friday, November 21, 1884, National Archives, London, FO 84, 1815, 150.

327. T. V. Lister, memo, November 23, 1884, National Archives, London, FO 84, 1815, 214.

328. T. V. Lister, memo, November 23, 1884, National Archives, London, FO 84, 1815, 214.

deeply sceptical. He regarded the constitution to be a rhetorical as much as a legal document—a "highly coloured sketch"—and not one, as a "Utopia," that would be realised. On this question he was correct—the Congo Free State never did adopt a formal constitution, although Twiss's draft of one did serve a purpose as part of the performance of the proofs necessary to the creation of the new person of the state.

Apart from stating that the territories of the new state had been acquired by cession from "indigenous Chiefs," Twiss's constitution declared that the sovereign of the new state was Leopold II, "Duc de Saxe, et Prince de Saxe-Coberg et Gotha" but not "Roi des Belges," as Lister observed. The administration of the state was to consist of a Governor General and other officers appointed by Leopold. The constitution established a legistlative council which could make laws, although any of those laws could be "revoked" by the king. The judiciary were also to be named by the king. The constitution made further provisions for public finance, defence, religion, commerce, and ports and for constitutional revision.

The British government continued to attempt to slow down the process of recognition, mainly because they did not accept, quite rightly, that the International Association possessed the attributes of a state. On November 24, Granville wrote a long despatch to Malet summarising the government position on the status of the Association. He noted Malet's previous telegrams on the subject: first, stating Bismarck's intention to recognise the Association as a state; and, in the second telegram, that "another source," namely Twiss, had revealed that the Germans had already given their recognition a week prior to the Conference. He restated his sympathy with the supposedly humanitarian aims of the Association. He then went on to note the United States' declaration recognising the flag of the Association. Extraordinarily, he added: "In the view of HMG the language of that Declaration hardly amounts to the recognition of the Association as a State. It would seem to import little more than the recognition of the Association as the representatives of certain native States which have placed in its hands the administration of their affairs."[329] There was no question that the United States had intended to recognise the Association as a state, but the British government strategy was now to deny that was the case. Granville therefore returned to his previous idea of adopting "a middle course" whereby the Association was not recognised as a state but was accepted as having administrative powers in the Congo. Such a middle course, he argued, "might be usefully examined by some of the Plenipotentiaries at Berlin, outside the Conference, and the result of their inquiries might lead to the adoption of unanimity among the Powers as to the character and extent of the

---

329. Granville to Malet, November 24, 1884, National Archives, London, FO 84, 1815, 216–221.

recognition which might legitimately be accorded to the Association without infringing well established Doctrines of International Law. The Association and the territories which it proposes to administer may be viewed as a state in course of formation and having regard to its benevolent aim HMG would subject to those inquiries."[330] Granville thought better of observing that the creation of the new Congo state would infringe "well established Doctrines of International Law," so he deleted the phrase, as shown, but that was the concern driving opposition to recognition.

Twiss had presented the case that transformation of a private association into a new state was consistent with the doctrines of international law, and it was his case that would have to be swallowed when recognition was finally forced. The law would follow the reality—the political reality, that is, that certain powers wished the state to exist; there was no reality about the state itself—although Granville was not yet ready to concede the realpolitik of the law. Granville continued on in his instructions to Malet to say that the British government "would be glad to be able to give to it [the Association] the greatest measure of support compatible with the well recognized doctrines of International Law. They would, for instance, be quite willing to recognize its flag, its territories, and its officials as appertaining to a state in course of formation and to give it their support for all practical purposes and in all matters which are calculated to promote the great objects of the enterprise."[331] He could only make a nebulous concession upon the recognition of "practical purposes" of the Association. Its flag, territories, and idea that it was a state in formation proved to be too much to swallow. He then asked Malet to make his case before Bismarck, suggesting he tell the prince that he would "perceive that HMG are not yet acquainted with the precise conditions under which the German Govt. consider that the territories of the Association are entitled to recognition as a State, if that should be the intention, but that they [HMG] are most willing to accede to his wishes in regard to the Association, so far as they can do with due regard to the Law and Practice of Nations." The British government did not believe that private associations could become states and furthermore did not believe that the Association in any way resembled a state. Telling Bismarck that Britain would accede to his wishes so long as they were consistent with the "Law and Practice of Nations" was to tell him that they would not accede to his foremost demand that they accord the Association recognition as a state.

Granville's instructions were a brilliant piece of dissimulation, calculated to maintain Britain's position while seemingly expressing sympathy with the

---

330. Granville to Malet, November 24, 1884, National Archives, London, FO 84, 1815, 216–221.

331. Granville to Malet, November 24, 1884, National Archives, London, FO 84, 1815, 216–221.

friends of the Association. Sophistry, however, was wasted on Bismarck. He was too cynical to be susceptible to it. He also knew exactly what he wanted and how to get it, so he brushed Granville's assurances aside while reminding him of his vulnerability. One of the main concerns for Britain going into the Berlin Conference was to establish support for British interests on the Niger River, which were maintained by the National African Company (from 1886 the Royal Niger Company).[332] The Niger Company, like the Borneo Company, was a revival of the chartered company method of imperial expansion, which the English and Dutch had pioneered in the seventeenth century, notably with their East India companies, but which had become unpopular after the 1857 Indian Rebellion. The National African Company was an aggressive and successful return to this model, but it faced competition from French and German interests on the Niger, despite its near-monopoly on trade. The leader of the Company, Sir George Goldie, attended the Berlin Conference in order to attempt to secure British interests over the Niger.[333] At the same time that Britain was opposing the claims of the International Association over the Congo, it was pushing for the NAC's control over the Niger. For the British government, there was no contradiction in simultaneously holding these positions. As Pauncefote had made clear, in January of the same year, in his memo concerning Twiss's second article on the Congo, there was, in his view, a strong difference between individuals and associations that carried sovereign authority with them, when making treaties, and those who did not. In 1881, Goldie had succeeded in convincing Gladstone's government to grant the NAC a charter that would permit it to make sovereign treaties.

Bismarck, however, was unconcerned by such distinctions and now stated that he would use the Berlin Conference to side with the French in their opposition to British control over the Niger if Britain did not agree to the claims of the International Association upon the Congo. The French were arguing for an international control over the Niger, which Bismarck said he could oppose, along with Britain, if they would recognise the Association as a state.[334] Bismarck met Malet on the morning of December 1 and told him that the only way that Britain "could be of use" to the International Association was "to give it such a measure of recognition as has been accorded to it by Germany and the United States."[335] He said the whole Conference would be imperilled if the Association did not have this "vitality." Malet assured Granville that failure to comply with Bismarck's request would result in

332. Robinson and Gallagher with Denny, *Africa and the Victorians*, 180–189; Roger Louis, *Ends of British Imperialism*, 100–101.

333. See Crowe, *The Berlin West African Conference*, 123–126. For Goldie, see Robinson and Gallagher with Denny, *Africa and the Victorians*, 166–168.

334. Bontinck, *Aux origines de l'État Indépendant du Congo*, 246.

335. "Decypher Telegram Sir E. Malet Berlin, Dec. 1, 1884," National Archives, London, FO 84, 1816, 116.

"a generally unfriendly attitude of Germany on the matters of the highest importance to us." The only concession Bismarck was prepared to make to the British position was that they could maintain "consular jurisdiction" in the Congo: that is, they could maintain an extra-territorial power similar to that which they maintained in many non-European countries. The Foreign Office immediately capitulated; their ambitions in the Niger outstripped their concerns over the observation of international law in the Congo. It is perhaps more surprising that, until this point, they had argued for a process that would conform to the conventions of international law than that they now abandoned those conventions.

On December 2, the day after receiving news of Malet's conversation with Bismarck, Pauncefote wrote to Malet to instruct him to say that Britain would recognize the International Association as a state: "You may inform Prince Bismarck that you are authorized to negotiate a Treaty with the Association under which we will recognize its flag as the flag of the Free States and of the government of those states."[336] Pauncefote added that this recognition would come "provided we are accorded" most-favoured-nation status in trade and "consular jurisdiction." His final instruction to Malet in this note was "Consult Twiss as to form of Document." Twiss, that is, was to be given responsibility for writing the treaty in which Britain recognized the International Association, recognition that would finally gurantee the creation of the new state. This is perhaps hardly surprising, given that he was the legal expert in Berlin advising the British delegation, but it nevertheless underlined not only his extraordinary position as a British advisor on questions dealing with the International Association, while at the same time being in the pay of the owner of that Association, but also the extraordinary fact that the Foreign Office had strongly suspected since at least January of the same year: namely, that he was in Leopold's pay.

Within the Foreign Office, however, scepticism of Leopold and his agents was now quickly put aside. On December 4, Henry Stanley visited the Foreign Office with Scottish shipowner William McKinnon, who had helped finance his expeditions. Stanley wrote to the Association's American agent, Henry Sanford: "I went to Foreign Office with Mackinonn. Saw Lister, Clement Hill [the Africa expert], Sir Julian Pauncefote ... Pauncefote then said: 'I have good news for you. All what you wanted is done.'"[337] Stanley boasted that he and Mackinnon had now arranged to dine with Lister, Hill, and Pauncefote at the Burlington Hotel, in Westminster, on December 9. "The English," he reported, "are now undoubtedly open-eyed to the Association now and welcome it."

---

336. Pauncefote to Malet, December 1, 1884, National Archives, London, FO 84, 1816, 120.

337. "Henry Stanley to Henry Sanford," in Bontinck, *Aux origines de l'État Indépendant du Congo*, 246–247.

Twiss, meanwhile, was busy drafting the treaty of recognition, and on December 5, he sent a copy of it to Pauncefote. In his letter accompanying the draft, he explained the sources were the German and American declarations of recognition, while Articles 3 to 9 were modelled on the articles regarding consular jurisdiction in "our treaty with Japan of the 18th of August, 1858."[338] He then noted that he had not included stipulations regarding consular jurisdictions in the constitution of the new state because "I ought to tell that the King of the Belgians had a strong objection to Consular jurisdiction, and I therefore did not include it in the constitution." In addition to confirming what had so far only been explicitly mentioned by Lister, that Twiss was the author of the constitution, his statement also reveals the degree to which he was directed by Leopold. He therefore declared rather duplicitously to Pauncefote: "If my hands had been quite free, I should have framed the constitution according to your ideas, but I was asked to draw it up after the model of our Crown Colonies"—albeit that Leopold's Congo state was no colony. Even Twiss now no longer concealed the contradictions of working for two competing masters.

The contents of the draft treaty of recognition were entirely concerned with the mechanisms of consular jurisdiction and guarantees of freedom of commerce for British subjects. The only exception was the opening declaration, which recognised the principle that the Association had been able to create a sovereign body through the treaties of cession made with African peoples: "By Treaties with legitimate sovereigns in the basins of the Congo and of the Naidi Kwilu, and in adjacent territories upon the Atlantic, there has been ceded to it territory for the use and benefit of free States established, and being established, under the government of the said Association."[339] In addition to recognising the principle that a non-sovereign body had been able to make sovereign agreements, this declaration also assumed, as Twiss had been arguing for several years, that African peoples possessed sovereignty that could be ceded. This claim is unremarkable in the twenty-first century, but it was contentious amongst nineteenth-century jurists.

The degree to which Twiss was torn between two masters, and the tendency for such conflicts to be resolved in Leopold's favour, became apparent the day after he sent the draft treaty to Pauncefote. He had had second thoughts about the provisions for consular jurisdiction in the treaty, either because he anticipated Leopold's objections, which had already been clear in the case of the constitution, or because of a further act of ventriloquism on Leopold's part when he saw a copy of Twiss's draft treaty. On December 6, Malet wrote to Granville to alert him to Twiss's concerns: "Twiss asks me to

---

338. "Draft Treaty of Recognition," National Archives, London, FO 84, 1816, 263.

339. "Draft Treaty of Recognition," National Archives, London, FO 84, 1816, 263. For the draft of this treaty in Twiss's hand, see "Draft Treaty of Recognition," National Archives, London, FO 84, 1816, 265-268.

say ... that he is of the opinion that it will be advisable to make two separate treaties. The one would be similar to the treaty with Germany while the other would deal with the question of consular jurisdiction."[340] Not leaving the matter to Malet, Twiss wrote a long letter to Pauncefote setting out his reasoning for removing consular jurisdiction from British recognition of the new state in the Congo.[341] Pauncefote summed up his reasoning in a letter to Selborne in which he asked for Selborne's views on leaving consular jurisdiction out of the "draft convention prepared by Sir Travers Twiss."[342] It might, Pauncefote argued, be better to "adopt one or two short and simple articles in preference to the clauses from our Japan Treaty, as it might give umbrage to the Association to be dealt with like Orientals." Pauncefote was reflecting the consciousness here that Britain was in the process of recognising something that was neither fish nor fowl. Leopold's state could not be called a colonial state because it was not established by any European sovereign state. It was not a European state, even though it had a European sovereign, but nor did it fit the conception of an "Oriental state" and could not therefore be included within consular jurisdiction. It was a legal person created using the ritual performances and legal arguments used to create states but not actually possessing the character of a state. All states were artificial creations, but they had some actual reified presence in their possession of the instruments of states—a bureaucracy, a financial system, a military, and so on. This one was almost entirely artifice, created by a master artificer. Its physical existence was no more than that of a filibustering enterprise, as Lister had observed earlier in the year.

Selborne responded to Pauncefote that he could accept the convention, although he was "unable to understand what Sir Travers Twiss may have intended" by Article 9, which stated that the Association could place "no restriction whatsoever" on British subjects in the employment of the "inhabitants of the said territories."[343] This, Selborne observed, "looks dangerously like a license to British subjects to have (under whatever name or pretext) domestic slaves," and he concluded, "I will not admit it." With Selborne's cut and Twiss removing the articles concerning consular jurisdiction, apparently under Leopold's instructions, the final treaty composed by Twiss, in which Britain recognised the Association as a state, was very short. It stated simply that the government of "Her Britannic Majesty" recognised the flag "of the

---

340. Malet to Granville: "International Association," December 6, 1884, National Archives, London, FO 84, 1816, 289 (for a clearer transcription, see 301–303).

341. Twiss letter to Pauncefote, December 6, 1884, National Archives, London, FO 84, 1816, 310–312.

342. Pauncefote to Selborne, December 10, 1884, National Archives, London, FO 84, 1817, 46–47.

343. Selborne to Pauncefote, December 11, 1884, National Archives, London, FO 84, 1817, 48–49.

Imperial Association of the Congo, and of the free states under its administration, as the flag of a friendly government."[344] It still contained some provisions for consular jurisdiction until such time as a system for the "administration of justice" had been established in the Congo, thereby recognising the absence of one of the most important attributes of a state. Malet, representing Britain, and Strauch, representing the Association, signed this treaty on December 16.

Britain's treaty of recognition, written by Twiss, became the model for all the subsequent treaties of recognition by the powers at the Conference which rapidly followed in its wake while the Conference continued. Recognition by Britain, the most powerful imperial state, was key to the acceptance of the Association as a state in international society. Following Britain's capitulation, there was a cascade of powers recognising the new member of international society. Italy gave its recognition on December 19, Austria-Hungry on December 24, Holland on December 27, Spain on January 7, Russia on February 5, Sweden and Norway on February 10, Portugal, which finally accepted the frustration of its claims, on February 14, and Denmark and Belgium on February 27.[345] Each of these treaties used the words Twiss had employed in the British treaty, except Belgium's, which entirely removed the reference to consular jurisdiction in a territory governed by its own king.[346] On February 26, the Berlin Conference convened for the last time, and the powers signed the General Act of the Conference, which codified the agreements on each of the three bases.[347] One of the signatories of the Act was the International Association of the Congo, which had began the Conference with only an informal presence because its claims that it had standing in international society, despite the treaties it had agreed with African sovereigns, were not recognised in international law.[348] By the end of the Conference, not only were those claims recognised, but the Association itself had been transformed into a sovereign power. Its signing of the Act was its first act as a sovereign power. In his closing speech, Bismarck was able to refer to the new sovereign as the "Congo State": "The new Congo State is called upon to become one of the chief protectors of the work that we have in view."[349]

---

344. *Convention between Her Britannic Majesty's Government and the International Association of the Congo*, December 10, National Archives, London, FO 84, 1817, 56–57.

345. Crowe, *The Berlin West African Conference*, 149.

346. See Crowe, *The Berlin West African Conference*, 147–149.

347. *General Act of the Berlin Conference*, in Stanley, *Congo*, Vol. 2, 440–458.

348. "Act of Adhesion of the International Association of the Congo to the General Act of the Conference of Berlin dated the 26th of February, 1885," *Protocols and General Act of the West Africa Conference, Presented to Both Houses of Parliament* (London, 1885), 302.

349. "Act of Adhesion of the International Association of the Congo . . . ," *Protocols and General Act of the West Africa Conference*, 303; Crowe, *The Berlin West African Conference*, 150.

Historians have debated the significance of the Berlin Conference for international law.[350] Some have argued that the Conference contributed nothing substantial in terms of the doctrines of international law.[351] More recently, post-colonial historians of international law have argued that the Conference was an important instrument in the harnessing of international law to the expansion of European empires.[352] This is unquestionably true. Moreover, the adoption of the principles of effective occupation at the Conference, in which Twiss played an important role, was not important for the development of new principles on occupation—these remained similar to arguments that had been prevalent since the sixteenth century—but it was important for the codification into positive international law, in the Act of the Conference, of what had in the past been recognised only as natural law principles.

The most important innovation in international law at the Conference, however, and one perhaps overlooked by most historians (despite the agitation it generated at the time), was the success of the idea that non-state actors could have a role in international society. Despite deep scepticism of Twiss's arguments supporting the claims of the International Association, by February 1885, his case had prevailed spectacularly. It would be true to say that the Association achieved recognition as a state largely because it received support from Bismarck, and that Bismarck was motivated more by his concern about the balance amongst European powers than he was by anything Twiss had said or written. Bismarck could not have prevailed, however, so long as the Vattel-like understanding of the membership of international society remained uncracked. For his pressure upon the other powers to succeed, there had to be some plausible account to which they could cling for why non-sovereign associations or individuals could be accepted as actors in international society, as well as a plausible account for how such associations could become states. What Twiss had made possible was a justification for Bismarck's position, as well as a justification for the new state in international society once all the powers at the Conference agreed to recognise it (with the exception of Turkey which granted recognition on June 25, 1885). Moreover, for some powers, such as the United States, Twiss's arguments were more than a convenient justification for political reality. At a time of strong liberal sentiment and expansion of the franchise, Twiss's proposals signalled the extension of liberalisation to international society beyond the rhetoric of the civilising mission and anti-slavery sentiment. They signalled a broadening of the franchise of international society itself. His arguments proved to be prescient. While

---

350. Matthew Craven critiques the various accounts in Craven, "Between Law and History: The Berlin Conference of 1884–1885 and the Logic of Free Trade," *London Review of International Law*, vol. 3, no. 1 (March 2015), 31–59.

351. For example, Crowe, *The Berlin West African Conference*.

352. See, for example, Anghie, *Imperialism, Sovereignty, and the Making of International Law*, 69.

contentious in the 1880s, the idea that membership in international society should be expanded beyond sovereign states was increasingly accepted by the early twentieth century.[353] The notion that a private association can become a state has fewer antecedents, unless we look to the manner in which large modern corporations, such as Apple and Google, established their own political communities and functioned, in some ways, as state-like entities.[354]

It was not because Twiss's arguments had prevailed, nor because the Congo Free State had been recognised, that the legitimacy of that state or the principles regarding non-state actors in international law would achieve wide acceptance. The issues continued to be debated after the Berlin Conference concluded, and both Twiss and Leopold understood that they would need to continue to make their case in order to ease the path of the new state. Conscious of this necessity, in April 1885, Leopold's agent, Henry Stanley, declared in his two-volume narrative *The Congo*: "The able and exhaustive statements of Sir Travers Twiss, the eminent English jurist, and of Professor Arntz, the no less distinguished [albeit dead] Belgian publicist, leave no doubt upon the question of the legal capacity of the African International Association in view of the law of nations."[355] The question which they had affirmatively answered, he said, was: "Can independent chiefs of savage tribes cede to private citizens (persons) the whole or part of their States, with the sovereign rights which pertain to them." Stanley and the Association had made 400 such treaties.[356] Twiss nevertheless continued to prosecute the case through a number of international forums. Although he had managed to prevail over diplomats and politicians at Berlin, he still had to convince jurists that what had happened in Berlin was consistent with the conventions of international law. At the same time, international lawyers, particularly through their forums, such as the meetings of the Institut de droit international, spent the years immediately following the Conference of Berlin raking over the General Act of the Conference and its deliberations and decisions, attempting to establish the consequences for international law.[357]

Just three months after the Berlin Conference terminated, Twiss wrote an article for the *Revue de droit international* in which he summarised the achievements of the Conference.[358] The article presented the Berlin Confer-

---

353. Lauterpacht, in the discussion following Idelson, "The Law of Nations and the Individual," 66; Wheatley, "Spectral Legal Personality," 755; Kjeldgaard-Pederson, *The International Legal Personality of the Individual*, 16–20.

354. These possibilities are explored in Joshua Barkan, *Corporate Sovereignty: Law and Government under Capitalism* (Minneapolis, 2013).

355. Stanley, *The Congo*, Vol. 2, 380.

356. Stanley, *The Congo*, Vol. 1, 18.

357. Fitzmaurice, *Sovereignty, Property, and Empire*, 271–301; Craven, "Between Law and History."

358. Travers Twiss, "Le Congrès de Vienne et la Conférence de Berlin," *Revue de droit international et de législation comparée*, vol. 17 (1885), 201–217.

ence in the tradition of the 1815 Congress of Vienna, which had been marshalled by his old friend Prince Metternich, and it celebrated the concert of powers which that Conference had established. Twiss argued that the Vienna Congress had abolished a world, created by the Peace of Westphalia, in which states pursued their narrow interests, and culminating in Napoléon's regime, which completely abandoned international law. The Vienna Congress replaced this individualistic regime in international relations with one which pursued the common interests of the European powers. Notably, one of the most important of those common interests was freedom of movement, particularly in the navigation of the rivers which separated and traversed countries. The Vienna Congress accordingly established free navigation of the Rhine, and the Congress of Paris, in 1856, continued this politics, Twiss observed, with the regime of free navigation of the Danube.[359] As we have seen from his correspondence with Metternich, Twiss regarded that regime on the Danube to be essential to the projection of power of Western European powers into the Black Sea and farther east.

The regime of international cooperation in order to establish free movement and free trade was, Twiss argued, the framework in which the Berlin Conference should be understood. The agreement achieved at the Conference for free navigation of the Congo would provide access to all European powers to the African interior. The creation of the Congo Free State, he added, "so usefully furthers the work of the conference" in establishing a regime of free movement and trade in Africa and would therefore "render precious service in the cause of humanity."[360] Whether or not Twiss believed these lofty ideals (and there are many reasons to suggest that he did), they were consistent with the arguments employed in the creation of the Congo Free State and with the liberal sentiment that Leopold exploited to his own ends. For Twiss, the arguments he had carried himself through various forums in order to gain recognition of the Association as a state were framed not simply by such high liberal ideals, including of freedom of movement, freedom of trade, and expansion of the franchise of international personhood; they were framed by the sense that those ideals belonged in a historical trajectory. That trajectory justified the continued movement to expand the franchise and to innovation in international law; the same historical trajectory expanded the franchise of individual persons, including who could be counted in the membership of Society. He knew that there were limits on that liberal movement: namely, his own wife's rejection by Society and the withdrawal of her recognition by the Court of St James. Nevertheless, despite the rejection of his wife by

---

359. In the same vein, on November 25, 1885, Twiss published "Le canal maritime de Suez et la Commission Internationale de Paris," *Revue de droit International et de législation comparée*, vol. 17 (1885), 615–630.

360. Twiss, "Le Congrès de Vienne et la Conférence de Berlin," 216–217.

Society, Twiss had not abandoned his commitment to the idea of transformation. As in the case of Pharaïlde Twiss's downfall, his colleagues in the community of international jurists were not entirely prepared to accept the expansion in the franchise of international society or, more precisely, presented with the fact of expansion, they struggled with its justification and the liberal apology.

On September 7, 1885, the Institut de droit international met, appropriately, in Brussels. The members convened in the Galerie de Marbre in the Palais des Académies, directly adjacent to Leopold's Royal Palace.[361] Leopold opened the meeting, and the President of the Institut then thanked him, offering the members' congratulations to the King on his new role as "head of state founded in Africa by the International Association of the Congo."[362] It was only through Leopold's "generous initiative," "elevated view," and "perseverance" that the "civilising mission" had been brought to the Congo. The recognition of that state, the President added, marked an "important date in the history of the law of nations," although just what that importance constituted was something the members would spend the next several years debating. He continued to point to the "vast regions" that had in the past been "abandoned to barbarity" and were now "open to humanity." The "old colonial politics" had been replaced by a "spirit of peace and good will for all," a fact underlined by the agreements on freedom of navigation and commerce.[363] At the same meeting in Brussels, the members of the Institut elected a new President, Belgian jurist and politician Gustave Rolin-Jaequemyns, who had been one of its founding members. The meeting also appointed two Vice Presidents; one was Russian jurist Friedrich, or Fyodor, Martens. The other was Twiss.[364] This was the first time Twiss had been appointed to an office (albeit a non-stipendiary one) since his marriage scandal in 1872. The appointment indicated that he had regained some measure of respectability and acceptance in Society. It was also recognition of the work he had performed in creating the new Congo state. This was not the only honour accorded to Twiss in the wake of his contribution to the creation of the Congo Free State and his services at the Berlin Conference. The following year, on August 25, 1886, Leopold named Twiss Commander of the Order of Leopold.[365] In truth, Leopold handed out numerous Orders of Leopold, but for Twiss this was nevertheless recognition of some

---

361. "Session de Bruxelles," *Annuaire de l'Institut de droit international*, huitième année (1886), 13.

362. "Vote d'une addresse à S.M. Léopold II, Roi des Belges, Souverain de l'État Indépendent du Congo," *Annuaire de l'Institut de droit international*, huitième année (1886), 17.

363. "Vote d'une addresse à S.M. Léopold II," 18.

364. "Élection d'un président et de deux vice-présidents," *Annuaire de l'Institut de droit international*, huitième année (1886), 16.

365. *The Times*, August 26, 1887, 3.

kind of redemption in the wake of his marriage scandal. He could hardly have guessed that the scandal surrounding his wife would soon engulf him again, undoing so much of his work.

Now that the creation of a new state from a private association was a reality, the jurists of the Institut struggled to bring their understanding of international law into line with that reality. They accordingly met Twiss's arguments with a mixed response. In 1886, the *Revue de droit international* published articles expressing support from jurists for Leopold's state. Friedrich Martens wrote an article on the realisation of Leopold's noble aspirations and Henry Stanley's extraordinary progress in civilising the Congo, despite the "pretensions" of the Portuguese.[366] By virtue of its treaties, the International Association had, he said, acquired "an immense territory" over which it exercised sovereignty. The French diplomat, Edouard Engelhardt, who had accompanied his country's delegation to the Berlin Conference, published an article in the same edition of the *Revue*, in which he examined the significance of the agreements upon effective occupation made in Berlin. Engelhardt noted that the Conference was obliged to accept a diversity of practices as constituting effective occupation. One such practice was the establishment of free trade, and this, he argued, might even be created by a "private consortium." "Isn't this close," he asked, "to the case of the International Association?"[367] For Engelhardt, therefore, the claim of the International Association to a status in international society had been based upon it having effectively occupied a vast territory in Africa.

In order to clarify exactly what were the rules of effective occupation established in Berlin, the members of the Institut de droit international agreed in Brussels to create a commission to examine the question. The commission was chaired by Ferdinand Martitz, a German jurist, but included Twiss, Martens, Engelhardt, and Emile de Laveleye. Twiss's presence was unsurprising, given his role in Berlin in chairing the sub-committee on effective occupation. His influence upon the commission was suggested by the participants adopting the term *territorium nullius* in their discussion of the different possible kinds of occupation. Jurists had always agreed upon the Roman law doctrine that it is possible to occupy, and claim title to, land that has not been occupied by anybody else. Twiss had introduced the term *territorium nullius* into discussions of international law, borrowing it from eighteenth-century descriptions of church land in ecclesiastical law, in articles he wrote in the 1870s, including the article on the "Applicability of the European Law of Nations to African

366. Friedrich Martens, "La conférence du Congo à Berlin et la politique coloniale des États modernes," *Revue de droit international et de législation comparée*, vol. 18 (1886), 141–144. Martens expanded on these arguments in Friedrich Martens, *The African Conference of Berlin and the Colonial Policy of Modern States* (1887).

367. Edouard Engelhardt, "La conférence de Berlin," *Revue de droit international et de législation comparée*, vol. 18 (1886), 96–98.

Slave States."³⁶⁸ In those articles, he used the term to point out that British naval ships possessed extraterritorial authority when in the waters of African slave states because the sea, he argued, was *territorium nullius*. In the discussions of the Institut's commission on occupation ten years later, *territorium nullius* was used to describe a lack of territorial sovereignty over land. By the sixteenth century, commentators on Roman law described such land as *res nullius*: that is belonging in the category of thing, *res*, that belonged to nobody, *nullius*. The principle was that the first person to take something would become the owner. What "taking" meant was the subject of some debate in Berlin in terms of the meaning of the term "effective." What Twiss introduced into this debate, however, was the idea that a particular piece of land could be vacant in different ways. It may not have had any kind of property established over it, and in this sense, it would be utterly vacant and unoccupied. It may, however, have been occupied by a people who had taken possession of the land insofar as they had established property over it, but at the same time failed to take possession of the sovereignty of that land. Or, Twiss argued, even if they had established personal sovereignty, as had existed in medieval Europe, they may have failed to seize the territorial sovereignty over the land in a manner that was characteristic of the modern state. Such land, he argued, would be *territorium nullius*. With this concept, he was able to justify the occupation of the Congo despite the fact that the peoples who lived there had undeniably established property relations and sovereignty that they could cede through treaties. The commission established by the Institut to discuss the question of effective occupation adopted Twiss's idea of *territorium nullius* to debate the territories occupied in Africa, including those occupied by the Association, although they proved unable to agree on what the appropriate terms and conditions should be for occupation. Nevertheless here Twiss could once again be seen shaping the terms of the debate over the legitimacy of the new Congo state—the failure of the jurists to agree on the nature of effective occupation could be as much an asset as a liability for Leopold.

In 1889, Leopold appointed Rolin-Jaequemyns as a member of the High Council of the Congo Free State, and in this same year, Rolin-Jaequemyns published a further article in the *Revue de droit international* in which he examined the place of that state in international law. The foundation of the Congo Free State, he noted, "is a new phenomenon until now unique in the history of international law."³⁶⁹ "There is something," he continued, "that at first glance disconcerts the jurist in the spectacle of this colony without apparent metropolis." In fact, the Congo state was, he argued, "an international

---

368. Twiss, "Applicability of the European Law of Nations to African Slave States," 436; Fitzmaurice, *Sovereignty, Property, and Empire*, 278.

369. Gustave Rolin-Jaequemyns, "L'année 1888 au point de vue de la paix et du droit international," *Revue de droit international et de législation comparée*, vol. 21 (1889), 168.

colony, sui generis." The state was a colony, he observed, insofar as it received its existence from "outside elements." But, he conceded, it was not a Belgian colony, nor one of any other state. Rather, it was created by all states. The new state was not created, he argued, by the acts of recognition by all the powers. The doctrine of international law, he observed, "does not allow private interests [*particuliers*], individuals or associations, to acquire territories with public title (*occupatione imperii*)."[370] Even Leopold's friends were unconvinced on this point. International law only permitted acquisition of territory "by virtue of a mandate, or delegation, from more or less under the authority or power of ratification of existing states." The situation of the new state, he argued with understatement, was "more or less ambiguous," even after it had received recognition from the powers at Berlin. What delivered it from that uncertain position was the final meeting, in which it was allowed to sign the treaty of the Conference. It was this sovereign act that transformed it into a sovereign state.

The aftermath of the Berlin Conference included such various attempts to rationalise the legality of the Congo Free State, including its effective occupation of the Congo, signified by the purported creation of free trade, and its signing of the act of the Berlin Conference. These attempts at justification merely underlined the continued uncertainty about the naissance of the new state. Not all jurists were as positively disposed to the events leading up to the creation of the Congo Free State. In 1889, the year that Rolin-Jaequemyns was appointed to the High Council of the Congo Free State and penned his own legal apology for that state, French jurist Charles Salomon wrote a treatise examining the principles established at Berlin. When he came to the elevation of the International Association, he asked whether territories in which "private interests" (*particuliers*), companies and individuals, had "established" themselves continue to be *res nullius* from the point of view of states and therefore "susceptible to occupation."[371] This was precisely the question that the French and Portuguese had considered in relation to the International Association. Salomon declared, "The State, and the State only, is capable of acquiring rights of sovereignty by acts of possession in territories without a master [*sans maître*]."[372] Given this fact, he argued, there are only two "hypotheses" for why a company could acquire sovereignty. In the first case, he observed: "Various political circumstances could lead to the recognition of a new state happening at a moment at which its political development was still so rudimentary that its quality as a state did not impose itself upon the eyes of the most disinterested observers." This, he continued, was what "is presented by the case of the Congo." In other words, as Salomon was quite rightly observing, the recognition of the International Association as a state was not a legal

370. Rolin-Jaequemyns, "L'année 1888," 169.
371. Charles Salomon *L'occupation des territoires sans maître* (Paris, 1889), 256.
372. Salomon, *L'occupation des territoires sans maître*, 256.

process; it was a political one. Proof of that political, rather than legal, creation of the state was the fact that it had "become a person in international law" at different moments depending upon the point at which it had been recognised by different states. Thus when the United States, for example, had recognised the International Association as a state, the territories of that state were still *res nullius* insofar as France was concerned and could therefore have been occupied by France while being barred to the United States.[373] What Salomon was saying was that neither the International Association, nor the Congo Free State, possessed a stable identity as a legal person in international society. Despite all the proofs and processes which Twiss and Leopold had employed to create that new legal person, it maintained a volatile character. "It is not recognition by other states," Salomon added wryly, "that robs a territory of its quality as *res nullius* if the political organism [of the new state] is at its base sufficiently developed to present to the uninitiated the character of a state."[374] The second scenario in which a company could become a state, he pointed out, is when the company in question occupies a territory and is then retrospectively licensed by a state to do so, although this case, of course, did not apply in the matter of Leopold's International Association.

The scepticism of the legal position of the Congo Free State endured into the 1890s, by which time it was accompanied by a growing knowledge that the new state was not even respecting the treaties by which it had been created. Free trade was not established in the Congo, and from 1887, a series of edicts increasingly restricted freedom of movement to a narrow zone alongside the lower Congo River. At the same time, the promises Leopold had made to bring a humanitarian regime to Congo peoples were increasingly being revealed as rhetoric which covered a spirit of plunder and abuse. Joseph Conrad began working in the Congo in 1890, and it was the moment that he met Roger Casement there, the British agent who would eventually reveal the true nature of the regime.[375] From its outset, Leopold had seen the Congo as a source of ivory. In 1887, exports of ivory from the Congo Free State were valued at 795,700 francs. By 1895, that figure had risen to 5,844,640 francs.[376] Conrad's *Heart of Darkness* was a dramatization of the abuses of that trade. The production of rubber, however, would have an even more devastating impact upon the Congo.

In 1887, John Dunlop, a Scottish veterinarian and inventor living in Northern Ireland, discovered that pneumatic rubber tires made bicycles faster and smoother to ride. In the 1880s, rubber was used for the first time, with cloth, to insulate electrical wiring, while it was also being applied to a number of other

373. Salomon, *L'occupation des territoires sans maître*, 257.
374. Salomon, *L'occupation des territoires sans maître*, 257–258.
375. Joseph Conrad, *Congo Diary*, in *Heart of Darkness*, 253.
376. "Congo Free State," *Encyclopedia Britannica* (1902), in Conrad, *Heart of Darkness*, 111.

industrial and domestic uses in Western economies. By the 1890s, demand for rubber was booming, and the most plentiful supplies, at this time, were the naturally occurring rubber vines in tropical forests, of which there was an abundance in the Congo (although they would later be supplanted by plantations of rubber trees in Malaysia and throughout Southeast Asia). In 1887, rubber production from the Congo was valued at 116,768 francs, a fraction of that of ivory; by 1895, it rivalled ivory at 2,882,585 francs, and by 1899, it had exploded in value to 28,100,917 francs, while ivory production remained static at 5,834,620 francs.[377] During the 1880s and '90s, the price of rubber rose sharply. As early as 1876, British explorer Henry Wickham took 70,000 rubber tree seeds from Brazil to the botanist Joseph Hooker, who was the director of Kew Gardens in London. Hooker succeeded in germinating the seeds and subsequently exporting the plants to Ceylon and the Malay Peninsula in 1877. The man who was director of the Singapore Botanic Gardens from 1888, Henry Ridley, then encouraged the use of those seedlings to establish rubber plantations throughout the Malay Peninsula. In the 1890s, however, plantation rubber was still in development, while the trees themselves take several years to reach a point where they produce rubber.

Leopold was aware of these developments and knew that there was a short window of opportunity to exploit the wild rubber vines of the Congo while prices remained high and before they could be overtaken by the more efficient plantations in Southeast Asia.[378] He therefore implemented a system that would extract as much rubber as possible from the Congo as quickly as possible. People living in the Congo basin had no interest in interrupting their existing economies for the purpose of farming rubber. Nevertheless, those people had the best knowledge of the forests where the rubber vines were located, and they lived in proximity to those forests. In order to persuade the reluctant people of the Congo, Leopold's agents would arrive in a village, take women, children, and old people hostage, and sell those people back to the village when their quota of rubber collection was met.[379] Villages that nevertheless refused to harvest rubber were massacred. The Force Publique—the army—was very conscious, however, of the cost of bullets. It did not want its soldiers wasting them in hunting, so it instituted a regime whereby, for each bullet used, a body part must be produced as proof of the purpose for which had been employed. Soldiers therefore took to amputating hands and limbs of villagers who they had not killed in order to account for the use of bullets.[380] Quotas could be filled either with rubber or with lives taken in lieu of

---

377. "Congo Free State," *Encyclopedia Britannica* (1902), in Conrad, *Heart of Darkness*, 111.
    378. Hochschild, *King Leopold's Ghost*, 159–160.
    379. Hochschild, *King Leopold's Ghost*, 161–162.
    380. Hochschild, *King Leopold's Ghost*, 165–166.

rubber, so the provision of hands proved the quota of lives. In consequence, both soldiers and villagers removed hands in order to prove they had fulfilled quotas. This meant that villagers would collect hands from amongst themselves or would raid neighbouring villages for hands in order to fulfil their quotas. The trade in rubber mutated into a trade in lives and limbs. The combined effects of massacres, dislocation of Congo society, mass amputations, and displacement of peoples produced a death toll of millions—precisely how many remains a moot point, although a number of sources estimate 10 million. Eventually, however, this human catastrophe came progressively to the attention of European observers, such as Conrad, Roger Casement, and Edmund Morel, who in turn brought to public attention the question of the legitimacy of the Congo Free State, leading to Leopold being obliged to hand over control of the Congo to the Belgian government in 1908.

In 1896, another French jurist, Gaston Jèze, wrote a treatise on occupation in which he examined at length the role of companies in colonisation. He argued that in the case where an "indigenous" people cede their sovereignty to an individual or a private company, their territory becomes "*nullius par derelictio*" (nobody's by dereliction). His reasoning was that it is impossible for a "*particulier,*" or private interest, to receive cessions of sovereignty because they are "*incapable*" of possessing an "*animus domini*" (intention to establish sovereignty).[381] Such an intention could only be possessed by a person, and private societies did not constitute legal persons in international society and so could not have intentions. Similarly, Jèze asked, what is the situation if an individual conquers a "barbarous state," destroying its armies and its government, "exterminating its inhabitants," and proclaims "himself sovereign"? Again, he argued, the "territory becomes *nullius* [nobody's] from the point of view of international law" because "an individual is incapable of proving an intention to establish sovereignty."[382] "Private societies," he concluded, could only become instruments of occupation from the point of view of international law when they were placed in the hands of a sovereign, never in their "own name."[383] He continually reiterated throughout this treatise that "from an international point of view, colonial companies do not exist."[384]

Although Twiss had, therefore, succeeded in a strategic battle to establish the Congo Free State, he had not succeeded in completely swaying legal opinion. He therefore republished, yet again, his most important work, *The Law of Nations Considered as Independent Political Communities . . . In Time of Peace*, which had been first published in 1861, then again in 1884 in the build-up to the Berlin Conference. In 1887, however, Twiss published his new edition

---

381. Gaston Jèze, *Étude théorique et pratique sur l'occupation* (Paris, 1896), 202–204.
382. Jèze, *Étude théorique et pratique sur l'occupation*, 205.
383. Jèze, *Étude théorique et pratique sur l'occupation*, 205.
384. Jèze, *Étude théorique et pratique sur l'occupation*, 344.

of this work in French, in the "traditional language," as he put it, "of European diplomacy," as well as the language with which Leopold was most comfortable.[385] In the new preface to this work, Twiss declared that the new edition had been justified by the advent of the Berlin Conference, which, he said, had "opened a new era in consecrating the principle that the indigenous people of the continent of Africa, constituted as independent states, have a juridical personality and should no longer be considered as being outside the community of the law of nations."[386] This was a bold statement of the argument Twiss had been developing since the 1870s. It was the argument that enabled peoples who did not conform to their duties in international society to be deprived of their sovereignty, and it was also the argument that allowed any people, in this case the "independent sovereigns" of the Congo, to cede their sovereignty to companies. "The most precious result of this conference," he continued, "was to resolve the problem of the circumstances in which the principles of the public law of Europe and America are applicable to the political associations of central Africa, organised in states under indigenous chiefs."[387] He was reminding international lawyers that no matter how much they wished to discuss the legitimacy of what happened in Berlin, the fact of the recognition of the International Association as a state at that Conference set a new precedent in international law.

Twiss added a whole new fifteenth chapter to this work devoted entirely to the question of the Berlin Conference and the creation of the Congo Free State, as well as an appendix which contained the General Act of the Conference. He therefore effectively reframed his entire general account of international law by terminating it with the transformation of the International Association into a state. He began this fifteenth chapter of his *Law of Nations* with the story of Henry Stanley's arrival at Boma, on the Lower Congo River, in 1877, after having traversed Africa from the East. He then moved to the diplomacy that led to the Berlin Conference and described the three bases that were to be negotiated at the Conference, and he gave an account of the discussions over each one of those bases: freedom of commerce, freedom of navigation, and conventions on effective occupation. In doing so, he slipped frequently from a third-person account to the first-person account of what "we" did.[388] He celebrated the agreements on free trade and free navigation, the indices of the new era in which states acted in their common interests—a regime, in the case

385. Travers Twiss, *Le droit des gens ou des nations considerées comme communautés politiques indépendantes. I. Des droits et des devoirs des nations en temps de paix* (Paris, 1887), vii. Twiss presented a copy of this work to the library of the Athenaeum in his last year of membership, after forty-four years as a member, writing *"Hommage de l'Auteur"* on the title page; see Athenaeum, Donations to the Library, 1887–1910, Lib 3/1/3.

386. Twiss, *Le droit des gens*, vi.

387. Twiss, *Le droit des gens*, vii.

388. See, for example, Twiss, *Le droit des gens*, 439.

of the Congo, that would be assured by an international commission.[389] He celebrated, also, the recognition achieved by the International Association as a state which had been established, he observed, by "separate conventions concluded with the majority of states."[390] He noted the importance whereby the new state was itself signatory to the General Act of the Conference, although, unlike Rolin-Jaequemyns, he did not argue that the signing of the Act was the measure that had created the new state. In fact, in this new edition of his treatise, Twiss did not so much argue for the legitimacy of the new state, as he had done up until 1884; rather, he simply presented the conditions that had led to its creation, while not disguising his own presence in that process.

In order that the importance of his continuing work for Leopold would not be lost on Leopold himself, Twiss sent to Paul de Borchgrave, the King's secretary, a copy of the new edition of his *Droit des gens*, asking that it be placed before the king. In his letter, he stressed that the work included: "the addition of a Special Chapter on the Berlin Conference and the General Act of the Conference."[391] On February 9, 1887, Borchgrave's draft reply to Twiss, whom he addressed as "Monsieur le Conseiller," noted the King's great pleasure on reading the work, and he conveyed the King's gratitude.[392] Whether gratitude included financial payments was not explicitly stated, but within two years, Twiss would reclaim Leopold's debt. In July of the same year, Twiss sent Borchgrave a brochure for the "hands of the King."[393] He did not give the title of the pamphlet, but it was almost certainly a copy of his *On International Conventions for the Neutralisation of Territory and Their Application to the Suez Canal*, which he had delivered earlier that year to the meeting of the Association for the Reform and Codification of the Law of Nations in the Guildhall of London. In 1882, Britain had extended military control over Egypt and the Suez Canal, but it remained a minority shareholder in the Suez Canal Company, which was controlled by the French. It was accordingly brought to the compromise of agreeing to a convention of neutrality for the canal which was being negotiated in Constantinople at the time Twiss wrote. Twiss had, for many years, been an enthusiast for the neutrality of the canal, beginning with his correspondence with Metternich, Strzelecki, and Gladstone on the subject, and his subsequent articles of the 1870s. In his 1887 pamphlet, he suggested the agreement reached in the Berlin Conference on the neutrality

---

389. Twiss, *Le droit des gens*, 440.

390. Twiss, *Le droit des gens*, 440.

391. Twiss to Borchgrave, [no date, but probably February 1887], Archives du Palais Royal, Brussels, *Commandements du Roi*, A154/40.

392. Borchgrave to Twiss, February 9, 1887, Archives du Palais Royal, Brussels, *Commandements du Roi*, A154/40.

393. Twiss to Borchgrave, July 29, 1887, Archives du Palais Royal, Brussels, *Commandements du Roi*, A 157/32.

of the Congo as a model that could be employed for Suez.[394] He pointed out that such conventions no longer contained meaningful clauses guaranteeing the obligation for powers to enforce the neutrality of a territory; they merely established a right to intervene, which might or might not be exercised in a crisis. He thereby anticipated the essential ambiguity of the neutrality of the canal established in the 1889 Constantinople Convention. Twiss's purpose in sending this pamphlet to Leopold was undoubtedly to demonstrate that the Congo Free State could be regarded as a model in international law rather than an exception. Borchgrave responded to Twiss, on August 8, that the King was grateful for the pamphlet and had read it with interest.[395]

394. Travers Twiss, *On International Conventions for the Neutralisation of Territory and Their Application to the Suez Canal* (London, 1887), 13–16.
395. Borchgrave to Twiss, August 8, 1887, Archives du Palais Royal, Brussels, *Commandements du Roi*, A 157/, 32–33.

PART 5

Civil Death

WITH THE TRIUMPH of the Berlin Conference and his participation in the life of international law, Travers Twiss and Pharaïlde Twiss also, it seemed, had put the nightmare of their marriage scandal behind them. Such was not, however, the case. Alexander Chaffers was a tenacious and obsessive adversary. He was seemingly motivated by hatred which proved to be more enduring than blackmail as he pursued the question of Pharaïlde Twiss for years beyond the point at which he could possibly hope for material gain. We have seen that, in the aftermath of the trial in 1872, Chaffers had sought a summons for perjury against Pharaïlde Twiss and her purported former maid, Louisa Hamilton. On that occasion, the magistrate, Mr Benson, who had also sat in the trial for libel, had "declined to accede" to the request. Ten years later, Chaffers discovered that Pharaïlde Twiss was once again living in the country, and he applied again at Southwark Police Court, this time before a new magistrate, Mr Bridge. Chaffers explained the circumstances of the original trial and pointed out that the case against him was discharged "owing to the absence of Lady Twiss." The magistrate asked, "How is it you have allowed 10 years to elapse before taking such proceedings?" Chaffers replied, "Lady Twiss left the country, and I have only recently ascertained that she is living at 37 Hamilton Terrace. I now wish for a warrant, not so much for her punishment as her extradition."[1] The 1881 census showed Twiss to be living at 71 Hamilton Terrace in St John's Wood—in the street, that is, in which he had lived as a boy, where his sister continued to occupy number 35 with her husband, George Marsden, until at least the 1860s, and around the corner from the house Twiss had rented for Agnes Willoughby in the late '50s. The same 1881 census revealed that Chaffers was an inmate of St Pancras Workhouse, where he had first been admitted on February 5, 1879.[2]

---

1. "The Twiss Libel Case," *Lloyds Weekly*, April 30, 1882, 8.
2. "Alexander Chaffers," in Frederic Boase, *Modern English Biography*, Vol. 4, 1908, 628.

The 1891 census showed Chaffers again to be in the St Pancras Workhouse, and he died in there in April 1899. Presumably, in 1882, he had temporarily regained his freedom during the previous twelve months because, according to his own account, he could not pursue litigation while in the workhouse. Indeed, from 1882 to 1889, Chaffers aided Georgina Weldon in preparation of the numerous lawsuits that had initially been launched by her husband's attempt to have her committed to an asylum. Although Weldon represented herself in court, by most accounts, Chaffers worked for her during these years in an office in Red Lion Court, near the Inns of Court, and it may well have been Weldon who kept him out of the workhouse.[3]

What Chaffers revealed in his testimony to the magistrate in 1882 was that Travers Twiss had moved during the previous year into number 37—that is, into the house next door to the family house. Pharaïlde Twiss was not named as also living at 71 Hamilton Terrace in the 1881 census, so it would appear that she returned to London following the 1881 census or in 1882 and that, with her return, the Twisses moved from number 71 to the slightly larger residence at number 37. This was a moment at which Twiss was beginning vigorously to promote Leopold's African plans, so it may, for that reason, correspond with an improvement in his finances. Certainly, he was recovering some of his professional status. Even if the scandal of his marriage continued to dog him in the press, he and Pharaïlde were apparently sufficiently optimistic to judge that she could return from exile on the continent. Strikingly, Chaffers was not seeking damages for libel against himself, but rather to have Pharaïlde Twiss deported. The magistrate advised him, however, that he would not grant a warrant or a summons and that, "in such a case after ten years," he advised Chaffers to set the facts before the Public Prosecutor. Chaffers responded that such a course would be "useless," and the magistrate commented, "Then I cannot help you." The report concluded: "Applicant then left the court with his papers." Although unsuccessful in his legal pursuit, Chaffers was succeeding in reminding the public, through newspapers reporting his efforts, of the scandal surrounding the Twisses.

He succeeded further in stirring such publicity just a few weeks later when, in July, he brought a case of defamation against Alexander Macmillan, one of the two brothers who had established Macmillan publishing. Alexander Macmillan duly appeared in Bow Street Police Court in answer to the summons from Chaffers claiming that he had published an account of the 1872 libel trial that defamed Chaffers. Macmillan's *Supplement to the Annals of Our Time: A Diurnal of Events, Social and Political, Home and Foreign from February 24, 1871, to March 19, 1874* had in 1875 published an account of the

---

3. "Alexander Chaffers," in Boase, *Modern English Biography*, Vol. 4, 628, claims that Chaffers also represented Weldon in court. See also Taggart, "Alexander Chaffers," 663.

1872 Twiss trial that once again brought the story back to public attention.[4] The account in *Annals of Our Time* was not only difficult for the Twisses but also for former friends such as Lady Rutherford Alcock, who was named as having presented Pharaïlde Twiss at the Court of St James. At the same time, the account accused Chaffers of having blackmailed the Twisses with sham actions, something he had consistently denied at the time of the trial. Chaffers had to wait seven years, until 1882, to sue Macmillan for defamation because he spent most of his time in the workhouse. His suit against Macmillan once again led to a full recounting of his charges against Lady Twiss. His account was heard again in court and then published in such popular newspapers as *Lloyds Weekly* in 1882. Not only were the embarrassing details for the Twisses retold, but Lady Alcock was once again named as the person who presented Lady Twiss at court.[5] Chaffers's case against Macmillan required that he read out in court the report in *Annals of Our Time*. That report contained lengthy passages from the trial, including the magistrate, Mr Benson's, concluding comments that Chaffers's conduct "will cling to you as a reproach to the end of your days, and you will live an object of contempt to all honest men." To this, the defending counsel remarked, "A prophecy that has been fully realised." Chaffers responded that no evidence had been cited to prove that he had brought sham actions. The magistrate asked him, however, to prove that he had been libelled—that is, to prove that he had not brought sham actions for the purpose of blackmail. With Chaffers floundering, the case was dismissed.

In 1884, Chaffers applied to the Master of the Rolls, the office responsible for admitting solicitors to practice, for a certificate to resume practice as a solicitor. The Master of the Rolls at this time was William Brett, Lord Esher. When Chaffers appeared at the hearing before Lord Esher, the counsel for the Incorporated Law Society, Mr Hollands, opposed the application on the grounds of Chaffers's "disgraceful conduct" in the Twiss case. Hollands read magistrate Benson's concluding remarks to Lord Esher, who refused Chaffers's application on the grounds of his being unfit.[6] Undeterred, Chaffers applied again to the Master of the Rolls in 1885 for readmission as a solicitor, and Lord Esher again refused the application.[7] Chaffers then applied in 1885 to the High Court of Justice for reinstatement as a solicitor. His case was heard by Lord Coleridge, who had defended Agnes Willoughby in the Windham lunacy trial and prosecuted in the Tichborne trial. It had been Coleridge who, in 1872, as Attorney General, in response to a question in parliament on the abuse of the law of statutory declaration in the Twiss case, refused to change the law,

---

4. *Supplement to the Annals of Our Time: A Diurnal of Events, Social and Political, Home and Foreign from February 24, 1871, to March 19, 1874*, 61.

5. *Lloyds Weekly*, July 23, 1882, 8.

6. "Action against the South London Press," *South London Press*, May 22, 1886, 4.

7. "Action against the South London Press," *South London Press*, May 22, 1886, 4.

as he put it, because of the abuse of "one scoundrel," namely Chaffers. Chaffers now sought from him the right to practice again as a solicitor. Coleridge and Justice Manistry, the judge accompanying him, agreed that they did not have jurisdiction to determine the question and referred Chaffers to the Master of the Rolls, apparently unaware that Chaffers had already explored that avenue.[8] Once again, this proceeding attracted the press, who were always happy to arouse prurient interest in the Twiss case through expressing moral indignation at Chaffers's exploits. The account in *The Times* was factual, but the *South London Press* published a sensational report celebrating Chaffers's failure. "'Alexander Chaffers, Gent.,'" the report began, "has got his well merited deserts. Any man who could pitilessly prosecute any lady as he did Lady Twiss deserves to be barred from the Rolls for ever."[9] The report then rehearsed the story of the Twiss trial in order to justify this judgement, and the newspaper stated that Chaffers had been barred by the High Court of Justice due to disgraceful conduct. The timing of this report could not have been worse for Twiss, who should have been celebrating the signing of the General Act of the Berlin Conference two days before, on February 26. For his part, Chaffers responded by suing the *South London Press* for defamation, arguing, correctly, that his application had not been refused by the High Court of Justice due to his disgraceful behaviour—that had been the basis for the refusal by the Master of the Rolls—but because the judges determined that they did not possess jurisdiction over the matter.

Chaffers's suit for libel and damages of £1,000 against James Henderson, the publisher of the *South London Press*, was heard in the Lord Mayor's Court, before a jury, on May 19, 1886.[10] The testimony in this case would produce the most detailed recounting yet of the Twiss trial, with the defence, in particular, attempting to use the details of the events of 1872 and the relations between Chaffers and Pharaïlde van Lynseele and Twiss prior to 1872 as a means of substantiating the claim that he deserved to be barred from the rolls. Henderson's lawyer, Mr Murphy, QC, defended him by arguing that he had made a minor error in reporting that the High Court of Justice had refused to reinstate Chaffers as a solicitor but that his newspaper's description of Chaffers's character, particularly of Chaffers as a blackmailer, and of the nature of the Twiss case was otherwise "fair and accurate." Murphy said that his client was prepared to pay for his error and had brought forty shillings to court to pay the plaintiff. Chaffers, who represented himself in court, as always, and who was seeking £1,000 in damages, responded that forty shillings was "not sufficient to satisfy his claim."[11]

8. "In the Matter of Chaffers, Once an Attorney," *The Times*, February 19, 1885, 3.
9. *South London Press*, February 28, 1885.
10. "Action against the South London Press," *South London Press*, May 22, 1886, 4.
11. "Action against the South London Press," *South London Press*, May 22, 1886, 4.

To win the case, therefore, Murphy set about demonstrating that Chaffers was the villainous person his client's newspaper had described. For his part, Chaffers began by arguing that he had never blackmailed Pharaïlde and Travers Twiss. *The South London Press*, Chaffers observed, had claimed that he had only made his accusations against Lady Twiss public when Travers and Lady Twiss had refused to pay him any more money. He said this was untrue and that he had never, at any time, accepted any payment for blackmail. Ingeniously, the witness he attempted to call to substantiate that fact was Sir Travers Twiss. Chaffers observed: "He had hoped to call Sir Travers Twiss a witness; but, unfortunately, after various attempts, he had been unable to find him." This failure was not for want of trying—he tried to find Twiss at the Inns of Court, at 3 Paper Buildings, Temple, the professional address he had used since he had resigned his offices in 1872: "He had called four or five times at the chambers of Sir Travers Twiss. On the first occasion, he was told he would be back at 5 o'clock, but he did not return. He called two or three times afterwards, and was told that Sir Travers Twiss was at Brussels, and would return the next day. On the following day, he was told Sir Travers had returned from Brussels, but had not come down to his chambers."[12] Chaffers was right, of course, that Travers Twiss could never testify that he had been blackmailed because to do so would be to admit the truth of the claims made against Lady Twiss. His account of the search for Twiss suggests some desperation to avoid Chaffers, but also that Twiss was still busy working for Leopold in Brussels in the year after the Berlin Conference. It was in August of this year, less than three months from this trial, that Leopold awarded Twiss the Commander of the Order of Leopold.

Mr Murphy now turned to questioning Chaffers, which, in turn, meant that the prosecution was obliged to step into the witness box, albeit not without a tussle: "Mr Murphy asked that Mr Chaffers should be sworn. / Plaintiff [Chaffers]: I ask them to produce these two affidavits [stating that Chaffers had blackmailed Twiss]. / Mr Murphy: I produce nothing. Will you, Mr Chaffers, go into the box? / Plaintiff: I am not afraid of that. / The Recorder [i.e., lower judge]: You are the plaintiff. / Plaintiff: Very well, I will go into the box." Chaffers swore that he never received money in the nature of blackmail from the Twisses. Murphy then asked him if his application to the Master of the Rolls for reinstatement as a solicitor had been refused on the grounds of "disgraceful conduct." Chaffers replied, "I think he did." After recounting how Chaffers had sent his statutory declaration to the Lord Chamberlain, Dr Tristram, the Archbishop of Canterbury, and others, Murphy turned to the trial itself: "Did you conduct your case in person?—I did. / Did you ask Lady Twiss, amongst other things, whether she had been suffering from a certain disease? / - I did. / Did you cross-examine her for two days about alleged intimacy with you and other men?—I did. / Did you allege that from April, 1859, until her marriage

---

12. "Action against the South London Press," *South London Press*, May 22, 1886, 4.

with Sir Travers Twiss in August, 1862, that she had been living the life of a common prostitute in London?—I did."[13] The cross-examination continued in this manner, keeping faithfully to the details of the original trial, often to the amusement of the court: "Did she say she was the daughter of an officer in the Polish army?—Either the Polish or the Dutch army, I don't know which. Sometimes it is one, and sometimes the other. / The Recorder: According to that answer it was both. (Laughter) / Witness: So it would appear from her."[14] Murphy then pointed out that Mr Benson's concluding remarks in the Twiss trial had been presented to the Master of the Rolls when Chaffers had applied for readmission as a solicitor. The Master of Rolls had observed: "I have seen this libel. I cannot conceive that it was within the bounds of the remotest idea of propriety or good conduct, even supposing the facts were true, that this libel should have been published in the way it was and acted upon, and I cannot think that the person so acting with regard to the libel in the substance and the way it was brought forward can now properly come to ask for indulgence or a renewed certificate, and I decline to grant it."[15] Chaffers conceded those were the words of the Master of the Rolls.

Murphy now turned to the matter of blackmail: "After Sir Travers Twiss's marriage were you received as a guest at his house?—I was. / By the woman you allege was a common prostitute?—I was. / Did that continue for some three or four years?—at all events, after the marriage?—I think about two years. / Did you make a claim for some money?—I made a claim for costs due to me. / For advising Lady Twiss?—Yes. / For business done for her as a 'prostitute'?—No. For several things—making the agreement of a house. / How much did you claim?—I think it was 175 pounds for work and for defending an action. / Did you first of all get 50 pounds that they might first of all be rid of you?—I got 50 pounds. / Did you give a receipt in full?—Yes, but it was obtained from me by fraud. / By Lady Twiss?—Yes. / A fraud on 'Chaffers, gent.' et cetera.?—Just so. (Laughter)."[16] Murphy then cross-examined Chaffers in detail on his further demands upon the Twisses and their payments, as well as the circumstances of Chaffers's own bankruptcy in 1866. He came to the statutory declaration: "It was on the 4th of April, 1871, that you filed a statutory declaration before Mr Vaughan?—Certainly. / Describing Lady Twiss as an abandoned woman?—The declaration speaks for itself. / Did you not do so, sir? / The declaration will speak for itself. I don't believe I used the word 'abandoned' in the declaration. / Did you allege that she had been immoral before her marriage? / Certainly. / And that you had slept with her over and over again? / Certainly. / Yes, I think you said so, and that you 'gave her a

---

13. "Action against the South London Press," *South London Press*, May 22, 1886, 4.
14. "Action against the South London Press," *South London Press*, May 22, 1886, 4.
15. "Action against the South London Press," *South London Press*, May 22, 1886, 4.
16. "Action against the South London Press," *South London Press*, May 22, 1886, 4.

sovereign' was, I think, the phrase used?—Certainly. / And that you had slept in bed with her when another woman was there also?—Certainly."[17]

Following Murphy's cross-examination, Chaffers switched roles from witness for the defence to prosecution of the case. He declined to call witnesses and instead made a statement to the jury defending his actions in the Twiss trial. He said he had been prosecuted for libel in the "most malicious" way. His letters to the Lord Chamberlain and the Archbishop of Canterbury had been, he said, "privileged communications." He had performed his duty because Lady Twiss's introduction to Court had been a "gross outrage on society." He had been "ruined and persecuted for years merely because I did a public duty." He had never blackmailed the Twisses, and he asked the jury for "damages for this gross and malicious libel."[18] Mr Murphy then summarised his case by stating that if the jury believed Alexander Chaffers's account of his motives in seeking "costs" against the Twisses, then they should award him damages against the *South London Press*. If, however, as a consequence of looking at the circumstances in which he made those demands, they concluded that he had other motives, then they would be obliged to agree with the Master of the Rolls, who had considered the matter twice, and the Incorporated Law Society, who had independently formed their own conclusions as to Chaffers's character.

Chaffers, Murphy argued, was far more insidious than a normal blackmailer. Blackmail usually entailed a threat such as "Pay me 1000 pounds, or I will bring some unpleasant things before the public." Chaffers, however, "in the position of a solicitor," clothed his "extortion under the name of a bill of costs." His method contained a "depth of cunning" that was "a thousand times worse." "In an unhappy moment," Murphy observed, "the weak husband—for weak he seems to have been—gives him £50 and Chaffers gives a receipt in full of all demands, showing whether this was an extortionate claim or an honest one. He has now got a taste of the blood, and he waits quietly for a month or two, and then out comes a claim again ... Chaffers had tasted blood money twice, they have not the pluck to refuse it—and £75 finds its way into his pocket, another receipt being given ... Sir Travers Twiss is about to be made, or is made, a Queen's Advocate ... What would you give for the character of such a man if there was nothing more or less than that in the case? He enjoys a woman's favours, becomes her guest when she is married, draws £50 and £75, and wants more ... Just imagine the advantage to the Archbishop of Canterbury of knowing that Chaffers had slept with Lady Twiss before her marriage! It is playing with you to put forward such a pretence as the public good ... And he has the hardihood to come here and ask you to say that the motive that actuated him was to keep her Majesty's Court clear of improper people! If there is any man in this country who is not entitled to complain of

---

17. "Action against the South London Press," *South London Press*, May 22, 1886, 4.
18. "Action against the South London Press," *South London Press*, May 22, 1886, 4.

improper people, I should think it is 'Chaffers, gent.' who cross-examined Lady Twiss as to whether he had not slept in the same bed with her and another woman, and who cross-examines her for two days. This is the man that pollutes the air of this court by coming forward and pretending that by what he did he was not endeavouring to levy blackmail, but only doing his duty as an honourable citizen of this country! (Applause in court)."[19] Murphy was certainly right about Chaffers's hardihood. He had an extraordinary determination to continue to pursue Pharaïlde Twiss, regardless of the consequences for himself. He had been vilified and rebuked in courts and newspapers already for fourteen years at this point. Murphy said his client had simply stated, following the judgement of the Master of the Rolls, "Let us have no more it. We have had too much of it." Chaffers, he argued, should be stopped from "perpetually raking up this matter." The Recorder summarised the case to the jury with overt sympathy for the defendant. The jury took ten minutes to reach their decision: namely, that no damages should be awarded and that the 40 shillings the defendant had offered should not be paid. Chaffers, however, was not finished with the Twisses.

There was seemingly no escape for Travers or Pharaïlde Twiss from their past. The new actions brought by Chaffers were widely reported, with the details of the history of the case. The May 1886 headline in *The Times* summarised the problem for the Twisses: "The Travers Twiss Scandal: Another Action for Libel."[20] Within three weeks of failing in his suit against Henderson, Chaffers appeared again, this time in the Lord Mayor's Court, applying for a new trial against Henderson on the grounds that he "was taken by surprise" in the previous trial when cross-examined on the question of the "costs due to him by Sir Travers Twiss."[21] What Chaffers called "costs," of course, were what his critics called blackmail. With interest, he declared, Twiss would now owe him £300 if it were not for the statute of limitations. The court Recorder told him that a trial on the "ground of surprise" would most likely fail and that, in any case, he was applying at the wrong time.

The stories of Leopold's corporation through which he ruled the Congo and the story of Pharaïlde Twiss had been linked through Twiss himself. They were linked simply because the Twisses' disastrous marriage scandal created the circumstances through which Twiss was forced to find employment outside Britain and so was driven into Leopold's arms. They were linked conceptually through the connection between the creation of new legal persons in civil law, particularly through marriage law, to the creation of new legal persons in international law—this was the process of analogical thinking through which

---

19. "Action against the South London Press," *South London Press*, May 22, 1886, 4.
20. "The Travers Twiss Scandal," *The Times*, May 22, 3; see also "Action for Libel," *The Times*, May 20, 1886, 10.
21. "Charge of Libel," *The Times*, June 10, 1886, 5.

international law developed new principles. In 1889, the paths of Pharaïlde Twiss and Leopold united as Pharaïlde came completely under the power of Leopold. Pharaïlde Twiss may well have met Leopold during the exiled years that she and Travers had spent in Brussels. Travers Twiss had worked closely with Leopold in the late '70s and '80s, and it possible his wife had accompanied him to social events in the royal palace in Brussels. Now, however, he brought his wife to Leopold's attention in a very painful way.

As we have seen, as recently as 1887, Twiss had reissued the first volume of his *Law of Nations* in French and had adapted it to the necessities of justifying the Congo Free State. He had also brought that service to Leopold's attention, as well as keeping him in touch with his latest pamphlets showing that the Congo Free State could be a model for international law. Having provided so much for Leopold, Twiss now sought a service in return. On April 17, 1889, Borchgrave, Leopold's Cabinet Secretary, wrote a note to the King which came with two enclosed letters. One was a dispatch from the Prince Chimay which had arrived late the previous evening. The other enclosed paper, Borchgrave related, was "a letter from Sir Travers Twiss which he asked me to bring to your majesty's attention."[22] Unfortunately, Twiss's letter of April 17 has not survived, but underneath Borchgrave's note, Leopold responded to his secretary, clearly having read the letter, by instructing him to "Demand very confidentially from Lord Vivian what has happened to Sir Travers Twiss, and ask if the English government can do nothing for him." Leopold added, "I don't know what I can do." Lord Vivian was Hussey Vivian, the 3rd Baron Vivian, a British career diplomat and plenipotentiary in Brussels, serving as Britain's representative to the slave-trade conference in Brussels in November 1889, a conference which Twiss also attended.[23] In April, Leopold was busy preparing for the conference on slavery, and he was seeking, with Prime Minister Auguste Beernaert, to coordinate Belgium's position at the conference with Britain. In particular, while the conference would serve his purpose in continuing to promote the Congo Free State as a humanitarian project, he was anxious, as he wrote to Beernaert, that it should not "restrain" his state's "recruitment of blacks."[24] In other words, he did not want the signing at the conference of the mooted treaty to suppress slavery and to interfere with the forced labour practices employed by his state. The colonial powers who signed the Act agreed with Leopold on this point, so the *Convention Relative to the Slave Trade and Importation into Africa of Firearms, Ammunition, and Spiritous Liquors,* signed in 1890, did nothing to change the conditions prevailing within African colonies. In order

22. Borchgrave to Leopold, April 17, 1889, Archives du Palais Royal, Brussels, *Commandements du Roi*, A168/16.

23. "Vivian, Hussey Crespigny, 3rd Baron Vivian," *Oxford Dictionary of National Biography* (Oxford, 2019).

24. Leopold to Beernaert, May 1, 1889, in Edouard van der Smissen, *Léopold et Beernaert d'après leur correspondance inédite de 1884 à 1894*, Vol. 1 (Brussels, 1920), 412.

FIGURE 18. Lord Vivian.*

to ensure the feebleness of the treaty, Leopold was in discussions with Lord Vivian over the British position in the last two weeks of April, and he wrote to Beernaert, on April 21, so that he, Leopold, and the Prince de Chimay could meet together and coordinate their written response to Vivian.[25] This was why news of Chimay's arrival in Brussels came with Twiss's own letter, but it also reveals that Leopold was in constant contact with Vivian at the time he asked Borchgrave to speak to him about Pharaïlde Twiss.

25. Leopold to Beernaert, April 21, 1889, in van der Smissen, *Léopold et Beernaert*, 411.
* Hussey Crespigny Vivian, 3rd Baron Vivian, National Portrait Gallery, London, Photographs Collection, NPG x13266

Indeed, Vivian had a working relationship with Leopold and the palace, and had been in Brussels for five years, so he would have had a good knowledge of eminent expatriates such Twiss, but he had also, as we shall see, became entangled in Pharaïlde and Travers Twiss's affairs. Before Borchgrave could complete his enquiry with Lord Vivian, the following day, on April 18, 1889, Leopold received another letter from Twiss which fortunately has survived. Twiss wrote in French from his Brussels address, 19 rue de la Chancellerie, across the park and almost next door to the Royal Palace. How long he had been at this address is uncertain, but he was cited as still being the tenant there four years later when the house was sold.[26] The letter was short:

> Sire, I beg your majesty to forgive my indiscretion in recommending to His Majesty's gracious kindness my wife Lady Twiss and in pleading with His Majesty to accord her his kindly protection. I have suffered so much misfortune, that I cannot come to her aid to meet certain very grave commitments that could compromise my honour.
>
> I beg your Majesty to believe that my heart is indeed broken to dare to hope for help in your kindness.
>
> I beg your Majesty will accept the respectful homage of his very faithful servant, Travers Twiss.[27]

The most obviously shocking aspect of this letter is that Twiss was handing his wife over to Leopold, placing her under Leopold's "protection" and thereby forgoing any further responsibility to her. Although Leopold had declared he did not know of any way he could assist Twiss in his predicament, Twiss had resolved on the best course himself. His conviction that Leopold would accept, as he did, underlined his sense of Leopold's debt to himself. Nevertheless, the dramatic nature of Twiss "recommending" his wife to Leopold's "protection" raises the question of whether such an act was legal. Under the Napoleonic code which prevailed in Belgium in the nineteenth century, the little power that women had over themselves they virtually lost upon marrying.[28] Speaking metaphorically, they were treated as chattels, but whether they could literally legally be passed between hands is another matter. It is surprising that Twiss could simply place his wife in the hands of the King, and strictly speaking, the act was probably not lawful. The 1807 Code Napoléon stated, "A husband has a duty of protection to his wife, and she a duty of obedience to him," and

---

26. *Indépendence Belge*, July 21, 1893, 3.
27. Twiss to Leopold, April 18, 1889, Archives du Palais Royal, Brussels, *Commandements du Roi*, A168/16.
28. René Piret, "Le Code Napoléon en Belgique de 1804 à 1954," *Revue internationale de droit comparé*, vol. 4 (1954), 753–791.

it did not state that the husband could alienate that duty.[29] Twiss's act suggests a rather feudal and aristocratic mentality—the mentality of the *Ancien Régime*—and, as such, is reminiscent of his appeal to the medieval precedents of the Teutonic Knights and the Order of Knights of the Hospital of St John of Jerusalem as a basis for a seemingly liberal expansion of the rights of non-state associations in international society. While the invention of Pharaïlde van Lynseele as Lady Twiss had a resonance with liberal visions of personal improvement, her loss of liberty through a seemingly feudal act underlines the limits of her transformation, as well as the limits of liberal improvements in the legal position of women.

Travers Twiss's letter to Leopold also hints at the life that Travers and Pharaïlde Twiss had led since the scandal of 1872, or at least in recent years. It would appear, according to Travers, that Pharaïlde, now 55 years old, had been implicated in a further scandal which had led to "certain very grave commitments," by which he probably meant blackmail. In saying his failure to meet those commitments would compromise his honour, he probably meant that the blackmailers would release new information concerning his wife. This aspect of the letter was clarified by further correspondence between Borchgrave and Leopold, following up on Borchgrave's interview with Lord Vivian.

Two days after Twiss's letter asking Leopold to take his wife off his hands, Borchgrave wrote to Leopold as follows:

> I saw Lord Vivian. He told me that Sir Travers Twiss is in financial embarrassments, but has been for quite a long time already. Certain people have for a long time been blackmailing him, threatening to publish certain matters, facts relating to Lady Twiss, a woman whose background does not recommend her. Lady Twiss has already paid, and frequently, but she is at the end of her means and we have already made in her favour a personal demand upon Lord Vivian. He told me that he would give nothing and he seems to be convinced that the English government will do nothing for Sir Travers Twiss. The person who came to the house of the English minister [i.e., Lord Vivian's house] on the part of Lady Twiss said that she needed several thousand francs. He said to me also, confidentially, that Lady Twiss was presented at the Court some years ago but that her name had subsequently been scratched from the list. / Sir Travers Twiss has just sent to the Palace his work "Le droit des gens ou des Nations considerée comme communautés politiques Indépendentes. Droits et devoirs en temps de guerre." New edition in French. The volume has on the first

---

29. *Code Napoléon. Édition originale et seule officielle* (Paris, 1807), Book 1, Titre 5, Ch. 6: "Des droits et des devoirs respectifs des époux," 213, 55.

page: Respectful homage from the author to His Majesty the King of Belgians.[30]

What Vivian was able to reveal was that Pharaïlde and Travers Twiss had once again been blackmailed and for a long time. Clearly, the Twisses had been bled dry. What precisely the new scandal relating to Lady Twiss was we do not know. Nor do we know the identity of the person who had visited Lord Vivian's house to request money to pay the blackmailers—it was not Travers Twiss, as he would hardly have dragged up Pharaïlde Twiss's more distant scandal in 1872. The several thousand francs that this person, possibly the blackmailer himself, requested from Lord Vivian, was equivalent to hundreds of pounds, or the annual earnings of a middle-class English gentleman. It was a sum which Twiss was able to pay when at the height of his career but was now well beyond his means. The refusal of Vivian or the English government to come to Twiss's aid was consistent with their position over the previous seventeen years, and his service in Berlin had changed nothing in that regard. Leopold, however, was sufficiently grateful to help, not only in making a financial claim upon Lord Vivian himself and the British government, but in terms of taking responsibility for Pharaïlde Twiss.

As if to underline the connection between the situation of his wife and his services for the Congo Free State, Twiss chose this moment also to send Leopold a gift of his French translation of the second volume of his *Law of Nations*.[31] The first volume, on the law of nations in times of peace, had been the subject of his correspondence with Leopold in 1887 when it was published. It was no coincidence that he abandoned Pharaïlde at the moment he published the second volume, in which his theory of the law of nations had been rewritten to justify the appearance of the Congo Free State in the society of nations. He was trading upon his capital, but more than that, there had always been in his mind the analogy between the natural person and the state, while matters of marriage and international law had always been closely bound in his legal practice.

There is no reason to suppose that Leopold would have thought Twiss to be guilty of moral turpitude for having married a prostitute. He did not share his cousin Victoria's attitude to such matters. In fact, Leopold was known for the openness with which he kept his mistresses. The most notorious of these, Caroline Lacroix, he had met ten years after Borchgrave wrote with Lord Vivian's news about Pharaïlde Twiss and, like Pharaïlde, Lacroix too was a prostitute. Lacroix was 16 when she met the 64-year-old Leopold in Paris.[32] At this time,

---

30. Borchgrave to Leopold, April 20, 1889, Archives du Palais Royal, Brussels, *Commandements du Roi*, A168/16–17.

31. Borchgrave to Twiss, April 20, 1889, Archives du Palais Royal, Brussels, *Commandements du Roi*, A168/16–17.

32. For a romanticised account, see *A Commoner Married to a King, as told by Baroness Vaughan to Paul Faure* (Binghamton, 1937).

she had been the mistress already for some time of a former French officer who paid his gambling debts with her sexual services.[33] Leopold became obsessed with her, showering her with gifts, jewellery, and clothing, as well as giving her the title Baroness Vaughan and installing her in a villa next to his Laeken residence, connected to his palace by an overpass.

During the last ten years of Leopold's life, Lacroix amassed a fortune of many millions. Public sentiment in Belgium turned against her, led by the socialists, as the relationship revealed the degree to which the riches Leopold was by now amassing from his African empire were being spent upon his own pleasure rather than the benefit of the country. Leopold and Lacroix finally married on his death bed, although the ceremony was not recognised in law because it was religious rather than civil. In the public imagination, Lacroix was identified with Leopold's African wealth, earning her the nickname *la reine du Congo*. Adam Hochschild comments upon the irony that, in Belgium, greater concern was aroused about Leopold's management of the Congo by the association with Lacroix than by the atrocities committed in his empire.[34] As we have seen with Pharaïlde Twiss, this was not the first time that a woman in such a position would become tied to the imagination of empire. The relations between gender and empire are so complex, and so contingent upon particular historical circumstances, that generalisation, as Mrinalina Sinha has observed, is "futile." Nevertheless, gender and empire were both built upon relations of power. In the nineteenth century, Europeans closely identified the nation with "a particular historical form of the family": namely, "the heterosexual, bourgeois, nuclear family—and the normative constructions of sexuality and gender identities that sustain this family-form."[35] Europeans were able to justify increasingly liberal regimes at home, while at the same time maintaining despotic regimes in their empires, by constructing both racial and gendered differences. One such difference was based upon the divergence of non-European societies from the ideal of the nuclear family. The reason Lacroix profiting from Leopold's African empire aroused such indignation in Belgium was that the very public nature of her role not only challenged the ideal of the nuclear family upon which the empire partially was justified—it was essential to the humanitarian imperial mission that intervention in non-European societies was based upon the moral superiority of European culture and the promise to extend that culture globally—but, moreover, her and Leopold's flaunting of their relationship recalled the "Oriental concubinage" that was believed to underpin the inferiority of non-European peoples.

33. Hochschild, *King Leopold's Ghost*, 221–224.
34. Hochschild, *King Leopold's Ghost*, 222.
35. Mrinalina Sinha, "Nations in an Imperial Crucible," in Philippa Levine, ed., *Gender and Empire* (Oxford, 2004), 187–188.

Pharaïlde Twiss found herself entangled in similar narratives, but her case was not the same. Empire and marriage were again connected. Empire was pursued through the law of nations, and the law of nations was a branch from the same body of law as ecclesiastical and marriage law. Ecclesiastical and marriage law provided principles upon which the law of nations could be extrapolated. The example of *territorium nullius*, applied to sacred land, is one such case of ecclesiastical law brought to the law of nations—a pertinent example because it was Twiss who drew that particular analogy. Another such case was the creation of legal persons. This was a practice particularly deep in ecclesiastical law—for example, in the creation of new bishops—and it is clear that the law of nations drew upon ecclesiastical law in this sense when it turned to the question of the nation as a legal person. Creating new persons was also, in ecclesiastical law, part of marriage. When a woman married, she was re-created as a new legal person with her husband. Given the deep links between ecclesiastical law and the law of nations, it was hardly surprising that, when Twiss began to think about the possibility of extending the existing understanding of the boundaries of the legal personality of states, he could look to marriage for new principles. The culture of the "age of extended of franchises," as Gladstone called it, was one that inspired the transformation in status, and aspirations for transformation in status, of numerous Victorians. It was this culture that Pharaïlde van Lynseele had exploited for her own metamorphoses—a transformation that exceeded the boundaries of even the expanded understanding of the period. It was also this culture, and his wife's transformation, that formed the background to Twiss's professional reflex of looking to private law analogies to create new possibilities in the law of nations, specifically for the Congo. It was not surprising, therefore, that Twiss would make a connection between his wife and Leopold.

When, however, Pharaïlde Twiss's metamorphosis unravelled, it posed a question about the legitimacy of the analogy that had been drawn from her example and others like it. It was also not surprising that Travers Twiss would turn to Leopold for a solution to that problem. If one metamorphosis that exceeded conventional boundaries could be an inspiration to another, the process could not be permitted to work in reverse: that is, the unravelling of Pharaïlde van Lynseele's reinvention could not be seen to throw a shadow upon another reinvention, that of the Congo, or upon the lawyer who had performed much of the work of transformation. In short, Leopold could not have the reputation of his new state tarnished by scandal attached to the lawyer who had achieved its transformation from a private company, particularly if such a lawyer was seen to have been involved in the dubious creation of new persons. Of course, the Twiss scandal had been public and had tarnished Twiss's reputation, which was partly the reason he found himself working for Leopold in the first place, but the scandal had always been generated by the claims of one eccentric man. The new scandal associated with Pharaïlde Twiss, to which Travers Twiss alluded in his letter to Leopold, would have established beyond doubt that hers had been a transformation beyond the bounds of convention, and Twiss would have been implicated in that scandal. Pharaïlde, therefore, had to be dealt with.

The consequences of Pharaïlde Twiss finding her destiny determined by Leopold could not have been graver for her. At this point, she lost the agency she had exercised throughout her life. In contrast, as we have seen, Agnes Willoughby succeeded in maintaining power over her affairs until the end of her life. We only learn of Pharaïlde Twiss's fate from a chance comment in English ecclesiastical correspondence three years later. Because Travers Twiss had held the post of Vicar General to the Archbishop of Canterbury until 1872, later occupants of the position consulted him from time to time on matters that had been determined under his tenure. The consultations were a source of income for Twiss. In 1892, John Hassard, the incumbent Vicar General, wrote to Twiss seeking his advice on matters relating to the fees charged by the clergy (for example, for marriages and funerals). On October 26, Twiss wrote to Hassard from "Riverside," in Middlesex, where he was now living: "I have enclosed a larger letter in answer to your questions as to the past . . . With regard to the Cheques which you kindly mention you may either send them payable to T.T. or Bearer and Crossed as last year or keep them until I come up to London which I propose to do either towards the end of 2nd week or towards the middle of the third week of November."[36] Twiss, it would seem, was now reclusive and receiving annual cheques for his consultation work, but the sums involved appear to have been minimal. Upon reading Twiss's letter, Hassard wrote to the Archbishop of Canterbury, who was now Edward Benson (Twiss's friend Archbishop Archibald Tait had died in 1882): "Your Grace asked me to send you any further information about 'The Clergy Fees.' / As Sir Travers Twiss is alive (at 83 or 84 years of age) and was the Vicar General of the Archbishop of Canterbury and was the advisor of Archbishop Sumner in 1857, I thought it well, to try and collect his views." Benson then wrote at length on the matter of the fees but included a postscript that reveals Pharaïlde Twiss's fate: "p.s. Riverside is at Ashford in Middlesex but Sir Travers Twiss does not care for the address to be known. His unfortunate wife (Lady Twiss) is, I hear, now, in a Lunatic Asylum in Belgium."[37]

Clearly, Leopold, upon receiving Lady Twiss from the hands of Sir Travers, wasted no time in determining her future. In Belgium, the law of June 19, 1850, had simplified the procedure for having purportedly insane people committed

---

36. Twiss to John Hassard, Vicar General, October 26, 1892, E. W. Benson Papers, Lambeth Palace Library, Benson 123, f.293.

37. John Hassard, Vicar General, to Archbishop Benson, October 31, 1892, E. W. Benson Papers, Lambeth Palace Library, Benson 123, ff. 291–292.

to asylums.[38] The Code Napoléon had stipulated that "all demands" for people to be committed to an insane asylum had to appear before a Court of First Instance, so that insanity was determined by the law.[39] As in Britain, in Belgium during the course of the nineteenth century, the determination of who was judged to be insane became increasingly a matter for medicine rather than the law. Accordingly, by the law of June 19, 1850, which superseded the code, all Leopold required was a medical certificate from a doctor stating that the mental condition of the person concerned merited committal, and a demand for the admission of the person either from a private individual—who, in this instance, might include Leopold—or from the mayor of the commune in which the person lived. Having already lost whatever liberty she enjoyed as a consequence of being placed in Leopold's hands, Pharaïlde Twiss now experienced the "civil death" that was the destiny of people who found themselves incarcerated as insane.[40] It is no coincidence that many of the stories of personal reinvention and transformation that characterised Victorian social life were closely tied to stories of insanity and the loss of liberty. We have seen such dual possibilities in the stories of Georgina Weldon, William Windham, and Agnes Willoughby. Emancipation and the civil death that accompanied committal to an asylum were two sides of the same coin of personal transformation. People who were socially mobile could be mobile in more than one direction, particularly when emancipation and liberty were understood to be contingent upon social condition rather than being natural.

It is possible, given her profession prior to 1862, that Pharaïlde Twiss suffered the long-term effects of syphilis. Although the mental atrophy associated with late-term syphilis was more common amongst men, many women in nineteenth-century asylums had syphilis.[41] If Lady Twiss was suffering from syphilis, Travers Twiss was almost certainly infected himself, and although he showed no signs of mental illness late in life, not all people infected, prior to its treatment with antibiotics starting in the 1930s, suffered from cerebral atrophy. At the same time, it is possible that Leopold incarcerated Lady Twiss in an asylum merely to solve the problem of what to do with her. Her behaviour was regarded as scandalous and was described as such not only by Borchgrave but also by her own husband in his letter to the King. As we have seen with the attempts to incarcerate William Windham and Georgina Weldon, scandalous or eccentric behaviour alone was sometimes considered by Victorians to provide enough substance to imprison a person in an insane asylum. Nevertheless, the incarceration of Pharaïlde Twiss in an asylum brings us back to

38. Mirella Ghisu, "*Malades mentaux, justice et libertés. Renverser l'entonnoir?*" *Mental'idées*, Brussels, vol. 17 (March 2012), 7.

39. *Code Napoléon*, Livre 1, Titre 11i, Ch. 2: "*De l'interdiction*," 492, 128.

40. On insanity and civil death, see Shanley, *Feminism, Marriage, and the Law in Victorian England*, 10–11.

41. Shorter, *A History of Psychiatry*, 53–58.

the extraordinary step Travers Twiss took in placing her, as he might with any other property, in Leopold's hands. If Pharaïlde Twiss was clearly insane with mental atrophy, Travers could have had her committed to an asylum without appealing to the King to take her off his hands. The act of "recommending" her to the King's "kindly protection" tells us a number of things. First, that Pharaïlde was a Belgian subject, as Chaffers had long maintained, because it was only by virtue of her being Leopold's subject that Travers could make his feudal appeal. Moreover, it was only by virtue of being a Belgian subject that Leopold could have her committed to a Belgian asylum. Second, that her behaviour was scandalous, rather than insane, or else Travers could have had her committed directly—the legal procedure was very simple. Third, it is striking that in Twiss's mind there was a connection between Pharaïlde's position and his work for Leopold in creating the Congo Free State.

Hassard's postscript note, apart from indicating the fate of Pharaïlde Twiss, also implied that the Archbishop would have been aware of her story. Although Hassard did not assume Benson knew Twiss was Vicar General in 1852, he did assume that Benson would know who Travers Twiss's wife was. Precisely because of this notoriety, it is not surprising that Hassard's postscript also reveals that Travers Twiss had by this time become reclusive. In 1889, when Travers Twiss abandoned his wife, he also made his last subscription to the Athenaeum, after forty-four years of membership, possibly because he was financially ruined but also because he no longer cared for the company.[42] Although he continued to send his publications to the club in the '70s and '80s, the dinner bills reveal no sign of him dining there after 1872. In the same year of 1889, according to the Electoral Register, Twiss was still resident at 71 Hamilton Terrace, St John's Wood, where he had been throughout the 1880s. At the same time that Pharaïlde and Travers lived in St John's Wood, Travers was also recorded as a tenant at the Brussels address, 19 rue de la Chancellerie. Apart from Pharaïlde's Belgian connections, the address was useful for Twiss's work for the King throughout the 1880s. He remained there until 1893, the year after Hassard's letter to Archbishop Benson.

The Brussels address also proved useful for Twiss in 1893, because in that year he published in Brussels a pamphlet on consular jurisdiction in Japan.[43] The pamphlet was an extract from an article he published in the same year in the *Revue de droit international*. He was now an honourary member of the Institut de droit international, rather than a full member. In this short article, he wrote to the *Revue* to complain that Italian jurist Alessandro Paternostro had misrepresented his views on Japanese membership in the society of nations. Paternostro had been employed by the Japanese government to assist

42. *Athenaeum: Rules and List of Members, 1890* (London, 1890), 104.
43. Travers Twiss, *La juridiction consulaire dans les pays de l'Orient et spécialement au Japon* (Brussels, 1893).

with their bid to be admitted to the international legal community.[44] Having been forced to open its borders to Western powers, the Japanese government undertook a programme of educating its elites in the law of nations in order to facilitate diplomatic relations and the admission of Japan to equality in the society of nations. Egypt had pursued a similar policy under Muhammed Ali Pasha in the 1830s and '40s in which Twiss had participated.[45] Paternostro made his case in a speech at an 1890 conference in Tokyo on law in Japan, which was published the following year in the *Revue de droit international*.[46] In this speech, Paternostro argued that international law was not simply the law that prevailed between European states, nor was it Christian. International law, he argued, was based upon "human nature" and took as its aim the organisation of all humanity.[47] No nation, therefore, could be excluded from membership in the society of nations or from possession of rights in international law. The sole qualification for entry into this society was the possession of civilisation, and Japan, amongst other "Oriental" nations, fulfilled that condition. All of these matters, Paternostro observed, had been placed under consideration by the Institut de droit international in 1874 and again in 1878 when they established commissions for examining the standing of "Oriental nations" in international law.[48] He favourably cited the conclusions of that commission, chaired by Twiss, which affirmed the "full equality of Oriental nations in full international rights."[49] Paternostro criticised Twiss, however, for having supported consular jurisdiction in Japan in a speech he said Twiss made to the Society for the Reform and Codification of the Law of Nations in London in 1890, as well as in his earlier report for the Institut on the status of Oriental nations in international law.[50] Having read this report in the *Annuaire* and also in the *Japan Daily Mail*, Twiss responded in the *Revue*, angrily pointing out that he had been too sick in 1890 to attend the conference of the Society for the Reform and Codification of the Law of Nations.[51] He also observed that he had never supported consular jurisdiction in Japan, but rather mixed tribunals, and that nobody had been prepared for the speed with which Japan would become one of the civilized nations.

44. Arnulf Becker Lorca, *Mestizo International Law: A Global Intellectual History 1842–1933* (Cambridge, 2014), 109.

45. For the Japanese government development of education in the law of nations, see Lorca, *Mestizo International Law*, 109.

46. Alessandro Paternostro, "La révision des traités avec le Japon au point de vue du droit international," *Revue de droit international et de législation comparée*, vol. 23 (1891), 5–29.

47. Paternostro, "La révision des traités," 6–8.

48. Paternostro, "La révision des traités," 8–10.

49. Paternostro, "La révision des traités," 9.

50. Paternostro, "La révision des traités," 5–29.

51. *Japan Daily Mail*, August 20, 1890.

This was the last occasion on which Twiss would be engaged in public debate over international law, but it is striking that the issue of legal personality and international franchise was one that remained central to his thought to the end of his life.

The year 1889 was traumatic for Travers Twiss. While he wrote to Leopold to say he had a "broken heart," he also withdrew from Society. He no longer had the financial means for the subscription of eight guineas at the Athenaeum, and it was the last year he was a full member of the Institut de droit international. From the time of the marriage scandal in 1872 until 1888, he had maintained his chambers at 3 Paper Buildings, Temple, in the Inns of Court, but in 1889, he had abandoned those chambers. Between 1887 and 1889, he also sold what appears to have been most of his remaining books through Hodgson's Book Auctioneers, raising a further £256.[52] He provided the *Annuaire* of the Institut with his new address in Riverside, Ashford, Middlesex, just west of London, the same address to which John Hassard, the Vicar General, wrote in 1892.[53] While Hassard mentioned that Twiss did not care for the address to be known, Twiss apparently saw no problem with publishing it in the *Annuaire*. Hassard was undoubtedly right that Twiss wished to avoid Society, but presumably Society did not read the jurists' *Annuaire*. The 1889 Electoral Register listed Twiss as resident at Hamilton Terrace, St John's Wood, so he moved to Riverside between 1889 and 1892.[54]

It was on June 17, 1892, that Twiss wrote from Riverside to James Franck Bright, the Master of University College, Oxford, congratulating him on the election of two new honorary fellows: namely, Sir Monier Monier-Williams, the Oxford Professor of Sanskrit (who received Twiss's vote for the position), and Edward Maunde Thompson, the first Director of the British Museum. Twiss segued in his letter from Thompson to the matter of British Museum manuscripts and the fact that "I have this very day put the last hand to my Preface of Glanvill for the Rolls Edition."[55] This was Twiss's translation of Ranulf de Glanvill's *Tractatus de legibus et consuetudinibus regni Anglie*, written, possibly at Henry II's behest, to outline legal practice in the King's court. Bright was a historian, and Twiss noted that his edition of Glanvill accorded with the claim Bright made in the first volume of his *History of England*—that

---

52. Twiss sold lots on February 12 and 16, and March 2, of 1887, and again on July 23, August 2, October 25, and November 25, of 1889, see "Sir Travers Twiss," in *Ledger, 1885– 1898*, vol. 58, Hodgson Papers, British Library, Add. MS 54637, 565.

53. "Noms et adresses des membres honoraires, membres, et associés de l'institut de droit international au 1er janvier 1892," *Annuaire de l'Institut de droit international*, vol. 11 (1892), vii.

54. London Metropolitan Archives, Electoral Register, 1889, 1, 10.

55. Travers Twiss to James Franck Bright, 17 June 1892, University College, Oxford, UC: GB6/1/A3/4/5.

to the reign of Henry II "can be traced the origin of trial by jury."[56] Twiss then added, "What a marvellous history that of Henry II is considering he had such a wife and such sons!" He was referring, ironically, to Eleanor of Aquitaine, who after twenty years became estranged and was then imprisoned by her husband for supporting his son's revolt against him. Twiss's enthusiasm for his edition of Glanvill was not shared by its publisher, the Deputy Keeper of the Public Record Office, Henry Maxwell Lyte, who wrote to eminent legal historian Frederic William Maitland to seek his opinion on its quality. Maitland condemned the work, and Lyte destroyed the printed copies. A generation later, Percy Winfield, writing on editions of Glanvill, made the following judgement: "An edition which fell still-born from the press was that by Sir Travers Twiss . . . It should be avoided . . . the Deputy-Keeper of the Rolls, acting on the advice of the author of this note [i.e., Maitland], destroyed all except a few copies of the book, because it fell below the standard of the Rolls Series." He added, sarcastically, "This has given the surviving copies a value to the book-collector which they never had for the reader. A remarkable consolation for literary damnation!"[57]

Twiss moved again back into London, between 1892 and 1896, to 6 Whittingstall Road, Fulham, a poor working-class suburb, well below the gentility he had enjoyed in St John's Wood, Oxford, the Albany, and Park Lane.[58] It was at this address that Twiss died on January 14, 1897. His death certificate stated the cause of death to be bronchitis and—unsurprisingly, after the life he had led—"exhaustion."[59] Charles Harper, the person noted in the certificate as present at his death, may have been a servant, but no family member was mentioned. He was buried six days later in Fulham Cemetery, in consecrated ground in an earth grave purchased for perpetuity by Michael Marsden, his nephew and the son of his younger sister, Ann, who had married George Marsden, from a family in North Wales near to where the Twiss family originated.[60] Twiss's tombstone recorded his professional accomplishments: "IN MEMORY OF / SIR TRAVERS TWISS / QC [Queen's Council] DCL [Doctor of Civil Law] FRS [Fellow of the Royal Society] & / FOR MANY YEARS REGIUS PROFESSOR OF CIVIL LAW / AT THE UNIVERSITY OF

---

56. Travers Twiss to James Franck Bright, 17 June 1892, University College, Oxford, UC GB6/1/A3/4/6. Franck Bright, *A History of England: Period I: Medieval Monarchy: From the Departure of the Romans to Richard III, 449–1485* (London, 1897), 108.

57. Winfield, *The Chief Sources of English Legal History*, 258. See also Fifoot, *Frederic William Maitland: A Life*, 132.

58. "Personnel de l'institut. Membres honoraires, membres, et associés," *Annuaire de l'Institut de droit international*, vol. 15 (1896), x.

59. *Certified Copy of an Entry of Death for Travers Twiss*, General Register Office: England and Wales Civil Registration Indexes.

60. Notice of Interment, Interment no.29504, Vestry of the Parish of Fulham in the County of London, Hammersmith and Fulham Archives.

FIGURE 19. The grave of Travers Twiss.*

OXFORD / ADMIRALTY ADVOCATE AND QUEENS ADVOCATE / DIED JAN 14 1897." It is a statement of his curriculum vitae, containing no personal expressions of family affection—"In loving memory of," "Beloved Husband," "Dear Father"—which are to be found on the neighbouring graves.

The funeral was attended by one family member, his niece, "Mrs Richard Marsden," the wife of one his other nephews. Otherwise, those present were professional associates, including Thomas Holland, professor of international law at Oxford, Sir George Sherston-Baker, a recorder in Cornwall, "Dr Stubbs of the Middle Temple," and Alfred Burton, a member of the Royal College of Surgeons.[61] The most important presence, however, was Twiss's friend Thomas Tristram, whose fortune Twiss had ensured many years earlier when he succeeded in having him admitted as the last civil lawyer to enter the Doctors' Commons just prior to its dissolution, thus ensuring not only Tristram's admission to office but also his share in the lucrative sale of the property upon which the College sat. Tristram would become the last surviving member of

---

61. For attendance at the funeral, see "The Late Sir Travers Twiss," *Law Magazine and Review*, vol. 112 (1896–97), 112–114.

* Author's photograph

the Doctors' Commons—the charter of the corporation survived the sale of its buildings and land—and when he died, in 1912, the college died with him. In 1897, Tristram still held Twiss's former position of Chancellor of the Diocese of London as well as Judge of the Consistory Court.

Twiss appears to have made only one bequest, and that was to Tristram. In 1935, Thomas Tristram's son, F. T. Tristram, wrote from a villa in avenue Albert 1er in Beaulieu sur Mer, on the seafront next to Nice, to the archivist in the Department of Manuscripts in the Bibliothèque Nationale in Paris, offering to sell forty letters written by Prince Metternich to Travers Twiss (all of Twiss's letters to Metternich were in the National Archives in Prague). F. T. Tristram wrote that Twiss had left the letters to his father, who had, in turn, when he died in 1912, passed them on to his mother. He said that his mother left them to him but that "she made me promise to transmit them to my son" upon his own death. Thomas Tristram's grandson, however, "was killed in the war [the Great War]." F. T. Tristram wrote that he now feared that, upon his own death, the letters would be dispersed and that he would be happy to have them preserved by the library in return for the modest sum of 5,000 francs. The library accepted and, underneath Tristram's letter, is a note from Travers Twiss, placed on top of Metternich's letters, which states, "The Metternich letters may be given to Dr T. Hutchinson Tristram, who will value them. 10 April, 1889." This note reveals that Twiss was preparing for his death eight years prior to the event. The date is significant—eight days prior to his letter to Leopold in which he placed his wife in the King's "protection." The timing suggests either that Twiss carried Metternich's letters about with him, which seems unlikely, or, more probably, that eight days prior to his letter to Leopold from his Brussels address, he had been in London, where he had put his affairs in order before he had travelled to Belgium with the express purpose of relieving himself of responsibility for his wife (a task that may have been more difficult in England).

Twiss's note directing Metternich's letters to Tristram would not fulfil its purpose for eight years, but it is important for the reason that it is the only surviving record of any kind of will or testament on Twiss's part. There is no probate record for Twiss. He had been one of the most eminent probate lawyers in England for fifty years, as well as a judge of probate, and yet he left no will. It must be the case that he simply had no property left to bequeath, because if he had still held property, probate would have to have been proved. Apart from the letters, the only other sign that property survived Twiss's death were two sales of his books and manuscripts at auction. The first of these was the sale of his books, along with those of another "gentleman," through auctioneers Puttick and Simpson from May 6 to May 10, 1897.[62] The second sale was of Twiss's collected legal opinions at auction from Hodgson and Co. Book Auctioneers,

---

62. "Sale by Auction," *The Times*, May 3, 1897, 18.

in Chancery Lane, who Twiss had used to sell his books in 1887 and 1889. The purchaser was the Harvard University Law Library, in June 1899, eighteen months after his death. These opinions bound all his cases in eight large folio volumes, plus two smaller volumes of notes on early cases in his career. No record survives of who put these books and manuscripts up for auction immediately after Twiss's death, although it is likely to have been the family of his sister, who had paid for the grave.

Travers Twiss's death and the settlement of his affairs was not the end of the controversy surrounding the metamorphosis of Pharaïlde van Lynseele into Lady Twiss. Curiously, Georgina Weldon's actions in the 1880s would have an impact upon the Twisses due to their common link with Alexander Chaffers. When Georgina Weldon had used the Married Women's Property Acts to protect her fortune, she frequently found herself before the Master of the Rolls, Lord Esher, with whom she developed a close rapport.[63] Perhaps encouraged by this rapport, after Chaffers had been assisting Weldon from 1882, he had applied to the Master of the Rolls in 1884 and 1885 to be readmitted to the Bar, but as we have seen, Esher had rejected the application due to Chaffers's conduct in the Twiss case (as a bencher in Lincoln's Inn, Esher would have at least been acquainted with Twiss).[64] In 1889, Georgina Weldon retired for some years to a convent in France, while in the same year, Lady Twiss found herself incarcerated in an asylum (a fate Weldon had fought off), and Chaffers turned his efforts elsewhere. He became involved in litigation in which he attempted to recover costs for work he said he had performed in finding a missing last will and testament.[65] He lost this case, as he usually did, but it gave cause for Lord Esher to refer to Chaffers in court in 1891 as an extortionist. Chaffers responded by suing Esher for slander and complaining, at the same time, that this slander was perpetrated by the same man who had previously refused his application to be readmitted to the Bar. Esher was protected to some degree, however, by judicial immunity. In fact, in the 1890s, Esher was sitting in judgement in cases establishing the limits of judicial immunity, a matter which touched him personally. Chaffers was not the only person to whom Esher had refused readmission to the Bar. John Pym Yeatman, described by Michael Taggart as a "wild man" of the Bar and also of Lincoln's Inn, held Esher responsible for the rejection of his application for readmission in 1894 and published a tract, the *Judicature Quarterly Review*, that denounced Esher's conduct of *Anderson vs Gorrie*, in which the matter of

---

63. [John Alderson Foote], *"Pie Powder," Being Dust from the Law Courts Collected and Recollected on the Western Circuit* (London, 1911), 188–189; Taggart, "Alexander Chaffers," 663.

64. On Esher and Twiss, see Taggart, "Alexander Chaffers," 664.

65. "Chaffers v. Williamson," *The Times*, May 2, 1890, 3; Taggart, "Alexander Chaffers," 666.

judicial immunity was being determined.⁶⁶ On appeal to the Court of Appeal, Anderson argued that Esher should have recused himself from *Anderson vs Gorrie* because he had a conflict of interest on the matter of judicial immunity and that *Anderson vs Gorrie* was used to stay a case against Esher. Yeatman reported in his tract that Esher had responded to this accusation by asking whose action was stayed. "Who is this plaintiff?," he asked, "Is it—? [naming an infamous person]."⁶⁷ It was Yeatman's action that was stayed, but he claimed to have been slandered by Esher because he had confused Chaffers with Yeatman. Chaffers read Yeatman's *Judicature Quarterly Review* and understood that "an infamous person" which Yeatman had inserted instead of a name referred to himself. Chaffers promptly sued Yeatman for defamation. Chaffers's infamy, of course, rested upon the Twiss case, and so the suit against Yeatman once again dredged up the details of that case.

Chaffers's case against Yeatman came before the Lord Mayor's Court when the matter reached an interlocutory stage in October 1896 while Twiss was still alive. Yeatman, however, was as hardened a litigator as Chaffers, and the argument was heated. Yeatman defended himself by saying that the interlocutory matter had been heard privately in the judge's chambers the previous day and that Chaffers had withdrawn, presumably because he had no case. Chaffers responded that he withdrew because he wanted the case to be heard publicly—he wanted his day in court—and, revealing his desperation to continue publicising the Twiss case, he observed that "reporters were not allowed to attend" the discussions in the judge's chambers. The judge agreed with Yeatman that the case had already been heard the previous day. His passion undimmed after twenty-five years, "Mr Chaffers, rising and gesticulating wildly said, 'And I also say this, that your Lordship has no more right to sit in this court than I have.'"⁶⁸ The judge walked out of the court. Nevertheless, on March 23 the following year, when Twiss had died, Chaffers's suit for £1,000 damages against Yeatman and his printer for damages went to trial. Yeatman conceded that the "infamous person" he had referred to was Chaffers, but he defended himself by reference to "a number of incidents connected to the past career of the plaintiff and his connexion with the Travers Twiss case."⁶⁹ The judge observed that if Yeatman could show that his report was a fair representation of the comments made by Lord Esher, that "would be an end to the matter." Chaffers responded that the trial he referred to was not the recent High Court actions dealing with judicial immunity but "a trial that took place 25 years ago; and therefore it would be necessary to go into the early matters." The jury said they "didn't want to hear anything of those matters" and found for the defendant.

66. Taggart, "Alexander Chaffers," 669.
67. Taggart, "Alexander Chaffers," 671.
68. "Mr Chaffers in the Lord Mayor's Court," *The Times*, October 17, 1896, 9.
69. "Libel Action," *The Times*, March 23, 1897, 3.

A week later, Chaffers was back in the Lord Mayor's Court, applying for a new trial and arguing that the jury had been misdirected and dismissed evidence. In one of his rare victories, the judge agreed, saying that he had previously been "under a misapprehension" as to the period to which Chaffers wished to address his testimony.[70] At the same time, the judge, Sir Forrest Fulton, commented: "He would point out to Mr Chaffers that he was getting an old man, and that he might as well let the action rest where it was. Sir Travers Twiss and Lady Twiss, whose names had been associated with the trial before the jury, were both dead, and the time was coming when Mr Chaffers, too, would be passing away. What was the good of keeping the matter up?" In Fulton's remark, two months after Travers Twiss's death, we learn for the first time of the death of Pharaïlde Twiss after her committal eight years earlier to a Belgian asylum. Fulton does not say how he had learned of Pharaïlde Twiss's death, any more than John Hassard explained how he learned of her committal, but presumably news of the Twisses would have circulated in the Inns of Court. The Belgian State Archives provide no death certificate for Pharaïlde Twiss, nor for Marie Twiss, nor Pharaïlde van Lynseele, nor Marie van Lynseele, so the precise moment and location of her death remains unknown.

70. "Mr Chaffers and the Common Sergeant," *The Times*, March 30, 1897, 11.

Conclusion

WRITING A SHORT TIME after Twiss's death, the English political theorist Harold Laski argued that the nineteenth century had witnessed a struggle of associations, notably in the form of the Catholic Church and the Church of England, at least from the perspective of the Tractarians, to free themselves from the control of the state.[1] For Laski, this was a struggle for pluralism, an understanding of the state that allowed other forms of societies to flourish alongside the sovereign. It was a struggle for a state that would have the confidence to allow such alternative forms of political organisation to pursue their own understandings of social and political fulfilment, as *perfecta societas*, without placing the authority of the state itself in question. Until the 1850s, Twiss had fought hard to prevent the flourishing of such corporations in a way that enabled them to be autonomous. He was Erastian on questions of religion, in regard to both Catholic emancipation and the Puseyites, as he termed them.

Twiss carried this conservatism regarding the emancipation of artificial persons into his understanding of the artificial persons of nations and states. Accordingly, he strongly opposed the outbreak of nationalism in the 1848 revolutions and the 1859 struggle for Italian unification, just as he had earlier opposed the creation of new states in the Oregon Territory in America. Each of these movements, as far as he was concerned, threatened to unbalance the international society that his friend Metternich had helped design at the Congress of Vienna. He was similarly resistant to any forms of broadening the franchise of natural persons, and resistant to all moves for personal improvement and transformation which would lead to an expansion in the political society of natural persons, as well as a change in "Society" itself. He expressed those concerns strongly again in relation to the revolutions of 1848 and in his many years of conversation and correspondence with Metternich. Twiss maintained these conservative positions on the status of both natural and artificial persons

1. Laski, *Studies in the Problem of Sovereignty.*

while always stressing the importance of covering his stance with liberal rhetoric. It was important, as he said, not to let the Devil have all the good tunes.

Between the late 1850s and the 1870s, Twiss progressively abandoned each of these conservative stances in relation to both natural and artificial persons. He presented a conservative face to the world, but the substance of his actions and arguments supported the dramatic transformation of persons who had previously been constrained by social codes. He changed at a time when English society as a whole was changing, and his own transformation should be placed in that context. His trajectory is in some ways emblematic of the rapprochement between liberals and conservative counter-revolutionaries in the decades after 1848. Twiss progressively adopted more liberal approaches to legal personality in the sense that he embraced a greater inclusion of natural persons in Society and artificial persons in international society. He also embraced the emerging liberal consensus upon the expansion of European empires. But he changed in response to some very specific circumstances within that broader social context, and his change initially came not in response to his dialogue with the many eminent intellectuals, clergymen, and politicians of his generation, but through his engagement with the other side of London society, and in his dialogue with Pharaïlde van Lynseele in particular. This same experiment in Lynseele's transformation into a "lady by blood," as Twiss put it, led to the unravelling of his professional life, but it left him as someone who was able to countenance even the most radical of personal transformations: namely, those that broke with social codes.

As an international lawyer, Twiss was accustomed to drawing innovations in international law from the lives of persons, as he stated himself, and he extended the practice of creating new persons in a way that broke with existing codes in international society, assisted in doing so by his long-standing practice of dealing with the law of nations and marriage law in the same legal practice. I would argue, therefore, that we must broaden the context for understanding the creation of artificial persons by considering conventions that bear upon the creation of natural persons, and vice versa. But this leaves us with the question of what benefits that richer understanding of context brings to our understanding of any particular person, natural or artificial.

In the case of artificial persons, the context of the emancipation of natural persons enables us to understand changes in the status of corporations in both national and international society as a similar movement towards emancipation. While perhaps not referring to the "emancipation" of artificial persons in international law, historians of international law have nevertheless represented the broadening of international society in the late nineteenth century in terms of the liberal values of international jurists at that moment.[2] That

---

2. There are numerous studies on liberalism and the creation of international law, but the classic study is Koskenniemi, *The Gentle Civilizer of Nations*. See also Karuna Mantena,

broadening is generally portrayed in terms of the debate over the inclusion of non-European societies, but it should also include non-state corporations, such as the International Association of the Congo.[3] I have described, however, two kinds of processes through which persons, natural and artificial, can be transformed. One is through emancipation: that is, by changing the rules that govern a society. The other is through changing persons so that they fit the rules, or so that they appear to fit. This was the strategy that Lynseele and Twiss used to transform her into a "lady by blood." Both strategies applied in the case of the creation of the Congo Free State. Twiss and Leopold sought to change the rules of international society so as to include the International African Association, but they also sought to represent that Association as something that it was not in order for it to become a state. While we are accustomed to thinking about the transformation of international society and the subjects of international society in terms of the rules governing that society, we are less accustomed to thinking about the transformation of international subjects in terms of the metamorphoses that natural persons used to change their membership in society within states. And yet, clearly, such techniques were used to make at least one international subject. Contemporary jurists objected to the creation of the Congo Free State because it violated the rules of the international order, even before it had started its violent existence.

It makes sense to consider conventions and behaviours of natural persons as part of the context for understanding artificial persons, given that philosophers and international lawyers themselves tell us that states draw their conventions from natural persons. It is perhaps less usual also to ask what benefit there could be to use the context of artificial persons to throw light upon our understanding of natural persons. Twiss, however, suggested one possible answer to that question. It is often argued that the liberal international order was one of fundamental inequality between Europeans and non-Europeans. For Twiss, it was more complex. He argued for the equality of "Oriental nations" in international society in order to impose duties upon those peoples. His expectation that they would fail in their duties would lead, he argued, to their dependence upon the great powers. Emancipation, therefore, was a premise of dependence in this ideological architecture of informal empire. It was with this paradoxical argument that Twiss was able to reconcile the formerly polarised liberal and conservative perspectives of 1848.

Alibis of Empire: Henry Maine and the Ends of Liberal Imperialism (Princeton, 2010); Casper Sylvest, *British Liberal Internationalism, 1880–1930* (Manchester, 2009); Pitts, *Boundaries of the International: Law and Empire*; Lorca, *Mestizo International Law*.

3. For attention to a non-state-centred account of international law and its historical obscurity due to the centrality of the state, see Doreen Lustig, Markus D. Dubber, and Christopher Tomlins, eds., *The Oxford Handbook of Legal History* (Oxford, 2018), 859–882; Doreen Lustig, *Corporate Regulation and International Law: A History of Failure?* (Oxford University Press, 2019).

The admission of non-European nations into international society was consistent with broader movements for the expansion of the franchise for natural persons. Male subjects of the British state were increasingly granted political standing—for example, in the Reform Act of 1867, which extended the vote to working-class men—and there were even arguments made to extend that standing to women. One might ask whether, in all such instances, the achievement of equality could also become a premise of dependence. The imperial race for Africa, including the occupation of the Congo by Leopold, was conducted in the name of the liberation of its people and the suppression of slavery, but the reality was very different. In this way, emancipation within states would establish informal empire, to adapt Robinson and Gallagher's term, over natural persons.[4] This was not empire in the classic sense of sovereignty, or *imperium*, but empire in the sense of dependent political relations. Twiss helped Leopold construct such a state: that is, he helped enfranchise artificial persons in international society, and in doing so, he helped create a repressive tyranny. Whether he knew that was what he was doing might be debated. Leopold certainly did. Twiss may have believed the humanitarian rhetoric, although the terms of the constitution that he wrote for the new state, and other acts, such as watering down the commitment to abolish slavery at the Berlin Conference, would suggest otherwise. Moreover, all such actions need to be placed in the context of his understanding that emancipation creates the conditions of dependence.

Once the principle was admitted that non-state persons could have a status in international society, the door was open to further broadening the membership of that society in the later years of the nineteenth century and throughout the twentieth century. Not only other corporations, such as the Red Cross, gained international standing, but even natural persons became subjects of international society through the flourishing of human rights discourse.[5] In the twentieth century, natural persons were perceived as subjects of international society, both when appeals were made to protect their rights from repressive regimes and when they were pursued in international tribunals— for example, for crimes against humanity. The principle for which Twiss and Leopold struggled, therefore, had some unexpected consequences. If, however, one recalls that their struggle was fought partly through the use of humanitarian rhetoric, as well as legal argument, a genealogy which links their arguments with the rise of human rights is less perverse, even if the reality behind that rhetoric was the creation of an extraordinarily brutal regime. As Mark Mazower has shown, the great powers of the twentieth century supported the rise of human rights discourse in part because of its weakness—a further

---

4. John Gallagher and Ronald Robinson, "The Imperialism of Free Trade," *Economic History Review*, vol. 6, no. 1 (1953), 1–15.

5. Kjeldgaard-Pederson, *The International Legal Personality of the Individual*.

illustration of the manner in which the recognition of rights and dependence could work hand in hand.[6]

Harold Laski's vision of emancipation leading to a pluralistic society in which individuals, natural and artificial, were able to pursue their own fulfilment did not take into account the possible connections between enfranchisement and dependence. Nor did it account for the way in which such fulfilment might be expressed by an aggressive, rights-bearing, autonomous individual such as the Congo Free State. Liberal subjects pursuing their own transformation could, like William Windham or Georgina Weldon, be very nearly deprived of their liberty or, like Pharaïlde Twiss, be so deprived and become civilly dead. In the metamorphoses of Pharaïlde van Lynseele into Lady Twiss and of the International Association of the Congo into the Congo Free State, she and Twiss had discovered the limits, as well as the possibilities, of the liberal world of personal transformation.

6. Mazower, "The Strange Triumph of Human Rights, 1933–1950."

BIBLIOGRAPHY

Primary Sources

MANUSCRIPT SOURCES

Belgium

Archives du Palais Royal, Brussels: *Commandements du Roi*, A96; *Commandements du Roi*, A136; *Commandements du Roi*, A154; *Commandements du Roi*, A157; *Commandements du Roi*, A168; Indicateur, 1863–1898, D.1.c.

Ministère des Affaires Etrangères, Brussels: *Correspondance et documents Afrique*, Association Internationale du Congo, 2, 1883; *Correspondance et documents Afrique*, Association Internationale du Congo, 3, 1884.

State Archives, Kortrijk, Civil Service, West Flanders: *Births* 1834 (Rijksarchief, Kortrijk, Burgerlijke stand, Vlaanderen, Geboorten, 1834).

Czech Republic

National Archives of the Czech Republic, Prague: *Correspondence between Travers Twiss and Klemens von Metternich*, RAM-AC/ 10/ 774–788.

France

Bibliothèque nationale de France, Paris: *Correspondence between Travers Twiss and Klemens von Metternich*, Fol/ R.D./13810; "F. T. Tristram to Monsieur le Conservateur," June 1, 1935, NAF 12629, 2; Travers Twiss, *Case of His Majesty the King of Oude: Copy Opinion of Dr Twiss*, Fol-NT-333.

United Kingdom

Athenaeum: *Ballots 1843*, Mem 1/4/1; *Book of Candidates*, 1841–1850, Mem 1/1/7; *Book of Candidates*, 1850–1858, Mem 1/1/9; *Book of Candidates*, 1858, Mem 1/1/11; *Candidates Book*, 1833–1840, Mem/1/1/5; *Donations to the Library*, 1887–1910, Lib 3/1; *Honorary Members*, Rule 13, 1830–1859, 14; *Letter Book*, Sec 1/3; *Letter Book*, Sec 1/4; *Marked Dinner Bills*, 1846–1850; *Minute Book*, 1848–1850; *Minute Book*, 1854–1855, Com 1/14.

British Library: "Egerton MSS," 2848, *Sir F. Madden Correspondence*, Vol. 12, 1863–1870; *Gladstone Papers*, Add. MS. 44369, Add. MS. 44370, Add. MS. 44397; *Hodgson Papers*, Add. MS. 54637; *Layard Papers*, Add. MS. 38988, Add. MS. 39034; *Literary Fund Anniversary Dinner Papers*, Loan 96; *Peel Papers*, Add. MS. 40586, Add. MS. 40686, Add. MS. 88906.

Denbighshire Archives, Ruthin, Wales: *Conveyance of Land in the Parish of Llanfair in the County of Denbigh*, 5 October 1877, DD/WY/347; Sir Travers Twiss Knight and the Honble E. Kenyon to United School District Board, *Conveyance of a Parcel of Land*, 18 December 1876, Denbighshire Archives, DD/CD/1; Edward Williams Esq to Sir Travers Twiss and the Honourable Edward Kenyon, *Conveyance of Abenbury Lodge*, 23 October 1884, Denbighshire Archives, Bdl 18, Box 3; Miss Jane Preston and Others to Sir Travers Twiss and the Honourable Edward Kenyon, *Reconveyance*, 13 February 1878, DD/CP/887; Messers Oswald, Bunbury, and Rainey to Dr Travers Twiss and the Honourable Edward Kenyon, *Reconveyance of the Cefn Estate*, 24 June 1859, Denbighshire Archives, Box 2 Bdl 4; J. B. Davies-Cooke and Others to Sir Travers Twiss and Capt. Kendall, *Conveyance*, 13 November 1895, Denbighshire Archives, Bdl 27, Box 4.

Hammersmith and Fulham Archives: *Notice of Interment, Interment no. 29504*, Vestry of the Parish of Fulham in the County of London.

King's College, London, Archive: *College Minutes*, 1849, MS KA/IC/M5; "Travers Twiss to Richard Jelf," January 20, 1849, KA/IC/T25; Travers Twiss, "Resignation letter," KA/ICT25, T33.

Lambeth Palace: MS. KKK/11/29; Doctors' Commons, "The Minute Book," MS. DC2; *Papers of Baroness Burdett-Coutts*, MS 1381; *E. W. Benson Papers*, Benson 123; *Jackson Papers*, MS 33; *Lee Papers*, MS 2876; *Tait Papers*, 48, 176, 184; *Tait Papers*, Official Letters London, 1858, Oct.-Dec., 111; *Tait Papers*, Official Letters London, Continental Chaplaincies, A-B 409, D 412, D-F 413; *Tait Papers*, Personal Letters 1874, 93; *Tait Papers*, Personal Letters Catharine Tait, 1850-1878, 103.

London Metropolitan Archives: *Board of Guardian Records*, 1834-1906; *Church of England Marriages and Banns*, 1754-1932; *Church of England Parish Registers*, 1538-1812; *Church of England Parish Registers*, 1813-1906; *Composite Register: Baptisms and Burials*, 1709-1812; *Electoral Registers*.

National Archives, London: *Census Returns of England and Wales*, 1861; *Census Returns of England and Wales*, 1861, Class: RG 9; *Census Returns of England and Wales*, 1871, Class: RG10; *Census Returns of England and Wales*, 1881; *General Register Office: Foreign Registers and Returns*, Class: RG 33; *General Register Office: Miscellaneous Foreign Marriage Returns*, Class: RG 34; Prerogative Court of Canterbury and Related Probate Jurisdictions: *Will Registers*; *Granville Papers*, PRO 30/29/23/10; In Her Majesty's Court for Divorce and Matrimonial Causes, October 28, 1862, *Windham v Windham and Guiglini*, C16/226/ Part 1.

National Archives, London, Foreign Office files: FO 84/ 1807; FO 84/ 1808; FO 84/ 1812; FO 84/ 1814; FO 84/ 1815; FO 84/ 1816; FO 84/ 1817; FO 84/ 1819; FO 84/ 1820.

Norfolk Records Office: *Windham Family Papers*, WKC 4/29/ 8, 464×7; WKC 4/29/11, 464×7; WKC 4/29/12, 464×7; WKC 4/29/8, 464×7; WKC 4/30, 465×1; 465×2 465×4; WKC 4/31, 465×5; MC 580/1.

Oxford University Archives, Bodleian Library, Oxford: *Minutes of the Hebdomadal Council*, HC 1/2/1; *Register of Convocation*, NEP/subtus/Reg Bu.

University College Archive, Oxford: Bursar's Ledger, 1840-41: BU3/F3/19; *Registrum*, Vol. 2, 1729-1842 UC/ GB3/A1/ 3/61; UC: "Travers Twiss to James Franck Bright," June 17, 1892, GB6/ 1/ A3/4.

United States

Harvard University: Houghton Library: *Louis Agassiz Correspondence*, MS. Am 1419.

Harvard Law Library Historical and Special Collections: [Travers Twiss], *Law Officer's Opinions, 1862-1886*, MS 1110, 8 vols.; Travers Twiss *carte de visite* by Maull & Co, Art 00.1885 F.

PRINTED PRIMARY SOURCES

A Commoner Married to a King, as Told by Baroness Vaughan to Paul Faure (Binghamton, 1937).

William Acton, *Prostitution, Considered in Its Moral, Social and Sanitary Aspects in London and Other Large Cities* (London, 1857).

Rutherford Alcock, *The Capital of the Tycoon: A Narrative of Three Years Residence in Japan*, 2 vols. (New York, 1863).

Annuaire de l'Institut de droit international, vol. 1, 1877; 1878; vols. 1 and 2, 1880; 1885; 1886; 1892; 1896.

The Annual Register: A Review of Public Events at Home and Abroad for the Year 1872 (London, 1873).

Anon., *Sir Travers Twiss et le Congo. Réponse à la Revue de droit international et de législation comparée et au Law Magazine and Review, par un membre de la Société Royale de Géographie d'Anvers* (Brussels, Office de Publicité, 1884).

M. E. Arntz, *De la cession des droits de souveraineté par des chefs des tribus sauvages* (Brussels, 1884).

Athenaeum, *Rules and Regulations, List of Members, and Donations to the Library, 1846* (London, 1847).

——. *Rules and Regulations, List of Members, and Donations to the Library, 1848* (London, 1849).

——. *Rules and Regulations, List of Members, and Donations to the Library, 1850* (London, 1851).

——. *Rules and List of Members, 1890* (London, 1890).

William Ballantine, *Some Experiences of a Barrister's Life* (New York, 1883).

Prosper Barante, *Questions constitutionnelles* (Paris, 1849).

Thomas Benton, *Speech of Mr Benton of Missouri on the Oregon Question*, delivered in the United States Senate, May 22, 25, 28, 1846 (Washington, 1846).

William Blackstone, *The Commentaries on the Laws of England*, 4 vols. (London, 1876).

Johann Kaspar Bluntschli, *Le droit international codifié* (Paris, 1874).

——. *The Theory of the State* (Oxford, 1895; first published in German in 1875).

François Bontinck, *Aux origines de l'État Indépendant du Congo. Documents tirés d'archives américaines* (Louvain, 1966).

Ernest Bowen-Rowlands, *Seventy-Two Years at the Bar* (London, 1924).

George Bowyer, *Observations on the Arguments of Dr Twiss respecting the New Catholic Hierarchy* (London, 1851).

——. *Commentaries on the Modern Civil Law* (London, 1848).

Franck Bright, *A History of England: Period I: Medieval Monarchy: From the Departure of the Romans to Richard III, 449–1485* (London, 1897).

William Brough, *Pygmalion; or, the Statue Fair* (London, 1867).

William Brough and Andrew Halliday, *The Pretty Horsebreaker* (London, 1861).

The Calendar of King's College London for 1849–50 (London, 1849).

The Calendar of King's College London for 1855–56 (London, 1849).

Lady Colin Campbell, *Etiquette of Good Society*, rev. ed. (London, 1893).

The Colin Campbell Divorce Case with Portraits (1886).

Robert Carter, *The Hungarian Controversy: An Exposure of the Falsifications and Perversions of the Slanderers of Hungary* (Boston, 1852).

Catalogue of a Portion of the Miscellaneous Library of Sir Travers Twiss, Removed from Park Lane (London, 1873).

Alexander Chaffers, *The Twiss Libel Case* (London, 1873).

Richard Cobden, *Speeches of Richard Cobden, esq., M.P., on Peace, Financial Reform, Colonial Reform and Other Subjects, Delivered during 1849* (London, 1849).

Code Napoléon. Edition originale et seule officielle (Paris, 1807).

Commission de Lunatico Inquirendo. An Inquiry into the State of Mind of W. S. Windham Esq. of Fellbridge Hall, Norfolk (London, 1862).

Joseph Conrad, *Diary*, in Conrad, *Heart of Darkness*, ed. Paul B. Armstrong (New York, 2006).

F. R. Cowell, *The Athenaeum: Club and Social Life in London 1824–1974* (London, 1975).

Randall Thomas Davidson and William Benham, *Life of Archibald Campbell Tait, Archbishop of Canterbury*, 3rd ed., 2 vols. (London, 1891).
Louis Delavaud, "La France et le Portugal au Congo," *Revue de géographie* (March 1883).
Frantz Despagnet, *Cours de droit international public*, 2nd ed. (Paris, 1899).
A. V. Dicey, *Lectures on the Relation between Law and Public Opinion in England during the Nineteenth Century*, ed. Richard VandeWetering (Indianapolis, 2008; first published 1917).
Charles Dickens, *David Copperfield* (Philadelphia, 1850).
———. *Sketches by Boz: Illustrative of Every-day life and Every-day People* (London, 1854).
———. *The Letters of Charles Dickens*, Vol. 12, ed. Graham Story (Oxford, 2002).
Benjamin Disraeli, *Letters: 1848-1851*, Vol. 5 (Toronto, 1993).
Sarah Ellis, *The Wives of England: Their Relative Duties, Domestic Influence and Social Obligations* (London, 1843).
Edouard Engelhardt, "La question du Danube," *Revue de droit international et de législation comparée* (1882).
———. "Le droit fluvial conventionnel," *Revue de droit international et de législation comparée*, vol. 16 (May 1884).
———. "La conférence de Berlin," *Revue de droit international et de législation comparée*, vol. 18 (1886).
———. "Du principe de neutralité dans son application aux fleuves internationaux et aux canaux maritimes," *Revue de droit international et de législation comparée* (1886), 159-167.
David Dudley Field, "De la possibilité d'appliquer le droit international européen aux nations Orientales," *Revue de droit international et de législation comparèe*, vol. 7 (1875).
Edmond Fitzmaurice, *The Life of Granville George Leveson Gower*, 2nd ed., Vol. 2 (New York, 1905).
Paul Pradier-Fodéré, *Principes généraux de droit, de politique et de législation* (Paris, 1869).
[John Alderson Foote], *"Pie Powder," Being Dust from the Law Courts Collected and Recollected on the Western Circuit* (London, 1911).
Joseph Foster, *Alumni Oxonienses*, Vol. 4 (Oxford, 1891).
———. *Oxford Men and Their Colleges, 1880-1892*, 2 vols. (Oxford, 1893).
Honoré Antoine Frégier, *Des classes dangereuses de la population dans les grandes villes, et des moyens de les rendre meilleures* (Paris, 1840).
Albert Gallatin, *The Oregon Question* (New York, 1846).
[William Gladstone], "War in Italy," *Quarterly Review*, vol. 105 (1859).
William Gladstone, *Bulgarian Horrors and the Question of the East* (London, 1876).
Charles Greville, *A Journal of the Reign of Queen Victoria from 1852 to 1860*, Vol. 1 (London, 1887).
Hugo Grotius, *Commentary on the Law of Prize and Booty*, ed. Martine Julia van Ittersum (Indianapolis, 2006).
Handbook for Northern Europe (John Murray: London, 1848).
Joseph Hatton, *Clytie: A Novel of Modern Life*, 3 vols. (London, 1874).
Thomas Hobbes, *Leviathan*, ed. Richard Tuck (Cambridge, 1991).
Henry Richard, Lord Holland, *Foreign Reminiscences* (New York, 1851).
Joseph Hornung, "Rapport," *Annuaire de l'Institut de droit international*, vol. 1 (1880).
House of Commons Hansard, Vol. 210 (1872).
House of Lords Hansard, Vol. 193 (1868).
Joseph Hume, *On Household Suffrage: The Speech of Joseph Hume in the House of Commons on the 21st of March 1839* (London, 1839).
Louis J. Jennings, ed., *The Croker Papers*, Vol. 3 (Cambridge, 2012; first published 1884).

Gaston Jèze, *Étude théorique et pratique sur l'occupation* (Paris, 1896).
The Jurist (London, 1842).
Schloss Johannisberg, http://www.schloss-johannisberg.de/en/history.htm.
Arthur Berriedale Keith, *The Belgian Congo and the Berlin Act* (Oxford, 1919).
Edward Kenealy, *The Trial at Bar of Sir Roger C. D. Tichborne* (London, 1877).
Russell of Killowen, Right Hon. Lord, "The Late Lord Chief Justice of England: Some Reminiscences," *The North American Review*, vol. 159, no. 454 (September 1894).
Jean-Louis [Johann Ludwig] Klüber, *Droit des gens moderne de l'Europe*, 2 vols, (Paris, 1834).
Richard von Krafft-Ebing, *Psychopathia Sexualis, with Especial Reference to Contrary Sexual Instinct*, trans. Charles Gilbert Craddock (London, 1894).
Harold J. Laski, *Studies in the Problem of Sovereignty* (New Haven, 1917).
"The Late Sir Travers Twiss," *Law Magazine and Review*, vol. 112 (1896-1897), 112–114.
John Knox Laughton, *Memoirs of the Life and Correspondence of Henry Reeve*, Vol. 1 (London, 1989).
Hersch Lauterpacht, *Private Law Sources and Analogies of International Law: With Special Reference to International Arbitration* (London, 1927).
The Literary Gazette, and Journal of the Belles Lettres for the Year 1842 (London, 1842).
James Lorimer, *The Institutes of the Law of Nations*, 2 vols. (Edinburgh, 1884).
[Samuel Lucas], *Dacoitee in Excelcis* (London, 1859).
F. W. Maitland, *The Collected Papers of F. W. Maitland*, ed. H.A.L. Fisher, Vol. 3 (Cambridge, 1911).
———. *State, Trust and Corporation*, eds. David Runciman and Magnus Ryan (Cambridge, 2003).
Joseph Marryat, *A History of Pottery and Porcelain* (London, 1850).
Friedrich Martens, "La conférence du Congo à Berlin et la politique coloniale des États modernes," *Revue de droit international et de législation comparée*, vol. 18 (1886), 141–144.
———. *The African Conference of Berlin and the Colonial Policy of Modern States* (1887).
A. Patchett Martin, *Life and Letters of the Right Honourable Robert Lowe Viscount Sherbrooke*, 2 vols. (London, 1893).
Henry Mayhew, *London Labour and the London Poor: Vol. 4: Those That Will Not Work* (London, 1862)
Thomas Mayo, *Elements of the Pathology of the Human Mind* (London, 1838).
Klemens von Metternich, *Mémoires, documents, et écrits divers laissés par le Prince de Metternich*, 8 vols. (Paris, 1884).
Princess Pauline Metternich, *My Years in Paris* (London, 1922).
Alexander Michie, *The Englishman in China during the Victorian Era: As Illustrated in the Career of Sir Rutherford Alcock, K.C.B, D.C.L*, 2 vols. (London, 1900).
Hamilton Murray, *Mildred Vernon: A Tale of Parisian Life in the Last Days of the Monarchy*, 3 vols. (London, 1848).
J. P. Neale, *Views of the Seats of Noblemen and Gentlemen, in England, Wales, Scotland, and Ireland*, 6 vols. (London, 1819–1823).
Occupation of the Congo Country in Africa, United States Senate, 48th Congress, 1st session, Report 393 (March 26, 1884).
Ovid, *Metamorphoses, Volume I: Books I to VIII*, trans. Frank Justus Miller, rev. by G. P. Goold, (Cambridge, Mass., 1916).
———. *Metamorphoses, Volume II: Books IX to XV*, trans. Frank Justus Miller, rev. by G. P. Goold (Cambridge, Mass., 1916).
Roundell Palmer, Earl of Selborne, *Memorials: Family and Personal 1766-1865*, 2 vols. (London, 1896).

Parliamentary Papers, *Reports from Committees* (London, 1843).
Arthur Parsey, "Inventors of Unconventional Forms of Motive Power," http://www.steamindex.com/people/unconventional.htm.
Alessandro Paternostro, "La révision des traités avec le Japon au point de vue du droit international," *Revue de droit international et de législation comparée*, vol. 23 (1891), 5–29.
Mark Pattison, *Memoirs* (London, 1885).
Proceedings of the Alaskan Boundary Tribunal, Vol. 3 (Washington, 1904).
Rowland E. Prothero and G. G. Bradley, *The Life and Correspondence of Arthur Penrhyn Stanley*, 2 vols. (New York, 1894).
Protocols and General Act of the West Africa Conference, Presented to Both Houses of Parliament (London, 1885).
J. S. Rarey's *The Art of Taming Horses* (London, 1859).
James Reddie, *Inquiries Elementary and Historical in the Science of Law* (London, 1840).
[Henry Reeve], "Kinglake's *Invasion of Crimea*," *Edinburgh Review*, no. 240 (April 1863).
Jesse Siddall Reeves, *The International Beginnings of the Congo Free State* (Baltimore, 1894).
Report of Her Majesty's Commissioners Appointed to Inquire into the Management and Government of the College of Maynooth (Dublin, 1855).
Report of the Royal Commission on the Laws of Marriage, Presented to Both Houses of Parliament by Command of Her Majesty (London, 1868).
Returns of All the Record Publications Relating to England and Wales Published since the Year 1866, House of Commons Parliamentary Papers, 1877.
Revere House menu, at NYPL Labs, "What's on the Menu?" http://menus.nypl.org/menu_pages/25827.
Revue des Deux-Mondes, 1850.
Gustave Rolin-Jaequemyns, "L'année 1888 au point de vue de la paix et du droit international," *Revue de droit international et de législation comparée*, vol. 21 (1889).
Auguste Romieu, *L'ère des Césars*, 2nd ed. (Paris, 1850).
George Augustus Sala, *Twice Round the Clock; or the Hours of the Day and Night in London* (London, 1859).
Charles Salomon *L'occupation des territoires sans maître* (Paris, 1889).
Charles Santley, *Student and Singer* (London, 1892).
Marmion Savage, *The Bachelor of the Albany* (New York, 1848).
Edouard van der Smissen, *Léopold et Beernaert d'après leur correspondance inédite de 1884 à 1894*, Vol. 1 (Brussels, 1920).
Goldwin Smith, *Reminiscences* (New York, 1910).
Henry Stanley, *The Congo and the Founding of Its Free State*, 2 vols. (London, 1885).
William Thomas Stead, "The Maiden Tribute of Modern Babylon," in Stephen Donovan and Matthew Rubery, eds., *Secret Commissions: An Anthology of Victorian Investigative Journalism* (Ontario, 2012).
Supplement to the Annals of Our Time: A Diurnal of Events, Social and Political, Home and Foreign from February 24, 1871, to March 19, 1874.
The Steeple Times, "The Badgers of Albany," November 15, 2012, http://thesteepletimes.com/opulence-splendour/the-badgers-of-albany/.
Baron de Syon, *Lettres de Beauséant* (Geneva, 1849).
Robert Stanley Thompson, *Fondation de l'État Indépendant du Congo* (Brussels, 1933).
Francis Henry Trithen, ed., *The Maha Vira Charita, or The History of Rama: A Sanscrit Play by Bhatta Bhavabhuti* (London, 1848).
Travers Twiss, *On the Amphitheatre at Pola in Istria* (Oxford, 1836).
———. *An Epitome of Niebuhr's History of Rome*, 2 vols. (London, 1836/1837).

A Tutor of a College [Travers Twiss], *Considerations of a Plan for Combining the Professorial System with the System of Public Exams in Oxford* (Oxford, 1839).
Travers Twiss, *On Money and Currency* (Oxford, 1843).
———. *The Oregon Territory* (London, 1846).
———. *View of the Progress of Political Economy in Europe since the Sixteenth Century: A Course of Lectures in Michaelmas Term 1846, and Lent Term 1847* (Oxford, 1847).
———. *The Relations of the Duchies of Schleswig and Holstein to the Crown of Denmark and the Germanic Confederation* (London, 1848).
[Travers Twiss], "The Germanic States," *Quarterly Review* (September 1848).
[Travers Twiss], "Austria and Germany," *Quarterly Review* (December 1848).
[Travers Twiss], "The German Confederation and the Austrian Empire," *Quarterly Review* (1849).
Corvinus [Travers Twiss], *Hungary: Its Constitution and Its Catastrophe* (London: John Murray, 1850).
Travers Twiss, *The Letters Apostolic of the Pope Pius IX Considered with Reference to the Law of England and the Law of Europe* (London, 1851).
———. *A Letter to the Vice-Chancellor of the University of Oxford on Law Studies at the University* (London, 1856).
———. *Two Introductory Lectures on the Science of International Law* (London, 1856).
———. *The Law of Nations Considered as Independent Political Communities: On the Rights and Duties of Nations in Time of Peace* (Oxford, 1861).
———. *The Law of Nations Considered as Independent Political Communities: On the Rights and Duties of Nations in Time of War* (Oxford, 1863).
———. *Monumenta Juridica: The Black Book of the Admiralty* 4 vols. (London, 1871–1876).
———. "La neutralisation du Canal de Suez," *Revue de droit international et de législation comparée*, vol. 7 (1875).
———. "Applicability of the European Law of Nations to African Slave States," *Law Magazine and Review* (May 1876).
———. "The Criminal Jurisdiction of the Admiralty of England: The Case of the *Franconia*," *Law Magazine and Review* (February 1877), 145–177.
———. "Collisions at Sea," *Albany Law Journal* (October 12, 1878).
———. "Collisions at Sea: A Scheme of International Tribunals," *Law Magazine and Review* (November 1878), 1–15.
———. *On International Conventions for the Maintenance of Sea Lights* (London, 1879).
———. "The International Protection of Submarine Telegraph Cables," *Association for the Reform and Codification of the Law of Nations: Report of the Eighth Annual Conference Held at Berne* (1880).
———. "De la sécurité de la navigation dans le canal de Suez," *Revue de droit international et de législation comparée* (November 1882), 572–582.
———. *An International Protectorate of the Congo River* (London, 1883).
———. "An International Protectorate of the Congo River," *Law Magazine and Review*, no. 250 (1883), 1–20.
———. "La libre navigation du Congo," *Revue de droit international et de legislation comparée*, vol. 15 (1883), 437–444.
———. "La libre navigation du Congo. Deuxième article," *Revue de droit international et de législation comparée*, vol. 15 (1883), 547–563.
———. "La libre navigation du Congo. Troisième article," *Revue de droit international et de législation comparée*, vol. 16 (1884).
———. *The Law of Nations Considered as Independent Political Communities: On the Rights and Duties of Nations in Time of Peace*, 2nd ed. (Oxford, 1884).

———. "Le Congrès de Vienne et la Conférence de Berlin," *Revue de droit international et de législation comparée*, vol. 17 (1885), 201–217.

———. "Le canal maritime de Suez et la commission internationale de Paris," *Revue de droit international et de législation comparée*, vol. 17 (1885), 615–630.

———. *Le droit des gens ou des nations considerées comme communautés politiques indépendantes. I: Des droits et des devoirs des nations en temps de paix* (Paris, 1887).

———. *On International Conventions for the Neutralisation of Territory and Their Application to the Suez Canal* (London, 1887).

———. *La juridiction consulaire dans les pays de l'Orient et spécialement au Japon* (Brussels, 1893).

Emer de Vattel, *The Law of Nations* (Northampton, Mass., 1805).

Henry Wellington Wack, *The Story of the Congo Free State* (New York, 1905).

Edward Walford, *Men of the Time: A Biographical Dictionary of Eminent Living Characters, including Women* (London, 1862).

John Westlake, "The Black Book of the Admiralty," *The Academy: A Weekly Review of Literature, Science, and Art*, vol. 5 (January 17, 1874).

Henry Wheaton, *Elements of International Law*, 6th ed. (Boston, 1855).

Montagu Williams, *Round London: Down East and Up West* (London, 1892).

Lyttleton S. Winslow, *Manual of Lunacy: A Handbook Relating to the Legal Care and Treatment of the Insane* (Cambridge, 1874).

Robert Charles Winthrop, *Speech of Mr Winthrop of Massachusetts, on the Oregon Question Delivered in the House of Representatives of the United States*, January 3, 1846 (Washington, 1846).

Edmund Yates, *Mr Thackeray, Mr Yates, and the Garrick Club: The Correspondence and the Facts* (printed for private circulation: London, 1859).

Newspapers: *Alnwick Mercury; Aris's Birmingham Gazette; The Athenaeum; The Bath Chronicle; The Belfast Newsletter; Bell's Life in Sydney and Sporting Reviewer; Bell's Weekly Messenger; Bermondsey and Rotherhithe Advertiser; Birmingham Daily Post; Brighton Gazette; Brooklyn Daily Eagle Bucks Herald; Cambridge Chronicle and Journal; Cambridge Independent Press; Carlisle Journal; Carlisle Patriot; Chelmsford Chronicle; Chicago Daily Tribune; Connaught Watchman; La Correspondencia de Portugal; The Daily News; Daily Telegraph; Dublin Evening Post; The Dundee Courier and Argus; Eastern Counties Journal; The Era; Essex Standard; Evening Mail; The Examiner; Exeter and Plymouth Gazette; Glasgow Daily Herald; The Globe; The Guardian; Hampshire Advertiser; Hampshire Chronicle; Hereford Journal; Hertford Mercury and Reformer; Illustrated London News; Indépendance Belge; Inverness Courier; The Ipswich Journal; Japan Daily Mail; Kentish Gazette; Lake's Falmouth Packet and Cornwall Advertiser; Lancaster Gazette; The Leader; Leeds Intelligencer; Liverpool Daily Post; Liverpool Mail; Lloyds Weekly; London Daily News; London Evening Standard; The London Gazette; Manchester Courier and Lancashire General Advertiser; Morning Chronicle; Morning Post; New Zealand Herald; Norfolk News; North Devon Journal; Northern Whig; The Norwich Argus; Norwich, Yarmouth and Lynn Commercial Gazette; Oxford Chronicle and Reading Gazette; Oxford Journal; Oxford Times; Oxford University and City Herald; Norddeutsche Allgemeine Zeitung; Pall Mall Gazette; Reading Mercury; Shields Gazette and Daily Telegraph; South Eastern Gazette; South London Press; Staffordshire Gazette and County Standard; Stamford Mercury; The Standard; Sussex Advertiser; Taunton Courier, and Western Advertiser; The Times; Trewman's Exeter Flying Post; West Kent Guardian; Western Daily Press; Westmorland Gazette; Windsor and Eton Express; Worcestershire Chronicle; Yorkshire Gazette; Yorkshire Post and Leeds Intelligencer.*

SECONDARY SOURCES

Maurice Agulhon, *The Republican Experiment, 1848–1852*, trans. Janet Lloyd (Cambridge, 1983).
Benedict Anderson, *Imagined Communities: Reflections on the Origins and Spread of Nationalism* (London, 2006; first published 1983).
Antony Anghie, *Imperialism, Sovereignty and the Making of International Law* (Cambridge, 2005).
Ian Anstruther, *The Scandal of the Andover Workhouse* (London, 1973).
David Armitage, *The Declaration of Independence: A Global History* (Cambridge, Mass., 2007).
David Armitage and Sanjay Subrahmanyam, eds., *The Age of Revolutions in Global Context* (Basingstoke, 2010).
Diane Atkinson, *Love and Dirt: The Marriage of Arthur Munby and Hannah Cullwick* (London, 2004).
Cemil Aydin, *The Idea of the Muslim World: A Global Intellectual History* (Cambridge, Mass., 2017).
J. H. Baker, *The Law's Two Bodies: Some Evidentiary Problems in English Legal History* (Oxford, 2001).
Joshua Barkan, *Corporate Sovereignty: Law and Government under Capitalism* (Minneapolis, 2013).
Chris Bayly, *The Birth of the Modern World, 1780–1914* (Oxford, 2004).
Duncan Bell, *The Idea of Greater Britain: Empire and the Future of World Order, 1860–1900* (Princeton, 2007).
Eugenio F. Biagini, *Liberty, Retrenchment and Reform: Popular Liberalism in the Age of Gladstone* (Cambridge, 1992).
Biographie coloniale belge (Brussels, 1948).
Alastair J. L. Blanchard, "Queer Desires and Classicizing Strategies of Resistance," in Kate Fisher and Rebecca Langlands, eds., *Sex, Knowledge, and Receptions of the Past* (Oxford, 2015).
Frederic Boase, *Modern English Biography*, Vol. 4 (Truro, 1908).
Asa Briggs, *The Age of Improvement, 1783–1867* (Harlow, 1959).
British Museum, "Harry Emanuel," https://www.britishmuseum.org/research/search_the_collection_database/term_details.aspx?bioId=87894.
W. L. Burn, *The Age of Equipoise: A Study of the Mid-Victorian Generation* (London, 1964).
J. H. Burns, "Happiness and Utility: Jeremy Bentham's Equation," *Utilitas*, vol. 17, no. 1 (March 2005), 46–61.
L. H. Dudley Buxton and Strickland Gibson, *Oxford University Ceremonies* (Oxford, 1935).
W. F. Bynum, Roy Porter, and Michael Shepherd, eds., *The Anatomy of Madness: Essays in the History of Psychiatry: Institutions and Society* (London, 1985).
Edward Cavanagh, "A Company with Sovereignty and Subjects of Its Own? The Case of the Hudson's Bay Company, 1670–1763," *Canadian Journal of Law and Society*, vol. 26, no. 1 (2011).
Kellow Chesney, *Victorian Underworld* (Harmondsworth, 1970).
Stefan Collini, *Public Moralists: Political Thought and Intellectual Life in Britain 1850–1930* (Oxford, 1991).
Philip Collins, *Dickens and Crime* (London, 1964).
Aurelian Crăiuţu, *Liberalism Under Siege: The Political Thought of the French Doctrinaires* (Lanham, 2003).
Matthew Craven, "Between Law and History: The Berlin Conference of 1884–1885 and the Logic of Free Trade," *London Review of International Law*, vol. 3, no. 1 (March 2015), 31–59.

Ketton Cremer, *Felbrigg: The Story of a House* (London, 1962).
Nigel Cross, *The Common Writer: Life in Nineteenth-Century Grub Street* (Cambridge, 1985).
S. E. Crowe, *The Berlin West Africa Conference, 1884-85* (London, 1942).
John Culme, *The Directory of Gold & Silversmiths, Jewellers & Allied Traders, 1838-1914* (London, 1987).
Robert Darnton, "The High Enlightenment and the Low-Life of Literature in Pre-Revolutionary France," *Past and Present*, vol. 51 (1971).
———. *The Great Cat Massacre and Other Episodes in French Cultural History* (London, 1984).
Robin Darwall-Smith, *A History of University College* (Oxford, 2008).
Saul David, *The Indian Mutiny 1857* (New York, 2002).
Natalie Zemon Davis, *The Return of Martin Guerre* (Cambridge, Mass., 1984).
———. "On the Lame," *American Historical Review*, vol. 93, no. 3 (June 1988), 572-603.
Natalie Zemon Davis and Peter N. Miller, "About an Inventory: A Conversation between Natalie Zemon Davis and Peter N. Miller," https://www.youtube.com/watch?v=hwiR3dz4Wg8.
István Deák, *The Lawful Revolution: Louis Kossuth and the Hungarians, 1848-1849* (New York, 1979).
———. *Beyond Nationalism: A Social and Political History of the Habsburg Officer Corp, 1848-1918* (New York, 1990).
Maksymilian Del Mar, "Legal Fictions and Legal Change in the Common Law Tradition," in Maksymilian Del Mar and William Twining, eds., *Legal Fictions in Theory and Practice* (Heidelberg, 2015).
John Dewey, "The Historic Background of Corporate Legal Personality," *Yale Law Journal*, vol. 35, no. 6 (April 1926).
Dictionary of National Biography, ed. Sidney Lee, Vol. 57 (London, 1899).
Arthur Herbert Dodd, "Trevor Family, of Trevalun, Denbighshire, Plas Têg, Flintshire, and Glynde Sussex," *Dictionary of Welsh Biography* (1959).
———. "Trevor Family of Brynkynallt, Denbighshire," *Dictionary of Welsh Biography* (1959).
Sos Eltis, *Acts of Desire* (Oxford, 2013).
The Encyclopaedia of Nineteenth-Century Photography (New York, 2008).
Frank Eyck, *The Frankfurt Parliament 1848-1849* (London, 1968).
Lucien Febvre, *Le problème de l'incroyance au XVIe siècle. La religion de Rabelais* (Paris, 1947).
C.H.S. Fifoot, *Frederic William Maitland: A Life* (Cambridge, Mass., 1971).
Norman J. Finkel, *Insanity on Trial* (New York, 1988).
Margot Finn, *After Chartism: Class and Nation in English Radical Politics, 1848-1874* (Cambridge, 1993).
Andrew Fitzmaurice, *Humanism and America: An Intellectual History of English Colonisation, 1500-1625* (Cambridge, 2003).
———. *Sovereignty, Property, and Empire, 1500-2000* (Cambridge, 2014).
———. "Scepticism of the Civilizing Mission in International Law," in Martti Koskenniemi, Walter Rech, and Manuel Jiménez Fonseca, eds., *International Law and Empire: Historical Explorations* (Oxford, 2017).
Richard Foulkes, *Church and Stage in Victorian England* (Cambridge, 1997).
Tibor Frank, "Marketing Hungary: Kossuth and the Politics of Propaganda," in László Péter, Martyn Rady, and Peter Sherwood, eds., *Lajos Kossuth Sent Word: Papers Delivered on the Occasion of the Bicentenary of Kossuth's Birth* (London, 2003).
John Gallagher and Ronald Robinson, "The Imperialism of Free Trade," *Economic History Review*, vol. 6, no. 1 (1953), 1-15.

Mirella Ghisu, "Malades mentaux, justice et libertés. Renverser l'entonnoir?" *Mental'idées*, no. 17, Brussels (March 2012).

Carlo Ginzburg, *The Cheese and the Worms: The Cosmos of a Sixteenth-Century Miller* (London, 1980).

David Goodway, *London Chartism, 1838-1848* (Cambridge, 1982).

Peter Gordon, "What Is Intellectual History," Harvard Colloquium for Intellectual History (2012), https://projects.iq.harvard.edu/harvardcolloquium/pages/what-intellectual-history.

Count Philipp Georg Gudenus, "Metternich as Ghostwriter," *Manuscripts*, vol. 40, no. 1 (Winter 1988), 41–42.

Szabad György, *Kossuth and the British "Balance of Power" Policy (1859-1861)* (Budapest, 1960).

Arthur G. Haas, "Metternich and the Slavs," *Austrian History Yearbook*, Vol. 4 (January 1968).

C. I. Hamilton, "John Wilson Croker: Patronage and Clientage at the Admiralty, 1809-1857," *Historical Journal*, vol. 31, no. 1 (2000), 49–77.

Ron Harris, "The Transplantation of the Legal Discourse on Corporate Personality Theories: From German Codification to British Political Pluralism and American Big Business," *Washington and Lee Law Review* (2006), 1421–1478.

F.J.C. Hearnshaw, *The Centenary History of King's College London* (London, 1929).

Tamar Herzog, *A Short History of European Law* (Cambridge, Mass, 2018).

Christopher Hibbert, Ben Weinreb, John Keay, and Julia Keay, "Regent Street," *The London Encyclopaedia*, 3rd ed. (London, 2010).

G. F. Hickson, "Palmerston and the Clayton-Bulwer Treaty," *Cambridge Historical Journal*, vol. 3, no. 3 (1931), 295–303.

Boyd Hilton, *A Mad, Bad, and Dangerous People? England 1783-1846* (Oxford, 2006).

———. "Moral Disciplines," in Peter Mandler, ed., *Liberty and Authority in Victorian Britain* (Oxford, 2006), 224–246.

Eric Hobsbawm, *The Age of Revolution: 1789-1848* (London, 2010).

Adam Hochschild, *King Leopold's Ghost* (Boston, 1998).

Lee Holcombe, *Wives and Property: Reform of the Married Women's Property Law in Nineteenth-Century England* (Toronto, 1983).

Vladimir R. Idelson, "The Law of Nations and the Individual," *Transactions of the Grotius Society*, vol. 30 (1944).

Ernst Kantorowicz, *The King's Two Bodies: A Study in Medieval Political Theology* (Princeton, 1957).

Astrid Kjeldgaard-Pederson, *The International Legal Personality of the Individual* (Oxford, 2018).

Cecil M. Knatchbull-Hugessen, *The Political Evolution of the Hungarian Nation*, 2 vols. (London, 1908).

Thomas Knowles and Serena Trowbridge, eds., *Insanity and the Lunatic Asylum in the Nineteenth Century* (Abingdon, 2014).

Martti Koskenniemi, *The Gentle Civilizer of Nations: The Rise and Fall of International Law 1870-1960* (Cambridge, 2001).

Seth Koven, *Slumming: Sexual and Social Politics in Victorian London* (Princeton, 2004).

Zsuzsanna Lada, "The Invention of a Hero: Lajos Kossuth in England (1851)," *European History Quarterly*, vol. 43, no. 1 (2013), 5–26.

Andrew Lambert, *The Crimean War: British Grand Strategy against Russia, 1853-1856*, 2nd ed. (London, 2011).

Randall Lesaffer, "Argument from Roman Law in Current International Law: Occupation and Acquisitive Prescription," *European Journal of International Law*, vol. 16, no. 1 (2005).

Michael Lobban, "English Approaches to International Law in the Nineteenth Century," in Matthew Craven, Malgosia Fitzmaurice, and Maria Vogiatzi, eds., *Time, History, and International Law* (Leiden, 2007).

———. "Legal Fictions before the Age of Reform," in Maksymilian Del Mar and William Twining, eds., *Legal Fictions in Theory and Practice* (Heidelberg, 2015).

Arnulf Becker Lorca, *Mestizo International Law: A Global Intellectual History, 1842–1933* (Cambridge, 2014).

William Roger Louis, *Ends of British Imperialism: The Scramble for Empire, Suez, and Decolonization* (London, 2006).

Doreen Lustig, *Corporate Regulation and International Law: A History of Failure?* (Oxford, 2019).

Doreen Lustig, Markus D. Dubber, and Christopher Tomlins, eds., *The Oxford Handbook of Legal History* (Oxford, 2018).

Martin Lynn, "British Policy, Trade, and Informal Empire in the Mid-Nineteenth Century," in Andrew Porter, ed., *The Oxford History of the British Empire: The Nineteenth Century* (Oxford, 1999).

Donald MacAndrew, "Mr and Mrs Windham: A Mid-Victorian Melodrama from Real Life," in *The Saturday Book: Being the Eleventh Annual Appearance of This Renowned Repository of Curiosities and Looking-glass of Past and Present*, ed. Leonard Russell (Watford, 1951), 191–210.

Peter Mandler, "'Race' and 'Nation' in Mid-Victorian Thought," in Stefan Collini, Richard Whatmore, and Brian Young, eds., *History, Religion, and Culture: British Intellectual History 1750–1950* (Cambridge, 2000).

———. ed., *Liberty and Authority in Victorian Britain* (Oxford, 2006).

Karuna Mantena, "The Crisis of Liberal Imperialism," in Duncan Bell, ed., *Victorian Visions of Global Order: Empire and International Relations in Nineteenth-Century Political Thought* (Cambridge, 2007).

———. *Alibis of Empire: Henry Maine and the Ends of Liberal Imperialism* (Princeton, 2010).

Mark Mazower, "The Strange Triumph of Human Rights, 1933–1950," *Historical Journal*, vol. 47, no. 2 (2004).

Kirsten McKenzie, *Imperial Underworld: An Escaped Convict and the Transformation of the British Colonial Order* (Cambridge, 2016).

Rohan McWilliam, *The Tichborne Claimant: A Victorian Sensation* (London, 2007).

———. "Unauthorised Identities: The Imposter, the Fake and the Secret History in Nineteenth-Century Britain," in Margot Finn, Michael Lobban, and Jenny Bourne Taylor, eds., *Legitimacy and Illegitimacy in Nineteenth-Century Law, Literature and History* (Basingstoke, 2010), 67–92.

Uday Singh Mehta, *Liberalism and Empire: A Study in Nineteenth-Century British Liberal Thought* (Chicago, 1999).

Frederick Merk, *The Oregon Question* (Cambridge, Mass., 1967).

Douglas Moggach and Gareth Stedman Jones, eds., *The 1848 Revolutions and European Political Thought* (Cambridge, 2018).

Jeanne Morefield, *"Covenants without Swords": Idealist Liberalism and the Spirit of Empire* (Princeton, 2005).

Samuel Moyn, *The Last Utopia* (Cambridge, Mass., 2010).

———. "Imaginary Intellectual History," in Darrin M. McMahon and Samuel Moyn, eds., *Rethinking Modern European Intellectual History* (Oxford, 2014).

Frank Lorenz Müller, *Britain and the German Question: Perceptions of Nationalism and Political Reform, 1830–63* (Basingstoke, 2002).

William Mulligan, "The Fugitive Slave Circulars, 1875–1876," *Journal of Imperial and Commonwealth History*, vol. 37, no. 2 (2009).
Deborah Epstein Nord, *Walking the Victorian Streets: Women, Representation and the City* (Ithaca, 1995).
Oxford Dictionary of National Biography (Oxford, 2019).
Alan Palmer, *Metternich: Councillor of Europe* (London, 1972).
Jonathan Parry, *The Politics of Patriotism: English Liberalism, National Identity, and Europe, 1830–1886* (Cambridge, 2006).
———. "Sir Austen Henry Layard," in the *Oxford Dictionary of National Biography* (Oxford, F2004–2019).
René Piret, "Le Code Napoléon en Belgique de 1804 à 1954," *Revue internationale de droit comparé*, vol. 4 (1954), 753–791.
Jennifer Pitts, *A Turn to Empire: The Rise of Imperial Liberalism in Britain and France* (Princeton 2005).
———. "Boundaries of Victorian International Law," in *Victorian Visions of Global Order*, ed. Duncan Bell (Cambridge, 2007), 67–88.
———. "Empire and Legal Universalisms in the Eighteenth Century," *American Historical Review*, vol. 117, no. 1 (February 2012).
———. *Boundaries of the International: Law and Empire* (Cambridge, Mass., 2018).
J.G.A. Pocock, *Virtue, Commerce, and History* (Cambridge, 1985).
———. "On the Unglobality of Contexts: Cambridge Methods and the History of Political Thought," *Global Intellectual History*, vol. 4, no. 1 (2019).
Mary Poovey, *Making a Social Body: British Cultural Formation, 1830–1864* (Chicago, 1995).
Roy Porter, *Mind-Forg'd Manacles: A History of Madness in England from the Restoration to the Regency* (London, 1987).
———. *London: A Social History* (London, 1994).
———. *Madness: A Brief History* (Oxford, 2002).
Roy Porter, Helen Nicholson, and Bridgett Bennett, *Women, Madness and Spiritualism: Vol. 1: Georgina Weldon and Louisa Lowe* (London, 2003).
Steven Press, *Rogue Empires* (Cambridge, Mass., 2017).
Mike Rapport, *1848: Year of Revolution* (London, 2008).
Jasper Ridley, *Lord Palmerston* (Basingstoke, 1970).
Michael J. D. Roberts, *Making English Morals: Voluntary Association and Moral Reform in England, 1787–1886* (Cambridge, 2004).
Ronald Robinson and John Gallagher with Alice Denny, *Africa and the Victorians: The Official Mind of Imperialism* (London, 1965).
Mina Roces, *Women's Movements and the Filipina, 1986–2008* (Honolulu, 2012).
Helen Rogers, "Women and Liberty," in Peter Mandler, ed., *Liberty and Authority in Victorian Britain* (Oxford, 2006).
Emma Rothschild, "Language and Empire, c. 1800," *Historical Research*, vol. 78, no. 200 (May 2005).
David Runciman, *Pluralism and the Personality of the State* (Cambridge, 1997).
Robert Saunders, "The Politics of the Reform and the Making of the Second Reform Act, 1848–1867," *Historical Journal*, vol. 50, no. 3 (2007), 571–591.
John Saville, *1848: The British State and the Chartist Movement* (Cambridge, 1987).
Miroslav Šedivý, *Metternich, the Great Powers and the Eastern Question* (Pilsen, 2013).
William Sewell, *The Logics of History: Social Theory and Social Transformation* (Chicago, 2005).
Mary Lyndon Shanley, *Feminism, Marriage, and the Law in Victorian England* (Princeton, 1989).

Edward Shorter, *A History of Psychiatry* (New York, 1997).
Elaine Showalter, *The Female Malady: Women, Madness, and English Culture, 1830–1980* (New York, 1985).
Wolfram Siemann, *Die deutsche Revolution von 1848/49* (Frankfurt, 1985).
———. *Metternich: Stratege und Visionär: Eine Biografie* (Munich, 2016).
Mrinalina Sinha, "Nations in an Imperial Crucible," in Philippa Levine, ed., *Gender and Empire* (Oxford, 2004).
Alan Sked, *Metternich and Austria: An Evaluation* (Basingstoke, 2008).
———. "The Nationality Problem in the Habsburg Monarchy," in Douglas Moggach and Gareth Stedman Jones, eds., *The 1848 Revolutions and European Political Thought* (Cambridge, 2018).
Quentin Skinner, *Visions of Politics: Vol. 1: Regarding Method* (Cambridge, 2002).
———. "A Genealogy of the Modern State," *Proceedings of the British Academy*, vol. 162 (2009), 325–370.
———. "Theories as Social Action: An Interview with Quentin Skinner," Collège de France, Books and Ideas, April 11, 2019, https://booksandideas.net/Theories-as-Social-Action.html.
Glenda Sluga, "Women at the Congress of Vienna," *Eurozine* (January 2015).
Philip Thurmond Smith, *Policing Victorian London: Political Policing, Public Order, and the London Metropolitan Police* (London, 1985).
Jonathan Sperber, *The European Revolutions, 1848–1851* (Cambridge, 1994).
G. D. Squibb, *Doctors' Commons: A History of the College of Advocates and Doctors of Law* (Oxford, 1977).
Gareth Stedman Jones, "Anglo-Marxism, Neo-Marxism and the Discursive Approach to History," in *Was Bleibt von Marxistischen Persepktiven in der Geschichtsforschung?* (Göttingen, 1997).
Philip J. Stern, *The Company-State: Corporate Sovereignty and the Early Modern Foundations of the British Empire in India* (Oxford, 2011).
Lawrence Stone, *The Family, Sex and Marriage in England 1500–1800* (Harmondsworth, 1977).
Judith Surkis, "Of Scandals and Supplements: Relating Intellectual and Cultural History," in Darrin M. McMahon and Samuel Moyn, eds., *Rethinking Modern European Intellectual History* (Oxford, 2014).
John Sutherland, *The Stanford Companion to Victorian Literature* (Stanford, 1989).
Casper Sylvest, "'Our Passion for Legality': International Law and Imperialism in Late Nineteenth-Century Britain," *Review of International Studies*, vol. 34, no. 3 (2008).
———. *British Liberal Internationalism, 1880–1930* (Manchester, 2009).
Michael Taggart, "Alexander Chaffers and the Genesis of the Vexatious Actions Act 1896," *Cambridge Law Journal*, vol. 63, no. 3 (2004).
Trudi Tate, *The Crimean War* (London, 2018).
Miles Taylor, "The 1848 Revolutions in the British Empire," *Past and Present*, vol. 166 (2000), 146–181.
Brian Thompson, *The Disastrous Mrs Weldon* (New York, 2000).
David Todd, "Beneath Sovereignty: Extraterritoriality and Imperial Internationalism in Nineteenth-Century Egypt," *Law and History Review*, vol. 36, no. 1 (February 2018), 105–137.
Robert Travers, "A British Empire by Treaty in Eighteenth-Century India," in *Empire by Treaty: Negotiating European Expansion, 1600–1900*, ed. Saliha Belmessous (Oxford, 2015), 132–160.
Richard Tuck, *The Rights of War and Peace: Political Thought and the International Order from Grotius to Kant* (Oxford, 1999).

Henry S. Turner, *The Corporate Commonwealth: Pluralism and Political Fictions in England, 1516-1651* (Chicago, 2016).
Jan Vandersmissen, *Koningen van de wereld: Leopold II en de aardrijkskundige beweging* (Leuven, 2009).
———. "The King's Most Eloquent Campaigner: Emile de Laveleye, Leopold II and the Creation of the Congo Free State," *Journal of Belgian History*, vol. 41 (2011).
Georgios Varouxakis, "1848 and British Political Thought on 'The Principle of Nationality,'" in Douglas Moggach and Gareth Stedman Jones, eds., *The 1848 Revolutions and European Political Thought* (Cambridge, 2018), 140–161.
Brian Vick, *Defining Germany: The Frankfurt Parliamentarians and National Identity* (Cambridge, Mass., 2002).
———. *The Congress of Vienna: Power and Politics after Napoléon* (Cambridge, Mass., 2014).
Judith R. Walkowitz, *Prostitution and Victorian Society: Women, Class, and the State* (Cambridge, 1980).
———. *City of Dreadful Delight: Narratives of Sexual Danger in Late-Victorian London* (Chicago, 1992).
John Manning Ward, *Colonial Self-Government: The British Experience, 1759-1856* (London, 1976).
The Wellesley Index to Victorian Periodicals, 1824-1900 (2006-2019).
Natasha Wheatley, "Spectral Legal Personality in Interwar International Law: On Ways of not Being a State," *Law and History Review*, vol. 35, no. 3 (August 2017), 753–787.
Percy Henry Winfield, *The Chief Sources of English Legal History* (Cambridge, Mass., 1925).
James Winter, *London's Teeming Streets: 1830-1914* (London, 1993).
Sarah Wise, *Inconvenient People: Lunacy, Liberty and the Mad-Doctors in Victorian England* (Berkeley, 2012).
Phil Withington, *The Politics of Commonwealth: Citizens and Freemen in Early Modern England* (Cambridge, 2005).
Ludwig Wittgenstein, *Philosophical Investigations*, trans. G.E.M. Anscombe (Oxford, 1953).
Ellen Meiksins Wood, "Why It Matters," *London Review of Books*, vol. 30, no. 18 (September 25, 2008), 3–6.
Margaret K. Woodhouse, "The Marriage and Divorce Bill of 1857," *American Journal of Legal History*, vol. 3 (1959).
The Workhouse, "Andover, Hampshire," http://www.workhouses.org.uk/Andover/.
Nigel Yate, *Anglican Ritualism and Victorian Britain 1830-1910* (Oxford, 1999).

INDEX

1848 revolutions, 10–11, 12; Austrian Empire at the heart of, 109–10; internationalisation of, 183; Twiss's response to, 112

Abbas I, 65
Abdul Hamid II, 412
absolutism, 196
Acton, William, 239, 245, 303
Adams, John Quincy, 90
Administration of Justice Act (1970), 80
Admiralty, 9, 35, 123, 326, 335, 414–15
Admiralty Courts, 53, 60, 70, 76–80, 88–89, 121, 139, 221–22, 327, 397–402, 422
Africa, 77, 164, 224–25, 414–19, 420, 423–26, 436, 533
African Exploration Fund, 425
Agassiz, Louis, 45
Age of Equipoise, 12
Albany, the, 74–75, 120; early residents of (including Lord Byron and Gladstone), 74; as the former home of Viscount Melbourne and Prince Frederick, 74; lampooning of in the novel *The Bachelor of the Albany* (Savage), 75
Albert, Prince Consort of England, 16, 46, 49, 75, 213, 219, 331
Alcock, Henrietta, 332
Alcock, Lucy, 16, 332, 336, 339–40, 342, 506
Alcock, Rutherford, 39, 74, 332, 333, 335, 339–40, 347, 425, 437, 449, 506; expertise of in Japanese culture, 334; as president of the Royal Geographical Society, 424
Ali, Hyder, 222
Ali, Muhammed, 64–65, 522
All Souls College, 333, 402–3, 405
All the Year Round (Dickens), 291
American Colonisation Society, 445–46, 456
Ancien Régime, 31, 153, 167, 188, 515
Anderson, Benedict, 167n261
Anderson, Mr. and Mrs., 360
Anderson, Percy, 461
Anderson vs Gorrie, 527–28

Angra Pequena, 458
Annales historians, 23
anti-slavery efforts, 228, 415, 423–24, 453, 491
"Aphorisms" (Metternich), 190
"Applicability of the European Law of Nations to African Slave States" (T. Twiss), 414, 495–96
Archbishop Laud, 58
Archbishop of Canterbury. *See* Sumner, John (Archbishop of Canterbury)
Archbishop of Westminster, 98
Arches Court, 76, 88
Argyle Rooms, 235
aristocracy, moral, 187
Armitage, George, 282
Armstrong, Eliza, 304, 305
Arndt, Ernst, 159
Arnold, Matthew, 9, 36
Arnold, Thomas, 57
Arntz, Egide, 429, 434–35, 451, 452–53, 454, 457
Arthur, Chester, 448
artificial persons, 1–2, 531–32; concept of among ecclesiastical lawyers, 2–3; concept of among international lawyers, 2–3; concept of revived in the late nineteenth century, 1; connection with natural persons, 3–4; debate concerning an independent existence for, 6; "family resemblances" between the creation of artificial and natural persons, 25; Hobbes's distinction between artificial and natural persons, 3; mystic fictions of, 4; non-state artificial persons, 7; rules governing the creation of, 6; widening recognition of the status of, 20
J. S. Rarey's Art of Taming Horses (Rarey), 242–43
Ascot Week, 253, 253–54n89, 300
Association for the Reform and Codification of the Law of Nations, 397; Twiss's addresses to, 414, 418, 422, 502

INDEX

Athenaeum, Twiss's membership in, 35–40, 35n36, 65, 74–75, 335, 390, 521, 523; Twiss's comments on dining at the club, 37, 37n44; Twiss's donations to the library of, 36, 36n42; Twiss's role in the selection of candidates for membership in, 35–36, 37–38n46, 38n51, 39–40, 39–40n57, 59, 63, 63n177; Twiss's ties and relationship building with members of, 37–38, 37–38n46, 38n47
Atlay, James, 38
Austen, Jane, 241
Austin, John, 2, 2–3n5, 125
Australia, 38, 151; universal manhood suffrage in, 38n50
Austria/Austrian Empire, 45, 72, 104, 108, 127, 128, 133n101, 136, 138, 142, 148, 154, 173, 179, 183, 215; alliance with England, 201; the "Austrian Cabinet," 161; the Austrian Constitution, 164–65; disintegration of under the forces of nationalism, 111–12; essential role of in Europe, 139; governmental organization of, 150; lack of will in for reform, 191; Magyar population of, 184–86, 188; Metternich's views concerning, 164–65, 165–66n257, 181–82; relations with England, 201; relations with Europe and specifically Germany, 161; revolution in, 111; and the rights of sovereignty, 144–45; struggle of Sardinia against, 167–68; on the types of monarchy that would be best for Austria, 140–41; war with France, 217–18, 220–21. *See also* 1848 revolutions, Austrian Empire at the heart of
"Austria and Germany" (T. Twiss), 128, 133n104, 134n106
Awadh, 225, 234, 437; annexation of, 226–27, 228; dependence of on the British East India Company, 226; the king of Awadh, 225–26; seizure of, 225; sovereignty of, 227; Twiss's defence of, 228

Bagehot, Walter, 36
Baker, J. H., 27
Balkans, the, 201
Ballantine, William, 382
Baraldi, Pietro Neri, 374
Barante, M. de, 171–72; Metternich's distortion of his views, 172–73

Barker, Ernest, 1
Barnard, Charles Townshend, 323, 359
Barnard, Francis, 293–94
Barnes and Bernard, solicitors to Twiss, 336, 347, 371, 372, 373, 375
Baron von Richtofen, 424
Batthyani, Lajos, 133, 188–89
Bavaria, 159
Bayly, Chris, 22–23
Belcher, Edward, 48–49
Belgian Association, 441, 442, 476
Belgium, 48, 423, 441, 443–44, 460; Belgian expansionism, 423. *See also* Leopold II (king of Belgium)
Bellot, Joseph René, 48–49
Benson, Edward, 357, 358, 363, 365, 369, 371, 373, 379, 389, 504, 521; reaction to the withdrawal of libel charges against Chaffers, 375–76
Bentham, Jeremy, 1, 2, 2–3n5
Berlin Conference (1884–1885), 20–21, 53, 435, 458–74 *passim*; aftermath of, 497–98; aims of, 467–68; Bismarck's role in, 473–74, 481–82, 486–87, 490; British attempts to slow the process of recognition of the International Association, 484–85; and British interests concerning the Niger River, 486; compatibility of Selborne's and Twiss's positions during, 469–70, 473–74; debates concerning the significance of, 491; Declaration of the Third Basis, 474; discussion on the rules of occupation, 466–68; first conference of, 461–62; on the free navigation of the Congo River, 464–65; General Act of the Conference, 474, 490, 502; and the idea that non-state actors have a role in international society, 491–92; and the issue of who exercised sovereignty over the Congo, 474; and the *Projet de declaration*, 463–64, 468–69, 470–72; on the recognition of the International Association of the Congo, 475–77; resumption of after the Christmas break, 466; on the sovereign status of the Congo, 459; stalemate concerning the third basis of, 472–73; three "bases" of, 459; on the transfer of sovereign rights, 466–67; Twiss's summation of the achievements of, 492–93

Bernard, Johann (Count von Rechberg), 327–28
Bernard, Montague, 402
Berry, Blaze de, 118–19n27
Bethel, Richard, 327
Bigge, Arthur, 37–38n46
Bille, M. de, 75
Binny, John, 245, 246
Bismarck, Otto von (Prince Bismarck), 20, 21, 458–59, 472, 475–76, 480. *See also* Berlin Conference (1884–1885), Bismarck's role in
Black Book of the Admiralty (T. Twiss, editor), 397, 399–402, 403–4, 406, 407
Black Sea, the, 73, 210–11, 212, 423, 493
Blackstone, William, 5, 26
Bleak House (Dickens), 76, 277
Bluntschli, Johann Kasper, 2–3n5, 440
Bocage, José Vicente Barbosa de, 476
Bonaparte, Charles-Louis-Napoleon (Napoleon III), 195, 197, 206, 208, 214, 217, 253; dispatching of troops to Lombardy, 213; intentions of on war, 214–15; success of, 199; Twiss's criticism of, 199–200
Bonaparte, Louis Lucien, 179n321, 183, 196
Bonaparte, Napoléon, 43, 64, 90, 108, 127, 131, 172, 190; civil code of, 62, 514, 520; system of government of, 150
Bonwell, James, 84–85, 299
Borneo, 437, 443, 467, 478
Bourbon Restoration (183–1840), 171
Bowen, George, 38n51, 63n177
Bowyer, George, 2–3n5, 62, 99–100, 379–80
Brazza, Pierre Savorgnan de, 428, 435
Brett, William (Lord Esher), 506, 527
Bright, James Franck, 523
British Foreign Office, 21, 315, 316, 324, 441, 476; scepticism of King Leopold II, 487
British North Borneo Company. *See* North Borneo Chartered Company (NBCC)
Brito Capelo, Guilherme Augusto de, 476–77
Brough, William, 237–38, 241
Brougham, William, 40, 49–50n109
Broun-Ramsey, James, 226–27
Brown, Charles, 253, 258, 273
Bruce, H. A., 349
Bruce, Knight, 291
Bruce, Thomas, 346
Brunel, Isambard Kingdom, 46

Buck, H J., 264–65, 268, 287
Bulgarian Horrors and the Question of the East (Gladstone), 412–13
Bundestaat (federal state), 169
Buol-Schauenstein, Ferdinand, 212–13
Burdett, Francis, 347
Burdett-Coutts, Angela, 347, 352, 356
Burke, Edmund, 110
Burshenschaft, 160
Bury, Henry Blaze de, 118–19n37
Bury, Marie Pauline Rose Blaze de, 118–19n37
Butler, Josephine, 304
Buxton, Thomas Fowell, 424, 425

Cairns, Hugh, 287–88, 319, 403, 417
Cameron, Verney Lovett, 425
Campbell, Colin, 331
Campbell, Gertrude (born Gertrude Elizabeth Blood), 330; presentation of to court, 330–31
Canning, Charles, 230
Capital of the Tycoon, The (R. Alcock), 332–33
Cardwell, Charles, 37–38n46
Cardwell, Edward, 75
Carter, Robert, 193
Casement, Roger, 481, 498, 500
Casino de Venise, 245, 246
Castro, Thomas, 354
Catholic "Emancipation" Act (1829), 99, 234
Catholic Relief Act (1829), 94–95, 98, 102
Catholics, 53, 97, 315; anti-Catholic fear, 98–99; anti-Catholic riots, 100; Catholic Church in England, 6; the Catholic Church as *perfecta societas*, 100; Catholic reform in England, 89; toleration of, 12. *See also* emancipation, of Catholics
Cavendish, Henry, 176
Cawnpore (Kanpur), massacre of the British in, 225
Chaffers, Alexander, 16, 306–8, 395, 507, 527–28; attempted blackmail of Twiss by, 336–39, 367, 380, 504, 506, 508–9, 511, 515, 516; attempt to have Lady Travers Twiss deported, 505; bills of cost presented by to Maria Gelas, 372–73; case of against Yeatman, 527–29; charges of perjury against Lady Twiss brought by Chaffers in the aftermath of the Twiss/Chaffers libel trial,

Chaffers (continued)
    389–90; damage to his reputation after the libel trial of, 383; defamation of Henry Williams by, 376–77; defamation case against Alexander Macmillan, 505–6; dire financial situation of, 336–37, 343, 351; as an inmate of St Pancras Workhouse, 504–5; libel case of against James Henderson, 507–11. *See also* Twiss/Chaffers libel trial
Chantrey, Francis, 36, 36n40
Chappell, Frederick, 274
Charles II (king of England), 43
Charles V (Holy Roman Emperor), 436
chartered companies, 19
Chartist movement/Chartists, 12, 146, 183–84, 186, 230
Chichele, Henry, 402
Chichele Professorship of International Law at Oxford, 397, 402; Twiss's attempts to be appointed to, 402–6
China, 74, 224, 335, 408, 410–11, 414
Christian VIII (king of Denmark), 124
Christians, Orthodox, 201
Christianity, 95, 203, 407, 409
Christmas Carol, A (Dickens), 44
Chronicles and Memorials of Great Britain and Ireland During the Middle Ages (T. Twiss, editor), 397–99
Church of England, 6, 26, 57, 59, 62, 81, 86, 96, 99, 100, 106, 316, 318, 323, 326–27, 346, 349, 530; Catholic titles to, 98
civil law, 68; institutional role of in English Ecclesiastical Courts, 70, 76; study of at Oxford as moribund under Phillimore, 69; Twiss's call for reform on the teaching and role of civil law, 69–71
Clark, Alan, 74n219
Clayton-Bulwer Treaty (1850), 469, 470
Clements, Rebecca, 374
Clytie: A Novel of Modern Life (Hatton), 390–91
Cobden, Richard, 35; Twiss's attack on, 129–30
Cockburn, Alexander, 49–50n109, 382
Code Napoléon (1807), 62, 514, 520
Coke, Edward, 70
Cole, Charles, 279–80
Cole, G.D.H., 6
Coleridge, John, 290–91, 380–81, 403, 506–7

Colombia Market, 348, 356
Colonial Church and School Society, 316
Comité d'Études du Haut-Congo (Society for the Study of the Upper Congo), 442, 443, 454, 455
Compagnie des Indes Orientales, 394
Compagnie de la Nouvelle-France, 394
Compiègne, Victor de, 424
Concert of Europe, 10, 12, 19, 40, 43, 108, 109, 144, 203, 207, 413; admission of the Ottoman Empire to, 211; justification of the suppression of liberty through, 209; Twiss's views concerning, 66–67
Congo/Congo Free State, 4, 28, 86, 87, 232, 311, 498, 512, 516, 532, 533, 534; case presented by Twiss for the transformation of the International African Association into the Congo Free State, 19; cessions of sovereignty in, 446–47, 452, 482; constitution of drafted by Twiss, 484; creation/formation of, 18–19, 20, 21, 25; establishment of European factories in, 430; foundation of, 496–97; ivory exports of, 498; Lower Congo, 432, 434, 439; Middle Congo, 430; rubber industry development and rubber exports of, 498–500; sovereignty of, 21; Twiss's arguments for the creation of the Congo as a new state, 429–30; Twiss's proposal for a regime of "*désintéressement*" for the Middle and Upper Congo, 431; Upper Congo, 426–27, 430, 431, 434, 438, 443, 446, 448, 454, 455–57. *See also* Berlin Conference (1884–1885); Congo/Congo Free State, diplomatic negotiations concerning
Congo/Congo Free State, diplomatic negotiations concerning: public campaign for the recognition of the International Association of the Congo, 449–50; scepticism concerning the legal position of, 498; specific scepticism and objections of America to the formation of, 448–49; Twiss's drafting of the constitution for the Congo Free State, 457–58
Congo River, 426, 456, 464–65, 493, 498; arguments concerning the free navigation of, 434–35; geography of, 420;

neutralisation of the Lower Congo River, 430, 431n130; Upper Congo River, 426–27; views of Twiss on the free navigation of, 435–36
Congress of Paris (1856), 493
Congress of Vienna (1815), 10, 11, 19, 34, 48, 90, 108, 109, 155, 202, 462, 530; guarantee of sovereignty by, 164–65; ratification of the Peace of Westphalia, 128; and rules governing the open navigation of the Danube River, 72–73; Twiss's re-evaluation of, 208
Conington, John, 56
Conrad, Joseph, 478, 498, 500
Conservatives, 10, 17
Constant, Benjamin, 171
Constant, Edmund, 370, 374
Constantinople Convention (1889), 503
constitutionalism, 215; liberal, 182
consular jurisdiction, 410, 480, 487–90, 521, 522
Consular Marriage Act (1849), 16, 318
Consular Marriage Act (1868), 322
Contagious Diseases Acts, 17, 243–44, 304
context: as fundamental to understanding the meaning of a particular act or event, 22, 22n64; linguistic context, 23n68; reconstruction of as micro-intellectual history, 23, 24–25
Convention Relative to the Slave Trade and Importation into Africa of Firearms, Ammunition, and Spiritous Liquors (1890), 512–13
Cook, Arthur, 371–73
Corn Laws, 12, 130; repeal of, 13, 36; Twiss's view of the "Corn Law question," 52
Corporation of London, 348, 351, 356
corporations, 3, 19–20, 89, 95, 167, 394, 427–28, 492, 530, 531, 533; bishops as, 86, 95; creation of, 166–67n257; local corporations, 197, 214; non-state corporations, 532; precedents for European corporations, 19; "private corporations," 19; "representative corporations," 145
Corporations Act, 102–3
Corvinus, 191, 193, 194
cosmopolitanism, "Utopian," 125
Count Colloredo, 39–40, 74
Countess Colloredo, 45, 50, 207

Countess D'Apponyi, 50, 332
Courcel, Alphonse Chodron de, 459
Court of Probate Act (1857), 71, 80
Coutts, Sophia, 347
Coutts, Thomas, 347
coverture, law of, 18
Crimean War (1853–1856), 11, 12, 66, 71, 200–212, 215; closer relations between England and Austria as a result of, 207; Twiss's skepticism concerning the justification for the war, 203–4; Twiss's view of as a "deplorable struggle," 209–10; Twiss's view of as a religious conflict, 208
Criminal Law Amendment Act (1885), 304
Crocker, John Wilson, 35, 123, 124
Crowe, Joseph Archer, 461
Crystal Palace (Chinese section of), 334
Czar Nicholas I (czar of Russia), 179

Dale, Henry, 315, 316–17, 323, 325, 358–59
d'Altena, Paul de Borchgrave, 423, 512, 515–16
Danube Commission, 461
Danube River, 48, 72–73, 205–6, 423, 430, 493; as European, 210–11
Darnton, Robert, 23
Dasent, George Webbe, 38n47
Davenport, John, 227
David Copperfield (Dickens), 77–78, 364
Davis, Natalie Zemon, 14
Dax, Edward, 373–74
Dead Heart (W. Phillips), 366
Deane, James Parker, 37–38n46
De la cession des droits de souveraineté par des chefs de tribus sauvages (Arntz), 451, 452–53
De Indiss, or Commentary on the Law of Prize and Booty (Grotius), 300
Delavaud, Louis, 428–29, 436, 452
De Legibus et Consuetudinibus Angliae (Bracton), 406
democracy, 143, 160
Democracy in America (de Tocqueville), 197
Denison, George, 105, 106
Denmark, 126, 227, 417, 460, 490; sovereignty over Schleswig-Holstein, 124–25
Des classes dangereuses de la population dans les grandes villes (Frégier), 244
Despagnet, Frantz, 2–3n5
despotism, 131, 175
Dewey, John, 2n3

Dicey, A. V., 27
Dickens, Charles, 29, 44, 76–77, 343, 347, 358, 364
Dignam, Eliza, 288–89
Disraeli, Benjamin, 56, 112–13, 114, 123, 128, 135, 412, 414, 417
divorce, 82; cost of, 81. *See also* law, divorce law
Divorce Act. *See* Matrimonial Causes Act (1857)
Doctors' Commons, 120, 526; as the civil law equivalent of the Inns of Courts, 76; dissolution/sale of, 79, 80; jurisdiction of lawyers in, 81; need for reform in, 78–79; reforms of, 80; shareholders in, 79; Twiss's admission to as a civilian lawyer, 74–75, 75–76n225; Twiss's career with, 75–76, 88; Twiss's plan to save the college, 80n241
doctrinaires group, 171
"doctrine of lapse," the, 226
Dodson, John, 83, 88
Dombey and Son (Dickens), 44, 241
Donkin, William, 56
Dore, Henry, 259
Doyle, Francis, 41
Droit des gens (T. Twiss), 502
Drouyn, Édouard de Lhuys, 446
Drummond Chair of Political Economy: competition for, 62–63; Twiss's lectures as, 63–64, 64n179
Duchy of Bremen, 125
Duchy of Holstein, 124–25; invasion of by Prussia, 126–27
Duchy of Schleswig, 124–25; invasion of by Prussia, 126–27
Duchy of Verden, 125
Duck, Betty, 247–48
Duke of Devonshire, 2433
Duke of Wellington, 30, 43, 49, 94, 123
Dunlop, John, 498–99
Dutch East India Company, 7, 19, 393, 394
Dyke, Francis Hart, 355, 356, 357–58

Earl of Carnarvon, 45
Earl of Clarendon, 315–16
Earl of Yarborough, 45
Ecclesiastical Courts, 81, 88; practice of civil law in, 76
Ecclesiastical Titles Act (1851), 100, 102
education, private, 187

Egypt, 64–66, 224, 410, 411, 414, 422, 502, 522
Eleanor of Aquitaine, 400
Elector of Hanover, 125
Elements of the Pathology of the Human Mind (Mayo), 284
elites, 14, 522; Muslim elites, 203n449
Ellis, Sarah, 329
emancipation, 17, 107, 216, 532, 534; arguments for, 166–67; connection between emancipation and nations, 167n261; emancipation of Catholics, 6, 62; women's emancipation movements, 17
Emanuel, Harry, 258–59, 264
Emperor Ferdinand, 112
enfranchisement: of African peoples, 464; of Catholics, 12; dangers of, 38; in England, 4
Engelhardt, Edouard, 495
England, 6, 104, 132, 163, 217; public support in for the Crimean War, 206; relations/ alliance with Austria, 201, 202. *See also* Victorian England
English/British East India Company, 7, 19, 54, 73, 155, 164, 222, 223, 225, 394; as responsible for the 1857 Indian rebellion, 228; Secret Committee of the Court of Directors of, 227
English Civil War, 232
Enlightenment, the, 196
Epitome of Niebuhr's History of Rome (T. Twiss), 60, 62, 400
Erastianism, 81, 97, 103, 104, 142
Erle, William, 75
Etiquette of Good Society (Campbell), 330–31
Eucharist, nature of: debates concerning, 105–6; process of, 106–7
Europe, 177–78, 188, 189, 404; Western Europe, 21, 170, 185, 203, 218, 423, 493
European Concert of Public Law, 414
"extraterritoriality": as a metaphor, 417–18; principles of, 418

Faure, Denis, 305–6, 347, 354, 360
Federal Act of the Confederation, 163; Article 57 of, 163
Federal System, 147, 160
Felbrigg Hall/Estate, 255, 256, 262, 268, 271, 272, 274; sale of, 293
Ferdinand I (king of Austria), 178
Ferdinand III (Holy Roman Emperor), 232

"Feudalists," 446
Field, Charles Frederick, 249, 249n62
Field, David Dudley, 397; on the applicability of the law of nations to non-European and "Oriental nations," 407–9
Field and Roscoe, 246–47, 277, 278, 278n178, 280, 281, 284, 288
Figgis, J. N., 6
Fitzmaurice, Edmund, 440, 457
Ford, Joseph, 272
Foreign Marriage Act (1892), 322
Foucault, Michel: "great confinement" thesis of, 5; "new" social theory of, 22
France, 108, 156, 167, 191, 206, 443, 468, 475; *coup d'état* in, 195–200; naval base at Cherbourg, 213–14; Second Republic of, 183, 195, 198; war with Austria, 217–18
Francis I (Holy Roman Emperor), 190, 214
Francis II (Holy Roman Emperor), 109, 132n101, 142, 215
Franco-Prussian War (1871), 397, 439
Frankfurt Parliament (1848), 112, 124, 127–28, 132n99, 135, 159, 173; and the desire to create an Imperial Constitution stipulating basic rights, 167; nationalist ambitions of, 168; proposed offer to Frederick William IV for the crown of the German Empire, 168–70
Franklin, John, 48
Frantzius (Herr Frantzius), 463
Franz Joseph I (king of Austria), 178, 182, 212–13, 217, 219
Frederick IV (king of Denmark), 125
Frederick William (prince of Prussia), 71
Frederick William IV (king of Prussia), 168–70, 171; rejection of the Imperial Crown by, 170
Free Traders, 35, 52
Frégier, Honoré Antoine, 244
Frelinghuysen, Frederick, 447–48, 451
Fremantle, William Henry, 314
French Revolution, 109, 171, 174, 190, 220
Frere, Henry Bartle, 424
Frère-Orban, Walthère, 443
Fulton, Forrest, 529

Gagern, Heinrich von, 169, 170
Gaius, 61
Gallatin, Albert, 91, 92
Garden, Jack, 250, 251; renewed "intimacy" with Agnes Willoughby, 252–53
Gardiner, George, 315
Gardiner, Jack, 276
Gelas, Marie (adopted name of Pharaïlde van Lynseele), 303, 323, 364, 370, 373–74, 386; as Twiss's mistress, 309–10. *See also* Twiss/Chaffers libel trial
Gentili, Alberico, 54
Gentz, Friedrich, 67–68
German Confederation, 109, 111–12, 127, 134, 144, 148, 150, 159; Metternich's views of 163–64; negotiations over the form of, 159–60; proposals for, 163; Twiss's apology for, 152; Twiss's criticism of Article 13 of the Act of German Confederation, 153n198
"German Question" (Metternich), 170–71
"Germanic States, The" (T. Twiss and Metternich), 126–27, 132–34
Germany/German Empire, 11, 129, 130, 170, 173, 213, 218, 227, 441, 458, 468, 475, 482; aggression of, 159; "Federal arrangement" adopted for, 158–59; German unification, 148; nature of the German political body, 148–49; North Germany, 215; revolution in, 112; romantic view of, 143n154; Twiss's view on German unity, 143–44, 160; Twiss's view on the political form Germany should take, 141–42
Gibson, Milner, 35
Gierke, Otto von 1
Gilbert, Ann, 241
Gilbert, William S., 235
Ginzburg, Carlo, 24
Girondists, 53
Gladstone, William, 17, 48, 51, 52, 74, 81, 100, 216, 238, 259, 412–13, 502; attachment of to courtesans, 239–40
Glanville, Ranulf de, 523, 524
Goldie, George, 486
Government of India Act, 233
Graham, James, 103, 104
Gray, Robert, 93
Great Britain/British Empire, 20, 62, 66, 90, 108, 125, 143, 151, 206, 221, 417, 443, 465, 469, 474; Bismarck's pressure on to recognize the International Association of the Congo, 476; military control of over Egypt and the Suez Canal, 502; political climate in (1850s), 200–201. *See also* British Foreign Office

Great Exhibition (Japanese section of), 334, 334–35n423
Greathed, Edward, 73, 229
Green, Elizabeth, 85n265
Green, Gretna, 85n265
Gregory, Robert, 354
Grey, Charles, 341
Grotius, Hugo, 93–94, 227, 300, 393, 409, 470
Gudenus, Philipp Georg, 110n3
Guerre, Martin, 380
Guibelei, Theodore Maine, 255
Guibelei, Theodore Victor, 255
Guiglini, Antonio, 259–60, 270–71, 277, 374
Guillaume, Edmond André, 382
Guizot, François, 43–44, 204
Guy Mannering (Walter Scott), 63

Halliday, Andrew, 241
Hampden, Renn, 96–97
Hansell, Peter, 269, 278, 279, 280, 281, 282, 283–84n207, 291, 294, 298
Hanworth Hall, 272, 293, 294–96, 298
Harding, John, 326
Harrison, Louisa, 370–71, 372
Hassard, John, 519, 521, 523, 529
Hatton, Joseph, 390–91
Havelock, Henry, 229
Haymarket, London, 239–40, 246, 257, 258, 287, 292; Haymarket Theater, 235, 238; music halls of, 243, 244, 362
Haynau, Jacob von, 188
Heart of Darkness (Conrad), 478, 498
Heathcote, William, 52
Heemskerck, Jacob van, 93; capture of the *Santa Caterina* by, 393
Heffter, Auguste-Wilhelm, 440
hegemony: of European powers, 65; liberal hegemony, 13
Hemming, A.W.L., 461
Hemyng, Bracebridge, 243, 244–45, 246, 249, 258; description of Agnes Willoughby, 250–51
Henderson, James, 507
Henry of Bracton, 406
Henry II (king of England), 400, 524
Herbert, Sidney, 35
Hero, 439–40
Hertslet, Edward, 439–40, 441–42
Higgins, Matthew James, 240–41
Hill, Clement, 468, 487

Hill-Trevor, Anne, 30
historicism, 61; legal historicism, 62
history: cultural history, 23; political history, 23. *See also* intellectual history/historians; micro-history
History of England (Bright), 523–24
History of England from the Accession of James the Second (Macaulay), 43
Hobbes, Thomas, 28, 93, 94, 146, 300; on the distinction between artificial and natural persons, 3; on sovereignty, 172; on types of persons excluded from natural persons, 4–5
Holden, James, 258n106, 273
Holland, 443, 490
Holland, Thomas, 490
Holstein, 124–28, 227
Holy Roman Empire, 127, 159, 169
Hooker, Joseph, 499
Hornung, Joseph, 409–10, 411, 417, 421; on the status of "Oriental nations" in international law, 412
House of Commons, 81
Household Words (Dickens), 45, 292, 343
Howard, George, 49–50n109
Hudson's Bay Company, 19, 90, 394
humanitarianism, 188
Hungary, 112, 113, 129, 132, 182, 190n381; constitution of, 190; future of, 189; nationalism of, 218; publications sympathetic to, 186; reform in, 187–88, 190n384; revolution in, 179–81, 183, 218
Hungary: Its Constitution and Its Catastrophe (T. Twiss), 51, 112, 192–93; reviews of, 193
Hyde, Edward, 43
Hyderabad, Nizam of, 222, 223
Hywel Dda (king of Deheubarth), 29

Importance of Being Earnest, The (O. Wilde), 74
India, Sikh and Hill states of upper India, 155, 164
Indian Rebellion (1857), 11, 12, 73, 205, 225, 228–29, 231–32, 342, 428
individualism, 178; logic of, 150
Inglis, John, 229, 319
Inglis, Robert, 52
Ionian Islands, 164; under the sovereignty of France, 156
imperialism, 421, 437

insanity/lunacy, 275, 283, 284, 291, 520; definition of, 5; moral insanity, 286, 287; proofs of in Victorian Britain, 5–6; as removing legal personality from people in the nineteenth century, 5; treatment of through "moral management," 284–85

Institut de droit international, 407, 494; annual meeting of (1883), 433–35, 439; commission of to examine the law of nations as applied to non-Christian and Oriental nations, 409, 414; commission of to examine the question of the rules of effective occupation, 495–96; dissenting report of Hornung to Twiss's report, 411–12; Twiss as honorary member of, 521; Twiss's questionnaire presented to concerning the non-Christian and Oriental nations question, 409–10

Institutes of Gaius (Gaius), 61, 400

Institutes of Justinian (Justinian), 61, 70

intellectual history/historians, 14, 22–23, 24; and the "linguistic turn," 22; micro-intellectual history, 24

International African Association, 1, 18–19, 89, 425, 427, 428, 431, 438, 443, 445, 454–55; case presented by Twiss for the transformation of into the Congo Free State, 19; as a filibustering entity, 478–79; formation of, 424, 429; and membership in the society of nations, 429; as a single-shareholder company, 442; transformation of into the Congo Free State, 19, 20, 25; Twiss's support of, 441

International Association of the Congo, 427, 437, 442, 445, 475–77, 494, 534; pretensions manifest in the treaties of, 476–78; recognition of by Britain, 487; recognition of by France, 459; recognition of by European powers, 490; recognition of by Germany, 482–83; recognition of by twelve world powers, 460; recognition of by the United States, 447–48, 453–54; sovereignty "*de jure*" of, 450–51; Twiss's drafting of the treaty of recognition for, 488–90

international/global society, 7, 20, 21; debates on whether non-European could be admitted to membership in, 7–8; expansion of, 8–9, 12

international law, 26, 65, 68, 396–97, 413; and the concept of occupation, 68; potential subjects of international law, 21–22; prevailing understanding of (the *ius publicum*), 125; professionalization of, 71; publishing work on the law of nations as Twiss's primary source of income for twenty years, 397–99; relationship with Roman law, 68. *See also* Twiss, Travers, and international law

internationalisation, 183, 421–22, 433; of the Congo, 429–31

International Protectorate of the Congo River, An (T. Twiss), 432, 448, 451

International Red Cross, 7, 21, 394, 397, 429, 533

Introductory Lectures on the Science of International Law (T. Twiss), 93

Ireland, 6, 102, 142, 151, 160; famine in, 12, 36, 100

Italy, 129, 167; unification of, 11

ius publicum, 125; *ius publicum Europaeum*, 67, 203

Jackson, John, 83–84, 87, 349, 350, 353, 354, 378; letter by Twiss to Jackson explaining his decision to withdraw the libel charges against Chaffers, 385–86; letter by Twiss to Jackson on the future in the aftermath of the libel trial against Chaffers, 385

Jah, Azam, 223

Jah, Azim, 223

Japan, 74, 224, 332–35, 339, 407, 410, 414, 522

Jastreuski, Felix Zerambe, 312, 355–56, 359, 368–69, 370–71, 372, 382

Jefferson, Thomas, 90, 91, 92

Jelf, Richard, 37–38, 38n51, 59, 64, 65

Jenner-Fust, Herbert, 83

Jesus Christ, interpretation of the creation of from the host, 26

Jèze, Gaston, 500

Johnson, George Henry Sacherval, 38n51, 59, 83

Johnson, Henry Charles, 263

Joseph II (Holy Roman Emperor), 131, 190

Justinian, 61

Kantorowicz, Ernst, 4

Karslake, John, 287–88, 351

Keith, Arthur, 457n233
Kenealy, Edward, 382–83
Kennedy, William, 48
Kepel, William, 380
Kielmansegge, Eduard von, 39
Kingdom of Piedmont-Sardinia, 212
Kinglake, Alexander, 205n461
King's College, London, 38, 64–69, 121, 152, 396, 406
King's Two Bodies, The (Kantorowicz), 4
Klüber, Jean-Louis (Johann Ludwig), 2–3n5
Knights of Jerusalem, 452
Knowles, James, 290
Koch, William, 66
Koler, August, 122
Komárom, 178–79
Kossuth, Lajos, 111, 133, 152, 179, 181, 182–83, 184, 188–89, 218
Kraft-Ebing, Richard von, 237
Krakow (Free City of Krakow), 154–56, 163–64

La Colonne, 298–99
Lacroix, Caroline, 516–17
Lalaing, Comte de, 457
"*La libre navigation du Congo*" (T. Twiss), 430, 431, 433, 451, 455–57
Lamb, Emily, 123
Lamb, Frederick, 123
Landseer, Edwin, 241
Laski, Harold, 1, 6, 95, 530, 534
Latitudinarianism, 96, 104
Laudism, 97
Lauterpacht, Hersch, 28, 394
Laveleye, Émile de, 429, 433, 495
law: Admiralty law, 77; approach of the German historical school to, 61, 62; divorce law, 81; "informal law" and legal fictions, 27–28; Law of Nature, 93, 94, 227, 445; public law of Europe (*ius publicum Europaeum*), 67, 203. *See also* civil law; international law; law of nations; marriage law; Roman Law
law of nations, 26, 32, 68, 94, 99, 154, 227, 396, 492; affinity of with marriage law, 80; applicability of to non-Christian and "Oriental nations," 407–9; as the European law of nations, 65, 435; Twiss's views concerning, 65–66, 77, 404, 416–17
Law of Nations, The (T. Twiss), 2–3n5, 72–73, 72n214, 300, 301, 406–7, 415, 445–47, 500–502, 512, 516

Lawrence, Henry, 229
Lawrence, John, 73, 229
Lawrence, Thomas, 116
Lawrence, William Beach, 440
lawyers: civil, 26; ecclesiastical, 2–3; international, 2–3, 22, 28, 62; Medieval lawyers, 62; natural lawyers, 62; Victorian lawyers belief in the connection between artificial and natural persons, 3–4
Layard, Austen Henry, 412–13
Leighton, Francis Knyvett, 333
Leopold II (king of Belgium), 1, 18–19, 20, 21, 426, 437, 448, 459–60, 479, 480, 493, 533; ambition of creating a state in the Congo, 428–29; attitude toward his mistresses, 516–17; conference organised by to a standard of civilization in Central Africa, 423–24; cynicism of, 481; developing interest of in Africa, 423; and the development of the rubber industry in the Congo, 499–500; linked story with Pharaïlde Twiss, 511–12
L'ère des Césars (Romieu), 195, 196
Letters Apostolic of the Pope Pius IX Considered with Reference to the Law of England and the Law of Europe (T. Twiss), 98–99, 102, 323, 380
Lettres de Beauséant (Syon), 195
Leviathan (Hobbes), 86
Leviathan (ship [later renamed *Great Eastern*]), 46–47, 47n95
Libel Act (1843), 351, 357
liberalisation, 4, 5, 11, 98, 491; of the Austrian constitution, 219
liberalism, 96, 137, 175, 177, 190, 201; high liberalism, 17; liberal hegemony, 13; liberal inclusiveness, 6; Victorian liberalism, 15
Liberals, 17, 212, 243
Liberia, 445–46, 454, 456
Liberty Trees, 104
Lister, Thomas Villiers, 458, 464, 478, 479, 483–84, 487; pro-Portuguese stance of, 481
Littlecote Hall, 40–41; ghost story associated with, 42; gifts from the library of given by Twiss to Metternich, 42
Livingston, David, 448–49
Llewellyn, David, 253–54n89, 259, 287, 288–89
Loiret, 439

Lombardy, 213, 217; Twiss's argument for the autonomy of, 214
London Labour and the London Poor (Mayhew), 243, 245, 250–51
London Straits Convention/Treaty (1841), 210, 423
London University (later University College London), 68
Longley, Charles, 49, 325, 345
Longman, Thomas, 35
Lord Aberdeen, 35, 52, 101, 206, 215
Lord Ampthill, 475–76
Lord Chelmsford, 321
Lord Derby, 53, 83
Lord Esher. *See* Brett, William (Lord Esher)
Lord Granville, 20, 206, 230, 231, 233, 341–42, 347, 432–33, 483; on Britain's position concerning the status of the International Association of the Congo, 479–81, 484–86; involvement of in the Berlin Conference, 458, 461, 462–63, 465, 468
Lord Holland. *See* Vassal-Fox, Henry (Lord Holland)
Lord Melbourne, 123
Lord Palmerston (Viscount Palmerston), 44, 49, 53, 64, 72, 123, 182, 216, 332, 433; and Charles Canning, 230; as leader of the "forward party," 206; and the Matrimonial Causes Act, 81–82
Lord Stowell. *See* Scott, William
Lord Wensleydale, 403
Lorimer, James, 2–3n5, 62, 66, 228, 411, 412, 421
Lowder, John Samuel, 332
Lowder, Lucy, 333
Lowe, Robert, 38, 38n48
Lucas, Samuel, 228
Lucknow, 225, 228–29, 274; siege of, 73
Lüderitz, Adolf, 458
Lunacy Act (1845), 5
Lynseele, Pharaïlde van (Lady Travers Twiss), 1, 13–14, 18, 87, 251, 302–3, 534; abandonment of by Twiss, 521; addresses/homes of, 305; adopted persona of, 14, 312–13, 323–24, 384; and the connection between empire and her marriage, 518; and the creation of new persons, 311–12, 335, 518; destiny/future of determined by Leopold II, 519–20; first meeting of with Twiss, 304; incarceration of in an asylum, 520–21; linked story with Leopold II, 511–12; long-term syphilis of, 520; placing of under Leopold's "protection" by Twiss, 514–16; as a prostitute, 13, 303, 304, 305, 310; public perception of, 382; relationship with her jeweler, 305–6; relocation of from London to Switzerland after the Chaffers libel trial, 378, 384; transformation (metamorphoses) of from streetwalker to a "lady of blood" in Victorian Society, 15–17, 25–26, 335, 395, 438, 461, 518–19, 527. *See also* Gelas, Marie (adopted name of Pharaïlde van Lynseele); Lynseele, Pharaïlde van (Lady Travers Twiss), presentation of to London Society; Twiss/Chaffers libel trial; Twiss/Lynseele marriage
Lynseele, Pharaïlde van (Lady Travers Twiss), presentation of to London Society, 16, 328–29, 338–39, 341; arrangements to have her presented to Queen Victoria, 330; cancellation of her presentation at court, 387–88, 493–94; challenges faced by, 331–32; and management of the news regarding the marriage to Twiss, 328; preparation for, 329–30
Lynseele, Pierre Denis van, 302, 346, 365, 370, 374
Lynseele, Raoul Felix van, 312
Lynseele, V., 325, 327
Lyte, Henry Maxwell, 524

Macaulay, Thomas Babington, 9, 43, 74
MacKinnon, William, 424
Macmillan, Alexander, 505–6
Madden, Frederic, 400
Magyars, 184–86, 188, 194; Magyar constitution, 189; sympathy for in Britain, 185
Magyar-Slavonian state, 191
Mahmud II, 202, 203
"Maiden Tribute of Modern Babylon, The" (Stead), 304
Maine, Henry Sumner, 9, 36, 62
Maistre, Joseph de, 195
Maitland, F. W., 1, 3, 6, 86
Makepeace, William, 330–31
Malay Peninsula, 499
Malet, Edmund, 460–61, 462, 463, 464, 465, 471–73, 474, 481, 482, 483, 484, 487
Malta, 436

Mandler, Peter, 132
Marie Thérèse, 190
Manning, Frederick, 358
Manning, Marie, 358
Maratha Confederation, 222
Mares, Paul Des, 371, 382
"Marriage of British Subjects in Foreign Countries" (Royal Commission on the Law of Marriage), 321
marriage law: affinity with the law of nations, 80; as a branch of ecclesiastical law, 26, 77; Catholic laws of, 81
Marriages Confirmation Act (1823), 320, 321–22
Married Women's Property Acts (1870), 17, 18, 26, 28, 421
Marquardsen, H. von, 434
Marquee of Northampton, 46
Marquess of Harington, 243
Marsden, George, 362, 504, 524
Marsden, Michael, 524
Marsden, Mrs. Richard, 525
Marsilius of Padua, 97
Martens, Friedrich (Fyodor), 494, 495
Martineau, Harriet, 17, 244
Marx, Karl, 176
Massachusetts Bay Company, 394
Matrimonial Causes and Probate Act (1857), 26, 71, 79, 80, 80n241, 84, 88, 292, 395; in the context of broader emancipations, 81–82; Twiss's opposition to, 234
Maull, Henry, 396n5
Maurice, John, 62–63
May, James Bowen, 251–52, 262, 265, 269, 337
Mayhew, Henry, 243, 245, 246, 249
Maynooth Commission, 100–101
Mayo, Thomas, 284, 286–87
Mazower, Mark, 533–34
McDougal, Colin, 247
McKinnon, William, 487
Meade, Robert, 461
Memoirs (Pattison), 57–58
mentalités, 24
Men of the Time (Walford), 30, 50–51
Merewether, John, 97
Merivale, Hermann, 62–63, 80
metamorphoses, 380; fascination of Victorians with the myths of metamorphosis, 17; of personhood, 1; Twiss's liberal interpretation of, 392–93. *See also* Lynseele, Pharaïlde van (Lady Travers Twiss), transformation (metamorphoses) of from streetwalker to a "lady of blood" in Victorian Society
Metamorphoses (Ovid), 235, 237
Metropolitan Board of Works, 80
Metternich, Klemens Wenzel von, 10, 28, 31, 34, 41, 48, 50, 139–40, 141n144, 327–28, 359, 422–23; as the architect of the Concert of Europe, 67; on the Austrian constitution, 165; as Chancellor of State, 109; disagreement with critics that he was a reactionary, 148–49; dispute with Gentz, 67–68; and Disraeli, 114; distrust of Palmerston, 44; flight from Vienna during the 1848 revolution, 39; German estate of (Johannisberg), 118; gifts given to by Twiss and Popham, 41–42n64, 42; as honorary member of the Athenaeum club, 39, 39n55; on nationalism, 181; as a notorious reactionary, 11; on the political form Germany should take, 141–42; portraits of, 115–17; properties of in Austria, 121; on public opinion, 180; resignation of as Chancellor, 111, 157; as "*sans reproche*," 150; on sovereignty, 173; suppression of the freedom of the press by, 158n226; views of concerning Twiss's *Two Introductory Lectures on the Science of International Law*, 66, 67; views on the German Confederation, 163–64; views on the Ottoman Empire, 413–14; warning to Twiss not to mention him by name, 149–50
Metternich, Klemens Wenzel von, friendship with Twiss, 108–24 *passim*, 122n51, 328, 493, 530; difficulty in characterizing the relationship between the two, 113; importance of gossip in their correspondence, 119; later years of their friendship, 117; as mentor to Twiss, 114–15. *See also* Twiss/Metternich correspondence
Metternich, Melanie, 117–18, 118–19n37
Michell, Richard, 71n207, 75, 117
micro-history, 18, 24; as biographical, 24–25
Mildred Vernon; A Tale of Parisian Life in the Last Days of the Monarchy (Murray), 118–19n37
Mill, John Stuart, 9, 36, 54, 204

INDEX [563]

Moldavia, 201
Molesworth, Andalusia, 35
Molesworth, William, 35
Monck, George, 43
Monier-Williams, Monier, 523
Monroe, James, 90, 91
Morel, Edward, 481, 500
Morgan, John Tyler, 450, 451
Morocco, 415–16
Morris, Jane, 290
Moynier, Gustave, 397, 429, 433, 434
Mubarak, Ali Pasha, 224
Mughal Empire, 73
Murphy, Mr, 507–11
Murray, Hamilton, 118–19n37
Murray, John, III, 44n75, 118–19n37, 134, 135, 136, 139, 185, 191–92
Musurus [Mousouros], Konstantinos, 71
Mysore, 222–23

Nachtigal, Gustav, 424
Napoleon III. *See* Bonaparte, Charles-Louis-Napoleon (Napoleon III)
Nash, John, 303
National African Company (NAC), 486
nationalism, 11, 125, 128, 137, 143, 166–67, 215, 216; Austrian, 111–12; blind nationalism, 150; dangers of, 130–32; German, 62; Hungarian, 218; Italian, 212; Metternich's view of, 181; rise of, 214; Romantic, 151, 159
nationalist separation, 111
natural persons, 1–2, 532; connection with artificial persons, 3–4; debate on the legal personality of outside the state, 6n15; "family resemblances" between the creation of artificial and natural persons, 25; Hobbes' distinction between artificial and natural persons, 3; liberation of, 22; widening recognition of the status of, 20
natural rights, 28
Nawabs of the Carnatic, 223
Nepal, 225
neutralisation, 48, 430, 434
New England Company, 394
Newman, John Henry, 57, 95; conversion to Catholicism, 98
New York Herald: funding of Stanley's expeditions by, 448–49; "Sovereignty Beyond Question" article in, 449

New Zealand Company, 427–28
Niebuhr, Barthold, 60–61, 400, 401
Niger, 465
Nightingale, Florence, 17, 244
non-Europeans, 7–8, 65, 413, 421, 532
non-state organisations, 7
non-state persons, 533
Norddeutsche Allgemeine Zeitung, 454
North Africa Company, 394
North Borneo Chartered Company (NBCC), 335, 437–38, 442–43, 449, 452, 453, 466, 486
notre homme, 112–13, 113n12
Novara, battle of, 167–68

Observations on the Arguments of Dr Twiss respecting the New Catholic Hierarchy (Bowyer), 99–100, 380
O'Connor, Arthur, 358
Ogle, James, 38n51
O'Hagan, Thomas, 319
Omar, Pasha, 71
On the Amphitheatre at Pola in Istria (T. Twiss), 45
"On International Conventions for the Maintenance of Sea Lights" (T. Twiss [address of]), 414
On International Conventions for the Maintenance of Sea Lights (T. Twiss [pamphlet of]), 418–20, 425, 426, 502
On Money and Currency (T. Twiss), 63
Order of Knights of the Hospital St John of Jerusalem, 4, 436, 515
Oregon Territory, 89–91, 93–94, 109, 301, 437, 445, 453, 456; and the issue of sovereignty, 92–93; migrants to, 90; Provisional Government of, 91
Oregon Territory, The (T. Twiss), 91, 465
"Oriental nations": on the applicability of the law of nations to non-European and "Oriental nations," 407–9; on the status of "Oriental nations" in international law, 412, 413–14, 415–16, 419; Twiss's arguments for the equality of "Oriental nations," 413, 423. *See also* Institut de droit international, commission of to examine the law of nations as applied to non-Christian and Oriental nations

Ottoman Empire, 48, 71, 185, 412; admission of to the Concert of Europe, 211; British policy toward, 64–65, 66; as a bulwark against Russia, 72; Metternich's view of, 413–14; perception of as failing, 201–2, 204–5; Russian intervention in, 409; as the "sick man of Europe," 201
Oude: the Oude dominions, 226; the "Sovereign of Oude," 226; Twiss's views concerning, 227–28. *See also* Awadh
Outram, James, 229
Owen, Richard, 334–35n423
Oxford Commission, 82
Oxford Encaenia, 334
Oxford Movement. *See* Tractarianism/Tractarians (Oxford Movement)
Oxholm, Marie Sophie Friderikke von, 41
Oxholm, Valdemar Tully von, 41

Palmer, Roundell (Lord Selborne), 53, 319, 432, 433, 468, 489–90
Panic of 1847, 37
Parre, Charlotte, 309, 336
Parsey, Arthur, 46
Parry, Jonathan, 215
Paternostro, Alessandro, 521–22
Pattison, Mark, 56; bitterness over and controversy concerning Twiss, 57–58
Pauncefote, Julian, 442–43, 458, 463, 468–69, 471, 482, 487, 488, 489
Peace of Westphalia (1648), 108, 125, 128, 301
Peel, Robert, 12–13, 51, 91, 100
Peelites, 35, 52, 53, 104
Penn, William, 452
Persia, 414
personality: fictitious, 2n3; "real personality," 2n3
personal transformation, 28
persons. *See* artificial persons; natural persons; non-state persons; Twiss, Travers, and personhood
Petre, George, 476
Petty-Fitzmaurice, Henry, 49–50n109, 327
Phillimore, Joseph, 69
Phillimore, Robert, 37–38n46, 326–27, 327n393, 335–36
Phillipps, Thomas, 36n40
Phillips, Henry Wyndham, 115–16, 117
Phillips, Watts, 366
Piedmont, 168, 217

Pierantoni, Augusto, 434
Pius IX (pope), 97, 104–5, 196, 323, 379–80
Plumptre, Frederick, 56
"pluralists," 6
Pocock, John, 24
Poland, Harry, 304, 357–63, 366, 367, 369–76
Police Act (1829), 230
political society, 4; expansion of in Victorian England, 8, 12; moral action of individuals as the basis of, 13
political thought, 24
political traditions, as self-referential, 24
Polk, James, 90
Ponsonby, John, 252
Ponsonby, Spencer, 340–41, 345
Popham, Alexander Hugh Leybourne, 41n61
Popham, Francis, 41–43, 41n61, 41–42n64; gifts given to Metternich by, 41–42n64
Popham, John, 41
Portugal, 441, 475, 476; alarm at European powers meddling in the Congo, 430; concerns of over the International African Association, 478–79; sovereign claims of to the Congo, 477–78; pretensions of sovereignty over the Lower Congo, 432, 438–39, 443; sovereignty of, 429
Powell, Baden, 63n178
Pradier-Fodéré, Paul, 2–3n5
press, the, censorship/abuse of, 184–85, 184n350
Preston, J., 276
Pretty, Horsebreaker, The (Brough and Halliday), 241
Pride and Prejudice (Austen), 241
Prince Albert, 46, 75, 331
Prince of Baden, 71
Princess of Wales, 16, 331–32, 333, 342
"principle of nationality," 129
Principles of a Sound Marriage Law (Royal Commission on the Law of Marriage), 319–20
Private Treaties with African Chiefs (Hertslet), 441–42
Privileges Committee, 232
Probate, Divorce and Admiralty Division of the High Court of Justice, 80
prostitutes/prostitution, 13, 14–15; 13n35, 17, 238–39, 239n12, 239n15, 347; as adept at creating multiple identities and personalities, 15; difference

between English and foreign prostitutes, 303–4; Hemyng's taxonomy of, 244–46; "pretty horsebreaker" image of, 240–43, 253, 258; and social transformation, 244–45; use of false names among, 248–49
Protestant Reformation, 96, 98; in England, 102
Prouhdon, Pierre-Joseph, 195
Providence Island Company, 394
Prussia, 108, 126, 128, 132, 143, 154, 170, 174; influence of in the Balkans, 201; invasion of Schleswig-Holstein by, 126–27; Prussian expansionism, 148
Pschopathia (Kraft-Ebing), 237
Pufendorf, Samuel von, 300
Pusey, Edward, 57, 95, 106
Puseyism, 95
Pusey party/Puseyites, 62, 95, 96, 103, 530
Pygmalion (Rousseau), 237
Pygmalion (Shaw), 238
Pygmalion and Galatea (Gilbert), 235, 237, 238
Pygmalion: or, The Statue Fair (Brough), 237–38, 241

Quarterly Review, 139, 157–58, 185, 191; Twiss's and Metternich's article in, 124, 130, 131, 132, 134–35, 135n115, 136, 138, 138n127
Queen Victoria, 99, 151, 213, 241, 387, 516
Questions constitutionnelles (Barante), 171–72

Radcliffe, Katherine, 379, 382
Radicals, 17, 186, 212
Rajah of Mysore, Twiss's *Opinion* concerning, 222–23
Rarey, John Solomon, 241–43
Rawlinson, Henry, 424
Reddie, James, 62
Reeve, Henry, 35, 42, 75, 197, 204–5, 204n455, 205n461
Reform Acts (1832, 1867, 1884), 8, 38, 244, 421
Relations of the Duchies of Schleswig and Holstein to the Crown of Denmark and the Germanic Confederation, The (T. Twiss), 112
Reminiscences (G. Smith), 349
Renault, Louis, 434, 439

Remarks on Certain Passages in the Thirty-Nine Articles, or *Tract 90* (Newman), 96
Republic of Cracow, 155
republics, 44, 91, 172–73, 189, 196; city republics, 214
Reuter, Rose, 371
Revue de droit international et de legislation compare, 397, 407, 411, 422, 435, 441, 455, 492–93, 495, 496, 521–22
Reynolds, James, 290
Rhodes, 436
Rhodian Laws of the Mediterranean, 400
Ridley, Henry, 499
Rimskaya-Korsakova, Sofya Vasilievna, 119
Rivier, Alphonse, 434
Roberts, James, 252, 253–54n89, 270, 272, 274, 278–79, 282, 284, 285, 287, 288
Roberts, Joseph, 446
Robins, Ronald, 273
Rogers, Agnes Ann, 247, 248, 310, 323; account of her early life in *Brief* (notes prepared by Windham family solicitors), 248
Rogers, Helen, 244
Rogers, Thiriza, 295
Rogers, William, 247
Rolin-Jaequemyns, Gustave, 397, 494, 502; as a member of the High Council of the Congo Free State, 496
Rolls of Oléron, 400
Roman Law, 3, 26, 60, 61, 495; as *ratio scripta*, 62; relationship with international and civil law, 68
Roman Republic, in the Papal States, 99
Romanticism, German, 1
Romieu, Auguste, 195
Rotten Row, London, 240, 243, 245, 251, 252, 253, 253–54n89, 259
Rousseau, Jean-Jacques, 237
Royal Commission on the Law of Marriage (1868), 16, 318–19, 335, 433; findings on the uniformity of the laws of marriage across various jurisdiction in Britain, 319–20
Royal Geographical Society, 424, 425
Royal Niger Company, 486
Russell, John, 46, 96, 97, 100, 102–3, 104
Russia/Russian Empire, 64, 66, 90, 108, 111, 129, 154, 201, 460; conflict with and defeat of Hungary, 179–81; Russian expansionism, 207

Russian American Company, 90
Russo-Turkish War (1877–1878), 412
Ryder, Dudley, 100, 349

Sacramental Test Act (1828), 102–3
Sala, George Augustus, 343
Salomon, Charles, 497–98
Sandor, Pauline, 117, 117n30
Sanford, Henry, 447–48, 487
Santa Catarina, 93
Sardinia, 217; struggle of against the Austrian Empire, 167–68
Savage, Marmion, 75
Savigny, Friedrich Carl von, 61, 400, 401; as a "cosmopolitan humanist," 62
Schleswig, 124–28, 227
Scotland, 104
Scott, Walter, 63
Scott, William (Lord Stowell), 59–60, 66, 415, 416
Scramble for Africa, 77
Seeley, J. R., 36
Select Committee on Legal Education (1846), 70
Seymour, Edward, 327
Shah, Wajid, Ali (the Nawab [king of Awadh]), 73
Shanley, Mary Lyndon, 17
Shaw, George Bernard, 238–39, 304–5
Shephard, John, 314
Shrew Tamed, The (1861), 241–42
Siemann, Richard, 110
Siemann, Wolfram, 110
Sir Travers Twiss et le Congo (anonymous), 444–45, 455
Sketches by Boz (Dickens), 76–77, 364
slavery/slaves, 416, 446, 463, 464–64, 512; Fugitive Slave Circulars, 415; slaves taking refuge on British ships in slave ports, 414–15; Twiss on the suppression of slavery, 463. *See also* anti-slavery efforts
Sloman, Abraham, 364; home of, 364, 364n530
Smith, Goldwin, 34, 56, 58, 349, 388–89
Smith, W. H., 304
Smith vs Windham, 295
socialism, 174
"social problem," the, 173–78
social theory, 23; "new" social theory, 23

societal expansion, processes of: the changing definitions of various kinds of society, 9; the emphasis on improvement and transformation of persons, 9
society: class-based concept of "Society," 4; London "Society," 12, 49; membership in "respectable society," 8; rules controlling membership in, 4–5; the society of nations, 6, 393–94; the society of natural persons, 8; transformations in the membership of artificial and natural persons, 8. *See also* international/global society; political society
Society for the Reform and Codification of the Law of Nations, 522
South Australia Company, 427–28
Southwell, Robert, 43
sovereigns, 8, 89, 93, 172; African, 490; British, 98; East Asian, 224–25; Indian, 222; sanctioning of "company-states" by, 19–20; sovereign domination of global society, 7; sovereign princes, 446–47; use of the mystic fictions of the artificial person to maintain authority, 4
sovereignty, 68, 154, 160, 162, 171, 198, 442, 464; artificiality of, 172; Austria and the rights of sovereignty, 144–45; conventional position concerning membership of the society of nations, 393–94; division of, 172; in the law of nations and ecclesiastical law, 89–94; of the people, 172; personal, 432; and private citizens, 480; rights of, 436; royal sovereignty, 171; subjective sovereignty, 161; of sub-Saharan Africa, 427; supremacy of, 100; in a system of modern states, 436; territorial, 432, 437; threat to by the established church, 94–95; and the transfer of sovereign rights, 466–67; Twiss's arguments concerning, 394–95, 440–41; Twiss's concept that private individuals or associations may exercise sovereign power and become states, 393, 452, 485; Twiss's fears concerning, 100; of the West Coast of Africa, 475
"Sovereignty of the People, The" (Metternich), 171–72
Spain, 89–90
Spooner, William, 346

INDEX [567]

Stanley, Arthur, 56–57, 58–59, 58n158, 88, 96, 345–46, 389
Stanley, Augusta, 346
Stanley, Henry, 424, 429, 476, 492; and the civilising of Africa, 495; explorations of, 425–27
states/nations, 28; artificial personality of, 2–3n5; "civilized states," 65; "company-states," 19–20; essential characteristics of, 2–3n5; formation of, 2–3n5, 4; hierarchy within the society of nations, 412–13, 421; liberation of, 22; nation-states, 167, 301–2; society of nations, 301; sovereignty in modern states, 436. *See also* Institut de droit international, commission of to examine the law of nations as applied to non-Christian and Oriental nations
Stead, William Thomas, 304, 357
Stein, Heinrich vom, 127, 159–60, 163
Stephen, Leslie, 36
Stepney Scandal, 84–85
Stewart, Robert Walter, 320, 321
Strauch, Maximilien, 448
Strzelecki, Paweł, 47–48, 73n215, 75, 502
Stuart, Rose, 118–19n37
Suez Canal, 201, 414, 420, 431, 502–3
suffrage, household, 184
Sultan, Tipu, 222
Sumner, John (Archbishop of Canterbury), 49, 107, 313, 326, 345, 403, 519; funeral of, 325, 328
Supplement to the Annals of Our Time: A Diurnal of Events, Social and Political, Home and Foreign from February 24, 1871, to March 19, 1874 (Macmillan), 505–6
Surkis, Judith, 14
Swaffield, Robert Hassall, 276–77
Swiss Confederation, 301
Switzerland, 48
Sydney, Earl, 387, 388
Symons, Benjamin, 96
Syon, Baron de, 195
Syria, 64
Système Metternich, 141–42, 141n6, 147–48, 149

Taaffe, Charles, 232, 342
Taaffe, Edward (Count Taaffe), 231, 232–33
Taaffe, Francis, 232
Taaffe, Louis, 232
Taggart, Michael, 527
Tait, Archibald, 49, 82–83, 96, 314, 315–16; attempts to help Twiss find work after the Twiss/Chaffers libel trial, 387–88, 402–6; as Bishop of London, 87, 345; involvement of in the Twiss/Chaffers libel trial, 346–47, 353, 356, 377–78
Tait, Catherine, 346
Taubman-Goldie, George, 460
Tennyson, Alfred, 47
territorium nullius, 495–96, 500
Teutonic Knights, 436, 454, 455, 515
Thirty-Nine Articles (1563), 96, 106
Thompson, Edward Maunde, 523
Thucydides, 146
Thurston, Anne, 290
Tichborne, Roger, 354
Tichborne case, 353–54, 379, 380, 382–83
Tocqueville, Alexis de, 162–63, 197, 204
Townsend-Farquhar, Minto, 43
Townshend, John, 340–41
Tractarians/Tractarianism (Oxford Movement), 6, 12, 81, 94–95, 100, 315, 346, 530; collapse of, 12; purpose of, 62, 95; Twiss's concerns over, 97–98
Tractatus de legibus et consuetudinibus regni Anglie (Glanville), 523
transformation, social, 10, 12, 17, 244, 294
transubstantiation, 106
Treaty Engagement of the European Powers, 153
Treaty of Gottorp (1715), 125
Treaty of Mysore, 223
Treaty of Paris (1856), 66, 203, 415; Twiss's view of, 72
Treaty of Utrecht (1713), 108, 125
Treaty of Vienna, 359
Treaty of Westphalia. *See* Peace of Westphalia (1648)
Trevor, Edward, 30
Trevor, John, 30, 41
Trevor, Richard, 30, 75–76n225
Trevor, Tudor, 29
Trevors of Trevalyn, 29; acquisition of estates by, 29–30
Tristram, F. T., 79n240, 526
Tristram, Thomas Hutchinson, 37–38n46, 79, 79n240, 120, 270, 349, 355, 356, 357, 526; as Chancellor of the Diocese of London, 385

Trithen, F. H., 222
Tuck, Richard, 28
Tufton, Richard, 40
Tuke, Edward, 289
Tuke, Thomas Harrington, 289
Turkey, 410, 414; British subjects in, 224
Twiss, Ann (born Ann Travers), 30
Twiss, Anne, 32n11
Twiss, Horace, 31
Twiss, Richard, 32n11, 308-9, 336, 337, 372
Twiss, Robert, 29; death of, 32; inheritance of, 30
Twiss, Travers, 1, 2-3n5, 4, 18, 26, 84n260, 87n273, 101n331; abandonment of Lady Twiss by, 521; advice given to Metternich to appear to be a "liberalist," 11-12; as an advocate of international order, 108-9; as apologist for Metternich, 136-37; arguments of for a tolerance of diversity, 104-5; attack on Cobden, 129-30; belief that Hungary should be maintained within the Austrian Empire, 181-82; "broken heart" of, 523; career of, 9; on the Church of England and the Catholic Church in England as subject to the will of the state, 6; concern of over liberation movements, 10; conservatism of, 12, 38, 56, 89, 109, 138, 176, 179, 346, 530-31; contact of with the Bishop of Dresden, 316-17; on the dangers of nationalism, 128, 130-32; death of, 524-25; as defender of the Austrian Empire, 45; defense of Metternich, 162; on the distinction between "unity" and "union," 147; diverse opinions concerning East Asian sovereigns, 224; ecclesiastical law practice of, 9; on *égalité*, 176-77; enthusiasm for the stability provided by the Congress of Vienna, 11; Erastianism of, 103, 104; expertise of concerning Africa, 20; explanation of the situation in Austria and Germany to Englishmen as an analogy with Britain and Ireland, 151-52; exploitation of the laws of marriage by, 27-28; on the faults of the papacy, 103; financial relationship with Leopold II, 442; and the formation of the Congo Free State as a type of artificial person, 18-19, 20-21; funeral of, 525-26; Hobbesian view of self-preservation, 146-47; involvement of with London's demi-monde, 10; issuing of marriage licenses by, 26, 82; knighthood of, 338-39; lessons learned from the Crimean War, 211-12; objections to German universities, 150; opinion of concerning Africa, 224-25; *Opinion* of concerning the "Rajah of Mysore," 222-23; opinions concerning jurisdiction and administration, 223-24; possible syphilis of, 520; progressive vision of history, 184; on public opinion, 180, 184; relations with the International African Association, 18-19; relationship with the Alcocks, 335; sale of his home's contents at auction, 388-89; sale of his library, 390, 523; on socialism, 174; on sovereignty, 173; speculation of on a "Counter Revolution" in Germany, 145-46; support of for reform and societal expansion, 12; support of for the war against the Indian Rebellion, 231-32; on treaties of guaranty, 126; transformation of, 12-13; on the types of monarchy that would be best for Austria, 140-41; view of daily newspapers, 95; views on of political union, 142-43; on the violation of treaty agreements, 163-64; writing habits of, 152-53n197. *See also* Berlin Conference (1884-1885); Metternich, Klemens Wenzel von, friendship with Twiss; Twiss, Travers, and international law; Twiss, Travers, as a lawyer; Twiss, Travers, offices held by; Twiss, Travers, at Oxford and King's College; Twiss, Travers, and personhood; Twiss, Travers, in society; Twiss/Chaffers libel trial; Twiss/Lynseele marriage; Twiss/Metternich correspondence
Twiss, Travers, and international law, 392, 461, 495, 523, 531; arguments for the creation of the Congo as a new state, 429-30; arguments of for the equality of non-European nations in international law, 418, 420-21, 423; arguments of for an "International Court," 422; drafting of the constitution of the

INDEX [569]

Congo Free State, 457–58; drafting of the treaty of recognition for the International Association of the Congo, 488–90; on "extraterritoriality" as a metaphor, 417–18; on the free navigation of the Congo River, 435–36, 441, 449; idea of for international jurisdiction over non-European nations, 414, 421–22; introduction by Twiss of the term *territorium nullius*, 77, 495–96; as one of the outstanding international lawyers of his generation, 406–7; pivotal role of in negotiating the status of the African Association, 482–83; on the possibilities of international regime, 422–23; recreation of himself as an international lawyer, 395–96; on slavery and the Fugitive Slave Circulars, 415, 416–17; on the suppression of slavery, 463; on the treaties between Muslim African nations and European states, 417–18

Twiss, Travers, as a lawyer, 9, 396; admission to the bar at Lincoln's Inn (1840), 74; auction of his collected legal writings, 526–27; as a barrister in the Court of Probate, 88; and the connection between marriage law and the law of nations as the heart of Twiss's story, 77; as Doctor of Civil Law at Oxford, 74; expertise of on overseas marriages, 320; flourishing practice and prosperity of in London, 74, 250; home of in the Albany, 74–75; practice of in the Admiralty Court, 88–89; practice of in the Court for Divorce, 88; practice of in the Ecclesiastical Court, 84n261; judgment of over cases that involved the nature of personification, 106–7. *See also* Doctor's Commons

Twiss, Travers, offices held by, 9; Bursar and Tutor at King's College, 55, 56; Chancellor of the Consistory Court of the Diocese of Hereford, 38–39, 83–84, 395; Chancellor of the Consistory Court of the Diocese of London, 9, 16, 97; Chancellor of the Diocese of Lincoln, 84, 87–88, 395; Chancellor of the Diocese of London, 314, 315, 316, 320, 395; as Commander of the Order of Leopold, 494–95, 508; Commissary-General of the city and diocese of Canterbury, 82; Drummond Professor of Political Economy at Oxford, 63–64, 74, 91, 395; Queen's Advocate General, 9, 16, 88, 221–22, 326, 336, 395; Professorship of the Law of Nations, 65–66, 396–97; Regius Professor of Civil Law at Oxford, 49, 54, 69, 71–72, 71n207, 395; resignation as the Chancellor from the Dioceses of London, Lincoln, and Hereford, 378; resignation as the Queen's Advocate, 378, 387; resignation as Vicar General to the Province of Canterbury, 378, 387; Vicar General to the Province of Canterbury, 26, 82, 83, 85–86, 105, 345, 395, 402

Twiss, Travers, at Oxford (University College) and King's College London, 152; call of for reform on the teaching and role of civil law at Oxford, 69–71; as a classicist, 60–61; constant presence of at University College events, 59, 59n163; controversy with Pattison, 57–58; earning of the Bachelor and the Doctor of Civil Law degrees, 68; and the Egyptian students at King's College, 64–65, 66; election of to the Bennet Scholarship and the Bennet Fellowship, 55; introduction of reforms by at University College, 58–59; in the key positions as Bursar and Tutor at University College, 55, 56; lifelong relationship with University College, 59–60, 59n164; presentation of honorary Doctorates in Civil Law (DCLs) by, 71–72, 73–74, 73n215, 333n418; as Public Examiner in classics, 55; reputation of as a polymath, 55–56; training of in the principles of international law at King's College, 68; various positions held at University College, 55

Twiss, Travers, and personhood: involvement of in the creation of new artificial persons, 17; public thoughts on the autonomy of persons, 299–300; radical flexibility of in the creation of new persons, 311–12, 392–93, 395; and the transformation and creation of persons, 26

Twiss, Travers, in society: alcoholic consumption of, 34, 34n27; annual holidays of, 44–45, 44nn75–76, 44n78; baptism of, 20; charitable contributions of, 40n58; childhood and family of, 29–32; contemporary accounts of his personality, 33–34; education of, 33, 33n23; election to the London Zoological Society, 47; election to the Royal Geographical Society, 47–48; eminent persons Twiss mixed with socially, 49–50; enthusiasm for technology, 46–47; extraordinary number of offices held by in various fields, 50–51; family homes of as a youth, 32; friendship with Francis Popham, 41–43, 41n61, 41–42n64; genteel background of, 30–31; home of in Park Lane, 32, 34, 75; home of in St John's Woods, 32, 33; income and prosperity of, 53–54; membership of in eminent societies, 45–49; membership in the Royal Society, 46–47; offices held by in the University of Oxford and the University of London, 34; participation in coursing (hunting) meetings, 40, 50n59; political allegiances of, 51–53; portrayal of an "extremist Whig," 52; puns on his name, 30n6; social dining of, 35, 40–41n60. *See also* Athenaeum, Twiss's membership in

Twiss/Chaffers libel trial, 511; abandonment/withdrawal of the libel charge against Chaffers by Twiss, 374–75; accusation of Chaffers against Lady Twiss, 340–41; Chaffers's appearance at the Southwark Police Court, 356–57; Chaffers's initial claims against Twiss and Lady Twiss, 337, 339; cross-examination of Jastreuski during, 368–69, 370; debate on whether to recall Lady Twiss to the stand, 369–70; examination of Arthur Cook by Chaffers, 371–73; examination of Lady Twiss by Chaffers, 363–67; examination of Lady Twiss by Harry Poland, 360–62; examination of Louisa Harrison by Chaffers, 370–71; examination of Mrs Harper by Chaffers, 374; examination of Rose Reuter by Chaffers, 371; financial and personal consequences to Twiss and Lady Twiss as a result of the trial, 383–85, 388–89, 390–91; inability of Twiss to placate Chaffers, 338; initial animosity that led to, 337; initial defence of Lady Twiss by Travers Twiss, 350–51; newspaper coverage of, 363; parallels of to the Tichborne case, 353–54, 382–83; preparations by Twiss for the libel case against Chaffers, 351–53, 355–56; public interest in, 363, 369, 374; removal of Chaffers to the Horsemonger Lane Gaol, 358, 376; representation of Twiss by the barrister Harry Poland, 357–63, 366, 367, 369–76; salacious account of the trial in *Trewman's Exeter Flying Post*, 381–82; on the slanders of Chaffers against Twiss and Lacy Twiss, 354–55; statutory declaration of Chaffers against Twiss, 342–43, 346–47, 348, 349; summonses by Twiss against Chaffers, 356–57; sympathy for Twiss in the aftermath of, 379; testimony of Archbishop Tait at, 367; Twiss's calling of Chaffers's bluff, 340–41; Twiss's explanation for withdrawing libel charges against Chaffers, 377; Twiss's views on the public reception of the trial and its aftermath, 386–87. *See also* Benson, Edward

Twiss/Lynseele marriage, 16, 310–11, 313, 315, 317–18, 320–21, 323–26, 345; exploitation of the laws of marriage by Twiss, 27–28

Twiss/Metternich correspondence: 110–11, 119–20, 121–22, 242, 392, 502, 526–27; concerning Austria and Germany, 128–38; concerning the *coup d'état* in France, 195–200; concerning the Crimean War, 200–212; concerning the German Confederation and the Austrian Empire, 129–67 *passim*; concerning global revolution, 221–34 *passim*; concerning Hungary and public opinion, 178–95 *passim*; concerning Napoleon III and Italian unification, 212–21; concerning Schleswig, Holstein, and Prussia, 124–28; on Prussia and Germany, 167–73; concerning the "social problem," 163–78; secrecy attached to the letters exchanged between Metternich and Twiss, 121–23

Two Introductory Lectures on the Science of International Law (T. Twiss), 66–67

Unitary System, 147–48n, 160
United States of America, 141, 163, 441, 460, 469, 482, 498
Universalis Ecclesiae (papal letter), 97, 379
Universities of Oxford and Cambridge Act (1877), 405
University College, Oxford, 9, 33, 34, 36, 38, 55–61, 69, 88, 345, 388–89, 415, 433, 523
Urania College, 347
utilitarians, 62
Utopians, 175

Vancouver Island, 90
Vanderschoore, Augustin, 303
Vanderschoore, Barbe Thérèse, 302, 303, 346
Vassal-Fox, Henry (Lord Holland), 123–24
Vattel, Emer de, 92, 125, 227, 394
Victoria Embankment project, 80, 80n243
Victorian England, 229–30; political polarisation in, 10; religious conflict in, 12
Victorians, 1, 8, 15; and the practice of "slumming," 257–58; Victorian liberals, 129; Victorian jurists, 1, 26
Vienna Note (1853), 207
View of the Progress of Political Economy in Europe since the Sixteenth Century (T. Twiss), 63–64
Villiers, Charles, 130
Virginia Company, 19, 394
Viscount Castlerosse, 344–45
Vitoria, Francesco de, 7–8
Vivian, Hussey, 512, 513–14, 516

Wack, Henry Wellington, 450n208
Waddilove, Arthur, 37–38n46, 63n177, 80
Wadiyar, Krishnaraja, III, 222–23
Wadiyars, 222–23
Walachia, 201
Wales, 98
Walford, Edward, 30, 50
Walker, Fanny (Fanny Twiss), 29, 30
Walker, George, 296
Walters, Catherine, 239–40, 242–43, 259; clients of, 243
Warren, Samuel, 282, 283, 283–84n207, 286
Watt, James, 176
Weldon, Georgina, 306–8, 505, 520, 527, 534
Wesley, John, 11
West, Henry S. W., 450n208

Westlake, John, 62
Weyer, Sylvain Van de, 197
Wheaton, Henry, 2–3n5, 300
Wheatstone, Charles, 46, 47
Whewell Professorship of International Law at Cambridge, 397
Whigs, 17, 35, 43, 52, 82
Wickham, Henry, 499
Wilberforce, Samuel, 82
Wild Dayrell, 42
Wilde, Oscar, 74
Wilde, Thomas, 49–50n109
Williams, B. B., 276
Williams, Fenwick, 71
Williams, Henry, 376–77
Willoughby, Agnes (Agnes Rogers; Agnes Windham-Walker), 13, 18, 241, 242, 283–84, 288, 296–98, 301, 303, 306, 309, 331, 337, 395, 520; arguments of with William Windham, 272–73; birth of her son, 294–95; claim that William Windham infected her with venereal disease, 265, 268; effect of their relationship on Twiss's marriage, 251; estates of, 296; as the first prostitute linked to Twiss, 246–47; home of, 250, 250n67; marriage of to William Windham, 270–72, 310; marriage of to George Walker, 296; marriage settlement of with William Windham, 269–70; payments of to William Windham's creditors, 295; purchase of jewelry for by William Windham, 258–59, 265, 272; relationship with James Bowen May, 251–52; relationship with James Roberts, 252; relationship with William Windham, 262–63; renewal of her relationship with Jack Garden, 252–53; separation from Twiss, 251; stories concerning Twiss and Willoughby after the Twiss/Chaffers libel trial, 386; Twiss as her best friend and lover, 249–50, 392; Twiss's involvement with when she was with Jack Garden, 250–51. *See also* Windham, William, insanity trial of
Wilson, Archdale, 73
Wilson, Horace, 222
Windham, Charles Ash (General Windham), 255, 268, 274–75, 295–96, 299; "peccadilloes" of, 278–79; role of in William Windham's insanity trial, 275–78

Windham, Frederick Howe Lindsay Bacon, 294–95, 296
Windham, Sophia, 255, 270, 274
Windham, William, 241, 319, 520, 534; arguments of with Agnes Willoughby, 272–73; bankruptcy of, 293–94; behavior of as consistent with the Victorian practice of "slumming," 257–58; birth of his son, 294–95; death of, 295; eccentric behavior of, 256–57, 286, 289; health of (examination of by Dr Buck), 264; ill health of, 295; inheritances of, 256–57; letter of to Agnes Willoughby at the Euston Hotel, 273–74; marriage of to Agnes Willoughby, 270–72, 310; prominent family of, 255; purchase of a coaching business by, 293; purchase of jewelry for Agnes Willoughby, 258–59, 265; relationship with Agnes Willoughby, 262–66; response to Agnes Willoughby's relationship with Antonio Guiglini, 259–60, 262; settlement of the claim he had infected her with venereal disease, 265, 268; suit of divorce brought by against Agnes Willoughby, 292–93. *See also* Felbrigg Hall; Windham, William, insanity trial of
Windham, William, insanity trial of, 18, 247, 248, 258, 269, 271, 275, 279–80, 281–83, 294, 403, 417, 506; closing arguments of, 290–91; costs of, 291; evidence presented at, 283–84; role of Charles Ash Windham (General Windham) in, 275–78; verdict concerning, 291, 295; Windham's defense team, 287–88; witnesses at, 284–87. *See also* Field and Roscoe
Windham, William Frederick, 255, 270, 296–98
Windham, William Howe, 255
Windham vs Guibelei, 255, 262, 269, 281–82
Windham vs Whidborne, 269–70
Windham vs Windham (1857), 255
Winslow, Forbes, 265, 284–86, 207
Winthrop, Robert, 91
Winton, Francis de, 476, 477, 478
Wiseman, Nicholas, 99, 103
Wittgenstein, Ludwig, 25
Wives of England, The: Their Relative Duties, Domestic Influence and Social Obligations (Ellis), 329
Wolff, Christian, 300
Wood, William Page, 295, 319
women: association of with scandal, 14–15; incorporation of their legal personality with their husbands after marriage, 5; as possessing personhood, 5; social mobility of, 17; women's emancipation movements, 17
Wurtemberg, 159

Yeatman, John Pym, 527, 528
Yorath, Elizabeth, 84–85

Zumpe, Hermann, 384, 386

A NOTE ON THE TYPE

THIS BOOK has been composed in Miller, a Scotch Roman typeface designed by Matthew Carter and first released by Font Bureau in 1997. It resembles Monticello, the typeface developed for The Papers of Thomas Jefferson in the 1940s by C. H. Griffith and P. J. Conkwright and reinterpreted in digital form by Carter in 2003.

Pleasant Jefferson ("P. J.") Conkwright (1905–1986) was Typographer at Princeton University Press from 1939 to 1970. He was an acclaimed book designer and AIGA Medalist.

The ornament used throughout this book was designed by Pierre Simon Fournier (1712–1768) and was a favorite of Conkwright's, used in his design of the *Princeton University Library Chronicle*.